The Luminous Way to the East

RELIGION IN TRANSLATION

SERIES EDITOR
John Nemec, University of Virginia

A Publication Series of
The American Academy of Religion
and
Oxford University Press

SACRED AND PROFANE BEAUTY
The Holy in Art
Garardus van der Leeuw
Preface by Mircea Eliade
Translated by David E. Green
With a new introduction and bibliography by
Diane Apostolos-Cappadona

THE HISTORY OF THE BUDDHA'S
RELIC SHRINE
A Translation of the Sinhala Thūpavamsa
Stephen C. Berkwitz

DAMASCIUS' *PROBLEMS & SOLUTIONS
CONCERNING FIRST PRINCIPLES*
Translated with Introduction and Notes by
Sara Ahbel-Rappe

THE SECRET GARLAND
Āṇṭāḷ's Tiruppāvai *and* Nācciyār Tirumoḻi
Translated with Introduction and Commentary
by Archana Venkatesan

PRELUDE TO THE MODERNIST CRISIS
The "Firmin" Articles of Alfred Loisy
Edited, with an Introduction by C. J. T. Talar
Translated by Christine Thirlway

DEBATING THE DASAM GRANTH
Robin Rinehart

THE FADING LIGHT OF ADVAITA
ĀCĀRYA
Three Hagiographies
Rebecca J. Manring

THE UBIQUITOUS ŚIVA
*Somānanda's Śivadṛṣṭi and His Tantric
Interlocutors*
John Nemec

PLACE AND DIALECTIC
Two Essays by Nishida Kitarō
Translated by John W.M. Krummel and
Shigenori Nagatomo

THE PRISON NARRATIVES OF
JEANNE GUYON
Ronney Mourad and Dianne Guenin-Lelle

DISORIENTING DHARMA
*Ethics and the Aesthetics of Suffering in the
Mahābhārata*
Emily T. Hudson

THE TRANSMISSION OF SIN
Augustine and the Pre-Augustinian Sources
Pier Franco Beatrice
Translated by Adam Kamesar

FROM MOTHER TO SON
*The Selected letter of Marie de l'Incarnation to
Claude Martin*
Translated and with Introduction and Notes by
Mary Dunn

DRINKING FROM LOVE'S CUP
Surrender and Sacrifice in the Vārs *of Bhai Gurdas*
Selections and Translations with Introduction and
Commentary by Rahuldeep Singh Gill

THE AMERICA'S FIRST THEOLOGIES
Early Sources of Post-Contact Indigenous Religion
Edited and translated by Garry Sparks, with
Sergio Romero and Frauke Sachse

GODS, HEROES, AND ANCESTORS
*An Interreligious Encounter in Eighteenth-Century
Veitnam*
Anh Q. Tran

POETRY AS PRAYER IN THE SANSKRIT
HYMNS OF KASHMIR
Hamsa Stainton

THE UBIQUITOUS ŚIVA VOLUME II
*Somānanda's Śivadṛṣṭi and His Tantric
Interlocutors*
John Nemec

FIRST WORDS, LAST WORDS
*New Theories for Reading Old Texts in
Sixteenth-Century India*
Yigal Bronner and Lawrence McCrea

THE LUMINOUS WAY TO THE EAST
*Texts and History of the First Encounter of
Christianity with China*
Matteo Nicolini-Zani

The Luminous Way to the East

Texts and History of the First Encounter of Christianity with China

MATTEO NICOLINI-ZANI

Translated by

WILLIAM SKUDLAREK

OXFORD
UNIVERSITY PRESS

Oxford University Press is a department of the University of Oxford. It furthers
the University's objective of excellence in research, scholarship, and education
by publishing worldwide. Oxford is a registered trade mark of Oxford University
Press in the UK and certain other countries.

Published in the United States of America by Oxford University Press
198 Madison Avenue, New York, NY 10016, United States of America.

© Oxford University Press 2022

All rights reserved. No part of this publication may be reproduced, stored in
a retrieval system, or transmitted, in any form or by any means, without the
prior permission in writing of Oxford University Press, or as expressly permitted
by law, by license, or under terms agreed with the appropriate reproduction
rights organization. Inquiries concerning reproduction outside the scope of the
above should be sent to the Rights Department, Oxford University Press, at the
address above.

You must not circulate this work in any other form
and you must impose this same condition on any acquirer.

Library of Congress Control Number: 2021044708
ISBN 978–0–19–760964–4

DOI: 10.1093/oso/9780197609644.001.0001

Contents

Foreword	ix
Preface	xi
Abbreviations	xvii

PART I: *A History of Encounters*

1. "The Luminous Breeze Blew Eastward": The Church of the
   East from Persia to China — 3
   The Missionary Dynamism of the Church of the East — 3
   Christian Archaeological Traces in Asia in the
       First Millennium — 17
   Christian Literature in the Languages of Central Asia — 31
   The Meeting of Religions on the Silk Road — 44

2. "The Brilliant Teaching Turned toward the Tang Empire":
   The Christian Presence in China between 635 and 845 — 59
   Chinese Designations of Tang Christianity — 59
   A Chronicle of the Events Attested by the Sources — 68
   The Composition and Structure of Christian Communities — 85
   The Geographical Location of Christian Monasteries — 106

3. "The Scriptures Were Translated": The First Christian Texts
   in Chinese — 117
   The 781 Xi'an Stele: A Monument "Celebrating the Eminent
       and Meritorious Events" — 117

vi   *Contents*

The 815 Luoyang Pillar: A Memorial Stone "Granting the
    Luminous Blessings"   137
The "Dunhuang" Manuscripts: A Summary of Research   146
The Production and Literary Form of the Texts   164
The Content of the Texts   177

PART II: *The Texts in Translation*

Notes on Sources   193
The Reference Editions of the Translated Texts   193
The Transcriptions of Foreign Names   195

Text A:

Stele of the Diffusion of the Luminous Teaching of Da Qin in China
(*Da Qin jingjiao liuxing Zhongguo bei* 大秦景教流行中國碑)   197

Text B:

1. *Hymn in Praise of the Salvation Achieved through the Three
Majesties of the Luminous Teaching* (*Jingjiao sanwei mengdu
zan* 景教三威蒙度讚)   222
2. *Book of the Honored* (*Zunjing* 尊經)   226

Text C:

Discourse on the One God (*Yishen lun* 一神論)   233
I. *Discourse on the One Godhead* (*Yitian lun diyi* 一天論第一)   233
II. *Metaphorical Teaching* (*Yu di'er* 喻第二)   246
III. *Discourse of the Honored One of the Universe on Almsgiving*
    (*Shizun bushi lun disan* 世尊布施論第三)   250

Text D:

Book of the Lord Messiah (*Xuting mishisuo jing* 序聽迷詩所經)   265

Text E:

Book on Profound and Mysterious Blessedness
(*Zhixuan anle jing* 志玄安樂經)   282

Text F:

Book of the Luminous Teaching of Da Qin on Revealing the Origin and Reaching the Foundation (*Da Qin jingjiao xuanyuan zhiben jing 大秦景教宣元至本經) 298

Bibliography 305

Index of Names, Texts, and Manuscripts 383

Foreword

THE DISCOVERY, NOW almost four hundred years ago, of the bilingual Chinese-Syriac monumental stele caused almost as great a stir in the world of learning at that time as did the discovery of the first Dead Sea scrolls in 1947. In both cases, so astonishing and unexpected were these two finds that at first some scholars refused to believe that the artifacts in question were genuine. Such doubts, however, were soon dispelled, but the newly gained information in both cases demanded a complete rethinking of previous perceptions, whether it was of the development of the Hebrew text of the Bible, or in the case of the Xi'an stele, of the history of the eastern expansion of Christianity. Who would ever have imagined that the year in which Damascus fell to the invading Arab armies was also the year when a group of monks from the Church of the East turned up at the seat of the Tang court? A precise date for this event, "the ninth year of the Zhenguan era," corresponding to 635 CE, is explicitly given in the beautifully inscribed text of the Xi'an stele, itself erected in 781.

With the subsequent discovery of Christian texts in Chinese from the Tang period, and the very recent discovery of a second stone monument, the Luoyang pillar dating from 815, a considerable amount of information about the presence and character of Chinese Christianity in the Tang period is now available, and quite a number of presentations of the documents for a wider public have been made. This textual evidence, provided by the two monuments and by a number of literary texts, is, however, no easy task for the historian to evaluate, and many of those who have attempted this have not always been true to the Latin author Tacitus's ideal for the historian that he or she should write *sine ira et studio*, instead doing so from the viewpoint of some particular Western perspective. This situation makes the appearance of the present English translation of Matteo Nicolini-Zani's *La via radiosa per l'oriente*, in its revised and expanded form, so very welcome. Being a scholar possessing a deep familiarity with both the primary sources and the (now very extensive) secondary literature, Matteo Nicolini-Zani is eminently well placed to provide a reliable and well-balanced introduction to, and translation of, the various materials in Chinese that are available. Furthermore, he has done this in a manner which very successfully caters both for a general readership and for an academic one: the general reader can skip the footnotes, while scholars will be immensely grateful for the richness of, and the wide learning displayed by, this annotation.

In the first half of the book the author has provided an excellent introduction to the wider background of the texts and their place both within the history of the Church of the East and within that of the Tang period. This is followed by a very helpful guide to the texts themselves and to the documents containing them, for some of which the provenance is problematic. Finally come authoritative translations of the Xi'an stele and of five further texts, the last of which is also to be found on the Luoyang pillar. All are provided with helpful annotation, and in many cases this illuminatingly brings out the ways in which Buddhist terminology was borrowed by the authors of the texts.

At a time when China is one of the places in the world where Christianity is expanding, it is particularly important that modern Chinese Christians should become aware of this earlier presence of an eastern—and Sinicized—form of Christianity in their country during the Tang period. For them, and for everyone else, the present book provides a reliable and comprehensive guide both to the texts themselves and to their historical and cultural background. May it be widely read!

Sebastian Brock
Oriental Institute, Oxford University

Preface

THE REPORT THAT Marco Polo (1254–1324) made of his travels in Asia between the years 1271 and 1295 includes a story "which is fitting to tell" about a meeting that took place around 1288 in Fuzhou (Fugiu in his account), a city in Southern China, with "a certain manner of people whose religion no one understands."[1] Marco and his uncle Maffeo visited them, talked with them, and questioned them about their customs and beliefs, and soon

> they found that they held the Christian religion. For they had books, and these Masters Mafeu and Marc reading in them began to interpret the writing and to translate from word to word and from tongue to tongue, so that they found it to be the words of the Psalter. Then they asked them whence they had that religion and rule. And they answered and said: "From our ancestors." And thus they had in a certain temple of theirs three figures painted, who had been three apostles of the seventy who had gone preaching through the world; and they said that those had taught their ancestors in that religion long ago, and that that faith had already been preserved among them for seven hundred years; but for a long time they had been without teaching and so were ignorant of the chief things. "Yet we hold this from our predecessors, namely that according to our books we celebrate and do reverence to these three, namely the apostles." Then Masters Mafeu and Marc said: "You are Christians and we are likewise Christians."[2]

---

1. Marco Polo, *Book of the Marvels of the World* 156, trans. Moule and Pelliot, 1: 349.

2. Ibid., 1: 350. About this specific passage of the work of Marco Polo, which was originally written in Latin, see "Un texte de Marco Polo" 1928; Duvigneau 1934, 473–83. The passages in the work of Marco Polo that deal with Christians can be found in Moule 1930, 128–43.

xii *Preface*

"Iam per annos septingentos apud eos erat fides illa servata." The faith of this group—if it really is the Christian faith, since we cannot exclude the hypothesis that what is referred to here is the Jewish faith[3]—would therefore go back to the end of the sixth century. There are sporadic but important reports of a certain continuity of the Christian presence in China, especially in the South, between the end of the Tang dynasty (618–907), the period on which this study focuses, and the beginning of the Yuan dynasty (1279–1368), the period in which the journey of the Venetian merchant travelers takes place.[4] For that reason it is not entirely unreasonable, but actually quite evocative, to introduce this study by recalling an event that takes us back to the historical period that is the subject of this study, namely, the centuries of the first millennium during which East Syriac Christianity—often improperly and hastily called Nestorian[5]—spread throughout Central Asia and from there to China.

I hope this work will provide a documented and helpful look at what was not only the first stage in the history of Christianity's dialogue with Chinese culture but also one of the most interesting and fruitful moments in that history. For this purpose, I believe it is essential to provide a translation of the documents that give direct witness to the first Christian presence in China and do so in the language of that culture (Part II). These texts therefore constitute the body of this book, to which the chapters preceding them serve as a long introduction (Part I).[6] I am perfectly aware that translating the Chinese Christian texts of the Tang era is an extremely challenging endeavor.[7] However, I believe it is important to embark on such a daring task for two main reasons.

The first is that the three existing English translations of the entire corpus of the Tang Christian literature are all defective in one way or another. P. Y. Saeki's translations (Saeki 1951; first edn, 1937), which for several decades

---

3. The book of the Psalter alone is not enough to clarify the question. Furthermore, the three characters depicted could be the patriarchs Abraham, Isaac, and Jacob. In the Yuan era, the Jewish presence is also well attested in Southern China, as is shown by Chinese historical sources, by Arabic and Persian authors, as well as by Christian writers (see Leslie [1998?], 41, 49–52).

4. In this regard, see Pelliot 1931–32, 1933; Wang Yuanyuan 2013a.

5. See Brock 1996. I will limit as much as possible the use of the appellation "Nestorian" in the following pages.

6. The titles of the three chapters that make up the first part of the volume are quotations of selected passages from the text inscribed on the 781 Xi'an Christian stele.

7. A useful introduction to this issue can be found in Deeg 2004, 2005, [2006b?], 2009.

Preface xiii

have been the only reference for English-speaking readers, are frequently debatable and today sound obsolete. Martin Palmer's translations (Palmer 2001) are often misleading and thus to be unconditionally avoided by those who demand a rigorous approach to the sources. Tang Li's translations (Tang Li 2002) are occasionally unconvincing. Moreover, these works do not include translations of the most recent archaeological findings and were unable to benefit from the most recent documentary research and contemporary philological studies.

The second reason is that the past translations into several different languages often show a partial and unacceptable approach to the sources. Some interpret the texts one-sidedly through a Christian lens, thus overly "Christianizing" their meaning and disregarding the cultural and religious references to the Chinese context in which they were shaped. Others interpret the texts one-sidedly through a Buddhist or Daoist lens, thus overestimating the Chinese cultural and religious "garment" of the texts and underestimating their original Christian contents. While my translations have benefited from the existing translations,[8] they are intended to offer new, more balanced interpretations of the texts. These interpretations take into account the background, mindset, and supposed intentions of the Christian authors in transmitting their message to their Chinese audience. They also suggest how the recipients who lived in the particular time and place that was Tang China were affected by the linguistic and ideological resources the authors drew upon, namely the Chinese language and the Buddhist, Daoist, and Confucian religious codes. To make my intentions clear, these new translations are accompanied by copious notes to help readers understand concepts, images, and expressions taken from the Chinese cultural and religious world, and also to indicate more or less direct references to Christian sources.

The Sino-Christian texts that have survived from this early period, albeit few in number, are extremely precious because they testify to Christianity's welcoming reception of the expressive forms of the Chinese cultural and religious world. As has been said,

The survival of Christian texts in Chinese from the Tang period demonstrates that the Nestorian Church in Tang China was conscious

---

8. These translations are indicated in the bibliography of this volume by putting them in square brackets at the end of the works in which they appear. For instance, "[trans. A]" at the end of the entry Xu Longfei 2004 means that this work contains a translation, in this case German, of the Xi'an Christian stele of 781 (Text A).

of its missionary duty, and its story therefore has an intrinsic interest which is lacking in the case of the later mission. It is a story of the meeting of two profoundly dissimilar cultures. . . . Although they failed to make a significant impact on Chinese ways of thought, the Nestorians in Tang China . . . at least tried to communicate with the Chinese among whom they lived.[9]

In the pages immediately preceding the translation of the texts (Chapter 3), I describe their form and content, highlighting and analyzing the most original elements and summarizing what published studies say about the origin of these documents and how they were discovered.

The documents, however, can only be read against the background of the historical and political events that the Christian communities experienced in the Chinese Tang Empire. Therefore, the preceding chapter (Chapter 2) offers a summary of the historical data that have come down to us and are attested to by the sources, together with my attempt to reconstruct the locations, organization, and denominations of Christianity in China between about 635 and 845.

Finally, I did not think it possible to isolate Tang Christianity in China from the place it originated, with which the Chinese periphery always maintained close ties. The Christian presence in China is in fact the point of arrival of the Church of the East's long process of expansion along the Silk Road from Persia, where it began, throughout Central Asia. For this reason I thought it useful to introduce a further chapter (Chapter 1) in which I briefly describe the extraordinary missionary dynamism of the Church of the East from the Middle to the Far East, presenting the archaeological and literary findings we possess and focusing on how East Syriac Christianity—significantly defined as "a Christianity of mission and cultural mediation"[10]—entered into dialogue with the religious traditions of Manichaeism, Zoroastrianism, and Buddhism encountered on the caravan routes of Central Asia.

This, in short, is the structure of the book, which deliberately does not end with a conclusion. The objective of this work is not to determine whether or not the encounter between Christianity and ancient Chinese culture described and evaluated in the following pages is a model for a truly Chinese Christianity. I hope that scholars in fields such as missiology and intercultural

---

9. Wilmshurst 1990, 49.

10. See Camplani 2011.

Preface

dialogue will find in this introductory study source material for developing new reflections. Their insights will undoubtedly echo the numerous questions that are raised by the dialogue between Christianity and Asian cultures and religions and that today are perhaps being addressed more consciously than they were in the past. I am convinced that the experience of Christians in the Tang period can stimulate contemporary theologians, particularly in China, to formulate a Sino-Christian theology, one that speaks a language that is genuinely Chinese.[11]

Some difficulties may be encountered in reading this book because of references to unfamiliar historical events within which Tang Christianity is located, the frequent use of terms in Asian languages (Syriac, Persian, Sogdian, Chinese, and Sanskrit), the cultural distance of the language used in the documents translated here, or the repeated references within these documents to philosophical and religious traditions which, despite studies that have been done on Chinese Buddhism, Daoism, and Confucianism, remain relatively unfamiliar in much of the West.

I hope, however, that curiosity, a willingness to listen, and a desire for knowledge and encounter (and therefore of empathy) will enable readers to surmount these difficulties. That same feeling of empathy, after all, was what prompted the Venetian merchants who traveled at the end of the thirteenth century to recognize their Chinese brothers, convinced that they were the heirs of the ancient East Syriac Christian tradition: "Vos estis christiani et nos sumus similiter christiani," said Marco and Maffeo to the Christians of Fuzhou. May this same feeling of empathy also be shared by those who now set out with me along the route of the "Luminous Way" in the first millennium.[12]

---

11. See Vermander [2006?].

12. The expression "luminous way" or "brilliant path" (*mingdao* 明道), which provides the title for this volume, is contained in the *Book on Profound and Mysterious Blessedness* (*Zhixuan anle jing*), where it refers to the Christian teaching (Text E, col. 149, p. 296).

Abbreviations

AoF	*Altorientalische Forschungen*
BCP	*Bulletin Catholique de Pékin*
BSOAS	*Bulletin of the School of Oriental and African Studies*
BTT	Berliner Turfantexte (Turnhout: Brepols, 1971–)
CSCO	Corpus Scriptorum Christianorum Orientalium (Louvain: various imprints, 1903–)
DF	*Dao Feng: Jidujiao wenhua pinglun* 道風：基督教文化評論 [Logos & Pneuma: Chinese Journal of Theology]
DJ	*Dunhuangxue jikan* 敦煌学辑刊 [Dunhuang Studies]
DMTC	Gunner Mikkelsen, *Dictionary of Manichaean Texts*, vol. 3.4: *Texts from Central Asia and China: Dictionary of Manichaean Texts in Chinese.* Corpus Fontium Manichaeorum; Subsidia 5 (Turnhout: Brepols, 2006)
DOT	Charles O. Hucker, *A Dictionary of Official Titles in Imperial China* (Stanford, CA: Stanford University Press, 1985)
DTY	*Dunhuang Tulufan yanjiu* 敦煌吐魯番研究 [Journal of the Dunhuang and Turfan Studies]
EIr	*Encyclopaedia Iranica*, edited by Ehsan Yarshater et al. (London et al.: Routledge & Kegan Paul et al., 1982–)
EIr Online	*Encyclopaedia Iranica*, online edition (<http://www.iranicaonline.org/>), edited by Ehsan Yarshater et al. (New York: Columbia University, Center for Iranian Studies, 1996–)
HdO	Handbuch der Orientalistik (Leiden: Brill, 1952–)
HX	*Huaxue* 華學 [Sinology]
JA	*Journal Asiatique*
LM	*Le Muséon*
MS	*Monumenta Serica*
OC	*Oriens Christianus*
OCP	*Orientalia Christiana Periodica*
OPOe	Orientalia-Patristica-Oecumenica (Münster: LIT, 2009–)
PG	Patrologia Graeca, 166 vols., edited by J.-P. Migne (Paris: Garnier, 1857–66)

xviii   *Abbreviations*

PO   Patrologia Orientalis (Paris: Firmin-Didot, 1903–66; Turnhout: Brepols, 1968–)
POC   *Proche-Orient Chrétien*
SC   Sources Chrétiennes (Paris: Éditions du Cerf, 1942–)
Sk.   Sanskrit
SRS   Silk Road Studies (Turnhout: Brepols, 1997–)
StIr C Studia Iranica: Cahier (Louvain: Peeters, 1982; Paris: Association pour l'avancement des études iraniennes, 1984–)
SZY   *Shijie zongjiao yanjiu* 世界宗教研究 [Studies in World Religions]
T   *Taishō shinshū daizōkyō* 大正新修大藏經 [The Buddhist Canon: New Compilation of the Taishō Era], 85 vols., edited by Takakusu Junjirō 高楠順次郎 and Watanabe Kaikyoku 渡邊海旭 (Tokyo: Issaikyō kankōkai, 1924–32)
TP   *T'oung Pao*
TY   *Tang yanjiu* 唐研究 [Journal of Tang Studies]
WB   *Wenbo* 文博 [Relics and Museology]
WS   *Wenshi* 文史 [Letters]
XY   *Xiyu yanjiu* 西域研究 [Western Regions Studies]
ZLJ   *Zhongyang yanjiuyuan lishi yuyan yanjiusuo jikan* 中央研究院歷史語言研究所集刊 [Bulletin of the Institute of History and Philology, Academia Sinica]
ZWL   *Zhonghua wenshi luncong* 中華文史論叢 [Collection of Essays on Chinese Literature and History]
*   collated text

Revised and enlarged English edition of the Italian original: La via radiosa per l'oriente: I testi e la storia del primo incontro del cristianesimo con il mondo culturale e religioso cinese (secoli VII–IX), *Magnano: Edizioni Qiqajon, 2006. The translation has been funded by the Yoga Science Foundation (Ashland, OR).*

PART I

A History of Encounters

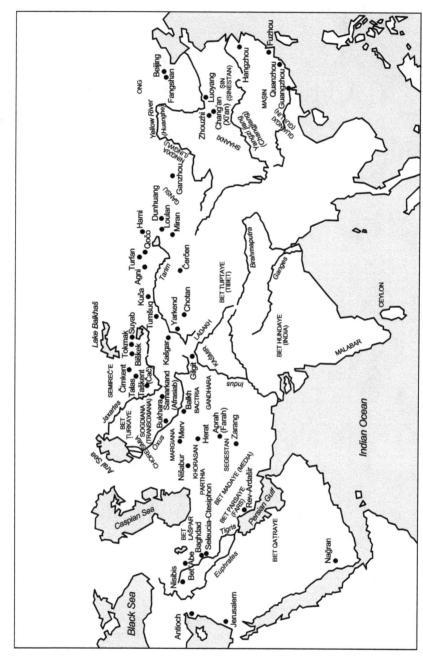

Figure 1.1 Map of the Near East, Central Asia, and the Far East.

I

"The Luminous Breeze Blew Eastward"

THE CHURCH OF THE EAST FROM PERSIA TO CHINA

The Missionary Dynamism of the Church of the East

> *It would be an attractive undertaking for the historian to be able to follow in the footsteps of those heralds of the Gospel, who went forth from Antioch with firmness and tenacity in those early days making their way to the East . . . building new centers of Christian irradiation, creating communities and spreading the doctrine of Jesus everywhere.[1]*

The interest would certainly grow if we were familiar with the challenges faced by these first evangelizers on their way to the Far East. Gaining that knowledge, however, is no easy task.

> Christ's teaching had to cover immense distances on its road from Antioch towards the East. . . . The details of this diffusion, however, remain obscure. There are no Acts of the Apostles, no Letters of Saint Paul, no contemporary or near-contemporary documents that might tell us how and when Christianity from the region of the Euphrates and the Tigris crossed over the mountainous regions of the Orient, how through Media and Parthia it went south to Herat and Segestan, and how it penetrated eastward, crossing the Margiana (Merv), into

---

1. Messina 1932, 535.

The Luminous Way to the East. Matteo Nicolini-Zani, Oxford University Press. © Oxford University Press 2022.
DOI: 10.1093/oso/9780197609644.003.0001

the region of the Oxus and the Jaxartes, and finally how it entered today's Russian province of Semireč'e, then Turfan, and then further south into the heart of China.[2]

For a number of reasons that will emerge in the course of this discussion, the Christianity that flourished in China in the first millennium cannot be studied apart from its Middle Eastern origin and its expansion throughout Central Asia. Here, then, is the itinerary that I will follow as I trace the footsteps of the missionaries of the Church of the East and give a brief introduction to the presence of Christianity "into the heart of China."[3]

To begin with, we must go, if only briefly, to the origin of this process, to the starting point of that "Luminous Way" that will cross the whole of Asia, enriching its cultural and spiritual traditions, but also—and perhaps even more—being enriched by them. This starting point is the territory in which a Syriac expression of Christianity was developed very early on, a territory geographically situated between Syria, Mesopotamia, and Persia that straddled two ethnic worlds (Semitic and Iranian), two linguistic worlds (Aramaic and Persian), and two political worlds (the Byzantine and Persian empires), worlds that were still strongly influenced by Hellenistic culture.

The main ecclesial body of this expansion was the Church of the East, one of the churches of the Syriac tradition.[4] Although it simply designated itself as the Church of the East (or, more recently, the Assyrian Church of the East),[5] one of the names by which it was also known in the West was the Church of Persia, a reference to the political affiliation of the territory where this church was independently configured from the fifth century on and where it had its center (Seleucia-Ctesiphon) for several centuries. It was succinctly described as follows:

> The Church of the East was ecclesiastically "Persian" in that it was, with minor exceptions, the officially recognized church of the

---

2. Sachau 1916, 958.

3. For a recent travel account of Christian traces along the Silk Road, see Courtois 2007.

4. For a brief historical and theological presentation of the Church of the East, I refer to the following studies: Tisserant 1931; Le Coz 1995; Baum and Winkler 2003; Baumer 2006; Wilmshurst 2011.

5. This definition is based on the historical-geographical criterion by which the Christian experience matured in the territories east of the Roman Empire. When a part of this eastern church united with Rome in 1553 (thus becoming one of the eastern Catholic churches), it became known as the Chaldean Church, while that part of this eastern church that did not enter into communion with Rome was referred to as the Assyrian Church.

Sasanian Empire. The church was politically "Persian" due to the role of Sasanian kings in the eleven synods from 410 to 775 CE. The church was geographically "Persian" in that it was coextensive with, but not limited to the orbit of the Sasanian Empire. The Church of the East was only secondarily "Persian" in terms of ethnicity.[6]

However, this description of the Church of Persia is restrictive, since it neglects both the incredible spread of what was the most missionary of the eastern churches and its primitive Aramaic matrix. The cradle of the Church of the East was the northwest region of Mesopotamia. The culture of this borderland between two political powers, the Byzantine and Persian, was primarily Semitic, but it was also influenced by Hellenistic culture. According to the reliable account of the evangelization of Mesopotamia and Persia by Addai, Aggai, and Mari at the end of the first and beginning of the second century, missionaries from Antioch established Christian communities in this region that were directly dependent on Antioch.[7]

That the Church of the East owes its birth to the church of Antioch has important implications for its subsequent expansion to the Far East. Pluralist from the beginning, the church of Antioch soon manifested itself as a missionary church (see Acts 13:1–3). Equally decisive for its missionary vocation was the abrupt confrontation between its primitive Semitic and Greek origins and Persian culture, as well as its encounter with Zoroastrianism, which became the dominant religious tradition of the Persian Empire, especially with the advent of the Sasanian dynasty (226–632).[8]

When Antiochene Christianity crossed the frontier of the Roman Empire and entered Persian territory, the absence of any explicit persecution of Christians allowed it to develop rapidly. The polytheistic Parthians (227 BCE–226 CE) were tolerant of foreign religions, thus ensuring an environment conducive to the growth of Christian communities. Even under the rule of the new Sasanian dynasty, there was relative religious tolerance. The Christian community continued to grow and became more organized, even though there were occasional periods of violent persecution, especially that of Šābuhr II between 339 and 379, those that took place in the last years of the reign of Yazdgird I (r. 399–421), and that of Yazdgird II (r. 439–57)

---

6. Buck 1996, 54.

7. See the *Acts of Mar Mari*; Jullien and Jullien 2002a.

8. Remarkable, in this regard, is Panaino 2004. See also William 1996; Buck 1996.

between 446 and 448.[9] It should be noted that the Acts of the Syrian martyrs include some Iranian names, which indicates that there were some Christians of Persian origin—or at least some Iranians who had converted from Mazdeism—who lost their lives during the persecutions of Šābuhr II. The Iranization of Syriac Christianity increased in later centuries, as witnessed by the names of Persian martyrs in the Syriac accounts of martyrdom.[10]

In addition, already in the second half of the third century, the deportation to Babylon and Persia of populations from the area of Syria subject to Rome was an important factor in the implantation of Christian communities in Persian territory. There were many Christians among the deportees, some of whom were priests and bishops. In these various transmigrations from the Greco-Roman West, there were Christians who arrived in the East either as fugitives or as deportees and who enlarged the ranks of the Christian communities that had already been established there or founded new ones. The *Chronicle of Se'ert* (early eleventh century), an important source for the religious history of this area, notes that this was the cause of the increased number of Christians in the region.[11]

As the tension between the Roman and the Sasanian empires increased, it was all the more necessary for the East Syriac communities to become independent. Their independence was clearly a response to political developments and not the result of a dogmatic schism. As one historian put it, "Having matured, Persian Christianity now becomes a national, autonomous, and autocephalous church."[12] In doing so, it also shows the king of Persia that it no longer has any ties to the Roman West and thus hopes to avoid future persecution.

The fourth century can be considered the initial period of the establishment of the self-identity and full ecclesiastical autonomy of the Church of the East. The following century marked an important stage in the evolution of its identity and autonomy. In the short space of fifteen years three synods took place: the Synod of Isaac (410), the Synod of Yahballaha (420), and the Synod of Dadišo' (424). These three synods, which dealt with questions of jurisdiction, ecclesiastical discipline, and liturgical customs of the Church of

---

9. See Becker 2014; Herman 2014b.

10. See Brock 2008, appendix, 77–125.

11. See *Chronicle of Se'ert* 2, ed. and trans. Scher and Périer, PO 4.3, 220–23.

12. Le Coz 1995, 38.

the East, might thus be considered as the events that actually "founded" this church.

Why, then, is there still so much talk of a "Nestorian" Church, especially in reference to the theology of the Church of the East? The question is all the more puzzling when we read the following statement by the East Syriac theologian ʿAbdišoʿ of Nisibis (ʿAbdišoʿ bar Brika; Ebedjesus, d. 1318) in his 1298 work entitled *The Pearl*:

> [East Syriac Christians] never changed their faith and preserved it as they had received it from the apostles, and they are called Nestorians unjustly, especially since Nestorius was not their patriarch and they did not understand his language.[13]

To summarize a rather complex question, we could say that the "Nestorianization" of the Church of the East took place only in the second half of the fifth century in reaction to the Council of Ephesus (431) and the Council of Chalcedon (451), the position of Ephesus being in opposition to that of Nestorius (patriarch of Constantinople, r. 428–31).[14] The Church of the East wanted to remain faithful to Antiochene theology and regarded the Alexandrian theological position as too radical. For this same reason, the Church of the East also opposed the Christology of the West Syriac Church, improperly called Jacobite, from the name of its "founder" Jacob Baradaeus, bishop of Edessa (r. 543–78). Barṣauma, metropolitan bishop of Nisibis (d. ca. 491–96), was mainly responsible for this "Nestorianization." It should also be noted, however, that the position taken by the Church of the East with regard to the Second Synod of Seleucia-Ctesiphon in 486, which was markedly dyophysite[15] in character, should be interpreted as a response to the political developments taking place between the Byzantine and Persian empires.[16] In short, the great breaks that occurred after the councils of Ephesus and Chalcedon were generated less by theological disagreements than by terminological and cultural misunderstandings, which were in turn aggravated by political rivalries.

---

13. ʿAbdišoʿ of Nisibis, *The Pearl* 3.4, in Mai 1825–38, 10 (pars II): 329 (text), 354 (trans.).

14. About the theological position of Nestorius, see Dickens 2020b.

15. The term dyophysitism, whose adherents are called dyophysites, refers to the doctrine that Jesus Christ has two natures, divine and human.

16. About the Christology of the Church of the East, see Brock 1999.

8   A HISTORY OF ENCOUNTERS

Throughout the sixth century and until the Arab conquest of Persia and the death of the last Sasanian ruler Yazdgird III (r. 632–51), the Church of the East was further consolidated. Internally, the catholicos Mar Aba I (r. 540–52) promoted a radical administrative and disciplinary reform by establishing new rules for the spiritual and intellectual formation of the clergy, the election of bishops, and the administration of eparchies and parishes. This reform was accompanied by the reform of monastic life carried out by Abraham of Kaškar (d. 586).[17] The church thus became more firmly established throughout Persia and intensified its efforts to expand outward.[18]

The first administrative action was the constitution of the so-called "interior" ecclesiastical provinces. They corresponded to the great administrative divisions of the Sasanian kingdom, which extended to present-day Iraq and to the regions of northwestern Iran immediately east of the Tigris. To these were soon added the so-called "exterior" ecclesiastical provinces, which were created and given their own bishops in the mission territories to the East as Christian communities continued to increase in number.

It is difficult to determine the exact number of these exterior ecclesiastical provinces at any given period of time. Some provinces were created and then disappeared. Others had metropolitans with multiple titles, indicating that they had jurisdiction over more than one province. Some had two different metropolitan centers, and still others were created for nomadic populations and therefore, in addition to having an itinerant episcopate, did not have well-defined sees. In this situation of permanent evolution, it is almost impossible to get an exact picture of the administrative organization of the Church of the East, all the more so in the period when missionary expansion became more intense.[19]

Syriac and Arabic historiographic, epistolary, and canonical sources offer important information about these exterior ecclesiastical provinces. For example, the canonical sources include synodal acts that are rich in information about the administrative situation of the provinces themselves, providing data on the dioceses, their hierarchy, and their administrative centers. From these sources we know that between the fifth and sixth centuries, the first

---

17. See Chialà 2005; Jullien, Florence 2008; Van Rompay 2011.

18. Reference works on the spread of Christianity in the territory that the Syriac chronicles call Bet Parsaye (the lands of the Persians) are the following: Labourt 1904; Fiey 1979; Chaumont 1988. Also useful are the summaries offered by Asmussen 1962; Brock 1982; Asmussen 1983; Widengren 1984; Rist 1996; Panaino 2010; Walker 2012; Poggi 2015; Jullien, Christelle 2019.

19. See Le Coz 1995, 235.

two provinces of Fars were created in the heart of Sasanian Iran and included the islands of the Persian Gulf and Bet Qaṭraye, that is, the eastern coast of the Arabian Peninsula. At this same time the province of Khorasan in the northeast of present-day Iran included the important centers of Nišabur, Merv, and Herat.[20] Shortly thereafter came the provinces of Segestan (south of Khorasan), Bet Madaye (the lands of the Medes) and, nearby, Bet Lašpar (the future Kurdistan). During the first half of the seventh century, the expansion of the Church of the East eastward led to the subsequent creation of the provinces of Bactria (today's northern Afghanistan), Sogdiana (with Samarkand as the metropolitan see), India, and China.[21] There are those who speculate about a later and further outreach of the mission of the Church of the East from China to Korea and Japan. The evidence for these claims, however, is very limited and open to doubt.[22]

The Islamic conquest of Persia certainly contributed to a further acceleration of the diaspora toward Central Asia, India, and East Asia. With the Islamic advance, in fact, the secular political fragmentation of the Central Asian kingdoms ended, and "the missionary work could regain momentum thanks to the unification, under Islam, of the trade routes. Monks, priests, and bishops accompanied the traders to the Far East."[23] The surrounding religious environment, which gradually became Islamic, would later become an obstacle to the spread of Christianity in Central Asia and to the relations of the more distant Christian communities with Seleucia-Ctesiphon, the center of the Church of the East. Another factor of the eastward expansion of Christianity was the missionary drive within the Church of the East that grew more intense from the eighth century onward and was better organized. The main animator of this dynamism was the catholicos Timothy I (r. 780–823), whose long patriarchate saw the various missionary enterprises of the Church of the East reach their apogee.[24]

---

20. On the important Christian community of Herat, which became a metropolitan see in 585, see Fiey 1990.

21. See Dauvillier 1948; Fiey 1993. This work will not deal with Syriac Christianity in India, a tradition that has had its own independent history, is still alive today, and has been the subject of many studies over time. The complex question of the creation of a metropolitan see in China will be dealt with in detail (see pp. 73, 86).

22. See Gordon 1914; Toepel and Chung 2004; Toepel 2005, 2009; Morris 2015a, 2015b, 2016; 2017, 255–64.

23. Fiey 1995a, 151.

24. On the figure of Catholicos Timothy I, see Tisserant 1946; Berti 2009; Bundy 2011. On the missionary policy of this patriarch, see Berti 2006; Platt 2016.

The metropolitans of the exterior ecclesiastical provinces were the major players in expanding the missionary activity of the Church of the East. In the *Book of Governors*, Thomas of Marga (ninth century) stresses that the main task of the metropolitan was precisely to be "shepherd and teacher to the barbarian nations . . . into whose country none of the preachers and evangelists of the kingdom of heaven had gone since the time of the apostles until the present."[25] A letter from Timothy I, dated 792/93, bears witness to this work of evangelization:

> For behold, in all of the lands of Babel [Baghdad], Pars [Persia] and Athur [Assyria], and in all of the eastern lands and amongst Bet Hinduwaye [the Indians or the lands of the Indians] and indeed amongst Bet Ṣinaye [the Chinese or the lands of the Chinese], amongst Bet Tuptaye [the Tibetans or the lands of the Tibetans] and likewise amongst Bet Ṭurkaye [the Turks or the lands of the Turks] and in all of the domains under this patriarchal throne—this [throne] of which God commanded that we be its servants and likewise its ministers—that one who is this hypostasis—who is from eternity, without increase, who was crucified on our behalf—is proclaimed, indeed in different and diverse lands and races and languages.[26]

According to Timothy's testimony, Indians, Chinese, Turks, and even Tibetans are people for whom the missionaries of the Church of the East were made servants and ministers by God. Unfortunately, very little is known about evangelization in the area of the Tibetan Empire, whose borders were much larger than those of present-day Tibet.[27] Some especially valuable information is provided by a letter of 795–98 addressed to Sergius, Metropolitan of Elam, that speaks of the intention of Patriarch Timothy to consecrate a metropolitan for Tibet: "The Spirit has anointed in these days a metropolitan for Bet Ṭurkaye and we are also preparing to anoint another one for Bet Tuptaye."[28]

---

25. Thomas of Marga, *The Book of Governors* 5.4, ed. and trans. Budge, 1: 260 (text), 2: 479 (trans.).

26. Timothy I, *Letters* 41 (to the monks of the Monastery of Mar Maron), in Bidawid 1956, 36 (text); Dickens 2010, 118 (trans.).

27. For a more detailed account of the Christian presence in Tibet in the first millennium, see Dauvillier 1941, 1950; Lalou 1957; Uray 1983, 1987; Fiey 1987; Zhang Yun 2017.

28. Timothy I, *Letters* 47 (to Sergius), ed. Braun, CSCO 74, 308; trans. Dickens 2010, 119.

The route we are interested in following more closely is the one that began in Merv, passed through Samarkand and Taškent (Sogdiana), and then continued along the high route of the Silk Road to arrive at Turfan, the gateway to China.[29]

The importance of Merv as the entry to Asia is due to the fact that it was the most likely starting point for the missions to the East. According to tradition, Baršabba was the evangelizer and the first bishop of Merv in the second half of the fourth century, although it is by no means certain that the two historical figures behind the name of Baršabba, namely, the first convert to Christianity in the city of Merv and its first bishop, are one and the same person.[30] The city very soon became an episcopal see (the bishop of Merv was already present at the Synod of Dadišoʿ in 424) and was then elevated to a metropolitan see. Various Syriac and Arabic chronicles contain stories about the conversion of Turkish people by various metropolitans of Merv.[31] There were also monastic communities near the city.[32] From here Christianity crossed the Oxus River and entered Transoxiana, reaching the oases of Bukhara and Samarkand, where it came into contact with Turks and Sogdians.

As far as the Turkish-Mongolian populations are concerned, some Hephthalite tribes appear to have been the first converts to Christianity. Around 549 the Hephthalite Huns, a people originally from the Altai Mountains who founded a great empire in Transoxiana and Bactria between the fifth and sixth centuries, asked for a bishop, and the catholicos Mar Aba I responded favorably.[33] The historian Theophylact Simocatta (seventh century) informs us that, around 570, some prisoners belonging to the tribe of the Turks had a cross painted on their forehead as a sign of protection.[34] It is also known that a *qaghan* of the Western Turks, most probably the Qarluqs,[35] was converted to the Christian faith. The catholicos Timothy I, in a letter to

---

29. A brief overview can be found in Nikitin 1984; Žukova 1994; Klein 1995; Gillman and Klimkeit 1999, 205–63; Borbone 2015b; Dickens 2015.

30. See Fiey 1973, 81; Brock 1995.

31. See Mingana 1925, 305–6, 308–11; Koshelenko, Bader, and Gaibov 1995.

32. On the history of Christianity in Merv, see Fiey 1979, 75–87; Hunter 1996, 131–34.

33. See *History of Mar Aba* 37, in Bedjan 1895, 266–69 (text); Braun 1915, 217–18 (trans.).

34. See Theophylact Simocatta, *History* 5.10, ed. Bekker, 225; trans. Whitby and Whitby, 146–47. See also Nau 1914, 245. About Christianity among the Hephthalites, see Tezcan, Mehmet 2020.

35. See Dickens 2015, 127–32.

the monks of the Monastery of Mar Maron, writes that the king of the Turks, with almost all his country, had abandoned "the godless error from antiquity," asking that a metropolitan be sent to his country. His request was granted.

> For behold, even in our days—prior to these ten years that I have been entrusted with the service of the administration of the church, for even now I have been thirteen years more or less in this service—the king of the Ṭurkaye [Turks], with more or less all of his territory, has left the godless error from antiquity, for he has become acquainted with Christianity by the operation of the great power of the Messiah, that by which all are subject to him. And he has asked us in his writings how he might appoint a metropolitan for the territory of his kingdom. This also we have done through [i.e., with the help of] God.[36]

In general, it can be said that the rule of the Western Turks over Central Asia in the sixth and seventh centuries greatly facilitated communication and the exchange of goods, ideas, and religious faiths, including Christianity, from one part of Asia to the other. Various sources attest to the presence of Christians among the Qirghiz, Qarluq, and Qangli Turks from the ninth to the eleventh centuries.[37]

As for the Sogdians, an eastern Iranian people, their role as diffusers of Christianity in Asia is closely linked to their early eastward migration from Sogdiana, their land of origin (broadly located in present-day Uzbekistan), to China.[38] Between the fourth and eighth centuries they controlled the overland trade routes between Merv and Chang'an (the Chinese capital) and between Gilgit (the upper Indus Valley) and India. It is very probable that they actively participated in maritime trade with Ceylon, Southeast Asia, and Guangzhou (Canton).[39] For a few centuries, the Sogdians acted as intermediaries between each of three cultural worlds—the Iranian, the Chinese, and the Indian—and it was precisely as intermediaries that they

---

36. Timothy I, *Letters* 41 (to the monks of the Monastery of Mar Maron), in Bidawid 1956, 46; Dickens 2010, 119 (trans.).

37. See Marazzi 1999, 269; Hunter 2002; Ōsawa 2017.

38. See Rong 2000a; La Vaissière and Trombert 2005; La Vaissière 2006.

39. A reference work on the Sogdians is La Vaissière 2005. See also Semenov 1996a; Sims-Williams 1996; Yoshida 1996; Skaff 2003; Rong 2018.

played a decisive role in the eastward spread not only of goods but also of religious doctrines.[40] At the same time that the Sogdians were migrating to the East, however, the Turks were advancing toward the West, with the result that the Sogdians came under the influence of the Turks sometime in the eighth and ninth centuries and were merged into the Turkish population, a development that is demonstrated by the name the Syriac sources of this period gave to Sogdiana: Bet Ṭurkaye, "the lands of the Turks." Nonetheless, the cultural heritage of Sogdiana remained strong and influenced many customs, personal names, and even the Old Turkic alphabet.

A lack of sufficiently informative historical sources makes it very difficult to reconstruct the history of the Christian community in Sogdiana. The exact timeline of the dissemination of Christianity in Sogdiana cannot be set out for certain, but in all probability it began in the fifth or sixth century. As suggested by its geographical location as well as by the material evidence datable to the earliest period, the principal starting point for Christian missions moving eastward from Persia into Sogdiana was the city of Merv in Khorasan. In addition, Herat and Balkh probably played an important role in the transmission of Christianity into Sogdiana from the South, although material evidence for this is limited.[41] However, by the sixth and seventh centuries Christianity was already well established in Sogdiana, which appears to correspond to the elevation of Samarkand, the capital city of Sogdiana, to a metropolitan see. The Syriac and Arabic primary sources disagree as to when this actually took place, pointing to a period between the fifth and the eight centuries.[42]

The evangelization of Sogdiana was accompanied by a progressive and evermore extensive translation of Christian texts into Sogdian.[43] Unfortunately, no Christian text in this Middle Iranian language has been discovered within Sogdiana. However, significant Christian archaeological evidence has been found in this region.[44] Even though the dominant religion in Sogdiana was Zoroastrianism,[45] the archaeological material found there, which dates back

---

40. The religious plurality of the Sogdian merchants is well attested in the colonies they established in the Chinese Empire (see Grenet 2007).

41. See Ashurov 2013, 22.

42. See Colless 1986, 51–52.

43. See Tremblay 2001, 56–65.

44. See pp. 19–21.

45. See Sims-Williams 2000; Mode 2003; Grenet 2006–10; Shenkar 2017.

only to the seventh and eighth centuries, testifies to a rather important position of Christianity in Sogdian society.[46] In particular, numismatic finds (coins with Christian iconography, mainly crosses) indicate that during the seventh and eighth centuries Christianity was fully integrated in the established socioeconomic fabric of Sogdian society.[47]

The evangelization of a part of the Sogdian population played a strategically decisive role in the missionary work of the Church of the East. The geographical position of Sogdiana, land of merchants, favored economic exchanges along the caravan routes that connected Persia to Central and Eastern Asia, and its geographic and economic position allowed it to become a new base for Christianity's further expansion to the East. The Sogdian merchants, traveling from Samarkand eastward and establishing their colonies as far as the Chinese Empire, brought Christianity to the Semireč'e region (the "Seven Rivers land," east of Sogdiana) around the eighth century, and to Eastern Turkestan, where it probably became consolidated with the vigorous policy of missionary expansion that characterized the patriarchate of Timothy I.

Kašgar, an important commercial center, must have been chosen as a convenient base for the ecclesiastical administration of the surrounding areas because of its strategic location. The jurisdiction of the city extended over a number of Christian centers that surrounded it. Among them was the oasis of Turfan to the north, dotted with Christian sites such as Qočo, where the ruins of a Christian church were found; Shuipang near Bulayïq, where in 1905 an expedition led by Albert von Le Coq (1860–1930)[48] discovered a library—probably part of a monastic settlement—with fragments of Christian literature in various Central Asian languages (mostly Sogdian and Syriac); and finally Toyoq, Astana, and Qurutqa, where some other Christian fragments were found.

The presence of an eighth- to tenth-century Christian community in Dunhuang, further to the east, will be mentioned in the following chapter in connection with the expansion of Christianity in China. At this point, I would simply stress that this Christian community also seems to have been closely linked to the presence of Sogdians.[49]

---

46. See Naymark 2001, 81–85.

47. See Ashurov 2013, 61–106; 2018.

48. On the expeditions made by various European countries to Central Asia (Chinese Turkestan) in the first quarter of the twentieth century, there is the lively account of Hopkirk 1980.

49. See pp. 113–14.

The Church of the East from Persia to China

In summary, therefore, "it is natural that these close relations with the Turks and the Sogdians contributed to a considerable expansion of the Christian presence not only in Central Asia but also in East Asia."[50] It is not possible, however, to conclude this summary without mentioning the presence, in the first millennium, of communities from two other eastern Christian churches—the West Syriac and the Melkite—which followed the steps of the Church of the East from Persia to the East.[51]

The sources do not provide much information about the presence of West Syriac communities in Persia and Central Asia, and there are few studies that treat of them.[52] It is certain, however, that in the first half of the seventh century some communities settled in the most distant regions of the Persian Empire. The historian Grigorios bar ʿEbroyo (Barhebraeus, 1225/26–86) and the *Chronicle of Seʿert* report that in the seventh century each of the regions of Khorasan and Segestan, with the centers of Herat, Aprah (Farah), and Zarang, had West Syriac bishops.[53] In the ninth century Herat became a metropolitan see, a sign that the West Syriac community present there had to be significant. This is confirmed by the concern of the East Syriac patriarch Timothy I, who wrote a letter asking for someone with rhetorical skills whom he could send to the metropolitan see of Herat precisely because of the presence of West Syrians in that city: "Send me that young rhetorician, perhaps I will make him metropolitan of Harew [Herat], in fact there are Severians there, and you need a strenuous fighter."[54]

In the first millennium, the West Syriac Church does not seem to have expanded any further. Apart from isolated cases of merchants who belonged to this church and who traveled along the Silk Road, ecclesiastical organization seems to have stopped at the borders of Khorasan and present-day Afghanistan. It was only later, in the Mongolian period, that this church expanded further to the east, an expansion to which Marco Polo also bears witness.[55]

---

50. Haussig 1979, 181.

51. A good summary can be found in Sims-Williams 1992a, 531.

52. A comparative chronological study of the creation of the see of metropolitans and bishops of the East Syriac and West Syriac churches is Hunter 1992.

53. See Fiey 1973, 96–102.

54. Timothy I, *Letters* 25 (to Sergius), ed. and trans. Braun, CSCO 74, 141–42 (text); CSCO 75, 96 (trans.). Severians refers to the followers of Severus the Great, patriarch of Antioch and head of the Syriac Orthodox Church from 512 until his death in 538.

55. See Dauvillier 1956b.

16 A HISTORY OF ENCOUNTERS

We are better informed about the Melkites.[56] They spread throughout the Sasanian Empire thanks to their commercial activities and because of prisoners who were deported to Persia during the frequent wars between the Byzantine and Persian empires. New cities were even founded for these prisoners, and they were often accompanied by their bishops.[57] Among the deportees and the "Greek" merchants (called *rūm*) there were certainly also some Melkites who intentionally or by the mere fact of their presence spread Christianity in Central Asia.[58] In Khorasan there were undoubtedly Melkite communities. In fact, according to the Arab historian al-Bīrūnī (973–after 1050), Merv was the seat of a Melkite metropolitan.[59]

There is probably a direct link between these ancient Christian presences in the region and the creation, already in the Sasanian era,[60] of the catholicosate of Rumagird ("city of *rūm*," Romagyris in Greek) located in Čač, the region of Sogdiana around Taškent.[61] This hypothesis seems more plausible than that which, on the basis of the information reported in the Arabic *Life of the Melkite Patriarch of Antioch Christopher* (d. 967) by Ibrahīm ibn Yuḥannā, explains that the origin of this catholicosate was prompted by the transfer of the Melkite colony of Ctesiphon and its alleged catholicos to distant Transoxiana around 762, when the caliph al-Manṣūr (r. 754–75) destroyed Ctesiphon and ordered the building of Baghdad.[62]

The sources of most of our knowledge of Melkites in Central Asia at that time come from Sogdiana and Khorasan. The evidence for a Melkite community in Chinese Central Asia is rather meager and not supported by archaeological and documentary evidence.[63] In this respect, two Sogdian fragments

---

56. Melkites (from the Syriac *malkā*, "king") are those Christians included in the patriarchates of Alexandria, Antioch, and Jerusalem who accepted the Council of Chalcedon and, consequently, the directives of the Byzantine court.

57. See Jullien, Christelle 2006.

58. See Dauvillier 1953; Nasrallah 1975, 1976, 1977; Parry 2012b.

59. See Abū Rayḥān Muḥammad Bīrūnī, *The Remaining Traces of Past Centuries* 15, ed. Sachau, 289; trans. Sachau, 283: "The residence of the *metropolita* of the Melkites in Khurasan is Marw." See also Messina 1952.

60. This is testified by the seal of the Sasanian era, preserved in the Bibliothèque nationale de France in Paris, of a "great catholicos" of Central Asia (see Fiey 1995b).

61. See Fiey 1977; Klein 1999.

62. See Ibrahīm ibn Yuḥannā, *Life of the Melkite Patriarch of Antioch Christopher* 2, ed. and trans. Zayat, 20–25. See also Edelby 1952; Nasrallah 1983.

63. See Parry 2016.

containing parts of Psalm 33 (32 in the numbering of the Septuagint) are of particular interest. On one fragment, the opening words of the psalm are written in Greek. This piece of evidence, which was found in Bulayïq (Turfan) and is dated to the eighth or ninth century, could be a product of the Melkite community in Sogdiana. It probably does not indicate significant Melkite presence in the Turfan oasis, which would be highly unlikely.[64]

At the end of this brief overview of Christian history in Central Asia, it is important to point out that the mediation and political influence of the Chinese Tang dynasty, which extended, directly or indirectly, over many of the Central Asian kingdoms, played an important, indeed decisive, role in the eastward expansion of Christianity. The cosmopolitan outlook of the Tang, their attraction to the exotic, and the religious tolerance manifested in their imperial policies improved contacts and communications in Eurasia, which reached their peak during the seventh to the tenth centuries and created an international sociopolitical climate that made this period a *kairos* for the encounter between cultures and religions in Central and Eastern Asia.[65]

Christian Archaeological Traces in Asia in the First Millennium

For the reconstruction of the religious history of Central Asia, archaeological findings are just as important as literary documentation.[66] Archaeological traces of the existence of Christianity in Central and Eastern Asia in the first millennium offer clues about the typology and organization of the Christian presence that was established in the vast territory between Persia and China (see figure 1.2).[67]

At the same time, as has been said, "to speak of Christian or Paleo-Christian archaeology in Central Asia may seem a bit excessive."[68] In fact, systematic research in this field is still rather sparse and is hindered by numerous

---

64. See Sims-Williams 2004, 2011b.

65. See Fairbank and Twitchett 1979; Lewis 2009; Hansen 2018.

66. See Jettmar 2003.

67. See Lala Comneno 1995, 1997. The following overview is mainly based on Lala Comneno's studies, and I refer to them for an exhaustive bibliography, including also a great deal of material in Russian. For a comprehensive survey of the archaeological evidence relevant to the question of the history of Christianity in Persia, Central Asia, and Chinese Turkestan, see also Gaibov and Košelenko 2002; Borbone 2013.

68. Lala Comneno 1998, 705.

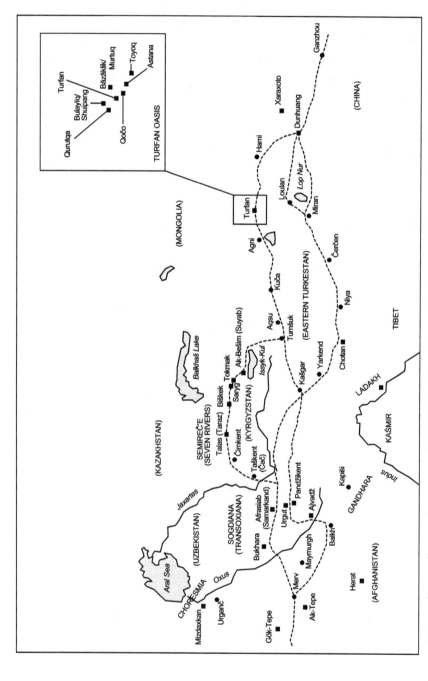

Figure 1.2 The northern and the southern routes of the Silk Road from Merv to Dunhuang, with the sites where Christian archaeological remains and literary documents were found (■).

difficulties, for instance, the lack of interdisciplinary studies; the different ethnic and political structures of the states in which the territory of Central Asia is divided today; the dispersion of documents; the fact that local residents have scarce interest in Christian archaeological remains in Central Asia; the non-specialized nature of some of the research done in the past, and the lack of interest of Western scholars who are more attracted by philological than archaeological surveys and more focused on a later historical period (Turkish and Mongolian Christianity).[69] However, in the former Soviet republics, the last thirty years have seen a revival of interest among scholars regarding Syriac Christianity in Central Asia.

This "patrimony without heirs," as Maria Adelaide Lala Comneno describes it, includes ruins of religious buildings (churches and monasteries, built of unfired bricks and therefore not very long-lasting); tombs and tombstones; crosses, reliefs, and graffiti with crosses, some of them accompanied by inscriptions; wall paintings and decorated fabrics; small tools, mostly in fragments; objects for liturgical use (jugs, censers, ossuaries); and coins with crosses. The Christian designation of some monuments and archaeological findings remains controversial to this day, and for reasons of brevity, we will not address this issue.

In the Merv region, several buildings have come to light, but it is uncertain if they were Christian.[70] The *naus*—a building intended to house ossuaries— of Mizdaxkan, dating from the end of the seventh century and the first half of the eighth, is the only building unanimously identified as Christian. The ossuaries found inside it have crosses painted on them. From this same area of Merv we also have a fragment of a jug with an engraved cross, a mold for crosses, terracotta Sasanian seals with Christian subjects (found in Ak-Tepe) from the fifth to the seventh centuries, and fragments of plates and medallions with crosses (found in Gök-Tepe).

From Sogdiana comes abundant material that is both varied and interesting.[71] Many coins with crosses come from Bukhara, Afrasiab (the pre-Mongolian Samarkand), and Pandžikent. From Afrasiab there is a small bronze necklace cross; a terracotta ossuary with at least three deeply hollowed-out crosses; and a Sasanian-type fabric, made in Sogdiana, with a biblical subject (the sacrifice of Isaac).

---

69. See ibid., 705–11.

70. See Hauser 2007.

71. See Semenov 1996b.

From Urgut comes a bronze censer with six scenes from the Gospel and an inscription in Syriac, dated to the eighth or ninth century. Urgut, a center located about thirty-five kilometers from Samarkand, is certainly the richest in archaeological finds in the Sogdian region.[72] Excavations conducted in the years 2004 to 2007 have unearthed a church—more likely a parish church than a monastic church—built according to the architectural traditions of the Church of the East. An analysis of the structural materials indicate that it was built in the late seventh century and then used from the eighth to the thirteenth centuries.[73] The Christian site of Qizil-qiya, located not far from the remains of this church, has a significant number of inscriptions in Syriac engraved on a rock wall. Many of these inscriptions are accompanied by a cross and include a person's name, sometimes followed by ecclesiastical titles, thus suggesting that pilgrims visited the site.[74]

A monastic complex of dozens of small rooms built of stone that probably dates from the sixth or seventh century has also been discovered at Ajvadž. From Pandžikent, we have an *ostrakon* dated to the first half of the eighth century, that is, a fragment of a vessel with two verses in Syriac taken from Psalm 1 and Psalm 2 and thought to be a Sogdian writing exercise;[75] a bronze necklace cross; and a fragment of a jug with an engraved cross. In Pandžikent, numerous wall paintings have also been preserved. The subjects of some of them suggest possible Christian influences. According to Aleksandr Naymark, the iconography of the agricultural deity that is the main figure in the painting of a harvest festival is modeled on the way Christian art presents Joseph ordering grain to be placed in the bags of his brothers (see Gen. 42:25), but now adapted to the artistic tradition of Sogdiana.[76] The conclusions in this regard are absolutely provisional, but in summary it can be said that on the basis of the evidence of East Syriac Christianity that has come to light throughout Sogdiana, it is possible to put forward a new interpretation of the wall paintings that is not entirely without foundation, namely, that the social and economic importance achieved by the followers of this religion during the seventh and eighth centuries is reflected in the choice of the subjects of these paintings.[77]

---

72. See Savchenko 2008.

73. See Savchenko and Dickens 2009; Ashurov 2013, 111–39.

74. See Savchenko 1996; Tardieu 1999; Dickens 2017.

75. See Paykova 1979.

76. See Naymark 2001, 345–88.

77. See Lala Comneno 1997, 39.

The analysis of the coins found in this site leads to the same conclusion: "The numismatic material certainly testifies for the greater role of Christianity in the religious life of early Medieval Sogdiana."[78] In the seventh or eighth century, a dynasty that ruled over one of the principalities of the Bukhara region even chose the cross as its distinctive symbol and had it placed on coins.[79] It is therefore reasonable to conclude this survey on the archaeological evidences for Christianity in Sogdiana with the words of Barakatullo Ashurov:

> When the Church of the East was planted in Sogdiana, it had to display conformity with its local socio-cultural and political setting in a tangible way. . . . Material culture (architecture and small objects) vividly illustrates the integration of Christianity into Sogdian society through a material expression that was both locally produced and imported. . . . These objects served as a means of visual identity for Christians in the multireligious milieu of Sogdiana.[80]

East of Sogdiana, in the region historically known as the "Seven Rivers land" (Semireč'e, in today's northern Kyrgyzstan and southern Kazakhstan), the heartland of the Qarluq kingdom, there is also significant archaeological evidence for the presence of Christianity in the first millennium.[81] In the cemeteries of Tokmak and Biškek more than five hundred tombstones with inscriptions in Syriac and Turkic have been found, but their dating is rather late (between the ninth and fourteenth centuries).[82] In Taraz (ancient Talas) and Krasnaja Rečka (ancient Saryg), the presence of Christianity is confirmed by the discovery of some Christian tombs dating from the ninth and tenth centuries; fragments of vases with crosses; inscriptions of Christian texts in Syriac and Sogdian; a silver jug, perhaps for liturgical use, with five impressions in the shape of a cross (found in Biškek); a plate engraved with biblical scenes from the Book of Joshua and inscriptions in Syriac; and a mortar with dove and cross, dated to the ninth or tenth century.

---

78. Naymark 2001, 295.

79. See ibid., 178–295.

80. Ashurov 2013, 151. See also Ashurov 2015a, 2019.

81. See Klein 2000.

82. The bibliography is extensive but, since these materials concern a historical period subsequent to the one dealt with in this work, they will not be mentioned here. For a summary, see Thacker 1966–67 (with an extensive bibliography in Russian); Klein 2004b; Dickens 2009c, 14–20; 2016b.

The most interesting archaeological discovery in this region of the Seven Rivers is certainly a building in Ak-Bešim (Suyab in medieval Arab sources) that is unequivocally identified as a church. The complex, which also includes Christian tombs and dates back to the eighth century, consists of a small chapel with two side rooms, at the entrance of which is a large portico. More recently, a second church whose main structure dates back to the tenth century was brought to light. Among the finds of the site are clay objects stamped with imprinted "Nestorian" type crosses, a jade cross, a ceramic plate with a cross, and several inscriptions in Sogdian and Turkic whose possible Christian attribution has yet to be ascertained. Especially interesting is a bronze cross with a Sogdian inscription.[83] The discovery of this second church and of the objects found there is proof that Christianity in the region of the Seven Rivers flourished continuously between the eighth and fourteenth centuries.[84]

In Eastern Turkestan, as already mentioned, the ruins of a church in Qočo (Turfan oasis) were discovered at the beginning of the twentieth century.[85] The wall paintings are especially interesting, and the most famous of these is what is commonly interpreted as a Palm Sunday scene that is dated from the ninth to tenth century (see figure 1.3).[86]

The painting portrays three orants, each holding a green branch. Two of them are male figures and wear a Central Asian or Uighur type of cloak, while a third is a female figure coiffed according to the Chinese fashion in vogue during the Tang dynasty. The three orants are turned toward a figure, most probably a priest, with Iranian features who is larger in size and who holds a cup in his right hand and a censer in his left. Clearly visible is the leg of an animal (a horse or a donkey) that presumably carried a Christ of considerable size, rendered in the so-called hierarchical perspective. Another painting, lost and known only through drawings, depicts a fragment of a haloed priest on horseback who holds a long staff with a "Nestorian" cross on top.[87]

Judging by the many texts on asceticism and the monastic life contained in the Sogdian manuscripts found in Bulayïq, on the outskirts of Turfan, there was

---

83. See Klein and Reck 2004.

84. See Semenov 2002; Klein 2004a.

85. See Chen Huaiyu 1999 (2012), 60–65.

86. This painting, 61 centimeters high and 67.5 centimeters wide, is now kept at the Museum für Asiatische Kunst, Berlin (MIK III 6911). It is reproduced in Le Coq 1913, plate 7 ("Wandbilder aus einer christlichen Tempel aus Chotscho").

87. See Parry 1996, p. 159 and fig. 7a, pp. 161–62 and fig. 9a; Chen Huaiyu 1999 (2012), 66–67; Mortari Vergara Caffarelli 2004, 15.

Figure 1.3 "Palm Sunday" (?), Christian wall painting from the ruins of a church in Qočo, Turfan (Xinjiang, China), 9th–10th century, Museum für Asiatische Kunst, Berlin.
(Source: Wikimedia Commons, <https://commons.wikimedia.org/wiki/File:Palm_Sunday_(probably),_Khocho,_Nestorian_Temple,_683-770_AD,_wall_painting_-_Ethnological_Museum,_Berlin_-_DSC01741.JPG>)

almost certainly a monastery on the Bulayïq site. Unfortunately, there are no archaeological findings or studies that can confirm this hypothesis.[88]

In 1908, the archaeologist Marc Aurel Stein (1862–1943) made another fascinating discovery in Dunhuang: a silk banner with a figure in ink and colors that is unfortunately greatly damaged (see figures 1.4 and 1.5).[89]

---

88. See Sims-Williams 1990b; Zhang Guangda and Rong Xinjiang 1998; Barbati 2015a, 92–97.

89. This hanging, 88 centimeters high and 55 centimeters wide, is now kept at the Asian Department of the British Museum in London (inventory no. 1919,0101,0.48). It is reproduced in Whitfield 1982–85, 1: plate 25. For a description, see Whitfield and Farrer 1990, 31, 33–34; Tang Li 2020a.

Figure 1.4 Silk banner with a figure in ink and colors from Dunhuang (Gansu, China), fragment, end of the 9th century, British Museum, London.
(© The Trustees of the British Museum)

Figure 1.5 Silk banner with a figure in ink and colors from Dunhuang (Gansu, China), end of the 9th century, British Museum, London, tentative restoration.

(Source: Saeki 1951, unnumbered page between 408 and 409)

The figure, represented according to Buddhist iconographic models of Central Asia and well attested to in Dunhuang, looks like a haloed bodhisattva in the gesture of argumentation (*vitarkamudrā*) who is adorned with jewels and Buddhist ornaments. Two minor features suggest that this painting dates from the end of the ninth century: the narrow flame border of the halo and the configuration of the mouth, which has a slight downward turn at the ends of the ink line between the lips. Unusual and surprising are the Western facial features (a fairly thick moustache and a slight beard), as well as the presence of a cross, each arm terminating in bead-like extensions, both in the headdress of the figure and hanging from the necklace he is wearing (like a pectoral cross). However, I do not believe these elements are sufficient to support the undoubted claim that "the figure is Christian in inspiration"[90] and that the portrait "was most probably an image of a saint or of a clergyman of a bishop level or above."[91] Rather, what we have here is a beautiful example of shared symbolism. The cross with arms of equal length, the halo, and the lotus flower are, in fact, symbols shared in the artistic representations of this period by Christians, Manichaeans, and Buddhists in Central Asia.[92] This figure also has very strong similarities with some Chinese Manichaean paintings depicting Jesus according to typically Buddhist iconographic canons, like the twelfth- or thirteenth-century "Buddha Jesus" from Southern China kept at the Zen Buddhist temple of Seiun-ji in Kofu, Japan (see figures 1.6 and 1.7).[93]

On the southern route of the Silk Road, a Christian cemetery was found in the area of Khotan (Yotkan).[94] According to information provided by Gardīzī, a Persian historian who lived in the first half of the eleventh century, there were two Christian churches there.[95] Ronald E. Emmerick does not exclude a priori the existence of Christian communities in Khotan, but

---

90. Parry 1996, 160.

91. Tang Li 2020a, 242.

92. See Klimkeit 1979.

93. See Izumi 2006; Gulácsi 2009.

94. Yotkan was the capital of the kingdom of Khotan (56–1006), an ancient Iranian Buddhist kingdom located on the branch of the Silk Road that ran along the southern edge of the Taklamakan Desert in the Tarim Basin (today's Xinjiang, China). The inhabitants of Khotan used Khotanese, an eastern Iranian language, and Prakrit, an Indo-Aryan language related to Sanskrit.

95. See Abū Saʿīd ʿAbd al-Ḥayy Gardīzī, *The Ornament of Histories*, ed. Ḥabībī, 270. See also Dauvillier 1948, 287.

Figure 1.6 "Buddha Jesus," Manichaean silk painting from Southern China, 12th–13th century, Seiun-ji, Kofu (Japan).
(Source: Gulácsi 2015, 418)

he has raised questions about the only presumed Christian literary testimony in Khotanese.[96]

Finally, the only archaeological evidence of a Christian presence in the region of historical Tibet is a few crosses carved on rock with inscriptions in Sogdian and other languages that were found near the village of Tangtse, in the area of Ladakh (a region of present-day Kaśmir, India), including one with the Sogdian word *'Yšw* (*Išu*), "Jesus" (see figure 1.8), and a longer one dated to 825/26. These crosses and inscriptions do not necessarily imply the

---

96. See Emmerick 1991.

Figure 1.7 "Buddha Jesus," Manichaean silk painting from Southern China, 12th–13th century, Seiun-ji, Kofu (Japan), detail of the golden cross (Cross of Light) that rests on a lotus pedestal in the left hand of the figure.
(Source: Gulácsi 2015, 418)

presence of a settled community of Christians in Tangtse. They do suggest, however, that Christianity entered Tibet from Central Asia rather than from China, and was brought by merchants or monks who came to Tibet from Sogdiana along the southern route of the Silk Road.[97] These traces "can be viewed within the larger context of travelers' marks along the road, either as a general petition for success and protection on the journey or, within a more specifically Christian context, as an invocation of Christ's blessing."[98]

In conclusion, some brief general observations emerge from an examination of these findings. As far as religious buildings are concerned, the layout of the ruins that have been excavated show, on the one hand, a connection to Middle Eastern models. For example, the Mesopotamian model is quite

---

97. See Benveniste 1937–39, 502–5 ("L'inscription sogdienne de Ladakh") and plates III, IV, V; Sims-Williams 1993.

98. Mullen 2016, 80.

Figure 1.8 Sogdian Christian inscription with a "Nestorian" cross, 825/26, Tangtse (Ladakh, Kaśmir, India).
(© Christoph Baumer, 2006, *The Church of the East: An Illustrated History of Assyrian Christianity*, I. B. Tauris, an imprint of Bloomsbury Publishing Plc)

evident in the case of the eighth-century church of Ak-Bešim, a rectangular building with openings on the two long sides. The sanctuary is on the eastern side, and alongside it is the baptistery, which has access to the outside, as is typical of Mesopotamian basilicas.[99] The room at the end of the nave, on the other hand, with its indented cruciform layout, does not belong to the Middle Eastern architectural tradition and may have been modeled on a type of plan characteristic of Buddhist temples and *stūpa*,[100] or on the Sasanian architecture of Zoroastrian religious buildings.[101]

We know, in fact, that such Christian buildings in Central Asia were always built in multiethnic and multireligious settings. So, for example, in Ak-Bešim there was a Buddhist temple with a large clay statue of the seated Buddha that was built during the eighth century and then plundered.[102] A large *stūpa* and a sanctuary, probably dating from the second century,

---

99. See Hambis 1961, 127–28.

100. See Mortari Vergara Caffarelli 2004, 14.

101. See Naymark 2001, 308–9.

102. See Lala Comneno 1997, 41–42.

have also been found in Merv.[103] In several places in Central Asia and Eastern Turkestan, including Turfan, there had been a strong Manichaean presence for several centuries, and in these centers the followers of Mani had their places of worship.[104] Finally, the *naus* of Mizdaxkan, already referred to, was probably a burial place that was even shared by Zoroastrians and Christians. In these and similar situations, it is therefore understandable that "Nestorian architecture is open to the influence of local constructions."[105]

Still on the subject of Christian buildings, their location within the layout of Central Asian cities of pre-Islamic times is revealing. The inhabited centers of those territories were characterized by a tripartite division: the *arg* (a sort of citadel, the seat of power, located on a natural summit and defended by walls), the *shahrustan* (the zone of nobles, located at the foot of the citadel and surrounded by a wall), and the *rabad* (the zone of traders and craftsmen, a suburb without walls). Archaeological findings and literary sources indicate that Christian churches were located in the *rabad* or even outside the city, these areas being the most appropriate for Christians who must have belonged to the class of traders and had to be in contact with people from different backgrounds.[106]

Among the representations of Asian Christian iconography in these centuries, the most common is undoubtedly the cross, specifically the so-called "triumphal" or "jeweled" cross (*crux gemmata*), or the "Nestorian" and Armenian cross of the parousia, which is a cross without a corpus. Its arms, mostly equal in length, are wider at the extremities and often had three pearls at the ends.[107] This kind of cross is found from Mesopotamia to Tibet, from Sogdiana to China, from Mongolia to India. The local artists, however, would enrich the cross with elements derived from the particular symbolism of their own cultures.[108] Three beautiful examples of this kind of cross from China in the first millennium are the one engraved on the Xi'an stele of 781 (see

---

103. See Koshelenko 1966. On the Buddhist artistic and architectural finds in Sogdiana, see Compareti 2008. More generally, on Buddhist art in Central Asia, see Rhie 1999–2002; Mkrtyčev 2002.

104. See Lieu 2008.

105. Mortari Vergara Caffarelli 2004, 14.

106. See Lala Comneno 1997, 27, 42–43.

107. See Badwi 2006.

108. See Dauvillier 1956a; Hage 1995–96; Wang Xinggong 2011.

figure 3.3) and the two engraved on the Luoyang funerary pillar of 815 (see figures 3.5 and 3.6). The tombstones of the Yuan period found in the coastal city of Quanzhou are the most numerous and interesting examples of this artistic creativity.[109]

To give a general idea of a very complex and fragmentary state of affairs, we could say in conclusion that

> the form and symbolism of the art and inscriptions show clearly that the Church of the East was able to express Christian truth in the art-forms and imagery of central and east Asian cultures. . . . The examples mentioned thus far, graphically show both how early Asian Christianity became rooted in local cultural contexts and yet maintained distinctive Christian features.[110]

Christian Literature in the Languages of Central Asia

There is no doubt that the use of Syriac (one of the Eastern Aramaic dialects) as a liturgical language was, over the centuries, a unifying element between the different local ecclesial bodies and the headquarters of the Church of the East in Seleucia-Ctesiphon. There are, however, those who say that "documents dating from the third to the eleventh century of our era leave no doubt that the first liturgical language of the Church of the East . . . must have been Middle Persian, the language of the Sasanian Empire."[111]

In addition to the system of centralized jurisdiction and the nomination of metropolitans and bishops among the Persian clergy, the use of Syriac as a common liturgical language soon became an important and effective contributor to the cohesion of the Church of the East as it was expanding. However, if this church had not at the same time encouraged the translation of the Scriptures, parts of the liturgy, and religious literary works into the indigenous languages of the evangelized peoples, its expansion would most probably not have been as extensive, and it could not have taken on some of the cultural elements proper to the peoples it encountered, cultural elements that were

---

109. See Lieu et al. 2012.

110. England 1996, 137–38.

111. Cereti 2003, 195.

32   A HISTORY OF ENCOUNTERS

expressed primarily through the vehicle of language.[112] The stringent need for this work of translation and the tension it caused is succinctly captured in a passage from the Syriac *Life of John of Daylam*, fragments of which have also been preserved in Sogdian. The text deals with a controversy between Christians of Iranian and Syrian provenance with respect to the language that must be used for worship, one group arguing that native Sogdian Christians should be able to understand the liturgical services, the other invoking the prestige of the Syriac language.[113]

The use of Syriac as a liturgical language in mission lands was maintained for several centuries. In the Far East it is certainly still attested in the thirteenth century, when the Franciscan Willem van Rubroek wrote about the Christians of Cathay (Northern China) he met on his journey to the East in the years 1253–55, noting that "They recite their office and have the Holy Scriptures in Syriac, a language they do not know, so that they chant like the monks among us who know no [Latin] grammar."[114]

We have evidence of Syriac as a liturgical language in the early settlements of Christians at the eastern end of the Silk Road. Among the documents found in the library of the East Syriac monastery of Bulayïq, north of Turfan, there are said to be around five hundred fragments in Syriac. They probably range in date from the eighth and ninth to the thirteenth and fourteenth centuries. There are some biblical and hagiographical fragments, but most of the texts are liturgical,[115] for example, a bilingual baptismal rite in Syriac with Sogdian rubrics.[116] Interestingly enough, among the hagiographical texts there is a *Life of Saint George*, which was also translated into Sogdian and Uighur in Turfan.[117] One of the longest manuscripts, MIK III 45 (formerly C14), contains part of the *Penqita*. This book, which was later known as the *Ḥudrā*, is a liturgical miscellany that comprises the variable parts of the daily offices and eucharist, to which have been appended some occasional services of the

---

112. On the relationship between the use of Syriac as an ecclesiastical language and the adoption of local languages, see Hage 1978.

113. See Brock 1981, 150.

114. Willem van Rubroek, *The Journey to the Eastern Parts* 26.12, in Wyngaert 1929, 238 (text); trans. Jackson and Morgan, 163.

115. See Maróth 1991b; Brock 2011. For a catalogue of the fragments, see Hunter and Dickens 2014.

116. See Brock and Sims-Williams 2011.

117. See Maróth 1991a.

Church of the East, including the burial service. The sixty-one folios that have come down to us were part of a manuscript that probably consisted of about 270 folios. It was most likely written in Merv in the eighth to ninth century (specifically 771–884).[118] Among the Syriac fragments found in Bulayïq are also a few prayer-amulets whose physical size indicates that they came from pocket-sized handbooks.[119]

In contrast to the manuscripts from the Turfan area, only two fragments in Syriac, both of them liturgical, have so far come to light in Dunhuang, which is further east. One is a fragment of a Pauline Lectionary,[120] while the other is a fragment of a Psalter.[121] The Syriac liturgical and exorcistic fragments found in Xaraxoto (or Khara-Khoto, Inner Mongolia) are very likely from a later period (thirteenth or fourteenth century).[122]

While Syriac was the common liturgical language, significant Christian literature was soon produced in the local languages. Fragments in Middle Persian not only from Persia but also from the mission territories of India and China tell us that Persian was also used for a certain time outside Persia. The extreme scarcity of material in this language, however, leads us to think that in the exterior ecclesiastical provinces Persian was used only by Christians of Persian origin, and that it was not used as a liturgical language. As has been said, this does not mean that some parts of liturgical services (hymns, biblical readings, prayers) were not translated and recited in the local languages, including Persian. In Turfan, the concurrence of Christian fragments in Syriac, Sogdian, Middle Persian, and New Persian leads us to assume that there had been an evolution in the use of these idioms in the Christian liturgies celebrated in Central Asia:

> Since the Nestorian mission to the East derived from the Syrian Church in Iran, it is probable that the newly-founded Christian communities initially employed Syriac and Middle Persian in their liturgy, the latter

---

118. As such, MIK III 45 is probably the earliest extant Syriac manuscript on paper and can be considered to be the earliest extant exemplar of the *Ḥudrā*. See Hunter and Coakley 2017. See also Hunter 2012, 2014, 2016, 2020.

119. For an example, see Hunter 2013.

120. See Kaufhold 1996; Wu Qiyu 2003, 2011.

121. See Duan Qing 2000a, 2000b, 2001.

122. See Pigoulewsky 1935–36; Smelova 2015; Mutō 2010, 2012, 2013a, 2013b, 2016.

34   A HISTORY OF ENCOUNTERS

being gradually displaced by the successive local vernaculars, firstly Sogdian and ultimately New Persian.[123]

In any case, tiny Syriac-Pahlavi bilingual inscriptions on the seals of Christian officials of both literary and liturgical texts attest that Christians in Persia made use of Pahlavi, a Middle Iranian language that became the literary language of the Sasanian Empire.[124] Christian authors such as John Chrysostom in the fourth century and Theodoret of Cyrus in the fifth century inform us of the existence of a possible translation of the Bible (or parts thereof) into Persian in ancient times:

> Syrians, and Egyptians, and Indians, and Persians, and Ethiopians, and ten thousand other nations, translating into their own tongues the doctrines introduced by him [i.e., John the Evangelist], barbarians though they be, have learned to philosophize.[125]

> We bring to light the strength of the teachings of the apostles and the prophets, because all the countries under the sun are filled with their words. Hebrew was translated not only into Greek, but into Latin, Egyptian, Persian, Indian, Armenian, Schytian, Sarmatian, in short, in all the languages that all peoples have always used.[126]

Further evidence of the literary activity of Christians in the Persian language can be adduced. The catholicos Maʿna (r. 420) translated some Syriac works into Persian, and fifty years later, another Maʿna, the metropolitan of Širaz, composed some hymns (*madrāše*), discourses (*memre*), and antiphons (*ʿonyātā*) for liturgical use in Persian. The catholicos Acacius (Aqaq, r. 485–96) translated from Syriac a compendium of the Christian religion written by Elišaʿ bar Quzbaye for the Sasanian king Kawād I (r. 488–531). Finally, around the year 600, Job of Rev-Ardašir translated into Persian the spiritual writings of his master Abraham of Natpar and the monastic rules of Abraham the Great.[127]

---

123. Sims-Williams 1990a, 207.

124. See Gignoux 1980; Maggi 2003; Orsatti 2003; Gyselen 2006b.

125. John Chrysostom, *Homilies on the Gospel of John* 2.2, PG 59: 32; trans. Schaff, 6.

126. Theodoret of Cyrus, *Cure of the Greek Maladies* 5.66, ed. and trans. Canivet, 1: 248 (text), 249 (trans.).

127. See Tisserant 1931, 264.

The Church of the East from Persia to China 35

It is necessary, however, to look elsewhere than Iran to find concrete traces of Christian literary and epigraphic texts in Middle Persian. There are Pahlavi inscriptions on a mid-eighth-century processional cross found in Herat,[128] and on seven crosses found in Southern India (one from Mount Thomas in Mylapore near Madras, four from Kottayam, one from Travancore in Kerala, and one from Goa), as well as on a cross on a pillar in the ancient royal city of Mantota, the port of the capital Anunadhapura, in Sri Lanka.[129] These Indian crosses with inscriptions in Pahlavi, dated to the sixth to ninth centuries, are evidence of the privileged links between the Christian communities of Fars and those of South India. Until the eighth century, Indian bishops were under the jurisdiction of the metropolitan see of Rev-Ardašir in Fars.

From the site of the Christian monastery of Bulayïq in the Turfan oasis comes a fragment of a Middle Persian translation of the Syriac Psalter consisting of twelve pages written on both sides. The preserved folios contain parts of Psalms 94–99, 118, and 121–136, written in archaic cursive. The manuscript was probably written in the sixth or seventh century, making this fragment the oldest textual testimony of Pahlavi literature. The text contains Middle Persian translations of Syriac forms that are part of the canonical liturgical additions composed by the catholicos Mar Aba I. The translation is literal and there are numerous *hapax legomena* and neologisms.[130] At Bulayïq, fragments of Psalms 131–132 and 146–147 in New Persian (in Christian Sogdian script) dated to the eleventh century have also been found.[131] There are also two fragments of a pharmacological text in New Persian (in Syriac script), one of them probably coming from Toyoq.[132]

Among the languages of Central Asia, Sogdian had an especially important place in Christian literary works.[133] In fact, this eastern Middle Iranian language[134] was the language of communication in the culturally and linguistically plural world of Central Asia. From the fourth century it served as a

128. See Gignoux 2001b; Jullien, Christelle 2011.

129. See Gropp 1970; Gignoux 1995; Cereti, Olivieri, and Vazhuthanapally 2002; Cereti 2003; Tang Li 2014.

130. Edition and translation in Andreas 1933. For a description, see Asmussen 1964; Gignoux 1969; Shaked 1990; Gignoux 2002.

131. See Müller 1915; Sundermann 1974.

132. See Sims-Williams 2011b.

133. For a preliminary bibliography on Christian Sogdian literature, see Nicolini-Zani 2006a.

134. For a concise and comprehensive presentation of this language and its morphological and syntactic characteristics, see Sims-Williams 1989; Yoshida 2016. A Sogdian dialect, called

language of exchange for trade, and from the sixth century as the *lingua franca* of the administration along the northern route of the Silk Road. This situation lasted for several centuries until, with the progressive Turkification of the Sogdians, Turkic became the language of exchange in Central Asia around the tenth to the eleventh century. In manuscripts from Turfan we notice the disappearance of Sogdian in the eleventh century.[135]

As already mentioned, no Christian text in Sogdian has been found in the region of Sogdiana itself nor in the surrounding areas, but it is reasonable to think that a certain amount of Christian literature was produced here and then lost. Christian texts in Sogdian may have been among those referred to by the Franciscan friar Willem van Rubroek in his account of Christians in the region of Choresmia (Khwarazm), a territory bordering the southern course of the Oxus River. Writing in the thirteenth century, he says:

> This country used to be known as Organum [Urganč, the capital of Choresmia] and to have its own language and script [i.e., Sogdian]; but by this time it was entirely occupied by Turcomans [i.e., Muslim Turks]. Its script and language were habitually used by the Nestorians of these parts for their services and for writing their books.[136]

The Armenian historian Het'um, writing around 1307, also mentions a language that was used as a liturgical language by the Melkite Christians of Choresmia and that could be Sogdian:

> A group of Christians who are called Soldains [Sogdians?] live in those lands [of Choresima]. They have their own letters and language, believe as the Greeks do, and obey the patriarch of Antioch. At church they sing in a different manner and celebrate as the Greeks do, but their language is not Greek.[137]

Yaghnōbī, is still spoken today in the valley of the Yaghnab River, north of the Pamir (today's Tajikistan).

135. See Krippes 1991.

136. Willem van Rubroek, *The Journey to the Eastern Parts* 23.7, in Wyngaert 1929, 226; trans. Jackson and Morgan, 148.

137. Het'um, *Flower of Histories of the East* 4, in Kohler 1906, 124.

The fragments of Christian Sogdian literature that have come down to us, both in the Syriac script (nearly five hundred fragments) and in the Sogdian script (about fifty fragments), come from the oasis of Turfan, and almost all from the site of the monastery of Bulayïq.[138] Today, most of these documents are part of the collection of materials found in Turfan (*Turfansammlung*, Berlin-Brandenburgische Akademie der Wissenschaften) during the four German Turfan expeditions conducted between 1902 and 1914, notably the second expedition (1904–5) and the third expedition (1905–7).[139] The extant Sogdian Christian texts vary in size and composition. There are manuscripts containing a single work or a collection of thematically related texts, as well as manuscripts containing various unrelated texts. The original manuscripts are extremely fragmentary, and often all that remains is only a few dozen lines.[140] Significant portions of just one manuscript (E27, formerly C2), which contains fragments of fourteen texts, have come down to us.[141]

None of the texts is dated, nor are there any colophons, signatures, or place indications useful for dating. These texts are written in a variation of the Syriac *esṭrangela* script, with the addition of three supplementary letters. This writing system was not used for recording Buddhist or Manichaean texts and therefore is usually referred to as the Christian Sogdian script. Its orthography reflects quite faithfully the phonetic structure of Late Sogdian and does not display the archaizing features of other Sogdian scripts. Precisely because of the script and of some elements of the content, these texts are probably translations that can be dated with a good deal of certainty to sometime between the eighth and eleventh centuries.[142]

Among the elements that characterize Christian Sogdian are stylistic and lexical peculiarities arising from the need to translate the texts of the Christian

---

138. For a general overview, see Sachau 1905; Dickens 2009a, 2013b.

139. About the Turfan expeditions and the resultant Turfan collection in Berlin, see Akademienvorhaben Turfanforschung 2007. An exception is the Sogdian Christian fragment Ōtani 2497, which was found in Bulayïq during the first expedition (1902–4) led by the Japanese Ōtani Kōzui (1876–1948) and is now kept in the Ōtani collection at Ryukoku University, Kyoto (see Yoshida 2017).

140. For a catalogue of the fragments, see Sims-Williams 2012 and Reck 2018. See also Tremblay 2001, 207–15.

141. All known Christian Sogdian texts from Turfan have now been published. For those in Syriac script, reference editions are Sims-Williams 1985, 2014b, 2015, 2017, 2019. For those in Sogdian script, Reck 2018.

142. See Yakubovich 2011, 382.

tradition into Sogdian. From a sociolinguistic point of view, it is also distinguished by its popular style. In fact, it would seem that while the Christian missionaries addressed their message to the common people, Manichaeans directed their teaching to the elite. Christian Sogdian frequently adopts syntactic structures, stylistic modules, and expressions that seem foreign to the strictly Sogdian linguistic heritage. In the majority of cases this is due to the fact that the texts were translated from a Syriac original, even though the original work cannot always be identified. The need for literal translations therefore influenced not only the lexicon but the very structure of the Christian Sogdian texts.[143] In addition to that,

> generally speaking, with particular regard to the Christian Sogdian religious terminology, it seems . . . that there is a trend consisting in the use of Syriac loanwords in the monastic and ascetic literature, i.e., in the texts in the East Syriac script used inside the monastic community, i.e., by people who were able to understand both Syriac and Sogdian and who were able to read the East Syriac script, whereas texts that were read during the Mass as well as texts in Sogdian secular script, i.e., texts presumably used outside the monastery, show a wide use of the corresponding Sogdian term.[144]

Christian Sogdian terminology thus makes use of a multiple lexical heritage that reflects the multiethnic and multilingual composition of the community that produced it—the community of the monastery of Bulayïq—and its history of inculturation in the oasis of Turfan where it was located. In fact, "if it could be possible that the Pahlavi Psalter testifies an early stage of inculturation, most probably the Christian Sogdian literature testifies a later stage where a clergy and a monastic community were perfectly able to use several languages, scripts, and terminologies depending on the kind of text, its use, its author, its readers, and its addressees."[145]

Sogdian took from Syriac all the properly ecclesiastical vocabulary. The technical terms of the liturgy and those indicating the different degrees of hierarchy are all loan words from Syriac. Even many proper names of persons and places (especially biblical) are modeled on the Syriac form. From the Iranian

---

143. See Panaino 1987–88, 24, 27.

144. Barbati 2015b, 452.

145. Ibid., 453.

languages (Parthian and Middle Persian) Sogdian borrowed many common terms, giving them a specifically Christian meaning. This is true, for example, of the term that in Sogdian designates the Christian faithful: *trs'q* (*tarsāk*), "one who fears [God]," derived from Middle Persian.[146] From the Iranian linguistic and cultural world, moreover, Sogdian took some religious terms common to other religions. In the Christian, Manichaean, and Buddhist texts we find a vocabulary of Mazdaic origin that constitutes the oldest nucleus of religious terminology in Sogdian. In reality, this Mazdaic heritage does not comprise a large number of terms, but they are the most general and often denote what is most important. For example, the Sogdian word *by* (*bagh*), a word of ancient Mazdaic origin that means "god," is well attested in the Sogdian texts belonging to the three different religious traditions.[147]

Despite this abundance of linguistic loans, which indicates the firm will of the Christian community of Turfan to maintain a close bond with the tradition of its mother church, the Sogdian Christians were the architects of remarkable linguistic creativity that demonstrates "the ability, or rather the will to adapt to an environment different from that of the mother church."[148] The development of indigenous Sogdian terms as Christian Sogdian *termini technici* signals the acculturation of the Church of the East into the local context through the use of language. For instance, from a detailed study of a Gospel Lectionary (E5, formerly C5), Chiara Barbati has shown "the attempt to create a liturgical terminology unique to Sogdian, rejecting loanwords and developing its own terms *ad hoc*, and even by stylistic choice, always with the respect for its source."[149]

In conclusion, with regard to Sogdian Christian literature, we see that

the textual evidence demonstrates the intellectually contextualized nature of "Sogdian Christianity." The entire surviving body of literature is translated from the Syriac. However, this literature, typologically speaking, can be perceived as an independent literary

---

146. This term is also present in Chinese phonetic transcription in the text of the 781 Xi'an stele (see Text A, col. 26, p. 214 and n. 112). This shows that Iranian Christian terminology was passed on to China. For an exhaustive discussion of this term, see Dickens 2020c.

147. See Benveniste 1964; Hansen 1966; Sims-Williams 1988; Ashurov 2015c. Precious tools for lexical research on the Christian Sogdian texts are the dictionaries Gharib 1995 and Sims-Williams 2016.

148. Barbati 2015a, 115.

149. Barbati 2014, 116.

work. The existing fragments display a variety of codicological and scribal traditions. In addition, the expression of Syriac concepts and expressions in Sogdian native vocabulary also demonstrates that Sogdian texts are not only a codification of what is translatable, but also a source of new vocabularies and concepts, which were formed in the process of interaction of Sogdian speakers with Syriac Christian literature. . . . Consequently, the varied vocabulary usage (loanwords, native words, etc.) observed in Sogdian Christian texts also shows the cultural-linguistic and cognitive contextualisation of a "Christian" worldview into Sogdian. . . . Sogdian translators, as well as Christian communities or individual Christians who had access to Christian literature, began, as a result of these newly translated texts, to express new ideas and concepts using both "new" and original words from their native language.[150]

What interests us most, however, is the type of texts translated into Sogdian.[151] First of all, manuscripts containing portions of biblical texts have been found. The only book of the Old Testament that we know for certain was translated into Sogdian is the Psalter.[152] Of the New Testament we have fragments of different lectionaries with portions of the Gospels (pericopes of Matthew, Luke, and John) and Pauline letters. The fragments are mostly bilingual, that is, made up of the original Syriac and its translation into Sogdian (but also, in some cases, Uighur Turkic and New Persian), the two languages alternating sentence by sentence.[153] With a few exceptions (including a fragment of Psalm 33 [32] that directly depends on the Greek text of the Septuagint),[154] all biblical translations into Sogdian depend to a massive extent on the Syriac version of the Peshitta (*Pšiṭtā*).[155] However, new research on Sogdian lectionaries reveals that occasional dependence on older Syriac versions (the

---

150. Ashurov 2013, 193–94.

151. For an overview, see Asmussen 1984; Sims-Williams 1991, 1992b, 1992c, 2009; Reck 2008; Băncilă 2009.

152. See Schwartz 1974; Sims-Williams 2011a.

153. See Metzger 1977; Asmussen 1984, 14–16; Sims-Williams 1990a, 2020a; Băncilă 2009, 241–42 (for references to identified biblical passages); Pittard and Sims-Williams 2013; Dickens 2016a.

154. See p. 17n64.

155. See Peters 1936; Asmussen 1975.

Diatessaron in particular) cannot be excluded.[156] From the insertion of intonation markers in the form of points above or under the text lines and from the composition of the manuscripts, we can deduce that the texts were meant to be chanted during the liturgy.[157] In conclusion,

> it is unclear whether or not the whole Syriac Bible was ever translated into Sogdian, . . . although portions of . . . [it were] used for reading in church services. The exception is the Psalter, one of the most important parts of the Bible for those living a monastic life, as is evident from the extant Psalter fragments in Syriac, Middle Persian, Sogdian, and New Persian.[158]

With regard to the fragments of the Turfan Psalter that have been found, Mark Dickens has remarked that they "are important for two reasons: first, no other Christian text found at Turfan was rendered in more languages and scripts than the Psalter; and second, the Syriac Psalter fragments from Turfan are amongst the earliest extant anywhere and can therefore be helpful in tracing the development of the Syriac Peshitta text of the Psalms."[159]

A second small group of manuscripts consists of liturgical texts: a Sogdian translation of the Niceno-Constantinopolitan Creed[160] and a version of the hymn *Glory to God in the Highest*.[161]

A third group, quantitatively significant, indicates that Bulayïq, a monastic center, was the origin of these manuscripts. They consist of admonitions, homilies, and treatises on topics such as the seven hours of daily prayer, withdrawal from the world, solitude, the fight against evil thoughts, silent contemplation in the cell, fasting, and humility, all of which presupposes that monks were readers. It is therefore the Sogdian version of those same ascetic texts and of texts dealing with the monastic life that nourished East Syriac monastic spirituality for centuries. What has come down to us of monastic literature in Sogdian includes fragments of the *Sayings of the Fathers*, works attributed to Macarius the Egyptian and to Abba Isaiah of Scetis, the

---

156. See Barbati 2016, 43–52.

157. See Wellesz 1918–19; Dickens 2013b, 14.

158. Dickens 2009b, 111.

159. Dickens 2013a, 358.

160. See Schwartz 1974, 257.

161. See Sims-Williams 1995a, 2013.

42   A HISTORY OF ENCOUNTERS

Antirrhetikos of Evagrius Ponticus, comments of Dadišoʿ Qaṭraya on some conferences of Abba Isaiah and on the *Paradise of the Fathers* of ʿEnanišoʿ, the *Profitable Counsels* of Simon of Ṭaibuteh, and the *Gnostic Chapters* of Isaac of Nineveh.[162]

A fourth group of texts, perhaps the most substantial, is made up of apocryphal and hagiographic literature, including fragments of such texts as the *History of Aḥiqar*, the *Acts of Peter*, the *Dormition of the Virgin*, the legend of the discovery of the Holy Cross and that of the Sleepers of Ephesus, the *Acts of Martyrs* (Sergius and Bacchus, Cyricus and Julitta, Eustace, George), and of many Persian martyrs (Pethion, Ādurhormazd, Nāhīd, and the martyrs during the rule of Šābuhr II), as well as several Lives of significant figures in the history of monasticism, such as Serapion, Eugene, and John of Daylam, founder of two monasteries in Fars, and an important fragment of the legend of Baršabba, evangelizer and martyr of Merv.[163]

In addition to the biblical, liturgical, ascetic, and hagiographic texts, there is a final group of texts that escapes a precise categorization. These are the *Apostolic Canons*, a commentary on the symbolism of the baptismal and eucharistic liturgies, translations of Syriac homilies into metrics, a collection of riddles on biblical themes, and anti-Manichaean polemical treatises.[164] Finally, there are two or three pharmacological texts and four calendrical texts, two of them concerning the dates for the beginning of Lent, Easter, Ascension Day, and Pentecost.[165] A text that was thought to be a fragment of the *Book of Life* or the *Book of the Living*, that is, the commemorative diptychs of the saints of the Church of the East, has been recently recognized as a prayer-amulet.[166]

The multireligious site of Dunhuang, where thousands of secular and religious (mainly Buddhist) texts have been preserved, has revealed a single Sogdian manuscript whose content is clearly recognizable as Christian. It is a small fragment of a popular text, oracular in nature, known in the West as *Sortes Apostolorum*.[167] However, several other documents of an epistolary and

---

162. Several of these texts are part of the manuscript E27 (formerly C2) and were published and translated by Nicholas Sims-Williams (1985). See also Sims-Williams 1981; Kessel and Sims-Williams 2011; Pirtea 2019, 2020.

163. In addition to the above edition of the manuscript E27 (formerly C2), see also Benveniste 1943–45; Gershevitch 1946; Sundermann 1976; Sims-Williams 1995b, 2014a.

164. Some of these texts can be found in the edition of the manuscript E27 (formerly C2). See also Brock 1980, 1986; Sims-Williams 1982, 1995c, 2002; Sundermann 1988.

165. See Dickens and Sims-Williams 2012.

166. See Schwartz 1991; Sims-Williams 2020b.

167. See Sims-Williams 1994.

commercial nature dating from the ninth and tenth centuries were written by Christians or contain references to Christians, including priests and monks.[168] Some linguistic characteristics of these texts reveal that although the authors wrote in Sogdian, they were more accustomed to think in Turkic. In fact, in these documents from Dunhuang one can observe, more clearly than in those from Turfan, the process by which Sogdian Christians were absorbed into the cultural sphere of the Turkic-speaking population that surrounded them.[169]

Old Turkic, or Uighur Turkic, is the language of the last group of Christian texts found in Eastern Turkestan (Bulayïq, Qočo, Qurutqa, and Xaraxoto). It consists of about sixty fragments, whose dating is not easily determined but seems decidedly later than that of the Sogdian manuscripts; most of them probably belong to the thirteenth or fourteenth centuries.[170] The most significant of them are fragments of a Creed; the history of the Magi who go to Bethlehem to adore the Christ child, which is based on the Syriac version of the *Protoevangelium of James*; the last page of the *Life of Saint George*, containing the prayer of the saint before his martyrdom;[171] a portion of the apocryphal *Acts of Paul*, whose literary form evokes the oracular genre;[172] a text that mentions a guest priest in a monastery who was treated unkindly; some prayers of praise and invocation asking the Savior to help the needy and the suffering, heal the sick, forgive sinners, and bless the believers;[173] a sermon on Matthew 10:42; and other fragments whose contents cannot be identified.[174] Some of the Old Uighur fragments are written in the Syriac script. These include a ritual text for the marriage liturgy,[175] a prayer booklet for personal use,[176] and a fragmentary text on the passion of Christ.[177]

---

168. See Sims-Williams and Hamilton 2015.

169. See Sims-Williams 1992c, 55–56.

170. For a catalogue of these fragments, see Zieme 2015a. For a survey, see Zieme 1974, 2015b; Asmussen 1984, 20–23; Gillman and Klimkeit 1999, 254–55; He 2019.

171. For these two texts, see Bang 1926.

172. See Arlotto 1970–71, in particular 693–96 ("Appendix: The So-called Christian Oracle-Book"); Zieme 1978.

173. See Zieme 1974, 662–65.

174. See Zieme [2006?], 2013.

175. See Zieme 1981.

176. See Zieme 2009; Dickens 2013c; Dickens and Zieme 2014.

177. See Pigoulewsky 1935–36.

44   A HISTORY OF ENCOUNTERS

Overall, it can be said that the majority of documents in Turkic do not have a properly religious content; they are mostly letters, administrative documents, and commercial contracts. However, they contain references to many people who have Christian names and thus are valuable sources for our knowledge of the life and presence of Christians in the oasis of Turfan.[178] Written in an uncultivated language, they attest that the religious and literary languages of Christians were Syriac and Sogdian, not Turkic.[179] Also, from a numerical point of view, the Turkic-speaking community of Turfan "had to be significantly smaller than the Sogdian community."[180]

From this overview of Christian literature in Central Asian languages it is clear that

> the importance of this literary tradition is remarkable, despite its de-
> pendence on Syrian sources. In fact, it testifies to the high cultural
> and religious level reached by the Christian communities in Eastern
> Iran and allows a better understanding of the kind of rootedness the
> Nestorian Church attained thanks to its missionary work in Central
> Asia.[181]

The Meeting of Religions on the Silk Road

As mentioned at the beginning of this chapter, the Church of the East, which came into being on a frontier, benefited from a thoroughfare that allowed it to become a missionary church. This thoroughfare was the Silk Road that connected the Persian capital Seleucia-Ctesiphon to the Chinese capital Chang'an. Under the umbrella of "Silk Road" are included a number of different caravan routes (see figure 1.2). One of them was a northern route that began in Merv, went through Bukhara and Samarkand (Sogdiana) to Kašgar, and then from there to Dunhuang through the oases north of the Tarim River

---

178. See Raschmann 2009.

179. See Tremblay 2001, 172–73n286.

180. Zieme 1974, 668. With regard to the ethnic composition of the Turfan Christian community as reflected by the languages used in the extant texts found in that oasis, see also Chen
Huaiyu 1999 (2012), 77–81. Since no text in Chinese has been found, it seems that the Christian
community in Turfan did not include ethnic Chinese or Chinese-speaking members.

181. Panaino 1987–88, 30.

basin, including Tumšuq, Kuča, Agni, Qočo, and Hami. A southern route went to Kašgar through Bactria and then continued on to Dunhuang passing south of Tarim and skirting, among others, the centers of Yarkend, Khotan, Čerčen, Miran, and Loulan. After the fourth and fifth centuries, the more arid and desert southern route was progressively abandoned, while an alternate northern route became more and more frequently traveled. It went from Samarkand and Taškent, arriving at Tumšuq through the region of the Seven Rivers (Čimkent, Talas, Biškek, Tokmak, and Suyab).[182]

Following these trade routes in the company of merchants who transported their goods on the backs of horses, donkeys, mules, and camels, Christian missionaries, together with Buddhist, Manichaean, and Zoroastrian missionaries, crossed a region that the British explorer Marc Aurel Stein named Serindia.[183] For several centuries it was a microcosm characterized by extreme political, linguistic, cultural, and religious plurality.[184]

From a political point of view, in the first millennium Serindia did not constitute a unitary and autonomous reality. Its individual city-state oases were characterized by acute particularism and small populations, and they never became a Central Asian confederation. As one author put it, "Central Asia was always an object and not a subject of political history."[185] Rather, the different city-states regularly assumed a passive role in the face of repeated foreign invasions and dominations. The immense territory of Central Asia was in fact the land of conquest of the great surrounding empires (Sasanian and then Muslim in the west, Chinese in the east, Tibetan in the south), and it was the destination of invasions by the various Turkish-Mongolian populations in the north. The wealth of the Central Asian oases and their key position as obligatory rest stops for the caravans on their journey along the

---

182. See Christian 2000; Graf 2018. Reference works on the Silk Road are Klimkeit 1988; Liu Xinru 1998; Hansen 2012; Whitfield 2018.

183. See Stein 1921, viii: "The term *Serindia*, as adopted (in the form *Sérinde*) by valued French fellow-scholars, is excellently suited for the designation of this region, well-defined by nature as well as by historical relationship. Significant brevity would amply justify its use even if the interpretation which derives Procopius' local name *Serinda* from a compound of the terms in Greek *Séres*, the classical name for the people of Serica or China and *Indoí* may prove to have no better foundation than 'learned popular etymology.'"

184. See Menges 1991; Liu Xinru 1995; Foltz 2010.

185. Petech 1992, 3.

Silk Road constantly attracted the sights of their powerful neighbors, who were always looking for ways to establish their control over the trade routes.[186]

As has already been noted, the city-states developed sophisticated material and artistic cultures but did not possess linguistic or religious unity. Fifteen different languages and four religions—Manichaeism, Zoroastrianism, Buddhism, and Christianity—coexisted.[187] To sum up, we can say that until the eleventh century, Indo-European languages—among them, Prakrit, Parthian, Sogdian, Bactrian, Khotanese, and two forms of Tocharian—were the principal languages for administrative, commercial, and religious purposes, while the progressive establishment of various Turkic dialects accompanied the subsequent Turkification and Islamization of Central Asia.

To better understand the special situation represented by Central Asian cities, two centers located at opposite ends of the Silk Road can be taken as examples and regarded more closely: Merv in the west, still in the sphere of Iranian political and cultural influence, and Turfan in the east, located in the area of Chinese influence.

Merv and its oasis (ancient Margiana) played an important role in the history of the ancient Iranian empires, not only for strategic reasons but also for their location at the crossroads of routes that once attracted traders, missionaries, and adherents of various religions and cults. Textual and archaeological evidence indicates that at least from the Parthian period onward, ancient Merv and the Merv oasis were home to peoples of various nationalities and faiths.[188]

In Merv, which continued to be a center of Parthian culture in the Sasanian era, Zoroastrianism was dominant, so in this city the confrontation between Christianity and Mazdeism must have been marked by the tensions and compromises that the sources, especially Persian, refer to in a general way. On one side, the Christians of Persia were responsible for the destruction of various fire-altars, and in their writings we repeatedly find polemical anti-Zoroastrian elements.[189] On the other hand, they also made an attempt

---

186. On the extremely complex history of Central Asia, see Sinor 1990; Litvinsky, Zhang, and Samghabadi 1996; Beckwith 2009; La Vaissière 2012; Baumer 2014. For the period following the Arab conquest (seventh to fourteenth centuries), see Starr 2013.

187. Tremblay 2001 is the best and most documented study for understanding the exceptional linguistic, cultural and religious coexistence in Central Asia before the Mongol conquest.

188. See Kaim and Kornacka 2016.

189. See Burns 2014. For two examples, see the *Martyrdom of Narseh* (martyr under Yazdgird I) and the *Acts of Adarparwa, Mihrnarseh, and Mahduxt* (martyrs under Šābuhr II).

The Church of the East from Persia to China 47

to adapt to the Iranian cultural and religious context.[190] An example is the positive approach of Christians to some elements of Mazdeism, as can be seen in the emphasis the Church of Persia placed on remembering and celebrating the visit of the Magi, who were considered to be Persian kings and therefore Zoroastrians. In the same way, while there are numerous passages in the Acts of the Persian martyrs and in the works attributed to Pseudo-Clement describing the repugnance felt by Christians for the worship of fire, which they considered idolatrous, other passages indicate a "tendency to give a Christian origin to the cult of fire and also to some of the major temples dedicated to it, and to connect it with the coming of the Magi to Bethlehem."[191]

This adaptation can be seen in some linguistic loans from Avestic terminology, which are found mainly in Sogdian, whose three variants—Christian, Buddhist, and Manichaean—contain some common words derived from the substratum of the ancient Zoroastrian religion. Examples are the words for God and paradise, the latter derived from an Avestic compound that means "the best existence," and the words for hell, Satan, and church.[192] Other examples of Christian adaptation to Zoroastrianism are the preservation by Christians of names whose origin was typically Mazdean and the use of formulas marked by Mazdean phraseology but adapted to Christian doctrine that can be found in some seals of Persian Christians. Finally, the negative criticism of the excessive ascetic rigor of some Christian circles that is found in much spiritual literature of the Church of Persia may have been prompted by the opposition of Zoroastrians to an a priori denial of material pleasures.[193]

On the one hand, the Christians of Persia had fairly good knowledge of Zoroastrianism. Some of them came from Zoroastrian families and certainly knew the Avesta very well, as evidenced by a sure and ancient witness of the Mazdean-Christian controversy in the Sasanid era, the *Acts of Mar Qardag*.[194] On the other hand, there is little information about how much the Zoroastrians knew about Christianity.[195] The texts of the Zoroastrian controversy with Christians are few in number and the only extended reference

---

190. See, for instance, Minov 2014.

191. Messina 1947, 112.

192. See Benveniste 1964, 86–88; Ashurov 2013, 152–89; 2015c, 5–13.

193. On the question of the relationship between Christianity and Zoroastrianism in Sasanian Persia, see Messina 1947, 101–13; William 1996; Gignoux 1999; Panaino 2004; Payne 2015.

194. See Walker 2006.

195. See Panaino 2000.

48 A HISTORY OF ENCOUNTERS

to them is in some passages in the Middle Persian apologetic text *Doubt-dispelling Exposition* (*Škand-gumānīg Wizār*), written by Mardānfarrox son of Ohrmazddād in the ninth century. In chapter 15 of this work, the Zoroastrian polemicist, citing numerous pericopes of the Gospels, shows that the annunciation to Mary is not plausible, that Mary's virginal conception of Jesus is to be rejected, and that Christ is not the Son of God. The author also sarcastically refutes the dogma of the Trinity.[196]

In Merv, Christians rubbed up against more than Zoroastrians. This great center at the gates of Asia, "due to its central geographical position, attracted the envoys of the world religions in a special manner."[197] Here the Buddhist, Manichaean, and Christian communities lived together and exchanged views for several centuries.

The presence of Buddhists in Merv is evidenced by several archaeological finds, including a Sanskrit manuscript containing a commentary on an ancient Buddhist sutra, the ruins of a *stūpa*, and a monastery with a *stūpa*.[198] This leads us to suppose that the Buddhist community must have been significant, all the more so because already in ancient times Buddhist missionaries of Parthian origin left this area for China and translated the first Buddhist texts from Sanskrit into Chinese.[199]

The legend of the conversion of the Merv region (Khorasan) to Manichaeism by Mar Ammō, a third-century disciple of Mani and founder of the eastern Manichaean church, speaks of an ancient Manichaean presence in the city. Although there are no subsequent written testimonies of Manichaean activity in Merv, there can be little doubt that it continued for a long time, given the location of this center and the certain presence of numerous Manichaean communities in the surrounding areas.[200]

The Christian community of Merv has already been mentioned.[201] In ancient times Merv constituted a great center of study, which certainly attracted the Christians of the eastern regions of Iran and allowed them to be educated and formed in both theological and secular sciences. It is therefore evident

---

196. See Mardānfarrox ī Ohrmazddād, *Doubt-dispelling Exposition* 15, ed. and trans. Menasce, 205–25. See also Gignoux 2008.

197. Gillman and Klimkeit 1999, 206.

198. See Koshelenko 1966; Callieri 1996.

199. See Compareti 2007.

200. See Lieu 1992, 219–25.

201. See p. 11.

The various centers that made up the oasis of Turfan provide another privileged setting for the study of the multireligious situation that characterized the pre-Islamic Serindia. An abundance of religious material belonging to the different religious traditions is found there. Furthermore, many scholars have dedicated themselves to the study of Turfan, which can be considered—albeit with due caution—representative of many other places where religions encountered one another in Central Asia, but of which there is little documentation.

In Turfan, in fact, as in many other centers, Christians formed a religious minority within a population that was mostly Buddhist and partly Manichaean.[203] The Uighur kingdom of Qočo, which was formed as a result of the diaspora of the Uighur tribes to the west, i.e., toward Chinese Turkestan (Xinjiang), adopted Manichaeism as state religion between 850 and 1008, after the invasion of the Kyrgyz, who destroyed the Uighur steppe empire (840). It did this not so much because Manichaeism was the religion of the majority of the population, but rather for political reasons. Qočo was the seat of the *mōžak* (master), a leading figure in the church of Mani, and in Turfan a Manichaean presence certainly existed since the beginning of the ninth century, as evidenced by the ruins of ancient Manichaean temples discovered there.[204] However,

> Manichaeism [in Qočo] was deprived of the sympathy of the local Buddhist population and limited to the Sogdians who also provided its clergy; it was supported only by the *qaghan* and finally became a victim of political turmoil. For these reasons, Manichaeism, in spite of the abundance of texts which reflects its influence and not the number of its adherents, did not last long. It knew neither how to propagate its

---

202. See Tubach 1998.

203. On the different religions present in Qočo (Turfan), see Tian Weijiang 2003.

204. See Chao 1996; Rong 2000b.

50 A HISTORY OF ENCOUNTERS

doctrines nor how to establish local communities capable of surviving when they no longer enjoyed the king's favor.[205]

What is remarkable, however, is the fact that Manichaeans diffused Christian texts in Central Asia. Among the thousands of Manichaean documents and fragments found mostly in Turfan, one notes a great interest on the part of the Manichaeans in Christian literature, mainly apocryphal. In addition to a certain number of apocryphal sayings of Jesus not attested elsewhere, the Manichaean texts contain direct quotations or allusions from the canonical and apocryphal Gospels (those of Peter, Nicodemus, Philip, Thomas, the Gospel of the Twelve Apostles, and, perhaps, the Gospel of the Seventy, as well as some Gospels of the infancy of Jesus), the apocryphal Acts of various apostles, and the apocryphal books of the Old Testament (*Book of Giants*). A fragment of the *Shepherd of Hermas* in Middle Persian was also found in Turfan.[206]

The peculiar Gnostic interpretation of the figure of Jesus was also transmitted to China in other Manichaean texts, among which are some hymns to Jesus and hymns to *parinirvāṇa*, a Sanskrit term that Buddhist literature used to indicate the "complete extinction" or "definitive uprooting" of any karmic residue at the moment of death.[207] Eastern Manichaean literature adopted this Buddhist expression and used it in the titles of hymns that recalled the earthly end of Mani or the passion of Christ, since the exit from this world of both Mani and Christ represented the liberation of light from the slavery of darkness and a return to its origin.

The Christology that emerges from the Manichaean *Hymnscroll* in Chinese (*Xiabu zan yijuan*, "Lower Section Hymns, in One Scroll") is of great interest. It presents, in summary, three representations of Jesus: Jesus the Judge, Jesus the Light, and, less explicitly, the Suffering Jesus (the latter two figures are also present in Manichaean literature in Sogdian). These representations are in continuity with the presentation of Jesus contained in the Manichaean texts of Central Asia, in which we find Jesus the Light, Jesus the Messiah, and the Suffering Jesus (*Jesus patibilis*). The Chinese Manichaean texts also invite believers to address Jesus as Physician, King, and Savior, and to him are applied such cosmological epithets as the Full Moon. He is also often called

---

205. Tremblay 2001, 120.

206. See Sundermann 1968; Klimkeit 1991; Lieu 1998, 36–39.

207. See Waldschmidt and Lentz 1926; Rose 1979; Morano 1982, 2010; Sundermann 1992; Franzmann 2003.

the Buddha, that is, the Enlightened One.[208] Chinese Manichaean hymns attribute many different titles to Jesus, most often applying to Jesus epithets originally used in Buddhist literature in reference to the Buddha, such as "Buddha of Harmony" (*hefo* 和佛), "Tathāgata" (*rulai* 如來), "King of the *Dharma*" (*fawang* 法王), and "Great Saint" (*dasheng* 大聖).[209] The last two titles are also found in contemporary Chinese Christian texts.

The Christian literature found in Turfan provides us with some information, albeit fragmentary, that enables us to make further comments on the situation of a small Christian community located in a non-Christian environment. If, in fact, this literature can and must be read within the Syriac literary and spiritual tradition in which it is fully inserted, it is also true that it expresses the Christian identity of the specific communities that produced and read this literature, an identity that was forged in direct relation to the surrounding cultural context.[210] It is this latter interpretative approach that is of greater interest in this study.

On the one hand, we have texts that indicate a great willingness to adopt indigenous models in presenting Christian content. This is especially true in ancient Turkic texts.[211] On the other hand, we have texts, Sogdian texts above all, in which apologetic or polemical terms indicate resistance to the dominant religious presence. In these texts we find, for example, a certain insistence on the bodily resurrection of Christ and of all who have died, which might also be explained as a reaction to both the Manichaean Docetist interpretation of the passion and death of Jesus and to the Buddhist conception of salvation, which implies the overcoming of corporeity.[212] This pivotal element of Christian preaching, emphasized in many pages of East Syriac literature, may have been given even greater prominence in the religious context of Central Asia.

A survey of the Sogdian Christian literature produced in Turfan gives evidence of this attitude of reacting or differentiating. Although some of the

---

208. In addition to the studies already mentioned in the preceding footnote, see also Klimkeit 1985, 1996a; Ma Xiaohe 1999.

209. See Klimkeit 1985; Mikkelsen 2002, 232–42; Yang Fuxue and Xue Wengjing 2019. For textual references to the terminological examples cited here and to others, see DMTC, ad loc. Here in particular, for *fawang*, see DMTC, 19; for *dasheng*, see DMTC, 13.

210. The dialectic between these two interpretative lines has been highlighted by Hage 1988a.

211. See Klimkeit 1998b, 138–39. A text studied by Peter Zieme, which insists on the effectiveness of the merits, could confirm this hypothesis (see Zieme [2006?]).

212. See Klimkeit 1985, 16. For considerations on the Sogdian terms designating resurrection, see Ashurov 2015c, 10.

52   A HISTORY OF ENCOUNTERS

Sogdian Christian terms used to translate Christian theological expressions are identical with those employed in Manichaean, Buddhist, or other Sogdian literature, this does not imply lexical syncretism. In contrast to the Manichaeans, who fully absorbed and widely integrated their teachings with Buddhist and Christian apocryphal writings, Sogdian Christianity remained aloof from this syncretistic religious atmosphere.[213] A further indication of the aloofness of Sogdian Christians is their choosing to use their own (modified) Syriac script for their strictly-religious literature as a mark of religious identity over and above linguistic identity—namely to distinguish their religious texts from texts of other religions existing in Sogdian, which were also identifiable by their scripts.[214]

In the literature discovered in Turfan we find the same dialectic between the rejection and the critical assimilation of Mazdaic elements, such as the symbolism and the cult of fire, that was already found in the eastern Iranian context of Merv. For instance, Hans-Joachim Klimkeit sees an allusion to the power of the Christian faith over the cult of fire in the following passage of the Sogdian version of the martyrdom of Saint George:[215] "Have mercy on us, and give us holy baptism, that we may no longer go to the burning fire and no longer see it."[216]

On the other hand, from this exact same region of Eastern Turkestan comes another extremely interesting fragment in Uighur Turkic in which the narrative of Matthew 2:1–12 is followed by the legend that gives a Christian justification for the adoration of fire by the Magi.[217]

The portrait of the community of Turfan that emerges from the Christian texts that have come down to us is summed up by Wolfgang Hage as follows:

> A small community, not only in a more passive manner possessing the assorted documents of a rich church tradition (with elements which, in the situation of Inner Asia, sound like apologetic-polemic ones), but also an active community with the theological experience and capacity not only to translate the Syriac prototypes into their vernaculars [i.e.,

---

213. See Ashurov 2015c, 13–14.

214. See Ashurov 2015b, 1–7.

215. See Klimkeit 1998b, 138.

216. Benveniste 1943–45, 99. The invocation is addressed to the martyr George.

217. See Bang 1926, 46ff. This legend is also handed down in Syriac and Arabic sources.

of the Christians living there], but also to actualize the Christian faith with regard to their present situation at Turfan.[218]

With regard to the expansion of Buddhism, Manichaeism, and Zoroastrianism in Central Asia,[219] I would simply call attention to what makes them similar to Christianity in the process of expanding eastward, namely, the Iranian influence over these different religious doctrines as they moved through Central Asia.

From the abundant literature preserved in the Middle Persian, New Persian, Parthian, and Sogdian languages found in Serindia,[220] it is evident that Manichaeism was initially brought to Asia by Iranians. This is also true for China, where translations, often literal, of Manichaean works into Chinese often included phonetic transcriptions of the Iranian originals.[221] In Turfan, Middle Persian and Gāndhārī Prakrit remained the liturgical languages of the Manichaean community for a long time.[222]

Very soon it was the same Iranian people from Kaśmir, Persia, Sogdiana, and Bactria, as well as the Indian people, who brought Buddhism to Central Asia, where it quickly spread, and from there to China.[223] In this regard, the intuition of the French sinologist Paul Pelliot (1878–1945) remains central:

The intervention of the Iranian and Iranized populations of the two Turkestans [Western and Eastern] in the propagation of the Indian religion [Buddhism] in China must no longer be lost sight of. . . . It is altogether reasonable to suppose that certain doctrinal aspects of

---

218. Hage 1988a, 54.

219. For a summary of the expansion of Buddhism in Central Asia, see Emmerick 1987 (with a reference bibliography); Puri 1987; Kōgi 2002; Tremblay 2007; Walter 2014. On Zoroastrianism, see Gignoux 1996; Grenet 2015. On Manichaeism, see Lieu 1992, 1998; Tremblay 2001.

220. See Lieu 1998, 207–37. For the editions of the texts, see Tremblay 2001, 215–45. Editions and translations of Manichaean texts in Iranian and Old Uighur languages from Turfan and preserved in the Berlin Turfan collection are currently being published in the "Berliner Turfantexte" (BTT) series by Brepols.

221. See Bryder 1985, 47–62 ("Middle Iranian Hymns Transcribed in Chinese Characters"), 63–74 ("Some Terminological Comparisons between Two Parallel Texts in Chinese and Parthian"); Sundermann 1996; Lieu 1998, 49–54, 59–75 ("From Parthian into Chinese").

222. See Tremblay 2001, 100.

223. On Buddhist literature in Sogdian, see Dresden 1983, 1221–24; Tremblay 2001, 203–6; Yoshida 2015.

54   A HISTORY OF ENCOUNTERS

Chinese Buddhism have been affected by this intermediary for too long unknown or underestimated.[224]

Subsequent historical and philological research on Buddhist texts from Central Asia has fully confirmed this intuition. The fact, moreover, that the vast majority of the first translators of Buddhist texts in China in the second and third centuries were of Iranian origin says much about Iranian influences on early Chinese Buddhist literature.[225]

As already mentioned, the Sogdians were the principal group among these Iranian populations. Between the sixth and ninth centuries, they were an effective agent for the diffusion of religious ideas in Central Asia and China.[226] Having establishing their colonies among the Turks, they practiced Buddhism and Manichaeism and introduced Christianity to them. On arriving in China, they brought Zoroastrianism, Christianity, and Manichaeism to the Chinese, as well as Western scientific knowledge (astrology, medicine, etc.). It is interesting to note that initially Buddhism was a typically colonial phenomenon, that is, a religion that for all intents and purposes was practiced by the Sogdians only in the colonies. The same was true of Manichaeism later on. Of all the foreign religions (i.e., religions other than Zoroastrianism), Christianity was the only one that was practiced in the homeland of those who bought it with them to the colonies.[227]

Having summarized such a varied picture, we can now return to the subject that interests us most: literature. As we have seen, the plurality of religions in Central Asia is well documented by the many literary testimonies that have been found, even if they are mainly fragmentary texts. Among the various religious literatures produced in Central Asia, the Christian writings described above are in the minority.[228] What is most surprising is the terminology used in these Central Asian texts, and that in turn prompts reflection on religious coexistence in Asia. The terminology, which in many cases is common to or strongly influenced by the lexical patrimony of others, undoubtedly speaks of

---

224. Pelliot 1912, 106.

225. See Deeg 2018a. A well-known figure for China is the Parthian An Shigao, who translated Buddhist texts into Chinese in the second half of the second century (see Forte 1995).

226. See Ribaud 2005.

227. See Tremblay 2001, 114–15.

228. Very useful in this regard is the table "Langues et religions de Sérinde jusqu'à l'arrivée des Mongols (IIe s. a.C.n.–XIIe s. AD)," in Tremblay 2001, 139, with notes on pp. 140–82.

The Church of the East from Persia to China   55

religious identities that are osmotic, permeable, and open to the assumption of linguistic categories and images different from their own.

This openness is especially evident in the Manichaean texts that often, so to speak, wear Buddhist garments; that is to say, they are replete with Buddhist terms and concepts. For example, the eastern Manichaean authors adopt the term *mokṣa*, which in Buddhism designates liberation from an existence conditioned by the cycle of birth-death-rebirth, to indicate salvation from this world dominated by darkness. They adopt the term *puṇya*, which in Buddhism indicates the virtues merited by good *karma*,[229] to designate the meritorious actions that contribute to the liberation of the particles of light imprisoned in bodies. They also make use of the term *saṃsāra*, which in Buddhism indicates the cycle of existence conditioned by *karma*, to designate earthly existence, where light is imprisoned by darkness. The Manichaeans even adopt the term *nirvāṇa*, a key concept of Buddhism that indicates the end of captivity to the law of *karma*, and thus a state of unconditioned existence, to speak of a life that has been liberated, brought back to its origin, and is now governed by the positive principle of light alone.[230]

Although this appropriation of Buddhist terminology clearly represents the manifestation of the method of adaptation proper to the Manichaean mission in Asia, it is still used selectively and not at all indiscriminately.[231] The technical Buddhist terms used in this eastern Manichaean literature "do not always carry their Buddhist meaning, but sometimes represent purely Manichaean ideas."[232] In the case of Chinese Manichaean literature, "the Chinese translator did not on every occasion seek the *interpretatio buddhica*."[233]

Christian literature (particularly Sogdian) certainly presents a vocabulary strongly dependent on Syriac and the ancient Iranian linguistic substratum, but quantitatively the words most used are drawn from the common Sogdian vocabulary and have then taken on a specifically Christian meaning. It is interesting, however, to note that these words do not belong exclusively to Christian

---

229. On the notion of *karma*, a term that is by now widespread in this form in the West but that would be more correct to use in the singular form (*karman*), see Text D, p. 278n95.

230. See Klimkeit 1986b, 1998a. For textual references to the terminological examples cited here and to others, see Durkin-Meisterernst 2004; Sims-Williams and Durkin-Meisterernst 2012.

231. See Scott 1985b.

232. Bryder 1985, 74.

233. Mikkelsen 1995, 100.

56   A HISTORY OF ENCOUNTERS

terminology, but "a significant proportion are common to Nestorianism and Manichaeism, and even to Buddhism ... Thus, Nestorian Christianity on the one hand, and Christian teaching reinterpreted in Manichaean Gnosticism on the other, have largely the same vocabulary."[234] An analysis of terms present in the same or similar form in Buddhist literature and in Christian literature in Sogdian has confirmed that the Sogdian language is the real link between these two linguistic and religious worlds, the Greek-Syriac world of Christian tradition and the Sanskrit-Chinese world of Buddhist tradition.[235]

Finally, we should not overlook the contemporary presence of Christian, Buddhist, and Manichaean iconographic elements in the archaeological and artistic findings of Central Asia, which further attest to a climate of mutual fertilization. Manichaean art, in particular, reveals a strong tendency to take on iconographic elements from other religious traditions.[236] Among the symbols shared by the three religions in Central Asia, that of the cross appears to be the most eloquent expression of mutual fertilization between Christology (Christian and Gnostic) and Buddhology.[237]

We can conclude that Syriac Christianity, from its very beginnings, was disposed to be open to diversity. Initially, this openness and interaction took place in the religious setting of Zoroastrian Persia in which Christianity was one of the several religious minorities. The best known ancient attestation of these coexisting religious minorities is an inscription (shortly after 276) by the Mazdean chief priest Kirdīr in Fars that mentions a campaign against Manichaeans (*zandīk*), Christians of Persian (*nāčārāy*) and "Greek" (*kristyān*) origin, Jews (*yāhūd*), and other religious groups that practiced a rite of baptism (*makdag*), as well as Hindus (*bramān*) and Buddhists (*šamān*).[238] The openness of Christianity to diversity and its encounter with other religious traditions took place then in the wide multicultural and multireligious space of Central Asia, where each religion was confronted and solicited by

---

234. Benveniste 1964, 88–89. See also Lin Wushu 2004; Piras 2011–12.

235. See Kaschewsky 2002.

236. Hans-Joachim Klimkeit is the author of numerous essays on the subject. I here need refer only to his major work *Manichäische Kunst an der Seidenstraße* (Klimkeit 1996b). See also Gulácsi 2005, 2015.

237. See Klimkeit 1979.

238. See Gignoux 1991, 60, 69–70. About the two terms for Christians that occur in the inscription, the first seems to be used of indigenous Christians in the Persian Empire, whereas the second refers to Christians deported from the Roman Empire and settled in the Persian Empire. For a discussion, see Jullien and Jullien 2002b.

The Church of the East from Persia to China   57

the others, each playing both an active and passive role in the exchange.[239] In this context Syriac Christianity proved to be "a malleable and dynamic religion."[240]

> The case of Central Asia demonstrates that translation meant more than just the mechanistic transferal of words from one language into another. It meant, for the East Syriac Christians, an attitude of mind. This attitude manifested itself in the willingness to see their texts, their liturgies, and even their lifestyles transmitted into foreign vernaculars. Across the Silk Routes, the manifestations of their attitude appeared in texts, inscriptions, and above all institutions.[241]

If this is true, we must suppose that Christianity, like Manichaeism, was not only influenced by other religious traditions (particularly the Buddhist), but that it also—and to some extent in ways still almost completely unknown to us—influenced Mahāyāna Buddhist doctrine and literature, despite the fact that Christians were a minority and that clear indications of such influence are rare. Ian Gillman and Hans-Joachim Klimkeit go so far as to speak of a possible "catalytic effect on Sogdian and Turkish Buddhism in that it served to stress and bring to the fore ideas that were already present in the Buddhist tradition, ideas that corresponded to basic Christian—and Manichaean—notions."[242]

Christianity thus arrived at the gates of China already shaped by otherness in the cultural transition zone that was Central Asia. It was therefore open to an encounter with a cultural reality and philosophical-religious traditions that were even more "other."[243] Christianity exposed itself without fear to the spiritual aromas of the East, letting itself be permeated by them. With specific regard to Buddhism, "One could almost speak of a Christian-Buddhist

---

239. A general reference work on the meeting of Christianity, Manichaeism, and Buddhism along the Silk Road is Klimkeit 1986a.

240. Johnson 2018, 206.

241. Ibid., 219.

242. Gillman and Klimkeit 1999, 259. For a study of the possible influence of Manichaean dualism on Mahāyāna Buddhism, see Scott 1995.

243. On the attitude of the Church of the East toward other religions present in Central Asia, see Hage 1982.

58 A HISTORY OF ENCOUNTERS

dialogue being conducted in Central Asia one thousand years ago, Christians and Buddhists not only living together, but being in constant interaction."[244]

In its eastward expansion, East Syriac Christianity succeeded in being open to otherness while maintaining its own peculiar identity. It did this to such a degree that we find Christians attacked as an easily identifiable group in the *Insādi sūtra*, a Uighur Turkic Buddhist sutra of Central Asian origin.[245] Reflecting on Christian literature in the languages of Central Asia, Wolfgang Hage also points this out when he states that "in spite of the overwhelming majority of the other religions, we cannot find any strong syncretism in the native versions of Christian texts compromising their own genuine Christian tradition."[246]

---

244. Gillman and Klimkeit 1999, 206.

245. See Tezcan, Semih 1974, 71.

246. Hage 1988a, 52.

2

"The Brilliant Teaching Turned toward the Tang Empire"

THE CHRISTIAN PRESENCE IN CHINA BETWEEN 635 AND 845

Chinese Designations of Tang Christianity

Any effort to interpret Tang Christianity would be pointless if we did not begin by calling it by its own name, that is, by the name it was given or by which it was known in the Chinese milieu of the seventh to ninth centuries. This endeavor is much more than a theoretical exercise of "rectifying names" (*zheng ming* 正名), a hermeneutical exercise dear to ancient Chinese philosophy.[1] Rather, it means approaching others with the desire to listen to them on the basis of *their* identity and not pigeonholing them in categories that in our case would be Western and, what is more, doctrinal.

In this sense, "to speak of Tang Christianity as 'Nestorian' [as has long been and still is often done][2] prejudices the discussion from the start. It is as if the discussion of Asian Christian history needs to be cast in light of the theological orthodoxies that emerged in the West."[3] There are two reasons why it is no longer possible to label Tang Christianity as Nestorian. The first is that the theology of the Church of the East, as seen in the previous chapter, is improperly defined as Nestorian. The second reason is that the theological

---

1. See Sun Zhenbin 2015, 17–20.

2. See Thompson 2013. For a Chinese perspective on the need to overcome misinterpretations of the true nature of the Church of the East in Tang China, see Wu Liwei 2010.

3. Wickeri 2004, 45.

The Luminous Way to the East. Matteo Nicolini-Zani, Oxford University Press. © Oxford University Press 2022.
DOI: 10.1093/oso/9780197609644.003.0002

60   A HISTORY OF ENCOUNTERS

content of the Chinese texts does not present any elements that are clearly identifiable as Nestorian. It will therefore be necessary to examine Chinese sources regarding the fundamental question of the way Christianity is designated in the Tang era with the conviction that "Tang Christianity must be understood on the basis of its own primary sources rather than on polemically driven notions of orthodoxy or in light of the ecclesiastical conflicts between the East and the West."[4]

The Chinese term *jingjiao* 景教, which means "luminous teaching" or "religion of light," is most likely the term Christians used to define their religious affiliation in Tang China. In the text inscribed in 781 on the Xi'an Christian stele, the origin of this denomination is clearly explained:

> This True and Unchanging Way is transcendent and difficult to define with a name. However, its effectiveness is manifested so brightly that we, striving to describe it, will call it the Luminous Teaching [*jingjiao*].[5]

The character *jing* 景, "light" or "luminosity," is found eighteen times in the text of the Xi'an stele, and it is always used to define something as Christian.[6] The most relevant expression is undoubtedly *jingri* 景日, "luminous sun," a term that refers to Jesus Christ. It is significant that it also occurs in the text carved on the 815 Luoyang Christian pillar.[7] From this we can infer that behind the choice to call Christianity the "Luminous Teaching" lies a clear, albeit symbolic, reference to Christ, the "Luminous Sun." By calling itself *jingjiao*, Christianity in China symbolically presented itself as the Teaching of Christ the Light. A second reference to the Messiah in the text of the stele as the "Luminous Honored One" (*jingzun* 景尊) provides further confirmation that light was the first attribute of Christ presented to the Chinese people.

Other examples of terms containing the character *jing* in the Xi'an inscription are *jingsi* 景寺, "luminous monasteries," to identify Christian monasteries; *jingmen* 景門, "luminous portals," and *jingfa* 景法, "luminous doctrine," to

---

4. Ferreira 2014, 3.

5. Text A, col. 10, p. 203.

6. See Zhu Qianzhi 1993, 130; Xu Longfei 2004, 114–15; Wu Changxing 2015b, 55–64.

7. ". . . Wishing that the Luminous Sun, fixed [on high] for long, may shine brightly in the dwelling of darkness, and that the true nature [of his teaching] may not be confused but may remain luminous . . ." (*Da Qin jingjiao xuanyuan zhiben jing chuangji*, "Note on the Pillar [Inscribed] with the *Book of the Luminous Teaching of Da Qin on Revealing the Origin and Reaching the Foundation*," col. 32, in Nicolini-Zani 2009b, 113 [text], 117 [trans.]).

The Christian Presence in China 61

indicate the space (physical and metaphysical) of the Christian teaching; *jingzhong* 景眾, "luminous multitude," to indicate the Christian faithful; *jingshi* 景士, "luminous gentlemen," to indicate the Christian monks; *jingfeng* 景風, "luminous breeze," to indicate the spread of Christian teaching; *jingli* 景力, "luminous power," *jingfu* 景福, "luminous blessing," and *jingming* 景命, "luminous mandate," to indicate the divine mandate emanating from the Christian God; and other similar terms. In the text carved on the 815 Luoyang pillar, we find the term *jingseng* 景僧, "luminous monk," which undoubtedly refers to Christian monks and clerics.[8]

The character *jing* is also present in the Chinese name adopted by several monks of the Church of the East in China. The most famous is Jingjing, "the luminous and pure one" or "luminous purity," the author of the text of the stele, whose birth name was Adam.[9] Moreover, Jingtong and Jingfu are included among the seventy Christian monks listed at the bottom of the same stele. It is also significant that in the epitaph of the Christian gentleman Li Su (741–817), who came from Persia and lived with his family in the Chinese capital between the end of the eighth and the beginning of the ninth century, the names of all his sons have *jing* as the first character (Jingshen, Jingfu, Jingliang, Jinghong, Jingwen, Jingdu).[10] It is thus reasonable to assume that the character for *jing* was chosen by Christians in Tang China as a distinctive emblem for their religion. Further evidence of this would be the fact that in Tang *jingjiao* sources, the Chinese character for *jing* is written in a variant form used almost exclusively by the followers of the Luminous Teaching.[11]

It is therefore evident that the symbolism of light lies at the very heart of the presentation of the Christian message brought by Iranian people to Chinese lands in these centuries. The centrality of light in the Christian proclamation can also be deduced from the fact that at this same period the Chinese referred to the Zoroastrian religion as *xianjiao* 祆教, "teaching of the fire god."[12] If the distinctive element of the Zoroastrian religion in China was the veneration of fire, the element that is more characteristic of the Christian

---

8. See Nicolini-Zani 2013c, 145.

9. About him, see Fang Hao 1970, 1:7–12.

10. See Chen Guoying 1981; Rong 1998.

11. See Wilmshurst 1990, 52; Lieu 2009, 243–44.

12. It is not possible to dwell here on the debated history of Zoroastrianism in ancient China, for which few historical documents are available for research. I therefore refer to the following works: Chen Yuan 1923; Drake 1940b; Liu Ts'un-yan 1976; Zhang Guangda 1994; Lin Wushu 1995a; Rong 1995; Lin Meicun 1996; Forte 1999–2000; Lin Wushu 2005c, 256–374, 421–31;

62 A HISTORY OF ENCOUNTERS

religion appears to be light.[13] It was chosen as the principal definition of the Christian religion and is at the heart of the way the Christian message was presented to the people of China during these centuries.

We have here, I believe, an instance of effective inculturation. As can be seen in the earliest Christian writings, light functions as a key symbol of the faith. The symbolism of light runs throughout the New Testament and is particularly recurrent in the writings of the evangelist John.[14] Light is also a central symbol in the theology and liturgy of the Church of the East, and as such is present in several theological and spiritual works, such as the *Odes of Solomon*; Aphrahat's *Demonstrations*; and especially Ephrem's *Hymns for Epiphany, Nisibene Hymns*, and *Hymns on Faith*.[15] Thanks above all to the contribution of Buddhism, the Chinese people could easily understand and relate to this symbol. In Buddhism, and particularly in the Pure Land school, light has a strong religious connotation, being the symbol of awakening, inner enlightenment, and true understanding of reality.[16] In the background of the Christian choice of this symbol there is, therefore, a deep knowledge of the milieu to which it is addressed, an appreciable evaluation of the spiritual sensitivity of the recipients, and a clear choice for the inculturation of the Christian message in the cultural and religious traditions of China. As has been remarked, the choice of Tang Christians to call their religion *jingjiao* "shows a determination to sinicize Nestorianism by approaching close to Chinese local religion,"[17] and *jingjiao* "is a local Chinese name that reflects the depth of Sinicization of this foreign religion."[18]

More recently, Samuel N. C. Lieu suggested that the character *jing* in the official title of the Church of the East in China could have originally been a calque for a Chinese word meaning "fear," since Christians in Central Asia had long been known by the term *tarsāk* (Sogdian) or *tarsāg* (Middle Persian), "[God-]fearer." Since the word *jing* in Chinese has several meanings

---

Zhang Xiaogui 2010; Zhang Xiaogui and Zeng Chaoying 2014; Aoki 2015. See also the bibliographical essays Rong 2000c and Lin Wushu 2005a.

13. See Mustafa 2001; Lin Wushu 2011a, 69–70.

14. See, for example, John 1:4–5, 7–9; 8:12; 9:5; 12:35–36, 46; 1 John 1:5, 7; 2:8–10. See also Tragan 1997.

15. See Beulay 1987, 69–73; Ferreira 2004, 144–46.

16. See Ingram 1974.

17. Zhang Xiaogui 2016, 303.

18. Ibid., 305.

The Christian Presence in China

other than "luminous"—among them, "reverence," "grand," "imposing," or "awesome"—Lieu speculates that *jing* was chosen not because it meant "light" or "luminosity," but rather because it meant "reverence" or "fear."[19] At any rate, the presence of *dasuo* 達娑, the phonetic transcription of the Iranian term *tarsāk* or *tarsāg*, in the text of the Xi'an stele has a strong symbolic value and further points to the Iranian identity of Christians in China—as well as in Central Asia—and their links with the mother church in Persia.[20]

A comparison with Manichaeism, another foreign religion present in China during this same period, is equally revealing. In this regard, we can make note, at least in passing, of three elements. First of all, the teaching of this Gnostic religion in China underwent a process of progressive and increasingly profound Sinicization, which can be seen in the evolution of the Chinese name for it. The oldest reports of Manichaeism in China speak of the arrival of the first *mōžak* ("master" in Sogdian) in 635. Chinese sources then record the spread of Manichaeism under the reign of Gaozong (650–83), the presentation of this religion to the court with the subsequent authorization of its presence in the imperial territory (694), and the official installation in the capital Chang'an of the *mōžak* (719).[21] The most commonly attested Chinese name for Manichaeism in the Tang sources is *monijiao* 摩尼教, which means "teaching of Mani." The figure of the master and founder, therefore, defined this religion in China too.[22] However, from the end of the tenth century onward, Manichaeism assumed a number of other names in China, among them, *mingjiao* 明教, "brilliant teaching," and *mingzun jiao* 明尊教, "teaching of the Brilliant Honored One," two terms close to *jingjiao*.[23] Moreover, in Chinese Manichaean texts from the Tang era, one of the epithets by which the founder is identified is "Mani the Buddha of Light" (*moni guangfo* 摩尼

---

19. See Eccles and Lieu 2020, 16–17; Lieu 2009, 241–46; 2013, 133–37; 2014, 374–76; 2020a, 129–31. See also Zhu Donghua 2021, 51: "As a broader category for religious practice and belief, *jing* should be holistically understood both from an objective perspective as 'shining' or 'universal,' and from a subjective perspective as 'venerating' or even 'fearing (of God).'"

20. On the connection between the ecclesiastical province of China and the church headquarters in Seleucia-Ctesiphon, see Wang Jing 2006.

21. See Lin Wushu 1996.

22. See Lin Wushu 2007 (2011e), 53–61; 2011a.

23. See Lin Wushu 1992, 347–49; 2007 (2011e), 61–75, 78–85; 2011a.

光佛).[24] Finally, in these texts, the Manichaean kingdom of light is described with the same terminology that is used to describe the Pure Land of Amitābha (Eternal Light) in the Buddhist texts of the Amidist school.[25] This confirms that both the Christian and Manichaean religions grafted symbolism that was part of their own tradition (the opposition of light and darkness is constitutive of Manichaean dualism) onto the Buddhist symbolism of light and thus found a way to gain access to the religious world of the Chinese.[26]

Reading some of the Christian texts of the Tang era, especially the *Book on Profound and Mysterious Blessedness* (*Zhixuan anle jing*), one can see that the symbolic and linguistic features found in Buddhism (particularly in Pure Land Buddhism) can also be found in these texts. Beyond any specific doctrinal or institutional affiliation, elements of Pure Land devotion can be found in all of Chinese Buddhism, and therefore these elements were not proper to a peculiar Buddhist school distinct from the others.[27] This fact leads one to think that it may have been all the more easy for the elements of Pure Land spirituality to influence the spirituality of the authors of the Tang Chinese Christian texts. In a few passages of the *Book on Profound and Mysterious Blessedness*, the Christian Way is called Luminous Teaching (*jingjiao*):

> Those who persevere in the supreme transcendent doctrine, put into practice the Luminous Teaching, and lead to salvation other living beings, they will share in blessedness in marvelous ways.[28]

> Only the supreme transcendent doctrine of this Luminous Teaching can protect living beings from the enemy [forces] that afflict them.[29]

> Only the supreme transcendent doctrine of this Luminous Teaching can lead living beings across the ocean of mortality to the other shore, the place of blessedness and precious scents.[30]

---

24. See Lieu 1992, 255–57. For *guangfo*, see DMTC, 24; for *Moni guangfo*, see DMTC, 105. A Manichaean manuscript discovered in 2008 in Xiapu County (Fujian) bears the title *Moni guangfo* (see Yang Fuxue and Bao Lang 2015).

25. See Mikkelsen 2002, 238–39.

26. See Holth 1968, 26–27. On the shared symbolism of light and radiance in some medieval Chinese Christian, Buddhist, and Daoist texts, see also Chen Huaiyu 2020, 98–101.

27. See Sharf 2002.

28. Text E, cols. 129–30, p. 294.

29. Text E, cols. 137–38, p. 295.

30. Text E, cols. 140–42, p. 295.

The Christian Presence in China 65

Only the supreme transcendent doctrine of this Luminous Teaching can ensure that living beings return to life [in which one has access] to the knowledge of truth, and every kind of sin and sorrow is eliminated.[31]

Christianity is called Luminous Teaching in the inscription on the Xi'an stele and in the Tang Christian manuscripts. In Chinese historiographic sources, however, the Christian religion was initially called *Bosi jiao* 波斯教, "the teaching of Persia"; and *Bosi jingjiao* 波斯經教, "the teaching of the scriptures of Persia" or, perhaps more properly, "texts and teachings of Persia."[32]

As Antonino Forte remarked, at a first glance it appears "rather curious that the term 'Persian' is applied to Christianity, which originated outside Persia, and not to Mazdeism or Manichaeism born in Persia. It is as if when Christianity was introduced into China, it was the 'Persian religion' *par excellence*."[33] Forte, however, cautiously asserted that the reason for this designation was not simply because Christianity was practiced in Persia, as the extant Tang sources state, but rather because Christianity was an important institution in Sasanian Iran and within its court, and also because it continued to be so among Iranians residing in the early Tang Empire after the collapse of Sasanian rule in 651.[34] More recently, R. Todd Godwin focused his study precisely on the Persian and courtly nature of the Church of the East's presence in Tang China, seriously taking into account the fact that the Church of the East moved with the fallen Sasanian royal house into Central Asia and China after the Arab conquest and carried the Sasanian royal house and its legitimacy with it.[35] Godwin has shown that the closeness existing between the Church of the East and the late Sasanian imperial court was carried into the Tang imperial setting and, though it changed over time, this closeness informed

---

31. Text E, cols. 144–45, p. 295.

32. See Nie 2011.

33. Forte 1996c, 363–64.

34. See ibid., 364, quoting Pelliot as support: "In Persia the Nestorians became in some sort a national Christian church. I do not mean by that that Christianity under the Sasanian dynasty was the official creed of Persia, but the Nestorian Church had taken some appearance of being a Persian national Nestorian Church. . . . It is this Nestorian Church of Persia which . . . in 635 finally reached the capital of the Chinese Tang dynasty at Hsi-an-fu [Xi'an fu]" (Pelliot 1930, 304–5).

35. On the relations between the last Sasanian sovereigns and the Chinese Empire, see Harmatta 1971; Humbach and Wang 1988; Compareti 2003, 2009; Pashazanous and Afkande 2014; Agostini and Stark 2016.

66 A HISTORY OF ENCOUNTERS

and shaped the relation between the Church of the East and the Tang court and emperors. The main reason this was possible was what Godwin calls the imperial charisma of the Persian courtly and ascetic elites living in China.[36]

The name *Bosi jiao* was used for most of the Tang era, but in 745 an imperial edict ordered that another geographical specification was to be preferred to define the region where Christianity originated, namely, Da Qin. Da Qin is the general term used by the Chinese sources to designate the eastern regions of the Roman Empire; it already occurs in the *Hou Han shu* (Annals of the Later Han, compiled in the fifth century).[37] This expression was coined by the peoples of Central Asia who had contact with both the Chinese and the Roman empires. For them China was the empire of Qin, from the name of the dynasty that first united it (221–206 BCE); the Roman Empire, which to their eyes must have seemed greater and more powerful, was the empire of Da Qin, that is, of "Great China." In East Syriac Christian texts in Chinese, Da Qin more likely indicates Syria, the place the Church of the East originated, rather than Persia, the land from which the monks of that church came to China, since for Persia already existed the designation Bosi.[38] This distinction is supported by the content of the edict of Emperor Xuanzong, dated 745, which ordered that the name of the Christian monasteries was to be changed:

> The texts and teachings of Persia originated in Da Qin; after being transmitted and practiced [in Persia], they came to China, where they have been circulating for a long time. Thus it was that when monasteries were built [in China], they were accordingly named [monasteries of Persia]. Wishing to show people that it is necessary to comprehend their origin, it is proper that the monasteries of Persia in the two capitals change [their names] to monasteries of Da Qin [Da Qin si]. As for those established in the superior prefectures and commanderies of the empire, they too should conform to this.[39]

---

36. See Godwin 2017.

37. See Leslie and Gardiner 1996; Lieu 2016a. For new insights on the interpretation of the name Da Qin, see also Godwin 2020.

38. See Daffinà 1983.

39. The basic text is found in *Tang huiyao* (Essential Regulations of the Tang) 49, 8: 864. It is also contained, with small variants, in *Tongdian* (Comprehensive History of Regulations) 40, 1: 1103; and *Cefu yuangui* (The Primary Divination Turtle of the Records Office) 51, fols. 2049–b2, 1: 575. The identical text of *Cefu yuangui* is found undated in *Quan Tang wen* (Complete

The choice of the name *Da Qin jiao* 大秦教, "the teaching of Da Qin," which explicitly indicates the land the Christian teaching came from, suggests that still in the mid-eighth century "the Church of the East was not only thought of as a foreign entity, but was to be reminded of this,"[40] at least on an official level. The real motivation for the decision to change the name, however, is unknown and continues to be the subject of debate. One proposal sees Christianity's adoption of the name "the teaching of Da Qin" as a skillful adaptation of the Church of the East to the political ideology prevailing in the Chinese imperial court in the first half of the eighth century, as well as to the changed international political climate of the time.[41] It seems likely that "the decision in 745 may have been adopted just because by that time official Persian backing of the religion had already ceased. This was quite normal given the collapse of the country and the loss of any hope that the Sasanian dynasty would be restored."[42]

Max Deeg believes that changing the identity of the provenance of Christianity from Bosi to Da Qin probably was a politically calculated move on the part of the Church of the East in China. At a time when the Persian (Sasanian) Empire had ceased to exist and the Chinese became increasingly suspicious of the intentions of Iranians in Tang China after the An Lushan Rebellion (755–63), "such a shift to a more neutral but at the same time more positive self-identity combined of different elements (culture, religion, language, ethnicity) may have proved potentially helpful to claim a partial Chinese identity."[43] According to Deeg, "adopting the identity marker Da Qin not only allowed a higher degree of Sinicization for Iranian Christians in the Tang Empire, but at the same time also allowed them to claim an origin from the wider region in which, according to their own tradition, their Messiah was born."[44] Moreover,

> to replace it [i.e., Bosi] with the more inclusive . . . toponym Da Qin had some advantages. It reflected a coherent community of Christians,

---

Prose Works of the Tang) 32, fol. 7a2–3, 1: 357, under the title *Gai Bosi si wei Da Qin si zhao* (Edict on the Change of Monasteries of Persia into Monasteries of Da Qin).

40. Godwin 2017, 70.

41. See Barrett 2002.

42. Forte 1996c, 364.

43. Deeg 2020a, par. 28.

44. Ibid., par. 29.

disregarding their linguistic, regional or cultural origin or affiliation such as Persian, Sogdian, Bactrian, etc., [and] it clearly demarcated Christianity from the Manichaeans. Da Qin also enabled Christians to distance themselves from the pejorative notions that were connected to the name Bosi as reflected in Buddhist and historiographical sources.[45]

In summary, therefore, according to the contemporary Chinese sources, the Christian religion in China during the Tang era was designated in three different ways: (1) "the teaching of Persia," which was the official denomination attested in official historical sources and which remained in use until 745; (2) "the teaching of Da Qin," the official denomination that in 745 replaced the previous one in the same sources; (3) "the Luminous Teaching," the name that seems to have arisen and been used within the Church of the East in China and that is testified to by "ecclesiastical" documents such as the inscription on the Xi'an stele, the *Hymn in Praise of the Salvation Achieved through the Three Majesties of the Luminous Teaching*, the *Book on Profound and Mysterious Blessedness*, and the *Book of the Luminous Teaching of Da Qin on Revealing the Origin and Reaching the Foundation*. David Wilmshurst went so far as to propose that Adam/Jingjing, the author of the Xi'an stele text, was a possible originator and propagator of the term *jingjiao*, a term that would position Christianity as a universal religion rather than as a religion first associated with a foreign land.[46]

A Chronicle of the Events Attested by the Sources

The years 635 and 845 officially mark the beginning and the end of the presence of East Syriac Christianity in Tang China in the sense that there is documentary evidence that there were Christian communities in the Chinese Tang Empire over the course of these two centuries.

The text of the Xi'an stele speaks to us of the arrival of the first official mission, which was recognized by the imperial court:

When the emperor of cultivated virtues Taizong [r. 627–49] inaugurated his glorious and splendid kingdom, he revealed himself to be an enlightened

---

45. Ibid., par. 27.

46. See Wilmshurst 1990, 65–66.

The Christian Presence in China 69

sage in the governance of his people. [At that time] in the kingdom of Da Qin there was a man of superior virtue whose name was Aluoben. Having scrutinized the signs of blue clouds, he took [with him] the true scriptures, and having examined the musical tones of the winds, he underwent difficulties and dangers. In the ninth year of the Zhenguan era [635], he arrived in Chang'an. The emperor sent his minister of state, Duke Fang Xuanling, with the Imperial Guard in the western suburbs of the city to welcome the visitor and introduce him to the Palace. The emperor had the scriptures translated in the [Imperial] Library and carefully examined that Way within the forbidden doors. He thus became deeply convinced of the orthodoxy and truth [of that doctrine] and gave special orders for it to be propagated.[47]

Aluoben is therefore the name of the first missionary of the Church of the East to come to China and be mentioned in the sources, and 635 is "the first certain point in our knowledge of Chinese Christianity."[48] In the text of the inscription, Aluoben is described as a missionary rather than a diplomat. However, the reception extended to Aluoben by the minister of state Fang Xuanling reveals that the visit drew the attention of the court. Aluoben's arrival must have been preceded by a diplomatic mission, implying that the Chinese court was already aware of the prominence and influence of Christianity. It is also possible that Aluoben could have been a "secret" diplomatic envoy sent by the collapsing Sasanian court to the Tang emperor.[49]

Of course, this does not prevent us from supposing that even before that date there was a Christian presence in the imperial territory, although it may not have been organized. Prior to the Tang dynasty, Chinese sources record the presence of an important (probably Uighur) Christian family of immigrants from the Western Regions, who settled in Lintao (Gansu) in 578.[50] Elsewhere we have only sporadic hints or legendary stories about

---

47. Text A, cols. 10–11, pp. 204–5.

48. Moule 1930, 24. Lin Wushu (2008) doubts the historicity of this date, since it is attested only by the inscription on the Xi'an stele.

49. About Aluoben, see Fang Hao 1970, 1: 4–6; Thompson 2009; Yeung 2019.

50. See Ma Qingxiang's biography in *Jin shi* (History of the Jin) 124, fols. 1–16, 2: 1212–19; Yuan Haowen, *Hengzhou cishi Ma jun shendao bei* (Stele on the Spirit-Way of Gentleman Ma, Prefect of Hengzhou), in *Yishan xiansheng wenji* (Collected Works of Mr. [Yuan] Yishan) 27, 3: 272–74. For an English translation of these sources, see Saeki 1951, 86, 479–89.

70 A HISTORY OF ENCOUNTERS

Christians in pre-Tang China.[51] According to a tradition whose antiquity cannot readily be established, Christianity was first introduced to China by Saint Thomas, the apostle of India.[52] There is a liturgical attestation of this tradition in a hymn in the Breviary of the Chaldean Church that reads:

> Through Mar Thomas the region of India has been converted from error to truth. Through Mar Thomas the darkness of idolatry has been illuminated and the darkness of idolatry has disappeared. Through Mar Thomas the error of idolatry by the Indians has ceased. Through Mar Thomas the Chinese, together with the Ethiopians, have also turned to the truth. . . . Through Mar Thomas the rays of the teaching of life have arisen throughout India. Through Mar Thomas the kingdom from above was spread and raised up in Bet Ṣinaye [the lands of the Chinese].[53]

The tradition that Saint Thomas was the apostle of China appears in other East Syriac sources, such as the *Law of Christianity* (*Fiqh al-naṣrāniyya*) by Ibn al-Ṭayyib (d. 1043)[54] and the *Nomocanon* by ʿAbdišoʿ of Nisibis (1290).[55]

Some Catholic missionaries working in the East at the end of the sixteenth and beginning of the seventeenth century also refer to this tradition and see themselves as the extension of Thomas's apostolate from India to China. Among them are the Spanish Jesuit Francis Xavier (1506–52), missionary in India and the Far East, in one of his *Letters*;[56] the Portuguese Dominican Gaspar da Cruz (ca. 1520–70), missionary in various countries of East Asia, in his *Tractado em que se contam muito por estenso as cousas da China*;[57] and the Belgian Jesuit Nicolas Trigault (1577–1628), missionary in China, in his work

---

51. See Latourette 1929, 48–51; Moule 1930, 1–26; Gillman and Klimkeit 1999, 265–67; Wang Weifan 2001, 2002; Ferreira 2007; 2014, 287–92.

52. In addition to the general works mentioned in the previous note, see the following specific contributions: "La question de l'apostolat de saint Thomas en Chine" 1925; Noyé 1934, 1935; Duvigneau 1936; Fang Hao 1970, 1: 1–3; Gu 1993; Tubach 1995–96, 2009; Conte 2013.

53. *Chaldean Breviary*, Office of Mar Thomas the Apostle (3 July), ed. Bedjan, 3: 476.

54. See Ibn al-Ṭayyib, *The Law of Christianity* VI.1.41, ed. and trans. Hoenerbach and Spies, CSCO 167, 2: 138 (text); CSCO 168, 140–41 (trans.): "The regions of Moṣul, al-Ahwaz, Fars, [Merv?], Gundešapur, India and China (al-Ṣin) belong to the mission of Thomas."

55. ʿAbdišoʿ of Nisibis, *Nomocanon* 9.1, in Mai 1825–38, 10 (pars I): 317 (text), 154 (trans.).

56. See Francis Xavier, *Letters* 56.16 (10 May 1546), in *Monumenta Xaveriana*, 1: 407, 414.

57. See Cruz 1569, fol. k iii (chap. 27).

De christiana expeditione apud Sinas suscepta ab Societate Jesu (1615). Trigault reports that "in these [Syriac] manuscripts [of the Malabar coast] . . . we read very plainly that the faith was carried to China by the same Apostle of Christ [i.e., Saint Thomas] and that several churches were founded [by him] in that kingdom."[58]

As evidence of Thomas's missionary activity in China, Trigault offers the Latin translation of two passages from the breviary in use in the Syro-Malabar Church in India.[59] These passages correspond to those from the Chaldean Breviary mentioned above. The same information is repeated a little later in some passages by other Jesuit missionaries in China: Álvaro de Semedo (1585/86–1658), in his *Relação da propagação da fé no reyno da China* (1641);[60] António de Gouvea (1592–1677), in his *Ásia Extrema* (1644);[61] Michał Piotr Boym (1612–59); and Athanasius Kircher (1602–80), in the well-known *China Illustrata* (1667).[62] This argument is repeated again by the Franciscan friar Carlo Horatii da Castorano (1673–1755) as late as the mid-eighteenth century in his "Brevi notizie della Cina" (1740). What he adds to the traditional argument are some curious details about Saint Thomas's apostolate to China:

The first time, therefore, that the Christian religion entered China was, we believe on the basis of various writers, through the Apostle St. Thomas. The first [witness] is given by various Indian monuments and by the *Office* and *Prayers* of St. Thomas, where it is said that he spread the Christian religion also in *Cathay*, that is, in Northern China. Secondly, among the many idols or figures of idols that are adored in the temples of China, one resembles the figure of St. Thomas the Apostle and is also called *Tomo*. Although the second syllable, *mo*, is pronounced in the northerly reaches of China with a rounded *e* or *o*, the proper and genuine tone and sound of the Chinese character 默 should be pronounced *me*, with a clear *e*, and not *o*; hence these two Chinese characters (used to write the name of this idol) 多默 should be read *Tome*, and it is certain that in India the Apostle St. Thomas

58. Ricci and Trigault 1615, 124.

59. Ibid., 124–25.

60. See Semedo 1655, 154–55 (part I, chap. 31).

61. See António de Gouvea, *Ásia Extrema* I.2.1, ed. Araújo, 2: 17–18.

62. See Kircher 1667, 9–10, 57.

is called *Tome*. Therefore, taking together the figure and the name of the said holy Apostle, we conclude and believe that among the other kingdoms of India where St. Thomas preached the Gospel, he also preached in *Cathay*, that is, in China.[63]

Quite recently, two French scholars have proposed an original but completely questionable interpretation of some archaeological evidence on rock in order to offer what they consider to be irrefutable proof of evangelization by the Apostle Thomas in China. This evidence consists of some scenes engraved on a rock face of the small mountain of Kongwangshan, not far from Lianyungang (Jiangsu), a port in Eastern China.[64] The largest of the engraved figures is thought to represent the Apostle Thomas. He wears a heavy coat that would have been appropriate for a long journey; his hand, at waist height, may have held a cross. To corroborate this fanciful Christian interpretation of these archaeological finds, the authors point to what they claim is a Christogram: a crouching female image, with a tiny and slightly bowed over person on her left, who is interpreted to be the Virgin Mary pointing to the child Jesus in the folds of her garment. The authors also claim there are scenes in which the Apostle Thomas can be seen preaching to Mingdi (r. 58–75), the emperor of the Eastern Han dynasty. From an iconographic, historical, and literary point of view, there is nothing to substantiate this Christian interpretation of Kongwangshan's rock engravings.[65]

Continuing our documentary investigation in search of traces of primitive Christian preaching on Chinese soil, we discover that the Latin rhetorician Arnobius in his work *Against the Heathen*, written around 300, intended to show that the extraordinary works of Christ and his apostles throughout the world "caused races, and peoples, and nations most diverse in character to hasten with one accord to accept the same faith." He speaks of events that have happened, among other people, even "among the *Seres*."[66] However, since the context of this statement is clearly apologetic, it is difficult to regard

---

63. Carlo Horatii da Castorano, "Brevi notizie della Cina," 544. The words in italics correspond to the underlined words in the manuscript. The Tomo mentioned by Castorano is actually Damo, the Chinese name of Bodhidharma (fifth to sixth century), traditionally credited as the transmitter of Chan Buddhism to China, and regarded as the first Chinese patriarch of this school.

64. See Perrier and Walter 2008; Perrier 2012.

65. See Cecchelli 2014, 653–55; Thompson, forthcoming.

66. Arnobius of Sicca, *Against the Heathen* 2.12, PG 5: 828; trans. Bryce and Campbell, 76.

The *Christian Presence in China*

it as historical testimony of a primitive Christian mission to the *Seres*, "the silk people," the name by which the Romans had referred to the Chinese.

Finally, a legend reported by Procopius of Caesarea (sixth century) makes mention of some individuals, probably East Syriac monks of Sogdian origin, who around 552 brought some silkworms to Byzantium and offered them to the emperor Justinian (r. 527–65), thus introducing silk production to the West. Judging by Procopius's text, however, the region from which the monks imported the silkworms—"the country north of the numerous nations of India, a country called *Serínda*"—seems to indicate Central Asia, perhaps specifically Sogdiana, and not China.[67]

To be considered more carefully, but with due caution, are the reports of Syriac authors that a metropolitan see for China had already been erected in very remote times.[68] According to tradition, Aḥai (r. 411–15) and Šila (r. 505–20), patriarchs of the Church of the East, created metropolitan sees in China. The early fourteenth-century historian ʿAbdišoʿ of Nisibis in fact states that "the catholicos Ṣaliba Zka [r. 714–28] created the metropolitan sees of Heria [Herat], Samarkand, and China, although some say they were established by Aḥai and Šila."[69] Ibn al-Ṭayyib in his work *The Law of Christianity* attributes to the catholicos Išoʿyahb III (r. 649–59) the erection of China as a metropolitan see.[70]

Returning to historical data, we know that in 638, only three years after Aluoben's presumed arrival in Chang'an, Emperor Taizong issued an edict officially approving the Christian cult in the imperial territory. This edict, according to the version contained in the inscription engraved on the 781 stele, states:

> The Way does not have an immutable name; the Saint does not have an immutable bodily appearance. Every region of the earth has its own teaching. Thus all living beings may be led mysteriously to salvation.

---

67. See Procopius of Caesarea, *On the Wars* 8.17, ed. and trans. Dewing, 5: 226–31.

68. For an account of these assumptions, see Latourette 1929, 46–51; Moule 1930, 10–23. Alphonse Mingana rightly states: "The oldest mention in Syriac literature of China in the form of Ṣin, Bet Ṣinaye, or Ṣinistan dates . . . from the eighth century, and the documents containing these appellations . . . are the Nestorian monument in China, the letters of Timothy the Patriarch, and the history of Thomas of Marga" (Mingana 1925, 327).

69. ʿAbdišoʿ of Nisibis, *Nomocanon* 8.15, in Mai 1825–38, 10 (pars I): 304 (text), 141 (trans.).

70. See Ibn al-Ṭayyib, *The Law of Christianity* VI.1.16, ed. and trans. Hoenerbach and Spies, CSCO 167, 2: 121 (text); CSCO 168, 123 (trans.).

74 A HISTORY OF ENCOUNTERS

> The Great Righteous One, Aluoben, of the kingdom of Da Qin, came from far away to present the scriptures and images [of his teaching] in our supreme capital. Having carefully examined the nature of his teaching, [we have found that] it is mysterious non-action. Having evaluated its essential elements, [we have concluded that] they concern the fundamental needs of human life and its perfection. Its language is simple and meagre, and its principles remain even after the occasion for which they were established has passed. [This teaching] leads creatures to salvation, and [from it] come benefits for humans. Its diffusion in the territories of the empire should be allowed, and the competent authorities should therefore build a Monastery of Da Qin in the Yining Ward of the capital and ordain twenty-one men as monks.[71]

In the following years, imperial favor guaranteed protection for the Christian community. Soon this favor took the form of a concrete and symbolically powerful action when "the competent authorities were instructed to produce a portrait of the emperor and to place it on the wall of the monastery."[72] Later, Gaozong (r. 650–83) "emulated the reverent deference of his predecessor" toward the Luminous Teaching.[73] Then Xuanzong (r. 713–55)

> ordered the prince of the kingdom of Ning and the other four royal princes to visit the places of worship in person and [re]build the altars there. The pillars of the doctrine, which for a moment had been torn down, were erected again, and the founding stones of the Way, which for a time had been removed, were put back in their proper position. At the beginning of the Tianbao era [742–55], [the emperor] ordered the general-in-chief Gao Lishi to take the portraits of the five saints to the various monasteries and place them inside, along with the gift of a hundred rolls of silk.[74]

The same Xuanzong "composed the vertical inscriptions that were placed in the monasteries, where the horizontal tablets with their calligraphy of the dragon

---

71. Text A, cols. 12–13, p. 205.

72. Text A, col. 13, p. 206.

73. Text A, col. 15, p. 206.

74. Text A, cols. 17–18, p. 208.

were [also] prominent."[75] The presentation of couplets of calligraphy from the emperor's own hand has been a mark of high imperial favor throughout Chinese history. The same benevolence was guaranteed by the successive emperors Suzong (r. 756–62) and Daizong (r. 763–79): "On every one of his birthdays he . . . offered food from his table to lend luster to the luminous community."[76] According to the text of the stele, the only period in which the Christian community suffered the hostility of imperial power was the long reign of Empress Wu Zetian (r. 690–705). In this period of great political unrest, "in the Shengli era [698–99] the sons of Śākyamuni, capitalizing on their position of strength, raised their voices [against the Luminous Teaching] in the eastern capital of Zhou, and at the end of the Xiantian era [712] some inferior scholars mocked and defamed [that teaching] in the western capital of Hao."[77] In the thirty years between 683 and 712 the Christian community evidently had to face much hostility, both because the Buddhists were favored by Empress Wu and because the Daoists were very influential at court during the successive reigns of Zhongzong (r. 705–9) and Ruizong (r. 710–12). The text inscribed on the stele that reports the Luminous Teaching's response and the efforts it made to reclaim its lost position reveals the strategy it used to negotiate a legitimate identity in China:

> There were [some persons] such as the head of the monks Luohan and the Great Virtuous Jilie, people of noble race in the Gold Region, eminent monks elevated above worldly things, who joined together to weave the mysterious net again and together they reconnected the knots that had been loosened. . . . The pillars of the doctrine, which for a moment had been torn down, were erected again, and the founding stones of the Way, which for a time had been removed, were put back in their proper position.[78]

In this rapid historical overview, we must also mention the arrival in the Chinese capital of several delegations that included bishops. This should not come as a surprise, since it was common practice to nominate culturally prepared bishops as ambassadors of the Persian Empire to foreign powers. The

---

75. Text A, col. 19, p. 209. The dragon is a symbol of the emperor.

76. Text A, col. 20, p. 210.

77. Text A, col. 16, p. 207.

78. Text A, cols. 16–17, pp. 207–8.

76   A HISTORY OF ENCOUNTERS

arrival of these delegations also confirms the fact that until the first half of the eighth century, diplomatic ties between the Chinese imperial court and Persia were still in force.[79]

In 719 a "great virtuous monk" (*dade seng* 大德僧) from Fulin (lit., "Rome," i.e., the Eastern Roman Empire), in all likelihood a bishop whose name is not mentioned in the sources, was sent to pay homage to the imperial court.[80] According to the *Cefu yuangui* (The Primary Divination Turtle of the Records Office), a Chinese historical source compiled in the early eleventh century, in 732 the king of Persia sent the chieftain Pannami, accompanied by a "great virtuous monk" (*dade seng*) named Jilie, who was probably a bishop, to the imperial court as an envoy from Persia.[81] The chief military leader Pannami was awarded military honors, while the monk Jilie "was presented with a set of purple colored robes and fifty bolts of silk."[82] It is significant that a "Great Virtuous Jilie" from the "Gold Region" (probably Bactria) is also mentioned in the text of the stele.[83] There are reasons to believe that these two Jilie are the same person. In 744, the Christian monk Jihe[84] left his homeland to reach China, as the text of the stele recounts:

> In the third year of the same era [744] in the kingdom of Da Qin there was the monk Jihe, who, upon observing the stars turned in the direction of the Transformation, and keeping before his eyes the sun, went

---

79. See Ecsedy 1979; Pulleyblank 1992; Rogers 1992.

80. See *Jiu Tang shu* (Old Annals of the Tang) 198, 16: 5315: "In an undetermined month [of the seventh year of the Kaiyuan era, 719] a great virtuous monk was also sent to offer tribute to the court."

81. See *Cefu yuangui* (The Primary Divination Turtle of the Records Office) 971, fol. 9b4, 12: 11409: "In the ninth month [of the twentieth year of the Kaiyuan era, i.e., September 24– October 23, 732], the king of Persia sent the chieftain Pannami and the great virtuous monk Jilie to offer tribute to the court." Some think that Jilie might be a phonetic transcription of the Syriac name Gabri'el, but from the phonological point of view it seems unlikely.

82. See *Cefu yuangui* (The Primary Divination Turtle of the Records Office) 975, fol. 13b1–3, 12: 11454: "On the Gengxu day of the eighth [read: ninth] month [of the twentieth year of the Kaiyuan era, i.e., October 3, 732], the king of Persia sent the chieftain Pannami and the great virtuous monk Jilie to the court. The chieftain was given [the title of] courageous [commandant, *guoyi duwei* 果毅都尉] and the monk was presented with a set of purple colored robes and fifty bolts of silk. Then they went back to the border."

83. Text A, col. 16, p. 207.

84. Two different interpretations have been proposed for the name Jihe: it could be the Chinese phonetic transcription of either the Syro-Iranian name Gigoy, or the Syriac Giwargis (George) or its diminutive Gigoe.

The Christian Presence in China

to pay homage to the Honored One. An [imperial] edict ordered that the monk Luohan, the monk Pulun, and seven others cultivate merits at Xingqing Palace along with the Great Virtuous Jihe.[85]

The historical narrative contained in the text of the stele ends at the year 781. Between that year and 845 we have no official account of events related to Christian communities. In 842, three years before the persecution of Buddhists, the Manichaeans were targeted,[86] and it is quite possible that this persecution included Christians. Since both came from Persia, they could easily be confused by the common people. According to various Chinese historical sources, the persecution of 845 was mainly directed against Buddhists for economic reasons,[87] but it also explicitly involved believers of other foreign religions, namely Christians and Zoroastrians. I quote the two interesting parts of the edict of persecution, as found in *Jiu Tang shu* (Old Annals of the Tang), in the section on Wuzong's reign (Huichang era, 841–46):

> As far as the forms of worship of Da Qin [Christianity] and the *muhu* 穆護 [Zoroastrianism] are concerned, just as appropriate measures have already been taken against Buddhism, neither can these heretical doctrines be allowed to survive. Monks of these cults, therefore, should also be induced to return to the lay state, move to their homes of origin, and pay taxes. If they are foreigners, they are to return to their own countries and be subject to their own jurisdictions. . . . Monks of Da Qin [Christians] and *muhu* [Zoroastrian] fire worshippers [*xian* 祆],[88] who number more than three thousand, are

---

85. Text A, col. 18, p. 209. "The Transformation" indicates China and "the Honored One" indicates the emperor; the expression "cultivate merits" is borrowed from Buddhist terminology and indicates the celebration of worship.

86. Li Deyu (787–850), an administrator of great distinction who was responsible for translating the imperial will into action, gave in a text dated April 842 a very guarded explanation of the closure of the Manichaean temples: see Li Deyu, *Ci huigu kehan shu yi* (The Purpose of a Letter Conferred to the *Qaghan* of the Uighurs), in *Li Deyu wenji* (Collected Works of Li Deyu) 5, ed. Fu and Zhou, 81 (text); Lieu 1998, 129 (trans.).

87. For an English translation of the relevant Chinese sources, see Foster 1939, 121–26, 158–62. On the context of the economic and moral crisis that lies against the background of persecution, see Ch'en 1956.

88. The edition of the text I consulted (Beijing: Zhonghua shuju, 1975) adopts the correction of the expression *muhufu* 穆護祓 to *muhu xian* 穆護祆. Some authors do not consider it necessary to correct the *muhufu* expression, seeing behind it the probable transcription of

78 A HISTORY OF ENCOUNTERS

to return to the lay state, so that they do not interfere with China's customs.[89]

For a minority community which, as we shall see, was formed around a largely foreign clergy, this persecution must have inflicted such a violent blow that it was no longer able to recover. Unlike the situation they faced on the central plain of China, Christians could continue living in peace in the northwestern sites such as Dunhuang and Turfan, where there were more tolerant political governments, namely, the Guiyijun Regime in Shazhou Prefecture (851–ca. 1036) and the Uighur kingdom of Qočo (ca. 850–1250). Chinese sources and Sogdian documents from both sites also reveal the existence of some sort of connection and exchange between the two Christian communities.[90] On the basis of documentary evidence, Sun Jianqiang argues that "Christians maintained a continuous presence in Dunhuang from the eighth century up to the eleventh century."[91]

Some Christians fled to the south of the country, where a number of (foreign) Christians involved in trade had already settled, believing that this region's more tolerant and open climate could guarantee their survival. However, the sociopolitical unrest that also existed in that location did not favor their stay. A rebellion led by Huang Chao in 877–78 devastated the southern provinces. In his work *Accounts of China and India* (*Aḫbār al-Ṣīn wa-l-Hind*), the Arab historian Abū Zayd al-Sīrāfī, who arrived in China in these same years, states the following in his description of the fall of Guangzhou (Canton):

Experts on Chinese affairs reported that the number of Muslims, Jews, Christians, and Zoroastrians massacred by him [i.e., Huang Chao], quite apart from the native Chinese, was 120,000; all of them had gone to settle in this city and become merchants there. The only reason the number of victims from these four communities

---

the Middle Persian *mowbed* (chief of the Magi). On this term and the previous one (*muhu*), indicating the Zoroastrians, see Leslie 1981–83, 279, 285. A detailed summary and discussion of the whole issue can be found in Lin Wushu 1999.

89. *Jiu Tang shu* (Old Annals of the Tang) 18A, 7: 605–6.

90. See Chen Huaiyu 1999 (2012), 86–90; Sun Jianqiang 2018b, 170–90.

91. See Sun Jianqiang 2018b, 189.

The Christian Presence in China

happens to be known is that the Chinese had kept records of their numbers.[92]

The Church of the East in China probably never recovered from these two blows. In this respect, it is significant that the ecclesiastical province of China (Bet Ṣinaye) was omitted from a detailed list of fourteen East Syriac metropolitan provinces and their suffragan dioceses compiled by Eliya of Damascus in 893.[93] When the patriarch 'Abdišo' I sent a delegation to the Far East in 980 to make contact with the surviving communities, one of its members, a monk from Nağran (a town in the south of the Arabian Peninsula), returned from the East and reported that Christianity was no longer in existence in China. The account of his report comes to us in the work of another Arab author, Abū-l-Farağ Muḥammad ibn Isḥāq (more commonly known as Ibn al-Nadīm, d. 996), whose *Catalogue* (*Kitāb al-Fihrist*), written in 987/88, tells us that

> the monk of Nağran, who returned from China in the year 377 of the hegira [987], told me that he had been sent to China, about seven years earlier, by the catholicos, along with five other Christians, among whom were doctors of the faith. Of this small group, the monk and one other returned six years later. I met him in Constantinople, behind the church. He was a young, good-looking man who spoke little, unless he was questioned. I asked him why he had left his country, and the reasons for his delay [in coming back]. He told me of the events that had forced him to linger for so long, and said that the Christians of China had disappeared and perished for various reasons, and that there was only one left in the whole country. He said that they had one church in that region, but it was in ruins. "When I saw that there was no one I could entrust with the interests of the faith, I returned in less time than it took me to go there."[94]

The causes of the decline and eventual disappearance of the communities of the Church of the East at the end of the ninth and beginning of the tenth

---

92. Abū Zayd al-Sīrāfī, *Accounts of China and India* II.2.1, in Mackintosh-Smith and Montgomery 2014, 68 (text), 69 (trans.).

93. See Eliya of Damascus, *List of the East Syriac Episcopal Sees*, trans. Assemani, 2: 458–60.

94. Ibn al-Nadīm (Abū-l-Farağ Muḥammad ibn Isḥāq), *The Catalogue* 9.2, ed. Flügel, Roediger, and Mueller, 1: 349.

century have been the subject of many studies over time, but there is still some speculation about the reasons the Christian presence in China came to an end. I believe they can be summarized in these three hypotheses.[95]

The first hypothesis postulates that Tang Christianity disappeared for political reasons. Having entrusted its survival to the imperial favor of the Tang court, on which the Church of the East in China relied for many years and from which it received protection and patronage, it perished when the dynasty was in crisis and came to an end.[96] The Muslim conquest of Persia, home of many Christian missionaries, and its later subjugation of Central Asia abruptly severed the many ties China had with the Persian Empire and the kingdoms of Central Asia. For several centuries these two empires had established an alliance through diplomatic missions, which occasionally included monks, and also through the presence of representatives of the courts of the Central Asian kingdoms at the Chinese imperial court in the capital Chang'an. In this respect, the presence of the so-called hostages (*zhizi* 質子) was significant. These hostages were members of the ruling family of an allied state who were held at the Chinese court as guarantors of the alliance. Some families of these guarantors appear to have been Christian.[97]

The second hypothesis highlights a missiological cause. According to some authors, the Church of the East in China never really became Chinese. Continuing to rely on an exclusively foreign hierarchy, it failed to take root among the Chinese people. When the Islamic advance in Central Asia made communication between the center (the catholicosate of Seleucia-Ctesiphon) and the periphery (the outer ecclesiastical provinces) extremely difficult, the vital channel for the survival of the churches in East Asia was interrupted and these communities found themselves isolated. Along the same line of a failed inculturation, another author claims that the use of Syriac as the common liturgical language in all mission territories to signify unity was a mistake because it hindered the process of situating the churches in Asian culture.[98] However, this claim can only be made by someone who does not consider or does not know how to interpret the documents available to us. Chinese

---

95. See Saeki 1955; Che 1971; Yang Senfu 1977; Cai 1983; Moffett 1992, 302–14; Lin Wushu 1998a, 2000b; Gillman and Klimkeit 1999, 282–85 ("The Decline of Christianity in T'ang China"); Chen Huaiyu 2000; Ge 2000; Deeg 2006a; Liu Boyun 2010; Ferreira 2014, 313–15.

96. See, in particular, Zheng Shulian 2012.

97. See p. 103.

98. This problem is debated in Hage 1978.

Christian sources indicate that Christianity in China in the eighth and ninth centuries was highly inculturated and that knowledge of the Syriac language in China during the Tang period was quite limited.[99]

The third hypothesis is that the cause was "theological." This hypothesis is based on a particular interpretation of the widespread acceptance of Buddhist and Daoist ideas and terminology in the Christian texts in Chinese that date back to this period. Some see in these texts evidence of extreme syncretism, that is, a "Buddhisizing" or "Daoization" of Christianity that caused the watering down of genuine Christian content and the Christian community's subsequent loss of identity.[100] Among the three reasons just presented, this seems the least defensible, both because the few texts that have come down to us do not seem to allow for such an interpretation, and because the example of the long survival of Manichaeism, which was strongly Sinicized, would indicate a contrary outcome.

A different hermeneutical approach is needed if we are to evaluate correctly the causes of the decline and ultimate disappearance of the communities of the Church of the East around the end of the Tang dynasty. There are two issues that have to be considered separately. On the one hand, there is the disappearance of Christian communities, with their places of worship and ecclesial structures. On the other hand, we need to consider the partial obscuring of the original Christian message or the way it was reformulated in the Chinese setting. Leaving aside the possibility that Christian concepts and images were absorbed into religious currents of a popular nature (Buddhist and Daoist)—a hypothesis that needs further study—I would like to clarify my view about what brought about the disappearance of Christian ecclesial structures in China.

In general, we can say that a change in imperial religious policy was certainly the main external factor that led to the decline and disappearance of Christian ecclesial structures from Chinese territory. However, a clarification is necessary. The Christian communities did not choose to rely on imperial

---

99. See Takahashi 2020, 39: "Viewed as a whole, the evidence for the knowledge of the Syriac language in China during the Tang period is relatively scanty. The Syriac text of the Xi'an stele indicates that at least a few members of the church in China had sufficiently good knowledge of Syriac to compose such texts in Syriac. As has been mentioned previously, we know that monks from monasteries in the heartland of the Church of the East in Mesopotamia were appointed metropolitans and sent to China. Such bishops and the monks who accompanied them probably made up the bulk of the people capable of using Syriac in China. . . . Thus, among the mass of the faithful there was probably only limited knowledge of Syriac at any time."

100. See, among others, Yu 2002.

82 A HISTORY OF ENCOUNTERS

power to obtain benefits or to gain favors from it, as Henri Leclercq claims. Referring to the numerous expressions of praise and deference to the emperors that are found in the text of the Xi'an stele, he says, "The praise lavished by the author [of the stele] on the Chinese emperors is too exaggerated."[101] The laudatory rhetoric of the Xi'an stele was not primarily an attempt to curry favor but an expression of submission or obedience to the rules that were prescribed for each religious organization in the Chinese Empire. In the traditional Chinese view, the power of state sovereignty is actualized through the integration of political and religious-cultural activities. Tang emperors turned this practice into a dominant political discourse to support royal legitimacy and the centralization of power. In this general framework, in which religions were in a position of absolute dependence on imperial power, Christianity also had to adapt to this policy.[102]

This relationship of dependence on political power is echoed in some passages of the Xi'an Christian stele, which mentions various honors that the different sovereigns bestowed on the Christian community and some of its members. In addition to the concession to build some Christian monasteries and the honors awarded to some Christian monks by the emperor, the close relationship between sovereign and Christian communities is evident in the decision made by Emperor Xuanzong to have the portraits of the emperors placed in the monasteries and in his gift of one hundred rolls of silk to these same communities.[103] R. Todd Godwin reminds us that we are here confronted with an "open imperial charisma" shared by emperors, courts, and ascetics. Christian "imperial monastics, through their asceticism and spiritual support for the Tang Empire, could participate in the personal charisma of the emperor himself."[104] This is made evident in the "rhetoric of imperial charisma participation"[105] that appears in the Xi'an stele and which can only be understood if we look at "the long durational and paradoxically imperial identity of the Church [of the East]"[106] rather than simply confining ourselves to the immediate context of the Xi'an stele. Under Sasanian rule and then under Muslim rule the Church of the East had learned that a persistent effort

---

101. Leclercq 1913, 1373.

102. See Lin Wushu 1998b.

103. For a discussion, see Text A, cols. 17–18, p. 208n82.

104. Godwin 2017, 16.

105. Ibid., 59.

106. Ibid., 189.

to build good relations with political authorities was the way to build a good relationship with the state. Working toward political and social integration while maintaining religious distinctiveness characterized *jingjiao*'s attempts to negotiate its place of belonging in Tang China.[107]

Buddhism experienced the same process of adaptation to the imperial political-religious vision. Like Christianity, Buddhism was initially foreign to China, arriving there in various stages in the first century of the Common Era. During the Tang dynasty, Buddhism seems to have already solved the difficult problem of the relationship between the monastic institution with its vision of salvation and the government with its policies regarding the use of power. Having adopted the theory of mutual dependence on the law of Buddha and the law of the sovereign, the monks accepted being subordinate to the government. They submitted to the control of the court and performed rites for the peace and welfare of the state. In turn the government sponsored the construction of important temples, founded monasteries in every province of the country, and exempted them from taxes. During the reign of Empress Wu Zetian, Buddhism even managed to become the official ideology, one based on the principles of pacifism and universalism.[108]

From this perspective, it is clear that the rise and fall of religious institutions in Tang China was indeed completely subject to the encompassing control of the central political administrative system. In other words, the strengthening or weakening of Tang religious institutions was determined by the active interference and rigorous application of imperial policies. For this reason, it might be more appropriate to consider the downfall of Tang Christianity from a political-religious point of view instead of a purely cultural one. Familiarity with Tang sovereign "political theology" will give us a more accurate understanding of the reasons for the demise of *jingjiao* in Tang China.[109]

At the same time, however, one should not overlook the great hardship inflicted on these small Christian communities in China—whose hierarchy, as far as we know, was foreign—by the loss of relations with the center of Syriac Christianity in Persia, whence they had come. Because of the geopolitical changes in Central Asia and the advance of Islam, it was no longer possible to repeat an external intervention similar to the sending of new missionaries from Central Asia which, according to the testimony of the

---

107. See Morrow 2019, 15–41.

108. See Ch'en 1972; Wright 1973; Forte 1976; Guisso 1978; Weinstein 1987.

109. See Zeng Qingbao 2011, 2019.

Xi'an stele, revived the Christian community in a difficult time between the end of the seventh century and the beginning of the eighth. The foreign head of the Tang Church was therefore cut off from his mother church and there was no Chinese leadership to replace him. In conclusion, we can say that

> To the extent that the vital nerve centre of the Nestorian Church was weakened, the distant ecclesiastical provinces and the Christian communities of Asia were also adversely affected. The difficulties of communication over such vast areas and the continuous wars that ravaged Asia also contributed to their decline. The communities were therefore left to fend for themselves. . . . When the Arabs occupied Bactria and went as far as Turkestan, and, above all, after the massive conversion of the Turks to Islam, only a few Christians remained in those regions. But it was precisely from Bactria and the Merv region that the missionaries had departed for Central Asia and China. Thus there was a lack of continuity in the work of the apostolate just when these communities were in such need of it because they now found themselves living among the followers of other religions.[110]

In this changing landscape of international geopolitical equilibrium, the Tang Church was faced with its own internal weakness. Over the two centuries it was present on Chinese soil, Christianity had failed, or simply had not had enough time and means, to penetrate deeply into the different strata of Chinese society. Even more significant was its failure to win the support of the cultural elites. Without this support, Christianity could not take root in the soil of the dominant culture of the time. Not having become an integral part of the Chinese cultural fabric, it could not withstand the impact of the sociopolitical changes at the end of the Tang era. This conclusion is shared by Kenneth T. Morrow:

> Without Chinese in clerical leadership, the *jingjiao* church forever felt foreign, not at home. Limited in its structure to a state-partner model . . . with weak indigenous support, the universal, supra-cultural part of church life failed to grow deep indigenous roots, so the church withered when state support became state opposition.[111]

---

110. Messina 1946, 126–27.

111. Morrow 2019, 189.

The Composition and Structure
of Christian Communities

When we try to describe as precisely as possible the Christian community of the Tang era, the first problem we have to deal with is its composition. To what extent was it a local community of Chinese Christians? To what extent was it a community of foreign Christians implanted in China? This problem essentially concerns the organization of the community itself.

We know that during the patriarchate of Timothy I special attention and support were given by the Church of the East to the missions in the exterior ecclesiastical provinces, and their organizational structure was put in place.[112] The metropolitans of these distant provinces were, for the most part, monks from the Monastery of Bet 'Abe. It was very rare for a metropolitan to be chosen from among the local clergy. Significantly, one of the rare cases of the election of an indigenous metropolitan occurred in a period later than the one being considered here. In 1280, to the great surprise of his contemporaries, the catholicos Denḥa I (r. 1265–81) chose the Öngüt monk Mark (Marqos), born near Beijing, to be metropolitan of Cathay (North China) and of Ong (the Öngüt country). One year later he became Catholicos Yahballaha III (r. 1281–1317).[113]

The practice of choosing metropolitans from among the Persian clergy was certainly a means of ensuring the link between the center and the periphery of the ecclesiastical territory. In most cases, the metropolitan chose and elected his bishops and chorepiscopi, but they too were Chaldean or Persian missionary monks. The consequence of this *modus operandi* was a strongly centralized top-down organization, even if the only concrete expression of the connection between the center and the periphery was in the form of written reports that the metropolitans sent to the patriarch. These reports took the place of their physical presence at the patriarchal synods every four years in Seleucia-Ctesiphon, which metropolitans from far distant lands were not required to attend.[114] A letter from the patriarch Išoʿyahb III confirms this for the whole of the East:

---

112. For a general description of the consistency and organization of the exterior ecclesiastical provinces, see Dauvillier 1948; Hage 1988b; Borbone 2015a.

113. See Borbone 2000; Amar 2011; Dickens 2020d.

114. See Dauvillier 1948, 272; Hage 2012.

86　　　　　　　　A HISTORY OF ENCOUNTERS

There are more than twenty bishops and two metropolitans in the East who have received and will receive the episcopal consecration of the church of God; and none of them have come to us for many years, nor have we asked them to come. Even though they are far away, they carry out the ministry of their episcopate in communion with the church of God, having received from us the office of their priesthood. They write to us, and we write to them.[115]

We have evidence that the same practice was used to provide hierarchical leadership for the ecclesiastical province in China. In one of his letters, Patriarch Timothy I states that "many monks cross the seas to India and China, with only a staff and a saddlebag."[116] Thomas of Marga reports that among the bishops ordained at the Monastery of Bet ʿAbe around 787, there was a certain David (d. 810) who "was elected to be metropolitan of Bet Ṣinaye [the lands of the Chinese]."[117]

Despite the fact that Syriac documents do not indicate the precise year the metropolitan see of China was erected, nevertheless there is solid evidence that at least since the time of Timothy I, the bishop of China had the important title of metropolitan, which means that there were suffragan dioceses dependent on him. This is attested to by Timothy's letter mentioning the death of a "metropolitan of Bet Ṣinaye."[118] In the precious semi-official list of the metropolitans of the Church of the East, which was compiled according to the hierarchical importance of the sees by ʿAmr ibn Mattā in the first half of the fourteenth century and is contained in the Arab chronicle known as *Book of the Tower* (*Kitāb al-Miğdal*), we find the metropolitan of China (al-Ṣin) in the fourteenth place.[119]

---

115. Išoʿyahb III, *Letters* 3.21, ed. and trans. Duval, CSCO 11, 280 (text); CSCO 12, 202 (trans.).

116. Timothy I, *Letters* 13 (to Sergius), ed. and trans. Braun, CSCO 74, 107 (text); CSCO 75, 70 (trans.).

117. Thomas of Marga, *The Book of Governors* 4.20, ed. and trans. Budge, 1: 238 (text); 2: 448 (trans.).

118. Timothy I, *Letters* 13 (to Sergius), ed. and trans. Braun, CSCO 74, 109 (text); CSCO 75, 72 (trans.).

119. See ʿAmr ibn Mattā, *Commentary on the Patriarchs of the Church of the East*, ed. and trans. Gismondi, 126 (text), 73 (trans.).

Once again, it is the Xi'an stele that provides us with some valuable information.[120] First of all, it gives us the name of the bishop who presumably was the immediate predecessor of Bishop David: John, designated as "Mar Yoḥanan *episqopā*" in Syriac, and in Chinese as "*dade* Yaolun," "Great Virtuous Yaolun." It does not specifically say that he was a metropolitan, but the fact that he is named first in the list of seventy monks at the end of the text of the stele suggests his primatial role. The name of the episcopal (or metropolitan) see that appears in the Syriac text of the stele is "Kumdan and Sarag," which Pelliot has identified as the Sogdian names (rendered in Syriac) of the two capitals of the Tang Empire, Chang'an and Luoyang.[121] Besides him, three other monks bear the title *dade* 大德, "Great Virtuous,"[122] which could indicate their episcopal dignity: Aluoben (arrived in China in 635), Jilie (arrived in China in 732), and Jihe (arrived in China in 744).

The inscription on the stele then bears the names of four chorepiscopi (*kore'pisqopā*), three of whom bear the honorary title of *mār*. Two of them are explicitly of Persian/Central Asian origin. For the remaining two, the fact that they both have a Syriac name (Sargis), suggests a non-Chinese origin. The four chorepiscopi are:

(1) "Mar Sergius, priest and chorepiscopus";
(2) "Mar Yazdbōzīd, priest and chorepiscopus of Kumdan," also called by the Chinese name Yisi, an approximate phonetical transcription of its Iranian original; his family was originally from Balkh, in the Central Asian region of Bactria. He quite likely fled from there during or after the final conquest of the city by the Arabs in the year 734 and settled in China sometime before the An Lushan Rebellion, during which he served under the Chinese general and high official Guo Ziyi (697–781). The Tang court granted him the titles of "Great Donor, Great Master of the Bright Prosperity with Golden [Seal] and Purple [Ribbon], concurrently vice military commissioner of Shuofang, probationary

---

120. For the following remarks I rely mainly on the commentary on the Syriac part of the 781 inscription of Jean Dauvillier and Antoine Guillaumont in Pelliot 1984, 63–80. See also the summary of the different interpretations of the names, titles, and events of the East Syriac monks mentioned in the stele contained in Zhou 1993 and Duan 2002.

121. See Pelliot 1928; Chen Fenggu and Yang Gongle 2018.

122. On this title, see p. 94.

director of the Palace Administration," and "honored [him] with the purple *kaṣāya*";[123]

(3) Another "Mar Sergius, priest and chorepiscopus, 'High-seated,'" whose Chinese name is "monk Jingtong";

(4) "Adam, priest and chorepiscopus and *p'apši* of Ṣinestan," the author of the text of the stele, whose Chinese name is Jingjing. We know of him thanks to a passage of a Buddhist work from the beginning of the ninth century that says he was "a Persian monk of the Monastery of Da Qin" (*Da Qin si Bosi seng* 大秦寺波斯僧).[124]

The stele then bears the names of two archdeacons (*arkedyaqon*): Gabriel, called "priest and archdeacon and head of the churches of Kumdan and Sarag," and Gigoy (whose Chinese name is Xuanlan), called "priest and archdeacon of Kumdan and reading master (*maqryānā*)." The two names, the first Syriac and the second Syro-Iranian, suggest a Persian or Central Asian origin. It seems unlikely that the position of reading master, that is, the person in charge of teaching the correct reading of scriptural and liturgical texts in Syriac, would have been entrusted to a Chinese.

All these data would confirm that also in China bishops and archdeacons were chosen from among the non-indigenous missionary clergy who came from Persia and Central Asia. A reflection on the possible identity of Aluoben, the first missionary of the Church of the East in China attested by sources, also supports this thesis. He appears to be from Persia or the Central Asian region of Sogdiana.[125] His original name, from which the phonetic transcription in Chinese was made, could be the Syriac epithet—also used in Sogdian[126]—*rabban* (our teacher), in its colloquial form *a-rabān*, modeled on

---

123. About Yisi/Yazdbōzīd, see Deeg 2013.

124. *Zhenyuan xinding shijiao mulu* (Catalogue of the Buddhist Teachings Newly Established in the Zhenyuan Era) 17, T 55: 892a8. The same passage discovered by Takakusu in the *Zhenyuan xinding shijiao mulu* is also found, as already noted by Pelliot, in the older *Da Tang Zhenyuan xu Kaiyuan shijiao lu* (Great Tang Zhenyuan Era Continuation of the Kaiyuan Era Catalogue of Buddhist Teachings) 1, T 55: 756a20. See also Takakusu 1896.

125. See Tubach 1992. From Chinese historical sources—*Jiu Tang shu* (Old Annals of the Tang) 3, 1: 45; and several others—we know that in 635 an embassy from the Samarkand region (Kangguo, in Chinese) came before the emperor, bringing a lion (or lions) as a gift. However, no mention is made of the presence of Christian monks among the members of the delegation (see Forte 1996c, 359–61).

126. See Sims-Williams 1988, 152.

similar forms present in Central Asian languages.[127] Another, perhaps more plausible hypothesis would confirm the Persian origin of Aluoben, seeing this Chinese name as the phonetic transcription of the Middle Iranian name Ardabān, whose meaning is "he who is protected by law" and which is also attested in Sogdian (*'rdb'n*).[128]

One last observation can be made about the names of the monks in the long list that closes the text of the stele, and about their translation into Chinese. We have no explicit information about the provenance of the monks mentioned. Although they also have Chinese names, their original names are Syriac or Persian, and this suggests that rather than being native Chinese who also had a Syriac name, they came from Persia or Central Asia. The Chinese scholar Rong Xinjiang has made a remarkable discovery in this regard. In the already mentioned epitaph of the Persian Li Su, it is written that his courtesy name (*zi* 字) is Wenzhen. This same name is also reported among the names of the monks that appear on the stele, where we find a "monk Wenzhen," next to the Syriac Luqa (Luke), without further titles. Not finding any chronological contradiction, the author proposes they are the same person.[129] This would also support the hypothesis of the Persian or Central Asian identity of the monk mentioned in the stele.

Further proofs of the Persian or Central Asian origin of many monks of the Church of the East present in China are three more epigraphic testimonies. The first is the epitaph of Mi Jifen (see figure 2.1), a Sogdian native of the kingdom of Maymurgh (Miguo in Chinese sources, corresponding to the current region of Panjikent), who lived in Chang'an at the end of the eighth century (d. 805). The epitaph says that of Mi Jifen's two sons, "the youngest is called monk Siyuan and lives in the Monastery of Da Qin," leaving no doubt that he was a Christian monk.[130]

The second testimony is the inscription engraved on a funerary pillar found in Luoyang and dated 815 (see figures 3.4 and 3.7).[131] The text clearly reports the different Sogdian origins of the four Christian monks of the

---

127. This is the hypothesis put forward by Barat 2002. The many other hypotheses, more or less well-founded, that have been put forward over time are summarized ibid., 192–93.

128. This is Max Deeg's view in Deeg 2018b, 110–11.

129. See Rong 1998.

130. See Ge 2001, 2004a.

131. For a description and discussion, see pp. 137–46.

Figure 2.1 Mi Jifen's epitaph from Xi'an, 805, Xi'an Beilin Museum, Xi'an (Shaanxi, China).
(Source: photo by Ge Chengyong)

Monastery of Da Qin in Luoyang mentioned in the inscription. One belongs to a family that came to China from the Sogdian region of Bukhara (Anguo in the Chinese sources); two bear the surname Mi, thus identifying them as members of families coming from Maymurgh; and one has the surname Kang, indicating that the origin of his family is the Sogdian region around Samarkand (known in Chinese sources as Kangguo).[132]

The third epigraphic testimony is the tomb epitaph of Hua Xian (d. 827), which was found in 2010 in Luoyang (see figure 2.2) together with that of his

---

132. See Nicolini-Zani 2009b, 119.

Figure 2.2 Hua Xian's epitaph from Luoyang, 827, private collection (China), rubbing.

wife, Lady An (d. 821), whose surname clearly indicates that she was from the Sogdian region of Bukhara.[133]

Some elements in the text of the inscription, composed by the Buddhist monk Wenjian of the Shengshan Monastery (Shengshan si) in Luoyang, indicate that this Sino-Sogdian family may have been Christian. The main reference is the sentence stating that the deceased Hua Xian, a prefectural governor of the Tang Empire,

> constantly cleansing his heart, served the Luminous Honored One [*jingzun*, i.e., Christ] and observed with a full purpose the principles of

---

133. See Mao 2014; Wu Changxing 2015a, 217–36; 2015b, 247–66; Tang Li 2016; Fukushima 2016; 2017, 260–303; Morrow 2019, 108–46, 221–40 (text and trans.).

the Teaching; being a pillar among those who practiced the Doctrine, he served as his fellow believers' reed organ. By inwardly devoting himself to the eight luminous [conditions, *bajing* 八景] and outwardly replete with the three constant [virtues, *sanchang* 三常], he bore witness to the One without Origin [*wuyuan* 無元] and venerated him with all his thoughts forever.[134]

The key expressions (the originals of which are contained in brackets) are also found with the same or similar forms in the inscription on the Xi'an stele and in the *jingjiao* text *Book of the Luminous Teaching of Da Qin on Revealing the Origin and Reaching the Foundation*. In another passage, the epitaph also alludes to the deceased's ties with a "luminous monastery" (*jingsi*), that is, a Christian monastery, most probably the one in Luoyang.

It is almost certain that only a few of the seventy-six Chinese names of monks and clerics engraved on the Xi'an stele are phonetic transcriptions of the Syriac names they are paired with. A small number of these Chinese names may have been intended to reflect the meaning of the names in Syriac.[135] Most of the Chinese names are constructed like Buddhist "*dharma* names" (*faming* 法名). That is to say, they are composed of two characters chosen from semantic spheres that are dear to Buddhists (like light, knowledge, virtue, peace, etc.) and therefore in Buddhist literature regularly appear in the names of monks and masters.[136] The Chinese names of the monks of the Christian monastery of Chang'an, as well as those of the monks of the Christian monastery of Luoyang mentioned in the inscription on the Luoyang pillar, all testify to a profound degree of inculturation in the Chinese religious milieu.[137]

The title that most frequently accompanies Syriac names is "presbyter" (*qašišā*). In addition to the already mentioned titles of "bishop" (*episqopā*), "chorepiscopus" (*kore'pisqopā*, lit., "bishop of the countryside"), "archdeacon" (*arkedyaqon*), and "reading master" (*maqryānā*), there are also the titles of "deacon" (*mšamšānā*), "monk" (*iḥidāyā*), "elder" (*sābā*), and "sacristan" (*qankāyā*), as well as two other titles that seem to be modeled on two Chinese Buddhist names. One is *p'apši*, which, according to the most reliable interpretation, appears as the transcription (most probably via the

---

134. Chinese original in Mao 2014, 85–86.

135. See Takahashi 2020, 28–29.

136. See Chen Huaiyu 2009b (2012), 36–38.

137. See Lin Wushu 2009b.

Sogdian *βapši*) of the Chinese *fashi* 法師, "Master of the Doctrine." The other is *ši'angtswa*, a transcription of the Chinese *shangzuo* 上座, which literally means "High-seated."[138] References to this term (Sk. *sthavira*) in Chinese-language Buddhist literature seem to imply that *shangzuo* was a term for an elder, that is, a high-ranking monk, in the canonical texts. Later on (from the beginning of the sixth century onward) it was a monastic title for one of the three leading administrative figures in a monastery other than the abbot.[139] The only passage in Tang Christian literature where this title is applied to a high-ranking priest and chorepiscopus shows that it is most likely an honorific title.

Among the Chinese titles, the most common is *seng* 僧, which also accompanies the names whose Syriac original is not followed by any title. This is the Buddhist term for the celibates of their *saṅgha* (*sengjia* 僧伽), whose particular religious status was "to have left home" (*chujia* 出家) and therefore to have renounced marriage in order to observe the Buddhist precepts in a monastic community. Christians too used this term as a general or common title for their monks, as is attested by all the Christian literature of the Tang dynasty that has come down to us. As the 781 inscription particularly testifies, Christians borrowed this Buddhist term to translate the Syriac terms for both monk (*iḥidāyā*) and priest (*qašišā*). Although the second Syriac term applies to both married and unmarried priests, the fact that it is translated into Chinese as *seng* leads one to think that it probably refers to the unmarried clergy. The use of *seng* seems to indicate that these Christians made a necessary adaptation to conditions in China in order to gain official legitimation as a tolerated religion in the territory of the empire, as has recently been pointed out with reference to the text of the Xi'an stele:

> The choice to call [Christian monks] *seng* in the *jingjiao* stele is not connected to their status within their church. What identified them as *seng* were not requirements placed upon them by Christian ecclesiastical authority but rules that the Chinese ecclesiastical province required them to comply with. . . . These rules were that they conform to the conditions that the Chinese required of the *seng* and to

---

138. These last two terms were identified by Paul Pelliot (1911). See also Eccles and Lieu 2020, 17–20; Lieu 2020b, 72–78. On the different interpretations of these two titles, see Zhou 1996.

139. See Deeg 2012, in particular 130–38.

be officially registered by having their names included in the monastic catalogues.[140]

The title *dade*, "Great Virtuous," occurs four times in the text on the 781 Xi'an stele and twice in the text on the 815 Luoyang pillar. This Buddhist title (Sk. *bhadanta*) was widely used in China by the Buddhists before the arrival of Christian missionaries. On the basis of the correspondence between these two titles in the Chinese-Syriac list of names at the end of the text on the stele, *dade* in Tang Christian literature is generally interpreted as the Chinese translation of the Syriac *episqopā*. However, the title *dade* does not seem to indicate a function. Rather, this Chinese epithet is more likely an honorific title, something like "Monsignor" or "Excellency." In Chinese Buddhist literature, this was actually the original meaning of this term as it was applied to senior monks. Since the Tang dynasty, "Great Virtuous" was also an official and honorary title that was bestowed or ratified by the emperor to show his high esteem for certain distinguished monks in the great monasteries of the empire.[141] In Syriac Christian terminology, *mār ḥasyā*, "Your Excellency" (lit., "the Holy One"), an honorific commonly applied to bishops, is closer to the Chinese *dade* than *episqopā*.

Sizhu 寺主, lit., "lord of the monastery," occurs once in the text on the stele and is the common Chinese Buddhist term (Sk. *vihārasvāmin*) for an abbot, that is, the spiritual leader of a monastery. If we look at the way monasteries (*dairā* or *ʿumrā*) were organized in the Syriac-speaking areas of Mesopotamia and Persia, which was a model for the organization of monasteries in China, we find that "superior" or "abbot" (*rišdayrā*, *rišʿumrā*, or *rišā*) is a likely equivalent of the "Christianized" Chinese title *sizhu*. The Chinese Buddhist title *laosu* 老宿, "Elder" (Sk. *sthavira*), also occurs once in the same text on the stele. It indicates a renowned senior monk, and as such it is often used as a synonym for *shangzuo*, "High-seated."

Finally, there is the interesting and puzzling title *fazhu* 法主, "Lord of the Doctrine," which occurs three times in the text of the Xi'an stele. It was borrowed from the Buddhist title "Lord of the *Dharma*" (Sk. *dharmasvāmin*). Buddhists gave this honorific title to officially recognized high-ranking

---

140. Lin Wushu and Yin Xiaoping 2009, 200. As a consequence of this opinion, Lin Wushu and Yin Xiaoping conclude that among the seventy names carved on the two sides of the Xi'an stele those which have only a Syriac name and are not qualified as *seng* in Chinese correspond to Christian monks not (yet) recognized as such by the Chinese imperial court (see ibid., 202).

141. See Forte 2003.

monks. It could be that Christians applied it within the *jingjiao* church to designate a kind of primate whose responsibility was similar to that of a metropolitan. It could then stand as a specifically Chinese Christian title that the church in China used to designate its chief representative, who was also recognized as such by the imperial court. The problem remains open, however, because two of the three occurrences of this term refer to the investiture of Aluoben by Emperor Gaozong, suggesting that this title was honorific, granted by the sovereign and not by the church.[142]

This analysis of honorifics in the text of the Xi'an stele shows us that with regard to ecclesiastical organization and hierarchical functions, the structure of the East Syriac ecclesiastical province of China is fundamentally the typical "Persian" structure of the Church of the East.[143] As Erica C. D. Hunter put it, the inscription on the Xi'an stele, and particularly the portions of it that are in the Syriac language,

> show the heart of the Church of the East [in China] to be "Persian," not only in the link that was maintained with the patriarchate in Mesopotamia, but also via the hierarchical organization and importation of titles that were integral to Syriac Christianity. And finally, the distinctly "Persian" components of several of the Syriac names listed on the stele intimate that some of the men had indeed travelled along the Silk Route from Mesopotamian "homeland" to China.[144]

The sources also make evident that the Church of the East in China adopted several honorific titles from Buddhism, some of which were titles of high rank granted to the Christian clergy by the imperial court. The text on the Luoyang pillar provides further evidence of this.[145] In addition to the titles that are also present in the text of the Xi'an stele, the inscription on the Luoyang pillar contains other intriguing titles for Christian clerics. One is *fahe* 法和, "Harmony of the Doctrine," an honorific title that, like the similar title *fazhu*, might refer to a position of primacy among the local ranks of the Church of the East in Luoyang.

---

142. See Duan 2002; Chen Huaiyu 2009b (2012), 38–39.

143. See Zhou 2003; Wilmshurst 2016.

144. Hunter 2009b, 83.

145. See Nicolini-Zani 2013c.

The honorific nature of the title *dade*, already detected in the text of the Xi'an stele, is confirmed in the text of the Luoyang pillar by being juxtaposed with the functional title *weiyi* 威儀. This Buddhist term means "respect-inspiring deportment," that is, dignity in walking, standing, sitting, and lying. It also refers to the comportment that is appropriate at a sacred rite or the right behavior according to proper rules of order. In this sense it is sometimes used as a synonym for *jielü* 戒律, "precepts." In Buddhist literature we can find a *weiyi seng* 威儀僧 or *weiyi fashi* 威儀法師, a "master of ceremonies," referring to the instructor (*weiyi shi* 威儀師) who teaches proper deportment during the ordination ceremony (*upasaṃpadā*). In the entire Chinese Buddhist canon, however, there is no trace of the compound title *weiyi dade* 威儀大德 with reference to a monk. Since its original meaning referred to an office in a Buddhist monastery, we can surmise that it was used by Christians to designate one of the following two offices: (a) a high-ranking monk in charge of proper discipline among the brothers, a responsibility usually entrusted to the prior (*rabbaitā*) in the Syriac monasteries (with the proviso that this possibility should be discarded if one assumes that the Syriac *rabbaitā* lies behind the term *sizhu*); (b) a virtuous monk in charge of the liturgy or liturgical discipline inside the Monastery of Da Qin. I am not aware of any offices in the Syriac monasteries that would correspond to this Chinese title.

The last title, *jiujie dade* 九階大德, "Great Virtuous of the Nine Grades," is a further specification of the honorific *dade*. While the term *jiujie* 九階 is absent from almost the entire corpus of Chinese Buddhist literature, another term very close to it, namely *jiupin* 九品 (nine grades, classes, or ranks), is attested hundreds of times in the Chinese Buddhist Tripiṭaka. It is variously applied, especially in the Pure Land texts, where it points toward the nine grades of accomplishment of beings in the Western Paradise of the Pure Land. These correspond to the nine grades of development of the practitioners in their previous life, upon which depends their closeness to Amitābha in the next life. On this basis, and supposing that in the pillar's text this term also applies to an office in a Christian monastery, I suggest that it might be used by Christians for a monastic elder who is in charge of the spiritual progress of the practitioners (novices) in the Monastery of Da Qin, or at least a virtuous monk who was himself well-trained in the spiritual life. If we were to look for a parallel in the internal organization of Mesopotamian and Persian monasteries, this elder monk might be a *sābā*, a monk proven by many years of monastic observance. Among the elders, the title *mešablānā*, which apparently referred to a guide for spiritual life and monastic observance in a Syriac monastery, best fits the meaning of the corresponding Chinese title, but the *malpānā*, a teacher, could also be the referent for this Chinese title. Another suggestion comes from a possible interpretation of the term *jiujie dade* as "Great Virtuous of the Ninth Rank." If we consider the hierarchical structure of the Church of the East, we discover that the ordained ministries are usually divided into three orders: episcopate, presbyterate, and diaconate. Each order is then divided into three categories: the episcopate includes patriarchs, metropolitans, and "simple" bishops; the presbyterate includes archdeacons, chorepiscopi, and priests; the diaconate includes deacons, sub-deacons, and readers.[146] The cleric who bears this title in the Luoyang stone inscription would belong to the ninth rank of this hierarchical division and therefore be a reader or a cantor.[147]

In conclusion, it is not clear if the titles mentioned in the text on the Luoyang pillar, like those in the text on the Xi'an stele, correspond to real offices or are merely honorific. No direct correspondence can be traced between the Chinese and Syriac titles attested in Syriac Christian literature. It is not excluded that some of the Chinese titles would apply to specifically Chinese offices within Christian monasteries in China.

A further consideration regarding the identity of the Christian missionaries and the communities they formed in China is that the "eminent monks elevated above worldly things," the "luminous ministers dressed in white," as the missionaries are referred to in the Xi'an stele, were mostly monks. From the limited information that has come down to us, we can deduce that the Christian communities that arose in the imperial Chinese territory during the Tang era were monastic communities. These communities were the fruit of a monastic Christian mission from Mesopotamia to the Far East that was undertaken by the Church of the East, as is attested by both archaeological discoveries and literary records.[148] This is not surprising if we remember that in the Church of the East, monasticism always occupied a central position and that the monastic movement became a driving force in Syriac Christian missions from very early on.[149]

---

146. See Maclean 1894. This division of the ecclesiastical hierarchy into orders, modeled on the celestial hierarchy, is attributed to Pseudo-Dionysius the Areopagite, whose writings were soon translated from Greek into Syriac by Sergius of Rešʿayna (sixth century).

147. Interpretation first proposed by Tang Li 2009a, 124n93.

148. See Nicolini-Zani 2013b, 2017b; Tang Li 2019.

149. See Vööbus 1958–88; Hendriks 1958, 1960; Mathews 2000; Chialà 2005.

98   A HISTORY OF ENCOUNTERS

For these same reasons it is even less surprising to discover that during this very first stage of the Christian presence in China, monastic literature already began to spread in the territory of the empire and to be translated into Chinese and at least one other language, namely Sogdian, which was spoken by some Christian monks and Central Asian immigrants who settled in China for reasons of politics or trade. Of the extant Chinese Christian literature of the Tang dynasty, two texts can reasonably be considered spiritual texts addressed to monks, namely the *Book on Profound and Mysterious Blessedness* (Text E) and the *Book of the Luminous Teaching of Da Qin on Revealing the Origin and Reaching the Foundation* (Text F). The spiritual and theological lexicon contained in these texts, extensively borrowed from Buddhist and Daoist terminology, testifies to early contacts between Christian and non-Christian monastic traditions in Eastern Asia.

The 781 Xi'an stele describes the ideal Christian community as one characterized by traditional monastic elements. Monks let their beards grow as a symbol of poverty and renunciation; ascetical practices, such as fasting, seclusion, meditation, vigilance (*népsis*), quietness of body and mind (*hesychía*), and absence of passions (*apátheia*) were fostered; liturgical services gathered the community seven times a day to chant the common monastic offices.

> The cross that [Christians monks] hold as an emblem makes the four horizons of the earth merge in its light, bringing together what was separated. Striking the wood, they diffuse a sound that rouses benevolent kindness. By rites facing the east they advance rapidly on the way of life and glory. They let their beards grow as a sign of their public ministry and they shave the top of their heads to signify that they do not have interior passions. They keep neither men nor women servants and hold in equal esteem people in high position and people of humble condition. They do not accumulate wealth or riches, but themselves offer an example of radical renunciation. They complete their fasting by solitude and meditation and reinforce their abstinence by quietude and vigilance. Seven times a day they chant liturgical praises, making great intercession for the living and the dead. Once every seven days they perform their worship, purifying their heart and thus restoring its purity.[150]

---

150. See Text A, cols. 8–10, pp. 202–3.

Two additional points should not be forgotten. First, this fundamentally monastic Christian presence in China is in full harmony with the strongly monastic type of Christianity that was present throughout Central Asia, as attested by both the genre of Christian literature translated into Central Asian languages and the kind of Christian buildings that archaeology has brought to light.[151] Second, this monastic Christian presence was particularly eloquent in the Chinese religious setting of the Tang era in which the Buddhist monastic community had become the most visible and prevalent religious institution, even influencing the configuration of Daoist monastic life.[152]

Finally, we need to ask if there is anything we know about the activities of individual Christians at this time and what can be said about the impact of Christian activity on Chinese society. Any attempt to answer these questions involves entering a treacherous terrain because there is little information that can be verified by reliable documentary evidence. As so often happens when we speculate about historical individuals of whom very little is known, we run the risk of transmitting opinions based on hypotheses more than on the data provided by historical, literary, and archaeological sources.[153]

This is what happened in the past with regard to the Persian leader known by the Chinese name of Aluohan (whose original name may have been Wahrām), an "ambassador" of the Sasanian court in China who was sent by Emperor Gaozong to the West. Between 691 and 695 he was involved in the construction of an imposing bronze monument in Luoyang in honor of Empress Wu Zetian. The belief that he was a Christian was undisputed for several decades, but it was not based on any documentary evidence. The only written record we have of him is his funerary inscription, which says nothing about his religious affiliation.[154]

Likewise, at present it cannot be said, as has been advanced in some quarters, that the monk Chongyi, who in 740 cured Emperor Xuanzong's older brother of his illness, was a Christian monk.[155] The religious affiliation of Qin

---

151. See pp. 17–44.

152. See Kohn 2003; Chen Huaiyu 2007.

153. As a latest example of this trend which lacks a critical approach see, for instance, Xu Xiaohong 2006.

154. A few years ago, Antonino Forte finally shed some light on this issue (see Forte 1984, 1996d). On Aluohan's epitaph, see also Lin Meicun 1995; Ma Xiaohe 2004.

155. The source reference is *Jiu Tang shu* (Old Annals of the Tang) 95, 9: 3012. Two articles by Cao Shibang have skillfully questioned the evidence, put forward by Chen Yuan and Wang

Minghe, another doctor in the service of the imperial court, has also been studied. In 683 Qin Minghe cured Emperor Gaozong's eye problems through the use of a technique that involved bloodletting.[156] While the family name of Qin may indicate that the doctor came from Da Qin, controversy remains surrounding the physician's origins and religious affiliation. Although we have more information about him than about Chongyi, it is still insufficient to allow us to conclude that he was a Christian. One should also consider that from its earliest days in China, Buddhism was dedicated to finding cures for various illnesses, and Buddhist monks, together with Daoist priests, practiced medicine at the Chinese court to a far higher degree than Christians.[157]

Another case of Christian attribution without sufficient documentary evidence is that of An Yena, whose funerary epitaph (dated 709) was discovered in Guilin (today's Guangxi), in Southern China. Both the name and the surname of the deceased point to his Sogdian origin. His surname An identifies him more precisely as a member of a family originally from Bukhara (Anguo in Chinese sources), while his given name Yena sounds like the Chinese phonetic transcription of the Sogdian Yānakk (*y'n'kk*).[158] The arguments given by Luo Xianglin (Lo Hsiang-lin, 1906–78), who first studied this epitaph, for a possible Christian religious affiliation of An Yena are unconvincing.[159] The burial site and the occurrence of the name Yānakk in a Buddhist Sogdian text would rather suggest that he was a Buddhist.[160]

On this basis, therefore, I think it would be a risky venture to state with certainty that the practice of Western medicine was one way the East Syriac Christians in China tried to ensure their survival and spread their religion.[161] This is not to deny that Christians of Persian and Central Asian origin who were present in China very probably possessed good medical knowledge and may have exploited it, as would be shown by the reference to the Bactrian

---

Zhixin in the 1930s, on which Chongyi's identification with a Christian monk was based (see Cao 1984, 1985).

156. The source reference is *Jiu Tang shu* (Old Annals of the Tang) 5, 1: 111. See Huang Lanlan 2002; Godwin 2017, 92–93.

157. See Salguero 2014; Yang Zengwen 2018.

158. See Yoshida 1996, 75.

159. See Luo Xianglin 1966, 87–96 and plate 14.

160. See Liu Yong and Chen Xi 2019, 68.

161. An opinion upheld by Lin Wushu 2003b (2005c), 361–66.

Yazdbōzīd/Yisi that is contained in the following text of the Christian inscription of Xi'an:

> Each year he gathered the monks of the four monasteries, served them with respect, and presented refined offerings for a period of fifty days. [On that occasion] . . . the sick were cured and healed.[162]

The possession and use of medical skills by Christians in China would also seem to be confirmed by the discovery in Turfan of some fragments of medical prescriptions and pharmacological works among the Christian materials in the Syriac, Sogdian, and New Persian languages.[163] Another confirmation could be the Syriac glosses in the description of medicinal plants preserved in the ninth-century *Youyang zazu* (Miscellaneous Morsels from Youyang), a Chinese miscellany of legends, accounts, tales, and notes on plants, by Duan Chengshi (d. 863). A section of this work contains a list of plants grown in Western Asia with their properties and their names in the languages of Bosi (Persia) and Fulin (Byzantine Empire) transcribed in Chinese. This information was probably conveyed to the compiler by a certain "Wan [or Luan], a monk from the kingdom of Fulin [*Fulin guo seng* 拂林國僧]," who is likely to have been a cleric of a Syriac-rite church.[164] Whether the monk was a Melkite (from the Melkite community in Central Asia),[165] or a member of the Church of the East, as would appear more likely, is a matter that will require further investigation.

In general terms and as background to this discussion, we should not forget that in the literature of the Tang period there are several references to Da Qin as a place that produced good physicians. This is stated, for instance, in *Tongdian* (Comprehensive History of Regulations): "In Da Qin [doctors] are good for eye and dysentery treatments, or for disease prevention and observation, or opening up the brain and releasing its ailments."[166] We also know that exchanges between Persians and Chinese regarding medical matters took place in medieval China, as is shown by the case of Li Xun, an ethnic Persian

---

162. Text A, cols. 25–26, p. 213. About this, see Nie 2008; Godwin 2017, 177–78.

163. See Maróth 1984; Sims-Williams 2011b.

164. See Duan Chengshi, *Youyang zazu* (Miscellaneous Morsels from Youyang) 18, ed. Cao Zhongfu, 696–98. See also Santos 2010; Takahashi 2020, 31–34.

165. As suggested by Lin Ying 2006b, 41–51; 2007, 24–42.

166. *Tongdian* (Comprehensive History of Regulations) 193, 5: 5266.

102   A HISTORY OF ENCOUNTERS

born in China, who combined foreign medicine with Chinese medicine in his work *Haiyao bencao* (Overseas Pharmacopoeia), a specialized *materia medica* work about remedies and prescriptions written in the Five Dynasties period (907–60).[167]

Finally, the practice of medicine was an integral part of the life of the Church of the East in Persia, the homeland of many of the missionaries in China from the Sasanid era onward. In fact, the teaching of medicine complemented theological studies at the renowned School of Nisibis as well as at other East Syriac centers of learning.[168] From the sixth century on, many lay people, monks, and Christian clerics in Persia were trained at the Xenodochium (*xenodochéion*) of Nisibis and other *bīmāristān*, that is, hospices or infirmaries attached to the schools. Moreover, medical practice was not foreign to East Syriac monasteries. Despite scant evidence, available accounts indicate that various medical treatments were familiar to and performed by monks. Some Syriac Christians even became influential figures in the Persian court precisely because of their medical and, more generally, scientific expertise. Syriac Christians living in Persia undoubtedly transmitted Greek, Syrian, Persian, and occasionally Indian medical traditions,[169] as well as other forms of cultural and scientific knowledge, to the Middle East, Central Asia, and beyond.[170]

With regard to the social status of individual Christians living in Tang China and their position in the society of the time, we should also call attention to the fact that they played significant roles in the political, cultural, and military administration of the Tang Empire. The number of individual figures whose position in society we know about through documented evidence is still quite limited, but among them there is a high percentage of foreigners with official positions in the imperial administration. As Eugène Tisserant (1884–1972) wrote, "Nestorian priests in China would gladly make themselves available to the government for public functions."[171]

Here I recall some individuals already mentioned. First of all, there is the Bactrian Yazdbōzīd/Yisi, who was "concurrently vice military commissioner of Shuofang [and] probationary director of the Palace

---

167. See Luo Xianglin 1966, 97–134; Chen Ming 2007.

168. See Becker 2006, 2008.

169. See Le Coz 1995, 103–5; 2004; Kessel 2019.

170. See Gignoux 2001a; Takahashi 2014a; Johnson 2017.

171. Tisserant 1931, 205.

The Christian Presence in China   103

Administration."[172] His high-ranking status made him a fitting candidate to erect the stone stele because "among all the styles of *bei* [碑, 'stele'], the most august form is one with a dragon-top [*chishou* 螭首] and a turtle-base [*guifu* 龜趺], reserved only for the highest officials. Sumptuary laws regulated who was entitled to erect a stele (based on social status and official rank) and the size and kind allowed."[173]

I also recall the married cleric Luke Li Su (Li Wenzhen). The biographical data on his tombstone informs us that the Li family was of Persian origin and had settled in Guangzhou (his grandfather came to China as a *zhizi*, "hostage"). Sometime during the years 766–79, Li Su was recruited as an officer in the Bureau of Astronomy (Sitian tai), which was in charge of astronomical reckonings for the compilation of the calendar, and relocated to the capital Chang'an. In the following Jianzhong era (780–83) of the Tang emperor Dezong, Li Su was appointed governor of Jinzhou in Hezhong Superior Prefecture (today's Shanxi).[174] As has been remarked, the political significance of his appointment in the Bureau of Astronomy is not to be disregarded:

> The role the foreigner astronomers played in the Tang court is noteworthy as it demonstrates the interest in foreign ideas within the multiethnic Tang society on one hand, as well as the special role the astral science played in Chinese politics on the other. Luke, like other skilled foreigners and Chinese with special talents, was recruited directly by the emperor and given special titles, bypassing the official imperial examination system. Due to the technical as well as the confidential nature of those working in the Bureau of Astronomy, who handled sensitive matters pertaining to state security, such arrangements, in particular with the foreigners who had fewer ties with the Chinese, would have been a politically sound choice.[175]

As the epitaph of Luke Li Su testifies, his sons were all employed in imperial administrative offices.[176] Other individual Christians also to be remembered are the different members of the Sogdian Mi Jifen's family, who held important

---

172. Xi'an stele inscription, Text A, col. 23, p. 212.

173. Wong 2004, 27.

174. See Wang Changming 2018.

175. Mak 2016, 89.

176. See p. 61n11.

military positions in the Chinese Imperial Army,[177] and the members of the An family, originally from the Sogdian area of Bukhara, who settled in Luoyang and who are remembered in the inscription carved on the 815 Christian pillar. They are said to bear high-ranking titles corresponding to important military and administrative posts in the two capitals of the empire.[178]

In conclusion, at the present stage of research we still know too little about Chinese individuals and communities who converted to Christianity during the Tang dynasty to be able to determine the degree to which the Christian faith attracted the Chinese people during this period. However, interpreting as best we can the evidence we have gathered, we can say that it is highly probable that the original nucleus of the Christian communities in the Tang era was constituted by more or less organized colonies of foreigners who had their own residential quarters, as was the case in the capital cities Chang'an and Luoyang. These foreigners came to the Chinese Empire from Persia and from at least three of the nine Sogdian states (known as *Zhaowu jiuxing* 昭武九姓 in the Chinese sources)[179]—Maymurgh, Bukhara, and Samarkand—with which the Tang Empire had established and maintained alliances for diplomatic and commercial reasons. Groups of monks and individual priests were at various times sent from the regions of Persia and Central Asia to China in order to support the religious and liturgical life of these immigrant communities, which, as they grew, also attracted a number of Chinese faithful. In short:

> Since the size of the colonies of foreigners [in China] was quite moderate, Christians were few in number, limited to people from Persia and some Sogdians from Central Asia. Since there were not many faithful, they could not form a large base for the spread of Christianity.... The Christian missionaries had to move about in a country, China, where the dominant cultures were Confucianism, Buddhism, and Daoism. Consequently, the difficulties they encountered are not hard to imagine.

---

177. See Ge 2001; 2004a. See also p. 89 and figure 2.1.

178. See Nicolini-Zani 2009b, 119.

179. *Zhaowu jiuxing*, lit., "the nine surnames of Zhaowu" or "Zhaowu consisting of nine surnames," is the name of the Sogdian allied states in Chinese historical accounts and therefore of the Sogdian families coming to China from those regions. They are Samarkand (Kangguo), Bukhara (Anguo), Sutrušana or Ušrusana (Dong Caoguo), Kaputana (Caoguo), Išitikhan (Xi Caoguo), Maymurgh (Miguo), Kušaṇiyya (Heguo), Kašana (Shiguo), Čač (Shiguo). See Xiang Da 1957, 12–24; Yoshida 2003.

They had only themselves to rely on, and great commitment was needed to be able to cope with the local Chinese situation.[180]

The prominent Iranian matrix of the Christian communities in Tang China is also confirmed by an analysis of the extant Christian literature of the time:

> Evidence such as the occurrence of Persian and Sogdian terms in transcription in Chinese documents serves to confirm the view that the majority of the Christians in China at this time were speakers, at least originally, of these Iranian languages. These transcriptions also suggest that the leaders among them made use of the materials available in Iranian languages (presumably mainly Sogdian) to compose the extant Chinese *jingjiao* texts (and other such texts as once existed).[181]

We know almost nothing about Chinese Christians of this time, except that—and this is not insignificant—they did not live out their Christian faith as mere bystanders. As evidence of this we possess a small but extraordinarily inculturated corpus of Christian literature in Chinese, of which individuals and communities were the beneficiaries and, at least in part, the producers. The sinologist Arthur C. Moule (1873–1957), who wrote in 1940, comments as follows:

> We are naturally anxious to know something about the Christian communities of the early church in the Tang dynasty. We read of nothing (then or later) but of monastic life; and I used to think that most if not all the monks were probably foreigners. But the survival of five actual documents written in Chinese without a letter of Syriac must be allowed to imply the existence of at least some Chinese Christians, yet not necessarily of many.[182]

This comment is very revealing, not so much in relation to the abstract question of what it means to root the Christian faith in Chinese culture, but rather in relation to a concrete mode of Christian ecclesial presence in the Chinese cultural, sociopolitical, and religious milieu. These documents testify to the

---

180. Ge 2004b [2006?], 167.

181. Takahashi 2020, 39.

182. Moule 1940, 33.

A HISTORY OF ENCOUNTERS

dialogical attitude adopted by the Church of the East in its mission in China and the willingness of this church to speak the language of the other.[183]

The Geographical Location
of Christian Monasteries

The indications of China's probable status as metropolitan see and the fact that the stele speaks of bishops and chorepiscopi and provides the names of about seventy monks support the hypothesis of the existence of different Christian communities in China. However, we have very little certain data that would make it possible to quantify the Christian presence in Tang China.[184] No source from the Tang era or later periods contains an inventory of the Christian monasteries in the country. The data that the text of the Xi'an stele provides us regarding this and other specific questions are the only information available to us and therefore must be considered with due caution. We must remember that the text is an encomium and thus incorporates celebratory rhetoric in the genre of the political-religious propaganda of the time. By its very nature it cannot be considered a purely historical account.[185] As Henri Leclercq has appropriately observed, "monumental epigraphy is not a model of sincerity; it gladly admits hyperbole."[186] One of the main concerns of Chinese epigraphy (and historiography more generally) is to inspire the current generation by recalling the meritorious events of former times and the exemplary deeds of past heroes, rather than to offer a strictly historical report.

What we do know is that the Christian presence in Tang China was monastic. An initial interesting observation concerns the way the Chinese designated Christian monasteries in the Tang era.[187] In the Chinese sources we find three different ways of referring to them: "monasteries of Persia" (Bosi si) or "foreign monasteries of Persia" (Bosi husi), "monasteries of Da Qin" (Da Qin si), and "luminous monasteries" (*jingsi*). As can be seen, the Buddhist term *si* is always present, manifesting the Christian choice to appropriate the Buddhist way of referring to this institution. It is significant to note that this choice

---

183. See Nicolini-Zani 2013a, 2014, 2017a, and forthcoming.

184. For an overview, see Lieu 2012.

185. See Deeg 2007; Tommasi 2017.

186. Leclercq 1913, 1373–74.

187. For a summary, see Leslie 1981–83; Lin Wushu 2000c.

was also a political one, since according to the Tang dynasty regulations, only state-sanctioned monasteries could be designated in this way.[188]

The first two terms for monasteries are the oldest (the seventh and the beginning of the eighth century), but their precise meaning in some sources is not clear. Since Persia was the common land of origin of the adherents of the three foreign religions that arrived in China during this period, it is not always evident if these terms refer to Christian monasteries, Manichaean sites, or Zoroastrian temples. This ambiguity could reflect the confusion that initially existed in the mind of the Chinese as they tried to understand the cults that the Iranian people brought from Persia. If, however, we take as our reference the text of the edict of 745, the ambiguity would appear to be resolved, making it possible to say with a good degree of certainty that the institutions called Bosi si between 638 and 745 were Christian places of worship.[189]

The designation *jingsi* is present only in the text of the Xi'an stele and therefore seems to be a designation that was neither popular nor official but originated and was used by the Christian faithful alone, at least before 745. Otherwise the edict promulgated in that year would have noted that the Christian monasteries were now to be referred to as *jingsi* rather than Da Qin si. The use of Da Qin si or *jingsi* would indicate how Christianity was known at the official level on the one hand, and at the ecclesial level on the other. The official character of the designation Da Qin si would also be confirmed by the fact that a seal, probably composed of the three characters constituting this way of referring to Christian monasteries at that time, is present at the end of the scroll "Pelliot chinois 3847," one of the ancient Christian manuscripts that have come down to us.[190]

With regard to the number of monasteries and their geographical distribution in China during the Tang dynasty, we need first of all to consider the references to Christian monasteries in the text of the Xi'an stele, even though they are sometimes not very clear.[191]

The first reference is that inserted in the aforementioned edict of 638, which refers to the construction of "a Monastery of Da Qin in the Yining Ward of

---

188. See Forte 1992.

189. Antonino Forte recalled that already around 1920 Pelliot seems to have been of this opinion (see Forte 1996c, 355).

190. See Wu Qiyu 1986, 411; Lin Wushu 2001c, 68.

191. A critical summary, which underlies these considerations, is Lin Wushu 2000e.

108   A HISTORY OF ENCOUNTERS

the capital."[192] The Yining Ward (Yining fang) was along the western wall of Chang'an, at the Kaiyuan Gate (Kaiyuan men), and not far from the Western Market (Xishi). Whereas the district near the Eastern Market (Dongshi) held the mansions of the noble and powerful, this area's inhabitants tended to be commoners and foreign merchants.[193]

The second reference describes the beginning of the construction of Christian monasteries during the reign of Gaozong:

> The great emperor Gaozong emulated the reverent deference of his predecessor [towards the Luminous Teaching]. Giving luster to true religion, he had luminous monasteries built in every prefecture. . . . [Thus] that doctrine spread throughout the ten provinces, and abundant blessings came down upon the [whole] country. Monasteries were built in all cities, and luminous blessings filled every household.[194]

The claim that a Christian monastery was built in every prefecture (*zhou* 州) must be critically evaluated. In fact, we know that the imperial territory at that time was divided into 360 prefectures. Therefore, if we were to take this statement literally, it would mean that at that time there were at least 360 monasteries in the empire. If they were really so numerous, however, we would have had traces of them in Chinese historical documents and local chronicles, and to this point, nothing of the kind has come to light. It is therefore more realistic to think that Emperor Gaozong had some monasteries built in certain prefectures, and that the text of the stele, written by a Christian monk in the style of a panegyric, has exaggerated historical facts. The other two passages—"That doctrine spread throughout the ten provinces [*dao* 道]" and "Monasteries were built in all [lit., 'one hundred'] cities"[195]—should also be interpreted in the same way. That is to say, the numbers ten and one hundred are to be understood symbolically to indicate a large number, a fullness. In short, these hyperbolic expressions are not exact figures corresponding to historical reality but an expression of the desire of the missionaries that the Christian faith be spread throughout every region of the empire, even outside

---

192. Text A, col. 13, p. 205.

193. See Xiong 2000, 170.

194. Text A, cols. 15–16, pp. 206–7.

195. Text A, cols. 15–16, p. 207.

The third reference concerns the action of Emperor Suzong (r. 756–62), who "rebuilt the luminous monasteries in five administrative divisions [*jun* 郡]: Lingwu [and four others]."[197] Lingwu is the ancient name of today's northwestern region of Ningxia. This region is close to Gansu, the territory where Dunhuang and Turfan are located, places where Christianity was definitely present, as has already been noted with regard to Turfan; more information about Dunhung will be provided later.[198] Since this was a region crossed by merchants moving along the Silk Road, there may very well have been a Christian monastery in Ningxia.[199]

The last reference on the stele states that

> [Yisi/Yazdbōzīd] brought some monasteries back to their former glory, while he expanded the rooms for worship in others, elegantly decorating their corridors and roofs, [whose inclines] were rising up [towards the sky] like pheasants in flight. . . . Each year he gathered the monks of the four monasteries, served them with respect, and presented refined offerings for a period of fifty days.[200]

For a number of historical and linguistic reasons and because of the encomiastic style of the text, the Chinese expression here translated literally as "four monasteries" should also be understood symbolically as referring to the four directions and therefore to a diffusion (real or desired) of monasteries throughout the region.

To sum up, on the basis of the data contained in the Xi'an stele, we can conclude that in the period of the Tang dynasty, there was at least one monastery in Chang'an, China's western capital; there were monasteries in the Ningxia region and in four other (probably neighboring) regions; there were Christians and probably a monastery in Luoyang, the eastern capital; and

---

196. See Lin Wushu 2000e (2003a), 35–36.

197. Text A, col. 20, p. 210.

198. See pp. 51–53 and 113–14.

199. See Chen Wei 2014.

200. Text A, col. 25, p. 213.

110   A HISTORY OF ENCOUNTERS

there were some (many?) monasteries in different parts of the empire, but we do not have much information about them.[201] However, as Pénélope Ribaud pointed out,

> if Christians were authorized to establish places of worship in the administrative districts at the prefectural and sub-prefectural levels, there is nothing to confirm that the generosity of the administration was followed up by actual effects. On the contrary, everything suggests that Christian missionary activity in China was concentrated in the two capitals, Chang'an and Luoyang, as well as in a few cities where merchants from Central Asia, Iran and the Arabian Peninsula lived.[202]

Some references in Chinese historical documents help to clarify other interesting data. First of all, several sources confirm the presence of a Christian monastery in the Yining Ward of the western capital Chang'an.[203] Furthermore, we can say that this is the first Christian monastery or church about which there is information in Chinese sources. Its construction was begun in the year 638. There is no evidence to support the hypothesis that it was constructed to welcome Aluoben, who arrived in China in 635. We can say with a good degree of confidence that since it was the center of the Christian mission in the Chinese Empire, this monastery in the capital had a prominent position, superior to that of all the other monasteries in China. The most plausible reasons for its dominance would be the status of Chang'an as the political center of the empire; its importance as a city with a large presence of foreign colonies that included some Christian faithful; and finally its prestige as seat of the *fazhu*, the "Lord of the Doctrine," perhaps a sort of primate, a position held by Aluoben (and probably others after him).[204] We can also hypothesize that "behind the edict of 638 allowing the foundation of a Nestorian monastery

---

201. See Drake 1936–37, 307.

202. Ribaud 2015, 56–57.

203. See *Tang huiyao* (Essential Regulations of the Tang) 49, 8: 864: "The competent authorities should build a Monastery of Da Qin in the Yining Ward"; *Chang'an zhi* (Description of Chang'an) 10, in Xin and Lang 2013, 341: "At the northwestern corner [of the Yining Ward], . . . the foreign Monastery of Persia [Bosi husi], which was built by Taizong in the twelfth year of the Zhenguan era [638] for Aluo[ben], a foreign monk [*huseng* 胡僧] from the kingdom of Da Qin." For other later sources, see Leslie 1981–83, 282n14.

204. See Lin Wushu 2000c.

in the Chinese capital there must have been a specific request by [the Sasanid sovereign] Yazdgird III."[205]

This is the only monastery whose community is known to us. At the end of the text of the edict of 638 authorizing the spread of Christianity in China, it is said that "the competent authorities should therefore build a Monastery of Da Qin in the Yining Ward of the capital and ordain twenty-one men as monks."[206] We still do not know for certain why the number of monks was set at twenty-one, but it is likely that the emperor simply applied to the Christian monastery a preexisting rule for institutions of other religions (Buddhist and Daoist).[207] It is in fact an indication that the Christian monastery in Chang'an was recognized as a monastery of the highest rank and, consequently, that Christianity received a high degree of recognition from the imperial authorities.[208]

Secondly, the documents mention the presence of a possible second Christian monastery in the Liquan Ward (Liquan fang), which was then transferred to the Buzheng Ward (Buzheng fang) of Chang'an.[209] This would be the "Foreign monastery of Persia" (Bosi husi) built in 677 at the request of the Persian Prince Pērōz (636–ca. 679), son of the last Sasanid ruler Yazdgird III, who fled to China to take refuge from the Muslim advance and was there recognized as "king of Persia" (Bosi wang 波斯王) by Emperor Gaozong in 662 (for which reason he should be regarded as Pērōz III).[210] Based on a passage in the stele that says that "an [imperial] edict ordered that the monk Luohan, the monk Pulun, and seven others cultivate merits at Xingqing

---

205. Forte 1996c, 363. Forte provides some valid elements on which it is possible to build such a hypothesis (see ibid., 363–67).

206. Text A, col. 13, p. 205.

207. See Forte 1996c, 358–59.

208. See Deeg 2018b, 120–21.

209. See *Chang'an zhi* (Description of Chang'an) 10, in Xin and Lang 2013, 337: "At the southwestern corner [of the Liquan Ward], . . . the old foreign Monastery of Persia [Bosi husi]. In the second year of the Yifeng era [677] the king of Persia Pērōz [Beilusi] petitioned the emperor that a Monastery of Persia [Bosi si] be built in this place. In the Jinglong era [707–10] the favorite courtier Zong Chuke [d. 710] built his residence on the location of this monastery, which was therefore moved to the southwestern corner of the Buzheng Ward, west of the Zoroastrian shrine [xianci]." For other later sources, see Leslie 1981–83, 282n17. Some believe it was a Zoroastrian temple, rather than a Christian monastery. Recently, however, Christian identification has prevailed.

210. See *Zizhi tongjian* (Comprehensive Mirror for Aid in Government) 200, 7: 6326: "On the Xinhai [day] of the spring first month of the second year [of reign, i.e., 14 February 622], [Gaozong] established the Persian commander-in-chief Pērōz [Beilusi] as king of Persia."

Palace along with the Great Virtuous Jihe,"[211] there has also been speculation about a possible third Christian monastery in Chang'an, near the Xingqing princely palace (Xingqing gong). However, there is no documentary or archaeological evidence to support this hypothesis.

Thirdly, an edict in *Tang huiyao* (Essential Regulations of the Tang) states that the name of the Christian monasteries had to be changed "in the two capitals," namely Chang'an and Luoyang.[212] This reference to the existence of a Christian monastery in Luoyang would be confirmed by Xu Song in his *Tang liangjing chengfang kao* (A Study of the Quarters of the Two Capitals of the Tang). This late historiographic work records that in the Xiushan Ward (Xiushan fang) of Luoyang there was a "Foreign monastery of Persia" (Bosi husi).[213] The recent discovery of a Christian funerary pillar from the Tang era in Luoyang is further confirmation not only of a Christian presence in Luoyang, but also of the existence of a monastery in this capital city. An explicit mention of it can be found in the "Note on the Pillar [Inscribed] with the *Book of the Luminous Teaching of Da Qin on Revealing the Origin and Reaching the Foundation*" (*Da Qin jingjiao xuanyuan zhiben jing chuangji*) engraved on the pillar.[214]

Fourthly, on the basis of historiographic works it is difficult to prove that the Monastery of Da Qin in Zhouzhi, not far from Xi'an, was Christian. The only evidence we have are a few references to it in the work of Su Shi (1036–1101)—notably a poem written in 1062 and entitled "Da Qin si"—and a couple of later poets.[215] The Chinese scholar Xiang Da (1900–66), who visited the site in 1933, gave a vague description of it.[216] Lin Wushu is of the opinion that the historical sources and archaeological ruins of this Monastery of Da Qin near Zhouzhi do not allow us to include this monastery among Christian places of worship. On the contrary, several elements would support identifying it as a Buddhist monastery.[217] Another Chinese scholar, Li Chongfeng, has confirmed that the present pagoda (Da Qin si ta, "Pagoda

---

211. Text A, col. 18, p. 209.

212. See *Tang huiyao* (Essential Regulations of the Tang) 49, 8: 864.

213. See *Tang liangjing chengfang kao* (A Study of the Quarters of the Two Capitals of the Tang) 5, fol. 21b9–10.

214. See Nicolini-Zani 2009b, 115 (text), 118 (trans.).

215. See Saeki 1951, 362–71. The Chinese text and a good English translation of Su Shi's poem "Da Qin si" is also found in Fuller 1990, 98.

216. See Xiang Da 1957, 93, 110–16 (abridged English trans. in Saeki 1951, 390–99). See also Drake 1936–37, 316–25, 332–34.

217. See Lin Wushu 2000f. See also Liang Yancheng 2010.

of the Monastery of Da Qin") can be dated to the early Song dynasty (tenth century) and its still visible decorative elements are typically Buddhist.[218] Thus, the hypothesis that there was a Christian monastery on this site in the Tang era does not appear to be supported by any archaeological findings. This conclusion counters the alleged rediscovery of Christian traces at this site by a team led by Martin Palmer, which was the subject of a highly criticized book.[219] However, the relationship between the identity of the monastic site and its name remains to be clarified.

Fifthly, an ancient administrative document found in Dunhuang (S. 1366), presumably from the year 980, refers to the presence of Persian monks (*Bosi seng* 波斯僧) in Ganzhou (near today's Zhangye), six hundred kilometers east of Dunhuang:

> To the Persian monks who came from Ganzhou, a monthly commission of seven *dou* 斗 of flour and one *sheng* 升 of oil. On the twenty-sixth day [of the month], to the Persian monks who came to collect drugs, one *shi* 石 of flour and three *sheng* of oil.[220]

As we have seen, the Christian monks were for some time actually called Persian monks. This would therefore confirm the statement on the Xi'an Christian stele that hints at a Christian presence, also linked to trade, in the region of present-day northwestern China (Ningxia and Gansu). In Dunhuang there was in fact a large drug emporium, and the monks employed as government officials in Ganzhou went to that city for the drug trade entrusted to them.[221] Moreover, the presence of an undisputable monastic community in Dunhuang from the eighth to the tenth century is suggested by a number of documents discovered by Marc Aurel Stein and Paul Pelliot in the Caves of the Thousand Buddhas, some of which testify to the Sogdian identity of some

---

218. See Li Chongfeng 2002.

219. See Palmer 2001. In the wake of Palmer's thesis, other works have appeared: Guan 2002; 2005; Wu Changxing 2002; Riegert and Moore 2003.

220. *Guiyijun yanei mianyou poyong li* (Calendar of the Flour and Oil Commissions for Government Officials during the Guiyijun Regime, S. 1366), in Tang Geng'ou and Lu Hongji 1986–90, 3: 284–85. See Sun Jianqiang 2018b, 188. It is interesting to note that the city of Ganzhou will be the seat of a suffragan bishop in the following Yuan era, with three churches (see Mechelen 2001, 109).

221. See Jiang Boqin 1994, 57–58, 64–65, 141.

of the Christians living there.[222] The presence of Chinese Christians then seems to be confirmed by the discovery in Dunhuang of at least one Christian text in Chinese, the scroll P. 3847, containing the Chinese adapted translation of the Syriac hymn *Glory to God in the Highest*. We also have fragments of a Sogdian translation of this hymn from Bulayïq (Turfan).

Sixthly, the presence of Christian monks in Turfan, already suggested by the ruins of a church in Qočo and the traces of a monastic library in Bulayïq, is witnessed to by a slightly later source (end of the tenth century). In his travel account, Wang Yande (939–1006), a Song dynasty envoy to the Uighur kingdom, reports that in Qočo "Manichaean monasteries and Persian monks (*Bosi seng*) hold their respective [religious] beliefs, which the Buddhist scriptures call heterodox ways."[223] From this we can deduce that, at the latest, Christian monks were already present in Qočo in the late Tang dynasty.

Unfortunately, archaeology is no help to us in locating a Christian presence in China in the first millennium. Apart from the Xi'an Christian stele of 781 and the funerary pillar of 815 found in Luoyang, no archaeological evidence clearly testifying to Christian places of worship in Tang China has come down to us.

The ruins of the so-called Monastery of the Cross (Shizi si) in Fangshan (about forty kilometers southwest of Beijing), where blocks of stone carved with crosses and an inscription in Syriac were found, also await further research *in situ* to ascertain the true identity of the complex, which was used as a Buddhist monastery for several centuries.[224] As far as we can tell, in the Chinese epigraphic documentation of the Fangshan site—two Buddhist steles, one from the Liao dynasty (960) and one from the Yuan dynasty (1365), copied and rewritten in the Ming dynasty (1535)—there is no explicit reference to a time when this worship site was used by Christians.[225] So was the Monastery of the Cross never anything but a Buddhist temple? The existence of a frieze on the Yuan stele in which the symbol of the cross appears,

---

222. This documentation consists of a fragment of a Christian manuscript in Sogdian (the content of which is an oracular text, known in the West as *Sortes Apostolorum*) and some Sogdian documents which are nonreligious, but which were written by Christians or which contain the names of Christian priests and monks (see Sims-Williams 1992a, 532–33).

223. Wang Yande, *Shi Gaochang ji* (Record of the Mission to Qočo) 4, fol. 5b4–5.

224. About the Fangshan site, see Irving 1919; Schurhammer 1930; Moule 1930, 86–89; Drake 1936–37, 334–36; Saeki 1951, 429–33; Xu Pingfang 1986, 1992; Shi 2000; Tang Xiaofeng and Zhang Yingying 2019.

225. See Guglielminotti Trivel 2005.

together with the presence of blocks with crosses and inscription in Syriac characters and language (Ps. 34:6 according to the version of the Peshitta), datable to the thirteenth to fourteenth centuries,[226] "constitutes tangible proof of a Nestorian phase of the site"[227] that can very likely be dated to the four centuries between the destruction of the Liao temple and its reconstruction at the end of the Yuan dynasty.[228] Therefore, even if this episodic Christian presence were to be confirmed in the future, the historical period to which this site would date would still be outside the chronological period that is the focus of this work.

In conclusion, the words of Shu Yuanyu, who writes around 824, probably best summarize the fragmentary picture that can be reconstructed from historical data. As he makes clear, although the presence of Christians in China was significant, they were—as were the Manichaeans and Zoroastrians—an absolute minority in relation to the Buddhists:

> Although our royal court was powerful from of old, yet it permitted miscellaneous foreign [religions] to enter [China]: the [religion] of Mani [*moni* 摩尼], of Da Qin [i.e., Christianity], and of the fire god [*xianshen* 祆神, i.e., Zoroastrianism]; but the monasteries of these three foreign [religions] throughout the whole empire are not equal in number to our Buddhist monasteries in one small city.[229]

As we did in the case of Central Asia,[230] we will briefly consider the presence in Tang China of Christians belonging to churches other than the Church of the East. To our great surprise, it seems that West Syriac and Melkite Christians did not join the East Syriac monks on their way to Chang'an. Speculation about their presence in China is not supported by reliable documentary evidence.[231]

---

226. See Saeki, Mueller, and Clément 1931; Borbone 2006.

227. Guglielminotti Trivel 2005, 455.

228. See Xu Pingfang 1992, 188; Marsone 2013.

229. Shu Yuanyu, *Chongyan si bei xu* (Preface to the Stele [Inscription] of the Chongyan Monastery, around 824), in *Quan Tang wen* (Complete Prose Works of the Tang) 727, fol. 27a6–9, 8: 7498. This passage is also quoted in Moule 1930, 69–70 (trans.); Drake 1936–37, 305 (trans.), 305n43 (text).

230. See pp. 15–17.

231. See, for instance, Lin Ying 2006a, 2007.

In the case of Melkites, except for the above-mentioned bilingual manuscript fragment of a psalm in Sogdian and Greek found in Turfan,[232] no other hint of their presence in China has come down to us. In the case of West Syrians, they were certainly aware of the mission of the Church of the East to China, and their communities in Khorasan and Segestan were well placed to follow East Syrians across the borders of the Chinese Empire, but there is no evidence that they ever did so. The comprehensive list of episcopal consecrations between the ninth and twelfth centuries compiled by the Jacobite patriarch Michael I Rabo (Michael the Syrian, r. 1166–99) mentions several West Syriac bishops in Khorasan and Segestan, but none in China.[233] A century later, the historian Grigorios bar 'Ebroyo made no mention of a Jacobite presence in China, and he would undoubtedly have done so had there been one. David Wilmshurst explains the absence of Jacobite and Melkite missions to China by saying that "the Nestorians were determined to keep China to themselves, and reacted as fiercely in the seventh century to competition as they did in the thirteenth century, when the cozy Chinese monopoly they enjoyed under Mongol protection was threatened by Latin missionaries."[234]

---

232. See p. 17.

233. See *Chronicle of Michael the Syrian*, appendix III, ed. and trans. Chabot, 4: 752–68 (text), 3: 448–82 (trans.).

234. Wilmshurst 2011, 122.

3

"The Scriptures Were Translated"

THE FIRST CHRISTIAN TEXTS IN CHINESE

The 781 Xi'an Stele: A Monument "Celebrating the Eminent and Meritorious Events"

Even though it is certainly an exaggeration to say that "the study of Nestorianism in China, as it began, ends with the [Xi'an] Nestorian inscription,"[1] it is still true that the discovery of this monument is what made Westerners aware of the presence of Christianity in China prior to the missions of the Franciscans in the thirteenth and fourteenth centuries and those of the Jesuits, which began at the end of the sixteenth century. The dozens of rubbings and copies of the eighth-century Xi'an stele found in various places around the world, including some important museums, have made this monument a sort of Christian Rosetta Stone, the object to which the stele has repeatedly been compared from the nineteenth century to the present day.[2]

Already in 1904, the French Jesuit and sinologist Louis Gaillard (1850–1900) made an important observation on how the Xi'an Christian stele is regarded:

It has become commonplace to refer to this stele as "the *Nestorian* monument of Si-ngan-fou [Xi'an fu]." Without entering into an arid textual analysis, I will simply point out that this expression is imprecise. Moreover, it wrongly and without proof makes a precipitous judgment

---

1. Saeki 1951, introduction, 7.

2. For a recent example, see Lu Yuan 2009, 11.

The Luminous Way to the East. Matteo Nicolini-Zani, Oxford University Press. © Oxford University Press 2022.
DOI: 10.1093/oso/9780197609644.003.0003

118   A HISTORY OF ENCOUNTERS

on an uncertain and unclear historical issue that is still the subject of dispute. It would be desirable to abandon the word "Nestorian" in favor of a qualifier such as *Sino-Chaldean* or *Syro-Chinese*. On the other hand, why not simply refer to it as the "Christian monument of Si-ngan-fou"? This expression is both accurate and precise, and would have nothing to fear from the possibility of future discoveries.[3]

More than a century later, one can detect behind this statement the existence of a long tradition of prejudicial readings of the 781 Xi'an stele and its contents. These readings will be mentioned later on in discussing the different ways of appropriating that "strange teaching from a strange land" as East Syriac Christianity was thought of in China over the centuries.[4] The "uncertain and unclear historical issue" Gaillard mentions is the alleged Nestorian (i.e., doctrinally unorthodox) nature of the Xi'an Christian inscription. This became the established position after the orientalists Athanasius Kircher and Giuseppe Simone Assemani (1687–1768) advanced their hypotheses between the second half of the seventeenth century and the beginning of the eighteenth century.[5] This erroneous understanding of the theological identity and doctrinal background of *jingjiao* Christianity then became common in later Western scholarship and also affected Chinese and Japanese scholars (with few exceptions),[6] as Johan Ferreira states:

> During the nineteenth century, the use of the term "Nestorian" in relation to Tang Christianity became general. Therefore, it can be seen that, because of the earlier works of Kircher and Assemani, the term "Nestorian" had become firmly associated with Tang Christianity in the nineteenth century. Most writers in the twentieth century, and up to the present day, reflect this erroneous perception of Tang Christianity. . . . The Nestorian appellation, and consequent disparaging estimation of Tang Christianity, has become fixed, not only in

---

3. Gaillard 1904, 113.

4. See, for an introductory overview, Thompson 2020a.

5. See Ferreira 2014, 12–16.

6. For the particular and comparatively more correct evaluation of the theological roots of *jingjiao* by the well-known philosopher Zhu Qianzhi (1899–1972) in his *Zhongguo jingjiao* (The Luminous Teaching in China), in particular 23–38, see Tang Kaijie 2019; Zhu Donghua 2019.

the minds of Westerners in general but also in the writings of most church historians, including writers in China.[7]

Anticipating what will become clear through the course of this study and what Johan Ferreira expressed in a clear and definitive manner, we believe that the following statement can be accepted with absolute certainty: "Contrary to common opinion, the theology of the Tang Chinese church was not an aberrant form of Christianity with only internal or syncretistic concerns, it was consistent with traditional orthodoxy."[8]

In the same line, the French orientalist Henri Cordier (1849–1925) wrote in 1908, "This inscription is generally considered to have come from the Nestorians, but this is supported only by circumstantial evidence. In fact it must be stressed that nothing in it is characteristic of Nestorianism."[9] This is echoed by the more recent words of John M. L. Young who, after reviewing and investigating the entire corpus of Tang Christian literature, rejects any interpretation of these documents as espousing a Nestorian theology:

> Throughout these documents, . . . a picture of "Nestorian" heresy does not appear, but only a picture of the traditional Antiochene theology. . . . The nature of the theology which appears in these seventh-and-eighth-century Chinese documents is that of the Antiochene tradition of the fifth century.[10]

If it is true that "there is virtually nothing in the documents that can be conclusively labeled 'Nestorian,'"[11] it follows that "there is no need to begin with Nestorianism when we study Christianity in Tang China."[12] Therefore, in our brief presentation of the "Stele of the Diffusion of the Luminous Teaching of Da Qin in China" (*Da Qin jingjiao liuxing Zhongguo bei*) we will not rely on past interpretative models that are reductive or disrespectful of its real identity. Instead, we will attempt a course that winds through three stages and is organized around three stories that have to do with this historic and

---

7. Ferreira 2014, 17.

8. Ibid., 337.

9. Cordier 1908, 669.

10. Young 1984, 89. See also Young 1969, 1970.

11. Moffett 1992, 306.

12. Wickeri 2004, 45.

almost mythical stone: (1) the story *of* the stone, (2) the story *on* the stone, and (3) the story *beyond* the stone.[13]

The first story of the Xi'an Christian stele, the story of the stone, recounts how this physical object remained hidden in the belly of the earth for several centuries and then was fortuitously restored to humanity at the beginning of the seventeenth century.[14] Before considering the history of its discovery, however, we need to focus our attention on this extraordinary stone itself, to look at it with a feeling of amazement similar to that felt by those who first saw it and tried to establish its identity. The Xi'an stele is not only a text to be read as we would read any page of history; it is also an object to be admired for its aesthetic and artistic features. This is true for every Chinese text. Because of the morphological characteristics of the Chinese language, the way it is written is not irrelevant. This is particularly significant for the Xi'an stele, which, as I would put it, materially and figuratively commemorates the "eminent and meritorious events" of the "diffusion of the Luminous Teaching in China," as the text of the inscription states.

The stele's visual appearance as well as the propagandistic rhetoric of its text follow the claim of the *jingjiao* church that as China was recovering from the devastation of the An Lushan Rebellion, and as Emperor Dezong (r. 779–805) began to institute reforms to restore a political structure similar to that of pre-rebellion times, the Christian God blessed China, whose wise emperors had honored the Luminous Teaching, and was ready to bless Emperor Dezong for following his predecessors and honoring God by securing the church's place before the court and, consequently, in Chinese society.[15]

Erecting a stone monument to describe, commend, and propagate its teachings was no small undertaking for the Tang Christian community. Putting up stone monuments was an expensive exercise because of the price of the stone and the fee of the expert artisan who engraved the text. Official government permission also had to be obtained for the erection of a stele. The reason for this was that stone monuments always had a clear sociopolitical function in Chinese history. They were set up in public spaces by communities or groups to commemorate the achievements and virtues of an individual or an institution. Their main function was to articulate the collective identity of

---

13. See Liang Yuansheng 2004, 1–18 (chap. 1: "Shitou ji: Yikuai xuanbei de jizhong gushi" 石頭記——一塊玄碑的幾重故事 [Notes on the Stone: Stories about a Mysterious Stele]).

14. For a summary of this first story, see Ribaud 2001, 12–15.

15. See Morrow 2019, 80–107.

the sponsors of the stone monument and thereby safeguard their status. They therefore had an important symbolic and rhetorical public function.[16]

For this reason, the specific content of the Xi'an stele inscription "should be read and understood as a discourse of political theology" or "a written manifesto in terms of political theology."[17] The monument itself makes an important statement about the place of Christianity within Tang society. "The setting up of a stately and solid monument . . . was a solemn occasion which represented the rare opportunity to dignify recognition and patronage granted by the imperial court to a foreign community,"[18] in this case, the Church of the East in Tang China. As Johan Ferreira reminds us, the monument was a symbol that Tang Christianity was an officially approved religion:

> By adopting the stone monument as the means by which to commemorate the spread of Christianity in China, the Tang Christian community made a significant statement on the place Christianity attained within Chinese culture and society. . . . The monument proclaims that Christianity has obtained official sanction. . . . The setting up of a stone in a public place, probably in the grounds of the Christian church in the Yining Ward in Chang'an, would have received official permission. The text would have been submitted to government censors, especially since it dealt with the Tang imperial house and history.[19]

Formed of black oolitic limestone, the stele is about 2 meters 80 centimeters high and about 1 meter wide (see figure 3.1). It is between 27 and 29 centimeters thick, weighs approximately two tons, and rests on a tortoise-shaped plinth, usual for Chinese epigraphy. Therefore, it appears majestic and distinctive, perhaps even a bit exotic, to our eyes. However, if we were to go to the Xi'an Beilin Museum where the original is kept, we might be surprised, perhaps even a little disappointed. The Christian stele is but one in a forest of hundreds of other Buddhist, Daoist, and Confucian steles similar in size and workmanship.

On the basis of its appearance we can draw a preliminary, though perhaps mundane, conclusion. The "container," that is to say, the material means by

---

16. See Wong 2004.

17. Zeng Qingbao 2019, 8, 17.

18. Ibid., 16.

19. Ferreira 2014, 143.

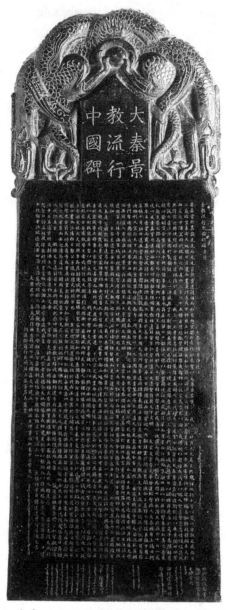

Figure 3.1 Christian stele from Xi'an, 781, plaster cast sponsored by Frits Holm in 1907–8, Musée Guimet, Paris.

(© RMN-Grand Palais / Art Resource, NY)

which the content of the Christian memorial is conveyed, is properly Chinese and was employed by the other religions present in China during the Tang dynasty. For that reason, the Chinese gazed—and still gaze—on such a "container" with a certain feeling of familiarity, of sympathy, that is very different from the feeling of estrangement that other Christian artistic "containers" in China sometimes aroused in later centuries. The Xi'an monument can be seen as an artistic attempt at contextualizing the proclamation of the Christian message within the Chinese cultural setting. It stands as an artistic demonstration that Christianity is compatible with Chinese culture.

The beauty of the stele—its decorative elements as well as the calligraphic style of its text—has been noted and appreciated by many. Representative in this respect are the words of Arthur C. Moule: "It is always pleasant to me to think that the Nestorians in China have given to the world one of its permanent treasures of beauty."[20]

From an artistic point of view, the ornamentation that surmounts the epigraphic panel and acts as a frame for the cartouche containing the nine characters of the title (see figure 3.2) is particularly interesting.[21]

The ornamental motif consists of two hornless dragons (called *chi* 螭 in Chinese) that are symmetrical and intricately intertwined. Saeki Yoshirō (P. Y. Saeki, 1871–1965) recognized these two dragons as *kumbhiras*, mythological animals of Indian origin. They were later used by Buddhists as a decorative element that already in ancient times became a common ornamental motif in China. In the center is a large pearl held in the claws of the hind legs of beasts. As Pelliot notes, "it is not necessary to look for any special symbolism in [the pearl of] our stele; it is an ancient and common theme of Chinese art."[22] A review of Tang-era steles in the Xi'an Beilin Museum shows that the auspicious motif of "two dragons playing with a pearl" (*erlong xizhu* 二龍戲珠) on the top of steles is a frequent ornamental flourish.

Engraved in a triangle on the upper part of the cartouche is a *crux gemmata* in the "Nestorian" style, that is to say, a cross whose four arms widen at the extremities, each one with three pearls at the end (see figure 3.3). The central pearl of the upper arm has a flame-like appearance and recalls the *maṇi* or marvelous pearl, one of the seven Buddhist jewels.

---

20. Moule 1930, 7.

21. For a description, see, for example, Pelliot 1996, 69–74; Saeki 1916, 12–14.

22. Pelliot 1996, 70.

Figure 3.2 Cartouche containing the nine characters of the title and a cross engraved in the upper ornamentation of the 781 Christian stele from Xi'an, rubbing.

The cross rests on a base of distinctive clouds, called *ruyi* 如意 in Chinese, a frequent decorative element, auspicious omen, and cosmological symbol in Daoist iconography. Clouds of *qi* 氣, the life force that, according to ancient Chinese cosmology, is the stuff of all being and the all-encompassing energy of the universe, effectively communicated to the Chinese people of the Tang era a sense of the Messiah's life-giving power.

This base, flanked by two flowering branches similar to lilies (traditional Christian symbols of purity and holiness), rests on a lotus flower (*padma*), a characteristic Buddhist element widely used in iconography as a support for various figures of the Buddhist pantheon. The fact that this flower rises out of mud alludes to the attainment of enlightenment via elevation from the opaqueness of this world. Used as a throne, the lotus retained the sense of transcendence, but its meaning was also expanded by becoming a symbol of the cosmos. As Dietrich Seckel explains, the lotus throne is

Figure 3.3 The *crux gemmata* resting on a lotus flower engraved in the cartouche in the upper ornamentation of the 781 Christian stele from Xi'an, rubbing.

the main symbol in Buddhism to denote the Buddha nature in man and all things that remained immaculate in its innermost essence, undefiled by the filth encountered in *saṃsāra*. At the same time the lotus is an ancient Indian symbol for the cosmos, and is thus associated with the Buddha in his capacity as spiritual ruler of the world and embodiment of the Absolute.[23]

Typically, the Buddha or a bodhisattva was depicted atop a lotus throne. In this case, however, the Buddha is displaced by a cross symbolizing Christ. The observer would thus understand that claims of honor, authority, and holiness were being made for the *jingjiao*'s Messiah.

The eclectic mix of symbols presented in the triangular field obviously draws on a symbolic vocabulary that a person of the Tang era would immediately understand as a statement about the divine or cosmic authority of the Messiah. Thus, certain authors came to the conclusion that, "as is provocatively hinted by this multiple framing of the cross, what makes the

---

23. Seckel 1964, 165–66.

126   A HISTORY OF ENCOUNTERS

so-called Nestorian monument itself so fascinating is that it is not, strictly speaking, a Nestorian monument at all, but rather a Daoist-Buddhist-Nestorian monument."[24] A similar but more evocative figure is carved in the 815 Christian pillar found in Luoyang (see figures 3.5 and 3.6).[25]

We can draw at least two conclusions from this symbolic concurrence. The first is that the adoption of properly Chinese decorative elements is an explicit choice and expresses a remarkable openness to local forms of artistic expression. The second is that this adoption does not conceal or disguise the centrality of the properly Christian element, the Cross. In addition to the depiction of the cross, the text of the stele contains two passages alluding to the cross. One passage speaks of "the cross that [Christian monks] hold as an emblem."[26] The other, which recounts the divine creation of the world, says that God, "drawing a cross, separated the four areas of space,"[27] an expression that has obvious cosmic symbolism.[28] While the text of the stele does not explicitly mention crucifixion in reference to Christ's sacrifice, in two of the Chinese Christian manuscripts of the Tang era—the *Discourse on the One God* and the *Book of the Lord Messiah*—the story of Christ's passion, crucifixion, and death is unequivocally present.[29]

These elements, taken as a whole, allow us to refute the thesis of those who say that there was no mention of the Cross and crucifixion in the preaching of the Church of the East during the Tang dynasty. It would be more appropriate to speak of a certain discretion, perhaps of a preparatory approach to the presentation of the Christian message, or of a precise choice of language that would be better understood by the Chinese. The subsequent experience of Jesuit preaching also seems to have moved in this direction.[30] In both cases, attention to the sensitivity of the other guided the choices of the missionaries in their preaching. In a general way, it is possible to say that a careful analysis of Tang Christian literature shows that Christ's work of salvation is faithfully

---

24. Billings 2004, 20.

25. See p. 140.

26. Text A, col. 8, p. 202.

27. Text A, col. 3, p. 199.

28. In this regard, see Jansma 1975; Stang 2017.

29. See Text C, cols. 250–85, pp. 254–56; Text D, cols. 145–70, pp. 278–81.

30. See Criveller 1997, 1998.

attested (the use of the term "Messiah" itself some seventy times in the texts attests to their Christocentric nature), and also that the Christology that emerges from it is expressed in a clear and orthodox way, with formulations that can be easily read in the tradition of the great Syriac Christological tradition.[31]

In 1663, only a few decades after the stele's discovery, the Jesuit historian Daniello Bartoli (1608–85) wrote admiringly of the stele's text, beginning with a description of its aesthetic and graphic components:

> Now in this province of Scensì [Shaanxi] and in this majestic metropolis of Sigan [Xi'an], the Fathers were preparing to bring the light of the Gospel, when a few months before their arrival, ... while excavating the ground to lay the foundations of a new building near Ceuce [Zhouzhi], a small town about thirty miles east of the metropolis, the excavators came across some ruins. Digging through them, they found a large slab of marble, which they removed. Having carefully cleaned it, they saw that it was incised with characters, some Chinese, others of a strange shape—nobody knew in what language—, but both of them carved by a most skillful hand.[32]

The unknown and undeciphered characters "of a strange shape" are Syriac letters in which are written some short portions of text and also the names of seventy Christian monks in a bilingual Chinese/Syriac list that is engraved on both sides of the stele. The first to decipher the Syriac script on the stele seems to have been the Jesuit Athanasius Kircher, in his work *China Illustrata* (1667, 42–45).[33] The main body of the text is written in Chinese in the "regular calligraphic style" (*kaishu* 楷書 or *zhengshu* 正書), arranged in columns like all ancient texts (34 columns corresponding to 1,780 characters), and elegantly carved by a skilled calligrapher, the scholar Lü Xiuyan.[34] An ancient

---

31. With regard to the Christology present in the Tang Christian texts, see Eskildsen 1991; Raguin 2002a, 2002b; Nicolini-Zani 2007; Zhu Donghua 2017. On the Xi'an stele in particular, see Suter 1938; Moffett 1992, 513–17 ("The Nestorian Monument's Theological Introduction"); Xu Longfei 2004, 167–256.

32. Bartoli 1663, 794.

33. The best study of the Syriac part of the 781 inscription remains that of Jean Dauvillier and Antoine Guillaumont in Pelliot 1984, 63–80.

34. On the calligraphy of the text carved on the Xi'an Christian stele, see Zhu Donghua 2011.

128   A HISTORY OF ENCOUNTERS

calligraphy expert, the Chinese Sun Chengze (1593–1675), observed with admiration that "the calligraphy of [Lü] Xiuyan in the *Stele of the Diffusion of the Luminous Teaching in China* is elegantly natural and powerfully vigorous. It is the most beautiful of the Tang stones."[35] The famous connoisseur Wang Wenzhi (1730–1802), in his remarks on the best specimens of calligraphic art in China, wrote that the Xi'an Christian stele "is distinguished among the examples of Tang calligraphy for its extreme clearness, softness, elegance, and richness. The strokes of the characters on the tablet are slender and shallow."[36]

This stone, which must have appeared familiar and at the same time mysterious to the first observers, was accidentally found, as described in the Bartoli chronicle mentioned above, just over a decade after the death of Matteo Ricci (1552–1610). During his twenty years as a missionary in China, his prolonged search for possible evidence of an ancient Christian presence in China yielded meager results.[37] After its discovery, the stele was soon placed inside the Chongsheng Buddhist monastery (Chongsheng si), in the western part of Chang'an, where it remained until October 2, 1907, the day the Chinese authorities moved the original stele from the grounds of the temple to the Beilin, or "Forest of Steles," a former Confucian temple in Xi'an that housed a number of steles from the area. That is where it is to be found today.[38]

Despite the large number of studies dedicated to the stele, some questions still remain open. First of all, the exact place where the stele was brought to light is not clear. It could have been near Zhouzhi, about seventy-five kilometers west of Xi'an, or, as is more likely, in the city of Chang'an (today's Xi'an, Shaanxi Province). There is also uncertainty about the date of its discovery.[39] The seventeenth-century material in Western languages,

---

35. Sun Chengze, *Gengzi xiaoxia ji* (Notes Written in the Summer of the Gengzi Year) 7, fol. 12a2–3.

36. Wang Wenzhi, *Kuaiyutang tiba* (Kuaiyutang Colophones) 3, in Lu Fusheng 2000, 10: 796 (text); Wylie 1856, 333 (trans.).

37. Matteo Ricci had established relations with some Jews in order to identify and then meet the so-called worshippers of the Cross, whose presence he had been informed of by a Jew from Kaifeng called Ai Tian (see Ricci and Trigault 1615, 119–24; see also Bernard 1932).

38. See Lu Yuan 1997. The Confucian temple became a museum in 1944 and was named the Shaanxi Provincial Museum in 1955. It was renamed the Xi'an Beilin Museum in 1992, when the new and separate Shaanxi History Museum was opened.

39. For a good account of the theories about the place and time of the discovery of the Xi'an stele, see Hong 1932; Saeki 1936; Li Hongqi 1985; Zhou 1994; Pelliot 1996, 5–57.

The First Christian Texts in Chinese   129

which, directly or indirectly, was very much influenced by the Jesuits, is almost unanimous in proposing the date of 1625. However, it seems more likely that 1623 was the actual year of its discovery, and that 1625 was the year in which the content of the stele was understood and disseminated in Jesuit circles, thanks to the intervention of Chinese scholars converted to the Christian faith.[40] Consequently, even the original location of the stele at the time of its erection in 781 is not clear. Was it the Christian monastery that stood in the Yining Ward of the capital Chang'an, or rather the district of Zhouzhi? Finally, the persecution that followed the imperial edict of 845 against religious communities of foreign origin present on imperial territory seems to have been the most likely reason for burying the stele, but historical documents do not allow us to verify with certainty the specific circumstances, intentional or accidental, that prompted its concealment.

We now move on to the second story, the story on the stone, which has to do with the translations and interpretations of the text written on the stele. It is first of all the story of how people reacted to the discovery of the stele. Finding it both marvelous and mysterious, their reaction reflected the dual nature of the stone. On the one hand, many were attracted to it; but at the same time, over the course of several decades, and especially in European circles, a certain skepticism reigned over its authenticity, based on the sharp accusation of "pious fraud" by no less a scholar than Voltaire (1694–1778), who penned this sarcastic observation:

> Some pretend that the Christian religion was known in China towards the eighth century, in the time of Charlemagne. It is affirmed that our missionaries have found in the province of Kingtching [?],[41] an inscription in Syriac and Chinese characters: this monument . . . mentions that a holy man named Olopuen [Aluoben] conducted by blue clouds, and observing the direction of the winds, came from Tacin [Da Qin] to China in the year 1092 of the era of the Seleucidae, which answers to the year 636 of Jesus Christ; that as soon as he arrived in

---

40. See Ji Xiangxiang 2002. According to this author, it was the Jesuits who transmitted, without any discussion, the date of 1625, probably so as not to increase the distrust of those who accused them of having fraudulently produced the stele in order to have at their disposal such remarkable proof of an ancient Christian presence in China.

41. An evident mistake. Most probably, the author wrongly took the name of the author of the Xi'an inscription, Jingjing, for the name of the province where the stele was found, Shaanxi.

130 A HISTORY OF ENCOUNTERS

the suburbs of the imperial city, the emperor sent a *colao* [*gelao* 閣老, "secretary of state"] to attend him, and built a Christian church for his use, etc.

It is evident by the very inscription itself, that this is one of those pious frauds, which have not been looked upon in so bad a light as they deserve. . . . This country of Tacin, this era of the Seleucidae, this name of Olopuen, which, they say, is Chinese, and resembles a Spanish name, these blue clouds, which serve as guides, this Christian church built all of a sudden at Pekin for a priest of Palestine, who could not set foot in China without running the risk of his life; all shows the story to be ridiculous. . . .

It is therefore very certain that in the time of Charlemagne, the Christian religion (as well as the people who profess it) were absolutely strangers to China.[42]

In-depth studies that were more thorough and not driven by ideological presuppositions gradually brought about a more balanced and correct evaluation of the authenticity of the stele. The debate regarding authenticity was finally laid to rest at the end of the nineteenth century.[43]

Returning to the question of when the stele was discovered, we know that the scholar Zhang Gengyu immediately realized the importance of the discovery. After making a rubbing of the inscription, he sent it to his Christian friend Li Zhizao (1565/71–1630), as reported by Daniello Bartoli:

[Zhang Gengyu] placed on the same stone one or two of those large sheets that are used for the art of stone printing in China and obtained a faithful copy of the writing in white characters on a black background. He then posted the rubbing to Doctor Lione [Leo Li Zhizao] his old friend and, as he well knew, a Christian, who lived in Hanceu [Hangzhou].[44]

---

42. Voltaire 1759, 1: 28–29.

43. A century after Voltaire's remarks, the American orientalist Edward E. Salisbury (1814–1901) wrote an article still aimed at supporting the authenticity of the stele (Salisbury 1853). For a good account of this debate, see Pelliot 1996, 147–66.

44. Bartoli 1663, 795.

The First Christian Texts in Chinese 131

Li Zhizao immediately had the text printed and published, with an explanatory note dated June 10, 1625.[45] The first European actually to see the stele was the Jesuit Nicolas Trigault in October of 1625, the year in which the first translation, in Latin, was made, probably by Trigault himself.[46]

From this moment on, commentaries by Chinese scholars and philological, historical, and theological studies on the text and the content of the inscription by Western scholars have followed one another without a break. On the Chinese side, the most authoritative commentary is that of Pan Shen (1917). On the Western side, the works of the French orientalist Paul Pelliot, abundantly cited in the course of these pages, certainly represent the most notable contribution (see bibliography, ad loc.). Moreover, numerous translations have been made in the principal languages[47] by prestigious sinologists (some of them also highly respected missionaries) such as Alexander Wylie (1815–87; Wylie 1856), Guillaume Pauthier (1801–73; Pauthier 1858), James Legge (1815–97; Legge 1888), Henri Havret (1848–1901; Havret 1895–1902, 1897), Saeki Yoshirō (1911, 1916; 1951, 53–112), Paul Pelliot (1996), and Max Deeg (2018b).

These studies approached the text of the stele from three different and complementary perspectives.[48] First, since this is a commemorative text by means of which the Tang *jingjiao* church wrote its first history, much of the research has moved in the direction of a historical investigation of the narrated events in order to reconstruct a synthetic picture of a minute ecclesial history situated in both the great imperial history of the Tang dynasty and the complex history of relations between China and West Central Asia.

Secondly, since the text of the stele is a rich and complex literary document, certainly equal to the most refined production of the Tang era, sinologists have undertaken philological studies in order to bring out the allusions and the direct and indirect quotations of literary, philosophical, and historical works used by the author of the text, thus highlighting the literary images and

---

45. See Li Zhizao, *Du jingjiaobei shu hou* (After Reading the Stone Inscription of the Luminous Teaching), in *Tianxue chuhan* (First Collection of Works about the Heavenly Studies), 1: 77–92.

46. For a more detailed excursus about the reception of the stele soon after its discovery, see Saeki 1951, 11–41; Pelliot 1996, 59–94.

47. For an account, see Pelliot 1996, 74–146; Lin Wushu 2000d; Geng 2001 (mostly based on Pelliot's work).

48. See Liang Yuansheng 2004, 10–13. It is impossible to mention here the individual works to which reference is made.

linguistic expressions borrowed from Buddhist, Daoist, and Confucian texts and terminology.

Finally, and thanks above all to the work of historians of Christianity in China, of theologians, and of missiologists, particular attention has been paid to the doctrinal and ideological content of the first part of the stele, that is to say the theological section that serves as a preamble to the narration of the historical events experienced by the Chinese community. In it the Christian God and the history of salvation realized in Christ are presented. Written with little more than four hundred characters and making use of a completely new Christian theological language forged from the philosophical-religious terminology of Chinese Daoism and Buddhism, this text is, in fact, the first theological synthesis produced in Chinese. The author evokes the transcendence of the Triune God, the divine creation of the world, the original goodness of human nature and its fall, the incarnation of the Messiah and his redemptive work, and the essence of Christian life.

Lastly, we can deal with the third story, the story beyond the stone, understood in two senses. The first deals with the use of everything on the stele and other sources to support wider studies that respond to particular questions linked to Tang Christianity. The main questions relate to the type of Christian community that existed in Tang China, relations between Christian believers and adherents of other religions, and the degree of inculturation of the Christian message in the Chinese milieu of the time. In this sense, the Xi'an stele is studied in conjunction with Tang Christian manuscripts and other Chinese historiographic sources as precious material for studies on the Luminous Teaching (*jingjiaoxue* 景教學 or *jingjiao yanjiu* 景教研究).

The second question concerns the conscious or unconscious appropriation of the stele, its content, and its symbolism for purposes external to it. By way of introduction, it is intriguing to note that interest in the Christian monument grew in the course of the centuries following its discovery to such an extent that at the beginning of the twentieth century there was even an attempt to bring the stele to the West. In 1907, fascination for this mysterious monument brought Frits V. Holm (1881–1930), a Danish adventurer, to China to examine it directly and, if possible, to purchase it. He failed in his attempt to buy it, but he succeeded in having a reproduction made that was identical in material and size to the original, and then, with enormous difficulty and considerable expense, in transporting it to New York.[49] After his

---

49. Reports on this expedition can be found in Carus 1909; Holm 1923. About Holm's "adventure," see also Pearce 2020.

The First Christian Texts in Chinese   133

expedition to Xi'an, Holm ordered many plaster casts of the monument to be made and to be placed in important museums all over the world. The replica of the stele brought by Holm to New York was exhibited in the Metropolitan Museum of Art for about ten years. Eventually, in 1917, a wealthy convert to Catholicism purchased it and sent it to Rome as a gift to Pope Benedict XV, who had it placed in the former Lateran Museum.[50] The stone's journey out of China was also symbolic in that from this moment on, it became the heritage of the whole of humanity.

There is a great deal of truth in a recent reference to the Xi'an stone as a mirror, "in the sense that every time it is interpreted, it is also interpreting the interpreter."[51] It has also "served as a kind of screen onto which Westerners could project their own self-image and this is what they were looking at, not China."[52] For this reason, the hermeneutical studies of the stele's text that have been carried out over time have produced different explanations and translations of its contents and different interpretations of Tang Christianity in general.[53]

The first and most influential way of interpreting the 781 Xi'an inscription was the approach taken by the Jesuits.[54] The discovery of the Christian stone was actually a major historical event for the Jesuit missionaries who entered China in 1582. For several decades they had looked for a way to ease open the closed door of Chinese culture. The discovery of the stele was an opportunity they could not miss. It was meaningful in two ways:

> As tangible evidence of the antiquity of Christianity, . . . the monument was the ideal prop for converting the people of China who would generally be less likely to revere a teaching that could be considered a novelty. In Europe, properly explicated, the stele could be appropriated as a providential sign of counter-reformation or pro-Jesuit polemics

---

50. This replica is now at the Ethnological Museum "Anima Mundi" within the Vatican Museums (inventory card no. 6075). See Pelliot 1996, 68, 490–91; Zheng Xiyuan 2006.

51. Wickeri 2004, 43.

52. Keevak 2008, 3. Michael Keevak adds: "When Westerners discussed the stone they were not really thinking about China at all. . . . The stone came to represent the empire and its history for many Western readers, but only because it was seen as a tiny bit of the West that was already there" (ibid.).

53. A good survey can be found in Wickeri 2004, 46–52.

54. For a more exhaustive exposition of this theme, together with reference to the sources, see Nicolini-Zani 2010b.

134 A HISTORY OF ENCOUNTERS

in the face of increasingly controversial and even endangered [Jesuit] missions in both India and China during the seventeenth century.[55]

Since the Xi'an stele appeared as a providential tool to prove the ancient and venerable presence of Christianity in China, both Jesuit missionaries and Chinese converts used it to make their missionary strategy more effective. First of all, they exploited the discovery of the stone to emphasize that Tang Christianity was a distinguished ancestor of their present Catholic missionary activity. Upon discovery of the stele, it was possible to identify the Catholic religion brought to China by Matteo Ricci and his Jesuit confreres, which was known in those years as Heavenly Studies or Heavenly Doctrine (*tianxue* 天 學), with the Luminous Teaching (*jingjiao*) that had entered China during the Tang dynasty. The inscription on the stele also served another aim, namely, to provide evidence of the support granted to the Luminous Teaching by emperors and ministers of the great Tang dynasty and thus to encourage Chinese rulers, ministers, and scholars of the Ming dynasty to grant official support to the Teaching of the Lord of Heaven (*tianzhujiao* 天主教), that is, Catholicism.

For these reasons, during some decades after the discovery of the stele, the Jesuits, together with those Chinese scholars who were the first to convert to Christianity, undertook to study, interpret, and translate the text of the inscription. The two major examples of the *interpretatio gesuitica* of the Xi'an Christian inscription are those of Manuel Dias Jr. (1574–1659), who in 1644 published the first commentary in Chinese on the text of the stele (*Tang jingjiao beisong zhengquan*, "Correct Explanation of the Tang *Stele Eulogy on the Luminous Teaching*"); and of Athanasius Kircher, who in 1667 published a critical edition of the epigraph that included a transcription of the Chinese text, a table of the pronunciation of the Chinese characters, a word-for-word translation into Latin (made by his Jesuit confrere Michał Piotr Boym), and a paraphrase, also in Latin (Kircher 1667, 1–45 [part I, chaps. 1–6: "Monumenti Syro-Sinici Interpretatio"]).[56] As a finely honed study of this work emphasized, "Kircher's edition is partly a sinological-doctrinal polemic aimed at figuring the stone as a proto-Jesuit historical relic by

---

55. Billings 2004, 18.

56. Based on Kircher's work, a few years later the Protestant theologian and sinologist Andreas Müller (1630–94) resumed the transcription of the Chinese text made by Kircher, adding a musical notation in order to make it easier for the Western reader to pronounce Chinese tones (Müller 1672; see Pang 2009).

The First Christian Texts in Chinese   135

strategically rewriting in translation everything that does not conform to the Jesuit identity that is positively projected onto it."[57]

As has been said, the stele also had a significant impact in European circles, thanks once again to the initiative of the Jesuits. To give just a few examples, in Italy the priest Matteo Ripa (1682–1746) "worked to spread the authentic testimony of the stele in the West,"[58] making a copy that was probably based on that of Kircher.[59] In Milan, Cardinal Federico Borromeo (1564–1631) acquired for his recently established Biblioteca Ambrosiana a rubbing of the Xi'an stele that was probably donated by Nicolas Trigault. This was one of the first rubbings of the Xi'an stele made after its discovery and is evidence of the cardinal's interest in the scientific and literary culture of China, as well as of the opening of his academic study program to distant Asian regions.[60]

Throughout history there was also a Protestant approach to the 781 Xi'an inscription. For example, in the nineteenth century the Protestant missionary Alexander Williamson (1829–90) considered the Xi'an stele to be a Protestant document *ante litteram*. He wrote:

> The preserving care of a wise Providence was the first thought in our minds, for this tablet not only enunciates all the leading doctrines of our holy religion, but is a most important witness in favour of our faith in opposition both to the heathen and Romanists, as it shows that the Protestant form of Christianity is not of yesterday.[61]

At the end of the same century a Chinese Protestant, Yang Rongzhi (1855–1919), wrote a commentary on the stele (1895) that "is especially concerned with showing what is of apostolic institution in the doctrine that the inscription makes known and denouncing what already smells of the 'innovations' of the 'Roman Catholics.' "[62] It is, Havret writes, "a Protestant counterfeit of the apologia of Father Emmanuel Diaz [Manuel Dias Jr.], emphasizing the

---

57. Billings 2004, 4.

58. Poggi 1985, 211.

59. See Albanese 2005.

60. See Fumagalli 2004.

61. Williamson 1870, 1: 381. See also Gaillard 1904, 118–19; Keevak 2008, 102–9.

62. Havret 1895–1902, 2: 408.

dogmatic content with numerous citations of Scripture texts, and overlooking all the historical section of the text."[63]

A third example is the cross-cultural approach to Tang Christianity, whose main representative is Saeki Yoshirō, a Japanese scholar and Anglican Christian. In Western countries, his pioneering works were for many decades the only way to approach the Christian documents of the Tang dynasty. While "placing the stone into a broader context of Chinese religious culture during the period, as well as . . . bringing together all the known documents regarding the Da Qin religion in both Chinese and English translation,"[64] his essays, books, and translations (not without reason accused of being examples of a "Christianized" or "Christianizing" translation)[65] interpret the Xi'an Christian monument mainly as a cultural bridge between East and West (e.g., Saeki 1911, 1916, 1935, 1951).

The most recent way of understanding Tang Christianity is the Daoistic approach represented by two books, one by Martin Palmer (2001), the other by Ray Riegert and Thomas Moore (2003).[66] Often misreading the Chinese sources, they present Tang Christianity as a creative Daoist-Christian reinterpretation of the faith, "a true blend of Christian and Daoist ideas,"[67] in which one can easily recognize "a New Age or post-modern Christianity."[68]

While these various interpretations of the Xi'an Christian stele and Tang Christianity in general can be considered partial and misleading, they suggest that these many different ways of looking at the same historical experience can also have ecumenical implications. In their path toward unity, the churches in China could perhaps one day consciously avail themselves of such an ecumenical appropriation of the experience of Chinese Christianity in the first millennium. That is to say, since the Xi'an stele is evidence of the presence of Christianity in China before the split between East and West, it could be regarded as a common ancestor whose symbolic heirs are the different Christian denominations flourishing in China today.

---

63. Ibid.

64. Keevak 2008, 127.

65. See Deeg 2004; [2006b?], 120.

66. Review of these two books in Keevak 2008, 129–41.

67. Deeg 2009, 136.

68. Wickeri 2004, 49.

The First Christian Texts in Chinese

The 815 Luoyang Pillar: A Memorial Stone "Granting the Luminous Blessings"

According to the text of the [Xi'an] stele, during the reign of Gaozong luminous monasteries [jingsi] were established in every prefecture. At that time the Luminous Teaching [jingjiao] was not limited to one monastery or to one stele. It is hence possible that in the future a second stele will be discovered![69]

Almost four hundred years after the discovery of the Xi'an Christian stele of 781 and more than half a century after the publication of the last discoveries of Tang Christian manuscripts, these words by the Chinese scholar Feng Chengjun (1885–1945) became reality.[70] In 2006 the academic world was stirred by the discovery in Luoyang, the eastern capital of the Tang since 657, of a new Christian stone from the Tang dynasty.[71] As is evident from the considerable amount of literature published in China within a short time after its reappearance, this Tang Christian inscription has aroused great interest among Chinese scholars[72] because of its importance for literary and historical research on East Syriac Christianity in Tang China.[73]

Actually, the pillar was brought to light already around 1976 by some farmers who were digging a well. It stood unnoticed in a public area for several years and then was stolen. In 2007 it was recovered and after being kept for some time in a storehouse of the Second Working Team for Cultural Heritage of Luoyang City, it is now on display in the Luoyang Museum.[74] Archaeologists were able to identify the original site where the pillar was unearthed, a flat area situated one kilometer southeast of Qi Village, Lilou Township, Luolong District, Luoyang City. Around this spot, ten tombs of

---

69. Feng Chengjun 1931, 60.

70. Actually, the last two documents that were published in the late 1940s, the so-called Kojima documents, have recently been recognized as modern forgeries (see pp. 154–55).

71. For a comparative study that analyzes the differences and similarities of the two Tang Christian stones discovered in China so far, namely the 781 Xi'an stele and the 815 Luoyang pillar, see Ge 2009b, 2013.

72. See Feng Qiyong 2007; Luo Zhao 2007a, 2007b; Zhang Naizhu 2007; Zhao Xiaojun and Chu Weihong 2007; Lin Wushu and Yin Xiaoping 2008; Yin Xiaoping and Lin Wushu 2008; Lin Wushu 2009a, 2009b; Tang Li 2009b; Xu Xiaohong 2009; Ge 2016.

73. See Moribe 2012.

74. See Luoyangshi dier wenwu gongzuodui 2009.

138 A HISTORY OF ENCOUNTERS

the Tang dynasty were also discovered. This area corresponds to what was the Gande Township in the Sui–Tang dynasties, thus corroborating what the text engraved on the pillar says about its location.

The Gande Township lies close to the area of the old city, called Southern Market (Nanshi) from the Sui to the Tang dynasties, where Sogdians had settled. The important role played by the Southern Market for international trade gradually led to the nearby establishment of a large settlement of foreigners (mainly Sogdians) who had moved to China for trading purposes and had gradually become Sinicized. It was in this area that the Gande Township was eventually established.[75] Generally speaking, the history of the Sogdian settlement in Luoyang resembles that of Chang'an, with merchants, government officials, emissaries, and diplomatic hostages all forming part of the community. Many tomb epitaphs found in Luoyang as well as inscriptions in the Longmen Buddhist grottoes give evidence of the settlement of the Sogdians in the city.[76] In 2009, a burial niche was discovered at the northwestern end of the Longmen grottoes. A cross and the character *shi* 石 that is visible above the niche have been taken to suggest a connection between those buried in the niche and Shiguo (Čač/Taškent). This discovery further confirms a Sogdian Christian presence in the Luoyang area,[77] although the religions most widespread among the different families of Sogdian residents in Luoyang seem to have been Buddhism and Zoroastrianism, as attested by the two or three Zoroastrian shrines (*xianci* 祆祠) within the city walls, located in the same areas as those inhabited by the Sogdians.[78]

The broken pillar is an irregular octagonal prism with a horizontal sectional diameter of 40 centimeters and a perimeter of 112 centimeters (see figure 3.4).[79] It is made of blue limestone rock and shaped like a typically Chinese Buddhist *dhāraṇī* pillar, known in Chinese as *jingchuang* 經幢, lit., "sutra pillar." A round stone tenon rises out of the middle of the round stone plate on top of the pillar, fitting into the stone plate just as it would

---

75. See Zhang Naizhu 2009, 2013. On the basis of abundant epigraphical material, Zhang Naizhu also clearly shows that during the Tang dynasty the same Gande area was used as burial ground by the non-Han communities who had settled in China.

76. See Rong 2000a, 142–44; Fukushima 2017.

77. See Jiao 2013; Zhang Naizhu and Zheng Yaofeng 2014, 2016; Wenzel-Teuber 2014.

78. About the location of these Zoroastrian shrines, see Leslie 1981–83, 286–90; Rong 2000a, 143. About the diffusion of the religious faiths practiced by the Sogdians to China, see Yan Wanjun 1988.

79. Sixteen high-quality photographs of the pillar can be found at the end of Ge 2009a.

The First Christian Texts in Chinese

Figure 3.4 Christian funerary pillar from Luoyang, 815, Luoyang Museum, Luoyang (Henan, China).

do on a Buddhist *dhāraṇī* pillar. The broken pillar we have is the upper section of the original structure, which, like most of the Buddhist *dhāraṇī* pillars, would have had a stone base. The eight sides of the broken prism are 14 to 16 centimeters wide and 60 to 85 centimeters high. The first and the eighth sides bear evident traces of intentional damage. Most scholars think that the damage was done during the persecution of foreign religions during the Huichang era of the reign of the Tang Emperor Wuzong. This may have been what happened, but there is no documentary evidence that the damage was done at that time.

Figure 3.5 The cross and *apsaras* decoration on the Christian funerary pillar from Luoyang, 815, Luoyang Museum, Luoyang (Henan, China), rubbing.
(Source: Ge Chengyong 2009a, plate 11)

Figure 3.6 The cross and *apsaras* decoration on the Christian funerary pillar from Luoyang, 815, Luoyang Museum, Luoyang (Henan, China), rubbing.
(Source: Ge Chengyong 2009a, plate 12)

The upper part of six of the eight sides of the pillar are carved with more or less square images, organized in two series (see figures 3.5 and 3.6). These square images occupy the part of Buddhist *dhāraṇī* pillars that is usually engraved with buddhas or bodhisattvas. In the two central images of both series is carved a "Nestorian" cross, namely a cross with four expanding and bifurcated arms of equal length, terminating in one or three pearls. Both crosses have a lotus flower as their base and are flanked by two *apsaras* or flying *devas* (*feitian* 飛天) that face the cross. They are seated on clouds and dressed in flowing robes adorned with floating ribbons. The lotus flower (*padma*), the precious pearl (*maṇi*), and the flying *apsaras* are typical components of Buddhist art. This borrowing of Buddhist iconographic motifs by Christian artists is a striking expression of the cross-cultural approach to religious iconography adopted by the Church of the East in China.

Another example from the same period of a cross on a lotus flower is the decoration on the Xi'an Christian stele of 781 (see figure 3.2). This pattern will subsequently become a common decorative element on Christian tombstones in Southern China and also in Inner Mongolia.[80] In contrast, the pattern of a cross flanked by two *apsaras* carved on the Luoyang pillar is the only example of this composition from the Tang dynasty. Nevertheless, it is very similar to several other carvings dating to the thirteenth and fourteenth centuries that adorn Christian tombstones in Quanzhou.[81] The similarity demonstrates the astonishing continuity of this iconographic model through time (from the Tang to the Yuan dynasty) and place (from Luoyang in the central China plain to Quanzhou on the southern coast of China). The discovery of the Luoyang pillar is also of great importance from an artistic point of view:

> The two series of images carved on the Luoyang *jingjiao* pillar are the most important *jingjiao* artistic products of the Tang dynasty. Formerly we could only admire the cross carved on the top of the Xi'an *Da Qin jingjiao liuxing Zhongguo bei* that had its base in the form of a lotus flower and was flanked by auspicious clouds and flowers. Although it is exquisitely carved, its decorative elements are rather small. The images on the Luoyang pillar are not only bigger and contain more figures, but the carving is more refined and there is an integral unity between the sober character of the figures and the movement of the floating lines into an integral unity, which makes us appreciate it as an even more precious example of *jingjiao* artistic forms and contents.[82]

The text engraved on the eight sides of the pillar (see figure 3.7) is divided into four sections: (1) an opening invocation of God that reads, "We implore [thee], Pure God, Pure Great Majesty, Pure . . .," most probably a Chinese version of the Trisagion ("Holy God, Holy Mighty, Holy Immortal");[83] (2) the text of the *Da Qin jingjiao xuanyuan zhiben jing* (Book of the Luminous

---

80. See Halbertsma 2005, 2008.

81. See Foster 1954; Parry 2005, 2012a. From the fourth century on, flying angels supporting the Cross were represented on sarcophagi as a symbol of Christ's victory over death, and this would be the reason for the presence of this motif on the Luoyang pillar and on Quanzhou tombstones (see Ge 2014). Other examples of flying angels supporting crosses come from the Caucasus region and others from the Middle East (see Van Esbroeck [2006?]).

82. Luo Zhao 2007a, 31.

83. I consider this more reasonable than an invocation of the three persons of the Holy Trinity, as suggested by Lin Wushu 2009a and Wang Juan 2018, 651–55.

142   A HISTORY OF ENCOUNTERS

Figure 3.7 Christian funerary pillar from Luoyang, 815, Luoyang Museum, Luoyang (Henan, China), rubbing.

Teaching of Da Qin on Revealing the Origin and Reaching the Foundation), consisting of 630 characters arranged in 35 columns; (3) the text of the *Da Qin jingjiao xuanyuan zhiben jing chuangji* (Note on the Pillar [Inscribed] with the *Book of the Luminous Teaching of Da Qin on Revealing the Origin and Reaching the Foundation*), consisting of 401 characters arranged in 23 columns; (4) a final annotation reporting on "a solemn commemorative ceremony" that "was performed as [the pillar] was moved with great reverence" in 829.

While the text of the *Da Qin jingjiao xuanyuan zhiben jing* carved on the pillar is extremely valuable for a comparison with the manuscript version of the same text that supposedly came from Dunhuang,[84] the *Note on the Pillar* offers precious historical information. The text explains why the pillar was engraved and erected:

> In order that all may be granted the luminous blessings by keeping [the practice] of intoning [the scriptures], they are also inscribed on

---

84. See pp. 155, 162.

The First Christian Texts in Chinese   143

pillars. . . . [I], who carry on the family and am the legal heir, vexed at not having been able as yet to express [my] sincere feelings of filial piety, so as not to disobey any longer the paternal instructions, . . . [with] deep emotions and humble feelings, I have now erected this pillar and have had it carved with a scripture . . . for the spirit-way[85] of [my deceased father?], the commandant . . ., my deceased mother, the lady of the An family from Bukhara, and for the deceased master's elder brother He . . .[86]

From these passages we learn the purpose for erecting and engraving the pillar: first, to obtain blessings by reciting the scripture engraved on the stone; second, to obtain these divine blessings for the souls of relatives. This is also clear by the way in which the text opens, namely, with the invocation of the thrice-holy God, expressed by the typical Buddhist formula of a prayer of entreaty *zhuyue* 祝曰, which means "to pray to someone and express one's wishes in his presence," followed by the name of the person to whom the entreaty is addressed and the object of the entreaty.[87]

The reason for erecting this Christian pillar is completely in line with the main overarching purpose that lies behind the custom of erecting Buddhist mortuary pillars, namely "to help the entombed deceased person be saved from the sufferings of hell and evil destinies,"[88] a practice that became widespread in China because it also fit in with the ancient Chinese concept of filial piety. Among the other reasons for erecting a mortuary pillar in the Buddhist tradition is one that also seems to apply to this Christian pillar, namely, to disseminate a particular scripture by engraving it in stone.[89] By making use of this Buddhist devotional and artistic object, the Christians in Luoyang probably wished to spread the contents of their own faith as it was described in the

---

85. The spirit-way (*shendao* 神道) is the passage that leads to the tomb.

86. *Da Qin jingjiao xuanyuan zhiben jing chuangji* (Note on the Pillar [Inscribed] with the *Book of the Luminous Teaching of Da Qin on Revealing the Origin and Reaching the Foundation*), cols. 28–31, in Nicolini-Zani 2009b, 113 (text), 116 (trans.).

87. This formula recurs more than one hundred times in the canon of the Chinese Buddhist scriptures. The Tang Christian text *Zunjing* (Book of the Honored) opens with a similar formula *jingli* 敬禮, "to pay homage reverently," addressed to the Trinity (Text B.2, col. 2, p. 226).

88. Liu Shufen 2003, 692.

89. See ibid., 727–33, in particular 728.

144 A HISTORY OF ENCOUNTERS

text of the *Book of the Luminous Teaching of Da Qin on Revealing the Origin and Reaching the Foundation*, which speaks of God and the Messiah.[90]

The text goes on to recount the circumstances, the place, and the time the tomb was constructed, as was often done in inscriptions on Buddhist mortuary pillars:[91]

> Successively [I] asked for permission to buy a grave plot in order to build a tomb, in the Bairen Village, Gande Township, Luoyang District, . . . then on the eighth day of the twelfth month of the ninth year of the Yuanhe era [January 22, 815], [I] bought a piece of land from the property owned by Cui Xing,[92] [with . . . as] guarantor . . . At the proper time of the year I offered libations of wine so that the will of heaven would agree with that of earth. After having polished the Nanshan stone[93] that [I] had bought, making it perfectly lustrous, I had it carved with the scripture . . . Feeling ashamed about my unpolished and poor style of writing, I took the brush and composed this account. May the future men of noble virtue excuse me [for my poor style]![94]

From this we may infer that the pillar was erected beside or within the tomb. Its close connection with the tomb is also confirmed by the fact that when the grave was transferred to another place fourteen years later, the pillar was also moved. This also appears perfectly in line with the fact that Buddhist mortuary pillars were mainly located beside or within a tomb, at least initially.[95]

The text that follows might contain the titles of the person responsible for the pillar's erection:

> [Nominated] by imperial decree martial commandant of the Mercenary Division of the Right Army of the Celestial Water Bearer at the

---

90. See Lin Wushu and Yin Xiaoping 2008, 335–43.

91. See Liu Shufen 2003, 693–94.

92. Another possible translation could be: "[I] bought a piece of land from Cui Xingben."

93. In ancient China this term referred to a kind of very precious and valuable stone, and not necessarily to the geographical origin of the stone.

94. *Da Qin jingjiao xuanyuan zhiben jing chuangji* (Note on the Pillar [Inscribed] with the *Book of the Luminous Teaching of Da Qin on Revealing the Origin and Reaching the Foundation*), cols. 34–37, in Nicolini-Zani 2009b, 114 (text), 117 (trans.).

95. See Liu Shufen 2003, 691–92, 700–3.

eastern capital [i.e., Luoyang], acting . . . [commandant?] of the Left Awesome Guard and of the Liangchuan Garrison [stationed] in the Ru Prefecture . . .[96]

The names of people belonging to both "the inner and outer circles of the family clan" (*zhongwai qinzu* 中外親族)[97] of the deceased appear at the conclusion of the text. The list includes some high Christian clergy of the Monastery of Da Qin, to which the family was supposedly attached because one of their relatives was the monk Qingsu:

> The younger brother, the Christian monk Qingsu; the paternal first cousin Shaocheng; the mother's brother An Shaolian; . . . father's younger adoptive brother, [who was] inactive general of the Left-Dragon Army at the capital [i.e., Chang'an], concurrently lackey, great pacificatory general, and acting general-in-chief of the Left Militant Guard assimilated to a governmental official; . . . [the clergy] of the Monastery of Da Qin: Xuanying, Harmony of the Doctrine, head of the monastery, whose secular family name is Mi; Xuanqing, Great Virtue of Respect-Inspiring Deportment, whose secular family name is Mi; Zhitong, Great Virtue of the Nine Grades, whose secular family name is Kang . . .; Chang'er, responsible for supervising the tomb and member of a peasant family.[98]

The fact that someone who bore an official title is mentioned before the name of the deceased mother leads me to infer that the persons chiefly

---

96. *Da Qin jingjiao xuanyuan zhiben jing chuangji* (Note on the Pillar [Inscribed] with the *Book of the Luminous Teaching of Da Qin on Revealing the Origin and Reaching the Foundation*), col. 38, in Nicolini-Zani 2009b, 114 (text), 118 (trans.).

97. The interpretation of this expression is difficult. I would discard the possibility that it means "the relatives from the Central Plain [i.e., China] and outside [China]," as suggested by Tang Li (2009a, 124 and 124n87), because the names that are listed above appear to be Sinicized and belong to members of families of foreign origin settled in China. Following Yin Xiaoping and Lin Wushu (2008 [2009a], 100–1), I tend to think that this expression refers to both the blood relatives and those who came to belong to the family clan through marriages, to the relatives from both the paternal and the maternal side. Moreover, since the list also includes some Christian clergy, I would guess that the expression might also refer to spiritual ties, namely those established on the basis of belonging to the same Christian faith.

98. *Da Qin jingjiao xuanyuan zhiben jing chuangji* (Note on the Pillar [Inscribed] with the *Book of the Luminous Teaching of Da Qin on Revealing the Origin and Reaching the Foundation*), cols. 39–42, in Nicolini-Zani 2009b, 115 (text), 118 (trans.).

146　　　　　A HISTORY OF ENCOUNTERS

commemorated by the inscription are two and not only one, as was implied by studies that have appeared thus far. We cannot fully know who this is because the pillar is broken off at this point. In a commemorative epigraphical text such as ours, the only person who can be recorded before a wife is her husband, that is, the deceased *paterfamilias*, the sponsor's father. For me this is also clearly confirmed by two omissions in the inscription: (1) if the sponsor's father was still alive at the time of the pillar's erection, he should have been mentioned in the first place among the persons dedicating the pillar; (2) all the members of the family from the paternal side are mentioned only by their given name, without the surname. This implies that the family name was clear to the reader, that is to say, it was already mentioned before as the "main" name in the text.

Unfortunately, the incomplete nature of the preserved inscription does not allow us to know the deceased father's family name. We know, however, that among the offspring of Sogdian families in China, marriage between persons of the same clan was very common. It was one of the foreign customs that was widespread in that era. This custom was a good way for the Sogdians to preserve their own national identity and their state's survival, and it is probable that these marriages were also political, because they united members of the royal family and officials of the upper ranks. They were most likely contracted between persons belonging to the same religious faith.[99] From this we can suppose that since the deceased mother was a certain "Lady An from Bukhara," the deceased father was also a member of the same An family or another family of the *Zhaowu jiuxing*, that is, the nine Sogdian family clans which had settled in China.

The "Dunhuang" Manuscripts: A Summary of Research

Until the early twentieth century, the only Christian literary source in Chinese that directly testified to the presence of the Church of the East in China during the Tang era was, as we have seen, the Xi'an stele. Other than a brief mention in two sources, there was no evidence that any Christian texts

---

99. Confirmation that this was also the practice among Christians is Mi Jifen's epitaph (see Ge 2001, 2004a). See also p. 89 and figure 2.1.

had been translated into Chinese. One source is the stele itself, which in one passage states:

> [At that time] in the kingdom of Da Qin there was a man of superior virtue whose name was Aluoben. Having scrutinized the signs of blue clouds, he took [with him] the true scriptures, and having examined the musical tones of the winds, he underwent difficulties and dangers. In the ninth year of the Zhenguan era [635], he arrived in Chang'an. The emperor sent his minister of state, Duke Fang Xuanling, with the Imperial Guard in the western suburbs of the city to welcome the visitor and introduce him to the Palace. The emperor had the scriptures translated in the [Imperial] Library and carefully examined that Way within the forbidden doors.[100]

The other mention of the translation of Christian texts into Chinese is the historical source *Tang huiyao* (Essential Regulations of the Tang), which, within the aforementioned edict of 638 authorizing the presence of the Christian religion in the imperial territory, states: "The Persian monk Aluoben, bringing the scriptures and the teaching [of Da Qin] from afar, has come to offer them at the supreme capital."[101]

In 1908 the so-called Dunhuang Nestorian documents, tangible evidence of Christian literary activity in Chinese, were first discovered and then studied and translated. The Mogao Caves in Dunhuang, in today's Chinese Gansu Province, is the place of their actual or supposed discovery, together with thousands of other religious and secular manuscripts, dating from the late fourth to the early eleventh centuries. A large number of religious documents are Buddhist, but other religions including Daoism, Christianity, and Manichaeism are also represented, giving witness to the multireligious nature of the site.[102] The majority of the manuscripts are in Chinese. Other languages represented are Khotanese, Sanskrit, Sogdian, Tangut, Tibetan, and Old Turkic (Uighur).[103]

---

100. Text A, cols. 10–11, p. 204.

101. *Tang huiyao* (Essential Regulations of the Tang) 49, 8: 864. The same edict, with a few variants, is also mentioned in the text of the Xi'an stele (see pp. 73–74).

102. See Yao Chongxin, Wang Yuanyuan, and Chen Huaiyu 2013.

103. See Akira 1966, 1969; Rong 1999b; Imaeda 2008.

148   A HISTORY OF ENCOUNTERS

The process of uncovering Christian texts began with French sinologist Paul Pelliot's discovery in the caves of Dunhuang of a manuscript (later catalogued as Pelliot chinois 3847 and abbreviated as P. 3847) containing two texts, the *Hymn in Praise of the Salvation Achieved through the Three Majesties of the Luminous Teaching* (*Jingjiao sanwei mengdu zan*) and the *Book of the Honored* (*Zunjing*), plus some final notes. This process ended in 1943 with the acquisition by the Japanese Kojima Yasushi of the manuscripts *Hymn of Praise to the Most Holy One of the Luminous Teaching of Da Qin, through Which One Penetrates the Truth and Turns to the Doctrine* (*Da Qin jingjiao dasheng tongzhen guifa zan*), the so-called Kojima manuscript A, and the *Book of the Luminous Teaching of Da Qin on Revealing the Origin and Reaching the Foundation* (*Da Qin jingjiao xuanyuan zhiben jing*), the so-called Kojima manuscript B. As we will point out, recent Chinese studies have highlighted the obscurity of the origin and transmission process of some of these documents. Our analysis of these studies will show that the claim—uncritically repeated in successive studies of these texts—that these manuscripts all come from the Dunhuang caves lacks documentary evidence.

Scholars were amazed to discover that in the four final columns of the manuscript Pelliot chinois 3847, the first manuscript found and the one that is still the most philologically and historically reliable, there are some annotations that speak of the translation of Christian texts into Chinese by Adam/Jingjing, the author of the text of the Xi'an stele.

A careful examination of the catalogue of all the writings shows that the writings of this teaching of Da Qin number one hundred and thirty in total and are written on *pattra*[104] in a foreign language.[105] In the ninth year of the Zhenguan era of the emperor Taizong of the Tang [635], the monk Aluoben, "Great Virtuous One" of the western lands, arrived in China and humbly presented a petition to the imperial throne in

---

104. *Beiye* 貝葉: palm leaves of the species Borassus flabelliformis. In ancient India and Central Asia Buddhist texts were written on these leaves, which were then strung together to form a book-like object called a *pothi* (see p. 149n107).

105. *Fanyin* 梵音: this expression indicated primarily Sanskrit, the original language of Buddhist texts; by extension, it came to mean all the foreign languages of lands to the west of the Chinese Empire. Here, therefore, it could indicate Syriac or an Iranian language. The Manichaean *Hymnscroll* in Chinese likewise presents a postscript that speaks of a Chinese translation of some sections of books written in the *fan* 梵 language, which evidently can be interpreted as a general term indicating one or more Central Asian Iranian languages (for which, it is true, there was a more precise name, *hu* 胡).

his native language. Fang Xuanling and Wei Zheng had the petition translated. In consequence, by imperial decree, the monk Jingjing, "Great Virtuous One" of that teaching, was summoned [to court] and the thirty scrolls mentioned above were produced [*yi* 譯]. The large number of the remaining [writings], contained in *pattra* manuscripts, have not yet been translated [*fanyi* 翻譯].[106]

It is certainly not easy to read the information provided to us by the compiler of these annotations. It is not clear, though it is possible, that the Christian scriptures that came to China were in the format known as *pothi*.[107] Among the Central Asian Christian fragments there is only one (E19, formerly C46) that appears in a format of this kind,[108] although "there is nothing to suggest that it ever had a string-hole like a real *pothi*."[109] It is bilingual (Syriac-Sogdian) and contains an unidentified New Testament passage. Are we to suppose that there were at that time many Christian texts of this type, which were then lost, or, more probably, that the compiler of the note had applied to the Christian scriptures a usage that was characteristic of the Buddhist manuscript tradition and was also adopted by the Manichaeans in Central Asia?[110]

What is certain, and what interests us more, is that these notes confirm the translation made by Adam/Jingjing from Syriac or from an Iranian language into Chinese, and that they affirm that the "aforementioned thirty scrolls" are translations. At the same time, two things must be considered. The first is that, as Chen Huaiyu rightly remarked, "because Jingjing held a high-ranking position in the *jingjiao* community in Chang'an, *jingjiao* translations produced under his direction would naturally have been attributed to him, as the leader of the community, and he may not have been personally involved in the translation process."[111]

---

106. Text B.2, cols. 19–22, pp. 231–32.

107. *Pothi* is the Oriya term (Sk. *pustaka*) for the narrow and long format of Buddhist books made of palm leaves (*pattra*), which were held together by means of a binding made by piercing the leaves at one end and passing a cord through them.

108. See Hansen 1968, 94n2.

109. Sims-Williams 1992b, 272. See also Sims-Williams 2012, 62.

110. A Manichaean *pothi* found at Murtuq was written in Tocharic and Uighur between the tenth and eleventh centuries; it contains two hymns to Mani, characterized by a typically Buddhist phraseology (see Clark 1982).

111. Chen Huaiyu 2020, 95.

150   A HISTORY OF ENCOUNTERS

The second thing to note is that the use of the Chinese term *yi* 譯 indicates an activity that goes beyond the limits of a mere translation in the strict sense of the word and includes the composition of new texts on the basis of the originals that are referred to. The titles of these thirty scrolls (there are actually thirty-five) that are listed in the manuscript P. 3847 just before the postscript and within a text that may have been for liturgical use certainly do not all appear to be translations, and if they are, it is not clear what texts have been translated.[112] The works translated include Old and New Testament books, liturgical texts, theological works, biblical stories, patristic works, secular books, and also works concerning the spiritual life that are clearly intended for those who followed the Christian monastic way of life in China.[113] Unfortunately, only three of the works listed in the manuscript P. 3847 (the section bearing the title *Book of the Honored*) have titles the same as or similar to those of the texts that have come down to us.[114]

Little is known about where Christian texts were written in Chinese or translated and how this was done. There can be no doubt, however, that the translation and composition of Christian texts took place in a setting where contacts between Christians and exponents of other religions were intense, that of the cosmopolitan Chang'an of the seventh to the ninth centuries, and most probably also in other places.

That the activity of translating Christian texts benefited from the collaboration of at least the Buddhists in the late Tang period can be deduced from a passage in the Buddhist catalogue compiled in 799–800 by the eminent monk Yuanzhao. It states that the Christian monk Adam/Jingjing helped the Buddhist monk Prajña (734–?), originally from Kapiśi in today's northern Afghanistan, in the translation of the *Sutra of the Six Perfections* (*Liu boluomi jing*, Sk. *Ṣaṭpāramitā sūtra*) from a Central Asian Iranian language (probably Sogdian) into Chinese. The two monks worked together after 782, the year when Prajña arrived in Chang'an, and in 787 they presented their translation to the emperor Dezong.[115] The passage reads:

---

112. See Text B.2, cols. 10–18, pp. 228–31.

113. See Wu Qiyu 2001, 31–48.

114. *Xuanyuan zhiben jing* could refer to the same text that came to us with the title *Da Qin jingjiao xuanyuan [zhi]ben jing* (Text F); *Zhixuan anle jing* corresponds exactly to the title of a work that has come to us (Text E); *Sanwei zanjing* could refer to the text that has come to us with the more extensive title *Jingjiao sanwei mengdu zan* (Text B.2).

115. See Takakusu 1896; Godwin 2016; 2017, 145–51.

The First Christian Texts in Chinese   151

[Prajña] together with Jingjing, a Persian monk of the Monastery of Da Qin, translated the *Ṣaṭpāramitā sūtra* in seven scrolls, on the basis of an Iranic text [*huben* 胡本]. But because at that time Prajña was not familiar with that Iranian language and did not understand the Chinese language, while Jingjing did not know Sanskrit and was not versed in the teaching of Śākyamuni, so, although they pretended to be translating the text, yet, in reality, they could not obtain a half of its gems [i.e., its real meaning].[116]

We should not forget that the Christian monastery of Da Qin in Chang'an was not far from the Chongfu Buddhist monastery (Chongfu si), which was the most important Buddhist institution in Chang'an. Between the end of the seventh and the end of the eighth century it was the center of the translation of sacred texts from Sanskrit into Chinese.[117] It therefore seems reasonable to think that in all probability Buddhist monks also helped Christian monks translate and compose Christian works in Chinese, although we have no clear evidence that this was the case.

This practice of encounter, collaboration, and dialogue is evident and unquestionable in the five documents we have today. Despite being obscure and difficult to interpret, they constitute precious literary testimonies to the process of inculturating the Christian message in the Chinese context, without which our knowledge of East Syriac Christianity in China in the first millennium would remain limited to the historical events and the brief theological exposition present in the text engraved on the Xi'an stele. For this reason, despite the small number of Sino-Christian texts of the Tang era, interest in them over time has been great and wide ranging:

> Of course, the Dunhuang manuscripts first attracted the interest of Dunhuangologists. However, since their content is the Luminous Teaching, it is only natural that they also attracted the interest of scholars of Christianity. Finally, since the Luminous Teaching is a foreign religion [in the China] of the Tang era, historians consider them, from the perspective of the history of culture, to be valuable material for the study of cultural exchanges between China and the West in

---

116. *Zhenyuan xinding shijiao mulu* (Catalogue of the Buddhist Teachings Newly Established in the Zhenyuan Era) 17, T 55: 892a8–9.

117. See Forte 1996b. On the many and varied monasteries of different religions in the capital Chang'an during the Tang era, see Xiong 2000, 235–76.

antiquity. Thus scholars, each from their own perspective, have offered their analyses of these manuscripts.[118]

Studies on these texts also show a certain variety in their typology. In brief,

> The specialized studies on these manuscripts are mainly concerned with two issues. Some, with a view to classifying the documents that have come to light, proceed to analyze the situation in which they were discovered and are preserved, their appearance, style, the time of composition, and the authenticity of the manuscripts. On the basis of the [original] text of the manuscripts, they also edit their transcription. Others, considering these texts as scriptures proper to the Luminous Teaching, provide explanatory notes and, on the basis of their content and literary genre, analyze the religious thought, the missionary strategy, etc. that are reflected in them. Looking at the published works, [it appears that] there are not few scholars who have conducted their research from both these angles simultaneously.[119]

A further overview of publications in this area reveals that the history of studies has evolved over three periods.[120] The fundamental work on early Sino-Christian texts was initiated by the Japanese scholars Haneda Tōru (1882–1955) and Saeki Yoshirō, who published, edited, and began interpreting the documents.[121] This was the golden age of the discoveries, and it coincides with the first half of the twentieth century, between 1918, when Haneda's first article was published[122] and 1951 when the second edition of Saeki's *The Nestorian Documents and Relics in China* came out. At the same time, Arthur C. Moule,[123] Francis S. Drake (1892–1974), and John Foster (1898–1973) offered their partial but valuable contributions to the understanding of these

---

118. Lin Wushu 2001b, 251.

119. Ibid.

120. For a brief overview of the history of research on Tang Christian literature and the related problems, see Lin Wushu 2001b; Nicolini-Zani [2006b?], 2009a; Zhao Jiadong and Nie Zhijun 2010; Ferreira 2014, 21–52; Iwamoto 2016; Wang Lanping 2016b, 1–30.

121. For a summary of the research conducted by Japanese scholars, see Zhang Jimeng 1969.

122. In fact, already in 1909 Luo Zhenyu (1866–1940) was publishing the *Jingjiao sanwei mengdu zan* (Luo Zhenyu 1909, 3: 45–47; repr. 2000, 5: 45–47). In 1916 Saeki mentioned this first text discovered in Dunhuang in his work on the Xi'an stele (Saeki 1916, 65–71).

123. For a review of Moule's research on the Church of the East in China, see Ding 2019.

texts and to the diffusion among Western scholars of what they had learned. This first period was exceptionally prolific, marked by great enthusiasm for the recent discovery of the texts and by a rigorous systematic approach to the work. The value of these works is limited, however, by occasional lack of care in examining the sources as well as by an insufficiently thorough investigation of the origin and transmission of the documents studied.

In a second period, which coincides roughly with the thirty years between the 1960s and the 1980s, studies were carried out mainly by Chinese scholars from Hong Kong and Taiwan who were interested in the history of Christianity in China, but, apart from rare cases, their work does not add many new elements to the achievements of the Japanese: "The studies on the scriptures of the Luminous Teaching in China that were undertaken after those of the Japanese were not carried out in an organic and exhaustive way: they are based on the achievements of Japanese scholars."[124] Although they contributed enormously to the spread of knowledge of these ancient texts among Chinese people, these works appear superficial at times and have made little headway in the area of research.

In 1969, Zhang Jimeng's remark that "more systematic work is what is expected of Chinese scholars"[125] was a prelude to the third period, which is being realized in the research of scholars such as Wu Qiyu (Wu Chi-yü, 1915–2011), Lin Wushu, Rong Xinjiang, Chen Huaiyu, Weng Shaojun, Tang Li, Wu Changxing (Wu Chang-shing), Wang Lanping, Nie Zhijun, and Zhu Donghua. This new phase of studies on Tang Christianity has certainly been facilitated by the reopening of areas for Chinese academic research that came about in the 1980s. Scholars with a more qualified philological, historical, and theological expertise are repositioning research on a more solid scientific basis, and their new analysis of the documents is producing excellent results.

Origin, Transmission, and Authenticity of Documents

As already mentioned, what the Franciscan Gabriele M. Allegra (1907–76) referred to as the *corpus "nestorianum" sinicum*[126] received its definitive form

---

124. Zhang Jimeng 1969, 51.

125. Ibid.

126. See Allegra 1973a, 312. I have added the quotation marks to indicate the inappropriateness of the adjective "Nestorian" when applied to *jingjiao* literature of the Tang era.

154 A HISTORY OF ENCOUNTERS

in the 1940s, when the so-called Kojima documents were published, and remained practically unchanged until the 1990s.

During the second half of the twentieth century, the vast majority of the publications that dealt with the *jingjiao* documents, despite their different methodologies and the depth of their research, was based on an uncritical acceptance and promulgation of the hypothesis that they were products of East Syriac Christianity of the Tang era and that they originated in Dunhuang. Over the last three decades the *corpus "nestorianum" sinicum* has been redefined, thanks to renewed investigations aimed at verifying precisely these specific points: the origin, transmission, and authenticity of the Tang *jingjiao* documents.[127]

The first documents whose authenticity was questioned were the last to be published, namely, the already mentioned Kojima manuscript A (*Da Qin jingjiao dasheng tongzhen guifa zan*) and Kojima manuscript B (*Da Qin jingjiao xuanyuan zhiben jing*).[128] In 1992, starting from the historical events related to these documents (i.e., the process of the dispersal of these documents from the collection of the Chinese book collector Li Shengduo, 1858–1937)[129] and a detailed analysis of the annotations and seals placed on them by Li Shengduo, as well as a careful study of their content in the light of the Christian faith and the history of Christianity in the Tang era, Lin Wushu and Rong Xinjiang (1992, 33–34; 1996, 13) came to the conclusion that the Kojima manuscripts are more likely than not forgeries executed by a knowledgeable antiques dealer. Soon thereafter, Chen Huaiyu (1997) confirmed the non-authenticity of these documents on the basis of further internal evidence—errors in understanding the history of Tang Christianity and its technical terms, as well as the author's lack of knowledge of the compositional and metric characteristics of the Tang era. Not all contemporary scholars agree with these conclusions,[130] but, at least for the Kojima manuscript B,

---

127. For a summary of the *status quaestionis* on the origin, transmission, and authenticity of the Tang *jingjiao* manuscript documents, see Rong 2014; Wang Lanping 2016b, 5–12.

128. See Haneda 1951; Nishiwaki 1988. Already in 1965 Zhu Qianzhi was suspicious of their authenticity: "With regard to what Saeki calls Kojima documents, published in *Shinchō kirisutokyō no kenkyū* 清朝基督教の研究 [Studies on Christianity during the Qing Dynasty], I suspect that they are forgeries" (Zhu Qianzhi 1993, 115).

129. About the Li Shengduo manuscript collection, see Rong 1997, 2002.

130. See, for instance, Zeng Yangqing 2005a, 7–38; 2005b; Eskildsen [2006?], 86–91 ("Appendix: On the Two Suspect 'Nestorian Documents'").

the comparison between this text and the one engraved on the Christian pillar found in Luoyang in 2006 definitively eliminated any residual doubt about it.[131]

The text of *Da Qin jingjiao xuanyuan zhiben jing* engraved on the Luoyang Christian pillar also led to another important assessment. This epigraphic text proved to be a faithful variant of another manuscript text with a similar title, *Da Qin jingjiao xuanyuan [zhi]ben jing*, which actually belonged to the Li Shengduo collection. Apart from a very few different characters, the preserved portions of the two versions of the text, the one carved on the pillar and the other in the manuscript, match and even complement each other almost perfectly. It is clear now that the content of the Li Shengduo manuscript is an original *jingjiao* text and that it can be edited, translated, and studied thoroughly. It is even possible to produce a reconstructed text of the **Da Qin jingjiao xuanyuan zhiben jing* by collating the two versions of it that we now have (Text F).

The other manuscript that belonged to the Li Shengduo collection, the *Zhixuan anle jing* (Book on Profound and Mysterious Blessedness), provides clear indications of how it was acquired. These are a final annotation—which reads: "Acquired from a gentleman from Suzhou on an autumn day of the Bingchen year [1916]. Recorded by [Li] Shengduo"—and five seals, all of them indicating that the manuscript belonged to the Li Shengduo collection. Rong Xingjiang (2014, 274–80) and Lin Wushu (2011c) have critically evaluated the history of the transmission and the content of this document on the basis of both external and internal elements, concluding that it undoubtedly belonged to the Li Shengduo collection of manuscripts from Dunhuang and that it is an authentic literary production of the Tang *jingjiao* community.

With regard to the so-called Tomioka and Takakusu documents—named after the Japanese collectors Tomioka Kenzō (1873–1918) and Takakusu Junjirō (1866–1945) who acquired them—namely the *Yishen lun* (Discourse on the One God) and the *Xuting mishisuo jing* (Book of the Lord Messiah), Saeki was still writing in 1951 as follows: "As far as we know, no scholars at home or abroad have ever expressed their opinion against the genuineness of these documents, while those who made a special study on the subject are all convinced of the genuineness of these Nestorian documents from both external and internal evidences."[132]

---

131. See Rong 2014, 272; Wang Lanping 2016b, 54–57.

132. Saeki 1951, 114.

156 A HISTORY OF ENCOUNTERS

This opinion remained unchanged among scholars until the research conducted in the last twenty years by Lin Wushu and Rong Xinjiang.[133]

As far as the Tomioka document is concerned, Lin Wushu points out first of all that there is no documentary evidence to date that it comes from Dunhuang. He goes on to say,

> All the various errors present in the text, . . . including wrong characters, confusion in the order of the parts, inconsistency between titles and content, etc., can only make us suspect that the entire document was composed by a non-Christian who collated some transcriptions made on the basis of garbled texts, and that it was not specifically created as a sacred text. However, the external appearance of the document is so beautiful and orderly, and the handwriting so scrupulously executed that it seems to have been composed with the devotion and piety typical of religious faith.[134]

On this basis, the scholar of Sun Yat-sen University in Guangzhou (Canton) formulates the following thesis:

> The Tomioka document is not an authentic Dunhuang document, but a twentieth-century transcription. However, it is not an *ex nihilo* forgery; it relied on an ancient original. . . . Among the Dunhuang documents that came to light in those years, in addition to the well-known Christian manuscripts, there may well have been some Christian texts whose content was similar to that of the *Discourse on the One God*. These texts then ended up in the hands of antique dealers, but, since they were so damaged, their value was unrecognized at the time, and thus copies were made by the skillful hands of a forger. The Tomioka document would therefore be one of the masterpieces of these skilled hands. It could be considered . . . a "refined forgery."[135]

As with the Tomioka document, so too for the Takakusu document, Lin Wushu (2001d, 151) shows that the claim that it comes from Dunhuang

---

133. For a summary of the research on the Tomioka and Takakusu documents, see Wang Lanping and Zhang Qiaosui 2019.

134. Lin Wushu 2000a, 81.

135. Ibid.

The First Christian Texts in Chinese

is not supported by the facts. He points out that there is already a stark contrast between the external appearance of the scroll (very neat and with very fine calligraphy) and the form and content of the text. On the basis of a careful analysis of the characters making up the title of the manuscript and those used in the text for the phonetic transcription of the name of Jesus, he concludes that the document can in no way be the work of the hand of a faithful Christian. Lin Wushu thus proposes the following thesis:

> Someone [unknown to us] may originally have owned an ancient Christian manuscript, but since it was very damaged, the owner, fearing that he would not be able to sell it at a good price, would have commissioned a new work based on that manuscript. Since the new manuscript was intended for profit and not for religious purposes, he naturally was only concerned about its outward beauty and was indifferent to errors and lacunae in the text. Moreover, since the new manuscript was the product of personal tastes and customs, the style of the text and wording was garbled, resulting in a counterfeit [that is characterized] by its extremely beautiful outward appearance but almost meaningless content.[136]

The author points out that this should not come as a surprise, considering that "the tendency of collectors of Dunhuang manuscripts was to give great importance to their external beauty and not pay attention to their intrinsic documentary value. Those who were in the business of selling manuscripts were certainly of the same mind."[137] To give further support to his view of the Tomioka and Takakusu manuscripts, Lin Wushu (2005b, [2006?]) has added the fact that some expressions in them do not correspond to the usage of the period in which they are supposed to have been composed.

Rong Xinjiang (2014, 280–88) supported and confirmed Lin Wushu's conclusions, providing further assessment of the manuscripts based on a comparison of the two Christian texts with the practice of composition and the rigidly imposed and observed canons for the production of religious texts of foreign origin in the Tang era. He also called attention to the unusual use

---

136. Lin Wushu 2001d, 152.

137. Ibid., 151.

of two different qualities of paper (one of which is very poor) for the packaging of the *Yishen lun* manuscript. He believes it is likely that these two manuscripts were made by copying Christian documents from a period subsequent to the Tang dynasty. As numerous writing errors make evident, a calligrapher who was unfamiliar with their contents would have copied them. Consequently, it would be better not to regard these two scriptures as Tang *jingjiao* documents.

Other Chinese scholars have been skeptical of some of the assessments made by Lin Wushu and Rong Xinjiang and have reopened the debate on the authenticity of the Tomioka and Takakusu documents (e.g., Zhang Xuesong 2016; Xiang Bingguang 2017). Of particular value are the studies of Wang Lanping (2015a, 2016a; 2016b, 57–123; 2017, 1–103), who reconsiders and refutes some of Lin and Rong's arguments, doing so mainly on the basis of a critical textual analysis. According to him, the presence of several phonetic transcriptions of Syriac names and some peculiar terminological choices undoubtedly point to the genuine Tang *jingjiao* content of those documents. The calligraphic style of the Chinese characters with their variants in the two manuscripts is common to other ancient Dunhuang manuscripts. For these reasons the two documents cannot be regarded as modern forgeries. On this basis, some Chinese scholars are now devoting their efforts to a more analytical study of the difficult points of the manuscripts (first of all the mistakenly written characters and the variant forms), with the hope of clarifying the origins of the texts and better understanding their nature (e.g., Nie 2010, 154–245; 2016, 1–23; Xiang Bingguang 2019).

A giant step toward the still unattained goal of having access to these and other original *jingjiao* documents and then verifying them was made in 2010, when the *jingjiao* manuscripts that were thought to be lost or hidden somewhere were unexpectedly located and made public in Osaka, Japan. From April 19 to 24, the Kyōu shooku, the library of the Takeda Science Foundation (Takeda kagaku shinkō zaidan) in Osaka, held a special exhibition of fifty-eight ancient Dunhuang manuscripts in its "Dunhuang Secret Collection" (*Tonkō hikyū*). This collection includes 758 manuscripts mostly collected in the years 1936–41 by Haneda Tōru, the outstanding orientalist, professor, and president (1938–45) of the Kyoto Imperial University (Kyōto teikoku daigaku). The nucleus of the *Tonkō hikyū* at the Kyōu shooku today consists of manuscripts that were once owned by the Chinese collector Li Shengduo and that Haneda purchased from his son Li Pang in the years 1935–36. This nucleus was then augmented through the acquisition of further manuscripts, including those that had been in the private collections of other Japanese scholars, such as Kiyono Kenji (1885–1955), Tomioka Kenzō, and Takakusu Junjirō.[138]

Among the seventeen documents displayed in the section "Life and Faith" of the exhibition were four *jingjiao* manuscripts. A year before the exhibition in Osaka, that is, in 2009, the Takeda Science Foundation had already started publishing a ten-volume series that comprised a catalogue of manuscripts from the *Tonkō hikyū* collection (one volume) and facsimiles of the manuscripts (nine volumes). In these volumes, the two *jingjiao* manuscripts that formerly belonged to the Li Shengduo collection, the Tomioka manuscript and the Takakusu manuscript, are described and reproduced with clear color pictures. Now that the two manuscripts have been unexpectedly relocated in Osaka, their authenticity as medieval documents and the precise date of their production can also be scientifically ascertained through the study of calligraphic style, age of paper, color of tint, chemical composition of ink, and carbon-dating of fragments of the manuscripts.[139] This has been carried out by the same Takeda Science Foundation in Osaka, which in 2020 sponsored the publication of a volume containing new material analysis and textual studies of the four *jingjiao* manuscripts kept at the Kyōu shooku, together with their color photographic reproductions and the transcription of their texts (Kyōu shooku 2020).

A Redefinition of the Corpus and Status of the Manuscripts

Thanks to the recent acquisition of the above-mentioned research, it is now possible to reformulate the real extent of the *corpus "nestorianum" sinicum*. I think it is preferable to do this on the basis of the manuscripts that have come down to us, rather than by isolating the individual texts contained in them, since their independence or mutual relationship is still an open question.[140]

(1) Manuscript BnF Pelliot chinois 3847, often abbreviated as P. 3847 (see figure 3.8). This manuscript was discovered in 1908 by the French sinologist Paul Pelliot in the Mogao "Library Cave" (Cave 17) in Dunhuang and today is kept at the Bibliothèque nationale de France in Paris. The text, written in

---

138. About the *Tonkō hikyū*, see Iwamoto 2010; Zheng Acai 2013; Takata 2014a, 2014b; 2016 (2018), 154–62.

139. For a more detailed report on the "re-appearance" of the four *jingjiao* texts in Japan, see Nicolini-Zani 2016.

140. A similar classification is proposed by Rong 2014, 288.

Figure 3.8 Manuscript "Pelliot chinois 3847" from Dunhuang (Gansu, China), Bibliothèque nationale de France, Paris, portion of the scroll.
(Source: BnF, Département des manuscripts, <https://gallica.bnf.fr/ark:/12148/btv1b8303183c/f5.item.r=pelliot%20chinois%203847>)

the *kaishu* or "regular calligraphic style" by the same hand, is made of 689 characters arranged in 46 columns. It is composed of three parts: (a) *Jingjiao sanwei mengdu zan* 景教三威蒙度讚 (Hymn in Praise of the Salvation Achieved through the Three Majesties of the Luminous Teaching), at the end of which the title is repeated in its complete form, *Da Qin jingjiao sanwei mengdu zan yijuan* 大秦景教三威蒙度讚一卷 (Hymn in Praise of the Salvation Achieved through the Three Majesties of the Luminous Teaching of Da Qin, in One Scroll); (b) *Zunjing* 尊經 (Book of the Honored); (c) a final explanatory annotation (the last four columns), written with characters of a smaller size.

The whole mulberry fiber paper scroll is 104.5 centimeters long; its height varies from 26.4 centimeters at the highest point to 25.9 centimeters at the lowest. It is made up of six sheets of unequal length that are glued together. The first sheet is 9.3 centimeters long and its function was evidently to join the right side of the roll to the frame. The second sheet, whose paper is of a lighter color, is 36.5 centimeters long and the third, on which there is

The First Christian Texts in Chinese 161

only text (a), is 20 centimeters long; the fourth is only 6 centimeters long and on it are written the first three columns of text (b); the fifth is 26.8 centimeters long and on it are written the remaining columns of text (b) together with text (c); the sixth sheet is 6.7 centimeters long and its function was evidently to join the left edge of the scroll to the frame. In the final part there is a seal, consisting of three incomplete characters in the typical *zhuanshu* 篆書 (seal script) calligraphic style; most probably the characters are "Da Qin si."[141]

Lin Wushu's direct analysis of the manuscript P. 3847 has shown how careful evaluation of calligraphic style, quality of paper, and size and composition of the sheets, can lead to a productive reconsideration of the structure of the document and the relationship of its three parts to one another:

> Analyzing the original manuscripts making up the scroll, it was noted that the two texts [*Hymn in Praise of the Salvation Achieved through the Three Majesties of the Luminous Teaching* and *Book of the Honored*] were [originally] independent manuscripts glued together to form a single scroll. Therefore, we can conclude with some certainty that the two texts do not constitute a single writing. . . . However, the annotations at the end of the *Book of the Honored*, in the original manuscript of the scroll are written on the same sheet on which the text of the *Book of the Honored* is written, and therefore there is no way they could be from a manuscript other than this latter one.[142]

However, there remains the problem of the relationship between the *Book of the Honored* and the eighty-five characters of the final notes. Looking at the manuscript, one can at least say that the four columns of the annotations have a more refined calligraphic style and smaller size than the previous text, which indicates that this part has the nature of an explanatory note and is not part of the body of the text.[143]

---

141. Description in Wu Qiyu 1986, 411, and Lin Wushu 2001c, 68. Digital images of the manuscript P. 3847 are available at <https://gallica.bnf.fr/ark:/12148/btv1b8303183c/f5.item.r = pell iot%20chinois%203847>.

142. Lin Wushu 2001c, 68–69.

143. See ibid., 69.

A HISTORY OF ENCOUNTERS

(2) Manuscript *Zhixuan anle jing* 志玄安樂經 (Book on Profound and Mysterious Blessedness). This manuscript once belonged to Li Shengduo and is now part of the "Dunhuang Secret Collection" (*Tonkō hikyū*) at the Kyōu shooku, the library of the Takeda Science Foundation in Osaka. It consists of a scroll of five dull-brown rough-paper sheets that is 26.2 centimeters high and 282.7 centimeters long. The text, written in the *kaishu* calligraphic style, has 2,596 preserved or partially preserved characters (of an estimated total number of 2,685), arranged in 159 columns. Five seals, all of them indicating that the manuscript belonged to the Li Shengduo collection, are stamped in three different places: two below the initial title on the first sheet, two below the end title on the last sheet, one below the final annotation. The first sheet is badly damaged and contains ten incomplete text columns.[144]

(3) Manuscript *Da Qin jingjiao xuanyuan [zhi]ben jing* 大秦景教宣元 ［至］本經 (Book of the Luminous Teaching of Da Qin on Revealing the Origin and [Reaching] the Foundation). This manuscript once belonged to Li Shengduo and is now kept at the Kyōu shooku in Osaka. One long sheet, 26.5 centimeters high and 47.7 centimeters long, is all that is left of a longer golden-oak rice-paper scroll. The preserved portion of the text, written in the *xingshu* 行書 (cursive) calligraphic style, consists of the first 26 columns (465 characters) of a longer text. Five seals are stamped in the area surrounding the title, all of which refer to the Li Shengduo collection.[145] The text preserved in this manuscript is the same as that carved on the Luoyang *jingjiao* pillar of 815, with the exception of a few variants.

(4) Tomioka manuscript *Yishen lun* 一神論 (Discourse on the One God). This manuscript is a single scroll, 25.4 centimeters high, 640 centimeters long, that consists of sixteen golden-oak high-quality hemp-paper sheets. The text, written in the *kaishu* (regular) calligraphic style, consists of 6,950 characters arranged in 405 columns. The manuscript has only a final title, *Yishen lun juan disan* 一神論卷第三 (Third Scroll of the *Discourse on the One God*), which traditionally gives the name to the whole document. It includes three tracts with no clear relation to one another: (a) *Yu di'er* 喻第二

---

144. Description in Kyōu shooku 2009, p. 7, no. 13; Kyōu shooku 2009–13, 1: 128; Sugimoto 2020, 110–11. Photographic reproductions in Kyōu shooku 2009–13, 1: 129–33; Kyōu shooku 2020, 71–85.

145. Description in Kyōu shooku 2009, pp. 149–50, no. 431; Kyōu shooku 2009–13, 5: 396; Sugimoto 2020, 111–12. Photographic reproductions in Kyōu shooku 2009–13, 5: 397; Kyōu shooku 2020, 87–90.

(Metaphorical Teaching, Second Part), cols. 1–60; (b) *Yitian lun diyi* 一天論第一 (Discourse on the One Godhead, First Part), cols. 61–206; (c) *Shizun bushi lun disan* 世尊布施論第三 (Discourse of the Honored One of the Universe on Almsgiving, Third Part), cols. 207–405.[146]

(5) Takakusu manuscript *Xuting mishisuo jing* 序聽迷詩所經 (Book of the Lord Messiah). The manuscript is a single scroll, 26.3 centimeters high and 276.8 centimeters long, that consists of eight golden-oak high-quality hemp-paper sheets, which are the first eight sheets of a longer manuscript. The complete title of the text as it appears in the manuscript is *Xuting mishisuo jing yijuan* 序聽迷詩所經一卷 (Book of the Lord Messiah, in One Scroll). The text is incomplete and only the first 170 columns (2,845 characters) are preserved.[147]

As shown by color photographic reproductions that are now available, the paper of these last two manuscripts is thick and the ink unfaded; despite some water stains, none of the glued sheets has deteriorated, crumbled, or become riddled with wormholes. Through a direct analysis of the paper and the format of the manuscripts, Tōno Haruyuki (2020, 11–12) has collected enough material evidence—such as the overlapping of old stains on the two manuscripts when they are laid one upon the other and rolled together, the perfect match in the shape of the last sheet of the manuscript *Yishen lun* and the first sheet of the *Xuting mishisuo jing*, and other elements—to confirm that the two manuscripts originally constituted one roll and were later cut apart.

As noted by scholars, the two sources also display some textual similarities. While their wording and style are similar, the contents of both are equally difficult. Many sentences are broken and do not lend themselves to straightforward readings. A number of characters, even some key theological phrases, were left out or incorrectly written. Furthermore, judging by the calligraphy, they were written within a reasonably short time of each other by the same hand.[148]

---

146. Description in Kyōu shooku 2009, pp. 161–62, no. 460; Kyōu shooku 2009–13, 6: 88; Sugimoto 2020, 109–10. Photographic reproductions in Kyōu shooku 2009–13, 6: 89–96; Kyōu shooku 2020, 21–54.

147. Description in Kyōu shooku 2009, p. 161, no. 459; Kyōu shooku 2009–13, 6: 83; Sugimoto 2020, 108–9. Photographic reproductions in Kyōu shooku 2009–13, 6: 84–87; Kyōu shooku 2020, 55–69.

148. See Haneda 1926 (1957–58), 2: 246–57; Drake 1935, 677–87; Lin Wushu 2001d; Tōno 2020.

The Production and Literary Form of the Texts
Dating and Authorship

The decision to deal with the issues of the dating and authorship of the Tang *jingjiao* documents jointly is motivated by the fact that they are strictly related to one another and also by the fact that these two issues have been closely associated in most of the specialized studies on the subject that have appeared. Reviewing the various published studies, it can be seen that, with minor variations, they arrange the documents into two groups: a first group of documents that can be attributed to Aluoben and his disciples and placed at the beginning of the Tang dynasty (around the 640s); and a second group of documents that can be dated to the mid-to-late period of the same dynasty (late eighth century) and attributed to Adam/Jingjing, "he who brought the church of the Tang dynasty to its classical period of literary production in the second half of the eighth century."[149] Among the few positions that depart from this perspective, it seems useful to call attention to that of Enoki Kazuo (1964, 71), even though we should note that his methodology is problematic. He addresses the issue of the dating of the documents by dividing them into three groups corresponding to the presence in them of the names Fulin, Da Qin, and *jingjiao*.

The Tomioka and Takakusu documents were considered to be the oldest because of a sentence in the *Discourse on the One God* that reads, "It has been but six hundred forty-one years since [the Messiah] took a body [made up] of the five aggregates."[150] Other elements were invoked in support of the early dating of those texts, including the abundance of writing errors and the content, which was still close to the biblical tradition and that of the Church of the East. From this followed the identification of Aluoben as the author since he is the only monk known by name who came to China on the first Christian mission. Since his name is linked to a primitive translation of the writings that was presented to the imperial court, the link between the period of composition and Aluoben as its author was all but automatic.[151]

---

149. Foster 1939, 107. For an example of what was the most common position among scholars regarding the dating of the documents during decades before the recent restriction and redefinition of the corpus, see Gong Tianmin 1960, 45. This opinion persists, more or less adapted, even in recent publications (see, for example, Ferreira 2014, 44–52; Zhu Donghua 2016a).

150. Text C, col. 366, p. 262 and n. 162.

151. This vision still persists in much contemporary literature (see, for instance, Tang Li 2004).

The First Christian Texts in Chinese

As we have seen, the studies of Rong Xinjiang and Lin Wushu (Lin Wushu 2000a, 81–82; 2001d, 145–52) delivered a severe blow to the fascinating myth of the antiquity of these documents. They drew a distinction between the manuscripts as material documents, which they believe to be the work of a contemporary; and their content, which they consider an authentic expression of a Christian of the Tang *jingjiao* church. The attribution to Aluoben as their author lacks any documentary evidence and is therefore totally arbitrary. Through a systematic critique of the traditional and common arguments, Sun Jianqiang (2018a; 2018b) has finally demonstrated that the conventional chronology for the Tomioka and Takakusu documents should be abandoned.

The Japanese scholar Tōno Haruyuki (2020, 12–16) has recently come to a completely different conclusion from that of Lin Wushu and Rong Xinjiang; he has provided definitive evidence for the antiquity of these two manuscripts. His direct analysis of the paper quality, the form of the characters used throughout the text, and its calligraphic style—namely, the style of Chu Suiliang (596–658), a renowned calligrapher active in the early Tang dynasty—led him to date these *jingjiao* manuscripts to the first half of the eighth century. The handwriting is judged to be the work of a scholar or a monk, not a professional copyist. The same Tōno also believes that there is no reason to doubt that these manuscripts come from Dunhuang.

Of the two Kojima documents, I would call attention to only one significant element when it comes to comparing them with the other documents. Prior to their recent identification as forgeries by most scholars, they provided what seemed to be a reliable way to solve the question of dating and attribution. As Jiang Wenhan remarked, "It should be noted that, among all the documents discovered, the two documents that Saeki obtained from Kojima are the only ones in which the date is clearly stated."[152] Obviously, that information is no longer reliable.

The other texts, *Hymn in Praise of the Salvation Achieved through the Three Majesties of the Luminous Teaching, Book on Profound and Mysterious Blessedness*, and *Book of the Luminous Teaching of Da Qin on Revealing the Origin and Reaching the Foundation*, are listed in the *Book of the Honored* among the works translated/edited in Chinese by Adam/Jingjing. On this basis, according to the traditional view, these compositions would be a work carried out under the direction of the great monk of the Church of the East Adam/Jingjing, the author of the text of the Xi'an stele, and therefore they

---

152. Jiang Wenhan 1982, 60.

166 A HISTORY OF ENCOUNTERS

would be produced in Chang'an and dated to the end of the eighth century. In support of this thesis, many scholars stress the fact that their content presents an evident evolution when compared to Aluoben's documents, testifying to a re-elaboration of the Christian message according to properly Chinese forms of expression and categories of thought.

A comparison made by Lin Wushu between the manuscript fragment of the *Book of the Luminous Teaching of Da Qin on Revealing the Origin and [Reaching] the Foundation* and that of the Xi'an stele has confirmed this view with regard to this specific document, while—as Chen Huaiyu noted—the other "three Chinese *jingjiao* texts, the *jingjiao* monument, the *Gloria in excelsis Deo* and the *[Zhixuan] anle jing* differ significantly in terms of style and vocabulary, and appear to be texts produced by three different writers and translators."[153]

> In addition to the similarity of terms, the Daoist and Buddhist nuances of expression and the writing style of the two texts [i.e., the *Book of the Luminous Teaching of Da Qin on Revealing the Origin and Reaching the Foundation* and the text of the Xi'an stele] also give the reader the impression that they come from the same source. So, we do not believe we go too far in saying that the author of the document we own [titled] *Book of the Luminous Teaching of Da Qin on Revealing the Origin and [Reaching] the Foundation* is Jingjing. Of course, in the case of both the Christian stele and the *Book of the Luminous Teaching of Da Qin on Revealing the Origin and [Reaching] the Foundation*, it is impossible that they are individual contributions of Jingjing alone. They have undoubtedly enjoyed the collaboration of Chinese scholars who helped perfecting them.[154]

For style and choice of terms, Lin also goes so far as to say that "the composition of the *Book of the Luminous Teaching of Da Qin on Revealing the Origin and [Reaching] the Foundation* cannot be placed after 781,"[155] the year of the stele's erection. Lin Wushu and Yin Xiaoping (2008, 343–52) also believe that the recension of this text preserved in the Li Shengduo manuscript (and most likely based on a lost Dunhuang manuscript) is probably older than the

---

153. Chen Huaiyu 2015a, 219.

154. Lin Wushu 1995b (2011b), 256.

155. Ibid., 257.

recension of the epigraphical text inscribed on the Luoyang pillar (before 815, the year of the erection of the pillar). As far as the *Book on Profound and Mysterious Blessedness* is concerned, the unanimous traditional view places this writing among the documents translated or written by Adam/Jingjing and his collaborators in the second half of the Tang dynasty. Recently, a study by the young scholar Bai Yu (2018, 35–53) narrowed the date of composition of the *Book on Profound and Mysterious Blessedness* to around 811. He did this by means of a textual comparison between this Christian text and the Chinese Buddhist text *Dasheng bensheng xindi guan jing* (Sk. *Mahāyāna mūlagata hṛdayabhūmi dhyāna sūtra*, "Mahāyāna Sutra of the Contemplation of the Mind Ground in this Life"), translated by the Buddhist monk Prajña presumably in 811.

As Haneda Tōru noted, the first element supporting the traditional view is the calligraphic style, which is similar to that of the *Hymn in Praise of the Salvation Achieved through the Three Majesties of the Luminous Teaching*:

> The style of the characters is different from that of the *Discourse on the One God* and the *Book of the Lord Messiah*; compared to them, the style of this one is crude, rather close to that of the *Hymn in Praise of the Salvation Achieved through the Three Majesties*. . . . It can undoubtedly be traced back to the late Tang period.[156]

The second element is the abundance of Buddhist elements in the text as pointed out, among others, by Gong Tianmin (K'ung Tien-min):

> The three writings, *Book on Profound and Mysterious Blessedness*, *Hymn in Praise of the Salvation Achieved through the Three Majesties* and *Book of the Luminous Teaching of Da Qin on Revealing the Origin and [Reaching] the Foundation*, all date back to the Dezong era in the late Tang dynasty, and were composed by Jingjing; moreover, I believe that they are later than the Christian stele of 781, since in these scriptures, even more than in the stele, Buddhist influences abound.[157]

The third element that proves that the text is a product of the same era as the stele and was probably written by the same hand that wrote the stele, namely,

---

156. Haneda 1929 (1957–58), 2: 272–73.

157. Gong Tianmin 1960, 60.

Adam/Jingjing, is the presence in the text of expressions similar to those contained in the Xi'an Christian inscription (e.g., *fanhun baoxiang* 返魂寶香, "precious scent that awakens the soul," and *baoshan* 寶山, "mountain of treasures"), as already pointed out by Luo Xianglin (1966, 33) and others.[158] This view was recently reiterated by Lin Wushu (2011c [2011b], 300–3).

On the basis of a careful analysis of the paper of the manuscripts, their calligraphic and literary style, and other elements, Tōno Haruyuki (2020, 12, 16–17) has recently concluded that the manuscripts containing the Christian texts *Book of the Luminous Teaching of Da Qin on Revealing the Origin and [Reaching] the Foundation* and *Book on Profound and Mysterious Blessedness* were produced in the late Tang dynasty (turn of the eighth to ninth century).

The firsthand analysis of the only publicly accessible manuscript, P. 3847, has laid new foundations on which it is possible to construct hypotheses that are more informed. Analysis of the calligraphy has revealed that the manuscript of the entire scroll, as it appears on the outside, is the product of the same hand in all three parts. From the style and content of the final notes, Lin Wushu does not hesitate to say that the manuscript, in the form in which it has come down to us, would have been transcribed and assembled between the tenth century (in the first decades after the fall of the Tang dynasty) and the early eleventh century (the time of the closure of the Dunhuang caves). On the identity of the possible copyist, he concludes:

> Looking in detail at the style of these notes, one can see that the author was no ordinary person, but an erudite monk who must have known the scriptures of that religion and the history of the mission of the Church of the East in China. His style is not different from the expressive forms of more refined works. The fact that the scroll contains these final notes leads me to suspect that the reason this scroll was composed is closely related to the care and preservation of the documents of this religion. If this deduction were proven correct, it would explain that until the tenth and eleventh centuries there were still Christians of the Church of the East who, in order to perpetuate the existence of their religion, continued to care for and transcribe the scriptures of this religion.[159]

---

158. For references to other authors, see Wang Lanping 2016b, 237n1.

159. Lin Wushu 2001c, 72.

The basic conviction is that at such a late period (the tenth to eleventh centuries) it seems very unlikely that the few Christians who escaped the great persecution ordered by Emperor Wuzong in 845 would have composed new scriptures or dedicated themselves to new translations. The two texts in the manuscript we possess would rather be copies of originals composed in previous decades. For the *Hymn in Praise of the Salvation Achieved through the Three Majesties of the Luminous Teaching*, Lin Wushu comes to the more precise conclusion that this liturgical text "is a translation, made by the Christian monk Jingjing, which saw the light of day during the reign of Emperor Dezong of the Tang."[160]

Mention should be finally made of the systematic attempt of Sun Jianqiang (2018b) to re-date the Dunhuang *jingjiao* sources. Through a historical linguistic and philological examination of the evolution of the Chinese passive voice and an analysis of the taboo names[161] and the variant forms of the characters used throughout the texts, this scholar proposes the following chronology of the documents: *Book of the Lord Messiah* and *Discourse on the One God*, 800–1010s; *Book of the Luminous Teaching of Da Qin on Revealing the Origin and [Reaching] the Foundation* and *Book on Profound and Mysterious Blessedness*, 745–87; *Hymn in Praise of the Salvation Achieved through the Three Majesties of the Luminous Teaching* and *Book of the Honored* (P. 3847), 907–1010s.

We can therefore say, in summary, that the traditional, decades-long approach to these manuscripts was based on the uncritical assimilation of some few but uncertain data that were available and on the uncritical transmission of many poorly founded assumptions. A reconsideration of the problem of authenticity and a reassessment of the external and internal data of these manuscripts has led to a careful reconsideration of and new hypotheses on the question of their dating and attribution.

Chinese Style Translations and Compositions

From the analysis of the *jingjiao* documents that have come down to us, one can see how, in their literary output, the monks of the Church of the

---

160. Ibid., 70.

161. The practice of name taboos (*hui* 諱, or *jinghui* 敬諱, "honorific taboos"), which originated in the Zhou dynasty (1122–255 BCE), was formally institutionalized in the Qin and Han (255 BCE–220 CE) dynasties and was most widely diffused in the Tang and Song (960–1278) dynasties. It was then exploited to the full by the Qing emperors (1644–1911). This peculiarity of Chinese culture proscribed writing the names of emperors and titles of reigns without modifying them in an approved way.

East adopted the literary forms used in China for centuries: *zan* 讚, "hymn of praise," also used in Buddhist texts (Sk. *stotra*); *jing* 經, "book," "canon," "scripture," also used in Buddhist texts (Sk. *sūtra*); *lun* 論, "discourse," "discussion," "treatise," also used in Buddhist texts (Sk. *śāstra*, *abhidarma*, *upadeśa*). Noting this, Weng Shaojun (1996, 10) divides the Tang Sino-Christian texts (including those that are now recognized to be forgeries) into *jingwen* 經文, "scriptural or canonical texts," and *songwen* 頌文, "laudatory or eulogistic texts."

In addition, Christian authors adopted and used two literary forms that were created or became very popular in the Tang era. The first is that of a text engraved on a stone stele (*beiwen* 碑文 or *beiji* 碑記), characterized by the high degree of formality and the marked political nature that we previously discussed. Recent scholarship has re-evaluated the former suggestion that the Buddhist inscription engraved on the "Stele of the Dhūta Monastery" (*Toutuo si bei*), composed by Wang Jin (d. 505), was the literary model for the text composed by Adam/Jingjing and his collaborators for the inscription on the Xi'an Christian stele.[162] Chen Huaiyu (2009b [2012], 31–35) reasonably points to contemporary eulogistic stele inscriptions (*beisong* 碑頌, lit., "stele eulogies"), such as the "Eulogy [Inscribed] on the Stele of the Great Tang [Commemorating the Erection] of the [Laozi's] Iron Statue at Yizhou, with a Preface" (*Da Tang Yizhou tiexiang beisong bing xu*, 739), composed by Wang Duan, or the "Eulogy [Inscribed] on the Stele of the Lingyan Monastery, with a Preface" (*Lingyan si beisong bing xu*, 742) and the inscription engraved on the "Stele of the Lushan Monastery" (*Lushan si bei*), both written by Li Yong, as the most probable models for the composition of the text on the Christian stone. Like other middle- and late-Tang stele inscriptions, the one carved on the 781 *jingjiao* stele indicates a strong revival in Chinese epigraphy of the writing style of ancient prose (*guwen* 古文) and a progressive transition from the style of parallel prose (*pianwen* 駢文) to that of free prose (*sanwen* 散文).

The second literary form, which is typically Buddhist, is the devotional text to be recited in honor of the dead (*dhāraṇī sūtra*) that was engraved on a stone pillar (*jingchuang*, "[*dhāraṇī*] *sūtra* pillar") in the form of a *stūpa* (*ta* 塔). The main reason Buddhists set up such a pillar was to perform a great meritorious deed, namely, the engraving of the powerful *dhāraṇī*

---

162. The text of Wang Jin's stele inscription is contained in *Wenxuan* (Anthology of Literature) 59, 6: 2527–42. See Mather 1963; Forte 1996a.

sūtra, which helps to free one from worldly sufferings and to deliver one from everything that hinders *nirvāṇa* in this and other existences. In addition, the erection of such a pillar was also intended to gain important social and religious merits for both the central state and the local community.[163] Among the *dhāraṇī* sutras, the one most often carved on these pillars was the *Foding zunsheng tuoluoni jing* (Sk. *Buddhoṣṇīṣa vijaya dhāraṇī sūtra*, "Sutra of the Honored and Victorious *Dhāraṇī* of the Buddha's Topknot"), which was widely diffused in both the urban and the rural society of Tang China thanks to a complex interaction of religious, political, and social factors. Besides being erected outside Buddhist temples, at town gates, or inside Buddhist pagodas, *dhāraṇī* pillars were also placed at *stūpas* that held the remains of members of the *saṅgha*, as well as beside the tombs of lay Buddhists. Mortuary pillars (*muchuang* 墓幢 or *fenchuang* 墳幢) were the most popular *dhāraṇī* pillars of the Chinese medieval era, erected mainly with the aim of gaining merits on behalf of the dead.[164] The merging of practices linked to mortuary pillars with indigenous Chinese concepts like filial piety (*xiao* 孝) served to enhance the overall function and significance of such *dhāraṇī* pillars.[165]

Since the Tang Christian texts are an expression of a religion originally foreign to Chinese culture, scholars immediately wondered if these texts were translations of originals that were written in Syriac, the liturgical language of the Church of the East, or original compositions in Chinese. According to Max Deeg, the texts are not

> a direct translation of an original Syriac text. . . . The texts were understood as vademecums or anthologies intended to transmit the basic notions of religion and . . . they were written in a language and style perfectly adapted to their Chinese intellectual, cultural and religious environment, using Buddhist, Confucian and Daoist terminology and concepts to express Christian ideas.[166]

One cannot but agree with this viewpoint. In a general sense, we could say that the surviving Tang Chinese Christian literature stands as a sort of

---

163. See Kroll 2001, 48–49.

164. See Liu Shufen 1996, 1997, 2003, 2008.

165. See Liu Shufen 2003, 711–14; see also Ge 2016.

166. Deeg 2015, 206.

172 A HISTORY OF ENCOUNTERS

"Chinese Gospel harmony" that was produced to present the Christian message to the Chinese audience and respond to its spiritual needs.[167] The most recent studies have confirmed what Drake had already recognized in 1935, namely that "the only manifest translation that has come down to us from Tang times is the *Gloria in excelsis Deo*."[168] This doxological hymn is part of the morning office on Sundays and feast days in use in the Church of the East, and its Chinese translation provides strong evidence that Chinese was used during the liturgy in Tang China. A later, presumably Yuan-dynasty Syriac hymnographic source gives an interesting hint of the use of Chinese as a language of worship:

> Receive, our Lord, the intercession of the Chinese and the Indians,
> for in the language of their country they exalt and worship your
>   name.[169]

As Tang Li remarks (2020b, 133), the author of these verses probably knew when he composed it that the Chinese and the Indians worshipped in their native languages. However, this may not necessarily mean that he was making a reference to what was done in the Mongol period. The writer may have drawn his information from the pre-Mongol period.

Translations of the Syriac hymn *Glory to God in the Highest* seem also to have been widespread in Central Asia, as evidenced by the discovery in Bulayïq (Turfan oasis) of some fragments of a translation of it into Sogdian, copied not later than the eighth century.[170]

Because of its unique feature as an undoubtedly genuine *jingjiao* text whose origin is clear and documented, the *Hymn in Praise of the Salvation Achieved through the Three Majesties of the Luminous Teaching* has been the most studied among the Tang *jingjiao* documents. These studies have focused on its form and style. The comparative analysis carried out by Wu Qiyu (Wu Chi-yü 1984; Wu Qiyu 1986) and supported by the work of Chen Huaiyu (1997, 46–49) between the Syriac original of the *Glory to God in the Highest*

---

167. See Foley 2008; Yao Zhihua 2009; Zhu Donghua 2021: 53–57.

168. Drake 1935, 741.

169. The Syriac source is the MS Cambridge Add. 1982, fol. 122/110r, as given in Tang Li 2020b, 133 (Syriac text and English translation).

170. See Sims-Williams 1995a.

(*Tešbuḥtā d-malakē*)[171] and its Chinese translation (most probably done from the Sogdian version of the Syriac text)[172] showed how the Chinese version is the adaptation of the original Syriac liturgical hymn to the metric of *zan*, a poetic hymnic genre characterized by the fixed structure of seven characters per verse (*qiyan shi* 七言詩), which sometimes led to some significant deviations from the original. Wang Juan (2018, 634–44) suggested that the Buddhist *gāthās* (lit., "songs" or "verses"; translated as *ji* 偈 or *jisong* 偈頌 in Chinese Buddhist literature) are a more specific model for the Chinese metrical structure of the Christian hymn. Chen Huaiyu (2006a, [2006b?], 2020) has highlighted the structural parallels, as well as the terminology, between the Christian Trinitarian hymn, the Chinese Buddhist text *Dasheng bensheng xindi guan jing* (Mahāyāna Sutra of the Contemplation of the Mind Ground in This Life), translated by the Buddhist monk Prajña, and the Chinese Daoist scripture *Taixuan zhenyi benji jing* (Book of the Original Bound of the Perfect Unity of Great Mystery). This indicates, *inter alia*, that in the Tang era, Buddhists, Daoists, and Christians used common expressive models to convey their religious teachings.

The *Book of the Honored*, which follows the Trinitarian hymn in the manuscript P. 3847, was judged to be a composition created in Chinese. In its expressive form it seems rather to take the Buddhist invocation texts as a model (*lichan wen* 禮懺文, lit., "texts for worship and repentance [rituals]"), such as the "Buddha-names" sutras (*Foming jing* 佛名經), as was already pointed out in a study by Matsumoto Eiichi in 1938, and more recently confirmed by Luo Xianglin (1966, 34), Gabriele M. Allegra (1973a, 302–3), Zhang Delin (1989, 32), Nie Zhijun (2016, 87–98), and Wang Juan (2018, 644–48). Recognizing in the first part of the *Book of the Honored* an invocation to the Trinity, in the second an invocation to all "kings of the doctrine" (*fawang*, i.e., saints), and in the third an expression of devotion to the different sacred scriptures, Matsumoto (1938) notes that the structure is the same as that of the Buddhist liturgical invocation texts, which consist of a supplication to the different buddhas, a supplication to the different scriptures, and a supplication to the different bodhisattvas; the only difference would be the order of the parts. As already noted by Saeki (1951, 277), the text could also be an

---

171. See *Chaldean Breviary*, Morning Office on Sundays and Memorial Feasts, ed. Bedjan, 1: 37–38.

172. Linguistic elements show that the Chinese translation is closer to the Sogdian version than to the Syriac version (see Chen Huaiyu 2020, 106).

174 A HISTORY OF ENCOUNTERS

adaptation of the commemorative diptychs of the saints of the Church of the East.

The view that "the literary form of the texts attributed to Jingjing is modeled on that of Daoist and Buddhist writings"[173] has become quite common among scholars. This seems reasonable when we look at the structure of the two certainly authentic works, the *Book of the Luminous Teaching of Da Qin on Revealing the Origin and Reaching the Foundation* and the *Book on Profound and Mysterious Blessedness*.

In the incomplete version we possess, the former presents the very common formal typology of Buddhist sutras, which provides an incipit consisting of the presentation of the one who offers the instruction or preaching (usually a buddha), his origin, and the identity of the listeners.[174] On this subject, Lin Wushu wrote,

> The style of the *Book of the Luminous Teaching of Da Qin on Revealing the Origin and [Reaching] the Foundation* is similar to that of Buddhist scriptures. It does not correspond to that of a translation of a [Christian] original document; there are, in fact, no documents similar to this in the Nestorian scriptures of the ancient eastern churches, including texts in Syriac and Central Asian languages such as Sogdian. We therefore conclude that the author of the Chinese text, adapting himself to Chinese practices, was himself the author of the text and took as his model Buddhist scriptures that had been translated into Chinese.[175]

A typical Buddhist form is even more recognizable with regard to the *Book on Profound and Mysterious Blessedness*. The evident parallelism between the expressive form of this text and that of the scriptures of the Pure Land school of Buddhism has been particularly emphasized by Gong Tianmin (1960, 61–62). The prologue and the epilogue of this Christian sutra closely follow the pattern, style, and language of popular Chinese Mahāyāna sutras:

> This treatise is the most Buddhistic in style of any that we have so far discussed. It opens in the style of a Buddhist scripture, such as the

---

173. Weng 1996, 118.

174. See Wang Juan 2018, 648–51.

175. Lin Wushu 1995b (2011b), 253.

Diamond Scripture (Jingang jing), with the Messiah surrounded by an assembly of disciples, listening to his teaching. . . . The thought is developed exactly in the manner of the Buddhist scriptures, by a leading disciple . . . rising and putting a question, to which the Messiah replies in length.[176]

The text closes with a formula, stereotypical in Buddhist texts, which emphasizes that putting into practice the words heard is a source of joy for the listeners. This "sutrafication" of a Christian text is an evident sign that the Christian author underwent a profound process of adaptation to the Chinese religious milieu. Not surprisingly, this "sutrafication" is common to the contemporary Manichaean literature, as remarked by Gunner B. Mikkelsen (2014).

It is therefore clear that the *Book on Profound and Mysterious Blessedness* "is undoubtedly . . . an original work"[177] and not a translation, as one might conclude from the fact that this writing is included in the list of works "translated" by Adam/Jingjing and his collaborators that is contained in the *Book of the Honored.* Further studies should carefully consider whether this text "was very much influenced by the *bianwen* 變文 style,"[178] the first form of popular fiction in which many (especially Buddhist) texts from Dunhuang have been written.

With regard to the quality of the Tang *jingjiao* literary production in its entirety, scholars do not always agree.

Tang Christianity, being able to count only on the strengths of some foreign missionaries and not enjoying the active work of Chinese literati, failed to produce works of refined literary quality. . . . Although the Christian documents in Chinese that have come down to us occupy a considerable place in the fields of epigraphy, archaeology, and religious studies, in the literary history of the Tang era only the stele and the *Hymn in Praise of the Salvation Achieved through the Three Majesties of the Luminous Teaching* can be counted among the literary jewels of that era. In reality even though these texts testify to high levels of refinement and elegance, they cannot be said to be

---

176. Drake 1935, 739.

177. Ibid., 741.

178. Tang Li 2002, 128.

176 A HISTORY OF ENCOUNTERS

"masterpieces" in relation to the entire literary and poetic output of the Tang era.[179]

Other scholars believe that Adam/Jingjing's literary work is qualitatively very significant. Consider, for example, what Zhu Weizhi says about the *Book on Profound and Mysterious Blessedness*:

> The style of this writing is the most beautiful of all the preserved writings of Luminous Teaching. We can say that it is an extraordinary exemplar of the literature that was translated in the Tang era and that it occupies an important place in the history of Chinese Christian literature.[180]

In my opinion, we do not yet have sufficient material to make a comprehensive and accurate analysis of the writing and translating done by monks of the Church of the East in Tang China. For this reason, thoughtful observations on individual texts are preferable to general conclusions.

Finally, there is a debate about the intended audience of these texts. A remark by Chen Huaiyu concerning what he calls a common textual community between Buddhists, Christians, and Daoists in medieval China provides a good summary of the question and introduces us to the next and final step in the study of the Tang *jingjiao* texts.

> Agreement is . . . elusive on the audiences for these texts. Were they aimed at the local *jingjiao* community in Chang'an or at *jingjiao* communities in China more generally? Were they aimed at the Tang rulers or the literati class? Were they aimed at the followers of other religions active in China, such as Buddhists and Daoists? Did these texts serve the families or individuals in the *jingjiao* community? Did they serve second or third generation *jingjiao* Persian and Sogdian immigrants who, it is sometimes assumed, could only read Chinese? The surviving sources do not contain enough information to allow us to give definite answers to these questions. . . . Given that the *jingjiao* texts employed a substantial amount of Buddhist and Daoist vocabulary, it is possible that they

---

179. Zhang Fengzhen 1970, 155–56.

180. Zhu Weizhi 1948 (1951a), 175.

The First Christian Texts in Chinese

were aimed at an audience in Chang'an and other urban centers in China which were familiar with such terminology. In other words, Buddhists, Christians and Daoists in medieval China seem to have shared the same textual community in the capital city, and perhaps in several other urban centers.[181]

The Content of the Texts

Transmission, translation, transformation? This question raised about the Manichaean texts in Chinese[182] can also serve as an appropriate guideline for evaluating the Sino-Christian texts of the Tang era. Since they are the first theological, spiritual, and liturgical works in Chinese, they have been the object of much attention by historians of Chinese Christianity and by missiologists.

Scholars interested in the doctrinal and theological content of these texts have adopted many different approaches in their investigations. One will notice, however, that their underlying question has thus far not been articulated all that clearly. We might put it this way: With their massive adoption of terms and ideas borrowed from Buddhism, Daoism, and Manichaeism, do these documents testify to an effective model of inculturation or do they rather confirm a drift toward unwarranted syncretism?

Already in 1939 John Foster had effectively expressed an important general opinion:

Terms belonging to the other religions are used throughout [the Tang Christian texts], the Buddhist being the most important. But it is not syncretism. Rather it is a borrowing of terminology, and a relation of doctrine to a familiar background of thought, as the only way of expressing Christian truth in its far-eastern environment.[183]

---

181. Chen Huaiyu 2020, 95.

182. See Lieu 1987; Bryder 1992; Sundermann 1996.

183. Foster 1939, 112. A similar opinion is found in Tang Li 2002, 142: "Even though Nestorians adopted many Buddhist and Daoist phrases in their texts, syncretism should not be considered a serious case."

178   A HISTORY OF ENCOUNTERS

Over time, numerous studies by Chinese[184] and Western[185] scholars have confirmed and corroborated this judgment. A particularly decisive contribution has recently been made by scholars engaged in lexical research, which is conducted with increasingly appropriate linguistic methodologies. These scholars have offered a careful etymological analysis of the vocabulary of Tang Christianity with its Confucian, Daoist, and Buddhist background, together with a study of the translation techniques used by the Christian authors.[186]

Similarly, beginning with the Christian vocabulary used in texts whose authenticity has been established, such as those on the Christian stele, the *Hymn in Praise of the Salvation Achieved through the Three Majesties of the Luminous Teaching* and the *Book of the Luminous Teaching of Da Qin on Revealing the Origin and Reaching the Foundation*, Chen Huaiyu concludes that "the Chinese translations of the scriptures of the Luminous Teaching are accurate and orthodox. Although they use many technical terms borrowed from the Buddhist scriptures, they strictly reflect Christian principles."[187] At least for the Christian Trinitarian hymn, the same scholar offered a convincing demonstration of his conclusion by carefully comparing the Syriac and Sogdian text of the hymn with the Chinese text.[188]

Huang Xianian also sees the Christian message of the *jingjiao* texts being conveyed by recourse to the terminology of other religions, primarily Buddhism. As he writes, "Buddhism became the vehicle for the entry of Christianity into China."[189] In other words:

---

184. See Gong Tianmin 1960, 52–66; Liu Weimin 1962; Luo Xianglin 1966; Yang Senfu 1969; Chen Zenghui 1987; Chiu 1987; Zhao Bichu 1990; Huang Xianian 1996; Chen Huaiyu 1997, [2006b?]; Zhang Xiaohua 1999; Tang Li 2002.

185. See Bundy 1985; Eskildsen 1991; Gillman and Klimkeit 1999; Palmer 2001; Raguin 2002a, 2002b.

186. See Liu Zhenning 2007; Nie 2010, 246–305; 2016, 24–63.

187. Chen Huaiyu 1997, 41–42.

188. "Thanks to the publication of the Syriac text and the Sogdian text of the *Hymn in Praise of the Salvation Achieved through the Three Majesties*, we can determine, through comparison with the Chinese text, the original Christian meaning of each term borrowed from Buddhism in the *Hymn in Praise of the Salvation Achieved through the Three Majesties*, such as *cifu* 慈父, *mingzi* 明子, *dasheng* 大聖, *dasheng zi* 大聖子, *fawang* 法王, etc." (Chen Huaiyu 1997, 41). As far as the comparative analysis of the Syriac and Chinese texts of the hymn is concerned, see also the valuable studies of Wu Qiyu already mentioned above (see p. 172).

189. Huang Xianian 1996, 84. Along the same line, see Hamada's studies (2005, 2007) specifically devoted to the *jingjiao* text *Yishen lun*.

The First Christian Texts in Chinese 179

With regard to the Nestorian experiment we see ... how a meta-cosmic religion [namely, Christianity] develops a new Asian identity within the idiom and the ethos of another meta-cosmic religion [namely, Buddhism]. Thus Christian soteriology was formulated within the terminological framework of the Buddhist or Daoist *Weltanschauung* by using the *Dao-* or Buddha/Avalokiteśvara/Guanyin-model to develop a "Buddho-Daoist" Christology.[190]

We have here an entirely modern Christian approach to other religions, a method of evangelization based on interreligious dialogue that was virtually unknown in the subsequent history of Christian missionary activity in China. Matteo Ricci and the first Jesuit missionaries of the seventeenth century introduced a form of dialogue that was primarily intercultural. Through a serious study of Chinese culture, they looked for a way to be accepted and to found Christian communities that were not cut off from Chinese culture. Their attitude toward religions was different from that of the missionaries of the Church of the East. Although they saw many similarities between Christianity and other religions, their attitude toward them was fundamentally negative. Thus, while they adapted Christian teaching and practice to other cultures (in the Chinese case, to Confucian culture), assuming the values and models of these cultures to the point of introducing them into their catechisms, they were strenuously opposed to their religious vision and practice. Daoism, Buddhism, and, even more so, Chinese popular cults were systematically attacked as idolatrous practices.[191] The reasons for their differing vision of culture and religion were theological: culture was seen as assimilable, as a means of evangelization; other religions, however, were considered superstitious cults without any salvific value. Christianity had surpassed them, and they were now obstacles to the search for truth.[192]

The positive view toward another religious vision and practice and occasional adoption of it by the Church of the East, which has been more properly called inreligionization (as opposed to inculturation), has produced texts, significantly the supposedly later ones, in which the key terms all belong to

---

190. Malek 2002, 36.

191. See Ricci and Trigault 1615, 104–16 ("Variae apud Sinas falsae religionis sectae"); Bertuccioli 1983; Kern 1984–85; Di Giorgio 1986, 2012; Shih 1998; Ma Xiaoyang 2003; Hsia 2009; Magone 2012; Littlejohn 2014; Liu Yu 2015; Rubiés 2020.

192. See Zhang Qiong 2017.

180   A HISTORY OF ENCOUNTERS

the religious sphere of Buddhism and Daoism, and their content features a strongly indigenized theology. It is therefore common to find in the historical studies of these texts the belief that the texts that were judged to be first— the *Discourse on the One God* and the *Book of the Lord Messiah*—"expound a Christology and a soteriology that are quintessentially Christian, while the later texts virtually ignore the crucifixion in favor of a Christology and soteriology that could be more aptly described as Daoist or Manichaean"[193]—or, I might add, Buddhist. That is, one notices in the texts an evolution from a type of "canonicalizing" transmission, one that tries to remain faithful to the original models and that is characteristic of the first period and marked by the preservation of biblical elements and Christian tradition, to a type of "indigenizing" transmission that is characteristic of the later period and marked by the abandonment of the original and canonical theological nucleus and by the tendency to rely more and more on the categories of thought proper to Buddhism and Daoism.[194] According to some authors, this seeming absorption of Christianity into Chinese religious systems was also one of the reasons for the disappearance of the Church of the East in China.[195]

One possibility worthy of consideration is that in the eyes of the Chinese, Tang Christianity, clad, as it were, in Buddhist robes, could appear as one of the many heterodox schools or heretical sects of Buddhist or Daoist derivation that had been flourishing in China for some centuries.[196] There are data that would support such a reading. One of these is the application of the name Messiah (*mishihe* 彌施訶) to one of the ninety-six "heterodox ways" (*waidao* 外道) listed in the *Laozi huahu jing* (Book on Laozi's Conversion of the Barbarians), a Daoist scripture completed in the Kaiyuan era (713–41) that has come down to us through a fragmentary manuscript created in Dunhuang (S. 6963) in the first half of the eighth century.[197]

Another intriguing text is a fragment (S. 6551), written around 930, that records the preaching of a Buddhist monk in Turfan. In this source too, Christianity, which is called the "Persian" heresy, is included among the ninety-six "heterodox ways":

---

193. Eskildsen 1991, 79.

194. See Weng 1996, 21–40.

195. See, for instance, Zhang Xiaohua 1999, 28.

196. See Rong 2007.

197. See *Laozi huahu jing* (Book on Laozi's Conversion of the Barbarians) 2, in Zhongguo shehui kexueyuan lishi yanjiusuo et al. 1990–95, 11: 237. See also Sun Jianqiang 2018b, 184–85.

The First Christian Texts in Chinese   181

Those who convert to Buddha, which Buddha do they convert to? He is neither the Mani Buddha [*moni fo* 磨（摩）尼佛], nor the Persian Buddha [*Bosi fo* 波斯佛], nor the Fire-God Buddha [*huoxian fo* 火祆佛], but the Śākyamuni Buddha. . . . In India [i.e., the West] there are ninety-six kinds of heterodox ways [*waidao*], among which are the [ways] of Persia [*Bosi*], of Mani [*moni*], of the fire god [*huoxian*, i.e., Zoroastrianism] . . .[198]

In addition, the imperial edict contained in the Yuanzhao's Buddhist catalogue of 799–800 that refers to the collaboration of the Christian monk Adam/Jingjing with the Buddhist monk Prajña was aimed at making a clear distinction between the two religious doctrines:

> Since the *saṅghārāma* of Śākyamuni [i.e., the Buddhist monasteries] and the monasteries of Da Qin [i.e., the Christian monasteries] are distinct from each other, and since their customs and doctrines are completely different, Jingjing shall hand down the teaching of the Messiah [*mishihe jiao* 彌尸訶教] and the *śramaṇa* sons of Śākyamuni [i.e., the Buddhist monks] shall spread the sutras of Buddha. We wish that the [two] doctrines be kept distinct and that people do not interfere with each other. Orthodoxy and heterodoxy are two different things, just as the rivers Jing and Wei have two different courses.[199]

In view of these assessments, however, a number of questions and observations may be raised. The fundamental questions we must always keep in mind are the following: Do we have sufficient data to evaluate the theological and doctrinal quality of the preaching of the monks of the Church of the East in China from the few documents that have come down to us, documents, moreover, that are not always reliable from the textual point of view? Do these same documents allow us to quantify the degree of the assimilation of Chinese cultural and philosophical-religious elements into the Christian theological system? In other words, our evaluation of the Church of the East's missionary activity in China must always consider the

---

198. Pan Zhonggui 1983–84, 1: 115. See also Sun Jianqiang 2018b, 186–87.

199. *Zhenyuan xinding shijiao mulu* (Catalogue of the Buddhist Teachings Newly Established in the Zhenyuan Era) 17, T 55: 892a8.

182   A HISTORY OF ENCOUNTERS

paucity and one-sidedness of the material available to us. Specific and precise studies on individual documents are therefore to be preferred to general reconstructions.[200]

More fundamentally, then, the evaluation of the content of the Christian texts of the Tang era must be brought back to the dialectic to which I referred at the beginning. That is to say, in every work of linguistic and cultural *transmission*, which results in the *translation* of original works and the *creation* of new texts, there is always a process of *transformation*, and transformation requires flexibility. As Max Deeg pointed out, the Chinese Christian texts of the Tang period "can help us better understand the degree of flexibility and cultural adaptation of the 'translation' of Christianity into another culture that had a high sense and pride in its own cultural level, which is not found . . . anywhere else in the history of religious translation."[201]

Above all, the discussion should be less influenced by Western hermeneutical models, as has been the case until now, and more open to hermeneutical models born in the East, that is, in the setting in which this form of Christianity developed and with which it interacted. In this regard, it has recently been wisely observed that

> doctrinal questions [linked with Tang Christianity] . . . cannot assume Western and European norms of heresy, orthodoxy and syncretism. Instead, we must begin with the East Syrian Christians' understanding of themselves and their mission, and relate this to the context from which they came, as well as the one in which they worked.[202]

To the extent that it became Chinese, Tang Christianity could not help inserting itself into, and to some extent making its own, a hermeneutical approach typical of all Asian religious experiences, but particularly evident in Buddhism, in which there is a tendency toward hybridization, that is, adaptation and deep interaction with the encountered cultural context and with experiences other than one's own, without fear of assuming those elements that a priori are seen as possible ways of enriching one's own tradition. To be more precise, this is a matter of selective integration: not everything is

---

200. A recent fine example of theological appreciation for two Tang *jingjiao* texts (the *Discourse on the One God* and the *Book of the Lord Messiah*) is Aguilar Sánchez 2021.

201. Deeg 2015, 206.

202. Wickeri 2004, 52.

assimilated, and such integration never occurs indiscriminately; it involves only those elements of other religious traditions that are felt to be compatible with one's own religious tradition.[203]

Thus, for example, Chinese Buddhism assimilated many Daoist philosophical and religious elements, considering them to be the expression of truth at a lower level than Buddhist truth, but useful for its adaptation to the Chinese context.[204] At the basis of this attitude is the so-called doctrine of skillful means (*upāyakauśalya*), that is, the adaptation of Buddhist teaching to the cultural, intellectual, and religious situation of its audience. This key doctrine of Mahāyāna Buddhism is one of the reasons for the rapid spread of Buddhism throughout Central and Eastern Asia, making it possible to reformulate the Buddhist message within cultures extremely different from those present in India, where Buddhism originated and first proliferated.[205]

This penchant for harmonizing diversity, which is a cultural constant on the Asian scene, is perhaps more clearly expressed in the culture of China, which is characterized by a pervasive "taste for harmony." By embracing this hermeneutical approach, it was possible to overcome the fear of diversity, the suspicion that the other's otherness is a threat to one's own idenity.

It has now become evident that within this hermeneutical scheme it is no longer possible to speak of an either/or with regard to the transmission or transformation of the Christian message in the Chinese cultural and religious context. Rather, both processes will always take place together. This being the case, the Western and Christian hermeneutical categories of syncretism, distortion, and heresy are no longer relevant.

Such was the case for Buddhism, which, having arrived in China, was receptive to Daoist philosophical experience and, by allowing itself to be greatly influenced by it, became a thoroughly Chinese Buddhism.[206] Such was the case for Manichaeism which, in its expansion toward the East, adopted the same Buddhist principle of adaptation to the linguistic, cultural, and philosophical context it encountered[207] and took on Buddhist dress in Tang

---

203. See Lopez 1988.

204. See Matsunaga 1969, in particular 98–138 ("Buddhist Assimilation in China").

205. See Schroeder 2001; Pye 2003; Williams 2009, 150–57.

206. See Zürcher 1972; Ch'en 1973.

207. Mikkelsen 1999 shows that by means of a detailed analysis of Manichaean technical terminology borrowed from Buddhism. He demonstrates how this missionary strategy was able to strike a balance between "skillful Buddhistization" and "faithful transmission."

184 A HISTORY OF ENCOUNTERS

China,[208] becoming a Chinese Manichaeism. As it penetrated into the life of the common people through a progressive "Daoization" of the figure of Mani,[209] this Sinicized Manichaeism survived in Southern China until the sixteenth century.[210] Something similar could well have happened with regard to Christianity. Having arrived in the Tang Empire, it was not afraid to open itself to the spiritual patrimony of Buddhism and Daoism, allowing them to shape it via osmosis and thus becoming a Chinese Christianity.

We should not overlook the fact that from the seventh to the ninth centuries Buddhist terminology was the dominant religious code in Central Asia and China. Daoists also incorporated Buddhist terms. They became a sort of Buddhist-Daoist *koinē*, with the result that medieval Buddhism and Daoism shared a great deal of common vocabulary and narratives. Given this state of affairs, the adoption of Buddhist and Daoist terms and forms of expression in Christian texts was virtually inevitable, at least in some cases. Since there was no preexisting Christian religious language in China that the missionaries of the Church of the East could rely on, they had to make use of the linguistic-religious code that was at hand. In other words, adoption of Buddhist and Daoist terminology was not, all things considered, a choice for the Tang Christians. As Zeng Qingbao (Chin Ken-pa) puts it:

> The *jingjiao* priests had little other option but to appropriate existing Buddhist and Daoist terminology in their translation of scriptures. As a foreign religion entering Tang China, it is quite feasible that *jingjiao* doctrines and theological teachings would first undergo a process of language and cultural appropriation. The canons needed to be rendered into the local language and dictions familiar to the locals in order to propagate. When *jingjiao* founders first settled in Tang China, the domineering religious terminology and dictions were those of the Buddhism and Daoism. If the pioneering *jingjiao* priests wished to propagate their faith in Tang China, they would have had no other alternatives but to appropriate the terminology used by the two established religions in the rendition of *jingjiao* canons and liturgies.

---

208. See Schmidt-Glintzer 1987.

209. See Lieu 1992, 257–61 ("The Taoicisation of Mani").

210. See Lieu 1992, 263–304 ("The Religion of Light in South China, Ninth–Sixteenth Centuries"); 1998, 177–95 ("Nestorians and Manichaeans on the South China Coast"); Palumbo 2003; Lin Wushu 2005c, 5–160.

Unless the initial *jingjiao* establishment only intended to serve the Tang Assyrian community exclusively, the clerical group would have needed to appropriate the existing local religions for their translation endeavor.... The appropriation of local religions' terminology seemed to be the most natural and reasonable decision for them.[211]

It is true that in some of the Tang Christian texts "the use of Buddhist terms is so extensive that one almost gains the impression of dealing with Mahāyāna texts."[212] However, if we compare Manichaean texts with contemporary Chinese Christian texts, the use of Buddhist terms in the latter is proportionately less frequent. As Samuel N. C. Lieu noted:

In translating their texts into Chinese, they [i.e., Christians] judiciously avoided the use of distinctive Buddhist terms although, like Manichaeans, they occasionally had to use the word *fo* (buddha) to denote divinity. Otherwise they coined many new terms and phrases to avoid borrowing from Buddhism.[213]

In any case, the assimilation of Buddhist as well as Daoist and Confucian terminology into the vocabulary of the Tang Christian literature was a selective integration, as it was for Christian literature in the languages of Central Asia.

The scriptures of the Luminous Teaching, in the process of their diffusion in China, adopted extensively terms, forms, and even the respective contents of the three teachings, Confucianism, Buddhism, and Daoism, of which Buddhism is the main one. However, this did not involve changes or transformations of [Christian] fundamental doctrines, but as regards certain details it resulted in the partial assimilation (imitation) of the vocabulary and style, contents and formulas of the other teachings. This assimilation was neither the reception [by Christianity] of the doctrines of the other religions, nor the wholesale adoption [of their lexical or other systems]; it was a process of transformation (only an external change) for its own use.[214]

---

211. Zeng Qingbao 2019, 6–7.

212. Klimkeit 1985, 18.

213. Lieu 1992, 261. An interesting study on the characteristics common to Christians and Manichaeans in the translation of their texts into Chinese is Mikkelsen 2005.

214. Wang Juan 2018, 633.

Read against this backdrop, the Tang Sino-Christian texts are more understandable and perhaps less disconcerting. They are an exceptional testimony to the fact that "Nestorians in China were involved in a . . . concrete and intimate interaction with this . . . living tradition [i.e., Buddhism],"[215] as well as with the other living tradition, Daoism.[216] The vocabulary and content of the *Book on Profound and Mysterious Blessedness* set it apart as the document that is most marked by Buddhist and Daoist terminology and thought.[217] As a meditation text, its form and content are very close to those found in Buddhist meditation texts.[218] Stephen Eskildsen (2006?) has found relevant parallel themes between this Christian scripture and several contemporary Daoist texts. Chen Huaiyu (2014, 2015a, 2020) has revealed that the Christian text *Zhixuan anle jing* shares some very similar sentences and vocabulary with the Daoist scripture *Taixuan zhenyi benji jing*. It is likely that the *jingjiao* community was very familiar with this Daoist text since the Qingxu guan, the Daoist temple in the Fengyi Ward (Fengyi fang) of Chang'an where the text was produced, was not far from the Da Qin si, the Christian monastery in the Yining Ward:

> Since the *jingjiao* community was located near the Daoist temple in Chang'an, we could speculate that the *jingjiao* translators and their assistants shared in the same intellectual and literary resources in Chang'an. In other words, the *jingjiao* translation team and the Daoist priests shared an intellectual and literary milieu. In this sense, the *jingjiao* priests and the Daoist priests in Chang'an area could use the same set of terms and vocabulary in their literary works, though these terms and vocabulary would have very different religious meanings and implications. . . . It seems that the "authors" of both Christian and Daoist texts knew a set of shared vocabulary and expressions, though they applied these terms in their own religious writings for their own religious purpose.[219]

---

215. Scott 1985a, 98.

216. See Chen Huaiyu 2015b.

217. See Wu Changxing 2007.

218. See Raguin 2001.

219. Chen Huaiyu 2015a, 219–20, 223.

The sharing of a religious linguistic heritage among Christians, Buddhists, and Daoists in the Tang era is therefore evident and increasingly proven by linguistic studies of Christian texts from this period. This sharing is also confirmed by occurrences of the terms "Messiah" and "Jesus Messiah" within three non-Christian documents from Dunhuang. In addition to the already mentioned Daoist scripture *Laozi huahu jing* (Book on Laozi's Conversion of the Barbarians), there are the *Lidai fabao ji* (Record of the Historical Transmission of the *Dharma* Jewel), a Chan Buddhist text extant in fragments,[220] and the manuscript Pelliot tibétain 351 (P. T. 351), a Tantric text of divination in Old Tibetan.[221] This element should be added to several others to prove, as claimed by Chen Huaiyu, that there were "organic dynamics between Nestorianism and Tantric Buddhism in medieval China":

> Nestorians and Tantric Buddhists in Chang'an benefited from each other during their mutual collaboration in translating Buddhist and Nestorian texts into Chinese. Some Tantric Buddhists might have shared Sogdian background with Nestorians, in kinship and in community. Nestorians and Tantric Buddhists all contributed to introducing Persian astronomical knowledge to the Tang court. Nestorian Christians adopted Tantric Buddhist scriptural pillars in their burial ritual, serving their Nestorian community. Nestorians and Tantric Buddhists in Dunhuang and Tibet might have had mutual relationship, textually and artistically.[222]

With regard to the question of possible Christian influence on some elements of Buddhist doctrine in the Tang era, there are no certain data we can rely on. Some scholars speculated about a possible Christian influence on Pure Land Buddhism (in particular the figure of Shandao, 613–81) and its theistic approach, especially evident in the cult of Amitābha.[223] Probably the first and best-known representative of this line of study was the British religious scholar Elizabeth Anna Gordon (1851–1925). Her joint study of Christianity

---

220. See Rong 1999a; Barrett 2003; Wang Lanping 2016b, 39–42 (with references to the editions of the related sources). See also Sun Jianqiang 2018b, 186–87.

221. See Uray 1983, 1987; Wang Yao 1991, 1994; Chen Jian 2016; Yan Fu and Gao Qian 2017.

222. Chen Huaiyu 2009a, 210.

223. See, for instance, Clemen 1920–22; Michihata 1927; Seah 1984; Hansbury 1993; Morita 2011; Hamada 2012.

188 A HISTORY OF ENCOUNTERS

and Mahāyāna Buddhism is believed to have been shaped by her interactions with scholars such as Saeki Yoshirō while she was in Japan.[224] Gordon's *The Lotus Gospel* (1911) and other works were published in Japan as a series in which she argues for a close relationship between and a common ancestry of Mahāyāna Buddhism and early Christianity. Her underlying argument was that the former had been directly influenced by the latter. As a symbolic image of her approach, in 1911 she erected a copy of the 781 Xi'an Christian stele at the entrance of the Inner Sanctuary (Okuno-in), the cemetery that houses the tomb of Kūkai (774–835), the founder of the Shingon school of Buddhism, on Mount Kōya (Kōya-san).[225]

All these speculations are still little more than conjectures. However, the slight evidence we have that Christians and Buddhists collaborated in the translation of their respective scriptures—and we still cannot say if this collaboration was occasional or ongoing—invites us to pursue this line of research.[226]

Within the dialectic between transmission and transformation, studies have so far mainly focused on transformation. An investigation of transmission, which only began in recent years, is particularly urgent. We need to ask what elements, themes, and images dear to the Syriac spiritual tradition were transmitted in the Tang Christian texts. In the light of the Syriac theological and spiritual context in which these texts are placed, as well as of the Syriac spiritual writers who nurtured the authors of these texts, what theological and spiritual thought is being transmitted through a vocabulary borrowed from Eastern religious traditions?[227]

Of course, "research on the Luminous Teaching cannot be said to be complete; indeed, much work remains to be done and many questions to be discussed."[228] Microtextual research on these documents is only at an early stage. A better philological and historical-textual study of the documents and more accurate methods of cultural translation will reveal how and to what degree the first Chinese Christians inculturated Christian doctrines in the Chinese cultural and religious world.[229] However, on the basis of the

---

224. See Koyama 2013; Okuyama 2018a.

225. See Okuyama 2017, 2018b.

226. See Inglis 1917; above, pp. 150–51.

227. See Ferreira 2004; 2014, 316–54.

228. Huang Xianian 2000, 460.

229. See Ribaud 2001, 37.

conclusions that have thus far emerged from studies on the Luminous Teaching in the Tang era, this early Christian presence in China can only be understood as a Sinicized Christianity, that is, a Christianity distinctly marked by specifically Chinese characteristics.[230] This tells us that the "Luminous Way" found a way to connect with the cultural and religious customs of the Chinese people.

---

230. See Gong Fangzhen 1992.

PART II

The Texts in Translation

Notes on Sources

The Reference Editions of the Translated Texts

TEXT A. We have accurate editions of the text of the "Stele of the Diffusion of the Luminous Teaching of Da Qin in China" (*Da Qin jingjiao liuxing Zhongguo bei*), as well as rubbings that allow us to verify their accuracy. The edition on which my translation of the Chinese text of the stele is based is the one Antonino Forte included in Pelliot 1996, 497–503. For the Syriac portions of the text, the edition I refer to is the one transliterated by Jean Dauvillier in Pelliot 1984, 53–61. An accurate reference edition of the complete Chinese-Syriac text of the stele has been recently made by Lance Eccles and Samuel N. C. Lieu (2020) and is easily accessible online.

The situation of the Tang Christian manuscripts is quite different. The main challenge is that of transcribing and editing the original manuscript texts, since these are the most direct sources for textual studies and translations. A text that has been transcribed and edited is easier to read and understand, but it is already an interpretation, especially if punctuation marks, which are absent in the ancient manuscripts, are introduced.

In the edited and published texts that are available to us, the methodologies employed for transcribing the text range from adhering to the original as closely as possible by maintaining the subdivision into columns and making only the most essential addenda, to editions that make use of punctuation marks and are enriched with explanatory notes, to those that neglect the original placement of the text in columns with a precise number of characters in each column in order to conform to the typographic standards required by modern publications, to editions using the simplified characters of mainland China. Among the most recent editions of all the documents, I recommend

The Luminous Way to the East. Matteo Nicolini-Zani, Oxford University Press. © Oxford University Press 2022.
DOI: 10.1093/oso/9780197609644.003.0004

194   THE TEXTS IN TRANSLATION

that of Nie Zhijun (2010, 330–66), in traditional characters, and that of Wang Lanping (2016b, 143–72, 192–235, 245–63, 267–75, 279–84, 287–92), in simplified characters.

TEXT B. With regard to document P. 3847, which contains the "Hymn in Praise of the Salvation Achieved through the Three Majesties of the Luminous Teaching" (*Jingjiao sanwei mengdu zan*) and the "Book of the Honored" (*Zunjing*), which is the only directly accessible manuscript, we can say that this is the text that seems to present the fewest problems for interpreting the characters with which it is written. However, a careful analysis of the different editions reveals that each of them contains errors that are the result of incorrect transcription or poor proofreading. Fortunately, we now have a new transcription by Lin Wushu (2001c, 60–61) that maintains the original's subdivision into columns and is expertly punctuated. My translation is based on this transcription, which corrects some erroneously written characters and includes explanatory notes that evaluate the explanations of doubtful passages that are found in previous editions.

TEXT C and TEXT D. The various transcriptions of the "Discourse on the One God" (*Yishen lun*) and of the "Book of the Lord Messiah" (*Xuting mishisuo jing*) all contain numerous obscure points and inadequate explanations of obscure passages, some of them related to the unreliability of the text itself. This is why my translations are primarily based on the xylographic reproduction of the documents, published in Japan in 1931 (Tōhō bunka gakuin Kyōto kenkyūsho 1931). The recent publication of new and clearer color photographic reproductions of the manuscripts kept in the "Dunhuang Secret Collection" (*Tonkō hikyū*) at the Kyōu shooku, the library of the Takeda Science Foundation in Osaka, Japan (Kyōu shooku 2009–13, 6: 83–96; Kyōu shooku 2020, 21–69), together with a careful transcription of their texts (Kyōu shooku 2020, 92–103), has made possible a better reading of the original characters. Among the various editions of the two documents, I occasionally refer to those of Luo Xianglin (1966, 194–212), since I find that they offer the most reasonable punctuation.

TEXT E. Until a few years ago, the editions of the "Book on Profound and Mysterious Blessedness" (*Zhixuan anle jing*) that are contained in various Chinese publications were still based for the most part on the transcription published in 1934 by Saeki Yoshiro (1934a, 122–32; repr. in Saeki 1951, appendix "Chinese Text," 77–95). However, a recent study by Lin Wushu (2001a) has revealed the numerous shortcomings of this transcription.[1]

---

1. For a review of this study by Lin Wushu, see Mikkelsen [2006?].

First of all, it is not based on the original but on the transcription made by Haneda Tōrū in 1929 (Haneda 1929). The additions made to it often appear arbitrary and the conclusions hasty. Moreover, the numerous interpolations are not accompanied by any explanatory notes. The partial photographic reproductions of the original document, published in 1958, unequivocally made known the obvious errors of Saeki's text, but also revealed the reliability of the first transcription made by Haneda in 1929. Haneda saw the manuscript the previous year, and on it he based his complete transcription of the text, which is very faithful to the original, respectful of the variable number of characters of each column of the text, sober in proposing corrections and additions, and cautious in solving uncertain points. The recent publication of new and clearer color photographic reproductions of the manuscript kept in the "Dunhuang Secret Collection" at the Kyōu shooku of the Takeda Science Foundation in Osaka (Kyōu shooku 2009–13, 1: 128–33; Kyōu shooku 2020, 71–85, with a careful transcription of its text, 103–6) has made it possible for Lin Wushu to revise Haneda's transcription and to produce a new, punctuated edition (Lin Wushu 2011c [2011b], 314–21). My translation is based on this edition.

TEXT F. The translation of the reconstructed text of the "Book of the Luminous Teaching of Da Qin on Revealing the Origin and Reaching the Foundation" (*Da Qin jingjiao xuanyuan zhiben jing*), a collation of the text carved on the Luoyang *jingjiao* pillar (edited transcription in Lin Wushu and Yin Xiaoping 2008, 329–31) and the Li Shengduo manuscript (transcription in Kyōu shooku 2020, 107; edited transcription in Lin Wushu 1995b [2011b], 248–49), is based on the edition I provided in Nicolini-Zani 2009b, 129–30.

The Transcriptions of Foreign Names

The Tang *jingjiao* documents contain a great number of foreign names (mostly proper names) transcribed in the Chinese language. In addition to a few Buddhist Sanskrit names, several Syriac and, to a lesser extent, Sogdian and Middle Persian (Pahlavi) names have been transcribed in the Chinese-language documents translated in the following pages.

For reasons of simplicity and since this is not a strictly philological study of the documents, in the footnotes to my translations the Chinese characters of these names are Romanized according to the standard modern pronunciation (the Pinyin system). The original, supposedly Tang-dynasty phonetic transcriptions, however, were based on the standard pronunciation at the time, which linguists have reconstructed and termed Middle Chinese

196 THE TEXTS IN TRANSLATION

pronunciation (Bernhard Karlgren) or Late Middle Chinese pronunciation (Edwin G. Pulleyblank), on the basis of the speech of Chang'an, the capital of the Sui and Tang dynasties.

For a list of the reconstructed pronunciation and linguistic consideration of each Syriac, Sogdian, and Middle Persian term transcribed in Chinese and contained in the following translated texts, I refer the reader to the articles of Takahashi Hidemi (2008, 2013, 2014b, 2020) and Samuel N. C. Lieu (2016b). Only by considering these reconstructed pronunciations is it possible to perceive the supposed phonetical correspondences between the original Syriac, Sogdian, and Middle Persian terms and their transcription in Chinese, and to understand the interpretations I propose. To give one example, the Chinese word 娑多那,[2] whose modern Pinyin pronunciation is *suoduona*, was presumably pronounced *satana* in the Tang era, according to the reconstructed pronunciation of Late Middle Chinese. It is thus easily recognizable as the Chinese phonetic transcription of the Syriac word *sāṭānā*, "Satan."

* * *

In order to facilitate reference to the original sources, in the following translations the numbers of the columns into which the Chinese text is arranged are given in square brackets using a bold-type face. In Text A, [**S** . . .] indicates the numbers of the columns of the original text of the 781 Xi'an stele inscription that are in Syriac, while other numbers enclosed in brackets indicate the numbers of the columns of the original text that are in Chinese. In Text F, [**P** . . .] indicates the numbers of the columns of the text carved on the 815 Luoyang pillar, while other numbers enclosed in brackets indicate the numbers of the columns of the same text but in the manuscript version.

The translation of Text F is a slightly revised version of the translation already published in Nicolini-Zani 2009b, 130–34.

---

2. Text C, col. 186, p. 244n58.

TEXT A

Stele of the Diffusion of the Luminous Teaching of Da Qin in China (*Da Qin jingjiao liuxing Zhongguo bei* 大秦景教流行中國碑)

[1] EULOGY WITH a Preface [Inscribed] on the Stele of the Diffusion of the Luminous Teaching in China[1]

---

1. The nine large characters of the title—*Da Qin jingjiao liuxing Zhongguo bei*—are engraved in the carved cartouche that is part of the decorative work above the stone slab on which is inscribed the actual text. For the origin and meaning of the geographical name Da Qin, see p. 66. About the use of *Zhongguo* (lit., "Middle Kingdom") for China, Samuel N. C. Lieu wrote: "I believe the decision to use the somewhat anachronistic term *Zhongguo* [instead of the more common, obvious, and respectful name of *Da Tang* 大唐 (lit., "Great Tang"), the name of the then reigning dynasty] to designate China by the Christian monks at Xi'an in the headstone and title of the Monument was arrived at after serious deliberation. . . . I believe the monks chose a term which was free from dynastic constrictions and suitably grandiose for it to be a parallel to Da Qin, viz. a timeless land with the same claim to mythological greatness as that of the land of origin of Christianity: *Christiana Romana*" (Lieu 2020b, 69). The main body of the inscription is divided into two parts: (1) The first part (*xu* 序, "preface") contains of two sections: (a) a "theological-doxological" introductory presentation, in which the creation of the world by God, the ensuing sin of man, and his redemption by the Messiah are described with a vocabulary strongly influenced by Confucian, Daoist, and Buddhist terminology; (b) a "historical" account of the diffusion of the Luminous Teaching in the Chinese Empire, which tells how the Christian missionary Aluoben came to Chang'an, how the Chinese emperors welcomed him and the other missionaries who entered China later, and how the Chinese court allowed the Christian teaching to be preached in China. (2) The second part (*song* 頌, "eulogy") is a lyrical encomium in praise of God and a poetic celebration of the events narrated in the preceding historical account. This pattern of a prose introduction to a poem appears frequently in Chinese literature. To this main body of the text is appended a final section, wherein the names of those donors responsible for the erection of the stele are mentioned. See Thompson 2020b; Chen Huaiyu 2009b (2012), 32–34.

The Luminous Way to the East. Matteo Nicolini-Zani, Oxford University Press. © Oxford University Press 2022.
DOI: 10.1093/oso/9780197609644.003.0005

THE TEXTS IN TRANSLATION

[2] A composition in prose and poetry[2]
by Jingjing, monk[3] of the Monastery of Da Qin[4]
[S1] Adam, priest and chorepiscopus and *p'apši* of Ṣinestan[5]

[3] It is said that [there is a being] constant in truth and tranquility, prior to every beginning and without origin, profound in intelligence and transparency; a transcendent and unlimited being, who, concentrating his mysterious power, creates and transforms [everything];[6] a supreme honored being,[7] who inspires all holiness—is this not properly God,[8] the transcendent person of our Three-One,[9] True Lord without origin?

---

2. *Shu* 述: a Chinese literary genre, in which after a first part in prose, there follows a second part in verse.

3. It is interesting to note that in the text the author always defines Christian monks and clerics with the generic term *seng* 僧, which in ancient Chinese literature usually indicates Buddhist monks. More specific titles found in the Syriac portions of the text, such as monk, presbyter, deacon, etc., are included in the Chinese title *seng*. See pp. 93–94.

4. On this expression (Da Qin si), which designated a Christian monastery or church in Tang China, see pp. 106–7.

5. Adam is the original name of Jingjing. The term *p'apši*, not attested elsewhere in Syriac literature, seems to be the transcription of the Chinese Buddhist title *fashi* 法師, "Master of the Doctrine." Ṣinestan or Ṣin is the Syriac term for Northern China (Southern China was called Maṣin).

6. The Chinese word used here, *zaohua* 造化, is a technical term that refers to a fundamental tenet of Daoist cosmology. To the original essence is attributed the movement of the world that perpetually regenerates itself and is constantly changing. It creates (*zao*) and transforms (*hua*) everything with a twofold operation (*zaohua*) in which the process of organization that generates something cannot be separated from the process of transformation, which implies a disintegration that is necessary for renewal. In this pairing, Chinese thought, in which transformation has primacy over creation, is combined with Semitic thought, which speaks more in terms of creation than of transformation. All the expressions used in this incipit of the inscription are common in Daoist literature and replicate the fundamental ideas of ancient Chinese cosmology.

7. The Chinese term used here, *zun* 尊, means "honored," "venerable," "worthy of honor and veneration," and is a recurrent title both in Daoist literature (in reference to Laozi) and in Buddhist literature (in reference to Buddha); it occurs several times in the text.

8. *Aluohe* 阿羅訶: Chinese phonetic transcription of the Syriac word *Alāhā*. It is also found in the text of the *Hymn in Praise of the Salvation Achieved through the Three Majesties of the Luminous Teaching* (Text B.1, col. 3, p. 222), of the *Book of the Honored* (Text B.2, col. 2, p. 226) and of the *Book of the Luminous Teaching of Da Qin on Revealing the Origin and Reaching the Foundation* (Text F, cols. 11/P7 and 18/P10, pp. 300 and 301).

9. The author renders the Christian concept of the Trinity with the Chinese term *sanyi* 三一, lit., "three-one." This is an expression that appears, with different meanings, in Daoist literature. For a discussion of the Daoist background of this term, see Muto 2020.

Drawing a cross,[10] he separated the four areas of space;[11] arousing the primordial spirit,[12] he produced [4] the two breaths.[13] Darkness and emptiness were transformed, heaven and earth were separated; the sun and the moon began to rotate, the day and the night began to alternate. After having forged and completed all things, he created the first human being. Differentiating [him from other living beings], he endowed him with every good quality in a harmonious whole and gave him dominion over the myriad creatures.[14]

Human nature at its origin was pure and lowly, and the [human] heart, simple and plain, was in its essence free from disordered passions. But then came Satan,[15] who used deceit and overlaid [humanity's] true essence with [alien] trimmings. At the heart of what was good, [5] he introduced [the presumption of] being as great [as God], and he interpolated an equivocal semblance [of good] within what was bad.[16] Then three hundred sixty-five sects[17] sprang up and spread in various directions, weaving a network of [different]

---

10. The cosmic cross that fixes the four cardinal points. It occupies a central place in Gnostic cosmogonic speculations that the author of the inscription must have known well.

11. According to Chinese cosmology, space—and therefore the earth—is square, and is divided into four *fang* 方, that is, "quadrants," "sectors," "areas," corresponding to the four directions or cardinal points: the west, the east, the north, and the south. This cross-shaped device has at its center the unity, totality and axis of the whole. God therefore appears here as the ordering principle of space and its very foundation.

12. Cf. Gen. 1:2: "spirit of God," "wind of God," hovering over the waters in the primordial void.

13. With the expression *erqi* 二氣, the author appears to refer to the *yin* 陰 and the *yang* 陽, the two forces, opposite and complementary, that interact and constitute the foundation of universal order. According to Chinese cosmology, these breaths are the materials or energies contained in a potential and undifferentiated state in the original matrix, the primordial chaos. By the principle of cyclical time, this matrix at a certain point comes to maturity and tears apart, giving rise to a bipolarity (*yin* and *yang*) and releasing the breaths that become separate: the lighter ones go up to form the sky, the heavier ones go down to form the earth.

14. The author here shows that he is well aware of the content of the biblical account of Genesis 1, and he uses this model for his account of the creation of the world. Nevertheless, in this initial scene recalling the primordial situation, the traditional Christian negative attributes of God (such as silence, stillness, perfection, eternity, anteriority, transcendence) intermingle with the pantheistic idea, widespread in Chinese thought, of a development and transformation from chaos. The result is a kind of "Sinicized Genesis 1."

15. *Suodan* 娑殫: Chinese phonetic transcription of the Middle Persian *sātān*.

16. Cf. Gen. 3:5. For the interpretation of this passage, which is one of the most difficult in the inscription, see Pelliot 1931; 1996, 193–99.

17. It is clear that this figure is inspired by the number of days of the year, indicating fullness. However, the origin of this image (Gnostic? Manichaean?) is not clear. This is also attested in the text *Book of the Luminous Teaching of Da Qin on Revealing the Origin and Reaching the Foundation* (Text F, cols. 4–5/P5, p. 299).

doctrines. Some of them designated material things as lords,[18] putting their trust in them; others [introduced] indistinctness between the two [principles of] non-existence and existence;[19] others [indicated] prayers and sacrifices as the way to obtain blessings;[20] others boasted of the goodness [of human nature] to deceive human beings.[21] With mind and intellect confused and thoughts and intentions enslaved, they, exhausted, [6] could no longer do anything. More and more consumed by their torment and oppression, sunk deeper into darkness, they lost their way and for long ages wandered astray, far from the excellent way.

And thus, the Luminous Honored Messiah,[22] distinct person of our Three-One,[23] depriving himself of and concealing his true majesty, appeared as a man.[24] An angel proclaimed the blessing to an unmarried girl, who gave birth to the Holy One[25] in Da

---

18. The reference could be to the followers of idolatrous cults in general, although Pelliot (1996, 201–2) suggests Daoist worship of "objects" like the sky, the earth, mountains, and rivers. It is more likely that the reference is to Manichaeans, whom Syriac heresiologists had already accused of worshipping the sun and the moon as gods (see Tardieu 2008, in particular 221).

19. All the interpreters have seen in this passage a reference to the Buddhist doctrine of the negation of both being and non-being (see Pelliot 1996, 202–3). More probably, however, the reference is to the followers of the Marcionite heresy (see Tardieu 2008, 221).

20. According to Pelliot (1996, 203), this reference is to the Chinese worship of ancestors. More likely, the reference is to those who prided themselves on their virtuous asceticism or to the followers of the Messalian or Euchite heresy, whose followers were reproached for despising work and ascetic practices under the pretext of continuous prayer (see Tardieu 2008, 221).

21. According to Pelliot (1996, 203), this reference is to Confucian morality. More probably, the text refers again to ancient Christian heretical groups.

22. *Mishihe* 弥施訶: Chinese phonetic transcription of the Syriac *mšiḥā* (or of its correspondent Sogdian form, modeled on the Syriac), which always occurs in this form throughout the text of the stele as well as in other Tang Sino-Christian texts (so it will not always be noted every time it appears). In these texts, it is the preferred term to designate Jesus Christ.

23. *Wo sanyi fenshen* 我三一分身: a very difficult expression from the linguistic as well as the theological point of view. For an account of the question, see Suter 1938. The expression *fenshen* (lit., "divided body") is used in the Buddhist Canon to indicate one of the three bodies of the Buddha, also called "the body of transformation" (*huashen* 化身, Sk. *nirmāṇakāya*), through which the Buddha manifests himself to sentient beings in order to instruct and save them. In one of the Christian texts of the Tang era, the *Hymn in Praise of the Salvation Achieved through the Three Majesties of the Luminous Teaching*, the term *yingshen* 應身 appears as a synonym (Text B.2, col. 2, p. 226 and n. 26).

24. Cf. Phil. 2:6–7. For a reading of this sentence on the background of the Syriac theology and the Antiochene exegesis, see Zhu Donghua 2021, 51–52.

25. The term *sheng* 聖, in general, describes a figure that is central to both the Confucian and Daoist traditions. In Confucianism, the term succinctly expresses the wise person who embodies every virtue on a personal, relational, and public level (the wise sovereign is

Qin.[26] A luminous constellation announced the happy event, and having glimpsed the brightness [of the star], from Persia some came to pay homage [to him] with gifts.[27] Fulfilling the ancient law [7] made known by the twenty-four saints,[28] [the Messiah] explained how we are to govern family and nation through his great plan. He established the ineffable[29] new teaching, based on the Pure Spirit[30] of the Three-One, to shape virtuous practice through the right faith.[31] Defining the norm of the eight conditions,[32] he purified the defiled and brought the truth to perfection. Opening the doors of the

---

its maximum historical concretization, the summit of all wisdom). In Daoism, the saint is the bodily expression, the visible manifestation of the invisible *Dao* 道, the one who fully participates in its movement, its breath. The term *sheng* occurs fifteen times in this text. It usually refers to the figure of the emperor, but sometimes to a more general figure of wisdom or holiness. This passage is the only time it refers to the Messiah. In order to seek as uniform a translation as possible, I have always translated the term as "holy," because it seems to me that the text in its entirety is more reflective of Daoist thought and language, and also because the figures to which it refers are presented as divinized figures. The reader should know, however, that there is no allusion here to the Christian concept of holiness.

26. Here we have further confirmation of the fact that Da Qin in Tang Chinese Christian texts must indicate the territory of the Syrian province of the Roman Empire, of which Judea was part at the time.

27. An account of the incarnation, the annunciation, the birth of Jesus, and the visit of the Magi (cf. Matt. 1:18–2:12; Luke 1:26–38; 2:1–7) is briefly presented here. It is interesting to note that in this relatively brief passage, a proportionally large place is occupied by the episode of the Magi, considered to be astrologers from Persia, the land of origin of some of the Christian religious who went to China.

28. The number of saints could correspond to the twenty-four authors of the books of the Old Testament.

29. Behind this expression we can glimpse the idea expressed by Saint Paul in 1 Corinthians 2:13. The Chinese wording *wuyan zhi jiao* 無言之教, "ineffable teaching," also closely recalls two passages of *Daodejing* (chaps. 2 and 43) that contain the synonymous expression *buyan zhi jiao* 不言之教.

30. *Jingfeng* 淨風: lit., "pure wind," indicates the Holy Spirit. This expression is present in other texts of the *corpus "nestorianum" sinicum*, such as the *Hymn in Praise of the Salvation Achieved through the Three Majesties of the Luminous Teaching* (Text B.1, col. 6, p. 223) and the *Discourse on the One God* (Text C, cols. 308, 311, 323–25; pp. 258–59). In the Christian literature in Sogdian, the equivalent expression *zprt w't* (*zpart wāt*, "Pure Spirit") is regularly used to indicate the Holy Spirit. See Lin Wushu 2014.

31. In this passage the author gives an interesting interpretation of the two Testaments, distinguishing them not only in their origin, but also in their essence. For him the Old Testament, that of the "letter," is a guide for family life and for the organization of society and the nation. The New Testament, on the other hand, the ineffable law of the Holy Spirit instituted by the Messiah, guides individuals through faith and teaches them how to live.

32. A possible allusion to the eight Beatitudes (cf. Matt. 5:3–10). For an explanation and other interpretations, see Pelliot 1996, 208–9; Deeg 2018b, 89–90.

202 THE TEXTS IN TRANSLATION

three constant [virtues],[33] he opened up life and abolished death. Hanging up the Luminous Sun,[34] he destroyed the abode of darkness. In this way the deceptions of the devil were completely swept away. Sitting at the oars [8] of the boat of mercy, he made the beings endowed with a soul ascend to the Brilliant Palace, and they were thus brought to salvation.[35] Having achieved his mighty work, he ascended to the Truth at noon.[36] He left the twenty-seven books of the Scriptures[37] which expound his great work of transformation, thus destroying the barrier to spiritual life. His doctrine requires immersion in water and in the Spirit,[38] thanks to which the human being is cleansed from vanity and purified, recovering thus his purity and his whiteness.

The Cross that [Christians monks][39] hold as an emblem makes the four horizons of the earth merge in its light, bringing together what was

---

33. The three theological virtues (faith, hope, charity) seem to be the most correct interpretation of this expression "the three constant [virtues]" (*sanchang* 三常), which closely recalls the Confucian *wuchang* 五常, "the five constant [virtues]," namely *ren* 仁, *yi* 義, *li* 禮, *zhi* 智, *xin* 信. For a comparison with the meaning and use of the same expression in Chinese Manichaean literature, see Lin Wushu 1995c.

34. The luminous sun is here the image of Christ (cf. Mal. 3:20; Heb. 1:3).

35. The use of Buddhist images and terms to describe salvation is explicit and evident in these passages. The Buddha, whose mission is to lead consciousnesses to enlightenment, to bring beings to salvation, does so by helping them to cross the ocean of human life on a boat. He brings humans from the shore of terrestrial existence to that of liberated existence, *nirvāṇa*. In addition, Guanyin (Sk. Avalokiteśvara), the bodhisattva of mercy, is called the "boat of mercy" (*cihang* 慈航) in the Buddhist tradition. However, this image of salvation as the "boat of mercy" or "oars of mercy" is also very prominent in Syriac Christian literature. It appears (but is conveyed with another term, *fa* 栿) in the *Hymn in Praise of the Salvation Achieved through the Three Majesties of the Luminous Teaching* (Text B.1, col. 17, p. 224).

36. This is clearly the Ascension, even if the temporal reference to noon time is not clear. In Daoist and Buddhist scriptures, the term *zhen* 真, here translated as "Truth," indicates the condition that is attained through the cultivation of self, the state of perfection, immortality, divinity. Through the use of this term, therefore, the return of the Son to the divinity of the Triune is being emphasized.

37. The allusion to the twenty-seven books of the New Testament seems evident, however the scarce knowledge we still have about the constitution of the biblical canon in the Church of the East does not allow us to verify this hypothesis with certainty. Already in the fifth century an "official" text of the sacred Scriptures, called the Peshitta, must have been in use. It included all the books of the New Testament except the Second Letter of Peter, the Second and Third Letters of John, the Letter of Jude, and the Book of Revelation.

38. Cf. John 1:33; 3:5.

39. Here begins a brief descriptive exposition of the East Syriac Christian monks, who are not, however, mentioned in the Chinese text as the explicit subject of these passages. The terminology and images chosen by the author clearly intend to define the Christian monastic community by differentiating it from the other monastic communities present in China during the Tang dynasty. See Deeg 2018b, 98–106.

Text A   203

separated.[40] Striking the wood,[41] they diffuse a sound that rouses benevolent kindness. By rites facing the east [9] they advance rapidly on the way of life and glory. They let their beards grow as a sign of their public ministry and they shave the top of their heads to signify that they do not have interior passions.[42] They keep neither men nor women servants and hold in equal esteem people in high position and people of humble condition. They do not accumulate wealth or riches, but themselves offer an example of radical renunciation. They complete their fasting by solitude and meditation and reinforce their abstinence by quietude and vigilance.[43] Seven times a day they chant liturgical praises,[44] [10] making great intercession for the living and the dead. Once every seven days they perform their worship,[45] purifying their heart and thus restoring its purity.

This True and Unchanging Way is transcendent and difficult to define with a name. However, its effectiveness is manifested so brightly that we, striving to describe it, will call it the Luminous Teaching.[46] The Way cannot

---

40. In this passage, the Cross, the radiant symbol of redemption, is given a more cosmological significance.

41. In place of bells, some Eastern Christian monasteries use a hanging wooden board (*nāqošā*, in Syriac), which is beaten to call the monks to the prayer.

42. Tonsure, which was introduced after the monastic reform of Abraham of Kaškar, was a peculiar element of monasticism in the Church of the East. See Thomas of Marga, *The Book of Governors* 1.4, ed. and trans. Budge, 1: 23 (text), 2: 40 (trans.): "He [i.e., Abraham the Great] invented this distinguishing mark of ours, and commanded that the disciples of this holy habit of life [i.e., the monastic life] should have their heads shaved like a crown."

43. The use of Buddhist terminology to define the ascetic practices of Christian monks, such as fasting, meditation, quietude (*hesychía*) and watchfulness of thoughts, abounds in this passage. See Deeg 2018b, 104–5.

44. This passage clearly refers to daily liturgical services, which gather the community seven times a day for chanting the common monastic offices. About the interpretation of the expression *qishi* as "seven times," see Duan 2003; Nie 2012a; 2016, 141–50 (with useful parallels with the use of the expression in the Chinese Buddhist texts). A similar practice was also used by Manichaeans in China (see Ma Xiaohe 2014).

45. *Jian* 薦: a specific cultural term indicating sacrifice without the offering of slaughtered animals, which are usually replaced by food offerings. Here it indicates the Sunday Divine Liturgy, the Eucharistic sacrament or mystery (*rāzā*, in Syriac).

46. Here the text of the Xi'an stele is patterned on what *Daodejing* says of the impossibility of defining the *Dao*: "I do not know its name, and I give it the designation of the *Dao* (The Way or Course). Making an effort (further) to give it a name I call it The Great" (*Daodejing* 25, trans. Legge, 67). The real name (*ming* 名) of the *Dao*, the "Way," cannot be known, because it defies any definition or classification, and while one strives (*qiang* 强) to define it more precisely, it can only be defined by means of the effects it produces. In like manner, the *Dao* of Christians cannot be defined in its absolute nature, but only in its actual manifestation.

204   THE TEXTS IN TRANSLATION

spread without a saint, and a saint cannot achieve greatness without the Way. [Only] when the Way and the Saint are bonded together as [the two parts of] an agreement is the world educated and enlightened.

When the emperor of cultivated virtues[47] Taizong[48] [r. 627–49] inaugurated his glorious and splendid kingdom, he revealed himself to be an enlightened sage in the governance of his people. [At that time] in the kingdom of Da Qin there was a man of superior virtue [11] whose name was Aluoben.[49] Having scrutinized the signs of blue clouds, he took [with him] the true scriptures, and having examined the musical tones of the winds, he underwent difficulties and dangers.[50] In the ninth year of the Zhenguan era [635],[51] he arrived in Chang'an. The emperor sent his minister of state, Duke Fang Xuanling,[52] with the Imperial Guard in the western suburbs of the city to welcome the visitor and introduce him to the Palace. The emperor had the scriptures translated in the [Imperial] Library and carefully examined that Way within the forbidden doors. He thus became deeply convinced of the orthodoxy and truth [of that doctrine] and gave special orders for it to be

---

47. Here and in the following references to Chinese emperors, their names are accompanied by expressions that are closely modeled on their respective posthumous names, that is, the honorary titles that were given to them after their death. See Pelliot 1996, ad loc.; Deeg 2018b, ad loc.

48. After Gaozu (r. 618–26), Taizong was the second emperor of the Tang dynasty. Here begins the historical part of the inscription, an account of the spread and reception of East Syriac Christianity in China via the different positions taken by the Tang emperors toward this religion.

49. Chinese phonetic transcription of a foreign name that is difficult to identify. Many hypotheses have been put forward over time (see pp. 88–89). The most plausible of them sees this Chinese name as the phonetic transcription of the Middle Iranian name Ardabān.

50. Images attested in ancient Chinese literature. Here, in particular, they seem to be based on those contained in the *Hainei shizhou ji* (Notes on the Ten Regions on This Side of the Sea), a mostly mythical geographical work attributed to Dongfang Shuo (154–93 BCE). See Pelliot 1996, 222–23; Deeg 2018b, 111–14.

51. In the Chinese imperial tradition, each emperor chose one or more titles for his reign (*nianhao* 年號). The only title Taizong chose was Zhenguan, which he adopted in the first year of his reign.

52. Fang Xuanling (578–648) was a celebrated official, advisor, and chancellor in the first decades of the Tang dynasty. He was an avid scholar and first rose to prominence in the ranks of the military. As a close supporter of Li Shimin (598–649) in the overthrow of the Sui dynasty, he became one of the eminent political figures of the Tang dynasty. He was also responsible for the compilation of the official dynastic histories. Fang Xuanling's biography is contained in several historical works, such as *Jiu Tang shu* (Old Annals of the Tang) 66, 7: 2459–67; and *Xin Tang shu* (New Annals of the Tang) 96, fols. 1a–3b (vol. 6). See Pelliot 1996, 224–27.

Text A   205

propagated. In autumn, [**12**] in the seventh month of the twelfth year of the Zhenguan era [638], the following imperial edict was promulgated:

"The Way does not have an immutable name; the Saint does not have an immutable bodily appearance.[53] Every region of the earth has its own teaching. Thus all living beings may be led mysteriously to salvation. The Great Virtuous[54] Aluoben, of the kingdom of Da Qin, came from far away to present scriptures and images[55] in our supreme capital. Having carefully examined the nature of his teaching, [we have found that] it is mysterious non-action.[56] Having evaluated its essential elements, [we have concluded that] they concern the fundamental needs of human life and its perfection. Its language is simple and meagre, and its principles remain even after the occasion for which they were established has passed.[57] [**13**] [This teaching] leads creatures to salvation, and [from it] come benefits for humans. Its diffusion in the territories of the empire should be allowed, and the competent authorities should therefore build a Monastery of Da Qin in the Yining Ward[58] of the capital and ordain twenty-one men as monks."[59]

---

53. Cf. *Daodejing* 1, trans. Legge, 47: "The *Dao* that can be trodden is not the enduring and unchanging *Dao*. The name that can be named is not the enduring and unchanging name."

54. For the meaning of this title, see p. 94.

55. *Jingxiang* 經像: this expression is common in Chinese Buddhist scriptures, where the Chinese monks returning from India are often described as bringing with them "scriptures and images." This Buddhist literary topos could therefore have been taken up by the author of the text of the stele (see Forte 1996c, 352n7). If "scriptures" reasonably refers to biblical scriptures and Christian spiritual texts, the question of what these "images" were cannot be answered with certainty. For a discussion of the possible Buddhist and Christian elements within the thinking that motivated and accompanied the gift of images, see Godwin 2018.

56. We have here the famous Daoist expression *wuwei* 無為, "non-action," a characteristic principle of the *Dao* (the Way). See *Daodejing* 37, trans. Legge, 79: "The *Dao* in its regular course does nothing (for the sake of doing it), and so there is nothing which it does not do." It is difficult to find a dynamic equivalent for this term. I have chosen to translate it literally, asking the reader not to take it in a negative sense.

57. The metaphorical expression used here, *li you wang quan* 理有忘筌, resembles a phrase contained in *Zhuangzi* 26, *de yu er wang quan* 得魚而忘荃, "When the fish have been caught, people forget the trap."

58. This quarter was located in the northwestern part of the capital, not far from the imperial palace. About this Christian monastery in Chang'an, see pp. 107–8 and 110–11.

59. About this number, see p. 111. The text of this edict is also reported, with slight variations, in *Tang huiyao* (Essential Regulations of the Tang) 49, 8: 864.

206   THE TEXTS IN TRANSLATION

The good fortune of the illustrious family of Zhou had come to an end and the black chariot was ascending toward the West,[60] but with the coming of the great Tang dynasty, the Way shone again as the Luminous[61] Breeze blew eastward. The competent authorities were instructed to produce a portrait of the emperor and to place it on the wall of the monastery. His heavenly beauty was shown by the bright colors, and his splendor shone [14] on the luminous portals. His features exerted a beneficial influence and ceaselessly illuminated the domain of doctrine.[62]

According to the *Illustrated Account of the Western Regions*[63] and the historical works of the Han and Wei [dynasties], the kingdom of Da Qin in the south is bordered by the Coral Sea, in the north it extends to the Mountains of Countless Treasures, in the west it looks toward the Land of the Immortals and the Flowering Forests, and in the east it faces the Strong Winds and the Shallow Waters. The country produces fabrics that are washed in fire,[64] scents that awaken the soul, pearls that glow like the moon, and gems that shine in the night. [15] Thefts and robberies are unknown: happiness and peace reign among the people. The only doctrine propagated is the Luminous [Teaching], and there are no rulers who are not virtuous. Its territory is vast and extensive, and the accomplishments of its civilization are splendid.[65]

The great emperor Gaozong [r. 650–83] emulated the reverent deference of his predecessor [toward the Luminous Teaching]. Giving luster to true religion, he had luminous monasteries[66] built in every prefecture, and he also

---

60. The author of the stele uses two figurative expressions to depict the moral decay that pervaded the Chinese Empire before the establishment of the Tang dynasty. In Chinese thought from Confucius on, the clan of the duke of Zhou was considered representative of a "golden age" in which virtue and morality were perfectly incarnated in the government of the nation. The image of a black chariot ascending to the West is a clear reference to Laozi's disappearance into Heaven, sitting on a black chariot driven by a black ox. These two expressions indicate the long absence of a moral doctrine in China to give guidance to the people.

61. The character *jing* 景, "light," or "luminous," that appears here and in other subsequent phases is undoubtedly a reference to *jingjiao* 景教, "Luminous Teaching."

62. The expressions "luminous portals" (*jingmen* 景門) and "domain of doctrine" (*fajie* 法界) are to be understood both concretely and metaphorically. They indicate the space (physical and metaphysical) of the Luminous Teaching. *Fajie* is a technical Buddhist term (Sk. *dharmadhātu*, "the realm of the *dharma*").

63. *Xiyu tuji*, a geographical work composed by Pei Ju around 605 and later lost.

64. I.e., asbestos fabrics.

65. For a more detailed understanding of this section, see Pelliot 1996, 243–50; Deeg 2018b, 128–37.

66. *Jingsi* 景寺, i.e., monasteries of the Luminous Teaching, namely, Christian monasteries.

Text A

honored Aluoben by making him Great Lord of the Doctrine, Guardian of the Kingdom.[67] [Thus] that doctrine spread throughout the ten [16] provinces,[68] and abundant blessings came down upon the [whole] country. Monasteries were built in all cities, and luminous blessings[69] filled every household.

In the Shengli era [698–99][70] the sons of Śākyamuni,[71] capitalizing on their position of strength, raised their voices [against the Luminous Teaching] in the eastern capital of Zhou, and at the end of the Xiantian era [712][72] some inferior scholars mocked and defamed[73] [that teaching] in the western capital of Hao.[74] But there were [some persons] such as the head of the monks Luohan and the Great Virtuous Jilie,[75] people of noble race in the Gold Region,[76] eminent monks elevated above worldly things, who joined together to weave the

---

67. For a treatment of this title, see pp. 94–95, and Deeg 2018b, 138–39.

68. During the Tang dynasty the empire was divided into ten administrative units.

69. *Jingfu* 景福, i.e., the blessings accorded by the Luminous Teaching.

70. The author here moves on to a later period, which was dominated by great unrest. Emperor Zhongzong, Gaozong's legitimate successor, was dismissed in 684 by Gaozong's concubine Wu Zetian, who replaced him with another son, Ruizong, and then reigned as empress herself until 705, when Zhongzong, the legitimate heir to the throne, regained power.

71. *Shizi* 釋子 (Sk. *Śākyaputra*), namely, Buddhists.

72. In the thirty years between 683 and 712, the Luminous Teaching faced great hostility, both because the Buddhists were privileged by Empress Wu and because in the subsequent kingdoms of Zhongzong (r. 705–9) and Ruizong (r. 710–12) the Daoists were very influential at court.

73. The expression *xiashi* 下士 occurs in *Daodejing*, where the attitude of people toward the Way is described as follows: "Scholars of the lowest class, when they have heard about the *Dao*, laugh greatly at it" (*Daodejing* 41, trans. Legge, 84).

74. One of the extravagant acts of the Empress Wu Zetian was changing the name of the Tang dynasty to Zhou, a reference to the mythical dynasty of Chinese antiquity, and creating a second capital, Luoyang, called the eastern capital of Zhou. In this period, the ancient capital Chang'an took on the name of the western capital of Hao, the name that the mythical King Wu (r. 1122–1116 BCE), founder of the Zhou dynasty, had given the capital.

75. From the transcription of these names in Chinese it is difficult to guess what the original was. Luohan has been identified by many scholars with the Syriac name Abraham, but it seems more reasonable to see there the Persian name Rahām, as suggested by Max Deeg (2018b, 147). Some think that Jilie might be a phonetic transcription of the Syriac name Gabri'el, but from the phonological point of view it seems unlikely. Jilie is called *dade* 大德 ("Great Virtuous One," Sk. *bhadanta*), a title used by Chinese Buddhists, which might perhaps correspond to the Christian title of bishop, as appears from the correlation between the Chinese *dade* and the Syriac *episqopā* in a name contained in the list of monks and clerics at the end of the inscription. Luohan is called the *sengshou* 僧首, "head of the monks," which may correspond to the Christian Syriac title *reš qašiše*, "head of the priests," namely, an archdeacon.

76. The region indicated by this expression remains unsolved. It may be Bactria. The name *jinfang* 金方 is composed of *jin*, which generally also means metal (therefore, the name of this

208   THE TEXTS IN TRANSLATION

mysterious net again and together they reconnected [**17**] the knots that had been loosened.[77]

Emperor Xuanzong [r. 713–55], the Perfect of the Way, ordered the prince of the kingdom of Ning and the other four royal princes[78] to visit the places of worship[79] in person and [re]build the altars there.[80] The pillars of the doctrine, which for a moment had been torn down, were erected again, and the founding stones of the Way, which for a time had been removed, were put back in their proper position. At the beginning of the Tianbao era [742–55], [the emperor] ordered the general-in-chief Gao Lishi[81] to take the portraits of the five saints[82] to the various monasteries and place them inside, along with the gift of a hundred [**18**] rolls of silk. [In this way], paying reverent homage to the imperial effigies, it is possible to reach the bow and the sword

---

region could also be translated as Metal Region). Of the five elements (along with wood, water, fire, and earth) *jin* is the one associated with the westerly direction (*fang*). The expression could then be a generic reference to the territories west of the Chinese Empire.

77. For literary, religious, and political references to this passage, see Pelliot 1996, 256; Deeg 2018b, 150–51.

78. The prince of the kingdom of Ning (Li Chengqi / Li Xian, 679–741) was the emperor's elder brother; the other princes were his younger brothers. All of them resided in the Xingqing Palace built for them by the emperor, and named a little later in the text.

79. Underlying the expression *fuyu* 福宇 is a reference to monasteries as places where religious services were offered (*fu* 福, Sk. *puṇya*) for the benefit of others, including the emperor and the imperial family (see Deeg 2018b, 153).

80. In Chinese sacred architecture the term *tanchang* 壇場 indicates a flat, usually circular, and raised space that is intended for worship—in other words, a kind of altar. Here the term could have been used to indicate the *bema* of the East Syriac Christian churches, which is a fenced platform placed in the center of the nave on which there were two ambos for the proclamation of the readings, a throne for the bishop, and some seats for the clergy. The altar was at the center of the *bema*.

81. According to the biography of the emperor contained in *Jiu Tang shu* (Old Annals of the Tang) 184, 16: 4757–59, in 742 he granted Gao Lishi (d. 762) the title of general-in-chief of the Right Palace Gate Guard (*you jianmen wei da jiangjun* 右監門衛大將軍). For this title, see DOT, p. 149, no. 847; p. 464, no. 5897.

82. Xuanzong's five predecessors, namely Gaozu, Taizong, Gaozong, Zhongzong, and Ruizong. The Tang dynasty exhibited a particularly strong political patronage of the arts, with sovereigns commissioning icons of themselves to be worshipped. During Emperor Xuanzong's reign, a particular kind of icon portraying the first five (or six, including Xuanzong) emperors of the Tang ruling house—the so-called five saints (*wusheng* 五聖) or six saints (*liusheng* 六聖)—was sponsored by the imperial court. Executed by the best artisans of the times, these images were enshrined in Daoist and Buddhist temples in the capitals and districts throughout the empire, serving as surrogates for the illustrious rulers they represented (see Liu Yang 2001; Lei 2003). From this passage of the inscription we see that the imperial custom was also applied to Christian monasteries, having them serve as sites for Christian worship as well as imperial ancestral shrines.

Text A 209

[of the emperors], even though the beard of the dragons is far away. Their solar protuberances spread light all around, and their celestial faces are intimately close [to those who reverence them].[83]

In the third year of the same era [744][84] in the kingdom of Da Qin there was the monk Jihe,[85] who, upon observing the stars turned in the direction of the Transformation, and keeping before his eyes the sun, went to pay homage to the Honored One.[86] An [imperial] edict ordered that the monk Luohan, the monk Pulun,[87] and seven others cultivate merits[88] at Xingqing Palace along with the Great Virtuous Jihe. In addition, [**19**] the celestial [emperor] composed the vertical inscriptions that were placed in the monasteries, where the horizontal tablets with their calligraphy of the dragon were [also] prominent. The precious ornaments sparkled like the plumage of a kingfisher, shone like flashes of rose-colored light at sunset. [With their radiance], the imperial inscriptions so pervaded the wide spaces that they were almost as bright as the sun. The imperial favor grew as high as the Southern Mountains, and the abundance of its benefits reached a depth like [that of] the Eastern Sea.

---

83. Here, as in the descriptive passage of the portrait of Taizong, the features of the emperor, identified with the dragon, are described with extraordinary images. During the Tang dynasty, classical signs of a Son of Heaven such as the solar protuberances or "sun horns" (*rijiao* 日角) on the brow were used in portraying the emperors' images. The portrait follows an iconographic typology typical of Laozi and Buddha in that their bodies were marked by seventy-two or eighty-one wonderful features, including, for example, a squared mouth, a solar protuberance and a crescent moon on the brow, three openings in the ears, two bones on the forehead. For references to the Chinese sources of these expressions, see Pelliot 1996, 260–62; Deeg 2018b, 156–59. The phrase in the inscription seems to mean that the Christian religious, despite their physical distance from the emperor, could be in contact with him by paying homage to him in front of the portraits placed inside the monasteries.

84. It was precisely in the year 744 that an imperial decree prescribed that the Chinese character for "year" be changed, from *nian* 年 to *zai* 載. Accordingly, the author of the inscription makes use of the second. This would be one of the internal proofs in favor of the authenticity of the stele.

85. Two different interpretations have been proposed so far for the name Jihe. It could be the Chinese phonetic transcription of the Syro-Iranian name Gigoy, or the Syriac Giwargis (George), or its diminutive Gigoe.

86. The Transformation refers to China, a country civilized by the righteousness of its sage sovereigns; the Honored One refers to the emperor.

87. Pulun appears as a Chinese original name. If it is a phonetic transcription of a foreign name, it is not clear to which Syriac or Persian name it could correspond.

88. *Xiu gongde* 修功德: a common term in Buddhism to indicate, among other things, the celebration of a service of worship whose merits benefited others. It here refers to a service in favor of the emperor and his family.

"There is nothing that the Way cannot accomplish, and [all] that it accomplishes can be given a name. There is nothing that the Saint cannot do, and [all] that he does can be described."[89]

The enlightened emperor of cultivated virtues Suzong [r. 756–62] [20] rebuilt the luminous monasteries in five administrative divisions: Lingwu [and four others].[90] Gifted with every good virtue, a period of prosperity and happiness began [during his reign]. Blessings fell abundantly and imperial power was consolidated.

The emperor of cultivated virtues and military merits Daizong [r. 763–79] brought the throne to even greater heights by applying the principle of non-action.[91] On every one of his birthdays he offered celestial incense in order to proclaim his meritorious actions. He also offered food from his table to lend luster to the luminous community.[92] [21] Heaven bestowed splendid favors on him, so that his action could be nothing other than the bearer of widespread blessings. The Saint embodied the original action [of heaven], thus bringing to completion and perfection [the favors heaven bestowed].[93]

---

89. Behind this "philosophical" passage, which introduces the way the Luminous Teaching and the imperial power in the reigns of Suzong, Daizong, and Dezong supported one another, there are echoes of expressions from the *Daodejing* (chaps. 1 and 2). See Pelliot 1996, 265–66; Deeg 2018b, 165–66. This four-line ode to "the Way" (*dao*) seems out of place both in content and in the flow of the text. Could it be that these sixteen characters are not from Jingjing, but are instead the couplets composed by Emperor Xuanzong to be placed in Christian monasteries? The vague reference to the religious teaching of "the Way" and the benevolent power of "the Saint" could well be the emperor's own poetic expression of his support for religious institutions. Taizong had used these same two words ("Way" and "Saint") in parallel in his decree quoted earlier in the stele text (cf. col. 12).

90. For this reference and for a summary of the hypotheses on the number and location of Christian monasteries in the Tang era, see pp. 109–10.

91. Cf. *Daodejing* 64, trans. Legge, 108 (with slight changes): "The one who acts (with an ulterior purpose) does harm; the one who takes hold of a thing (in the same way) loses hold of it. The sage does not act (so), and therefore does no harm; he does not lay hold (so), and therefore does not lose his hold. (But) people in their conduct of affairs are constantly ruining them when they are on the eve of success. If they were careful at the end, as (they should be) at the beginning, they would not so ruin them. Therefore the sage desires what (others) do not desire, and does not prize things difficult to get; he learns what (others) do not learn, and turns back to what the multitude of humans have passed by. Thus he helps the natural development of all things, and does not dare to act (with an ulterior purpose of his own)." About *wuwei*, see p. 205n56.

92. *Jingzhong* 景衆, i.e., the community of the Luminous Teaching, namely, the Christian community of the Church of the East.

93. For the expression "bringing to completion and perfection" (*tingdu* 亭毒), see *Daodejing* 51, trans. Legge, 94: "Thus it is that the *Dao* produces (all things), nourishes them, brings them

Text A

In the present period of Jianzhong's reign [r. 780–83],[94] our holy and august emperor of cultivated virtues and military merits propagated the eight principles of government, so that the unworthy were degraded and the worthy promoted. He spread [the great plan of government divided into] nine sectors, thus giving new vigor to the illustrious [imperial] mandate.[95] Innovations [brought by him] led to deep understanding of the most mysterious principles; the hearts of his invokers[96] are not shamed.

That [human beings] should pursue the highest moral stature but remain humble; that they should aim for calmness but remain sensitive [to others]; that they should seek, with expanded **[22]** compassion, to alleviate the pains of others; and that, in their goodness, they should share the life of all the living—this is the Great Way that we practice, this is the gradual ascent through which we rise. And furthermore, that the winds and rains come at the right time, that peace reigns in the world, that justice prevails among the people, that beings keep themselves uncorrupted, that the living prosper and the dead have joy, that thoughts are born and an echo responds to them, that feelings pour out and the eyes are sincere—these are the meritorious effects that our luminous power[97] is able to produce.

The monk Yisi,[98] Great Donor,[99] **[23]** Great Master of the Bright Prosperity [decorated] with Golden [Seal] and Purple

---

to their full growth, nurses them, completes them, matures them [*ting zhi du zhi* 亭之毒之], maintains them, and overspreads them."

94. Jianzhong is the title of reign assumed by Emperor Dezong (r. 779–804) for the first period of his government.

95. *Jingming* 景命: this expression seems deliberately ambiguous. Since the term *jing*, "luminous," throughout the text of the stele refers to the Luminous Teaching coming from God, the imperial mandate evoked here appears closely linked to the divine mandate emanating from the God of the Luminous Teaching.

96. Here the "invokers" are most likely the Christian monks who offer prayers for the emperor, as mentioned above.

97. *Jingli* 景力, i.e., the power of the Luminous Teaching, namely, of Christianity.

98. The Persian Yazdbōzīd, priest and chorepiscopus, mentioned in the final, Syriac part of the inscription. About him, see pp. 87–88; Deeg 2013.

99. The Buddhist title of *dashizhu* 大施主 (Sk. *dānapati*) means "the one who offers" the gift of the Buddhist *dharma*. The title certainly refers to the function of Yisi/Yazdbōzīd as sponsor of the erection of the stele and to his beneficent actions described in the following section of the text. However, in addition to indicating the specific donations of Yisi/Yazdbōzīd, one can probably assume that this title also refers to Yisi/Yazdbōzīd's general religious function in performing what has been described in detail in the previous section. He thus appears as the paradigmatic purveyor of what leads to order and harmony in the world and what makes it possible to achieve salvation (see Deeg 2018b, 185–87).

212   THE TEXTS IN TRANSLATION

[Ribbon],[100] concurrently vice military commissioner of Shuofang,[101] probationary director of the Palace Administration,[102] honored with the purple *kaṣāya*,[103] was a mild and benevolent [man]. As soon as he heard of the Way, he began to practice it with zeal. From the far-off City of the Royal Residence[104] he arrived in China. His erudition surpassed [that of] the three dynasties,[105] and his knowledge extended to all fields. He first served the Red Court, then wrote his name in a princely [**24**] tent.[106] When Duke

---

100. *Jin[yin] zi[shou] guanglu daifu* 金［印］紫［綬］光祿大夫 was one of the highest ranks awarded to an officer. In the Tang dynasty it was one of the ranks of independent civil mandarins, that is, the levels of the mandarin hierarchy that did not correspond to real charges. For a more detailed description of this title, see DOT, p. 168, no. 1159; Pelliot 1996, 277–79.

101. For this title, see DOT, p. 144, no. 777. Shuofang was the name of the military headquarters in the extreme northwest of the empire during the time of the An Lushan Rebellion (755–63). Guo Ziyi was appointed military commander of these headquarters after the end of the rebellion.

102. For this title, see DOT, p. 193, no. 1616.

103. The term used here is *jiasha* 袈裟 (Sk. *kaṣāya*), which is the word for the robe of a Buddhist monk. The emperor's custom of giving the purple *kaṣāya* to Buddhist monks as a mark of special recognition is attested from the end of the seventh century, and shortly afterward was extended to Christian and Manichaean monks.

104. This identification of the "City of the Royal Residence" (*wangshe zhi cheng* 王舍之城) with the western city of the Little Royal Residence (*xiao wangshe cheng* 小王舍城), namely Balkh in the country of Bactria (a region south of the Oxus/Amu Darya River, in today's northern Afghanistan), was first made by the Jesuit Manuel Dias Jr. (Yang Manuo, 1574–1659) in his *Tang jingjiao beisong zhengquan* (Correct Explanation of the Tang *Stele Eulogy of the Luminous Teaching*, 1644), fol. 48b, p. 578. This identification has been ignored by almost all modern translators of the Xi'an stele, who identify the royal residence with the northern Indian city of Rajagṛha (see Pelliot 1996, 80, 280; Deeg 2018b, 190–92). "The close relationship of Jingjing and especially his father Yisi with the Tang court may have prompted the author of the text . . . to emphasise the significance of the place of origin of the family for the sake of the person for whom the inscription was committed in the first place—Jingjing's father (and his grandfather Milis)—as a royal city in the Chinese text, although the glory days of Balkh were long over when the first generation of the family had emigrated to China, which is reflected in the Syriac part of the text where Balkh is just called *medina*. The use of the name then would, in a certain way, reflect and symbolize the Persian Christian family's position in the Tang hierarchy: while the imperial city Chang'an (Khumdan) is called the 'Royal (or Imperial) City' (*medinat malkuta*), the city of origin of Jingjing's/Adam's father Yisi, who held a relatively high position as a direct advisor of the *wang* ('prince') of Fenyang, Guo Ziyi, was appropriately and aptly designated by its well-known Chinese name: the city of the 'Residence of a Prince'" (Deeg 2014, 352–53).

105. The first three Chinese dynasties—Xia, Shang, and Zhou—governed China over a period of about two millennia, ca. 2100–256 BCE.

106. The Red Court (*danting* 丹庭) indicates the Imperial Palace; the princely tent (*wangzhang* 王帳) was the seat, under the Tang, of the military chancellery of a prince during a campaign.

Text A 213

Guo Ziyi,[107] state secretariat director and prince of Fenyang Prefecture, was initially in charge of military operations in Shuofang, Emperor Suzong ordered Yisi to follow him. Although he was admitted to the [emperor's] bedroom, he never differed [from the troops] in their march. He proved to be "claw and tooth" for the duke, and "ear and eye" for the army. He distributed the gifts given to him by the imperial favor as well as his salary, so that he [never] accumulated anything for himself. He offered the glass [jars] of the approaching benefit, and he laid **[25]** the gold [brocade] carpets on which one rests after taking leave. He also brought some monasteries back to their former glory, while he expanded the rooms for worship[108] in others, elegantly decorating their corridors and roofs, [whose inclines] were rising up [toward the sky] like pheasants in flight. By further promoting the Luminous Teaching,[109] he used all his rental income in acts of charity. Each year he gathered the monks of the four monasteries,[110] served them with respect, and presented refined offerings for a period of fifty days. [On that occasion], the hungry ran to him and were satisfied; the naked came to him and were clothed; the sick were cured and **[26]** healed; the dead were buried resting in peace.[111] No one had ever heard of such perfection among the pure

---

This sentence, which introduces the one that follows, means that Yisi/Yazdbōzīd had to give up his duties at court to follow Guo Ziyi in the military campaign.

107. Guo Ziyi (697–781) was one of the most skilled commanders of the Tang dynasty, holding the highest positions during the reigns of Xuanzong, Suzong, and Daizong. He played an important role in the repression of the An Lushan Rebellion by the Tang loyalists. He was given command of the northern divisions (Shuofang) in 764, at the end of the revolt. A biography of Guo Ziyi can be found in *Jiu Tang shu* (Old Annals of the Tang) 120, 15: 3449–67; and *Xin Tang shu* (New Annals of the Tang) 137, fols. 1a–7a (vol. 7).

108. *Fatang* 法堂: lit., "hall of doctrine." A technical Buddhist term (*dharma* hall), it indicates the room where the monastic *saṅgha* gathers to receive the teachings of the abbot. In the text of the stele it is adopted as a stylistic variant and is synonymous with "monastery."

109. *Jingmen*: see p. 206n62.

110. Translators differ in their rendering of the expression *sisi* 四寺: some translate it literally as "four monasteries," as I have done; others think it means "all the monasteries" or "the monasteries scattered in the four directions," and still others translate it as "the surrounding monasteries." The question of identifying Christian monasteries in Chang'an in these centuries still remains open (see pp. 106–16).

111. See Matt. 25:31–46. Some scholars see here an indication of the medical knowledge and surgical activities of the East Syriac Christians in Tang China, with particular reference in this case to Yisi/Yazdbōzīd (see pp. 99–102).

214 THE TEXTS IN TRANSLATION

tarsāg,[112] but now we see such a man among the luminous ministers dressed in white.[113]

To celebrate all these eminent and meritorious events, we wish to engrave on this august stele the following lyrical encomium:[114]

> *To the one who is True Lord without origin,*[115]
> *deeply quiet and eternal.*
> *Commencing with primordial matter, the universe was forged and*
>   *transformed,*
> *the earth established, the sky fixed.*
> *The Distinguished Person was made manifest,*
> *and salvation spread beyond all borders.*
> *The sun arose and the darkness* **[27]** *was destroyed,*[116]
> *and everyone knew the True Mystery.*
>
> *Glorious emperor of cultivated virtues,*[117]
> *[Taizong] surpassed all previous rulers in [sustaining] the Way.*

---

112. *Dasuo* 達娑: phonetic transcription of the Middle Persian term *tarsāg* (New Persian *tarsā*) or the Sogdian term *tarsāk*, meaning "[God] fearer" and used to indicate Christians in Persia and Central Asia.

113. The "luminous ministers" (*jingshi* 景士) are the clerics of the Luminous Teaching, that is the Christian clergy. It seems that at that time the (married) secular clergy dressed in white, while the (celibate) monks dressed in black (see Moffett 1992, 300; Godwin 2017, 109–10).

114. *Ci* 詞: a type of lyric poetry in the tradition of classical Chinese poetry. It uses a set of poetic meters derived from certain basic patterns. Formal types or models are characterized by fixed-rhythm, fixed-tone, and variable line-length. The rhythmic and tonal pattern of the *ci* is based upon set melodies. In the following stanzas we find varying forms of terms and expressions already used in the main section, which is prose. For the several references to the Chinese classics that lie behind these poetic expressions, see Pelliot 1996, 293–308; Deeg 2018b, 209–46. This poetic eulogy (*song*), although appearing at the end of the stele text, is the central element of the honorary inscription. The introduction (*xu*) which precedes the eulogy is some six times as long as the text it is introducing. Thus, it would be appropriate to call it a commentary. Each part of the concluding poetic ode has a corresponding and usually much longer equivalent in the previous section. The only anomaly is the three-column accolade to the Christian military leader, benefactor, and clergyman Yisi who is not mentioned in this poetic eulogy.

115. The same expression (*wuyuan zhenzhu* 無元真主) is found in the *Da Qin jingjiao xuanyuan zhiben jing chuangji* (Note on the Pillar [Inscribed] with the *Book of the Luminous Teaching of Da Qin on Revealing the Origin and Reaching the Foundation*), col. 23, in Nicolini-Zani 2009b, 112.

116. The same expression (*ri sheng an mie* 日昇暗滅) is found in the *Book of the Luminous Teaching of Da Qin on Revealing the Origin and Reaching the Foundation* (Text F, col. P21, p. 303).

117. Here begins an encomium to the glorious works of the various emperors of the Tang dynasty on behalf of the communities of the Church of the East present in China. It takes up and summarizes what had already been said, beginning with the emperor Taizong.

Knowing how to seize the right time, he overcame every disorder,
[so that] the sky became wider and the earth more extensive.
The brilliant Luminous Teaching turned toward our Tang [Empire],
the scriptures were translated and monasteries built.
The living and the dead were transported by the boat [of mercy],[118]
[causing] blessings to descend abundantly, and peace to abound
*   everywhere.*

Gaozong succeeded his predecessor,
and rebuilt the pure buildings.[119]
The palaces of harmony[120] shone everywhere,
and filled every region [28] of China.
The True Way spread its light everywhere,
and a Lord of the Doctrine was appointed.
Happiness and peace reigned among the people,
and the world knew neither misery nor suffering.

Xuanzong increased holiness,
and pursued and fostered truth and integrity.
The imperial inscriptions spread their splendor all around,
and the celestial calligraphies shone in their elegance.
The imperial portraits shone like gems,
and all the lands gave him great honors.
Various activities flourished everywhere,
and everyone benefited from [Xuanzong's] profitable action.

Suzong then restored [the imperial throne],
and the heavenly majesty led [29] the [imperial] procession.
The sacred sun spread its crystalline rays around it,
and the favorable wind swept away the darkness.
Renewed blessings descended upon the royal house,
and the omens of calamity vanished forever.

---

118. *Zhouhang* 舟航: see p. 202n35.

119. *Jingyu* 精宇: this term is close to *jingshe* 精舍, which refers to the "pure abode" for the spiritual cultivation of Daoist or Buddhist practitioners. It is, therefore, a place of meditation for Daoist ascetics or a monastery (Sk. *vihāra*) for Buddhist monks. Here it refers to Christian monasteries or churches. See also the similar term *fuyu* 福宇 (p. 208 and n. 79), which also refers to Christian places of worship.

120. *Hegong* 和宮: like the preceding term, this one also refers to Christian monasteries or churches.

216 THE TEXTS IN TRANSLATION

Riots were quenched and the disorder subsided,
[so that] the empire was finally re-established.

Daizong was a man of great filial piety and exceptional moral righteousness,
and his virtue was united with heaven and earth.
He dispensed benefits for human life and its perfection,
and all creatures were abundantly invested with such excellent favors.
He offered incense to proclaim his meritorious deeds,
and in his benevolence acted as a great benefactor.
The valley of the rising sun came [to pay homage] to his majesty,
and the lunar caverns gathered in great numbers.[121]

In the [present] Jianzhong era [30] our emperor succeeded to the throne,
and from the beginning of his reign he has fostered the illustrious virtues.
The might of his military action extends to the four oceans,
and its erudite action shines on all lands of the world.
Like the light of a candle, it penetrates the innermost part of human beings,
and, as in a mirror, it reflects the appearance of [all] things.
The six regions of the universe[122] are enlightened and enlivened [by his deeds],
and even the barbarian peoples take [his government] as their model.

How vast is the Way, and yet it remains impenetrable in its secrets!
By striving to give it a name, we will employ the expression Three-One.
May that which the Lord has accomplished be [worthily] narrated by
*   his servant!*
With the erection of this noble stele we praise [the Lord] for his
*   bountiful blessings.*

[LOWER PART]

[31] Erected in the second year of the Jianzhong era of the great Tang dynasty, in the year under [the sign] Zuo'e,[123] in the month of

---

121. The valley of the rising sun represents the East, and is the image used to designate the most distant populations in Eastern China. Paralleling this image, the lunar caves represent the West, and therefore the people who came to China from the extreme western regions. The general meaning of this phrase, therefore, is that Daizong's great virtue attracts people to his court from all over the world.

122. The four cardinal points plus the zenith and the nadir.

123. That is the tenth year of Jupiter's cycle, according to the Chinese astrological calendar in use at that time.

Taicu,[124] in the seventh day, day of the great *ēwšambat*.[125] The monk Ningshu, current Lord of the Doctrine,[126] presided over the luminous communities[127] of the East.[128]

[S2] In the days of the father of the fathers, Mar Ḥenanišoʿ, catholicos-patriarch.[129]

---

124. Name of the third of the twelve sound-tubes, corresponding to the first month of the calendar year.

125. *Yaosenwen* 耀森文: phonetic transcription of the Middle Persian term *ēwšambat* (New Persian *yakšambah*) or the Sogdian term *ʾywšmbyd* (*ēwšambid*), meaning "Sunday." The date corresponds to February 4, 781, in the Western calendar.

126. *Fazhu* 法主: for more on this title, see pp. 94–95.

127. *Jingzhong*: see p. 210n92.

128. I.e., the Chinese Empire. Ningshu stands as the approximate Chinese transcription of the Syriac Ḥenanišoʿ. Ningshu/Ḥenanišoʿ is here presented as the higher representative of the Church of the East in China. In the corresponding Syriac passage below, however, he is presented as the catholicos of the whole Church of the East. As suggested by Max Deeg, the reason for such hierarchical "downgrading" of the title belonging to Ningshu/Ḥenanišoʿ and the reduction of his jurisdiction could be that the Christian author wanted to avoid anything in the text of the stele that would give the impression that Christianity had powerful ambitions and would thus be seen as a threat to the strong political and economic power of the Buddhist and the Daoist religious communities. In this context, the official claim to the hierarchical position of a patriarch, who was moreover a resident of the potentially hostile, Abbasid-controlled foreign country (Iran), a position that exceeded the usual Buddhist clerical titles, would have offered sufficient reason for friction. A conflict could be avoided by claiming a comparatively modest position for its own church leader and by assigning to the head of the community of the Luminous Teaching a territory and a jurisdiction that did not exceed the dominion of the Tang emperor (see Deeg 2018b, 247–48).

129. Ḥenanišoʿ II, catholicos of the Church of the East from 773/74 to 779, the year of his death. Since the stele was erected in 781, that is at a time when Timothy I (elected and consecrated in May 780) would have succeeded the office of patriarch, a problem arises: why is Ḥenanišoʿ II still mentioned in the text and not Timothy I? A solution, now considered weak, is that at the time of the writing of the inscription, sometime before February 4, 781, news of the death of Ḥenanišoʿ had not yet arrived in China. Max Deeg has recently offered a more plausible solution, one that takes into account the broad political context and that sees a matter of political and ecclesial convenience, behind this chronological inconsistency: "A disputed patriarch like Timothy I—if this knowledge really had come to China by then—who was supported by the caliph and whose election had created an ongoing schism by the time of the erection of the stele, would probably not have met the acceptance of the Tang imperial court nor have made a vast portion of the Christian Iranian and Central Asian community in China content, some of whom may still have harboured fond memories of the Sasanian past before the Muslim conquest, and some of whom came from a region where there was substantial resistance to the central Abbasid power in Baghdad at the time. . . . This may have triggered or at least encouraged the 'authors' of the stele to put down the name of a patriarch that was already dead at the time of the erection of the stone slab instead of a successor that may not have been fully recognised outside the sphere of influence of the Abbasid caliphate, and by a community whose loyalty, inside China, had to be with the Tang Empire, and who outside China was rather linked to the

218 THE TEXTS IN TRANSLATION

[32] Calligraphy executed by Lü Xiuyan,[130] Court Adviser,[131] formerly acting administrative adjutant of [the prefect of] Taizhou.[132]

[S3] In the year 1092 [S4] of the Greeks[133] Mar Yazdbōzīd, priest [S5] and chorepiscopus of Kumdan,[134] [S6] the Royal City, son of the [S7] late Milis, priest [S8] from Balkh,[135] a city of Taḥurestan,[136] [S9] erected this stone stele [S10] on which are written [S11] the economies of our Savior and the preaching [S12] of our fathers to the emperors [S13] of the Chinese.

[33] Monk Lingbao.

[S14] Adam, deacon, [S15] son of Yazdbōzīd, chorepiscopus; [S16] Mar Sergius, priest and chorepiscopus.

[35] Monk Xingtong, [34] superintendent of the erection of the stele.

[S17] Sabrišoʿ, priest; [S18] Gabriel, priest and archdeacon, [S19] and head of the churches of Kumdan and [S20] Sarag.[137]

[38] Monk Yeli, abbot of the monastery,[138] [37] honored by the purple kaṣāya, [36] probationary master of the [imperial] ceremonies,[139] assistant superintendent [of the erection of the stele].

---

north-eastern Iranian places from where they themselves or their family had hailed than to the church's centre in the heart of the Abbasid caliphate" (Deeg 2016, 248).

130. Since no reference to a Christian office or Syriac name is given, we can assume that Lü Xiuyan was not a Christian, but was chosen and hired for his exceptional calligraphic skills.

131. *Chaoyilang* 朝議郎: honorary title corresponding to the highest class of the highest grade of the sixth mandarin rank. See DOT, p. 118, no. 325, where this title is translated as "Gentleman for Court Discussion."

132. For this title, see DOT, p. 455, no. 5761; pp. 517–18, no. 6876. See also Nie 2016, 99–109.

133. Corresponding to the period from October 1, 780, to September 30, 781.

134. See below, n. 137.

135. See p. 212n104.

136. Syriac rendering of the toponym Tocharistan (also known in Syriac sources as Bet Taḥoraye), the name by which the region of Balkh (the ancient Bactria) was designated in these centuries.

137. Kumdan and Sarag are the Sogdian names—ʾxwmtʾn or ɣwmtʾn (*axumdān*) and *sry* (*saragh*), here rendered in Syriac—of the two capitals of the Tang Empire: Chang'an, the western capital, and Luo (or Luoyang), the eastern capital.

138. *Sizhu* 寺主: lit., "lord of the monastery" (Sk. *vihārasvāmin*), is the common term in Chinese Buddhism to indicate the post of abbot, the leader of the monastic community.

139. For this title, see DOT, p. 476, no. 6138, where this title is translated as "chamberlain for ceremonials."

Text A

[*LEFT SIDE*]

[**S21**] Mar John, bishop[140] [**39**] Great Virtuous Yaolun

[**S22**] Isaac, priest [**40**] Monk Rijin

[**S23**] Joel, priest [**41**] Monk Yaoyue

[**S24**] Michael, priest [**42**] Monk Guangqing

[**S25**] George, priest [**43**] Monk Heji

[**S26**] Mahdadgušnasp,[141] priest [**44**] Monk Huiming

[**S27**] Mšiḥadad,[142] priest [**45**] Monk Baoda

[**S28**] Ephrem, priest [**46**] Monk Fulin

[**S29**] Abay,[143] priest

[**S30**] David, priest

[**S31**] Moses, priest [**47**] Monk Fushou

[**S32**] Bacchus, priest [and] monk [**48**] Monk Chongjing

[**S33**] Elijah, priest [and] monk [**49**] Monk Yanhe

[**S33**] Moses, priest and monk

[**S34**] ʿAbdišoʿ, priest and monk

[**S35**] Simeon, priest of the tomb[144]

[**S36**] John, deacon and monk [**50**] Monk Huitong

[**S37**] Aaron [**51**] Monk Qianyou

[**S38**] Peter [**52**] Monk Yuanyi

[**S39**] Job [**53**] Monk Jingde

[**S40**] Luke [**54**] Monk Lijian

[**S41**] Matthew [**55**] Monk Mingtai

---

140. On top of the Syriac and Chinese names on the left side of the stele is inscribed the following text in Chinese: "One thousand and seventy-nine years later, in the Jiwei year of the Xianfeng era [1859], I, Han Taihua of Wulin [Hangzhou], came and saw [this stele]. Fortunately, the lettering is still perfect. I rebuilt the pavilion that houses the stele. Sadly, my late friend, the treasurer Wu Zibi, was unable to accompany me on my travels, which I greatly regret."

141. Middle Persian name of Zoroastrian origin. For a discussion of this and other Middle Persian and "composite" Syriac-Middle Persian names, which point to the Iranian origins of several of the clerics mentioned in this list, see Hunter 2009b, 80–81; 2010.

142. Syriac-Middle Persian compound name (whose meaning is "given by the Messiah"), not common in the Church of the East.

143. Name of Iranian origin.

144. Cemetery caretaker seems to be the most plausible interpretation of this designation.

THE TEXTS IN TRANSLATION

[S42] John [56] Monk Xuanzhen

[S43] Išoʿemmeh[145] [57] Monk Renhui

[S44] John [58] Monk Yaoyuan

[S45] Sabrišoʿ[146] [59] Monk Zhaode

[S46] Išoʿdad[147] [60] Monk Wenming

[S47] Luke [61] Monk Wenzhen

[S48] Constantine [62] Monk Juxin

[S49] Noah [63] Monk Laiwei

[S50] Izadspas[148] [64] Monk Jingzhen

[S51] John [65] Monk Huanchun

[S52] Anoš [66] Monk Lingshou

[S53] Mar Sergius [67] Monk Lingde

[S54] Isaac [68] Monk Yingde

[S55] John [69] Monk Chonghe

[S56] Mar Sergius [70] Monk Ningxu

[S57] Pusay[149] [71] Monk Puji

[S58] Simeon [72] Monk Wenshun

[S59] Isaac [73] Monk Guangji

[S60] John [74] Monk Shouyi

[RIGHT SIDE]

[S61] Jacob, priest [75] Elder[150] Yejumo

[S62] Mar Sergius, priest and chorepiscopus, "High-seated"[151] [76] Monk Jingtong

---

145. Syriac compound name that means "Jesus with him."

146. A very common Syriac name that means "hope of Jesus."

147. Syriac-Middle Persian compound name that means "given by Jesus."

148. Middle Persian name.

149. Name of Iranian origin that was very common in the Church of the East.

150. *Laosu* 老宿: a title that in Buddhism indicates an elderly and eminent monk (Sk. *sthavira*).

151. The Syriac term *ši'angtswa* seems to be the transcription of the Chinese *shangzuo* 上座, lit., "the one who sits on high" (Sk. *sthavira*); see p. 93.

Text A 221

[S63] Gigoy,[152] priest and archdeacon of Kumdan, and reading master [77] Monk Xuanlan

[S64] Paul, priest [78] Monk Baoling

[S65] Samson, priest [79] Monk Shenshen

[S66] Adam, priest [80] Monk Fayuan

[S67] Elijah, priest [81] Monk Liben

[S68] Isaac, priest [82] Monk Heming

[S69] John, priest [83] Monk Guangzheng

[S70] John, priest [84] Monk Neicheng

[S71] Simeon, priest and elder

[S72] Jacob, sacristan [85] Monk Chongde

[S73] ʿAbdišoʿ [86] Monk Taihe

[S74] Išoʿdad [87] Monk Jingfu

[S75] Jacob [88] Monk Heguang

[S76] John [89] Monk Zhide

[S77] Šubḥalmaran[153] [90] Monk Fengzhen

[S78] Mar Sergius [91] Monk Yuanzong

[S79] Simeon [92] Monk Liyong

[S80] Ephrem [93] Monk Xuande

[S81] Zechariah [94] [Monk] Yiji

[S82] Cyriacus [95] Monk Zhijian

[S83] Bacchus [96] Monk Baoguo

[S84] Emmanuel [97] Monk Mingyi

[S85] Gabriel [98] Monk Guangde

[S86] John

[S87] Salomon [99] Monk Qushen

[S88] Isaac

[S89] John [100] Monk Dejian

---

152. Name of Iranian origin.

153. Syriac compound name that means "glory/praise to our Lord."

TEXT B

1. Hymn in Praise of the Salvation Achieved through the Three Majesties of the Luminous Teaching (*Jingjiao sanwei mengdu zan* 景教三威蒙度讚)

[2] THE HIGHEST heavens adore thee with deep deference,

the whole earth meditates continuously on thy universal peace and harmony.
Human beings, in their original [3] *true nature, find in thee support and rest,*
God,[1] Merciful Father of the three domains.[2]

All who are good[3] [4] *honor thee in perfect sincerity,*
all who have wisdom[4] raise hymns and songs of praise to thee.

---

1. *Aluohe* 阿羅訶: phonetic transcription of the Syriac term *Alāhā*. It is also found in the text of the Xi'an stele (Text A, col. 3, p. 198), of the *Book of the Honored* (Text B.2, col. 2, p. 226), and of the *Book of the Luminous Teaching of Da Qin on Revealing the Origin and Reaching the Foundation* (Text F, cols. 11/P7 and 18/P10, pp. 300 and 301).

2. *Sancai* 三才: technical term that indicates the three domains of creation, that is, heaven, earth, and humanity, invoked in the three previous verses and summarized here in a single expression.

3. *Shanzhong* 善眾: lit., "the good," "the multitude of the good"; it is a Buddhist term for those who adhere to the law of the Buddha.

4. *Huixing* 慧性: lit., "[those endowed with] a wise/intelligent nature"; in the Buddhist tradition the term (Sk. *prajñāsvabhāva*) indicates those who, enlightened, possess true understanding and true discernment about the essence of reality.

The Luminous Way to the East. Matteo Nicolini-Zani, Oxford University Press. © Oxford University Press 2022.
DOI: 10.1093/oso/9780197609644.003.0006

All those who are in truth unanimously turn to thee,

[5] *so that, in receiving thy holy and merciful light, they may be saved and freed from the evil one.*[5]

Unfathomable and inaccessible, immutable in thy reality,

[6] *Merciful Father, Bright Son, Pure Spirit, King.*[6]

In the midst of all the sovereigns thou art Master and Supreme Sovereign,

[7] *of all the Honored Ones of the Universe, thou art the Emperor of the Doctrine.*[7]

From thy eternal dwelling thou canst mysteriously illuminate that which is infinite,[8]

[8] *with thy shining majesty, penetrate that which is finished.*[9]

No human being has yet been able to contemplate thee,

[9] *and never will be able to see thy real image through apparent forms.*

Thou alone art absolute depth, pure power,

[10] *thou alone art divine majesty, unparalleled strength.*

Thou alone art immutable, always the same,

[11] *thou art the root of all goodness, thy bounty is infinite.*

---

5. *Mo* 魔: the spirit of evil, the devil.

6. The epithets *cifu* 慈父, "Merciful Father," *mingzi* 明子, "Bright Son," and *jingfeng* 淨風, "Pure Spirit" that make up this triple invocation can also be found in some contemporary Manichaean hymns (see Bryder 1985, 88–90; DMTC, 11, 45). To be noted in particular is the use of the expression *jingfeng* to define the Holy Spirit (see also Text A, col. 7, p. 201 and n. 30), which in the Manichaean texts is frequently attested in the variant *jing fafeng* 淨法風, "Pure Spirit of the Doctrine" (see DMTC, 34). In the Chinese Manichaean *Hymnscroll* the whole tripartite formula *Cifu, mingzi, jing fafeng*, "Merciful Father, Bright Son, Pure Spirit of the Doctrine" occurs twice (see DMTC, 11). Within this verse, it is difficult to interpret the title *wang* 王, "king." Most translators attribute it only to the Pure Spirit. For my part, I think that the title refers rather to the whole Trinity, to which majesty is attributed.

7. The last two verses make abundant use of Buddhist terminology.

8. *Wu panjie* 無畔界: lit., "without boundaries." In Buddhist thought it indicates the world of intangibility.

9. *You jiejiang* 有界壃: lit., "with boundaries." In Buddhist thought, it indicates the world of tangibility. The meaning of these two verses is clear: God, despite living in a mysterious and inaccessible light, reaches, by means of the divine shining majesty, every reality, visible and invisible, material and spiritual.

Now we all meditate[10] on thy mercy and grace,
and we call upon thee [12] that this marvelous joy [which is with thee] may
   enlighten this land.
Messiah, most holy Son, Honored One of the Universe,[11]
[13] thou, through this world of pain, hast saved countless beings.

King of eternal life, merciful and blessed Lamb,
[14] to repel all the pain [of the world], thou hast not rejected suffering.
Wanting to redeem the accumulated sins of all living beings,[12]
[15] goodness has returned to being part of true human nature, which has
   [thus] been able to be freed [from evil].[13]

Holy Son, who worthily sits on the throne at the right hand of the Father,[14]
[16] thy throne is so sublime that nothing can surpass it.
Great Master,[15] we implore thee: listen to the pleas of all,
and send [17] [thy] boat[16] from above that we may not be swept away by the
   river of fire.[17]

---

10. *Nian* 念: lit., "recognize," "remember."

11. *Shizun* 世尊: for an explanation of this title, see p. 250n87.

12. These three verses are undoubtedly modeled on the description of the Messiah as a suffering servant in Isaiah 53.

13. The verse, in its totality, is a remarkable expression of the Christian doctrine of redemption, using biblical images as well as expressions and ideas that are typically Buddhist. In particular, liberation from the law of evil recalls the work of the Buddha, who put forth the way of enlightenment as the means to escape the cycle of *karman* (for an explication of this term, see p. 278n95). It is interesting to compare this verse with the part of the inscription on the Xi'an stele in which the redemptive action of the Messiah is spoken of (Text A, cols. 6–8, pp. 200–2).

14. Cf. Ps. 110:1, which is cited in the New Testament (Rom. 8:34; Heb. 10:12; 1 Pet. 3:22; etc.).

15. *Dashi* 大師: this title, which occurs six times in the text, is attributed in Buddhist literature to a buddha or a bodhisattva.

16. The same image occurs twice in the text of the Xi'an stele (Text A, col. 8, p. 202; col. 27, p. 215), with the difference that the Chinese term used here is different (*fa* 栿) and properly means "raft." In Buddhist literature, the raft is a metaphor for the teaching of the Buddha, which takes people from ignorance to enlightenment. Moreover, the bodhisattva Guanyin (Avalokiteśvara) is often presented at the helm of a boat, in the act of saving people, transporting them from the world of suffering to that of bliss. However, "this symbol may come from the images of Syriac Christianity" (Ferreira 2014, 276n55), since "the image of the raft of salvation is also very prominent in Syriac Christianity" (ibid., 329).

17. In the Bible, fire is often a metaphor for the wrath of God that flares and burns as well as for the tribulations that beset people. It is also a sign of eschatological judgment. In Buddhism,

Great Master, thou art our Merciful Father,
Great Master, [18] thou art our Holy Lord.
Great Master, thou art our King of the Doctrine,
Great Master, thou canst [19] save the whole world.

Great Master, the power of thy wisdom[18] will help all the weary,
[so] the eyes of all are reverently turned to thee, never [20] having looked
  away from thee.
Send thy sweet dew from above over what is dried up and
  shriveled,[19]
so that everything be drenched in it, and [21] the root of good draw
  nourishment from it.

[Through] the Messiah, the most holy Honored One of the Universe,
we invoke the mercy of the compassionate Father, [22] [extended] like the
  sea,
in the most holy Spirit, whose nature is discreet and pure,
whose doctrine, clear and profound, [23] surpasses all understanding.

[24] "Hymn in Praise[20] of the Salvation Achieved[21] through the Three
  Majesties[22] of the Luminous Teaching of Da Qin, in One Scroll."[23]

---

as in many other religious traditions, fire is the constituent element of hell, where the damned are tormented. It is therefore closely connected with the symbolic complex of destruction, evil, and punishment. The similar metaphor of "the sea of fire" (*huohai* 火海) is well attested in the contemporary Chinese Manichaean literature (see DMTC, 29; Kósa 2011).

18. *Huili* 慧力: a Buddhist term (Sk. *prajñābala*) that indicates the power of true intelligence, the strength that comes from the knowledge of the true reality of the world.

19. In the biblical tradition dew and rain are symbols of God's saving intervention (cf. Deut. 32:2; Ps. 72:4; Isa. 45:8; Hos. 6:3). The symbol of water (or dew, rain, etc.) is also used as a positive metaphor in the Syriac Christian writings, where it denotes enlightenment and salvation (see Ferreira 2014, 329–30). For a parallel image found in the Chinese Daoist medieval text *Taixuan zhenyi benji jing*, which was very much influenced by Buddhism, see Chen Huaiyu 2020, 103.

20. *Zan* 讚: the literary genre of the *zan*, "hymn of praise" (Sk. *stotra*), is attested in other manuscripts found in Dunhuang. The meter is that of seven characters for each line, for a total of forty-four lines.

21. *Mengdu* 蒙度: this Buddhist term, in its meaning of "obtaining liberation," "receiving salvation," is here spoken of as the result of the action of the Trinity invoked in this hymn.

22. *Sanwei* 三威: an expression clearly allusive to the Trinity.

23. *Juan* 卷: a division of a traditional Chinese manuscript or book.

2. Book of the Honored (*Zunjing* 尊經)

[2] Let us reverently pay homage to:

God,[24] *Transcendent Person,*[25] *Supreme Father,*
the Messiah, Manifest Person,[26] *Son of the Most High,*
[3] *the Holy Spirit,*[27] *Testifying Person.*[28]
　　　　　　　— These three persons[29] consist of one substance.[30]

[4] *The King of the Doctrine*[31] *John,*[32]
the King of the Doctrine Luke,[33]

---

24. *Aluohe* 阿羅訶: Chinese phonetic transcription of the Syriac word *Alāhā*. It is also found in the text of the Xi'an stele (Text A, col. 3, p. 198), of the *Hymn in Praise of the Salvation Achieved through the Three Majesties of the Luminous Teaching* (Text B.1, col. 3, p. 222), and of the *Book of the Luminous Teaching of Da Qin on Revealing the Origin and Reaching the Foundation* (Text F, cols. 11/P7 and 18/P10, pp. 300 and 301).

25. *Miaoshen* 妙身: lit., "mysterious body." It indicates the unknowable, absolute quality of the person of God the Father. In Chinese Buddhist literature the character for *miao*, "mysterious," "inconceivable," "wonderful," or "excellent," often denotes the quality of a buddha or of everything that has to do with the dimension of Buddhahood.

26. *Yingshen* 應身: lit., "response body." In Buddhist texts it is the Chinese term that translates the Sanskrit *nirmāṇakāya*, "transformation body," and indicates the body through which the Buddha manifests himself to living beings; an example of *nirmāṇakāya* is the very Buddha Śākyamuni. Here it was adopted by Christians to refer to Jesus Christ, in whose body, through the incarnation, God was made manifest to people in compassionate response to their situation of sin and for their salvation (see Zhu Donghua 2013, 2016c).

27. *Luhe ningjusha* 盧訶寧俱沙: phonetic transcription of the Syriac *ruḥā d-qudšā*.

28. *Zhengshen* 證身: lit., "testifying body."

29. *Sanshen* 三身: the terminology used here to describe the three persons of the Trinity clearly reflects the tripartition of the Buddha's body (Sk. *trikāya*)—*fashen* 法身 (Sk. *dharmakāya*), *yingshen* 應身 or *huashen* 化身 (Sk. *nirmāṇakāya*), and *baoshen* 報身 (Sk. *saṃbhogakāya*)—but introduces significant lexical variants that reflect differences in theological content.

30. *Ti* 體: the Chinese word used here is also used in Buddhism to designate the substantial essence of all realities. In the manuscript this sentence is written in smaller characters than the previous ones and appears as a sort of gloss, an explanatory note on the previous doxology.

31. *Fawang* 法王: this title, used in Buddhist literature as an epithet for a buddha (Sk. *dharmarāja*), here seems to translate the Christian title of "saint." It is a title also used in contemporary Manichaean literature in Chinese (see DMTC, 19; Wang Yuanyuan 2013b).

32. *Yuhannan* 瑜罕難: phonetic transcription of the Syriac name Yoḥanan.

33. *Lujia* 盧伽: phonetic transcription of the Syriac name Luqa.

the King of the Doctrine Mark,[34]
the King of the Doctrine Matthew,[35]
[5] the King of the Doctrine Moses,[36]
the King of the Doctrine David,[37]
the King of the Doctrine Jingtong,[38]
the King of the Doctrine Paul,[39]
[6] the King of the Doctrine Qianyan,[40]
the King of the Doctrine Daniel,[41]
the Queen of the Doctrine Mary,[42]
the King of the Doctrine Mar Sergius,[43]
[7] the King of the Doctrine George,[44]
the King of the Doctrine Mar Bacchus,[45]
the King of the Doctrine Simon Peter,[46]
the twenty-four Holy Kings of the Doctrine,[47]

---

34. *Mojuci* 摩矩辭: phonetic transcription of the Syriac name Marqos.

35. *Mingtai* 明泰: phonetic transcription of the Syriac name Mattay.

36. *Moushi* 牟世: phonetic transcription of the Syriac name Moše.

37. *Duohui* 多惠: phonetic transcription of the Syriac name Dawid.

38. *Jingtong* 景通: Buddhist-style epithet that occurs also in the *Book of the Luminous Teaching of Da Qin on Revealing the Origin and Reaching the Foundation* (Text F, cols. 2/P4, 6/P6, and P19; pp. 298, 299, and 303) and in the text of the Xi'an stele, where it is the Chinese name of a Mar Sergius (Text A, col. 76, p. 220). To whom it refers is not clear.

39. *Baolu* 寶路: phonetic transcription of the Syriac name Pawlos.

40. *Qianyan* 千眼: lit., "Thousand Eyes." The identification of this individual is not clear. Perhaps Qianyan refers to the seraphim, since in Christian literature they are often described this way.

41. *Nuoningyi* 郍寧逸: phonetic transcription of the Syriac name Dani'el.

42. *Minyan* 珉艷: perhaps the phonetic transcription of the Syriac name Maryam (or its correspondent Sogdian form, modeled on the Syriac). The identification remains doubtful, since the Chinese masculine title *fawang* would not really suit a female figure.

43. *Mo Sajisi* 摩薩吉思: phonetic transcription of the Syriac name Mar Sargis.

44. *Yihejisi* 宜和吉思: phonetic transcription of the Syriac name Giwargis.

45. *Mo Meijisi* 摩沒吉思: phonetic transcription of the Syriac name Mar Bakkos. Sergius, George, and Bacchus are likely to have been the holy martyrs who died in 303 under the persecution of Maximian (286–305).

46. *Cenwen seng* 岑穩僧: see p. 283n11.

47. As in the text of the Xi'an stele (Text A, col. 7, p. 201), here too the number of saints could correspond to the twenty-four authors of the books of the Old Testament.

228   THE TEXTS IN TRANSLATION

[8] *the King of the Doctrine Hananiah,*[48]
[the King of] the Doctrine Azariah,[49]
the King of the Doctrine Mishael,[50]
the Queen of the Doctrine Sarah,[51]
[9] *the King of the Doctrine Cyrus,*[52]
the King of the Doctrine Baoxin.[53]

[10] *Let us reverently pay homage to:*

the "Book on the Eternal Light and the Excellent Joy,"[54]
the "Book on Revealing the Origin and Reaching the Foundation,"[55]
the "Book on Profound and Mysterious Blessedness,"[56]
[11] *the "Collection of Heavenly Treasures,"*[57]
the "Book of the Holy King David,"[58]
the "Book of the Gospels,"[59]

---

48. *Xiannanye* 憲難耶: phonetic transcription of the Syriac name Ḥananya.

49. *Hesaye* 賀薩耶: phonetic transcription of the Syriac name ʿAzarya.

50. *Mishaye* 彌沙曳: phonetic transcription of the Syriac name Mišaʿel.

51. *Suoluo* 娑羅: perhaps the phonetic transcription of the Syriac name Sara. The Sarah intended here may be the fourth-century (?) Persian martyr and sister of Behnām rather than the biblical wife of Abraham. Her identification with the Persian martyr remains doubtful for the reasons given at p. 227n42.

52. *Qulu* 瞿盧: phonetic transcription of the Syriac name Qureš or Qiyore. A possible identification could be the sixth-century East Syriac author Cyrus of Edessa.

53. *Baoxin* 報信: lit., "the Announcer [of the Gospel]," that is, "the Evangelizer." It could be Addai, the great evangelizer of Edessa (first to second century).

54. *Changming huangle jing* 常明皇樂經.

55. *Xuanyuan zhiben jing* 宣元至本經: a text with a similar title, the *Da Qin jingjiao xuanyuan zhiben jing* 大秦景教宣元至本經 (Book of the Luminous Teaching of Da Qin on Revealing the Origin and Reaching the Foundation), has come down to us (Text F).

56. *Zhixuan anle jing* 志玄安樂經: a document with the same title has come down to us (Text E).

57. *Tianbao cang jing* 天寶藏經: this may be the breviary, the book that contains the liturgical compositions for the office of vigils, called *Gazā*, which means "treasure." Another possibility is that the *Collection of Heavenly Treasures* refers to the *Cave of Treasures*, or to the *Book of Treasures*, attributed to Barḥadbšabba ʿArbaya (sixth century) and listed by ʿAbdišoʿ of Nisibis in his *Catalogue of Authors* (late thirteenth century), trans. Badger, 2: 372.

58. *Duohui shengwang jing* 多惠聖王經: this could be the book of Psalms, whose composition is traditionally attributed to King David.

59. *Aenqulirong jing* 阿恩瞿利容經: *aenqulirong* could be the phonetic transcription of the Syriac *ewangelyōn* (correcting *si* 思 in the original manuscript with *en* 恩).

Text B
229

[**12**] *the "Book of the Origins,"*[60]
the "Book on the Penetration of the Truth,"[61]
the "Book on the Precious Light,"[62]
the "Book of Traditions,"[63]
the "Book on the Radical Renunciation,"[64]
[**13**] *the "Book on the Original Spiritual [Life],"*[65]
the "Compendium,"[66]
the "Book on the Three Steps,"[67]
the "Book on Demonstrations,"[68]

---

60. *Hunyuan jing* 渾元經: *hunyuan* is traditionally defined as "the *qi* 氣 of the sky of the earth," that is, the vital principle within all creation, present since the origin of the world. This same term is present at the beginning of the text of the Xi'an stele, where it describes human beings in their original nature (Text A, col. 4, p. 199). The *Book of the Origins* could therefore mean the book of Genesis.

61. *Tongzhen jing* 通真經.

62. *Baoming jing* 寶明經.

63. *Chuanhua jing* 傳化經: could refer to apostolic traditions, and thus identify the Acts of the Apostles or works such as the *Apostolic Constitutions*.

64. *Qingyi jing* 磬遺經: in the text of the Xi'an stele (Text A, col. 9, p. 203), in a descriptive passage on the way of life of Christian monks, the same expression used here (*qingyi*) recurs. For Christians in Tang China it must therefore have been a technical term.

65. *Yuanling jing* 原靈經.

66. *Shulüe jing* 述略經: this could indicate a catechism, given that many Syriac authors wrote works of this kind.

67. *Sanji jing* 三際經: the oft-repeated and almost unanimously accepted thesis is that this is a Manichaean text (abbreviated form for *Erzong sanji jing* 二宗三際經, "Book on the Two Principles and Three Times"; see DMTC, 18), since the Manichaean doctrine is strongly based on a cosmogony and a soteriology in three times. Following Yang Senfu (1971) and Lin Wushu (2011d, 141–43), I believe that the presence here of a Manichaean text is difficult to justify and we should regard it as a Christian scripture. Since different references to this theme of the "three steps" can be found in the Christian tradition, I think it is useful to note the following two points. First of all, in some ascetic-spiritual Christian texts of the Syriac tradition, the spiritual life is described as a journey in three moments (the finding of an anonymous Christian fragment in the Sogdian language indicates that texts on this subject were translated in Central Asia: see Sims-Williams 1981). Moreover, many of the great East Syriac spiritual authors (e.g., John the Solitary, Simon of Ṭaibutheh, Isaac of Nineveh, Joseph Ḥazzaya, Dadišoʿ Qaṭraya) speak of three "orders" (*ṭakse*) or "steps" (*mušḥātā*) of the spiritual life: corporal, psychic, and spiritual (see Beulay [1987], 95–125). Since there is no reason to doubt that the Chinese work in question deals with this subject, I therefore believe that the work in question may be the *Liber graduum* or *The Three Steps of the Monastic Life* by Joseph Ḥazzaya.

68. *Zhengjie jing* 徵詰經: this could be the twenty-three *Demonstrations* of Aphrahat, the Persian Sage (first half of the fourth century).

the *"Book on the Mastery of Thoughts,"* [69]

[**14**] the *"Book on the Disclosure of the Meaning,"* [70]

the *"Book of the Apostles,"* [71]

the *"Book of the King of the Doctrine Paul,"* [72]

the *"Book of Zechariah,"* [73]

[**15**] the *"Book of Gregory,"* [74]

the *"Book of Testament,"* [75]

the *"Disciplinary Book of Rules,"* [76]

the *"Book of Benedictions,"* [77]

[**16**] the *"Hymn to the Three Majesties,"* [78]

the *"Book of the King of the Doctrine Moses,"* [79]

---

69. *Ningsi jing* 寧思經: this could be a work on combating evil thoughts, such as, for example, the *Antirrhetikos* of Evagrius Ponticus, which was translated into Syriac. Some fragments of it have come down to us in the Sogdian language (see p. 42).

70. *Xuanyi jing* 宣義經.

71. *Shilihai jing* 師利海經: *shilihai* is a phonetic transcription of the Syriac *šlīḥā* (apostle). It could refer to the Acts of the Apostles or to a liturgical book, since in the Church of the East the lectionary containing the readings from the Epistles is called the "Apostles" (*Šlīḥe*).

72. *Baolu fawang jing* 寶路法王經: this could be a way of identifying the Pauline corpus.

73. *Shanhelu jing* 刪訶律經: *Shanhelu* is probably a phonetic transcription of the Syriac name Zkariya. Rather than a reference to the Old Testament prophet, this Zechariah could perhaps be Zechariah the Rhetor (end of the fifth century), who was then bishop of Mytilene and author of a *Church History*.

74. *Yiliyuesi jing* 藝利月思經: *Yiliyuesi* could be the phonetic transcription of the Syriac name Grigoriyos. However, in the absence of additional information, it is difficult to determine which Gregory is being referred to. A possible candidate would be Gregory of Nazianzus, whose works are known to have been translated into Syriac, and who, of the three Greek Fathers by the name of Gregory (i.e., Gregory of Nazianzus, Gregory of Nyssa, and Gregory Thaumaturgus), is the one most frequently cited by authors of the Church of the East.

75. *Ningyeyi jing* 寧耶頤經: *ningyeyi* could be the phonetic transcription of the Syriac *diyaṭiqi*, "covenant" or "testament."

76. *Yize lüjing* 儀則律經: the reference could be to monastic rules. However, it could also be a phonetic transcription of an unidentified Syriac term.

77. *Pi'eqi jing* 毗遏啟經: a possible phonetic transcription of the Syriac *brāke*. It is plausible that it is a liturgical book.

78. *Sanwei zanjing* 三威讚經: the hymn that constitutes the first part of this manuscript P. 3847 (*Jingjiao sanwei mengdu zan* 景教三威蒙度讚) is most probably the work mentioned here.

79. *Moushi fawang jing* 牟世法王經: a possible reference to the Pentateuch, the composition of which is traditionally attributed to Moses.

the "Book of Elijah," [80]
the "Book of Ephrem," [81]
[**17**] the "Book of the King of the Doctrine Baoxin," [82]
the "Book of the Messiah, the Almighty in Heaven and on Earth," [83]
the "Tetrabiblos," [84]
the "Book on the Revelation of the Truth," [85]
[**18**] the "Book of Mar Sergius," [86]
the "Book of the Cross," [87]
the "Book of the Hosannas." [88]

— [**19**] A careful examination of the catalogue of all the writings shows that the writings of this teaching of Da Qin number one hundred and thirty in total and are written on *pattra*[89] in a foreign language.[90] [**20**] In the ninth year of the Zhenguan era of the emperor Taizong of the Tang [635], the monk Aluoben, "Great Virtuous One" of the western lands, arrived in China and humbly presented a petition [**21**] to

---

80. *Yiliye jing* 伊利耶經: *Yiliye* is the phonetic transcription of the Syriac name Eliya. It is not clear who is being identified (the biblical Elijah, Elijah of Nisibis, or Elijah of Merv?).

81. *Efulin jing* 遏拂林經: *Efulin* is a phonetic transcription of the Syriac name Aprem. It is likely to be Ephrem the Syrian (306–73), one of the greatest spiritual authors of the Church of the East.

82. *Baoxin fawang jing* 報信法王經: see p. 228n53. This work could be identified with the *Doctrine of Addai* or the *Acts of Addai*.

83. *Mishihe zizai tiandi jing* 彌施訶自在天地經: probably a work of Christology. Note the use here of the Buddhist technical term *zizai*, which is generally rendered "omnipotent," but which is difficult to translate. It indicates the ability of a buddha to pervade all of reality thanks to his supernatural powers, which are derived from his attained perception of true reality.

84. *Simen jing* 四門經: Ptolemy's *Tetrabiblos*, translated from Greek into Syriac by Severus Sebokt, is the most plausible identification.

85. *Qizhen jing* 啓真經.

86. *Mo Sajisi jing* 摩薩吉思經: see p. 227n43. The work alluded to could be the *Acts of Sergius and Bacchus*.

87. *Cilipo jing* 慈利波經: *cilipo* is a phonetic transcription of the Syriac *ṣlibā*, "cross." This work could be one of the stories about the events surrounding the Cross of Christ (a fragment of the legend of the finding of the Holy Cross is significantly attested in Sogdian: see p. 42) or a liturgical book for Holy Week.

88. *Wushana jing* 烏沙那經: this could be a liturgical book for the liturgy of Palm Sunday, called "Hosanna (*ušaʿna*) Sunday" in the Church of the East.

89. See p. 148n104.

90. See p. 148n105.

232   THE TEXTS IN TRANSLATION

the imperial throne in his native language. Fang Xuanling and Wei Zheng[91] had the petition translated. In consequence, by imperial decree, the monk Jingjing, "Great Virtuous One" of that teaching, was summoned [to court] [22] and the thirty scrolls mentioned above were produced. The large number of the remaining [writings], contained in *pattra* manuscripts, have not yet been translated.[92]

---

91. According to his biography contained in *Jiu Tang shu* (Old Annals of the Tang) 71, 8: 2545–63, Wei Zheng (d. 642/43) was appointed by Taizong first Assistant Director of the Left in the Department of State Affairs (*shangshu zuocheng* 尚書佐丞, see DOT, p. 412, no. 5053; p. 522, no. 6951) in 627 and then Director of the Palace Library (*bishu jian* 秘書監, see DOT, pp. 376–77, no. 4588) in 628.

92. This paragraph is a sort of final annotation, a gloss on the list of "the thirty scrolls mentioned above."

TEXT C

Discourse on the One God
(*Yishen lun* 一神論)

I. Discourse on the One Godhead
(*Yitian lun diyi* 一天論第一)

[**61**] Question[1]: "What did human beings create?" Answer: "Of both visible and invisible things, [**62**] what could ever have been created [by humans]? The visible things, that is, those created from the four elements—earth, water, [**63**] fire, and air—were all created by the power of God."[2]

Question: "What was created [from] the four elements?" Answer: [**64**] "There is nothing in the world that has not been created [from them], and there is nothing that has not been created by the One God; [though] the One God is not [**65**] of this world,[3] nor is he subordinate to the world,[4] as [is the

---

1. The manuscript does not have an initial title, but it can be deduced from what is indicated at the end of the manuscript. The three sections that make up the manuscript are arranged in the following order:

    I. "Discourse on the One Godhead" (cols. 61–206);

    II. "Metaphorical Teaching" (cols. 1–60);

    III. "Discourse of the Honored One of the Universe on Almsgiving" (cols. 207–405).

The relationship between the parts is not clear nor is the reason why they follow one another in this order in the original manuscript. It may perhaps have been an assembly error on the part of the scribe. In my translation I have arranged the parts in what I suppose to have been the most likely original order. The title of this first section, not present in the manuscript, can be deduced from what is indicated at the end of the section.

2. The "power of God" or "divine power" (*shenli* 神力) is the dominant theme of the following portion of the text.

3. Lit., "is not in the world."

4. Lit., "he does not seek the world."

The Luminous Way to the East. Matteo Nicolini-Zani, Oxford University Press. © Oxford University Press 2022.
DOI: 10.1093/oso/9780197609644.003.0007

234 THE TEXTS IN TRANSLATION

case] with someone who wants to build a house; such a person is subordinate first of all [66] to the place where it is to be built. The One God accomplishes [everything] he wants."

The One God is visible in the world [67] in his compassion for all living beings; he is clearly recognizable in his mercy for [all] living creatures. In the heavens, on the earth, and [68] in [all] that he has created one can discern the One God.

Divine power, in its volition, is like the wind: it has no body or [69] spirit,[5] and therefore cannot be seen at all by the human eye; yet what divine power commands and disposes of [70] can be known by all. No other being acts like this: what other being, then, is like him? If most [71] realities exist in a stable way, it is because the One God supports the world with divine power. Living creatures, such as insects, deer, [etc.], [72] cannot communicate in words nor do they have intelligence, so it is [only] through that [divine power that they can subsist].

Think of any reality: a second reality will share with this first one [its divine origin], [73] and a third one will share [the same divine origin] with the second, [and so on]. Therefore, although [the different realities of] the world are not similar, they cannot be considered independent of each other. [And yet], people doubt this, and in their mind think [74] that there are different gods who have created the different visible realities and made them distinct. But [if it is stated that] there are such gods, who would then have created the different realities [75] that are not distinctly visible? [They say] that it would be the different gods who [also] created the different realities that were not clearly visible.

Therefore, [76] multiple realities can be traced back to only two typologies: the visible ones and the invisible ones, and this can be clearly discerned by everyone. Thus, for example, [77] there are two types of humans: one can be spoken of, the other not.[6] [78] There are not however two types of gods: a God who would have made human beings and a God of whom one could not speak. And although the world [79] makes a distinction between two types of gods, [in reality] a single God has created

---

5. The comparison with the wind, also present in the *Book of the Lord Messiah* (Text D, cols. 6–7 and 11–15, pp. 266–67), aims to make the transcendent character of the presence and will of God comprehensible through an image. For the same purpose—that is, to describe the immaterial nature of God—the expression "has no body or spirit" was also chosen.

6. Philologically, at this point the text of the manuscript is very problematic. The repetition of some characters leads one to suspect that the scribe has made a mistake, and the translation therefore remains provisional. In any case, the meaning of this passage remains obscure.

and permanently established [80] the two worlds.[7] For example, the body endowed with spirit belongs to the first world, while [81] the second world completes [the first] with the addition of the soul. Thus, whoever in the world is endowed with a body, [82] is also endowed with a soul, which can dwell intact [in the body] without abandoning it for a long time. So, for example, if the soul does not die out it is because [83] its nature is divine,[8] and it returns [to God].[9]

It is [only] thanks to [the body made up of] the five aggregates[10] that the soul and the spirit [84] can see and hear distinctly, speak, and move. For the soul, by its very nature, if there were no eyes, [85] could not see, if there were no hands, could not function, if there were no feet, could not walk.[11]

Let us consider, for example, two things that are dependent on each other, [86] such as the sun and fire. They are two distinct things that share the same nature, and from this one understands how fire can have its origin in the sun. Although they share the same unique [87] nature, the sun does not burn [anything] and yet it radiates light autonomously. On the other hand, fire needs fuel [88] if it is to radiate light. It is evident, therefore, that it does not radiate its light autonomously. Therefore, just as the sun and the fire, though possessing the same nature, radiate light differently—one doing so autonomously [89] while the other cannot do so without fuel—so the divine power can be distinct [from the object with which it shares its own nature] and at the same time similar to it, [90] and vice versa.

---

7. Namely, that of the visible realities and that of the invisible realities. Both, the author says, reiterating what had been said previously, were created by the One God.

8. Lit., "its nature is [that which is] proper to the divine power."

9. The brevity and difficulty of the text at this point does not allow one to make any definite judgments about its meaning, but it does seem to reflect belief in the immortality of the soul. If this is the case, it could be interpreted as a strong attack on Buddhist thought, which absolutely denies the existence of an immutable and eternal personal element that would survive death. The core of Buddhist doctrine is that everything is constantly changing. Therefore, each of the elements that make up human reality is also subject to continuous transformation. The text returns to this later on.

10. *Wuyin* 五蔭: "five aggregates" or "five attributes" (Sk. *pañcaskandha*). A technical Buddhist term that, at the level of the individual, designates the five constituent aggregates of the psychophysical reality of personal existence, namely: (1) form; (2) sensations; (3) perceptions; (4) mental formations, that is, discursive thought, volition, imagination, and emotion; (5) consciousness. The different occurrences of this expression in our text show that it is used here to emphasize the physicality of the body, its concreteness.

11. Lit., "eyes of flesh," "hands of flesh," and "feet of flesh."

236   THE TEXTS IN TRANSLATION

Divine power does not make use of human strength, and what human strength achieves autonomously is [only] due to the power [91] of the One God. The same is true for the [human] soul. By means of the [body made up of] five aggregates alone, it could not achieve anything; but in the same way it could not achieve anything [92] without it.

Since there are no other gods, [it is the One God who], having control over [the body made up of] the five aggregates, [93] guarantees that the world will not be extinguished, and that nothing will prevent multiple realities from being realized.

To better grasp the [reality of the] soul, one could compare [94] the five aggregates [making up the body] to five flavors,[12] with the soul giving something like the tastiest flavor to the world.[13] [95] Or one could also say that the soul in the body is comparable to a wheat sprout planted in the ground that in its time [96] produces seed. The five aggregates [making up the body and] endowed with a soul could be said [to be comparable] to the seed produced by the wheat sprout. From the seed, in turn, a sprout [97] can be born, and both grow autonomously, without need of fertilizer and water, until the wheat is harvested [98] and placed in barns. [All of this takes place] without need of fertilizer, water, and heat.[14] Likewise, the soul in the body does not seek [99] food or drink, nor does it need clothing.

Even when heaven and earth pass away and other *kalpas*[15] follow, [100] the soul will return [again] to the body [made up] of the five aggregates. By subsisting autonomously, it will not seek clothing [101] or food, it will dwell

---

12. *Wuwei* 五味: the five flavors are sweet, sour, bitter, spicy, and salty.

13. *Meiwei* 美味: this expression, which designates food that has an exquisite, excellent, refined flavor, is presumably used here to designate the result of the right balance between the five aforementioned flavors. The purpose of such a comparison would be to suggest that the soul gives creatures a certain quality ("the soul constitutes that which gives taste to the body," as is said a little further on), a quality derived from the proper balance between the different parts that make up the person, namely, the five aggregates compared to the five flavors.

14. Lit., "warm wind," or "warm breeze."

15. *Jie* 劫: to express the duration of time in relation to the evolution of the different existing worlds, Hindu cosmological thought has elaborated the notions of *kalpa* and *yuga*, later also taken over by Buddhism. Four cosmic cycles (*yugas*) follow each other in the life of the universe: production or formation, duration or maintenance, destruction, and emptiness or reduction, leaving a "remnant" necessary for the activation of the next cycle. Four *yugas*, together, form one *mahāyuga*; one thousand *mahāyugas* form one *kalpa*, or twelve hours of Brahmā's life. A second occurrence of the concept of *kalpa* is present in the final part of the text.

permanently in blessedness,[16] it will delight in wandering [from one place to another] thanks to its supernatural powers,[17] it will not disperse into [different] realities, nor will it be linked to [different] bodies. We can compare this [102] to the blessedness of flying immortals[18] who, in their body of blessedness,[19] delight in wandering [from one place to another]: [103] the blessedness proper to the other world is similar to the blessedness proper to the soul that wanders above the body.[20]

[104] The soul dwells as a guest in the blessedness proper to the other world, and [in the same way] dwells as a guest in the body [made up] of the five aggregates that is [situated] in this world and participates in the blessedness proper to the other world. [105] Using [this same] metaphor, we can say that if the soul is a guest of this world—that is, a guest of this world [insofar as it is] in the body [made up] of the five aggregates—and [106] if it is free from anguish and enjoys blessedness in the other world, this is only possible thanks to the divine power [107] of the Honored One of Heaven.[21]

As [we have already said] above, the soul constitutes that which gives taste to the body.[22] In it, the Honored One of Heaven is revered. [Thanks to it], [108] it is clearly seen how all the realities of the world are subject to the [law

---

16. *Kuaile* 快樂: lit., "happiness [and] joy," this condition is the fundamental characteristic of the divine space, even in Buddhism, where these terms indicate the condition proper to the Pure Land of Ultimate Bliss (see p. 283n8).

17. *Shentong youxi* 神通遊戲: this expression is present in Chinese Buddhist literature (mostly by inverting the two constituent terms: *youxi shengtong*; Sk. *vikrīḍita ṛddhi-sākṣātkriyā*), where it indicates the supernatural powers in which the buddhas and bodhisattvas delight. These powers include appearing in different places at will and moving freely in space without obstacles.

18. *Feixian* 飛仙: this word is proper to Daoism but has also become common in Buddhism. It is used here to refer to the celestial being that in the Jewish-Christian tradition is called an angel.

19. *Kuaile shen* 快樂身: see above, n. 16.

20. Here the idea of the immortality of the soul seems to be strengthened. Freed from the body, it has a life independent of it, thanks to the power of God.

21. *Tianzun* 天尊: synonymous with *Shizun* 世尊, "Honored One of the Universe." This title appears as another Chinese translation of the Buddhist epithet *Bhagavat*. Later it will also be used in Daoist literature as a derivation of *Yuanshi tianzun* 元始天尊, "Primordial Honored One of Heaven," the supreme divinity of the Daoist pantheon, the personification of the *Dao*, the transcendent and all-pervasive principle of the universe. In the Christian texts translated here, the appellation designates the Christian God.

22. That is, the essence (see p. 236n13).

238 THE TEXTS IN TRANSLATION

of] retribution.[23] Just as the soul constitutes the reference [for the body], the soul being its host and [the body made up of] the five aggregates [109] being the master of the house,[24] so [the Honored One of Heaven is the reference] for the world in which it dwells permanently.

Do your best to ensure that the soul is sufficiently rich, so that [the body made up of] five aggregates, [110] however poor it may be, may without delay borrow [from the soul]. In this way, even though [the body made up of] the five aggregates is poor and therefore unable to pay [111] any debt, the soul, being rich, will be able to provide a loan for [the body made up of] the five aggregates.[25] There is no doubt that [the body made up of] the five aggregates, being poor, [112] cannot pay off its debt without the wealth of the soul. Therefore we affirm that [the body made up of] the five aggregates [113] is miserable while the soul is rich, but the true reality of the two is not [often] discerned. [The body made up of] the five aggregates [114] is mud, but the soul [alone] could hardly constitute anything like a person. Both [components] together—[body made up of] the five aggregates and soul— form a person.

[115] [This is a matter of] surpassing knowledge.[26] If you have this knowledge, then you will not know this world [alone]. Besides knowing both worlds—this and the previous one—[116] you will also know the other world, and, even more, the future will be like the present and the past. Only when one is no longer [117] in the mother's womb can one become aware that one has previously lived in the mother's womb.[27] If this is true, then we must consider [the relationship between] this [118] world and the beyond as the

---

23. *Baochang* 報償: a term that in Buddhist soteriology refers to karmic retribution, and which here is used by the Christian author to describe the moment of judgment. This sentence is not clear in relation to its immediate context.

24. Reading the character *zhu* 主, "master," as an error in place of the homophone *zhu* 住, "dwelling," which has a very similar script, one could instead translate the passage as follows: "As the soul constitutes the reference for [the body made up of] the five aggregates, dwelling in it as a guest, so . . ."

25. The meaning of this metaphor could be that the soul constitutes the true wealth of the person, whose qualities can make up for any deficiencies in the physical body. The superiority of the soul over the body is also the theme of the following discourse.

26. *Shenzhi* 神知: lit., "divine" or "spiritual knowledge."

27. This comparison, which is also discussed a little further on, is intended to illustrate the relationship between the previous existence and the present one. Although the relationship is characterized by unconsciousness, it is still very close. The womb is a metaphor for the source, for what precedes and from which one has originated. It is interesting to observe that, in Buddhist literature, the image of the womb (Sk. *garbha*) is also what gives rise to the name of the world's matrix (Sk. *garbhadhātu*), the place where all realities are generated. The allusions

Text C 239

world of future existence. Now we live in this world; [119] however, we will not dwell there forever. If we consider this, then in [this] life we will be able to cultivate every good fruit,[28] [120] and in the other world the seeds planted in one's previous existences will be transferred to a future existence. [121] Wherever the afterlife is, the afterlife is dependent on[29] the mother's womb, for it generates all reality. [122] The afterlife is dependent on this world, [and this world] is dependent on previous existences. However, we must speak of them separately.

[123] Eyes are clearly needed in the world so that the objects looked at can be seen. [In the world] there are countless [124] words and sounds, but ears are needed to hear them. There are countless scents, but the nose [125] is needed to distinguish them. There are countless foods, but the mouth is needed to taste their flavor. There are countless [126] actions, but hands are needed to perform them.

[The body made up of] the five aggregates is not the work of this world but of the mother's womb. [127] Even if [the body made up of] the five aggregates is generated without realizing it, it could not have happened without [a mother's womb]. [128] Those who leave their mother's womb are all generated by it and could not be created by anything else. [129] [Everything] that is generated in this world can be considered to be generated by the mother's womb.[30]

This world cooperates with what will be in the other world. [130] If this world were not to collaborate, there would not even be an afterlife. All [131] meritorious actions should be carried out in this world and not in the other.[31]

---

to it that are present in our text could legitimately be read in the light of this detail of Buddhist cosmogony.

28. *Guobao* 果報: a Buddhist technical term (Sk. *vipāka*, lit., "ripening," thus "maturation," "fruition," or "result") that indicates remuneration for good or evil actions and expresses the firm belief that the different conditions in this life are the fruit of seeds planted in other previous lives.

29. Lit., "needs."

30. See p. 238n27.

31. *Zuo gongde* 作功德: "doing meritorious and virtuous [actions]," "accumulating merits," is one of the main means of achieving salvation in Buddhist teaching. The author of our text, adopting this expression central to Buddhist doctrine, shows that in his mind, Christian theology accepts, at least partially, the value of Buddhist praxis and its reward on the day of judgment. This section of the text deals extensively with the theme of meritorious actions, emphasizing that they are effective only if accompanied by faith in the One God, and that, for the purpose of salvation, there is no meritorious action except that of the redemption brought about by God through Christ.

240   THE TEXTS IN TRANSLATION

Do not bow in worship to spirits, [132] but rather perform meritorious actions in this world, not in the other. The One God has disposed that he should not be disobeyed, and he desires that [meritorious actions] be carried out in this world, [133] and not in the other. So, if meritorious actions are carried out, they should be carried out first of all in this world, and not [134] in the other. The meritorious action of giving alms[32] to others should be carried out in this world. In fact, in the other world, even though [135] one [would like to] give alms, it will not be possible [to do so]. A generous heart[33] is one that is wide and large; it cannot be narrow and small. [The heart] is able to expand [136] in this world but not in the other. Let us reflect on this. It is necessary to eradicate from the heart the poison of bad thoughts [137] and the revenge that increases hatred. In this world, it is possible to eradicate all that poisons the heart but not in the other. [138] To keep one's heart pure, to venerate and worship [the Honored One of Heaven], and to act without transgressing the precepts, [all these things] should be realized in this world [139] but not in the other. Let us wholeheartedly worship the Honored One of Heaven, [thanks to whom] all sins[34] [140] will be eliminated, and let us worship [him] in this world, since it is not possible to do so in the other world.

When people leave this world, [141] the fruits [they] sow in this world will be fully brought to maturity, [while] in the other world, no matter how much you sow, [142] you will not be able to bring it to maturity. In the other world one only knows blessedness; one encounters nothing else.[35]

The One God is a God whose action is holy.[36] [143] The power of the God whose action is holy first established the world, but then was driven into the other. [144] This is not a good time to explain that. Suffering has taken hold among people, and each of them, [caught up] in their own suffering, [145]

---

32. *Bushi* 布施: in Buddhism generosity (Sk. *dāna*) is one of the six "perfections" (Sk. *pāramitā*) that the one who aspires to become awakened must practice. The others are morality (Sk. *śīla*), patience (Sk. *kṣānti*), energy (Sk. *vīrya*), meditation (Sk. *dhyāna*), and wisdom (Sk. *prajñā*). In the Christian faith almsgiving is a concrete sign of fervent love for God and for neighbor.

33. *Faxin* 發心: a synonymous expression (*fa shanxin* 發善心) is used in the text of the *Book of the Lord Messiah* (Text D, cols. 86 and 106, pp. 273 and 275). At p. 273n55 I give an explanation of its meaning in Buddhism.

34. *Zuiye* 罪業: Buddhist term that properly indicates the negative *karman* produced by sin, and the fruit of suffering that comes with it. It occurs several times in the text.

35. The entire section insists very strongly on the unique value of this present life, in which everything is being definitively prepared, in relation to the future life, which is described as absolute blessedness and no longer shares anything of the features of this world.

36. *Zi shenghua* 自聖化: that is, whose holiness is operative and effective (see p. 254n119).

Text C

241

is no longer concerned [about performing] meritorious actions. [However], this is important: that, as in the beginning, people should acknowledge what the Honored One of Heaven has established, [146] serve only the One God, worship the One God, and submit to the orders of the One God. [147] If the meaning of this is not understood, then there will not be any meritorious actions. Neither this nor other worlds [148] will be places [in which to foster] meritorious actions.

To make use of a simile, someone who is building a house first has to lay the foundations. [149] First of all, the foundations have to be solid, for if they are not, the house will not stand. The same happens when one wishes [150] to perform meritorious actions. First of all, one must correct one's own actions[37] and be perfectly vigilant. Furthermore, one must be aware that the One God has established [151] that all people offer worship to and accept the grace of the One God. Only in this way can they then perform meritorious actions.

[152] These are the meritorious actions that we consider[38] in our discourse, and there is no need to know other merits. [153] If we claim that it is necessary to do what is good, but the Honored One of Heaven is unknown to our own intelligence, then we will also exempt ourselves [154] from being zealous in meritorious actions. We would be like a foolish[39] person who, wanting to build a house, [155] does not lay the foundation in the ground, and thus the wind takes the house away. If the foundations of the house are solid, the wind cannot [156] lift it.[40] Likewise, if meritorious actions are not founded in the Honored One of Heaven,[41] they are ineffective.

If one wishes to be able to see [157] the One God, the heart must be pure,[42] and serious reflection must follow to be sure that this is so.

Just as [158] there are innumerable blood vessels in the [body made up of] the five aggregates, and each one is different from the other, so too the body

---

37. *Xiuxing* 修行: this typically Buddhist expression indicates the action of amending one's own conduct, performing good deeds. Hence it also has the meaning of being faithful, devoted to religious teachings.

38. Lit., "we praise and lament."

39. *Wu yizhi* 無意智: lit., "without intelligence," "lacking wisdom."

40. Cf. Matt. 7:24–27; Luke 6:47–49.

41. *Tianzun zheng* 天尊證: God is the cause that validates and the foundation that makes possible every meritorious action. Works cannot exist if they are not rooted in God, that is, if there is no faith in God. This is the central point of the whole discourse.

42. *Qingjing* 清淨: lit., "limpid and pure," i.e., free from evil and corruption, it is a recurrent term in Buddhist texts (Sk. *pariśuddhi* or *viśuddhi*). Cf. Matt. 5:8.

242   THE TEXTS IN TRANSLATION

[made up of] the five aggregates and the soul [159] are independent of each other, [but, like] the blood vessels, they are closely related to each other.

In the world there are many [160] species [of different things], and all should resemble the One God who created, nourishes, [161] and sustains each of them. Everyone should also worship [the One God]. The divine word is eternal and does not fail, and time is subject to the divine dispositions. [162] Springs give way to autumns, winters alternate with summers; these four seasons form the years. [163] Days follow nights, until they form [successive] *jiachen* 浹辰.[43] [And of all this] the cause is the One God. The wisdom of the one who is the Wise and the Holy[44] is by nature [164] stable and immutable.[45]

To use a metaphor, just as a pleasant sound only exists because it is an autonomous entity with the capacity to resonate, [165] so the One God only exists because he is a fully autonomous entity whose doctrine can spread out [166] to all celestial creatures.[46]

Human beings, because of the presence of the Adversary[47] among them, have been diverted[48] by the spirit of evil, [167] so that their ears have become deaf and their eyes blind, unable to accept the precepts and rules of life [of the One God]. At one time all people in their goodness were [as] God. At one time [168] they had in themselves goodness,[49] but then, in their foolishness,[50] they were diverted by the spirit of evil, unable [169] to understand things in

---

43. According to the computation of time based on the system of celestial trunks and terrestrial branches used in ancient China, a *jiachen* corresponds to a cycle of twelve days, from the first to the twelfth terrestrial branch.

44. *Xiansheng* 賢聖: this compound indicates two types of virtuous and excellent people, the wise (*xian*; Sk. *bhadra*) and the holy (*sheng*; Sk. *ārya*).

45. *Wukui wuying* 無虧無盈: lit., "does not decrease and does not increase"; it is therefore constant.

46. *Zhu tianzi* 諸天子: lit., "all the children of heaven." *Tianzi*, "Son of Heaven," is the title given to the sovereign in ancient China. Here, however, I believe that the plural indicates celestial creatures.

47. *Yuanjia* 怨家: interestingly, one of the biblical terms for Satan, the "Adversary," has been faithfully translated into Chinese.

48. *Mihuo* 迷惑: the term that occurs most frequently in the final part of this section of the text and always indicates the spirit of evil's work of diverting, misleading, and deceiving.

49. *Shanye* 善業: lit., "a good *karman*." On the Buddhist concept of *karman*, see p. 278n95.

50. *Yuchi* 愚癡: Buddhist term (Sk. *mūḍha*) that indicates one of the "three poisons" (Sk. *triviṣa*) that hinder awakening and are the cause of all passions and all evils, that of foolishness, ignorance, non-intelligence of the truth of things and of the teaching of the Buddha. In Chinese this term also has the nuance of "madness."

their truth. Using a metaphor, just as people copy [a text] by their own hand, so people—good and bad [indifferently]—consciously allowed themselves to be misled, neither [170] awakening[51] nor recognizing God's blessings, and thus becoming like quadrupeds. Being like quadrupeds, [171] their hearts have become like those of quadrupeds—the reason is difficult to explain—and as a result they can hardly obtain liberation,[52] and they lack discernment. [172] It is known, however, that quadrupeds are what they are because of their lack of intelligence.[53] They do not understand that they are to venerate the One God. [On the other hand, we also recognize that], even though they do not understand [173] that they are not to offer sacrifices to the spirits of evil, they refrain from doing it.

In order to mislead humanity, evil then took the form [174] of the Adversary, but even so, it could not [alone] overcome [what] the spirit of evil [had brought about]. In their foolishness, [175] people were diverted by the spirit of evil, which caused them to fall into the path of evil. The Adversary [alone] [176] could not have overcome the spirit of evil in its work of deception, but some people, in their foolishness, wrote the name "god" [177] on wood and stone, and for this reason it is said that the spirit of evil is called the adversary of humanity. [178] This is how we know the name with which people discuss [good and evil], and this allows people to discern good and evil.[54] If [179] any do not come to this discernment and continue to let themselves be distracted by the spirit of evil without being able to foster [180] what is good, they will, thanks to these [words], certainly come to discern the spirit of evil. If any succeeds in silencing the spirit of evil, this will lead them [181] to be awakened.

The spirit of evil was [originally] like the other flying immortals[55] in heaven, but because of its deliberate [182] choice for evil, it turned to the path of evil. To make use of a simile, the spirit of evil is like a foolish person who

---

51. *Juewu* 覺悟: Buddhist technical term to indicate the understanding of the true essence of things thanks to *bodhi*, that is, "awakening" or "enlightenment." In the *Book on Profound and Mysterious Blessedness*, the synonyms *juezhi* 覺知 and *jueliao* 覺了 are used (Text E, col. 131, p. 294n76; col. 135, p. 295n81).

52. *Jietuo* 解脫: the cornerstone of Buddhist soteriology is liberation (Sk. *mokṣa* or *mukti*) from the illusion and suffering caused by *saṃsāra*, thanks to the supreme understanding of the intimate reality of things, and therefore the achievement of the state of *nirvāṇa*.

53. *Shijie* 識解: lit., "comprehension."

54. Lit., "to know the different depths of good and evil."

55. *Feixian*: see p. 237n18.

244 THE TEXTS IN TRANSLATION

[originally] was good, but who, because of a deliberate [183] choice for evil, turned aside to falsehood. Because of the evil [that is in this person], [184] there is no difference between this one and the evil opponent of the One God and of all living beings, who ended up falling, abandoning [185] the highest place [of blessedness].[56]

Since God and the wicked are not one reality, it was not possible to drive [the wicked] out of the three spheres,[57] but it abandoned [186] all its relationship with what is good. That is why it is called the spirit of evil. Another name is Satan.[58] [187] Thus do the [Iranian] foreigners[59] designate the spirit of evil, and in this one name [188] they include the various evil spirits who turn to the way of evil, and also those who mislead others [189] by making them turn to evil.

The foolish ones who, distracted by the spirit of evil, turn their hearts to evil, [190] are called by the same name as the spirits are called; [in fact] they are like the *wangliang* 魍魎 spirits,[60] who, turning to the way of evil, have ended up leaving [191] the Heavenly Hall[61] and making the desolate places of the world their dwelling place. After [Satan] had broken off his relationship with God, [192] it is said that his negative influences[62] also affected the world and that his evil action became like that of spirits. These adversaries of humankind [193] are pleased to dwell in desolate places. Among those who

---

56. *Dachu* 大處: lit., "great place." In the light of the following, this may refer to the Heavenly Hall.

57. *Sanjie* 三界: in Buddhist cosmology, each of the countless worlds consists of three spheres (Sk. *tridhātu*), namely, the sphere of desire (*yujie* 欲界; Sk. *kāmadhātu*), in which people and all beings moved by desire live, the sphere of pure form (*sejie* 色界; Sk. *rūpadhātu*), where the gods whose bodies are made of subtle matter reside, and the sphere of the without-form (*wusejie* 無色界; Sk. *arūpadhātu*), which escapes all material representation and is inhabited by pure immaterial spirits.

58. *Suoduona* 娑多那: phonetic transcription in Chinese of the Syriac word *sāṭānā*. In the next section of this same text ("Discourse of the Honored One of the Universe on Almsgiving") and in that of the Xi'an stele another Chinese transcription has been used (*suodan* 娑殫, see p. 199n15).

59. In Chinese historiographic works the term *hu* 胡 indicates the foreigners who live in the territories west of the Chinese Empire. In the Tang era it designates more specifically the Iranian people (particularly the Sogdians) from Central Asia.

60. In ancient Chinese tradition, the evil spirits of mountains and rivers were called *wangliang*.

61. *Tiantang* 天堂: this recurrent term in Christian texts of the Tang era, which is borrowed from Chinese Buddhist literature to designate the abode of God, here seems to indicate more properly the divine reality in its transcendent dimension.

62. Lit., "wind."

Text C 245

inhabit these desolate places, the main [spirit] is called [**194**] the devil,[63] and the others are called the spirits,[64] according to their hierarchy. These different spirits, together with the spirit of evil, [**195**] have abandoned the Heavenly Hall and its light and have also set out on the path of evil.

Because of the manifold evil trickery [**196**] that the devil has used to deflect humankind, there is no escape for them. The spirit of evil is jealous [**197**] of the goodness of humanity, and because of this jealousy it does not allow people to worship the One God. So the spirit of evil, [**198**] having evil as its only thought, and desiring to mislead living beings, leads people to fall into the path of evil. Because of this [**199**] deception by the spirit of evil, foolish people do not turn their hearts to worship the One God, and believing the lie, [**200**] they err. In this way they will first meet the three unfortunate destinies,[65] together with the spirits of evil, and [only] then [**201**] will they be reborn in the world as human beings, but in distant lands[66] and among inferior people, until a *kalpa* has passed, since the law [**202**] of the *kalpa* is constant and immutable forever.[67]

Since evil is caused by the spirit of evil, no matter how much one reflects upon evil in order to recognize it [**203**] as evil, one is drawn into it by the [spirit of] evil. Instead the One [God] is the one who in the four directions of the world constantly makes one meditate on what is good [**204**] so that one can become a better [human being]. No matter how much the spirit of evil is the one who in the four directions of the world[68] [makes people] reflect upon evil, deflects people, and makes them fall into [**205**] the path of evil, the One God has the eternal power to make them wise.

[**206**] *Discourse on the One Godhead*[69] (first part).

---

63. *Shennu* 參怒: phonetic transcription of the Sogdian term *šmnw* (*šmanu, šimnū*), attested in the Sogdian Christian literature of this period with the meaning of "demon," "devil," "fiend."

64. *Gui* 鬼 is the Chinese term for spirits in general, without distinction of class or species.

65. *San edao* 三惡道: lit., "the three evil ways" (Sk. *tridurgati*). In Buddhist teaching, this refers to the three possible lower fates after death, namely the states of existence in purgatory, the condition of a ravenous spirit, and animal life. The destinies of rebirth in the world of human beings and in that of the gods (Sk. *deva*) are considered superior fates.

66. *Biandi* 邊地: lit., "borderlands."

67. For the meaning of *kalpa*, see p. 236n15.

68. *Si tianxia* 四天下: a term used in Buddhist literature (Sk. *cāturdvīpa* or *cāturdvīpaka*) to indicate the four sectors or quarters of the world, which extend in the four directions (north, south, east, west).

69. *Tian* 天 (Sk. *deva*) is synonymous with *shen* 神 (see pp. 296n88 and 299n10).

II. Metaphorical Teaching (*Yu di'er* 喻第二)

[1] All realities[70] reveal the One God.[71] It is the One God who made all realities. [2] There is no distinction between contemplating the created realities and contemplating the One God. From this, one [3] understands that it is God who made all realities. Both what is visible and what is invisible [4] are created by God. Over the course of time until the present it has been possible to contemplate the realities created by the One God.

[5] [The One God] so fixed heaven and established the earth that they would remain unchanged until today. Heaven does not have pillars to support it. If the One God did not [6] support it, how could it have stayed in place so long without collapsing? This is only possible thanks to [7] the power of the One God, whose ways are mysterious. If it were not the One God who acted, who could sustain [heaven] to keep it from collapsing? [8] From these words we can understand that it is only thanks to the power of the One God that heaven is held in place. By means of an example, [9] it is possible to understand the mysterious[72] power of the One God. It is only this divine power that allows us to understand how heaven can stand [10] without pillars of support. Since heaven is held up without pillars, we understand that heaven does not stand by itself [11] but only thanks to the power of the One God. Therefore, since the power of the One God has the same function as visible pillars, one understands that [12] thanks to it [heaven] does not need pillars or retaining walls.

Some are aware that they are in a world[73] established[74] [by the One God], [13] while others are not, and therefore say, "There is no place established [by anyone]; [14] [the world] has simply been established above the waters." And where, then, would the waters have been established? [They say], "They have been established above the winds."[75] A long time has passed and [the heavens

---

70. *Wanwu* 萬物: lit., "the ten thousand things."

71. The title of this section, not present in the manuscript, can be deduced from what is indicated at the end of the section.

72. *Shenmiao* 神妙: this term, also frequent in Buddhist literature, indicates the mysterious and wonderful quality of the divine.

73. *Tiandi* 天地: lit., "heaven and earth."

74. *Anzhi* 安置: this verb expresses the idea of "fixing in a stable way." It is the recurrent keyword in the portion of the text that follows and expresses the creative action of God.

75. There seems to be an attack here on the cosmological and cosmogonic conceptions elaborated by Buddhist thought. In particular, one can see a reference to the structure of one of the three spheres into which each of the innumerable worlds in which humans also dwell

and the earth] have not [15] collapsed. Even though the One God[76] was not visible in the events that ensued, nevertheless the divine power was present, making [16] all realities conform to his will.

Consider, by way of example, someone who shoots an arrow, but only the falling arrow can be seen and not [17] the archer. Even though the archer is not visible, there is no way the arrow has moved by itself. There has to have been an archer. [18] [From this example] we can understand that it is because of the power exerted by the One God that heaven and earth do not collapse or fall into ruin. Through divine power [heaven and earth] can remain [19] stable over time. Even though the one who supports[77] them is not visible, it is certain that they are mysteriously supported by God. [20] To return to the example of the archer, if that person were not strong, the arrow would fall to the ground. [In the same way], if the divine power were not exercised, heaven and earth would fall into ruin. [21] It is only thanks to the divine power that heaven and earth are not destroyed. Therefore, if it is thanks to the power of the One God [22] that heaven and earth do not collapse, then one can understand that the mysterious power of the One God cannot fail.

His divine power [23] is not shared by other gods; the One God alone possesses it. [God] is invisible, and at the same time also has a visible aspect. To illustrate, [24] there is no [apparent] difference between the left hand and the right hand, or between the left foot and the right foot, or between the front and the back, or between the top and the bottom. [25] Now, if the One God is manifested within [all things] as a force [that makes them exist], then, from the point of view of the One God, one can understand [26] that there is neither left nor right, neither front nor back, neither above nor below, but the One God supports all. [27] There is only one reality, not a second nor a third. [The one reality sustained by the One God] cannot have been created [by others]: it could not have been created by anyone else as master, [28] sustainer, or creator. So, if one considers God as the ruler and supporter of heaven and earth, it is in his invisible aspect [29] that he sustains them.

---

is divided, namely, the sphere of desire (Sk. *kāmadhātu*; see p. 244n57). It is made up of five cylinders, placed on top of one another in the following way: the empty space where the winds swirl, the cylinder of the waters resting on the previous one, the earth floating on the water, the celestial residences of the gods, and the caves dug under the cylinder of the earth, where the damned endure unspeakable torments.

76. I propose the following correction: *yishen* 一神, "one God," in place of *yiwu* 一物, "one thing."

77. The Chinese verb used here, *chizhuo* 持捉, means "to have in hand," "to hold."

248 THE TEXTS IN TRANSLATION

However, [if one considers that] God nourishes and brings to life all living beings, it is here that the visible aspect of God is manifest.

[Another] simile: Just as in a house [30] there is only one master, so in a person[78] there is only one soul.[79] If there were more than one master in the house, there would be no prosperity in that house. [Likewise], if there were more than one soul [31] in a person, that person would not be able to act well. Therefore, a person does not have two or [32] three souls. Similarly, just as in a house there is only one master, and not two or three, so in heaven and on earth there is only [33] one God, and not two or three.

In heaven and on earth the One God cannot be seen, so also in a person the soul [34] is invisible to human eyes. Just as the soul that is present in a person cannot be perceived in a tangible way[80] or seen, so too [the One God who is present in] [35] the world cannot be seen. Everyone would like to see and touch the soul that is present in the person. Like the air, the Holy One who is great in wisdom[81] [36] cannot be perceived in a tangible way or seen, and yet the One God fills every place. The soul exercises government [37] over the person, and so does the One God govern heaven and earth.

In the Heavenly Hall there are no [38] spatial boundaries; the One God is everywhere, not residing in or dominating any one place. [39] Since there are no spatial boundaries between one place and another, in a moment God can pass over to other places. [40] For example, it is as if there were no spatial boundaries or it took no time to travel between here and Persia, or between Persia and "Rome."[82] [41] Like an outstanding sage whose influence

---

78. *Shen* 身: indicates the human body as a person, in its fundamental components (physical, intellectual, and affective).

79. *Hunpo* 魂魄: a term that recurs many times in this text. As Huang Xianian (2000) has shown through an analysis of the passages containing this expression and at the same time rereading the most widespread Chinese philosophical and religious texts in the Tang era and before, the choice of this word is very interesting and revealing. By adopting a word that was very infrequent in contemporary religious literature, Christian monks showed that they wanted to preserve and communicate the specificity of this key concept of Christian anthropology. They did not rely on concepts already existing in the religious traditions present in China (as they had done in several other cases).

80. The Chinese term used here, *zhi* 執, properly means "to grab," "to grasp," "to touch."

81. *Dazhi zhi sheng* 大智之聖: "the holy/wise one of great wisdom." *Dazhi* (Sk. *mahāmati*) is an epithet of the Buddha in his wisdom and omniscience. It is also a title of the bodhisattva Mañjuśrī, an apotheosis of transcendent science and wisdom. In our text it becomes an epithet for God.

82. *Fulin* 拂林: transcription of the Middle Persian *hrwm* (*hrōm*) or the Sogdian *frwm* (*frōm*, *frūm*), "Rome." It is a geographical term attested in various Chinese historiographic sources. The most common opinion among scholars is that Fulin indicates the territories subject to

Text C 249

is felt down to the present and transcends spatial boundaries, [42] who has no beginning and is unique, so too is the One God who transcends [43] the boundaries of space, has no beginning, and is unique. The fact that [the One God] transcends the boundaries of space, has [44] no beginning, has no abode, and transcends temporal limits cannot be investigated. Nonetheless, even without [45] investigating them, they can be deduced.

Where is the One God? The place where the One God is located has no spatial boundaries [46] or starting point. The existence of the One God cannot be determined in temporal terms. However, even if it cannot be investigated, [47] one can [deduce] it.

What is permanent is not extinguished, what is extinguished in time is not permanent. The One God is [48] permanently present in all realities. There is no moment when [this presence] began; it was permanent for all eternity. The place where [the One God] [49] is located is that of the Eternal Honored One,[83] who is not [visible] yet is the Eternal Honored One.[84] The One God has established his norms and laws, and [50] there are no others. In his infinite wisdom the Honored One of Heaven has also created what is not [visible] in the world. [51] [In fact], the Honored One of Heaven dwells in the world, both in visible and invisible things.

Consider for example the soul. [52] Despite the human desire to be able to see it, it is invisible. So it is with the human spirit.[85] To all human beings [soul and spirit] appear to be [53] two distinct things, but [in reality] they have the same origin. To use a metaphor, they are like two shoots [sprouting] from the same root. Every human being [54] is made up of soul and spirit. Humans cannot exist without a body, nor can they exist [55] without the soul, nor can they exist without the spirit.

Byzantine authority, the Eastern Roman Empire (see Aalto 1975; Lin Ying 2006b; Zhang Xushan 2009; Lieu 2016a).

83. *Changzun* 常尊: this title was used in ancient China to designate those who held eminent positions, sometimes even the sovereign. Like the other titles *Tianzun* (see p. 237n21) and *Shizun* (see p. 250n87), in this Christian text it becomes an epithet for God.

84. The insistence on the permanent character of God's presence and action, as the eternal foundation of all reality, sounds like a strong criticism of the Buddhist conception of the impermanence of all things, of the instantaneous character of each phenomenon, which is particularly emphasized by the Yogācāra school of Mahāyāna Buddhism.

85. *Shenshi* 神識: designates the human soul, understood as a complex of psychic, intellectual, and affective faculties; therefore, it indicates both the rational part of human beings (mind, intellect, knowledge) and their volitional and emotional part (spirit, conscience, heart).

250 THE TEXTS IN TRANSLATION

The visible realities in the world [56] cannot exist autonomously, nor can the invisible realities in the world exist autonomously. [57] If therefore these two categories [of reality] in the world have the same origin, someone could ask, "In what [category of] reality is it possible to know the One God?" Or again, [58] "Where are the invisible realities?" To this we answer that these realities, though invisible, are in the world. [59] And if it is the One God who has arranged them in such great quantity, what great number [proportionately speaking] of humans [would have been necessary] to give rise [to all this]!

[60] All realities of the world can all be traced back to the four elements.[86] *Metaphorical Teaching* (second part).

III. Discourse of the Honored One of the Universe on Almsgiving (*Shizun bushi lun disan* 世尊布施論第三)

[208] Word of the Honored One of the Universe.[87]

When you give alms, let it not be done in the sight of others. [Rather] take care [209] that [this act] be known [only] to the Honored One of the Universe. Only then go and give alms. If the left hand gives alms, do not let the right hand know about it.[88]

[210] When you pray,[89] do not hope to be seen by others, or for others to know about it. [Rather] take care [211] that it be seen by the One God alone. Only then go and pray.[90]

When you invoke [the One God], do not inundate him with your requests.[91]

---

86. *Sise* 四色: as it was already explained (see p. 233), the four elements are earth, water, fire, and air.

87. *Shizun* 世尊: this name is an epithet, recurrent in the Buddhist lexicon (Sk. *Bhagavat*), to designate a buddha. In our text it is used to designate God and also Christ. It therefore corresponds well with the title of "Lord of the Universe" in the Christian tradition. Occurring twenty-five times in the entire text of the *Discourse on the One God*, it is one of its key terms (see Tan 2018; Tam 2019).

88. Cf. Matt. 6:2–3. The curious inversion of the text of Matthew 6:3 is worth noting: "But when you give alms, do not let your left hand know what your right hand is doing."

89. *Libai* 禮拜: lit., "worship."

90. Cf. Matt. 6:5–6.

91. Cf. Matt. 6:7.

Text C 251

When you invoke [the One God], **[212]** first forgive the others for their sins.[92] If you do so, whenever you have sinned, your sins **[213]** will [also] be forgiven. If you forgive, then the One [God] will forgive you.[93] For you know that **[214]** Jesus,[94] who forgives all things, was the one who forgave the faults of his own.[95]

If you have riches, do not accumulate them on earth [where] they **[215]** can be consumed and plundered, or stolen by thieves. [Instead], take care to destine all of them for the Heavenly Hall [where] they **[216]** will not be consumed or lost.[96]

When one considers human beings, [one can see] that two [distinct] principles of life govern everything under heaven. The first is **[217]** the Honored One of Heaven,[97] the second is wealth.[98] Without wealth, food and clothing are lacking. However, you should not **[218]** be concerned. Rather, be like a child who, if it were a victim of thieves, would not worry about no longer having **[219]** anything to eat or to put on. When you ask for something, why do you not ask for it from the One God? **[220]** Surely you would not be wrong [in doing so], for you will have all that you desire in accord with your desire. Even more you, **[221]** disciples[99] of the One [God], do not be concerned. Whoever [among you] insistently asks to be near the Honored One of Heaven **[222]** [shall know that] it is already so. All that you want to eat and wear belongs to the One God. At birth, a person **[223]** is clothed with only

---

92. *Jie* 劫: lit., "thefts."

93. Cf. Matt. 6:14.

94. *Yishu* 翳數: phonetic transcription of a non-Chinese word, most likely the Syriac name Išoʿ (or the correspondent Sogdian form, modeled on the Syriac).

95. The expression composed of the two characters *kenu* 客怒 (which has no meaning as a compound and does not seem to have a sufficiently well-founded origin as a phonetic transcription from a foreign term) seems totally meaningless. I interpret it as a writing error in place of two other very similar characters: *rongshu* 容恕, "to forgive." The translation of the entire sentence containing this term remains uncertain. Since it is not a reference to the Gospel passage of chapter 6 of Matthew, it might perhaps be a gloss on the text.

96. Cf. Matt. 6:19–20.

97. *Tianzun*: an epithet for God (see p. 237n21).

98. In the background there seems to be the evangelical opposition between God and money (cf. Matt. 6:24).

99. *Dizi* 弟子: in the text two different terms are used to indicate the disciples, *dizi*, lit., "the younger brothers"; and *xueren* 學人, lit., "those who learn." In the translation it was decided always to use the term "disciples" since English does not have synonyms that adequately express these two shades of meaning.

252 THE TEXTS IN TRANSLATION

one soul and [a body made up of] the five aggregates,[100] but at the appropriate time, the One [God] grants both food and drink, [224] and clothing.[101] None of the other [gods] has the power to grant [all of this]. Look at the birds. They do not sow [225] or reap, nor do they have barns or warehouses to care for. As was the case in the desert,[102] the One [God] does not allow them to want for food and drink. [226] They do not plough and do not work, nor do they worry about their clothes. Now your position exceeds that of all of them, so do not worry [227] about yourselves.[103]

Even if you are a luminous person, do not look at the sins of others, but look only at their [228] righteousness. If what you cannot correct [in yourself] you want the others to correct [in themselves], [229] it would be as if you, having a beam in your eye, were to say to another: "You have [230] something in your eye that needs to be removed." So your correction would be hypocritical: first remove the beam in your own eye![104]

[231] Do not give what is pure to those who are like dogs,[105] and do not give your words away as if you were [tossing] pearls in front of those who are far away,[106] [232] lest they, like pigs,[107] trample on them and [your words] become worthless.[108] The sufferings that you will suffer [233] will be innumerable. You will be tested with violence. Did you not know this?

---

100. *Wuyin*: see p. 235n10.

101. The overall meaning of this phrase is that humans are born naked, and that God gives them everything they need at the right time.

102. In this obscure passage, there seems to be an allusion to God's care for the people of Israel in the desert, when they were nourished daily with manna (cf. Exod. 16). An appropriate comparison here would be with the passage about the lilies of the field in Matt. 6:28.

103. Cf. Matt. 6:25–32.

104. Cf. Matt. 7:1–5.

105. Here I interpret the character *gou* 苟, "negligent," "bad," "illicit," as an error of the scribe in place of *gou* 狗, "dog," a homophone whose character is similar in appearance to the character for the former.

106. *Liaoren* 遼人: "people of Liao." Behind the use of this expression is the association of the people of Liao (Liaodong) with swine, contained in a famous story recounted in *Hou Han shu* (Annals of the Later Han) 33. In the years when this text was probably written, Emperor Taizong (r. 627–49) sent a military expedition against the inhabitants of the Liaodong region, who were considered to be enemies because they were vicious savages, not at all like the civilized Chinese people. This image would thus have been used by the author of this text to indicate outliers, barbarians, pagans.

107. I here interpret the character *du* 睹, "observe" or "look at," as an error of the scribe in place of *zhu* 豬, "pig," which is similar in appearance to the former.

108. Cf. Matt. 7:6.

Text C 253

Make your invocation to the One [God]. Knock, [234] and the door will be opened for you. Everything you ask for from the One God, you will receive. Knock, and it will be opened to you. [235] If you ask and do not receive or knock and [the door] is not opened, it is because what you asked for [236] was not appropriate. Even if you ask, you will not get what would harm you. If you [237] ask your father for bread, you will receive it, [but] if you ask for a stone, you will not receive it because it could be harmful. [238] If you ask for a fish, you will have it, [but] if you ask for a snake, it will not be granted to you, because you could be poisoned. [239] [If] you do this, [you who] are foolish and wicked, all the more expect the Father, the merciful and good,[109] [240] to have such discernment. Everything depends on his discernment. Therefore, when you ask for [something] [241] and it is possible to grant it to you, it can[not] be that it will not be given to you. Whether it is granted to you or not depends in both cases [242] on what it is that [the Father judges is for your good]. To the son who asks, he will grant [what he needs]. In the wisdom of the One [God] there is no distinction between the intelligent and the foolish, [243] nor between the righteous and the sinful. Those who exalt themselves—[244] it should not even be necessary to say this—will not get what they ask for; nor will they get anything when they ask for impossible [245] or excessive things.

What you expect of others, others also expect [of you]. [246] [Therefore] what you want others to do to you, do to them in return.[110]

Abandon the evil way and, as [247] it has been said by the King's mouth, strive to pass through the [narrow] gate that will lead you to the heavenly dwellings, which only a few [inhabit].[111] If you [248] walk the wide way, you will find many pleasures, but it will lead you to the prisons of the earth.[112] There will be some who will confuse others, [249] saying that this [evil] is like good,[113] but you know that I have come precisely so that your lives may hear the [true] doctrine.

---

109. Cf. Matt. 7:7–11.

110. Cf. Matt. 7:12.

111. This is an obscure sentence, from both the philological and hermeneutic points of view, whose translation therefore remains conjectural.

112. Cf. Matt. 7:13–14. *Diyu* 地獄 is a term borrowed from Buddhism to designate the underworld, the Christian hell.

113. A possible allusion to false prophets (cf. Matt. 7:15).

254   THE TEXTS IN TRANSLATION

[250] The Messiah acted as had been preordained.[114] The manifestation of his way took place through [a period of] three years and six months,[115] [251] during which he lived as a disciple [lives with his teacher],[116] accepting that he had to be hung up high[117] and was going to die, [252] and that the Jews[118] from the beginning would try to raise their hand [against him]. Three days before his death, [the Messiah] had already predicted his imminent end, [253] so that all people would later rise from the dead and ascend to heaven. And this is precisely what his sanctifying action brought about in this world.[119] [254] He set a time of three years and six months for the proclamation of these things under heaven. [255] Now it is up to you to judge what happened.

The Jews captured him and [256] discussed the fact that he had said he was the son of the Honored One: "[He says], 'I am the Messiah,' [257] [but] who can say such a thing? He is not at all the Messiah. He lies, and we want him to be arrested! [258] It is up to you to do the right thing."

That is why they went to "Rome."[120] At that time the Caesar[121] was there, but even if the Caesar [259] had not consented to his arrest, [the Messiah] could not have escaped death. In fact, he was captured and arrested in accordance with [the judgment of] the doctors of the law, [260] was meticulously interrogated by them and, [as expected] from the beginning, [condemned to be] hung up high. Since the law had been applied, there was no further

---

114. *Chufen* 處分: a term that occurs many times in the text, almost always referring to the Messiah and to God, indicating divine plans, wishes, and judgments.

115. Probable allusion to the public ministry of Jesus.

116. I think that this means that Jesus submitted himself completely to God's plan for him, just as does a student vis-à-vis his teacher.

117. An expression that recurs several times in the text, indicating the crucifixion.

118. *Shihuren* 石忽人: the Chinese term *shihu* is the phonetic transcription of the Sogdian word *cxwd* (*čaxud*), which is derived from the Middle Persian *yāhūd*, meaning "Jewish."

119. *Shenghua* 聖化: lit., "holy transformation," "sanctification," a key term in this portion of the text that may be intended to describe the marvel of God's glory, the divine omnipotence that accomplishes salvation.

120. On the interpretation of this geographical term, see p. 248n82. Here it seems to indicate more specifically the Roman political authority.

121. *Jixi* 寄悉: phonetic transcription of a term of foreign origin, probably the Sogdian *qysr* (*kēsar*) or the Syriac *qesar*. The fact that the use of this title was at one time also extended to some rulers of Central Asia could explain the choice of such an appellation (see Haussig 1979, 189–90). The figure of Pilate, to whom this appellation seems to allude, is presented more extensively in the *Book of the Lord Messiah* (Text D, cols. 153–61, pp. 279–80), where the name of Pilate is rendered with the phonetic transcription *Piluodusi* 毗羅都思.

Text C   255

consideration [**261**] of what was fitting; he would be hung up high. [The Caesar had said], "You say that among you there is a law according to which [**262**] he must die because of what he said about himself, [because] who can say, 'I [**263**] am the Honored One of the Universe'? Let us therefore cease to argue."[122]

Verily, this temptation is not only yours; [**264**] it originated with Adam.[123] Let all know that it is present in human beings [from the beginning]. [**265**] Whoever, by lying, claims to be the Honored One of the Universe will immediately be unmasked. [Adam] ate [**266**] of that tree, and thus disobeyed the command of the Honored One. [That act of] eating was like "eating with the heart."[124] From the moment he ate [of the tree], [**267**] he felt like the Honored One, enlightened in his knowledge as if he were the Honored One of the Universe. In this way he and humans were no longer [**268**] in communion.[125]

Whoever, by lying, claims that he is God deserves death. For this reason the Messiah was not [recognized as] [**269**] the Honored One. [However], in his human body he revealed the Honored One to people through his unlimited sanctifying action. His work was not [**270**] of human origin, but divine. [Nonetheless], he took a body subject to the passions,[126] and this is precisely the place of the temptation that he shares [**271**] with Adam, [and therefore also] with you. Temptation has been present since the earliest times. Without the work of the Messiah, [**272**] no one could ever have anticipated the declaration [that we have been freed from it].

Like a sheep that makes no sound, nor does it raise its voice when brought to the slaughterhouse, [**273**] so [the Messiah] silently bore in his body the

---

122. The background is the account of the condemnation of Jesus by the Sanhedrin and Pilate (cf. Matt. 26:57–66; 27:11–26). It should be pointed out that the insistence that the Jews misunderstood the identity of Jesus as the Son of God is more properly a Johannine theme (cf. John 19:7).

123. *Atan* 阿談: phonetic transcription of a term of foreign origin, probably the Syriac name Adam (or its correspondent Sogdian form, modeled on the Syriac).

124. This means that this act of transgression of God's commandment produced an inner change in the human heart.

125. Cf. John 3.

126. *Aishen* 愛身: I read this term, proper to Buddhism, as the Chinese equivalent of the Sanskrit *tṛṣṇākāya*, "body of desire" or "body of lust," that is, a body subject to passions. Adopting this expression, the text here seems to place particular emphasis on the full humanity of Jesus, who shared the human condition in fullness.

[condemnation of] the law. In his love he bore [all things] for you,[127] [274] desiring to free you from the nature of Adam. That is how the Messiah died in [his body made up of] the five aggregates.[128] [275] That did not, however, mean the end of his life. It was the way temptation came to an end [276] and Adam's nature escaped the [power of] death. Passing through death, the Messiah did not avoid it, [277] but with the help of holy wonders he managed to escape the [power of] death. This was [in fact] the way it should be: that the Messiah [278] should suffer, and that he should act in weakness so that others would [no longer] be subject to weakness.

[279] Applying the law, he was hung up high at the appointed time, and thus gave up his life. The earth shook and the mountains [280] collapsed, the rocks crumbled and the fabric[129] that was hung next to the wall in that place was torn into two parts by the intervention of sanctifying action. [281] The tombs in that place opened and illustrious, holy, and virtuous persons rose from the dead, [282] returning to the places of human habitation.[130] [Although] the moon was in its fourteenth day, and therefore there was no time when [283] a place was in darkness,[131] the sanctifying action caused everything to be in darkness for three hours. [284] The human eye could not see [anything], [but] the sanctifying action could be heard and seen. The Messiah was hung up high [285] and prayed that he would be acknowledged in his true identity as the Honored One of the Universe. As is said in the Scriptures, it was necessary for him to pass through the darkness. The Messiah

---

127. Cf. Isa. 53:7. The same image is present in the *Hymn in Praise of the Salvation Achieved through the Three Majesties of the Luminous Teaching* (Text B.1, cols. 13–14, p. 224).

128. That is, his physical body did not escape death in the flesh.

129. *Qushu* 氍毹: in Chinese sources this term indicates a fabric, perhaps wool, from the West. It was used by the author of this text to designate the veil in the temple of Jerusalem that separated the Holy of Holies from the rest of the cultic space.

130. Cf. Matt. 27:51–53.

131. That is, being a full moon day (or, by extension, full moon days), there could be no complete darkness anywhere on earth, neither during the day nor at night. This insertion in the text would serve to bring out the extraordinary nature of the prodigious fact that Jesus' death was accompanied by darkness over the whole earth for three hours (cf. Matt. 27:45). The translation of this passage remains doubtful and provisional, but it seems to echo John's account of the passion, which places the death of Jesus on the fourteenth of Nisan (cf. John 19:14). The later tradition, in fact, continued to refer to the fourteenth of Nisan as the day of Jesus's crucifixion. An interesting passage in a Manichaean hymn from Turfan in the Parthian language (preserved in the manuscript fragments M 104, M 459, M 734), reads as follows: "On this day [came] salvation for souls; in the month of Mihr, the fourteenth [day], when into *parinirvāṇa* went Jesus, the Son of God" (Morano 1998, 134). The Persian month of Mihr corresponds to the Jewish month of Nisan (March–April).

Text C 257

[286] was indeed a man with [a body made up of] the five aggregates, but he was also the Honored One of the Universe.[132]

Then Joseph, [a man] who was known, a follower who had authority over the law,[133] [287] asked [for the body of the Messiah]. He wrapped it in a new linen cloth and laid it in a new sepulcher, [288] recently excavated in the mountain. A large stone was placed there, and the tomb was sealed.[134] [289] Those who sympathized with the Jews had [the tomb] guarded, saying: [290] "The Messiah said that on the third day he would rise from the dead. Do not let yourselves be deceived. His disciples will go to [the grave], so do not allow [291] the body to be stolen, [lest] they say that he has returned to life from among the dead." And so it was: [292] the Jews had the [Messiah's] tomb guarded for three days, watching over the seal from outside.[135]

[293] The women who had followed [the Messiah] even after hands had been raised [against him], testified to what they had seen, and then also some other followers [did the same]. [294] A flying immortal[136] clad in garments as white as snow[137] was sent by the Honored One of the Universe. [295] He appeared from the heavens, approached the guards, went to the great stone, rolled away the rock that had been placed on the door [of the tomb], [296] and sat on it.[138] The guards, recognizing [that figure] as a flying immortal, entered the tomb [297] and searched for the body,[139] but did not find it. They discussed [the matter] among themselves and then abandoned the tomb, [298] going to report to the Jews everything they had seen. From the Jews [the guards] received great wealth, so that [299] they would not respond to the questions [of the disciples] and would not say what they had seen.[140] But

---

132. Here too the meaning is that Jesus had a body of flesh, and therefore he was truly a man.

133. Joseph of Arimathea (in the Chinese text Yaoxi 姚霫, phonetic transcription of a foreign name, perhaps the Syriac Iawsep), a member of the Sanhedrin.

134. Cf. Matt. 27:57–60.

135. Cf. Matt. 27:62–66.

136. *Feixian*: see p. 237n18.

137. *Shuangxue* 霜雪: lit., "frost and snow." This compound is used to indicate blinding light, like the one reflected by snow in sunlight, hence purity.

138. Cf. Matt. 28:2–3.

139. Here, too, the concept of the physical body is rendered with the Buddhist expression *wuyin*, "the five aggregates."

140. Cf. Matt. 28:11–14.

258 THE TEXTS IN TRANSLATION

the guards said, [300] "Everything was as it had been proclaimed: the Messiah rose from the dead as he had said."

Then the women [301] went there according to the law, and some Jews also went to the tomb on the third day [302] to make sure [of the end of the Messiah]. There, [the women] clearly saw that the Messiah had departed, and together they went to inform the disciples.[141]

[303] As once it was a woman who transmitted to Adam the deception that had been introduced into the world, [304] and was responsible for the spreading of the sins to [the whole] world,[142] so [now] it was some women who went to the tomb, [305] [recognized] that the words spoken by the Messiah were true and went to report it to the disciples. Thus, [through them] the Good [News] reached [the whole] world. [306] Immediately afterwards [the disciples] came to that place and then went to report [what they had seen].

The disciples of the Messiah [307] had been clearly instructed: "Go into every place and proclaim my words to all nations; [308] make them be baptized with the sign of water,[143] in [the name of] the Father, of the Son, and of the Pure Spirit.[144] Teach them all that I have transmitted [to you]. [309] I am with you unto the end of the world."[145]

It is said that the Messiah [appeared] on earth for thirty days,[146] [310] and then ascended [to heaven] from the land of mortals. [He said], "I give you power [311] over every creature and every tongue, and as promised, I will send you the awaited Pure Spirit God."[147] [312] The Messiah was seen resplendent in the air. In the sky there was a figure [313] sitting in the midst of the Spirit of great mercy.[148] In order to accomplish his great sanctifying action, he manifested himself to the world.

---

141. Cf. Matt. 28:8.

142. Cf. Gen. 3; Rom. 5:12.

143. The text of the Xi'an stele states, with reference to the Luminous Teaching, that is to say to Jesus's teaching: "His doctrine requires immersion in water and in the Spirit" (Text A, col. 8, p. 202), a clear baptismal expression.

144. *Jingfeng* 淨風: lit., "pure wind"; it indicates the Holy Spirit (see p. 201n30).

145. Cf. Matt. 28:19–20.

146. Cf. Acts 1:3. Note that the number of days given here is different from the forty days given in the Acts of the Apostles.

147. *Jingfeng tian* 淨風天: cf. Acts 1:5.

148. Lit., "wind of great mercy." This description of Christ's ascension into heaven, whose figure appears to be enveloped in a cloud, is very close to that of Acts 1:9.

Text C

The spirit of evil exercised its evil [314] action, attracting people with its [seductive] offerings, and tossing on the ground what the Honored One of the Universe had obtained. [315] [The Messiah] underwent every kind of suffering, and taking his stand alongside human beings, raised his hand against the spirit of evil. [316] But it was useless. His sufferings were so great that fear caused people to distance themselves from the Honored One of the Universe [317] and provoked their action against the Messiah.

All who believe will stand before the presence of the Honored One of the Universe. If one does not [318] believe these words, one's eyes will not be able to see the Creator [319] and Perfecter of all things. If one believes, one already sees his presence now. The living [therefore] shall not doubt [320] and in their feelings shall not fear death. Like their predecessors, they too will die, [but] those among the dead [321] who believed in the Messiah must not doubt. All of them will rise [322] from the Yellow Springs.[149]

Ten days after he had ascended to heaven, the Messiah [323] sent the Pure Spirit upon the disciples in order to strengthen their faith. He looked down from heaven and clearly [324] saw the disciples receive the Pure Spirit coming down and resting on their heads as the light of fire [325] in the form of tongues.[150] From the Pure Spirit they received the power to teach all people and nations [326] [that which concerns] the Messiah, so that the whole world could clearly see the plan of the Honored One of the Universe. That is, that he who was with your Father [327] came down from heaven and did his sanctifying deed; that in order to assume in his divine nature[151] our condition of sin,[152] [328] he suffered death; that on the third day [his body made up of]

---

149. *Huangquan* 黃泉: in traditional Chinese cosmology, the underground world of water is the dwelling place, the land of the dead. This concept appears very close to the Jewish, and therefore biblical concept of Sheol. Perhaps this is also the reason it was chosen and used by the author to define the place and the condition of death.

150. The description of Pentecost is faithful to the account in Acts 2:1–3.

151. *Ziyou shen* 自由身: this compound does not seem to be attested in the Chinese Buddhist literature and could have been coined in an original way by the Christian author, but on the basis of Buddhist influences. I interpret it as a possible synonym for *zixing shen* 自性身 (Sk. *svabhāvakāya*, "body of essential nature"), the first aspect of *dharmakāya*, "*dharma*-body" or "true body." It designates the first of the "three bodies" (Sk. *trikāya*) of a buddha, that is, that of an awakened being, and specifically the dimension of emptiness proper to awakening, not subject to birth or death, pure potentiality, imperceptible, aformal, timeless. I think the author of the text has adopted this Buddhist term to express the Christian concept of Christ's divine nature. There may also be an allusion to the freed, transfigured body of Christ, his glorified body.

152. *Zuiye*: see p. 240n34.

260   THE TEXTS IN TRANSLATION

the five aggregates rose from death, thanks to the energies[153] of the Honored One of Heaven, [329] and went up to heaven.[154] No one has ever heard [anything like this] before!

All that is in the world be to the praise of the Messiah. [330] No one has ever heard of a dead man returning to life, but it was precisely this [331] that the Messiah achieved in the world. Rising from the Yellow Springs and turning to true doctrine, he has given life [332] to all humankind.

This will be the case at the time of judgment, [when] there will be retribution[155] for the whole world. Those who believe [333] will be where the Messiah is; those who adore the Honored One of the Universe will live forever in the Heavenly Hall [334] with the Messiah and the Father and will enjoy eternal happiness. [335] Where the Messiah is, there is no behavior that is not perfect. [Everything] is subject to the will of the Honored One of the Universe. [336] However, if you have not worshipped the Father, if you have turned to the worship of evil spirits, you will [then] be in a condition of impurity [337] and will have sadly drawn down upon yourself condemnation to the dark prisons of the earth. There you will dwell eternally [338] with demons, forever distancing yourself from the good.

Appearing in the world, [the Messiah] proclaimed [339] the [divine] judgments and his teaching was brought to completion [by him].

In the nature of his disciples there was not [only] a human seed, there was also the seed of the Honored One of the Universe. [340] For this reason they could heal the sick in the name of the Messiah, [341] and in his name demons were driven out and the dead returned to life. [However], as these deeds [342] spread throughout the world, people everywhere began to hate the disciples of the Messiah. [343] These [adversaries], the first [of whom] were the Jews, got the better of the disciples of the Messiah. [344] [The disciples] suffered countless and uninterrupted sufferings. [However], not even [345] the Jews escaped [from all this]. "Rome" made its voice heard around their great city in Judea[156] [346] with shocking destruction and the killing of [many] Jews, while the rest of the people [347] were plundered and sent into

---

153. *Qili* 氣力: lit., "strength of *qi*." For a general definition of *qi*, "breath" or "vital energy," see p. 266n13. As a dynamic aspect of the *Dao*, it here indicates the power of God's intervention.

154. This last part appears as a credal statement.

155. *Baochang*: see p. 238n23.

156. *Shiguo* 石國: probable contraction of *Shihu guo* 石忽國, "the country of the Jews." The "great city" is Jerusalem.

Text C   261

exile throughout the world. The disciples of the Messiah, [348] who preached and served the Honored One of the Universe, [also] became [349] the object of hatred of all, of both the great and the small, and only a turn of fate[157] could [change their destiny]. [350] By killing the disciples of the Messiah, the blessings [they brought] were also annulled, [but in this way] they were able to receive the result of all their deeds.[158] For [the Messiah] said, [351] "When you proclaim the Honored One of the Universe, know that you will have to defend yourselves countless times.[159] [352] Those among you who serve the Honored One of the Universe, consider carefully [353] and keep away from false doctrines. This is how you serve [the Honored One of the Universe] righteously, even if it does not always satisfy your desires."

The Honored One of the Universe [354] considers all people fairly, [while] all kings violate the freedom of the people. From "Rome" to Persia, [355] the law was thus a cause of tribulation and death [for the disciples of the Messiah]. All those who spoke [against the law] were killed. Dead and buried, [356] they could never be released and return to their country again. But there was [still] someone who served the Messiah, so that [357] the name of the way could still be clearly manifested.

This was done on earth by the Honored One of the Universe with his wonders, [358] performing sanctifying work in the midst of all nations. Consider this carefully, [and you will see that] this is what [the Honored One of the Universe] himself has done. Nothing but [359] the will of the Honored One of the Universe is completely fulfilled. All kings and wise people [of this world] long to [be able to do] this.

In both "Rome" [360] and Persia some died because of evil laws. Those who openly professed [their faith] were persecuted [361] unto death.[160] But today in all of "Rome" the Honored One of the Universe is worshipped. [362] In Persia, [on the other hand], there are still a small number of people who,

---

157. *Yunye* 運業: a Buddhist term indicating a change in *karman*, a reversal of fate.

158. *Shouye* 受業: a Buddhist term that indicates the act of receiving the results of the *karman* of one's actions, remuneration at the moment of death.

159. Cf. Matt. 10:16–23.

160. Lit., "they suffered tribulations to the point that they were no longer able to bear them." The Church of the East has always been a foreign minority in Sasanian Persia, with alternating periods of tolerance and persecution. Our text testifies to this by mentioning the numerous and severe persecutions of Christians in that land. Among the darkest periods are the reigns of Šābuhr II (r. 309–79), Wahrām IV (r. 388–99), Yazdgird II (r. 439–57), Xusraw I (r. 531–79), and Xusraw II (r. 591–628). See, in this regard, Panaino 2004.

262   THE TEXTS IN TRANSLATION

misled by evil spirits, [363] worship clay figures. All the others, however, worship Jesus the Messiah[161] [364] [as] the Honored One of the Universe.

As has been said, the Honored One of the Universe did not delay in bringing to pass [365] his sanctifying action in the world. By appearing in the world, the Messiah made manifest the plan [of the Honored One of the Universe]. [366] It has been but six hundred forty-one years since [the Messiah] took a body [made up] of the five aggregates,[162] [but] now [367] those who have intelligence, wherever they may be, can come to understand what these wonders consist of. [Such a thing] has rarely been heard of in the world [368] and does not fall within human possibility. In fact it is the work of the divine power of the Honored One of Heaven. [369] From this everyone can understand how all things exist for the divine power of the One God.

[370] The Messiah chose and sent his disciples: "Go [371] into the whole world and teach and proclaim all my words."[163] He did not choose his disciples from among the wise lords and kings [of this world], [372] or from those who consider themselves rich and worthy of honor. [Rather], he chose them from the poor, [373] the weak, and the unimportant.

This is the doctrine of the will of the Messiah; [374] this is what you devote yourselves to. If you observe it, you will be heard in all things. So all will know what the work [375] of the One God consists of, and all will know that the promises of the One God are in the doctrine that you preach. All [376] who desire to be saved[164] will be heard according to the judgments of the One God. For the soul to go up to the Heavenly Hall, [377] it is necessary to follow the path of doctrine step by step: not to be false or deceive [others], [378] not to speak lies or commit sins. This is what the doctrine asks of you. All those who, wandering [far from the true way], [379] are sinners and follow wrong

---

161. *Yishu mishihe* 翳數弥師訶: phonetic transcription of the Syriac compound expression *Īšōʿmšīḥā*, which is very frequent also in the Sogdian Christian literature in the correspondent Sogdian form.

162. As suggested by Hidemi Takahashi (2020, 25n6), it should be noted that the Syriac Christians, as a rule, placed the date of Christ's birth some years before the year reckoned as 1 CE according to the computation made by Dionysius Exiguus (d. ca. 544). The Christians of the Syrian Orthodox tradition usually placed it in 309 of the Seleucid era (4/3 BCE), but others sometimes placed it even earlier, especially in the case of Christians living in, or originating from, Central Asia. What the seventh-century Christians in China reckoned to be the year "641 after the incarnation" is, therefore, likely to be a few years earlier than 641 CE (e.g., 635/36 CE).

163. Cf. Matt. 28:19–20.

164. *Jie* 解: lit., "to be freed." Here this Buddhist term (Sk. *mokṣa*; see p. 243n52) is used to express the salvation brought about by the death and resurrection of Christ.

Text C

paths [but] desire to turn from their sins to the Truth, [380] must walk on the way of the One God and accept his judgments. There is [381] no other way humans can reach the Heavenly Hall [than by] recognizing [as God] the only Honored One of Heaven. [382] As for other people, they will be subjected to the judgment of the One God. Among those who wander [far from the true way], fear those [383] who worship the sun, the moon, and the stars or adore the fire god.[165] Fear also those who worship [384] evil spirits, such as the *yakṣas*[166] and the *rākṣasas*.[167] They will go to the burning prisons of the earth and there dwell forever. [385] This is because they have not believed with great faith the Truth and have not obeyed the judgments of the One God. [386] For them there will be only [one lot], that of the demons, of the *yakṣas*, of the *rākṣasas*, and of the other spirits.

[And it will come to pass] as is written in the Scriptures [387] [that contain] the doctrine of the One God. At the end of time, there will be catastrophes in the world, and evil spirits will come. [388] They will appear on earth in human form and with their deceptive cunning [389] will cause [people to commit] innumerable sins, and in this way they will harm them all. Distanced [390] from the One God, people will be brought closer to evil spirits. But [the Messiah] spoke these words to you: "I am [391] the Messiah. My work of restoration will take three years and six months,[168] [392] after

---

165. These are clear references to Zoroastrians and their religion, which in Chinese was called *xianjiao* 祆教, from the main object of its worship, i.e., the fire god (*xian* 祆 or *huoxian* 火祆). Chinese historical sources contain descriptions similar to those presented here. For example, *Jiu Tang shu* (Old Annals of the Tang) 198, 16: 5311, reports: "It is their [i.e., the Persians'] custom to worship various spirits: of the sky, of the earth, of the sun, of the moon, of water, of fire. The different [Iranian] foreigners [*hu* 胡] of western countries who worship the fire god [*huoxian*], have all learned this religion after having been in Persia." Similarly, *Xin Tang shu* (New Annals of the Tang) 221B, fol. 8b4–5 (vol. 10), reports: "They offer sacrifices to the sky, to the earth, to the sun, to the moon, to water, to fire.... The different [Iranian] foreigners of western countries have received [from Persia] the rules for sacrificing to the fire god [*xian*]."

166. *Yakṣas* are a broad class of nature-spirits, usually benevolent, but sometimes mischievous or capricious, connected with water, trees, mountains, and wilderness. In Hindu, Jain, and Buddhist texts, the *yakṣa* has a dual personality. On the one hand, a *yakṣa* may be an inoffensive nature-fairy, associated with woods and mountains; but there is also a darker version of the *yakṣa*, which is a kind of ghost that haunts the wilderness and waylays and devours travelers, as does the *rakṣasa* (see the following n. 167).

167. In Hindu, Jain, and Buddhist mythology, *rākṣasas*, which means "those from whom one must protect oneself," are terrifying evil spirits who consume raw flesh and wander in the night, taking on the likeness of animals or human beings.

168. The time of three years and six months reminds us of the figure that recurs several times in the Book of Revelation in different forms: forty-two months (Rev. 11:2), one thousand two hundred sixty days (Rev. 11:3; 12:6), one time, two times and half of a time (Rev. 12:14).

264 THE TEXTS IN TRANSLATION

which all creatures, [even] those whose nature and behavior are evil,[169] will be able to make a clear distinction between those who, having turned to the Truth, [393] accumulated merits,[170] and those who, not having believed in the judgments of the Honored One of Heaven, [394] are nothing more than demons in human form."

The Messiah and the One God [395] will be seen clearly in heaven. At the end of the world all the dead will rise according to the judgment [of the One God]. Therefore, [396] those of you who believe, who have accumulated merits, and who have walked the path of integrity, [397] will go up to the Heavenly Hall, to the place of eternal joy, [but] all those who know [398] the righteous path of the One God, but do not walk on his righteous paths,[171] who do not accept the judgments of the One God, commit [399] sins. Furthermore, those who worship evil spirits, *yakṣas*, and all other spirits, will immediately go to the prisons of the earth, [400] along with all hellish demons. [401] Eternally burned by a great fire, they will dwell there forever in great tribulation.

If you desire to obtain [salvation], listen to these words [402] and you will obtain it. All that you have heard will be fulfilled. Those who are not pleased with these words should think [403] about the fate of their own soul. Those who are not pleased [with these words] and do not listen to them [404] will share the fate of the demons, the prisons of the earth, from which there is no escape.

[405] Third scroll[172] of the *Discourse on the One God*.

In Revelation it coincides with the eschatological time and designates the time of trial and persecution, in which perseverance is required of believers. This symbolic figure, present in Revelation but coming from Daniel (cf. Dan. 7:25; 12:7), could have been present in the imagination of the author of our text, even though the Book of Revelation did not seem to fall within the first biblical canon of the Church of the East.

169. *Eye exing* 惡業惡性: compound expression, with a strong Buddhist flavor. *Eye* is actually negative *karman*, about which see p. 278n95.

170. *Zuo gongde*: see p. 239n31.

171. The structure of this sentence and the previous one, as well as the context in which they are inserted, leads me to read the character *jing* 經, "book," "scripture," "canon," as a scribal error in place of the character *jing* 徑, "path," a homophone of the previous word but having a different radical. If we were to maintain the character that we find in the text, the translation then could be: "but they do not act according to the good [i.e., true] scriptures."

172. See p. 225n23.

TEXT D

Book of the Lord Messiah
(*Xuting mishisuo jing* 序聽迷詩所經)

[2] AT THAT time,[1] the Messiah preached the doctrine of the Lord,[2] the Honored One of Heaven,[3] saying:[4]

Who can say how many different visions [concerning the Honored One of Heaven] there are? [3] To interpret the meaning of the Scriptures is difficult

---

1. *Book of the Lord Messiah* is a preliminary translation proposal for the title of this manuscript. I advance the hypothesis that *xuting* 序聽 may be the phonetic rendering in Chinese of the Sogdian *xwtw*, *xwt'w*, *xwd'w* (*xutāw*), and *mishisuo* 迷詩所 a corruption (i.e., a mistake in writing made by the copyist of the manuscript) for *mishihe* 迷詩訶 (or other homophonic transcriptions, such as those attested in the Tang Christian documents: 弥施訶, 弥師訶). In Sogdian Christian texts, this term for translating "Lord" is regularly used in connection with Jesus's name. For problems related to the interpretation and translation of the title, see Lin Wushu 2001d, 146–49; Deeg 2015, 211–12; 2020, 111–16. The complete title as it appears in the manuscript is *Xuting mishisuo jing yijuan* 序聽迷詩所經一卷 (Book of the Lord Messiah, in One Scroll).

2. *Xusuo* 序娑: all the hypotheses proposed thus far for the interpretation of this term, which appears to be a phonetic transcription, are unconvincing. One hypothesis is that this term, which is not found in the Buddhist texts in Chinese as a transcription from Sanskrit, may be a transcription from some other foreign language (Syriac, Sogdian, or Middle Persian). Moreover, several scholars think that we are faced with one of the various writing errors of the copyist and have proposed the correction of the second character of the term, which would give us *xupo* 序婆. Adopting this correction, I advance the hypothesis that it could be the phonetic rendering in Chinese of the first part (*xypϑ*) of the Sogdian term *xypϑ'wnt* (*xēpthāwānd*), another term for translating "Lord" and attested in fragments of Sogdian Christian literature. For a discussion of the problems surrounding the translation of this term, see Deeg 2020, 116–18.

3. *Tianzun* 天尊: see p. 237n21.

4. The literary structure of this incipit is frequent in Chinese Buddhist sutras that propose to pass on the words of the Enlightened. The expression "preaching the law" (*shuofa* 説法) is commonly used to describe the activity of teaching and transmitting the Buddha's *dharma*. Here it designates the preaching of God's teachings by the Messiah.

The Luminous Way to the East. Matteo Nicolini-Zani, Oxford University Press. © Oxford University Press 2022.
DOI: 10.1093/oso/9780197609644.003.0008

266　　　THE TEXTS IN TRANSLATION

to accomplish in a comprehensive way, so who can speak about it? What is the existence that is manifested [4] under the presence of the Honored One of Heaven? How far does his presence extend? Among all the divine beings,[5] among the beings that do not belong to the human race,[6] the spirit-guardians,[7] [5] the *arhats*,[8] who has ever been able to see the Honored One of Heaven? Among all living beings,[9] no one has ever seen the Honored One of Heaven.[10] [6] Who has the power to see the Honored One of Heaven? In fact, the Honored One of Heaven is like [7] the wind. Who can see the wind? In less than an instant, the Honored One of Heaven travels the whole world,[11] dwelling in every place.[12] [8] Since everyone holds within himself the breath[13] of the Honored One of Heaven, everyone can keep himself alive from the beginning, and from the beginning [9] he can thus, being in the peace of his house, reach [the state of] perfect mind and thought. From the rising of the sun to its setting, dwelling [in his house], he sees [10] his mind abandoning him and arriving everywhere. His body attains light, joy and quietness and dwells in heaven, in peace. [11] All divine beings move from one

---

5. *Zhufo* 諸佛: to name the divine creatures, and also God himself, the author uses here and in other passages in the text the term *fo*. This term (lit., "buddha") seems to have widened its semantic sphere in the Tang era, becoming a sort of "trans-religious" term for the gods, the divinity, the divine in general. Evidence of this usage is the fact that it was also chosen by the Manichaeans in the translation of their texts into Chinese (see DMTC, 100).

6. *Feiren* 非人: lit., "non-human." In Buddhist literature this term (Sk. *amanuṣya*) indicates the beings of the Buddhist pantheon, especially the evil spirits, such as *devas, kinnaras, nāgas, māras, rākṣasas*, and other creatures.

7. *Pingzhang tian* 平章天: the "*devas* guardians [of the universe]." Perhaps heavenly spirits in general are meant here.

8. This term (lit., "the worthy one") indicates, in general, the one who, completely freed from *saṃsāra*, has reached the last stage of spiritual development, i.e., has reached *nirvāṇa*. This liberation, however, is only personal and individual. It does not contribute to the liberation of others, as does the bodhisattva.

9. *Zhongsheng* 眾生: this word, common in Buddhist texts (Sk. *sattva*) and repeatedly used in this document, indicates the multitude of sentient beings immersed in *saṃsāra*.

10. Cf. 1 Tim. 6:16; John 1:18; 1 John 4:12.

11. *Shijian* 世間: this term, common in Chinese, in Buddhist texts (Sk. *loka*) assumes the specific meaning of the finite and ephemeral world, which consists of material (non-sentient) beings and sentient beings.

12. Cf. Ps. 139:7–10.

13. *Qi* 氣: a term that in traditional Chinese thought indicates a very complex concept. It is cosmic energy, but also primordial matter in which, at the beginning, *yin* and *yang* were mixed. Physical and spiritual balance is given by the proper flow of *qi*. Here it seems to indicate a sort of vital breath (that of Genesis 2:7?) with which God shares life with the first man.

Text D 267

place to another like the wind, and there is no place in the world that they do not reach. The Honored One of Heaven [**12**] is constantly in peace, in a place of happiness and joy, yet there is no place that is not reached by the effects[14] [of his existence]. Among the people of the world, [**13**] who knows the movements of the wind? One can only hear its voice,[15] but one cannot see its shape at all. No one can discern [**14**] the true reality of its appearance. Whether it be yellow, white, or the color of jade, no one knows. The wind dwells [**15**] in a powerful place; the Honored One of Heaven, given his divine power, lives in the same place. The place in which he lives [**16**] is inaccessible to human beings; in it there is no mortality,[16] nor are there magnificent figures.[17]

From the moment heaven and earth were created, [**17**] it is not possible for divine power to be absent from the world, and everyone is in a good position to [obtain] lasting joy and immortality. [**18**] When one is in tribulation, invoke the name of God.[18] There are many ignorant people who call on the gods as [**19**] if these were the Honored One of Heaven, addressing them as "Supreme Honored One" or "Highest Joy." According to their local traditions, people say, [**20**] "Our Honored One of Heaven is the Eternal One, different [from all others]."

The Honored One of Heaven has given humans [**21**] intelligence and knowledge in abundance. Whoever you are who express gratitude for God's compassionate mercy,[19] consider [this] carefully, and you will clearly see that the [Honored One of Heaven], [**22**] who knows neither sin nor evil, nourishes the human person and makes it grow to maturity, thanks to his divine power. Moreover, all living beings [**23**] should consider that what is in a human being—body, life, organs, and breath—are all things that have their

---

14. *Guobao* 果報: a technical Buddhist term (see p. 239n28).

15. Cf. John 3:8.

16. *Sisheng* 死生: lit., "death and birth," a Chinese translation of the Buddhist concept of *saṃsāra* (see p. 268n21).

17. I have interpreted the two characters *lisuo* 麗娑, which have no meaning as a compound, as a scribal error for *lizi* 麗姿, "beautiful things" or "beauties." With regard to the content of this last paragraph, it should be noted that the themes of the immortality of God, of the inaccessibility of his dwelling place of light, and of the impossibility of seeing God closely recall 1 Tim. 6:16.

18. *Foming* 佛名: here again the term *fo*, "buddha," is used for God (see p. 266n5).

19. *Fo ci'en* 佛慈恩: lit., "Buddha's compassion and mercy." Synonymous with *cibei* 慈悲 (Sk. *karuṇā*, "compassion"), *ci'en* designates a key concept of Buddhist doctrine.

268   THE TEXTS IN TRANSLATION

cause in the Honored One of Heaven.[20] [24] All living beings are subject to the cycle of rebirths.[21] They take a body and inhabit the earth, which is why they are transformed and formed [25] into [new] molecules. All living beings should improve their minds for perfect enlightenment and inwardly reflect, [that] all living beings [26] die, all living beings perish.

The personal destiny of all living beings is determined by the spirit.[22] At the moment life ceases to exist and their destiny approaches, [27] the spirit abandons living beings.[23] There is no spirit for the mind and thought, but they too are kept alive by the spirit. The moment the spirit abandons living beings [28] is the moment of passage. But why do people not see the spirit depart? And what color is the spirit? [29] Red, green, or some other color? It is not possible to see what the spirit is like.

Living beings say, [30] "Where is the Honored One of Heaven?" They also say, "Why do we not see the Honored One of Heaven? Why [31] do living beings find themselves in sin, [far] from [any ability] to see the Honored One of Heaven?" The Honored One of Heaven is not like a human being. [32] So [we say] once again, "Who can see him?" Among the living beings there is no one who dares to approach the Honored One of Heaven. [And yet] the beings whose actions bring about what is good[24] [33] can already begin to see the Honored One of Heaven.[25] In the world, from the beginning, the Honored One of Heaven has never been seen, nor has it been possible [34] to recognize him. For this reason, living beings do not see the [Honored One of] Heaven.[26] But if they cultivate merits,[27] they will not fall into the evil

---

20. Cf. Ps. 139:13–16; Job 10:8–12; Acts 17:25.

21. *Liuzhuan* 流轉: a technical term (Sk. *saṃsāra*, "transmigration") that in Buddhism indicates the cycle of births and deaths determined by birth; it is a source of suffering. The believer therefore aims to free himself from it and thus extinguish pain.

22. Previously used in the text to describe the transcendence of God, the same character *feng* 風, "wind," is here used to describe the spirit that inhabits humans, who is also transcendent because it is of divine nature.

23. Cf. Ps. 104:29–30; Job 34:14–15.

24. *Shanfu shanyuan* 善福善緣: a Buddhist expression that, against the background of the general conviction that each cause always corresponds to an effect, seems to indicate the good causes (positive *karma*) that give rise to the good fruits of liberation, and therefore to bliss.

25. Cf. Matt. 5:8. If the condition of sin prevents the vision of God, the way to blessedness and the contemplation of God is open for the one who acts correctly.

26. Cf. John 1:18; 1 John 4:12.

27. As above (see n. 24), here recourse is made to the Chinese *fu* 福 (Sk. *puṇya*), which in Buddhist terminology indicates positive *karman*.

way [that leads] to the prisons of the earth [35] but reach [the way that leads to] heaven.[28] But if there are wicked people[29] who let themselves fall into the evil way, they will not see [36] brilliant fruit[30] and will not reach the way of heaven. Therefore, let the living creatures pay close attention [to this].

The heavens and the earth [37] are pervaded by numerous and powerful forces of evil.[31] [It happens that] those who serve and promote them are solicitous for the country and thus are given many official titles [38] and are offered the greatest variety of foods in huge quantities. [On the contrary, it happens that] those who do not serve [39] the many powerful forces of evil [and then] do not submit to the imperial orders are not given official titles, nor are they offered any reward. [40] Driven away, they die in exile. But none of this is the result of the independent action of the many powerful forces of evil [41] but is due to the cycle of causes and effects resulting from previous births. [For this reason], let living beings think first of all of the remuneration [they will receive] [42] for the actions they have performed.[32]

It was the Honored One of Heaven who originally expended great effort to raise up living beings.[33] Let the living beings [43] keep in mind that God[34] is not far away; he has raised human beings to their responsibility.[35]

Good bears good fruits, while evil carries its causes on its back.

---

28. *Tiandao* 天道: this Buddhist word (Sk. *devagati*, "the kingdom of the gods") indicates a place of happiness and joy where the deserving enjoy the fruits of their positive *karman*. The author of this text seems to use it to describe the way of salvation, which leads to the blessedness and vision of God, in antithesis to the evil way (*edao* 惡道, Sk. *durgati*), which leads to hell, to perdition. This part is very reminiscent of the final part of the third section ("Discourse of the Honored One of the Universe on Almsgiving") of the *Discourse on the One God* (Text C, cols. 396–404, p. 264).

29. Lit., "negative-*karman* beings." On the Buddhist concept of *karman*, see p. 278n95.

30. That is, the reward intended for those who, on the other hand, have sown positively.

31. *Tianda zhue* 天大諸惡: lit., "all the wicked things as big as the sky."

32. In these last lines the author makes extensive use of Buddhist terminology, expressing in Chinese the key concepts of the teaching preached by the Buddha: the doctrine of causes and effects, more properly called the "law of dependent origination" (see p. 270n39), of the cycle of birth-death-birth, of remuneration on the basis of one's conduct in a previous life. It is interesting to point out the Chinese expression *yuanye zhongguo* 緣業種果, lit., "cause and effect, seed and fruit," to indicate the Buddhist law of dependent origination. The situation described in this paragraph aims to explain that what we can experience as an apparent contradiction is actually the result of unknown causes that shape the present.

33. See the creation account of Genesis 1–2.

34. The term *fo*, "buddha," is also used here to refer to God.

35. See the creation account of Genesis 1, which portrays Adam as a human being invested by God with responsibility for creation, that of Genesis 2–3, which portrays Adam and Eve and

270　　　　THE TEXTS IN TRANSLATION

[44] Ignorant beings make for themselves camels, elephants, oxen, donkeys, horses, and other animals out of clay and wood; they even make roe and deer. [45] Although [people] give them a form, they cannot give them life.[36]

Let those who possess knowledge reflect, and [the relationship between] cause and effect[37] [46] will become evident to them. Once more, they will know that this is the truth.

In this world there are many [47] who make for themselves a great number of manufactured figures and serve them the same way they serve the Honored One of Heaven, [48] but they cannot give them life. All people are deceived, and make for themselves metal images, silver [49] and bronze idols, as well as idols of clay and wood. Moreover, they make [statues of] numerous [50] domestic animals and human [images] resembling [real] people, images of horses resembling [real] horses, of oxen resembling [real] oxen, of donkeys resembling [51] [real] donkeys. Only they cannot walk, talk, eat, or breathe.[38] They have no flesh [52] or skin, no organs or bones.

The interlinking of the causes of all things[39] is not a question about which we [can] speak exhaustively. [However], with a few words one can grasp many aspects [53] of the intrinsic organization of this interlinking. It is for the benefit of all that we speak of it, that [all] may be led to discern good and evil. [The situation is similar to] our ability to determine whether or not the food and drink [54] offered in a plentiful banquet are tasty or insipid by sampling only a few of the dishes. Any effort, however, on the part of the servants of the Honored One of Heaven [55] to interpret the meaning of the Scriptures and to accomplish all that is contained in them will be very commendable.

---

their freedom in the face of evil, and that of Genesis 4, which portrays Cain and Abel and human responsibility toward another human being.

36. The theme of idolatry, which is taken up a little later, is a purely biblical theme. The living and true God, the giver of life, is contrasted with false idols, objects made by human hands. Those who fabricate idols are therefore described primarily as ignorant (cf. Isa. 44:9–20).

37. Another allusion to the law of dependent origination (see below, n. 39).

38. Cf. Ps. 115:4–7; Deut. 4:28.

39. The law of dependent origination (Sk. *pratītyasamutpāda*), central to Buddhist thought, sets out the conditions and connections necessary for the appearance or disappearance of phenomena and existence. Quite simply, this law states that acts are always followed by an effect, by retribution, and this is ultimately equivalent to a rebirth by virtue of the cycle of *saṃsāra*, itself governed by the law of dependent origination. Acts are conditioned by certain factors that always proceed in a precise order of succession in relation to each other: that is, there is an interlinking, an interdependence, which is well rendered here in Chinese with the expression *youxu* 由緒, lit., "thread [of connection] of the causes."

Text D 271

[56] But if the details were more numerous, the [comprehensibility of the] interlinking of causes would be less.

However, among those who serve the Honored One of Heaven and interpret the heavenly will, there are some [57] who fear the law of the Honored One of Heaven, show a good heart in their conduct, do good works, and exhort others to good works. These are they [58] who have accepted the teaching of the Honored One of Heaven and who have accepted his precepts.[40] The fate of those who often do evil and teach it [59] to others, who have not accepted the teaching of the Honored One of Heaven and have fallen into the evil path will be in the hands of King Yama.[41] [60] There are others who have accepted the teaching of the Honored One of Heaven and who repeatedly say, "I have accepted the precepts," and teach others to accept them,[42] showing that they too fear [61] the Honored One of Heaven. Every day they warn them against error, so that each living person will fear the Honored One of Heaven. [These] exercise dominion [62] over all beings, living and dead, and have authority and dominion over all divine creatures.

If living beings fear the Honored One of Heaven, [63] [they must] also fear the holy sovereign.[43] Blessings abound in the life[44] of the holy sovereign. The Honored One of Heaven supports his government, [64] which is not his own undertaking, but that of the Honored One of Heaven. Since they are subject to the one who proclaims himself a holy sovereign, [65] everyone [must] submit to his orders. If there is anyone who does not accept [the orders] of the holy sovereign and obey his decrees, [66] that one is a rebel. Those who accept the orders of the holy sovereign [67] become persons who have a right understanding of all things. Those who obey the decrees are good; they

---

40. *Shoujie* 受戒: an expression used by Buddhists to indicate the act of receiving the teachings of the Buddha, of accepting his precepts, of submitting to the discipline of the Buddhist community. It therefore means becoming a disciple of the Buddha. The beginner receives the first five precepts; the novice and the laypeople who are more zealous receive the first eight precepts; and finally the monk, at the time of his ordination, receives all ten precepts. In our text the author uses this expression many times to indicate becoming a believer in God.

41. *Yanluo wang* 閻羅王: King Yama (Sk. *Yamarāja*). He is the Lord of Death, the supreme judge of the dead in Hindu mythology. In China he does not rise to the level of supreme sovereign of the underworld, but is only one of the ten kings of the lower regions and judges only the actions of men; judgment of the actions of women is reserved to Yamī, his sister.

42. Cf. Matt. 5:19.

43. Cf. Rom. 13:1–7. "Holy sovereign" (*shengshang* 聖上) is an appellation that designates the Chinese emperor.

44. *Qianshen* 前身: a technical Buddhist term that literally indicates previous existences, previous incarnations.

272 THE TEXTS IN TRANSLATION

exhort [68] others to do good and not to do evil. They become the dwelling place that receives the precepts. If [69] any accept the precepts but do not fear the Honored One of Heaven, [or, on the contrary], conform their whole life to the divine doctrine[45] but do not become [70] the dwelling that receives the precepts, they are rebels.[46]

Thirdly, [living beings] must fear and honor their parents [71] as [they fear and honor] the Honored One of Heaven and the holy sovereign. Those who do not fail to serve first the Honored One of Heaven, [72] then the holy sovereign, and finally also their parents, will receive a blessing from the Honored One of Heaven. [73] These three things alone [are required]: first, to serve the Honored One of Heaven; [74] second, to serve the holy sovereign; third, to serve one's parents.

In heaven and on earth, [75] [all beings come into existence] through the action of their parents. This also applies to the holy sovereign. [Actually], his origin is divine, even though he has [76] parents in this world. People should consider [this] wisely, and fear the Honored One of Heaven, [77] the holy sovereign, and their parents.

[First vow]: Those who truly accept the teachings of the Honored One of Heaven do not transgress his precepts.[47] [78] Those who accept the Honored One of Heaven and his teaching first of all lead other living beings to honor all celestial creatures[48] [79] and to endure all tribulation for God,[49] for it is only through the pure[50] power [of God] that heaven and earth have been established. [80] All the holy sovereign has to do is exhort the community of believers[51] to perfection and in his palace implore all the divine beings. [81] The holy sovereign has the power to do so. The Honored One of Heaven says,

---

45. *Fofa* 佛法: lit., "the law of Buddha" (Sk. *buddhadharma*). Here again, the term *fo*, "buddha," is chosen by the author to mean God.

46. Here the author seems to be saying that faith and works must both be affirmed (cf. Jas. 2:14–26).

47. *Pojie* 破戒: lit., "breaking the precepts," is a common expression in Buddhist literature (about receiving the Buddhist precepts, see p. 271n40).

48. *Zhu tianfo* 諸天佛: a recurrent expression in the Buddhist texts.

49. *Fo* 佛, "buddha," in the Chinese text.

50. *Qingjing* 清淨: see p. 241n42.

51. This is my interpretation of a difficult passage. The character *jia* 伽 seems to be the second character of a compound word, *sengjia* 僧伽 (Sk. *saṅgha*), which indicates the Buddhist monastic community. The first character of the compound has most probably been omitted or forgotten by the scribe.

Text D 273

"Those who [82] return to all sorts of evil, [these] rebel against the Honored One [of Heaven] and show no filial piety."

Second vow:[52] [83] Those who show filial piety towards parents and respect all living beings, who do not fail to take care of parents and honor them, [84] will obtain the way to their dwelling place in heaven when they reach the end of their life. Therefore, parents [85] should be cared for, since, without parents, which of the living beings would have come into existence?[53]

Fourth[54] vow: [86] Those who have accepted the precepts show themselves benevolent[55] in their relationship with other beings and have no evil feelings.

Fifth [87] vow: Living beings do not kill other living beings, nor induce others to kill; in fact, [88] living beings and human beings share the same life, without any difference.[56]

Sixth vow: Do not urge someone else's wife to commit adultery, [89] nor abandon yourselves [to it].[57]

Seventh vow: Do not commit theft.[58]

Eighth [vow]: Do not be envious [90] when you see those who have money and riches, or see others—owners of fields, houses, and servants— surrounded by riches and honors.[59]

Ninth vow: [91] Towards those who have a good wife, money, and houses in great numbers, [do not] produce false documents to deceive them.[60]

---

52. The Chinese term used here and later is *yuan* 願 (Sk. *praṇihita* or *praṇidhāna*), which in Buddhism indicates a vow, that is, the firm will, the firm decision to observe the discipline that the vow imposes. We may have here a sort of (incomplete) decalogue, partially adapted to the Chinese context. There is no explicit mention of the first vow, but it can be implicitly recognized in the previous paragraph, which speaks of the acceptance of the teachings of the Honored One of Heaven. On these "ten vows," see Tian Haihua 2009; Wang Lanping 2009; Li Zhu 2016; Li-Layec 2019.

53. Cf. Exod. 20:12.

54. The text does not mention a third vow between the second and fourth. Some translators propose that the second part of the second vow ("Therefore, parents . . .") might be a third vow.

55. *Fa shanxin* 發善心: lit., "show a good heart." In Buddhism this expression, which occurs twice in the text, indicates an inner attitude of benevolence, which outwardly manifests itself in helping those in need and in the practice of almsgiving.

56. Cf. Exod. 20:13.

57. Cf. Exod. 20:14.

58. Cf. Exod. 20:15.

59. Cf. Exod. 20:17.

60. Cf. Exod. 20:16.

274 THE TEXTS IN TRANSLATION

Tenth [92] vow: If you receive goods from others in consignment, [do not] squander them for your advantage.[61]

The Honored One of Heaven has commanded [93] many [other] things to be observed.[62] If you see a weak person, do not take advantage [of his weakness] to oppress him. If you see someone who is poor, do not turn away your face, and [if you see] an enemy of yours [94] who is hungry, feed him and give him plenty to drink[63] so as to stifle and extinguish the resentment caused by your enmity. If you see a man toiling, [95] toil with him, and offer him the drink he needs. If you see someone without clothes, give that person something to wear. If an employee [of yours] is needy, [96] do not wait even one day [to give him clothes to wear];[64] he and his family could not otherwise escape the cold. If you see a servant, do not rant against him: the divine creatures have the power to do worse [to you], because they can cause you [97] great misfortunes. If a poor man asks you for money and you have it, give it to him.[65] But if you have no money to give him, [98] dismiss him quietly, since you are not in a position to give him alms. If you see someone who has been sick for a long time, do not [99] mock him,[66] because such an illness is not his fault. [If you see] a poor man without clothes or with his clothes shredded, [100] do not mock him. Do not take advantage of others by taking away [what they own].[67] Do not do injustice to others. If anyone is accused, [101] let him be judged according to truth and not given an unjust sentence. [102] If a defenseless and abandoned person, whether that be a man or a woman, or a widowed woman, [103] is brought to trial, do not give in to injustice, do not allow the truth to be distorted.[68] Do not be haughty, do not [104] brag, do not talk behind someone's back so as to set two people against

---

61. On the subject of the custody of others' property, cf. Exod. 22:6–14.

62. This is followed by a very interesting passage that lists various situations in which believers are asked to give concrete witness to their faith by showing love to a neighbor in need. In the background one can easily detect similar biblical themes, in particular some ethical norms contained in the Pentateuch. However, here we shall only point out a few of the scriptural references that lie behind these passages.

63. Cf. Prov. 25:21.

64. Cf. Deut. 24:14–15; Lev. 19:13.

65. Cf. Matt. 5:42.

66. Cf. Lev. 19:14 (against contempt for the deaf and the blind).

67. Cf. Lev. 19:11.

68. Cf. Lev. 19:15; Exod. 23:1–3, 6.

Text D

one another. [If that happens], seek [a solution] among yourselves, and do not [105] appeal to the local magistrates, because you do not know [what] their sentence [might be].[69]

None of those who have accepted the precepts should do any harm to others [but] [106] let them always be benevolent to all living beings.[70] Even if something bad happens to you, do not wish misfortune on others. [107] Of the many [precepts], only a few are essential: let everyone always do good to all living beings. If anyone [108] desires to know [these precepts], [they should know] that those who have received them have written them down. Thus, whoever acts in accordance with these Scriptures will be one who has accepted the precepts.[71] [109] Whoever does not act in accordance [with these Scriptures] will be one who has not accepted the precepts. [All these] provisions come from the Honored One of Heaven and are addressed [110] to all, the old, the great, and the insignificant, so that all may receive them and exhort one another in goodness before anything else. The Honored One of Heaven has arranged [111] for living beings to obey him. Those who obey him will not allow living beings to be killed, not even for sacrifice.[72] [112] Those who do not obey this teaching kill living creatures and sacrifice them, and then eat their flesh. [113] They rely on false gods and kill lambs and other [animals]. Those who do not do good do not obey this teaching; [114] those who order [others] to do the same return to do evil, and consequently turn their backs on the Honored One of Heaven.

Seeing human beings in this situation, [115] the Honored One of Heaven felt great compassion. [Since] people did not obey him,[73] even though they had been encouraged to do good, the Honored One of Heaven sent the Sweet Spirit[74] [116] to a virgin whose name is Mary.[75] The Sweet Spirit entered Mary's womb and, [117] as had been ordered by the Honored One of Heaven,

---

69. Cf. 1 Cor. 6:1–6.

70. Cf. Ps. 34:15; Rom. 12:17–18.

71. That is, a disciple.

72. Respect for all forms of life, a Buddhist precept already stated previously in the more general context of the prohibition of killing, is here taken up in its application to sacrifices and in the more specific context of idolatry.

73. It is interesting to note that God's intervention is moved by his compassion for humans, and that the birth of the Messiah is yet another act of God's love for people who do not recognize him and do not walk along his ways.

74. *Liangfeng* 涼風: lit., "cool breeze," indicating the Holy Spirit. In other texts another expression recurs: *jingfeng* 淨風, lit., "pure wind" (see p. 201n30).

75. *Moyan* 末艷: phonetic transcription of the Syriac name Maryam (or of its correspondent Sogdian form, modeled on the Syriac).

THE TEXTS IN TRANSLATION

Mary immediately became pregnant.[76] This happened because the Honored One of Heaven had sent the Sweet Spirit; [118] no man was responsible for the pregnancy of the virgin. Seeing that no [119] man was responsible for the pregnancy, people said to one another, "The Honored One of Heaven is powerful indeed!" [120] [This event] also led people to return[77] with faith and purity[78] to the cause of good.[79]

When Mary's pregnancy came to term, [121] she gave birth to a son, whose name is Jesus.[80] Paternity is to be attributed to[81] the Sweet Spirit, but there were some ignorant people [122] who said, "If this is the way things are, then the responsibility for the pregnancy and birth rests with the Spirit. But in this world [it cannot be like that], [for in it] there is [123] a holy sovereign who issues rulings. All he has to do is decide, and people are driven into exile. For this reason, everyone submits to his rulings."[82]

[124] The Honored One of Heaven makes his light shine from above in heaven and on earth. At the moment of the birth of Jesus the Messiah in this world, [125] its brilliant effect was seen in heaven and on earth. [126] A star[83] as big as the wheel of a chariot appeared. It lit up the dwelling place of the

---

76. Cf. Matt. 1:18.

77. *Huixiang* 迴向: in the Buddhist lexicon, this term (Sk. *parinnāmanā*) indicates a change in direction and orientation, that is, the movement proper to conversion.

78. *Xinxin qingjing* 信心清淨: lit., "sincere heart and purity."

79. *Shanyuan* 善緣: Buddhist word perhaps used here to speak of God as the first cause, source of all that in the world manifests itself as goodness.

80. *Yishu* 移鼠: phonetic transcription of the Syriac name Išoʿ (or of the correspondent Sogdian form, modeled on the Syriac). See Nie 2012b; 2016, 76–87. The same choice of rendering the name Jesus in Chinese through a phonetic transcription, but using two other homophonic characters (翳數), is present in the third section ("Discourse of the Honored One of the Universe on Almsgiving") of the *Discourse on the One God* (Text C, col. 214, p. 251 and n. 94; col. 363, p. 262 and n. 161). Cf. Matt. 1:25.

81. Lit., "comes from."

82. A possible meaning of this passage is that the conception of Jesus could not be understood by ignorant people, that is, people without faith, who did not go beyond the logic of the world, its laws, and its customs.

83. *Xinxing* 辛星: the character *xin* designates the eighth of the so-called celestial stems (*tiangan* 天干), corresponding in Chinese tradition to astrological cycles. The identification of this star with such an astrological sign could indicate the time in which it appeared. The allusion to the star is present in Matthew's Gospel, but linked to the visit of the Magi (cf. Matt. 2:1–12), of which the author of our text makes no mention. The annunciation to the Virgin and the birth of the Messiah accompanied by the rising of a star are also briefly narrated in the text of the Xi'an stele (Text A, col. 6, pp. 200–201).

Text D

277

Honored One of Heaven. At that moment [**127**] [the Messiah] was born in the city of Jerusalem,[84] in the country of "Rome."[85]

[**128**] After five years[86] had passed since his birth, the Messiah began to speak and preach his doctrine, and to do good to all the living.

[**129**] Twelve years later,[87] [the Messiah] went to the place of purification called Jordan,[88] to be marked and immersed in the river by John.[89] John, [**130**] who from the beginning was a disciple of the Messiah, prostrated himself before the Holy One. [John] lived in a cave [**131**] all his life and did not eat meat or drink wine[90] but only raw vegetables and honey, the honey of the earth.[91] [**132**] At that time, many went to John for the ceremony of immersion, thus returning to adhere to the precepts.[92] [**133**] Then John let the Messiah enter the Jordan to be washed clean.[93] The Messiah, [**134**] after entering the river, came out of the water, and it came about that the Sweet Spirit descended from heaven. Its appearance [**135**] was similar to a small dove that came to rest on

---

84. *Wulishilian* 烏梨師斂: phonetic transcription of the Syriac place name Urišlem (or of its correspondent Sogdian form, modeled on the Syriac). It is worth noting that there is a divergence from the Gospel stories, which speak more precisely of Bethlehem as the place of Jesus's birth.

85. See p. 248n82.

86. There is no trace of this time period in the Gospel accounts.

87. The age of Jesus at the time of his baptism is not mentioned in the Gospels. An allusion to the age of twelve is present in Luke, but it refers to the age of Jesus when he conversed with the teachers in the temple of Jerusalem (cf. Luke 2:42).

88. The proper noun that is thought to indicate the Jordan River is rendered in the Chinese text in two different ways: here with Shunan 述難, later with Duonan 多難. If it refers to the Jordan, as the context would suggest, it seems that the rendering Duonan is to be considered the correct one since it calls to mind the Syriac name [Yur]denan (or the correspondent Sogdian form, modeled on the Syriac). Shunan could therefore be considered an error of the scribe, who chose the wrong character for the first character of the compound.

89. *Ruohun* 若昏: I interpret this as *yuhun* 谷昏, since this form is attested twice in two subsequent passages and since the first character *yu* can be easily confused with the similar character *ruo*. It appears to be the phonetic transcription of the Syriac name Yoḥanan (or its correspondent Sogdian form, modeled on the Syriac). Cf. Matt. 3:13.

90. Cf. Luke 7:33.

91. Matt. 3:4 and Mark 1:6 speak of "wild honey." The expression used here could therefore indicate wild honey, that is, honey produced by wild bees and collected in the cracks of rocks in the desert of Judah (cf. Ps. 81:17: "honey from the rock").

92. *Fu shoujie* 復受戒: this expression is perhaps used to indicate conversion. Cf. Matt. 3:5–6; Mark 1:5.

93. What seems to be implied here is the initial resistance of John to baptize Jesus, as described by Matt. 3:14–15.

278 THE TEXTS IN TRANSLATION

the Messiah. In the air [a voice] said, "The Messiah [136] is my son. Let all the living in the world be subject to the will of the Messiah. [137] What he commands is that all should do good."[94]

As was predisposed by the Honored One of Heaven, the Messiah has shown the living the way to heaven. [He, in fact], [138] has disposed that all who live in the world cease to serve [false] gods. [139] Since those who have listened to these words are no longer subject to [false] gods and have ceased to do evil, let them place their faith in good actions.[95]

[140] The Messiah, from the age of twelve to the age of thirty-two,[96] implored all those who are evil[97] [141] to turn to the way of goodness and good deeds.[98] The Messiah had twelve disciples,[99] [142] who later underwent suffering. The dead were brought back to life, the blind were given their sight, those whose appearance [143] was deformed[100] were later healed, the sick were cured and [their illnesses] eradicated, those who were subdued by demons were freed from them, [144] even the lame were cured.[101] All the sick approached the Messiah and, [145] by taking hold of his *kaṣāya*,[102] were cured.[103]

But even at that time there was no lack of those who did evil, who did not turn to the way of goodness, [146] who did not believe in the teaching of the Honored One of Heaven, who were impure and eager for profit. [147]

---

94. Cf. Matt. 3:16–17; Mark 1:10–11; Luke 3:22.

95. Lit., "in a positive *karman*." Here and in the following lines, the author makes explicit use of the Buddhist concept of *karman*, lit., "action," and the Chinese terms expressing it. The doctrine of *karman* (commonly known by the word *karma*, the plural of *karman*), according to which every act done intentionally creates a karmic "seed" that will ripen and bear fruit at the appropriate time in accordance with its positive (*haoye* 好業) or negative (*eye* 惡業) nature, seems to be used here to speak about the effects that can be produced when someone converts from idolatry and sin to the teachings of the Honored One of Heaven.

96. Luke's Gospel reports that "Jesus, when he began his ministry, was about thirty years old" (Luke 3:23).

97. Lit., "beings with negative *karman*."

98. Lit., "positive *karman*."

99. *Dizi* 弟子: common term in Buddhist texts to designate the disciples of the Buddha.

100. That is, the crippled.

101. Cf. Matt. 4:24; 10:8; 11:5; 15:31.

102. See p. 212n103.

103. Cf. Matt. 9:21; 14:36; Mark 6:56; 5:27–29.

Text D 279

There were [even] some well-educated persons[104] who loved wine and flesh-meat, who served [false] gods, and who, [148] in their slander and jealousy,[105] wanted [the Messiah] killed. But many [149] believed in his teaching, making it impossible to kill him. So those evil people[106] joined together [150] and stirred up people who were faithful and pure, managing to induce even the rulers to want the Messiah killed. [151] For him there was no way to escape the great king.[107] People whose words and actions were evil slandered the Messiah, [152] presenting as wickedness the fact that he had done good and also taught others to do good. When he was thirty-two years old, [153] [the Messiah] was brought to trial before the great king Pilate[108] by those whose deeds were evil.[109] [154] Before Pilate they said, "The Messiah deserves the death sentence." The great king [155] investigated all the accusations of wickedness [that were leveled against the Messiah]. [156] In the presence of the great king Pilate, the advisability of condemning the Messiah to death was considered. The great king, as he was about to give orders as to whether that man [157] should be sentenced to death, [said], "Verily I neither see nor judge there [to be any fault]; this man does not deserve death." [158] [In fact], this had been organized by those evil people. The great king said, "I cannot kill this man." But the evil people [159] said, "If this man is not put to death, our men and women [will suffer harm]." The great king Pilate [160] asked

---

104. *Wenren* 文人: the reference here is probably to the scribes.

105. For the emphasis placed on the jealousy of the authorities, cf. Matt. 27:18; Mark 15:10.

106. In the following part of the text, concerning the condemnation of the Messiah, the emphasis is placed on the responsibility of the "evil people." I thus translate three different Chinese forms used in the Buddhist texts that define these people: *e'ren* 惡人, "evil people"; *eye ren* 惡業人, "people with negative *karman*"; and *eyuan ren* 惡緣人, "people with a negative condition (Sk. *pratyaya*)." The allusion could refer, on the basis of the Gospel accounts, to the high priests and the elders of the people, that is, to the Jewish religious authorities. The amount of space devoted in the account to the plotting of the unbelieving Jews appears to be excessive. However, the reason for this emphasis may be the catechetical purpose of the author rather than any supposed anti-Semitism. One of the many "stumbling blocks" for Chinese to believe that the Christian Messiah was a worthy figure of worship was his condemnation and death as a criminal. Thus, a detailed account had to be provided to show that his death was not due to any crimes of his own but that it was rather a miscarriage of justice that was still part of God's plan of salvation.

107. It is interesting to note that Pilate is designated as *dawang* 大王, "great king," a title that the author of this text has chosen to translate the office of governor into Chinese.

108. *Piluodusi* 毗羅都思: phonetic transcription in Chinese of a foreign term, probably the Syriac name Pilaṭos.

109. Cf. Matt. 27:2 and parallels. The allusion to the thirty-two years of age of Jesus at the time of his arrest is not attested in the Gospels.

280 THE TEXTS IN TRANSLATION

for water and washed his hands. [Then] in the presence of those evil ones, [he said], "There is no way I will execute this man." [161] But the wicked insisted on demanding [condemnation], so that it was no longer possible for [the Messiah] to be spared from death.[110]

The Messiah [162] delivered himself to the wicked for the benefit of all the living. So that the inhabitants of the world might know that their lives [163] are like a candle about to become extinct, he gave his life and suffered death as a ransom for the living of this world. The Messiah [164] delivered himself up and suffered death.[111] The evil people led the Messiah [165] to another place, to the place of execution,[112] which is called Golgotha[113] and bound him to the wood.[114] [166] They also brought two thieves [there], putting one on his left and one on his right.[115] The day when [167] the Messiah was bound to the wood for five hours was the fast of the sixth day.[116] They tied

---

110. A large part of the text is devoted to Pilate's judgment. What most characterizes this narrative, read in the light of the Gospel accounts (cf. Matt. 27:11–26; Mark 15:1–15; Luke 23:1–6, 13–26; John 18:28–19:16), is the emphasis placed on the planning and responsibility of the religious authorities, the absence of any dialogue between Pilate and Jesus, and the lack of any mention of the consequences the condemnation or absolution of Jesus would have for the people. One should also note the allusion to the gesture of Pilate washing his hands, which within the canonical tradition is reported only by the Gospel of Matthew (cf. Matt. 27:24).

111. Here the purpose of Christ's death is made explicit: first of all, that he freely gave his life as a ransom for all—this is clearly the teaching of the New Testament (cf. Matt. 20:28; Mark 10:45; John 10:17–18; 1 Tim. 2:6; Titus 2:14)—but also that Jesus wanted to show people that their life is mortal and in God's hands (and in this also lies salvation, the author seems to say). The latter purpose is clearly an emphasis proper to our text. A brief description of the crucifixion follows, in which many elements present in the Gospel accounts are omitted. This version is closer to the Matthean account than to that of the other Gospels.

112. This is my proposed interpretation of a difficult passage. Literally, according to my reading of the characters allegedly written incorrectly by the scribe: "The neighborhood where the wood [i.e., the Cross] was raised up."

113. All translators recognize in the Chinese expression *Qiju* 訖句 the phonetic rendering of the foreign name Golgotha. Even if there are strong doubts about such an identification, mostly due to our ignorance of the precise term that lies behind it (the Syriac Gagulta?), here I too adopt the common interpretation, not finding for the moment other possible solutions.

114. Cf. Acts 5:30; 10:39; 13:29; 1 Pet. 2:24.

115. Cf. Matt. 27:38.

116. *Liuri zhai* 六日齋: the practice of fasting, attested to very early in the ancient church, was immediately put in relation to the two main moments of the Lord's passion, namely, the betrayal of Jesus (Wednesday), and his crucifixion and death (Friday). In the Church of the East, fasting was particularly stressed, and perhaps for this reason the text highlights this element. It is interesting to note that the Chinese term used, *zhai*, is a technical word that Buddhist

Text D 281

him up at dawn,[117] and until **[168]** dusk there was darkness everywhere.[118] The earth trembled and the mountains collapsed. All the tombs of the earth were opened, **[169]** and life was restored to all the dead.[119] Having seen this, those present, as well as all the living and the dead who had not believed **[170]** the Scriptures and the teaching, recognized [Jesus] as the Messiah. Among those present was a man with a heart rich in faith[120] who said, . . .[121]

---

monasticism adopted in China to designate its practice of fasting, which consisted mostly of a few days or periods of abstinence and limitation to a single meal before noon.

117. Mark instead speaks of "the third hour" (cf. Mark 15:25), that is, nine o'clock in the morning.

118. The chronological data relating to the persistence of darkness does not agree with the synoptic tradition (cf. Matt. 27:45; Mark 15:33; Luke 23:44).

119. Cf. Matt. 27:51–53. A similar description of the death of Jesus Christ can also be found in the third section ("Discourse of the Honored One of the Universe on Almsgiving") of the *Discourse on the One God* (Text C, cols. 279–85, p. 256).

120. Probable allusion to the Roman centurion, described as the first believer (cf. Matt. 27:54).

121. The text is interrupted here, and it is obviously unfinished.

TEXT E

Book on Profound and Mysterious Blessedness (*Zhixuan anle jing* 志玄安樂經)

[2] WHEN SUCH sublime words were heard, the supreme . . .[1] [3] river, inside the Hall of Pure Emptiness,[2] together with all . . . [4] those who were around, left and right, standing deferentially side by side. . . . [5] [Simon] Peter [?] [and the other] followers stood up and huddled around . . . [saying]: [6] "We are completely confused,[3] . . . [7] with what skillful means[4] save[5] sentient beings[6] . . ."

---

1. Since the first part of the manuscript is damaged, the first ten columns of the text are incomplete.

2. The term *tiantang* 天堂, "heavenly hall," recurrent in Buddhist texts to indicate the place of bliss and the extinction of all desire and suffering, was borrowed by Christians to designate in all probability the Christian paradise, as evidenced by the Sino-Christian texts of the Tang era that have come down to us. The similar expression that is present at the beginning of this text (*jingxu tang* 淨虛堂), which is still within the terminology used by the Buddhists, may have been chosen to designate this same immaterial reality. This is the place where the Messiah instructs his disciples.

3. *Mihuo* 迷惑: this Buddhist term (Sk. *saṃmūḍha*) indicates the deception of *māyā*, the illusion that leads away from the truth of reality.

4. *Fangbian* 方便: this Buddhist technical term (Sk. *upāya* or *upāyakauśalya*) refers to a method that is convenient to the place or situation, therefore opportune, appropriate. It means teaching according to the capacity of the hearer, by any suitable method, including that of a device or stratagem that would benefit the recipient. The notion of skillful means is something distinctive to Buddhism as compared with other religions. It is related to the fundamental view, expressed in the earliest Buddhist teachings, that the actual content of the Buddha's enlightenment cannot be conveyed through ordinary language. In this sense of the term, any sort of teaching that occurs through language can be seen as a skillful method.

5. *Jiuhu* 救護: a Buddhist term that literally means "save [and] protect."

6. *Youqing* 有情 (Sk. *sattva*) is a Buddhist term to indicate sentient beings endowed with consciousness.

The Luminous Way to the East. Matteo Nicolini-Zani, Oxford University Press. © Oxford University Press 2022.
DOI: 10.1093/oso/9780197609644.003.0009

Text E 283

[8] The Messiah replied by saying, "Well! . . . [9] [living] beings . . . if you try to scrutinize the transcendent doctrine,[7] sit back and discipline your spirit . . . [10] all species [of beings] have a nature [characterized] by blessedness,[8] so . . . [11] like the moon in the water: if the water gets cloudy, it no longer reflects the image [of the moon]; or like the straw [burning] in the fire: [12] if the straw gets wet, you will no longer see the brightness of the fire. The same is true of living beings[9] immersed [in ignorance].[10]

Simon [13] Peter,[11] [along with] all those who follow the transcendent way,[12] first of all abandon emotions and passions. [Indeed], without emotions and passions there will be no yearning or [14] [mental] activity.[13] Without yearning or [mental] activity, one can be limpid and pure.[14] Being limpid and

---

7. *Shengfa* 勝法: recurrent expression in the text that in Buddhism indicates the inscrutable law that is beyond any description and surpasses any understanding (Sk. *abhidharma*), thanks to which you can realize the true essence of reality, and then *nirvāṇa*.

8. The term *anle* 安樂 (Sk. *sukha*), lit., "peace [and] joy," in Buddhism means the condition of (bodily and mental) beatitude proper to the awakened beings who have purified their mind and their bodies from spiritual hindrances and physical pollutions, have realized the true reality, and have been therefore liberated from suffering. It is the condition proper to the Pure Land of Ultimate Bliss (*jile jingtu* 極樂净土; Sk. *sukhāvatī*). Influenced by Buddhism, we find this term also in later Daoism (see Yamada 2015). Different compounds with *anle* are present also in the Chinese Manichaean *Hymnscroll* (see DMTC, 1).

9. *Hansheng* 含生: a Buddhist term for beings endowed with life. Two synonyms of this term, *youqing* (see p. 282n6) and *zhongsheng* 眾生 (see p. 266n9), are also used throughout the text.

10. *Chenmai* 沉埋: lit., "immersed [in the cycle of birth and death] and plunged [into ignorance]," i.e., not released from *saṃsāra*.

11. *Cenwen seng* 岑穩僧: an expression composed of two terms of foreign origin. On the basis of a hypothetical phonetic reconstruction, they seem to be the Chinese transcription of the Sogdian *Šmywn sng* (*Šamghōn sang*), the name by which, in Christian literature, Simon Peter is translated into Sogdian. It should be noted that in the *Book of the Honored* a certain *Cenwen seng* is named in a list of saints (*fawang* 法王, "kings of the doctrine") who are to be venerated (Text B.2, col. 7, p. 227).

12. *Shengdao* 勝道: the path that leads to the realization of the true essence of reality (see also p. 282n6).

13. Emotions (*dong* 動), passions or desires (*yu* 欲), lust (*qiu* 求), and the mental activity that produces attachment to existence (*wei* 為), are seen as the four main obstacles on the way to blessedness.

14. *Qing* 清 (Sk. *amala*, "limpid") and *jing* 淨 (Sk. *vimala*, "pure") are two recurrent terms in Buddhist texts. The compound *qingjing* (Sk. *pariśuddhi* or *viśuddhi*) is also very frequent and designates a state of mind free from evil and corruption.

pure, one can be enlightened[15] and [15] realize [the truth],[16] and having been enlightened and having realized [the truth], one will make all reality shine [with its true essence]. Making all spheres of reality shine [with their true essence] is precisely what brings about [16] blessedness.[17]

Simon Peter, consider the extraordinary appearance of my body and how different is my will [from that common to human beings]. The ten [17] principles [behind reality][18] can be summarized in 'four acquisitions.'[19] I do not know the 'four acquisitions' through an experience [of sensible knowledge], and I do not contemplate the ten principles through [18] an experience [of sensible vision]. In order to instruct people, I [now] use fictitious names.[20] But if one really cannot have knowledge or vision of the true teaching [about the true essence of reality], [19] then what should one do? If there were knowledge and vision, then there would be a body. If there was a body, [20] then there would be sentient beings.[21] If there were sentient beings, then there would be craving and [mental] activity. Having what you crave and what you work for, that is what is meant by emotions and [21] passions. Those who have emotions and passions will not be able to avoid finding themselves in all sorts of sufferings and anguish, and they will be far from being able [22] to obtain the fullness of blessedness! For this reason, I affirm the absence of desire and the absence of [mental] activity, the abandonment of the sphere of corruption[22] [23] and

---

15. *Wu* 晤（悟）: "to be enlightened," "to be awakened," "to realize" the truth of reality; it is a central technical term in Buddhism.

16. *Zheng* 證: in Buddhism this term indicates the experience of the realization of truth, and the consequent entry into the state of Buddhahood; like the previous term *wu*, it is a central technical term in Buddhism.

17. *Anle yuan* 安樂緣: the attainment of blessedness is described here as the entry into the true essence of reality, characterized by an all-pervasive state of light.

18. *Shiwen* 十文: the "doctrine of the ten realities to be discerned" (*shizhong guan fa*), which is described later in the text (see p. 290n58), is here evoked with a synonymous expression.

19. *Sida* 四達: this expression seems to anticipate the "four transcendent principles" (*sizhong shengfa* 四種勝法; also abbreviated as *sifa*), which are described later in the text (see pp. 293–95).

20. In Buddhist doctrine, the sense-world is only appearance and has no existence of its own. Therefore, the names given to the phenomena known by the senses serve only to understand their fictitious, unreal aspect, which must be surpassed.

21. *Huai shengxiang* 懷生想: lit., "[beings] containing life and thought," therefore living and sentient beings.

22. *Ranjing* 染境: it indicates that part of the universe that contains life and is therefore subject to corruption, that is, to the cycle of births and deaths. *Ran*, "contaminated" or "corrupt," is the opposite of *jing*, "pure." This idea is taken up later in the text (see p. 296n87).

Text E   285

the immersion in the uncontaminated source. By abandoning corruption, it is possible to become pure, which corresponds to emptiness.[23] By emanating grace and light, [24] it is possible to make all reality shine out. To make all reality shine out, this is what is called the way of blessedness.

[25] I will tell you once again, Simon Peter. I am in heaven, and yet I am also on earth. I protect and support all beings whose actions have good effects; those who are on the way of God [26] and those who, on the contrary, are among people; those who belong to the same species as I and those who, on the contrary, belong to different species; those who possess [true] knowledge and those who, on the contrary, do not possess it.[24] I protect and assist [27] all those who [have done] good deeds that bring about goodness, and I save and set free all those who would be destined for punishment for the evil [they have done].[25] As for salvation and protection, in reality [28] it has never been heard that they coincide with emptiness and the abandonment of merits. What does that mean? If there are merits, [29] then there will also be fame; if there is fame, then there will also be pride; if there is pride, then [30] there will also be a worldly mind.[26] Those who have a worldly mind will experience pride and arrogance. They will be unable to free themselves[27] and will be far removed [31] from a deep understanding[28] of blessedness! For this reason I say that those who have no merit or fame but rather assume[29] [32]

---

23. *Xukong* 虛空: in Buddhism this term (Sk. *śūnyatā*) indicates the true essence of every phenomenon.

24. An evocative series of opposite images to describe the human-divine nature of the Messiah.

25. Here are opposed the good deeds that bring about goodness (*shanyuan* 善緣) and the bad deeds that will produce negative effects at the time of remuneration (*ebao* 惡報).

26. *Xin* 心: in all Buddhist schools, the importance of *citta*, "consciousness," the last of the five aggregates that make up the psychophysical reality of the human person, is emphasized. Translated into Chinese by *xin*, it includes both the emotions (heart) and the intellect (mind), the place of all mental activity. The decision always to translate this term with "mind" was dictated by a need for uniformity of translation and should always be understood in the aforementioned dual dimension of mind-heart.

27. *Dutuo* 度脫: a Buddhist technical term that signifies being led from the wheel of transmigration to liberation, and then being saved.

28. *Yuantong* 圓通: a Buddhist word that indicates total penetration to the true nature of all things, thanks to an enlightened mind.

29. Lit., "bear the responsibility for."

286 THE TEXTS IN TRANSLATION

a compassionate mind[30] toward all sentient beings will be completely freed. If you rely on [my] divine powers[31] you will be enlightened [33] about the exact truth, and enlightenment about the exact truth is precisely the way to blessedness.

I will tell you once again, Simon Peter. Thanks to my [34] way of looking at things, I can see every form without hindrance. Thanks to my way of hearing, I can hear every sound without hindrance. Thanks to my way of smelling, [35] I can detect every aroma without hindrance. Thanks to my way of tasting, I can distinguish every flavor without hindrance. Thanks to my way of touching, [36] I can perceive every form without hindrance. Thanks to my way of mental [perception], I can penetrate every object of knowledge without hindrance. If these six modes [of perception][32] [37] are fully implemented, then the results will be remarkable.

All [my] truthful and luminous teaching[33] has its origin in infinite[34] causes, [38] and these, over time, have accumulated without limit. The merciful[35] blessings [granted by my teaching] are abundant, incessant, and innumerable.[36] To make a comparison, [39] [the grandeur of the blessings] is even greater than that of the imperial mountain.[37] From this point of view,

---

30. *Beixin* 悲心: the character *bei* translates into Chinese the Sanskrit *karuṇā*, "sympathy" or "compassion" for the sufferings of others, a central concept of Mahāyāna Buddhism.

31. *Shentong* 神通: supernatural powers, especially of a buddha.

32. *Liufa* 六法: through a typically Buddhist way of speaking, the potential of the Messiah to overcome the hindrances linked to the formal and sensory world is here described. It is summarized in the "six inputs" (*liuru* 六入) that correspond to the six senses: eye (sight), ear (hearing), nose (smell), tongue (taste), body (touch) and mind (knowledge, intellectual perception). Like a buddha, that is, an awakened being, the Messiah is liberated and therefore free of the obstacles (*wuai* 无礙, Sk. *apratihata*) and of the limits of the phenomenal world. In the background there seems to be also that particular, undistorted knowledge (Sk. *abhijñā*, "deep knowledge") of the true characteristics of all phenomena that is obtained by practicing the eightfold path and mental attentiveness. The six canonical forms of "deep knowledge" (*liutong* 六通) are magic power, divine eye, divine hearing, knowledge of the thoughts of others, memory of previous existences, and knowledge that causes the overcoming of human passions.

33. *Jingjiao* 景教: on this name, by which East Syriac Christianity was known in China from the seventh to the ninth centuries and which occurs five times in this text, see pp. 60–65.

34. Lit., "without beginning or end."

35. *Luojimei* 囉稽浼: I propose that this term, which occurs twice in the text, is the phonetic transcription in Chinese of the Syriac word *raḥmā*, "mercy."

36. Lit., "a billion."

37. *Dishan* 帝山: it is not clear which mountain is meant. It could be Mount Sumeru (or Mount Meru), the kingdom of the gods and buddhas (the Buddha is also called by the title of

Text E

all good things can conform [40] to the exact truth, and therefore, thanks to their light and grace, they can make everything shine out. Understanding in depth[38] [the true reality of all things], they can ascend to the land of blessedness.[39] [41] Once [this goal] has been reached and full [knowledge] achieved, there is no longer any change.[40]

Simon Peter, if that is so, then [the mind] [42] cannot conceive the vast benefits brought by these countless and merciful blessings. Now, I reflect on this: If this is really [43] unattainable [by the mind], then what should be done? If I speak of achieving [something] and then cannot achieve it, then I cannot say that there are no obstacles.[41] [44] Therefore I affirm the absence of desire, the absence of [mental] activity, the absence of merit, and the absence of realization.[42] If these four principles are present, it is no exaggeration [45] [to say] that it is possible to leave behind all discussion of everything else: being mild and humble, free and patient, and having great compassion.[43] All those [46] who are free of unrestrained passions will have full access to the law [governing] all things,[44] and will obtain what is absolutely transcendent. To obtain what is absolutely [47] transcendent is what is called the way to blessedness."

At that moment Simon Peter stood up again, bowed, and burst forth in words of praise, [48] saying, "Great is the Supreme and Only Honored One![45] The Supreme and Only Honored One is truly great! He is able to expose the mysterious [49] and transcendent doctrine. This is indeed a profound, inconceivable mystery. I have not yet fully realized its meaning. [50] [For this reason] I would like to be instructed again. You, Honored One, claimed the absence of desire, the absence of [mental] activity, the absence of merits, and

---

fadi 法帝, "Emperor of the *Dharma*"), center of the universe, and axis of the world in Buddhist cosmology, or another of the nine sacred mountains of Buddhism.

38. *Xuantong* 玄通: an expression similar to the previous *yuantong* (see p. 285n28).

39. *Anle xiang* 安樂鄉: this is the goal of the way to blessedness (*anle dao* 安樂道).

40. Behind this seems to be the idea of the cessation of *saṃsāra*, i.e., the cycle of rebirths.

41. The concept of non-impediment, mentioned above, returns here (see p. 286).

42. *Wuyu* 无欲, *wuwei* 无為, *wude* 无德, and *wuzheng* 无證: the four principles listed here will be described in more detail in the final part of the text.

43. Lit., "to bring compassion into one's depths."

44. *Zhufa* 諸法: a Buddhist term (Sk. *sarvadharma* or *sarvabhāva*) which indicates the multiplicity of phenomena and their relationships.

45. *Wushang yizun* 无上一尊: Buddhist epithet, which here designates the Messiah.

288   THE TEXTS IN TRANSLATION

the absence of realization. [51] [You also claimed that] these four principles are what is called the way of blessedness. [But], not yet having gone more deeply into the [question of] the denial of existence, I ask: How can there be any joy in it?"

[52] The Messiah, the Only Honored One, said, "Excellent question! A really excellent question! Since you would like to go more deeply into [this question], [53] I will explain it to you once again. In fact, it is only by denying existence that phenomena[46] can occur. But if existence is affirmed, then there can never be [54] blessedness. What follows? Let us consider, for example, the trees of the forest on an imaginary mountain. Their abundant branches and leaves [55] provide shade. Now, this mountain forest does not seek birds and wild beasts [intentionally]. Rather, all the birds and wild beasts spontaneously [56] take refuge in it. Or let us consider, for example, the waters[47] of the ocean. They are vast and unlimited, and their depths [57] are unfathomable. However, the water of the sea does not seek aquatic beings [intentionally], but all aquatic beings live in it spontaneously. [58] It is not the same with well-disposed[48] living beings, who [take the initiative] in searching for blessedness and do so insistently? What they should do, however, [59] is pacify their mind, dwelling in quietness, and constantly cultivating [themselves]. Since my teaching does not seek blessedness [intentionally], blessedness will come spontaneously. [60] For this reason [I say that it is only] from the denial of existence that existing things[49] can occur."

The Messiah instructed Simon Peter and [61] all the others again, saying, "What is set forth in this book is profound and difficult to understand. None of the doctrines transmitted by various holy and virtuous persons [62] is based on this true and profound teaching. Consider this example. [63] If beings with sight wish to walk, the light of the sun enables them to see far and wide. [64] Simon Peter, the same is true of this book. Now and in the future, it allows those who are endowed with an apt [65] mind to discern the way of blessedness, and this can thus form the basis for all the doctrines of

---

46. *Youti* 有體: a philosophical term that, in Buddhism, indicates everything that has a real or mental form.

47. Lit., "springs of water."

48. *Youyuan* 有緣: a Buddhist term that literally means "having a cause/bond," and often refers to beings who, touched by the Buddha and his doctrine, respond by turning to his teachings; hence, believers.

49. *Youfa* 有法: a Buddhist term that indicates existing things, as opposed to nonexistent things (*wufa* 無法).

Text E 289

the different sages. If so, [66] then others who hear the teaching of this book will take pleasure in it. They will examine it closely and draw nourishment from it; they will recite it and draw support from it.

[67] You should also know that they, as well as their forebears and their ancestors down through the generations, are oriented to good through a string of positive causes.[50] [68] In previous times, the good root passed through the generations, and veneration for my teaching has grown. [69] Therefore, thanks to the benefits it bestowed, one can aspire to joy. Compare, by way of example, [this situation to that of] the spring rain that falls and moistens [the soil], and all plants that have roots [70] produce shoots. If they were without roots, they could never grow. Simon Peter, [71] the same is true for you. If you are able to look to me for the transcendent doctrine, it is because your many previous generations—[72] forebears, ancestors, and relatives bound to you by marriage—have acted wisely in accumulating good deeds, and [the merit] has been transmitted to you."

Simon Peter, [73] overcome by emotion, prostrated, stood up again, then bowed and addressed him saying respectfully, "Supreme and Only Honored One, great in mercy, compassion,[51] and power, [74] show yourself benevolent towards me, that my foolishness not lead me to distort [your words] [75] and that I not be misled. If it is [as you say], then it is our parents [76] and the hundreds of thousands[52] of previous generations—and so, not just people in the present—who have achieved for my benefit and that of all people what it is that generates blessedness.[53] However, we have long been plunged into confusion,[54] [77] and although we wish to redeem ourselves, we have not yet succeeded. We have not [yet] fully understood what is needed [78] to progress towards what brings about [blessedness]."

The Messiah, the Only Honored One, said, "It is so, it is so, it is just as you say. [79] Compare, by way of example, [this situation to that of] the

---

50. *Shan jieyuan* 善結緣: a technical expression that, in the Buddhist soteriological doctrine, indicates a string of positive causes that will produce good effects, resulting in future liberation.

51. *Daci dabei* 大慈大悲: in Buddhist literature, these two characteristics of "great mercy" and "great compassion" (Sk. *mahākaruṇā*) proper to a buddha and a bodhisattva have become frequent epithets, mainly used for Guanyin Bodhisattva and Maitreya Buddha.

52. Lit., "one hundred, one thousand, and ten thousand," which means a huge number.

53. *Anle yuan* 安樂緣: lit., "the cause of blessedness."

54. *Hunzhuo* 昏濁: this term also means "ignorance" and "corruption."

mountain of treasures, where the fruits of the jade forest[55] shine like pearls in their splendor. With their delicious fragrance they can [80] satisfy hunger and quench thirst; they can also cure many diseases. Once upon a time there was a sick man who, having heard of this, never ceased thinking, day and night, [81] about the forest [in which] those fruits were found. However, the mountain was high and the road [that led to it] long. His body was frail, and he had little energy. [82] Moreover, since he had accumulated impure desires, he could not have his aspiration satisfied. However, since he could count on a wise and virtuous relative who offered him a ladder, [83] helped him to climb up, and sustained him, he was able to pick the desired fruit, and thus his illness was eradicated.

Now, Simon Peter, [84] the minds of many have long been deceived and they have been misled. Although they have heard [of it], they do not want to get the fruit on the mountain of blessedness, [85] and although they think about cultivating [their minds], their faith is still weak. Therefore, if they could count on a good friend[56] who would do the same for them as the relative [of the story] did, [that is], who would instruct them with intelligent words [86] that would become a 'ladder' for them, then they would be able to know the way,[57] and all the accumulated deceptions would be eradicated.

For this reason, the doctrine of the ten realities [87] to be discerned[58] is necessary as a path of gradual cultivation [of the mind]. To this you will ask, 'What is meant by this doctrine of the ten realities to be discerned?'

The first reality to be discerned [88] is that the life of human beings, because they have a physical body,[59] gradually declines and cannot escape death. Compare, by way of example, [this situation to that of] [89] an inn that provides a dwelling and a roof and offers food but does so only for a time. Why should [the guest] worry about these things, not being the owner [of

---

55. Places and images of Buddhist mythology. As before (*dishan*, see p. 286n37), here too the "mountain of treasures" (*baoshan* 寶山) could refer to Mount Sumeru or another of the nine sacred mountains of Buddhism.

56. *Shan zhishi* 善知識: a Buddhist expression (Sk. *kalyāṇamitra*) which often designates a disciple of the Buddhist teaching who is well versed in sacred scriptures and erudite.

57. *Wudao* 悟道: that is, to be enlightened about knowledge of the way to blessedness.

58. *Shizhong guan fa* 十種觀法: central in the section of the text that begins here is the Buddhist concept of *guan* 觀 (Sk. *vipaśyanā* or *vidarśanā*). It indicates contemplation, the careful discernment of reality through the faculties of the mind in order to distinguish what is illusory from what is real, and thus understand its true essence, i.e., penetrate the truth. For more on the presence of this concept in the text, see Wang Lanping 2008, 2009.

59. *Roushen* 肉身: lit., "body of flesh."

Text E 291

the inn]? [90] And if he has to leave [the inn, will he think] he can stay there for a long time?

The second reality to be discerned [91] is that people love their own families, but at some point they will have to part from them, and they will find it difficult to remain united [with them]. Compare, by way of example, [this situation to that of] [92] all the leaves that appear on a tree. When it is stricken by wind and frost, the branches become bare, the leaves fall and disperse, [93] and not even one remains.

The third reality to be discerned is that there are people who are eminent and honored, [but] their glory and prosperity [94] cannot last long. Compare, by way of example, [this situation to that of] the light of the moon. At night it illuminates everything in every direction, but when the mist is raised, [95] darkness takes the place [of light].[60] [The moon] may be bright, but how long can one rely on its light?

The fourth reality to be discerned is that among people [96] there are those who are despotic and selfish. They may think they are acting for their own benefit, but they are actually hurting themselves. Compare, by way of example, [this situation to that of] a moth [97] that sees a fire at night and flies rapidly toward it, thinking it is doing something good, unaware that its life is about to be consumed [98] by the fire.

The fifth reality to be discerned is that people expend great energy and exhaust themselves accumulating treasures and riches, [99] but all for naught. Compare, by way of example, [this situation to that of] a small vessel that holds only a little [liquid]. If one tried to pour all the water of the rivers and seas into it, [100] the vessel, once full, would overflow, unable to contain more.

The sixth reality to be discerned is that human [101] passions are an obstacle. They originate from the corporeal nature [of human beings], but they are enemies of that corporeal nature. Compare, by way of example, [this situation to that of] the caterpillar[61] [102] that lives[62] inside [the trunk] of a tree

---

60. Lit., "The last day of the moon and the first day of the moon exchange places." The last day of the moon corresponds to the darkest night of the lunar month, while the first day of the moon corresponds to the brightest night (full moon).

61. *Hechong* 蝎蟲: indicates a particular type of larva that, creeping into the trunk of trees, devours them from the inside, thus causing them to die.

62. *Huasheng* 化生: the verb that is specifically used for insects that are born and live by transformation, developing from the egg to the larva and from the larva to the butterfly.

and is able to destroy it. Even if it devours nothing but the innermost core of the tree, the tree eventually dries up [103] and progressively falls apart.

The seventh reality to be discerned is that when people drink intoxicating drinks, they are filled with happiness. [However], when they get drunk and [their minds] become clouded, [104] they are no longer able to distinguish the real from the unreal. Compare, by way of example, [this situation to that of] clear water which reflects everything like a mirror, and through it everything having a shape [105] can be seen. But if mud contaminates [the water], the reflected images vanish, and if it becomes very dirty, nothing [106] can anymore be seen.

The eighth reality to be discerned is that people enjoy theatrical performances and the like, but they are a waste of time and [107] dull the spirit.[63] Compare, by way of example, [this situation to that of] a madman whose blurred eyes see confusedly and whose limbs[64] are frenetically agitated. [108] He cannot sleep by day or by night, his strength is diminished, and in the end he can do nothing.

The ninth reality to be discerned is that [109] practicing their various doctrines, human beings [in reality] serve illusory realities[65] and thus remain far from the truth. Compare, by way of example, [this situation to that of] a gifted artist who creates [110] oxen by painting them with such splendid colors that they look real, but if he were to use them in the work of the fields, they would certainly be no help in bringing in [111] the harvest.

The tenth reality to be discerned is that when people do something to foster good in themselves, what they [really] seek is the admiration of others, unaware that [in so doing] [112] they deceive themselves. Compare, by way of example, [this situation to that of] the oyster that contains a pearl. The fisherman breaks open the oyster to retrieve the pearl, causing the oyster to die. [113] [The oyster with its pearl] can adorn people but is unaware of the suffering [it will meet].

By reflecting on these ten realities with the goal of understanding them, by disciplining body and mind, [114] and matching words with action, you will not err. Only in this way will you be able to penetrate the above

---

63. *Jingshen* 精神: this term refers to the "spiritual" part of man, distinct from his physical body; it can therefore indicate the spirit, the vital energy, the mental faculties, etc.

64. Lit., "hands and feet."

65. The original Chinese term (*youwei* 有為) is a Buddhist technical term for everything that is plunged into *saṃsāra*, namely, every phenomenon connected with karmic processes. It therefore refers to the illusionary world as opposed to true reality.

four transcendent principles. [But] you will say, 'What are [**115**] these four principles?'

The first is the absence of desire.[66] The emotions are in what is called the inner mind. They lead [us] to do all sorts of evil[67] by making it look like something noble. [**116**] [For this reason], it is necessary to control the emotions until they are extinguished and not allowed to awaken. But how is this accomplished? [**117**] Consider, by way of example, a plant that has its roots hidden in the soil. One cannot see from the outside whether or not [the roots] are diseased [**118**] and will only realize that they are when the plant's withered shoots are seen. The same is true for humans as well. The passions they have within them are not visible [**119**] from the outside. However, if good breath[68] does not circulate through their four limbs and seven openings,[69] all sorts of wickedness will increase [within them] and their blessedness [**120**] will fade. Therefore [people] should put into practice in their inner mind the principle of the absence of desire.

The second [principle] is the absence of [mental] activity.[70] What are called external forms[71] [**121**] have their own movements and realizations. They do not follow a natural law, and therefore are unreal.[72] For this reason it is necessary to reject them and not [**122**] allow them to come close. But how does one do that? Consider, by way of example, a passenger on a ship that is buffeted by the wind [**123**] and tossed by the waves as it crosses the ocean. Fearing that the ship will sink, the passenger is agitated. The same is true for all people. [**124**] Their external form has its own existence that shapes its own worldly principles. Only by progressing towards the cause of good [**125**] and not giving in to fatigue will it be possible to forget [all the efforts] that one has made. Precisely because of their external form, [human beings must] follow the path of the absence of [mental] activity.

---

66. *Wuyu* 无欲.

67. *Eyuan* 惡緣: "negative cause," which, according to the doctrine of karmic retribution, will produce negative effects.

68. *Qi* 氣: on the concept of *qi* in traditional Chinese thought, see p. 266n13.

69. *Sizhi qiqiao* 四支七竅: "four limbs" means hands, feet, arms, and legs; "seven openings [of the head]" means ears, eyes, nostrils, and mouth.

70. *Wuwei* 无為.

71. *Waixing* 外形, that is, apparent realities.

72. *Xuwang yuan* 虛妄緣: "cause of falsehood," in the sense of unreality (as opposed to reality, *shi* 實 or *shixiang* 實相).

294 THE TEXTS IN TRANSLATION

[126] The third [principle] is the absence of merit.[73] If you gain merit, do not be pleased with the fame [that comes from it], [but rather] show great mercy [127] and bring to salvation every kind [of living creature].[74] In this way, without having called anyone's attention to you, you will finally have fulfilled what was possible for you. But how can this be achieved? Consider, by way of example, [128] the earth, which makes everything grow according to its own nature and in accordance with what is proper to it, so that each thing [that grows] produces its own fruit. [129] There are no words to describe this exhaustively. The same is true for those who persevere in the supreme transcendent doctrine, put into practice the Luminous Teaching, and lead to salvation [130] other living beings; they will share in blessedness in marvelous ways. [In all of this] there is nothing to be praised. This is what is called absence [131] of merit.

The fourth [principle] is the absence of realization.[75] We cannot understand[76] anything about the true realization of all things. Therefore forget [the false distinction between] what is right and what is wrong, [132] break every [pre-constituted] order, and abandon all merit. Even with regard to the sun, although its existence is evident, [think about the fact that] its deep nature is emptiness.[77] So what are we to do? Consider, by way of example, [133] the mirror. It reflects everything: green, yellow, and every other color. Though we do not know how it does it, it reflects what is long, what is short, [134] and any other form. The same is true for human beings. For them realizing the nature of the true way,[78] having a blessed mind,[79] [135] scrutinizing the cause of everything, being able to penetrate in depth[80] every reality—these are

---

73. *Wude* 无德.

74. Behind these words one can recognize the ideal of the bodhisattva, who, motivated by compassion (Sk. *karuṇā*) and guided by the perfection of wisdom (Sk. *prajñāpāramitā*), vows to help other beings reach awakening.

75. *Wuzheng* 无證, that is, the conscious effort to renounce to discern the true nature of reality in apparent and contradictory phenomena.

76. *Juezhi* 覺知: a common word in Buddhism to indicate the understanding of the true essence of things through *bodhi*, that is, awakening, enlightenment.

77. *Xukong*: see p. 285n23.

78. *Zhendao* 真道: as *shengdao* before (see p. 283n12), this expression also indicates the way to blessedness, that is, the way that leads to the realization of the true essence of reality.

79. *Anle xin* 安樂心.

80. *Tongda* 通達: similar to two terms previously used (*yuantong* and *xuantong*, see p. 285n28; and p. 287n38), this Buddhist word also indicates the total penetration of the true nature of all things, thanks to an enlightened mind.

all things whose understanding[81] has been completely lost; nothing remains. This is [136] what is called the absence of realization."

The Messiah went on to say, "So then, those who enlist in the army must be provided [137] with armor for bodily protection. If the armor is good, they will not fear the enemy. [Likewise] only [138] the supreme transcendent doctrine[82] of this Luminous Teaching can protect living beings from the enemy [forces] that afflict them, just as the aforementioned armor [139] protects the body.

Those who sail across the ocean must be equipped with a vessel [140] that can handle the wind and the waves. If the vessel is in good shape, they can reach the opposite shore. [Likewise] only the supreme transcendent doctrine [141] of this Luminous Teaching can lead living beings across the ocean of mortality to the other shore, the place of blessedness [142] and precious scents.[83]

If, during an epidemic in which many are sick and even more are dead, [143] one breathes the wonderful breath of the precious scent that awakens the soul,[84] then the dead will return to life and the disease [144] will be eradicated. [Likewise], only the supreme transcendent doctrine of this Luminous Teaching can ensure that living beings return to life [in which one has access] to the knowledge of truth,[85] [145] and every kind of sin and sorrow is eliminated.

---

81. *Jueliao* 覺了: similar to the previous *juezhi* (see p. 294n76), this too is a technical Buddhist term that indicates being clearly and completely enlightened about the true reality of things.

82. *Shengshang fawen* 勝上法文: variant of *shengfa* and *shengshang fa* used previously (see p. 283n7).

83. Although the same images are present in Syriac Christian literature, the explicit use of Buddhist terms to describe salvation is evident here. The Buddha, whose mission is to lead the sentient beings to enlightenment, does so by helping them to cross the ocean of human life on a boat. He brings people from the shore of terrestrial existence, immersed in *saṃsāra* (to which the image of the "ocean of mortality" refers, *shengsi hai* 生死海), to that of liberated existence, *nirvāṇa*. In addition, Guanyin (Sk. Avalokiteśvara), the bodhisattva of mercy, is called the "boat of mercy" in the Buddhist tradition. These images are also present in the text of the Xi'an stele (Text A, col. 8, p. 202; col. 27, p. 215) and in that of the *Hymn in Praise of the Salvation Achieved through the Three Majesties of the Luminous Teaching* (Text B.1, col. 17, p. 224).

84. *Fanhun baoxiang* 返魂寶香: the allusion to this particular type of perfume is also present in the text of the Xi'an stele, where it describes Da Qin (corresponding to the eastern provinces of the Roman Empire), the land of origin of the Luminous Teaching (Text A, col. 14, p. 206).

85. *Zhenzhi* 真智: Buddhist term for true wisdom or knowledge of the ultimate truth.

If a man or a woman relies on my words, [146] if they resolutely follow my supreme doctrine, if they reflect[86] [on it] day and night, if they abandon every kind of corruption,[87] if they purify their true nature, reaching deep [147] and complete enlightenment, know that they will be liberated. Know too that heavenly creatures[88] [also] recognize the benefits of this book [148] [even if] they too do not come to the point of penetrating ultimate reality fully.[89]

Those who sincerely love [this teaching] and rarely neglect to improve their own conduct[90] [149] will be able to follow the brilliant path. Fearing no difficulty at all, they will be able to follow [even] dark ways; refraining from committing evil, [150] they will be able to reach a totally different place and there enjoy blessedness for a long time. [Knowing these things], how much more decisively will one devote oneself to improving [one's own conduct]!

You, disciples,[91] [151] and all those scattered under the sky who are listening, put into practice this book of mine, and you will become like a king who protects [152] his territory. Consider, by way of example, a high mountain on which a great fire breaks out. All the inhabitants of that country will see it. [153] The king and the dignitaries [who govern a country] are comparable to that mountain, and the benefits that this teaching of mine [can bring] are comparable to that great fire. If [154] it is put into practice, it naturally enlightens [the rulers and the whole country] as does the light [of fire]."

Simon Peter stood up again to ask [155] for more information, [but] the Messiah said, "It is better for you that I stop here, and that I do not add any more words. Consider, by way of example, a wonderful well, [156] whose water is inexhaustible, and a newly healed patient who cannot [yet] drink

---

86. *Siwei* 思惟: in the Buddhist lexicon indicates the action of carefully considering something, of reflecting with discernment on a (real or mental) object.

87. *Ranwu* 染污: in Buddhism indicates everything that is contaminated, false, diverted by adherence to illusory reality. It translates the Sanskrit *kleśa*, a broad term that designates corruption or contamination resulting from attachment to the pleasures of the senses, to false interpretations of reality, to moral and ascetical practices considered sufficient for salvation, to faith in the existence of a self that in reality is a cause of suffering, etc.

88. *Tian* 天: a term that in Buddhist literature indicates the *devas*, divine creatures divided into numerous classes.

89. *Zhenji* 真際: a technical Buddhist word that indicates the realm of true reality, the ultimate truth.

90. *Xiuxing* 脩行: this idea, which returns several times in the text, is frequently used in Buddhism to indicate ethical discipline, action, or conduct (Sk. *caryā*) in accordance with Buddhist law. By extension, it also indicates the one who practices it, i.e., the Buddhist disciple.

91. *Dizi* 弟子: see p. 278n96.

Text E 297

very much. If you do not limit the [amount of] water the patient drinks, there will again be problems. [**157**] Your situation is similar. Since your good nature has just been awakened, listening to too many words might confuse you.[92] That is why it is better not to add anything else."

[**158**] Then, having listened to those words, everyone was filled with joy. They politely took their leave and put them into practice.[93]

[**159**] *Book on Profound and Mysterious Blessedness.*[94]

---

92. Lit., "would cause doubts in you."

93. The text ends like many Buddhist sutras.

94. At the end of the manuscript there is a final annotation, which reads: "Acquired from a gentleman from Suzhou on an autumn day of the Bingchen year [1916]—recorded by [Li] Shengduo."

TEXT F

Book of the Luminous Teaching of Da Qin on Revealing the Origin and Reaching the Foundation

(*Da Qin jingjiao xuanyuan zhiben jing 大秦景教宣元至本經)

[2/P4] AT THAT time in the town of Nazareth[1] in the kingdom of Da Qin[2] the King of the Doctrine Jingtong,[3] whose throne is the precious clouds of the doctrine[4] in the Brilliant Palace,[5] [3] began to consider the various

---

1. *Nasaluo* 那薩羅: a phonetic transcription of the Syriac place name Naṣrat.

2. For this geographical term, which in the Chinese historical sources designates the eastern regions of the Roman Empire, see p. 66.

3. *Jingtong* 景通: an epithet whose identification is not clear. It also occurs once in the *Book of the Honored* (Text B.2, col. 5, p. 227) and in the text of the Xi'an stele, as the Chinese name of one Mar Sergius (Text A, col. 76, p. 220).

4. *Fayun* 法雲: a Buddhist term (Sk. *dharmameghā*) for the clouds that distill the gentle and fertile dew of Buddhist law; in Buddhist cosmology they characterize the location of the last stage of the spiritual progress of a bodhisattva toward illumination.

5. *Minggong* 明宮: a term borrowed from Chinese Buddhist literature, where it designates the place of beatitude and of the extinction of every desire and all suffering. It is a synonym for the terms "Heavenly Hall" and "Hall of Pure Emptiness," found in two other Chinese Christian texts of this period, the *Discourse on the One God* (Text C, col. 191, p. 244 and n. 61) and the *Book on Profound and Mysterious Blessedness* (Text E, col. 3, p. 282 and n. 2).

The Luminous Way to the East. Matteo Nicolini-Zani, Oxford University Press. © Oxford University Press 2022.
DOI: 10.1093/oso/9780197609644.003.0010

visions[6] concerning the True Origin,[7] so that this might be properly evaluated.[8]

[News of this] sounded everywhere like music, and [all] gathered like clouds from the seven directions. [4] All the brilliant and pure[9] were there, all the heavenly creatures[10] and the kings [P5] of the wonderful doctrine,[11] the countless awakened ones, and people having three hundred [5] and sixty-five different visions.[12] These countless and boundless peoples, suffering from illusion and [6] darkness [proper to their minds], and having long ago lost the True Origin, gathered all together in the Brilliant Palace and looked up[13] [towards the King of the Doctrine] with all their heart. [P6] At that moment the King of the Doctrine Jingtong, [7] raising his eyes towards the Lord of all reality[14] and having received [from him] the seal of his will, proclaimed solemnly and announced to the crowd:

"Welcome,[15] [8] all of you faithful of the doctrine,[16] you have not [yet] reached the peak [of comprehension]. This norm [of mine] is constant, it discloses life and abolishes death.[17] Since every system has its own elements that

---

6. *Erjian* 二見: lit., "two [opposite] visions."

7. *Zhenyuan* 真源: lit., "the authentic source."

8. *Liaojue* 了決: a Buddhist expression that means being clearly and completely illuminated concerning the true reality of things. It is a synonym for similar Buddhist expressions found in two other Chinese Christian texts of this period, the *Discourse on the One God* (Text C, *juewu*, col. 170, p. 243n51) and the *Book on Profound and Mysterious Blessedness* (Text E, *juezhi*, col. 131, p. 294n76; *jueliao*, col. 135, p. 295n81).

9. *Mingjing shi* 明淨士: a term that designates illuminated beings, that is, those whose mind, free from evil and corruption, penetrates the true essence of reality.

10. *Shentian* 神天: the heavenly creatures (Sk. *deva*) in Buddhist literature.

11. *Miaofa* 妙法: in Mahāyāna Buddhism this term (Sk. *saddharma*) refers to the teaching of the Buddha.

12. Clearly, this number, based on the number of days in a year, signifies fullness and the totality of different positions. The same numerical expression is found in the text of the Xi'an stele (Text A, col. 5, p. 199).

13. The verb used here means literally "to look up towards," from which is derived the meaning "to place one's confidence in," "to believe in."

14. *Konghuang* 空皇: a synonym for *kongwang* 空王, "king of immateriality," is one of Buddha's epithets, "Lord of all things." In the present context it appears to refer to God the Father.

15. *Shanlai* 善來: a recurring formula in Chinese Buddhist texts (Sk. *svāgata* or *susvāgata*).

16. *Fazhong* 法眾: a technical term that in Buddhist literature indicates the assembly of monks.

17. A similar expression occurs in the text of the Xi'an stele: "[The Messiah], opening the doors of the three constant [virtues], opened up life and abolished death" (Text A, col. 7, p. 202).

300 THE TEXTS IN TRANSLATION

constitute it, therefore, [9] calmly examine my teaching. If one understands that [God] is without origin, then every obstacle will disappear."

[P7] And he proclaimed the true and constant decree concerning the mysterious Sovereign Creator.

[10] "[God] is without origin, ineffable, inaccessible, and without cause: existing in his transcendence yet not existing, profound and still,[18] [11] the High God,[19] in whom we place our trust. In what he undertakes there is no contradiction;[20] his life is not subject to the corruption proper to the [human] mind; he preserves the intimate principle of the life of the world,[21] [12] gives rise to [realities] but himself is not originated, is not of human nature, is imperturbable.[22] All living beings[23] have been drawn out of emptiness[24] thanks to him, [P8] and he is the cause and axis [of reality]. As the nature [of the world], [13] he is manifest as the foundation of [all] forms. As the cause [of all phenomena], he acts as the means that arouses them. He separates and holds together the three births and the seven states of existence.[25] [14] No name can do him justice, and there is no force that can compete [with his power]. It is he who causes all things to mesh with each other, to be mutually integrated, and who teaches the way of return to the Origin, to one's own true nature. [P9] In his act of creation, [15] should anything not be in accord with his decrees, he transforms it without waiting for favorable conditions. Putting an end[26]

---

18. This passage is reminiscent of the beginning of the Xi'an stele: "It is said that [there is a being] constant in truth and tranquility, prior to every beginning and without origin, profound in intelligence and transparency; a transcendent and unlimited being . . .—is this not properly God, the transcendent person of our Three-One, True Lord without origin?" (Text A, col. 3, p. 198).

19. *Aluohe* 阿羅訶: phonetic transcription, occurring twice in this text, of the Syriac *Alāhā*. It also occurs in the text of the Xi'an stele (Text A, col. 3, p. 198), in the *Hymn in Praise of the Salvation Achieved through the Three Majesties of the Luminous Teaching* (Text B.1, col. 3, p. 222), and in the *Book of the Honored* (Text B.2, col. 2, p. 226).

20. Lit., "In what is carried out there is nothing different from what he carries out."

21. This expression in Chinese cosmology designates the *qi* of heaven and earth.

22. *Wudong* 無動: "imperturbable," "calm," "serene," "not agitated"; in Buddhist literature this is one of the characteristics attributed to the Buddha (Sk. *akṣobha*).

23. *Shengling* 生靈: more precisely, this term indicates sentient beings with the gift of intelligence.

24. *Xukong* 虛空: see p. 285n23.

25. *Sansheng qiwei* 三生七位: this is likely another Buddhist expression, composed of *sansheng* ("the three births," that is, the past, the present, and the future) and *qiwei*, possibly a synonym for *qiyou* 七有, which indicates the seven conditions or states of existence, the seven destinies (Sk. *gati*) after death: purgatories, the animal condition, the condition of a ravenous spirit, of *asura*, of *deva*, of man, and an intermediate condition.

26. Lit., "closing."

Text F 301

to non-existence he makes it become existence, destroying existence he makes it become non-existence. [**16**] Of all things that have been created,[27] there is nothing that does not lean on [God as] cause. For this reason, he is called the mysterious Sovereign Creator, the unknowable Lord of all reality.

[**17**] Living beings, both hidden and manifest, are prompted to respond [to him] with grateful acknowledgment. It is truly strange that later on [**P10**] living beings, dazzled by creation, became confused, [thus] losing the Foundation, [that is], the Sovereign Creator, [**18**] and not understanding that God acts efficaciously without showing anything [of his action] openly and operates without anything of his benevolence being seen. In his purity he is capable of scrutinizing [everything] minutely [**19**] and nurtures all living beings alike. In the sight [of God] all corruptible existence is like a speck of dust, and this speck of dust is as nothing.

[**20**] As for his visibility, he is not visible, yet, [**P11**] if one scrutinizes attentively, he is seen. Being formless,[28] [his voice] cannot be heard, yet, if one listens attentively, it is heard. Formless, he is without [**21**] [evident] power, yet he holds every power. Formless, he is wrapped in silence,[29] does not have an image, does not look like a being. What we can contemplate is [only] his being without limits and without [**22**] bounds, his uniqueness and his independence. His good government [of the world] has no equals, and his stable dwelling has no borders. The wonders worked [by him] occur everywhere, [**23/P12**] and all things mesh together.

Some living beings, however, go astray. [Over them] darkness gathers and they lose their way. Because of this he nurtures them with his goodness, [**24**] governs them with his justice, and saves them with his mercy. For the one who desires to convert [to God] there is no sin that ought not to be abandoned; [nevertheless], only he whom we call [**25**] Sovereign Creator can bring to completion the conversion of all the living, something they cannot achieve on their own, [**P13**] since such a conversion is extremely difficult to implement.[30]

---

27. *Zaohua* 造化: this indicates creation in its perpetual becoming through a process of creation and transformation. See p. 198n6.

28. Lit., "without limits [of form]."

29. *Wuxiang* 無嚮: lit., "does not emit sound." In Daoism this expression indicates the state of silent tranquility.

30. This sentence is obscure, philologically and hermeneutically, and the translation therefore remains conjectural.

302 THE TEXTS IN TRANSLATION

The Sovereign Creator alone [26] lacks nothing and [at the same time] has nothing in excess, is not clouded but [at the same time] is not limpid,[31] holds all reality,[32] exists perpetually, without change . . .[33]

. . . [P14] the Messiah is the one who fulfilled with great blessings the original spiritual [life] and [through him] wisdom was therefore brought to perfection. He made people become aware of what is unreal and what is real.[34] What is real[35] has nothing to do with what is unreal; what is of no hindrance . . . [P15] Through his spiritual substance[36] [he revealed] what is absolutely true and deep, the life of immutable joy. It was he who revealed that the Sovereign Creator is without limits and that he does not . . . [P16] People [should have] understood [this revelation] and [should have been] greatly enlightened to their general benefit . . . [?]. But people were prevented from recognizing [this revelation] or were led to disregard it, and their spiritual source became clouded. . . . [P17] For this reason, [the Messiah] endured this [refusal] to the point of dying. Acknowledged as the Lord, he was reverently recognized in the spirit, and the perception that he had abandoned [the world] was not prolonged . . . [P18] [The Messiah] established the eight conditions. The norm of the three constant [virtues] that disclose life and of the eight conditions that abolish death[37] aroused deep repentance [among the people] and was a warning [to them] . . ."

---

31. I think that these images serve to express that God is beyond all definitions.

32. *Zhenkong* 真空: lit., "true emptiness." Like the preceding term *xukong* (see p. 285n23), it conveys a central concept of Mahāyāna Buddhism, according to which all reality, in its substantial essence, is emptiness (Sk. *śūnyatā*).

33. The manuscript ends here. Lacunae in the following part of the translation are due to the fact that from this point on the only source is the text carved on the Luoyang stone pillar, the lower part of which is broken, cutting off columns of the Chinese.

34. *Kongyou* 空有: a Buddhist term that designates what is nonexistent and what is existent and therefore also true or false views about what is real and unreal.

35. Lit., "what is not unreal."

36. *Luhena ti* 盧訶那體: two interpretations of this expression seem possible. The one I prefer reads *luhena* as the phonetic transcription of the Syriac adjective *ruḥānā*, which means "spiritual." The other interpretation reads only the first two characters *luhe* as a phonetic transcription of the Syriac word *ruḥā*, "spirit." As for *ti*, the Tang Christian document *Book of the Honored* clearly distinguishes the two theological terms of "substance" (*ti*) and "person" (*shen*) in the fourth line—which shall be considered an annotation—of the opening Trinitarian doxology: "These three persons [*shen*] consist of one substance [*ti*]" (Text B.2, col. 3, p. 226).

37. Parallel expressions are found in the inscription on the Xi'an stele (Text A, col. 7, pp. 201–2). The "three constant [virtues]" might refer to the three theological virtues, while the "eight conditions" might refer to the eight beatitudes of the Gospel.

Text F 303

... [**P19**] When the King of the Doctrine Jingtong finished his sermon, all entered in contemplation and were enlightened.[38] He [then] explained with wisdom to the assembly... [**P20**] in every region. If people will but hold on to[39] the recitation [of this book], understand it in faith, and conduct themselves diligently [in accordance with it],[40] if their virtue surpasses... [**P21**] as the sea overflowing its shores. The sun rose and the darkness was destroyed,[41] so that every people knew [God's] profound stillness and understood his absolute immutability. Joyfully cleansing...

---

38. This is a common phrase with which most of the Buddhist sutras close.

39. *Shouchi* 受持: a term that in Buddhist literature means "to receive [and] retain," "to keep" the Buddha's teaching and precepts.

40. This is a common phrase found at the end of many sutras (a variant is *xinshou fengxing* 信受奉行, "in faith receive and reverently put into practice").

41. The same expression (*ri sheng an mie* 日昇暗滅) is found in the text of the Xi'an stele (Text A, cols. 26–27, p. 214).

Bibliography

Some of the works listed in the following bibliography contain transcriptions or editions of the Chinese originals of the documents translated in Part II of this volume, as well as translations into several European languages. These documents are indicated in square brackets at the end of the works in which they appear.

PRIMARY SOURCES

ʿAbdišoʿ of Nisibis (ʿAbdišoʿ bar Brika, Ebedjesus), *Catalogue of Authors*. Translated into English by George Percy Badger, *Index of Biblical and Ecclesiastical Writings*. In Badger 1852, 2: 361–79.

ʿAbdišoʿ of Nisibis, *Nomocanon*. Edited and translated into Latin by Angelo Mai, *Ebediesu Collectio canonum synodicorum*. In Mai 1825–38, 10 (pars I): 191–331 (text) and 23–168 (trans.).

ʿAbdišoʿ of Nisibis, *The Pearl*. Edited and translated into Latin by Angelo Mai, *Domini Ebediesu Liber margaritae*. In Mai 1825–38, 10 (pars II): 317–41 (text) and 342–66 (trans.).

Abū Zayd al-Sīrāfī, *Accounts of China and India*. Edited and translated into English by Tim Mackintosh-Smith. In Mackintosh-Smith and Montgomery 2014, 1–161.

Acts of Adarparwa, Mihrnarseh, and Mahduxt. Edited and translated into English by Sebastian P. Brock, *The Martyrs of Mount Berʾain*. Persian Martyr Acts in Syriac: Text and Translation 4. Piscataway, NJ: Gorgias Press, 2014.

Acts of Mar Mari. Edited and translated into French by Christelle Jullien and Florence Jullien, *Les Actes de Mār Mārī*. CSCO 602–3; Scriptores Syri 234. Louvain: Peeters, 2003. Also translated into English by Amir Harrak, *The Acts of Mār Mārī the Apostle*. Writings from the Greco-Roman World 11. Leiden: Brill, 2005.

Acts of Mar Qardag. Translated into English by Joel Thomas Walker, *The Legend of Mar Qardagh: Narrative and Christian Heroism in Late Antique Iraq*. Berkeley: University of California Press, 2006.

ʿAmr ibn Mattā, *Commentary on the Patriarchs of the Church of the East*. Edited and translated into Latin by Enrico Gismondi, *Maris, Amri et Slibae De patriarchis nestorianorum Commentaria. Pars altera: Amri et Slibae textus; textus versio latina.* Rome: C. De Luigi, 1896–97.

Arnobius of Sicca, *Against the Heathen*. PG 5: 713–1290. Translated into English by Hamilton Bryce and Hugh Campbell, *The Seven Books of Arnobius Adversus Gentes*. Ante-Nicene Christian Library 19. Edinbourgh: T&T Clark, 1871.

Bartoli, Daniello. 1663. *Dell'historia della Compagnia di Giesù: La Cina, terza parte dell'Asia*. Rome: Stamperia del Varese.

Bīrūnī, Abū Rayḥān Muḥammad, *The Remaining Traces of Past Centuries*. Edited by Eduard Sachau, *Chronologie orientalischer Völker*. Leipzig: Brockhaus, 1878. Translated into English by Eduard Sachau, *The Chronology of Ancient Nations or "Vestiges of the Past": An English Version of the Arabic Text of the Athâr-ul-Bâkiya of Albîrûnî*. London: William H. Allen, 1879.

Carlo Horatii da Castorano, "Brevi notizie della Cina: Come e quando e da chi e quante volte è stata predicata la religione cristiana in Cina, e dove quali e quanti PP. Missionari sono attualmente in Cina." 1740. MS BAV Vat. lat. 12871, 529–97.

Cefu yuangui 冊府元龜 [The Primary Divination Turtle of the Records Office]. 1000 *juan*. Compiled by Wang Qinruo 王欽若 and others in 1005–13. Beijing: Zhonghua shuju, 1960.

Chaldean Breviary. Edited by Paul Bedjan, *Breviarium iuxta ritum syrorum orientalium id est chaldaeorum*. 3 vols. Rome: apud S. Congregationem "Pro Ecclesiae Orientali," 1938.

Chang'an zhi 長安志 [Description of Chang'an]. 20 *juan*. Compiled by Song Minqiu 宋敏求, preface dated 1076. Edited in Xin and Lang 2013, 117–610.

Chronicle of Michael the Syrian. Edited and translated into French by Jean-Baptiste Chabot, *Chronique de Michel le Syrien, patriarche jacobite d'Antioche (1166–1199)*. 4 vols. Paris: E. Leroux, 1899–1924.

Chronicle of Se'ert. Edited and translated into French by Addaï Scher, Jean Périer, and Robert Griveau, *Histoire nestorienne (Chronique de Séert)*. PO 4.3: 215–313; 5.2: 219–344; 7.2: 99–203; 13.4: 437–639. Paris: Firmin-Didot, 1908–18.

Cruz, Gaspar da. 1569. *Tractado em que se contam muito por estenso as cousas da China*. Évora: Andre de Burgos.

Da Tang Zhenyuan xu Kaiyuan shijiao lu 大唐貞元續開元釋教録 [Great Tang Zhenyuan Era Continuation of the Kaiyuan Era Catalogue of Buddhist Teachings]. 3 *juan*. Compiled by Yuanzhao 圓照 in 794. T 55: no. 2156.

Daodejing 道德經 [The Book of the Way and Its Virtue]. Translated into English by James Legge, *The Sacred Books of China: The Texts of Taoism*, vol. 1: *The Tâo Teh King; The Writings of Kwan-tze (Books I–XVII)*. The Sacred Books of the East 39. Oxford: Clarendon Press, 1891.

Duan Chengshi 段成式, *Youyang zazu* 酉陽雜俎 [Miscellaneous Morsels from Youyang]. 30 *juan*. Written in the mid-ninth century. Edited by Cao Zhongfu 曹中孚. Shanghai: Shanghai guji chubanshe, 2012.

Bibliography

Eliya of Damascus, *List of the East Syriac Episcopal Sees*. Translated into Latin by Giuseppe Simone Assemani, *Tabula Eliae Metropolitae Damasci*. In Assemani 1719–28, 2: 458–60.

Francis Xavier, *Letters*. In *Monumenta Xaveriana: Ex autographis vel ex antiquioribus exemplis collecta*, vol. 1: *Sancti Francisci Xaverii Epistolas aliaque scripta complectens*. Madrid: Typis Augustini Avrial, 1899–1900.

Gardīzī, Abū Saʿīd ʿAbd al-Ḥayy, *The Ornament of Histories*. Edited by ʿAbd al-Ḥayy Ḥabībī, *Zayn al-akhbār*. Tehran: Intishārāt-i Bunyad-i Farhang-i Irān, 1968. Translated into English by C. Edmund Bosworth, *The Ornament of Histories: A History of the Eastern Islamic Lands AD 650–1041*. London: I. B. Tauris, 2011.

Gouvea, António de, *Ásia Extrema: Entra nella a Fé, promulga-se a Ley de Deos pelos Padres da Companhia de Jesus*. 1644. Edited by Horácio P. Araújo. 4 vols. Lisbon: Fundação Oriente, 1995–2018.

Guiyijun yanei mianyou poyong li 歸義軍衙內麵油破用歷 [Calendar of the Flour and Oil Commissions for Government Officials during the Guiyijun Regime, MS. S. 1366]. Reproduced in Tang Geng'ou and Lu Hongji 1986–90, 3: 281–86.

Hetʿum, *Flower of Histories of the East*. Edited by Charles Kohler, *La flor des estoires de la terre d'Orient*. In Kohler 1906, 111–253.

History of Mar Aba. Edited in Bedjan 1895, 206–74. Translated into German in Braun 1915, 188–229.

Ibn al-Nadīm (Abū-l-Faraǧ Muḥammad ibn Isḥāq), *The Catalogue*. Edited by Gustav Flügel, Johannes Roediger, and August Mueller, *Kitāb al-Fihrist*. 2 vols. Leipzig: F. C. W. Vogel, 1871–72.

Ibn al-Ṭayyib, *The Law of Christianity*. Edited and translated into German by Wilhelm Hoenerbach and Otto Spies, *Fiqh an-naṣrānīya: "Das Recht der Christenheit."* 2 vols. CSCO 161–62, 167–68; Scriptores Arabici 16–19. Louvain: Imprimerie orientaliste L. Durbecq, 1956–57.

Ibrahīm ibn Yuḥannā, *Life of the Melkite Patriarch of Antioch Christopher*. Edited and translated into French by Habib Zayat, "Vie du patriarche melkite d'Antioche Christophore († 967) par le protospathaire Ibrâhîm b. Yuhanna: Document inédit du Xe siècle." *POC* 2 (1952): 11–38 and 333–66.

Išoʿyahb III, *Letters*. Edited and translated into Latin by Rubens Duval, *Išōʿyahb patriarchae III Liber epistularum*. CSCO 11–12; Scriptores Syri, 2nd ser., 64. Paris: C. Poussielgue; Leipzig: Harrassowitz, 1904–5.

Jin shi 金史 [History of the Jin, 1115–1234]. 135 *juan*. Compiled by Tuotuo 脫脫 (Toghto) and others, completed in 1344. Taipei: Yiwen yinshuguan, 1956.

Jiu Tang shu 舊唐書 [Old Annals of the Tang, 618–907]. 200 *juan*. Compiled by Liu Xu 劉昫 and completed in 945. Beijing: Zhonghua shuju, 1975.

John Chrysostom, *Homilies on the Gospel of John*. PG 59: 23–482. Translated into English by Philip Schaff in Saint Chrysostom, *Homilies on the Gospel of St. John and the Epistle to the Hebrews*. A Select Library of the Nicene and Post-Nicene

308 *Bibliography*

Fathers of the Christian Church, 1st ser., 14. New York: The Christian Literature Company, 1890.

Kircher, Athanasius. 1667. *China Monumentis, qua Sacris qua Profanis, Nec non variis Naturae & Artis Spectaculis, Aliarumque rerum memorabilium Argumentis Illustrata.* Amsterdam: apud Joannem Janssonium a Waesberge & Elizeum Weyerstraet.

Laozi huahu jing 老子化胡經 [Book on Laozi's Conversion of the Barbarians]. 10 *juan* (only 4 juan preserved in the MS S. 6963). Completed in the Tang Kaiyuan era (713–41). Reproduced in Zhongguo shehui kexueyuan lishi yanjiusuo et al. 1990–95, 11: 234–40.

Li Deyu wenji 李德裕文集 [Li Deyu's Collected Works]. 34 *juan.* Compiled in the first half of the ninth century. Edited by Fu Xuancong 傅璇琮 and Zhou Jianguo 周建國, *Li Deyu wenji jiaojian* 李德裕文集校箋 [Li Deyu's Collected Works, Collated and Annotated]. Zhongguo lishi wenji congkan 中國歷史文集叢刊. Beijing: Zhonghua shuju, 2018.

Mardānfarrox ī Ohrmazddād, *Doubt-dispelling Exposition.* Edited and translated into French by Pierre Jean de Menasce, *Škand-Gumânîk Vicâr: La solution décisive des doutes.* Collectanea Friburgensia, n.s., 30. Fribourg: Librairie de l'Université, 1945.

Martyrdom of Narseh. Edited and translated into English in Herman 2016, 2–27.

Müller, Andreas. 1672. *Monumenti Sinici.* Berlin: ex officina Rungiana.

Polo, Marco, *Book of the Marvels of the World.* Translated into English by Arthur C. Moule and Paul Pelliot, *The Description of the World.* 2 vols. London: George Routledge & Sons, 1938.

Procopius of Caesarea, *On the Wars.* Edited and translated into English by Henry Bronson Dewing, *History of the Wars.* 7 vols. The Loeb Classical Library. London: W. Heinemann; New York: G. P. Putnam's Sons, 1914–40.

Quan Tang wen 全唐文 [Complete Prose Works of the Tang]. 1000 *juan.* Completed in 1814 under the direction of Dong Gao 董誥 and others. Beijing: Zhonghua shuju, 1983.

Ricci, Matteo, and Nicolas Trigault. 1615. *De christiana expeditione apud Sinas suscepta ab Societate Jesu.* Augsburg: apud Christophorum Mangium.

Semedo, Álvaro de. 1655. *The History of That Great and Renowned Monarchy of China.* London: John Crook.

Sun Chengze 孫承澤, *Gengzi xiaoxia ji* 庚子銷夏記 [Notes Written in the Summer of the Gengzi Year]. 8 *juan.* 1660. Available online at China Text Project (<http://ctext.org>).

Tang huiyao 唐會要 [Essential Regulations of the Tang]. 100 *juan.* Compiled by Wang Pu 王溥 and completed in 961. Taipei: Shangwu yinshuguan, 1968.

Tang liangjing chengfang kao 唐兩京城坊考 [A Study of the Quarters of the Two Capitals of the Tang]. 5 *juan.* Compiled by Xu Song 徐松 in 1848. Available online at China Text Project (<http://ctext.org>).

Bibliography

Theodoret of Cyrus, *Cure of the Greek Maladies*. Edited and translated into French by Pierre Canivet, *Thérapeutique des maladies hélleniques*. 2 vols. SC 57. Paris: Les Éditions du Cerf, 1958.

Theophylact Simocatta, *History*. Edited by Immanuel Bekker, *Theophylacti Simocattae Historiarum libri octo*. Bonn: Weber, 1924. Translated into English by Michael Whitby and Mary Whitby, *The History of Theophylact Simocatta*. Oxford: Clarendon Press, 1986.

Thomas of Marga, *The Book of Governors*. Edited and translated into English by E. A. Wallis Budge, *The Book of Governors: The Historia Monastica of Thomas, Bishop of Marga*. 2 vols. London: Kegan Paul-Trench-Trübner, 1893.

Tianxue chuhan 天學初函 [First Collection of Works about the Heavenly Studies]. Edited by Li Zhizao 李之藻 in 1626. Taipei: Taiwan xuesheng shuju, 1965.

Timothy I, *Letters*. Edited and translated into Latin by Oskar Braun, *Timothei patriarchae I Epistulae*. CSCO 74–75; Scriptores Syri, 2nd ser., 67. Paris: Gabalda, 1914–15. Letter 41 edited and translated into Latin in Bidawid 1956, 89–125 (trans.) and 1–47 (text).

Tongdian 通典 [Comprehensive History of Regulations]. 200 *juan*. Written by Du You 杜佑 and completed in 801. Beijing: Zhonghua shuju, 1988.

Voltaire. 1759. *An Essay on Universal History, the Manners, and the Spirit of Nations: From the Reign of Charlemaign to the Age of Lewis XIV*. Translated by Mr. Nugent. 4 vols. London: J. Nourse.

Wang Wenzhi 王文治, *Kuaiyutang tiba* 快雨堂題跋 [Kuaiyutang Colophones]. 8 *juan*. 1831. Edited in Lu Fusheng 2000, 10: 783–818.

Wang Yande 王延德, *Shi Gaochang ji* 使高昌記 [Record of the Mission to Qočo]. Written after 984. Edited by Wang Mingqing 王明清, *Wang Yande lixu shi Gaochang xingcheng suo jian* 王延德歷敘使高昌行程所見 [Wang Yande's Account of What He Saw during His Mission to Qočo]. In Wang Mingqing, *Huizhu lu: Qianlu* 揮塵錄·前錄 [Records of a Horse Tail Wisk: First Part], 4: fols. 3b–7b. Sibu congkan xubian 四部叢刊續編 351. Shanghai: Shanghai yinshuguan, 1934. Available online at China Text Project (<http://ctext.org>).

Wenxuan 文選 [Anthology of Literature]. 60 *juan*. Edited by Xiao Tong 蕭統 and completed in 530. Shanghai: Guji chubanshe, 1986.

Willem van Rubroek, *The Journey to the Eastern Parts*. Edited by Anastaas van den Wyngaert, *Itinerarium Willelmi de Rubruc*. In Wyngaert 1929, 164–332. Translated by Peter Jackson and David Morgan, *The Mission of Friar William of Rubruck: His Journey to the Court of the Great Khan Möngke, 1253-1255*. Works Issued by the Hakluyt Society, 2nd ser., 173. London: The Hakluyt Society, 1990.

Xin Tang shu 新唐書 [New Annals of the Tang]. 225 *juan*. Compiled by Ouyang Xiu 歐陽修, Song Qi 宋祁, and others in 1043–60. Taipei: Zhonghua shuju, 1971.

Yang Manuo 陽瑪諾 (Manuel Dias Jr.). 1644. *Tang jingjiao beisong zhengquan* 唐景教碑頌正詮 [Correct Explanation of the Tang *Stele Eulogy on the Luminous*

Teaching]. Wulin [Hangzhou]: Tianzhutang. Reproduced in Zhang Xiping et al. 2014, 27: 447–582 [text A].

Yishan xiansheng wenji 遺山先生文集 [Mr. Yuan Yishan's Collected Works]. 40 *juan*. Compiled after 1257. Shanghai: Shangwu yinshuguan, 1937.

Zhenyuan xinding shijiao mulu 貞元新定釋教目錄 [Catalogue of the Buddhist Teachings Newly Established in the Zhenyuan Era]. 30 *juan*. Compiled by Yuanzhao 圓照 in 799–800. T 55: no. 2157.

Zizhi tongjian 資治通鑒 [Comprehensive Mirror for Aid in Government]. 294 *juan*. Written by Sima Guang 司馬光 and others, presented to the throne in 1084. Beijing: Guji chubanshe, 1956.

SECONDARY SOURCES *(INCLUDING EDITIONS)*

Aalto, Pentti. 1975. "Nomen Romanum." *Ural-Altaische Jahrbücher* 47: 1–9.

Agostini, Domenico, and Sören Stark. 2016. "Zāwulistān, Kāwulistān and the Land Bosi 波斯—On the Question of a Sasanian Court-in-Exile in the Southern Hindukush." *Studia Iranica* 45.1: 17–38.

Aguilar Sánchez, Victor Manuel. 2021. *Corpus Nestorianum Sinicum: "Thus Have I Heard on the Listening of Mishihe (the Messiah)"* 序聽迷詩所經 *and "Discourse on the One-God"* 一神論: *A Theological Approach with a Proposed Reading Structure and Translation*. Analecta Gregoriana 331. Rome: Gregorian & Biblical Press [text and trans. C, D].

Akademienvorhaben Turfanforschung. 2007. *Turfan Studies*. Berlin: Berlin-Brandenburg Academy of Sciences and Humanities, <http://turfan.bbaw.de/bilder/Turfan_engl_07.pdf>.

Akira, Fujieda. 1966. "The Tun-huang Manuscripts: A General Description, Part I." *Zinbun: Memoirs of the Research Institute for Humanistic Studies, Kyoto University* 9: 1–32.

Akira, Fujieda. 1969. "The Tun-huang Manuscripts: A General Description, Part II." *Zinbun: Memoirs of the Research Institute for Humanistic Studies, Kyoto University* 10: 17–39.

Albanese, Andreina. 2005. "La stele di Xi'an, i gesuiti e Ripa." In *Caro Maestro. . . Scritti in onore di Lionello Lanciotti per l'ottantesimo compleanno*, edited by Maurizio Scarpari and Tiziana Lippiello, 73–83. Venice: Cafoscarina.

Allegra, Gabriele M. 1973a. "Due testi nestoriani cinesi." *Euntes docete* 26.2: 300–19 [trans. B].

Allegra, Gabriele M. 1973b. "La Sutra del Messia." *Rivista Biblica* 21, no. 2: 165–86 [trans. D].

Alzati, Cesare, and Luciano Vaccaro, eds. 2015. *Dal Mediterraneo al Mar della Cina: L'irradiazione della tradizione cristiana di Antiochia nel continente asiatico e nel suo universo religioso*. Storia religiosa Euro-Mediterranea 2. Vatican City: Libreria Editrice Vaticana; Gazzada: Fondazione Ambrosiana Paolo VI.

Bibliography

Amar, Joseph P. 2011. "Yahbalaha III." In Brock et al. 2011, 429.

Ammassari, Antonio. 2003a. "La soteriologia della stele di Xian-Fu e il sutra pneumatologico *Riposo e gioia*." *OCP* 69.2: 381–428.

Ammassari, Antonio. 2003b. "La struttura carismatica della Comunità Siro-Cinese a Xian-fu (635–845) e il suo Tempio di Daqin: Tradizioni proto-evangeliche del *Sutra di Gesù Messia*." *OCP* 69.1: 29–71.

Andreas, Friedrich Carl. 1933. *Bruchstücke einer Pehlevi-Übersetzung der Psalmen*. Edited by Kaj Barr. Berlin: Verlag der Akademie der Wissenschaften. Offprint from *Sitzungsberichte der Preussischen Akademie der Wissenschaften* (1933): 91–152.

Aoki, Takeshi. 2015. "Zoroastrianism in the Far East." In Stausberg and Sohrab-Dinshaw Vevaina 2015, 147–56.

Arlotto, Anthony. 1970–71. "Old Turkic Oracle Books." *MS* 29: 685–96.

Ashurov, Barakatullo. 2013. "Tarsākyā: An Analysis of Sogdian Christianity Based on Archaeological, Numismatic, Epigraphic and Textual Sources." PhD diss., SOAS, University of London, London.

Ashurov, Barakatullo. 2015a. "Inculturation matérielle de l'Église d'Orient en Asie centrale: témoignages archéologiques." In Borbone and Marsone 2015, 161–84.

Ashurov, Barakatullo. 2015b. "Sogdian-Christian Texts: Socio-Cultural Observations." *Oriental Archive* 83.1: 1–18.

Ashurov, Barakatullo. 2015c. "Sogdian Christian Texts: The Manifestation of 'Sogdian Christianity.'" *Manuscripta Orientalia* 21.1: 3–17.

Ashurov, Barakatullo. 2018. "Coins Convey a Message: Numismatic Evidence for Sogdian Christianity." *Central Asiatic Journal* 61.2: 257–95.

Ashurov, Barakatullo. 2019. "'Sogdian Christianity': Evidence from Architecture and Material Culture." *Journal of the Royal Asiatic Society*, 3rd ser., 29.1: 127–68.

Asmussen, Jes Peter. 1962. "Das Christentum in Iran und sein Verhältnis zum Zoroastrismus." *Studia Theologica* 16: 1–22.

Asmussen, Jes Peter. 1964. "The Pahlavi Psalm 122 in English." In *Dr. J. M. Unvala Memorial Volume*, 123–26. Bombay: Kanga.

Asmussen, Jes Peter. 1975. "Iranische neutestamentliche Zitate und Texte und ihre textkritische Bedeutung." *AoF* 2: 79–92.

Asmussen, Jes Peter. 1983. "Christians in Iran." In Yarshater 1983, 924–48.

Asmussen, Jes Peter. 1984. "The Sogdian and Uighur-Turkish Christian Literature in Central Asia before the Real Rise of Islam: A Survey." In *Indological and Buddhist Studies: Volume in Honour of Professor J. W. de Jong on His Sixtieth Birthday*, edited by Luise Anna Hercus, Franciscus B. J. Kuiper, Tissa Rajapatirana, and Edmund R. Skrzypczak, 11–29. Bibliotheca Indo-Buddhica 27. Delhi: Sri Satguru.

Assemani, Joseph Simonius. 1719–28. *Bibliotheca Orientalis Clementino-Vaticana . . .* 4 vols. Rome: Typis Sacrae Congregationis de Propaganda Fide.

Badger, George Percy. 1852. *The Nestorians and Their Rituals*. 2 vols. London: J. Masters.

Badwi, Abdo. 2006. "Iconography of the Holy Cross in the Syriac Tradition." *The Harp* 20: 447–58.

Bibliography

Bai, Yu. 2018. "The Messiah's Dharma: A Transcultural and Philological Approach to *Zhi xuan an le jing*." Master's thesis, Heidelberg University, Heidelberg.

Băncilă, Jonuţ Daniel. 2009. "Christian Sogdian Literature: An Overview." *Studia Asiatica* 10.1–2: 233–62.

Bang, Wilhelm. 1926. "Türkische Bruchstücke einer nestorianischen Georgspassion." *LM* 39: 41–75.

Barat, Kahar. 2002. "Aluoben, a Nestorian Missionary in 7th Century China." *Journal of Asian History* 36.2: 184–98.

Barbati, Chiara. 2014. "Notes on Christian Sogdian Terminology with Special Reference to the Sogdian Gospel Lectionary C5." *Nāme-ye Irān-e Bāstān* 12.1–2: 105–20.

Barbati, Chiara. 2015a. "La documentation sogdienne chrétienne et le monastère de Bulayïq." In Borbone and Marsone 2015, 89–120.

Barbati, Chiara. 2015b. "Syriac into Middle Iranian: A Translation Studies Approach to Sogdian and Pahlavi Manuscripts within the Church of the East." *Open Linguistics* 1: 444–57.

Barbati, Chiara. 2016. *The Christian Sogdian Gospel Lectionary E5 in Context*. Veröffentlichungen zur Iranistik 81. Vienna: Verlag der Österreichischen Akademie der Wissenschaften.

Barrett, Timothy H. 2002. "Buddhism, Taoism and the Eight-Century Chinese Term for Christianity: A Response to Recent Work by A. Forte and Others." *BSOAS* 65.3: 555–60. Repr. in Malek [2006?], 45–53.

Barrett, Timothy H. 2003. "Tang Taoism and the Mention of Jesus and Mani in Tibetan Zen: A Comment on Recent Work by Rong Xinjiang." *BSOAS* 66.1: 56–58.

Baum, Wilhelm, and Dietmar W. Winkler. 2003. *The Church of the East: A Concise History*. London: Routledge Curzon.

Baumer, Christoph. 2006. *The Church of the East: An Illustrated History of Assyrian Christianity*. London: I. B. Tauris.

Baumer, Christoph. 2014. *History of Central Asia*, vol. 2: *The Age of the Silk Roads*. London: I. B. Tauris.

Becker, Adam H. 2006. *Fear of God and the Beginning of Wisdom: The School of Nisibis and the Development of Scholastic Culture in Late Antique Mesopotamia*. Philadelphia: University of Pennsylvania Press.

Becker, Adam H. 2008. *Sources for the History of the School of Nisibis*. Liverpool: Liverpool University Press.

Becker, Adam H. 2014. "Political Theology and Religious Diversity in the Sasanian Empire." In Herman 2014, 17–36.

Beckwith, Christopher I. 2009. *Empires of the Silk Road: A History of Central Eurasia from the Bronze Age to the Present*. Princeton, NJ: Princeton University Press.

Bedjan, Paul, ed. 1895. *Histoire de Mar-Jabalaha, de trois autres patriarches, d'un prêtre et de deux laïques, nestoriens*. Leipzig: Harrassowitz.

Benveniste, Émile. 1937–39. "Notes Sogdiennes [IV]." *BSOAS* 9.3: 495–519. Repr. in Benveniste 1979, 163–86.

Benveniste, Émile. 1943–45. "Fragments des Actes de saint Georges en version sogdienne." *JA* 234: 91–116. Repr. in Benveniste 1979, 190–215.

Benveniste, Émile. 1955. "Études sur quelques textes sogdiens chrétiens [I]." *JA* 243: 297–335. Repr. in Benveniste 1979, 228–66.

Benveniste, Émile. 1959. "Études sur quelques textes sogdiens chrétiens [II]." *JA* 247: 115–36. Repr. in Benveniste 1979, 267–86.

Benveniste, Émile. 1964. "Le vocabulaire chrétien dans les langues d'Asie Centrale." In *Atti del Convegno Internazionale sul tema: l'Oriente cristiano nella storia delle civiltà (Roma 31 marzo–3 aprile 1963, Firenze 4 aprile 1963)*, 85–92. Problemi attuali di scienza e di cultura 62. Rome: Accademia Nazionale dei Lincei. Repr. in Benveniste 1979, 308–14.

Benveniste, Émile. 1979. *Études sogdiennes*. Beiträge zur Iranistik 9. Wiesbaden: L. Reichert.

Bernard, Henri. 1932. "Chrétiens nestoriens et missionnaires catholiques à la fin du XVIe siècle." *BCP* 19, no. 224: 176–78, 241–51.

Berti, Vittorio. 2006. "Cristiani sulle vie dell'Asia tra VIII e IX secolo. Ideologia e politica missionaria di Timoteo I, patriarca siro-orientale (780–823)." *Quaderni di storia religiosa* 13: 117–56.

Berti, Vittorio. 2009. *Vita e studi di Timoteo I patriarca cristiano di Baghdad: Ricerche sull'epistolario e sulle fonti contigue*. StIr C 41. Paris: Association pour l'avancement des études iraniennes.

Bertuccioli, Giuliano. 1983. "Matteo Ricci and Taoism." In *Jinian Li Madou lai Hua sibai zhounian Zhongxi wenhua jiaoliu guoji xueshu huiyi lunwenji* 紀念利瑪竇來華四百週年中西文化交流國際學術會議論文集 [*International Symposium on Chinese Western Cultural Interchange in Commemoration of the 400th Anniversary of the Arrival of Matteo Ricci S.J. in China*]. Xinzhuang: Furen daxue chubanshe, 52–74.

Beulay, Robert. [1987]. *La lumière sans forme: Introduction à l'étude de la mystique chrétienne syro-orientale*. L'Esprit et le Feu. Chevetogne: Éd. de Chevetogne.

Bidawid, Raphael J. 1956. *Les lettres du patriarche nestorien Timothée I: Étude critique avec en appendice "La lettre de Timothée I aux moines du Couvent de Mār Mārōn."* Studi e testi 187. Vatican City: Biblioteca Apostolica Vaticana.

Billings, Timothy. 2004. "Jesuit Fish in Chinese Nets: Athanasius Kircher and the Translation of the Nestorian Tablet." *Representations* 87: 1–42.

Billings, Timothy. 2008. "Untranslation Theory: The Nestorian Stele and the Jesuit Illustration of China." In *Sinographies: Writing China*, edited by Eric Hayot, Haun Saussy, and Steven G. Yao, 89–114. Minneapolis: University of Minnesota Press.

Borbone, Pier Giorgio. 2000. *Storia di Mar Yahballaha e di Rabban Sauma: Un orientale in Occidente ai tempi di Marco Polo*. Turin: Zamorani.

Borbone, Pier Giorgio. 2006. "I blocchi con croci e iscrizione siriaca da Fangshan." *OCP* 72.1: 167–87.

Borbone, Pier Giorgio. 2013. "Les églises d'Asie centrale et de Chine: état de question à partir des textes et des découvertes archéologiques. Essai de synthèse." In *Les églises en monde syriaque*, edited by Françoise Briquel Chatonnet, 441–65. Études syriaques 10. Paris: Geuthner.

Borbone, Pier Giorgio. 2015a. "Les 'provinces de l'extérieur' vues par l'Église-mère." In Borbone and Marsone 2015, 121–60.

Borbone, Pier Giorgio. 2015b. "I siri orientali e la loro espansione missionaria dall'Asia centrale al Mar della Cina." In Alzati and Vaccaro 2015, 279–304.

Borbone, Pier Giorgio, and Pierre Marsone, eds. 2015. *Le christianisme syriaque en Asie centrale et en Chine*. Études syriaques 12. Paris: Geuthner.

Botta, Sergio, Marianna Ferrara, and Alessandro Saggioro, eds. 2017. *La Storia delle religioni e la sfida dei pluralismi: Atti del Convegno della Società Italiana di Storia delle Religioni. Roma, Sapienza, 8–9 aprile 2016*. Quaderni di Studi e Materiali di Storia delle Religioni 18. Brescia: Morcelliana.

Braun, Oskar, ed. 1915. *Ausgewählte akten Persischer Märtyrer, mit einem Anhang: Ostsyrisches Mönchsleben*. Kempten: Verlag der Jos-Köselschen Buchhandlung.

Brock, Sebastian P. 1980. "Some Early Syriac Baptismal Commentaries." *OCP* 46.1: 20–61.

Brock, Sebastian P. 1981. "A Syriac Life of John of Dailam." *Parole de l'Orient* 10.2: 123–89.

Brock, Sebastian P. 1982. "Christians in the Sasanid Empire: A Case of Divided Loyalties." *Studies in Church History* 18: 1–19. Repr. in Brock 1984, chap. 7.

Brock, Sebastian P. 1984. *Syriac Perspectives on Late Antiquity*. Collected Studies Series 199. London: Variorum Reprints.

Brock, Sebastian P. 1986. "An Early Syriac Commentary on the Liturgy." *Journal of Theological Studies*, n.s., 37.2: 387–403.

Brock, Sebastian P. 1995. "Bar Shabba/Mar Shabbay, First Bishop of Merw." In *Syrische Christentum weltweit: Studien zur syrischen Kirchengeschichte. Festschrift Wolfgang Hage*, edited by Martin Tamke, Wolfgang Schwaigert, and Egbert Schlarb, 190–201. Studien zur orientalischen Kirchengeschichte 1. Münster: LIT.

Brock, Sebastian P. 1996. "The 'Nestorian' Church: A Lamentable Misnomer." *Bulletin of the John Rylands University Library of Manchester* 78.3: 23–35.

Brock, Sebastian P. 1999. "The Christology of the Church of the East in the Synods of the Fifth to Early Seventh Centuries: Preliminary Considerations and Materials." In *Doctrinal Diversity: Varieties of Early Christianity*, edited by Everett Ferguson, 281–98. Recent Studies in Early Christianity 4. New York: Garland Publishing.

Brock, Sebastian P. 2008. *The History of Holy Mar Ma'in: With a Guide to the Persian Martyr Acts*. Persian Martyr Acts in Syriac: Text and Translation 1. Piscataway, NJ: Gorgias Press.

Brock, Sebastian P. 2011. "Turfan, Syriac Texts from." In Brock et al. 2011, 420–21.

Brock, Sebastian P., and Nicholas Sims-Williams. 2011. "An Early Fragment from the East Syriac Baptismal Service from Turfan." *OCP* 77.1: 81–92.

Brock, Sebastian P., Aaron M. Butts, George A. Kiraz, and Lucas Van Rompay, eds. 2011. *Gorgias Encyclopedic Dictionary of the Syriac Heritage*. Piscataway, NJ: Gorgias Press.

Bryder, Peter. 1985. *The Chinese Transformation of Manichaeism: A Study of Chinese Manichaean Terminology*. Löberöd: Plus Ultra.

Bryder, Peter. 1992. "Transmission, Translation, Transformation: Problems Concerning the Spread of Manichaeism from one Culture to Another." In Wießner and Klimkeit 1992, 334–41.

Buck, Christopher. 1996. "The Universality of the Church of the East: How Persian Was Persian Christianity?" *Journal of the Assyrian Academic Society* 10.1: 54–95.

Bundy, David D. 1985. "Missiological Reflections on Nestorian Christianity in China during the Tang Dynasty." In *Religion in the Pacific Era*, edited by Frank K. Flinn and Tyler Hendricks, 14–30. Studies in the Pacific Era Series. New York: Paragon House.

Bundy, David D. 2011. "Timotheos I." In Brock et al. 2011, 414–15.

Burns, Peter. 2014. "Antizoroastrische Polemik in den Syro-Persischen Martyrerakten." In Herman 2014, 57–76.

Cadonna, Alfredo, ed. 1992. *Turfan and Tun-huang: The Texts. Encounter of Civilisations on the Silk Route*. Orientalia Veneziana 4. Florence: Olschki.

Cadonna, Alfredo, and Lionello Lanciotti, eds. 1996. *Cina e Iran da Alessandro Magno alla dinastia Tang*. Florence: Olschki.

Cai Jingmei 蔡晶玫. 1983. "Tangchao jingjiao xingshuai yuanyin zhi tantao" 唐朝景教興衰原因之探討 [Inquiry into the Causes of the Rise and Decline of the Luminous Teaching during the Tang Dynasty]. *Shixue huikan* 史學會刊 [Journal of the Society for Historical Studies] 12: 64–82.

Callieri, Pierfrancesco. 1996. "Hephthalites in Margiana? New Evidence from the Buddhist Relics in Merv." In *Convegno internazionale* 1996, 391–400.

Camplani, Alberto. 2011. "La Chiesa siro-orientale: un cristianesimo di missione e di mediazione culturale." In *A Oriente: Città, uomini e dei sulle Vie della Seta*, edited by Francesco D'Arelli and Pierfrancesco Callieri, 52–55. Milan: Electa.

Cao Shibang 曹仕邦. 1984. "Tangdai de Chongyi fashi shi 'jingjiao seng' ma? Zheng Chen Shou'an xiansheng de lunshuo" 唐代的崇一法師是「景教僧」嗎？靜陳授菴先生的論說 [Was Chongyi, Master of the Law in the Tang Dynasty, a Monk of the Luminous Teaching? A Discussion with Mr. Chen Shou'an]. *Xianggang fojiao* 香港佛教 [Buddhism in Hong Kong], no. 292: 16–20.

Cao Shibang. 1985. "Tangdai de Chongyi fashi shi 'jingjiao seng' ma?" 唐代的崇一法師是「景教僧」嗎？ [Was Chongyi, Master of the Law in the Tang Dynasty, a Monk of the Luminous Teaching?]. *Youshi xuezhi* 幼獅學誌 [The Youth Quarterly] 18.3: 1–8.

Carus, Paul, ed. 1909. *The Nestorian Monument: An Ancient Record of Christianity in China, with Special Reference to the Expedition of Frits V. Holm*. Chicago, IL: The Open Court [text and trans. A].

Cecchelli, Margherita. 2014. "Note sul primo cristianesimo in Cina." In *L'officina dello sguardo: Scritti in onore di Maria Andaloro*, edited by Giulia Bordi, Iole Carlettini,

Maria Luigia Fobelli, Maria Raffaella Menna, and Paola Pogliani, vol. 1: *I luoghi dell'arte*, 649–59. Rome: Gangemi.

Cereti, Carlo Giovanni. 2003. "Le croci di San Tommaso e la letteratura cristiana in lingue medioiraniche." In *Studi in onore di Umberto Scerrato per il suo settantacinquesimo compleanno*, edited by Maria Vittoria Fontana and Bruno Genito, 1: 193–206. Series Minor 65. Naples: Università degli Studi di Napoli "L'Orientale"; Istituto Italiano per l'Africa e l'Oriente.

Cereti, Carlo Giovanni, Luca M. Olivieri, and Joseph Vazhuthanapally. 2002. "The Problem of the Saint Thomas Crosses and Related Questions: Epigraphical Surveys and Preliminary Research." *East and West* 52.1–4: 285–310.

Chao, Huashan. 1996. "New Evidence of Manichaeism in Asia: A Description of Some Recently Discovered Manichaean Temples in Turfan." *MS* 44: 267–315.

Chaumont, Marie-Louise. 1988. *La christianisation de l'empire iranien des origines aux grandes persécutions du IVe siècle*. CSCO 499; Subsidia 80. Louvain: Peeters.

Che Weikun 車煒堃. 1971. "Tangchao jingjiao zhi weinan shiqi ji qi shuaiwang yuanyin chutan" 唐朝景教之危難時期及其衰亡原因初探 [A Preliminary Discussion of the Critical Period of the Luminous Teaching in the Tang Dynasty and the Reasons for Its Decline]. *Guoli bianyiguan guankan* 國立編譯館館刊 [Journal of the China National Editing and Translating Bureau] 1.1: 59–71.

Chen Fenggu 陈凤姑 and Yang Gongle 杨共乐. 2018. "*Da Qin jingjiao liuxing Zhongguo bei* zhong de 'Khumdan' yu 'Serag' kaoxi" 《大秦景教流行中国碑》中的 "Khumdan" 与 "Serag" 考析 [Analysis of "Khumdan" and "Serag" in the *Stele of the Propagation of the Luminous Teaching of Da Qin in China*]. *Henan shifan daxue xuebao (zhexue shehui kexue ban)* 河南师范大学学报（哲学社会科学版）[Journal of Henan Normal University: Philosophy and Social Sciences Edition], no. 5: 85–87.

Chen Guoying 陈国英. 1981. "Xi'an dongjiao sanzuo tangmu qingli ji" 西安东郊三座唐墓清理记 [Clarifying Notes on Three Tang Tombstones in the Western Suburbs of Xi'an]. *Kaogu yu wenwu* 考古与文物 [Archaeology and Cultural Relics], no. 2: 25–31.

Chen Huaiyu 陳懷宇. 1997. "Suowei Tangdai jingjiao wenxian liangzhong bianwei bushuo" 所謂唐代景教文獻兩種辨偽補說 ["Supplementary Notes on the Authentication of Two So-called Tang Nestorian Documents"]. *TY* 3: 41–53. Repr. in Chen Huaiyu 2012, 1–10.

Chen Huaiyu. 1999. "Gaochang huigu jingjiao yanjiu" 高昌回鶻景教研究 [Research on the Uighur Luminous Teaching in Qočo]. *DTY* 4: 165–214. Repr. in Chen Huaiyu 2012, 58–103.

Chen Huaiyu. 2000. "Jingjiao zai zhonggu Zhongguo de mingyun" 景教在中古中國的命運 [The Fate of the Luminous Teaching in Medieval China]. *HX* 4: 286–98. Repr. in Chen Huaiyu 2012, 41–57.

Chen Huaiyu. 2006a. "Cong bijiao yuyanxue kan *Sanwei mengdu zan* yu *Dasheng bensheng xindi guan jing* de lianxi" 从比较语言学看《三威蒙度赞》与

《大乘本生心地观经》的联系 [Connections between the *Hymn in Praise of the Salvation Achieved through the Three Majesties* and the *Mahāyāna Sutra on the Contemplation of the Mind Ground in This Life* from the Perspective of Comparative Linguistics]. *Xiyu wenshi* 西域文史 [Literature and History of the Western Regions] 1: 111–19. Repr. in Chen Huaiyu 2012, 11–22.

Chen, Huaiyu. [2006b?]. "The Connection between *Jingjiao* and Buddhist Texts in Late Tang China." In Malek [2006?], 93–113.

Chen, Huaiyu. 2007. *The Revival of Buddhist Monasticism in Medieval China*. American University Studies, Series VII: Theology and Religion 253. New York: P. Lang.

Chen, Huaiyu. 2009a. "The Encounter of Nestorian Christianity with Tantric Buddhism in Medieval China." In Winkler and Tang 2009, 195–213.

Chen Huaiyu. 2009b. "Tangdai jingjiaoshi yanjiu santi: Yi jingjiaobei wei zhongxin" 唐代景教史研究三题—以景教碑为中心 [Three Questions about Research into the History of the Luminous Teaching in the Tang Dynasty That Are Raised by the Stele of the Luminous Teaching]. *Xiyu lishi yuyan yanjiu jikan* 西域历史语言研究集刊 [Journal for the Reseach on the History and Languages of the Western Regions] 2: 166–79. Repr. in Chen Huaiyu 2012, 23–40.

Chen Huaiyu. 2012. *Jingfeng fansheng: Zhonggu zongjiao zhi zhuxiang* 景风梵声—中古宗教之诸相 [Christian Wind and Buddhist Sounds: Various Aspects of Medieval Religions]. Beijing: Zongjiao wenhua chubanshe.

Chen Huaiyu. 2014. "Cong liangjian decang Tulupan wenshu kan jingjiao yu daojiao zhi lianxi" 从两件德藏吐鲁番文书看景教与道教之联系 [The Relationship between the Luminous Teaching and Daoism on the Basis of Two Documents from Turfan in a German Collection]. In Zhang Xiaogui 2014, 290–311.

Chen, Huaiyu. 2015a. "The *Benji jing* and the *Anle jing*: Reflections on two Daoist and Christian Manuscripts from Turfan and Dunhuang." *Studies in Chinese Religions* 1.3: 209–28.

Chen Huaiyu. 2015b. "Tangdai jingjiao yu fo dao guanxi xinlun" 唐代景教与佛道关系新论 [New Views of the Relationship between the Luminous Teaching and Buddhism and Daoism during the Tang Dynasty]. *SZY*, no. 5: 51–61.

Chen, Huaiyu. 2020. "Shared Issues in a Shared Textual Community: Buddhist, Christian, and Daoist Texts in Tang China." In Lieu and Thompson 2020, 93–109.

Chen Jian 陈践. 2016. "P. T. 351 hao jingjiao zhanbu" P. T. 351 号景教占卜 [A Divination of the Luminous Teaching in the Manuscript P. T. 351]. In *Dunhuang tufan wenxian xuanji: Zhanbu wenshu juan* 敦煌吐蕃文献选辑—占卜文书卷 [Selected Documents in Old Tibetan from Dunhuang: Divination Documents], edited by Zheng Binglin 郑炳林 and Huang Weizhong 黄维忠, 249–54. Beijing: Minzu chubanshe.

Ch'en, Kenneth K. S. 1956. "The Economic Background of the Hui-ch'ang Suppression of Buddhism." *Harvard Journal of Asiatic Studies* 19.1–2: 67–105.

Ch'en, Kenneth K. S. 1972. *Buddhism in China: A Historical Survey*. Princeton, NJ: Princeton University Press.

Ch'en, Kenneth K. S. 1973. *The Chinese Transformation of Buddhism*. Princeton, NJ: Princeton University Press.

Chen, Ming. 2007. "The Transmission of Foreign Medicine via the Silk Roads in Medieval China: A Case Study of *Haiyao Bencao* 海葯本草." *Asian Medicine* 3: 241–64.

Chen Wei 陈玮. 2014. "Gongyuan 7–14 shiji jingjiao zai Ningxia quyu fazhan shi yanjiu" 公元 7–14 世纪景教在宁夏区域发展史研究 [A Study of the Development of the Luminous Teaching in the Region of Ningxia from the Seventh to the Fourteenth Century]. *Dunhuang yanjiu* 敦煌研究 [Dunhuang Research], no. 1: 109–14.

Chen Yuan 陳垣. 1923. "Huoxianjiao ru Zhongguo kao" 火祆教入中國考 [A Study of the Entry of Zoroastrianism into China]. *Guoxue jikan* 國學季刊 [The Journal of Sinological Studies] 1.1: 27–46. Repr. in Chen Yuan 1980–82, 1: 303–28.

Chen Yuan. 1924. "Jidujiao ru Hua shilüe" 基督教入華史略 [History of the Entry of Christianity into China]. *Zhenli zhoukan* 真理周刊 [Truth Weekly] 18. Repr. in Chen Yuan 1980–82, 1: 83–92.

Chen Yuan. 1930. "Jidujiao ru Hua shi" 基督教入華史 [History of the Entry of Christianity into China]. *Qingnianhui jikan* 青年會季刊 [Bulletin of the Young Men's Christian Association of China] 2.2. Repr. in Chen Yuan 1980–82, 1: 93–106.

Chen Yuan. 1980–82. *Chen Yuan xueshu lunwenji* 陳垣學術論文集 [Chen Yuan's Collected Scholarly Essays]. 2 vols. Beijing: Zhonghua shuju.

Chen Zenghui 陈增辉. 1987. "Dunhuang jingjiao wenxian *Zhixuan anle jing* kaoshi" 敦煌景教文献《志玄安乐经》考释 [Notes on the Document of the Luminous Teaching *Book on Profound and Mysterious Blessedness* from Dunhuang]. In *1983 nian quanguo Dunhuang xueshu taolunhui wenji* 1983 年全国敦煌学术讨论会文集 [Papers Presented at the 1983 Dunhuang National Academic Symposium], 2: 371–84. Lanzhou: Gansu renmin chubanshe [text E].

Chialà, Sabino. 2005. *Abramo di Kashkar e la sua comunità: La rinascita del monachesimo siro-orientale*. Spiritualità orientale. Magnano: Qiqajon.

Chiu, Peter C. H. 1987. "An Historical Study of Nestorian Christianity in the T'ang Dynasty between A.D. 635–845." PhD diss., Southwestern Baptist Theological Seminary, Fort Worth, TX [trans. F].

Christian, David. 2000. "Silk Roads or Steppe Roads? The Silk Roads in World History." *Journal of World History* 11.1: 1–26.

Clark, Larry V. 1982. "The Manichaean Turkic *Pothi-Book*." *AoF* 9: 145–218.

Clemen, Carl. 1920–22. "Christliche Einflüsse auf den chinesischen und japanischen Buddhismus." *Ostasiatische Zeitschrift* 9.1: 10–37; and 9.2: 185–200.

Colless, Brian E. 1986. "The Nestorian Province of Samarqand." *Abr-Nahrain* 24: 51–57.

Compareti, Matteo. 2003. "The Last Sasanians in China." *Eurasian Studies* 2: 197–213.

Compareti, Matteo. 2007. "Buddhist Activity in Pre-Islamic Persia According to Literary Sources and Archaeology." *Transoxiana* 12, <http://www.transoxiana.org/12/compareti-iranian_buddhism.php>.

Compareti, Matteo. 2008. *Traces of Buddhist Art in Sogdiana*. Sino-Platonic Papers 181. Philadelphia: University of Pennsylvania.

Compareti, Matteo. 2009. "Chinese-Iranian Relations XV. The Last Sasanians in China." In EIr Online, <http://www.iranicaonline.org/articles/china-xv-the-last-sasanians-in-china>.

Conte, Rosa. 2013. "Tommaso e l'Oriente: La questione dei cristianesimi cinesi." *Rivista di Studi Indo-Mediterranei* 3, <http://archivindomed.altervista.org/ASIM-3_TOMMASO_in_CINA.pdf>.

Convegno internazionale sul tema: La Persia e l'Asia centrale da Alessandro al X secolo. 1996. Atti dei Convegni Lincei 127. Rome: Accademia Nazionale dei Lincei.

Cordier, Henri. 1908. "China." In *The Catholic Encyclopedia*, edited by Charles G. Habermann, Edward A. Pace, Condé B. Pallen, Thomas J. Shahan, and John J. Wynne, 3: 663–88. New York: R. Appleton.

Courtois, Sébastien de. 2007. *Chrétiens d'Orient sur la route de la Soie: Dans les pas des nestoriens*. Paris: La Table Ronde.

Criveller, Gianni. 1997. *Preaching Christ in Late Ming China: The Jesuits' Presentation of Christ from Matteo Ricci to Giulio Aleni*. Variétés sinologiques, n.s., 86; Annali 10. Taipei: Ricci Institute for Chinese Studies; Brescia: Fondazione Civiltà Bresciana.

Criveller, Gianni. 1998. "Jésus-Christ annoncé en Chine à la fin de la dynastie Ming." In *Le Christ chinois: Héritages et espérance*, edited by Benoît Vermander, 57–97. Christus 87. Paris: Desclée de Brouwer; Bellarmin.

Daffinà, Paolo. 1983. "La Persia sassanide secondo le fonti cinesi." *Rivista degli Studi Orientali* 57: 121–70 (1–50).

Dauvillier, Jean. 1941. "Témoignages nouveaux sur le christianisme nestorien chez les Tibétains." *Bulletin de la Société archéologique du Midi de la France*, 3rd ser., 4: 163–67, 276. Repr. in Dauvillier 1983, chap. 2.

Dauvillier, Jean. 1948. "Les Provinces Chaldéennes 'de l'extérieur' au Moyen Âge." In *Mélanges offerts au R. P. Ferdinand Cavallera*, 261–316. Toulouse: Bibliothèque de l'Institut Catholique.

Dauvillier, Jean. 1950. "L'expansion au Tibet de l'Église chaldéenne au Moyen Âge et le problème des rapports du bouddhisme et du christianisme." *Bulletin de l'Université et de l'Académie de Toulouse* 75: 218–21. Repr. in Dauvillier 1983, chap. 4.

Dauvillier, Jean. 1953. "Byzantins d'Asie centrale et d'Extrême-Orient au Moyen Âge." *Revue des études byzantines* 11: 62–87. Repr. in Dauvillier 1983, chap. 16.

Dauvillier, Jean. 1956a. "Les croix triomphales dans l'ancienne Église chaldéenne." *Eléona* (October 1956): 11–17. Repr. in Dauvillier 1983, chap. 10.

Dauvillier, Jean. 1956b. "L'expansion de l'Église syrienne en Asie centrale et en Extrême Orient." *L'Orient syrien* 1: 76–87. Repr. in Dauvillier 1983, chap. 13.

Dauvillier, Jean. 1983. *Histoire et institutions des Églises orientales au Moyen Âge*. Collected Studies Series 173. London: Variorum Reprints.

Deeg, Max. 2004. "Digging out God from the Rubbish Heap: The Chinese Nestorian Documents and the Ideology of Research." In Takata 2004, 151–68.

Deeg, Max. 2005. "Verfremdungseffekt beim Übersetzen und 'Wieder'-übersetzen der chinesischen Nestorianica." In *Das Christentum aus der Sicht der Anderen: Religionswissenschaftliche und missionswissenschaftliche Beiträge*, edited by Ulrich Berner, Christoph Bochinger, and Klaus Hock, 75–104. Beiheft der Zeitschrift für Mission 3. Frankfurt am Main: Lembeck.

Deeg, Max. 2006a. "The 'Brilliant Teaching': The Rise and Fall of 'Nestorianism' (*Jingjiao*) in Tang China." *Japanese Religions* 31.2: 91–110.

Deeg, Max. [2006b?]. "Towards a New Translation of the Chinese Nestorian Documents from the Tang Dynasty." In Malek [2006?], 115–31.

Deeg, Max. 2007. "The Rhetoric of Antiquity: Politico-Religious Propaganda in the Nestorian Stele of Chang'an." *Journal for Late Antique Religion and Culture* 1: 17–30.

Deeg, Max. 2009. "Ways to Go and Not to Go in the Contextualisation of the *Jingjiao* Documents of the Tang Period." In Winkler and Tang 2009, 135–51.

Deeg, Max. 2012. "Sthavira, Thera and '*Sthaviravāda' in Chinese Buddhist Sources." In *How Theravāda is Theravāda? Exploring Buddhist Identities*, edited by Peter Skilling, Jason A. Carbine, Claudio Cicuzza, and Santi Pakdeekham, 129–62. Chiang Mai: Silkworm Books.

Deeg, Max. 2013. "A Belligerent Priest—Yisi and His Political Context." In Tang and Winkler 2013, 107–21.

Deeg, Max. 2014. "A Note on the Place Name 'City of Royal Residence' (*Wangshe-zhi-cheng*) in the Xi'an Stele." In Zhang Xiaogui 2014, 338–59.

Deeg, Max. 2015. "La littérature chrétienne orientale sous les Tang: un bref aperçu." In Borbone and Marsone 2015, 199–214.

Deeg, Max. 2016. "An Anachronism in the Stele of Xi'an—Why Henanisho?" In Tang and Winkler 2016, 243–51.

Deeg, Max. 2018a. "The Spread of Buddhist Culture to China between the Third and Seventh Centuries." In Di Cosmo and Maas 2018, 220–34.

Deeg, Max. 2018b. *Die Strahlende Lehre: Die Stele von Xi'an*. OPOe 12. Münster: LIT [text and trans. A].

Deeg, Max. 2020a. "The 'Brilliant Teaching': Iranian Christians in Tang China and Their Identity." *Entangled Religions* 11.6. doi: 10.46586/er.11.2020.8674.

Deeg, Max. 2020b. "Messiah Rediscovered: Some Philological Notes on the So-called *Jesus the Messiah Sutra*." In Lieu and Thompson 2020, 111–19.

Di Cosmo, Nicola, and Michael Maas, eds. 2018. *Empires and Exchanges in Eurasian Late Antiquity: Rome, China, Iran, and the Steppe, ca. 250–750*. Cambridge: Cambridge University Press.

Di Giorgio, Franco. 1986. *Comprendere e convertire: Il dialogo di padre Matteo Ricci con le religioni cinesi*. Milan: Istra.

Di Giorgio, Franco. 2012. "Confucianesimo, Buddismo e Taoismo nelle Opere di P. Matteo Ricci." In *Scienza, ragione, fede: Il genio di Padre Matteo Ricci*, edited by Claudio Giuliodori and Roberto Sani, 199–240. Macerata: EUM.

Dickens, Mark. 2009a. "Multilingual Christian Manuscripts from Turfan." *Journal of the Canadian Society for Syriac Studies* 9: 22–42. Repr. in Dickens 2020a, 96–119.

Dickens, Mark. 2009b. "The Syriac Bible in Central Asia." In Hunter 2009a, 92–120.

Dickens, Mark. 2009c. "Syriac Gravestones in the Tashkent History Museum." In Winkler and Tang 2009, 13–49. Repr. in Dickens 2020a, 25–64.

Dickens, Mark. 2010. "Patriarch Timothy I and the Metropolitan of the Turks." *Journal of the Royal Asiatic Society*, 3rd ser., 20.2: 117–39. Repr. in Dickens 2020a, 65–95.

Dickens, Mark. 2013a. "The Importance of the Psalter at Turfan." In Tang and Winkler 2013, 357–80. Repr. in Dickens 2020a, 149–72.

Dickens, Mark. 2013b. "Scribal Practices in the Turfan Christian Community." *Journal of the Canadian Society for Syriac Studies* 13: 32–52. Repr. in Dickens 2020a, 189–215.

Dickens, Mark. 2013c. "Syro-Uigurica. 2, Syriac Passages in U 338 from Turfan." *Hugoye: Journal of Syriac Studies* 16.2: 301–24. Repr. in Dickens 2020a, 173–88.

Dickens, Mark. 2015. "Le christianisme syriaque en Asie centrale." In Borbone and Marsone 2015, 5–40.

Dickens, Mark. 2016a. "Biblical Fragments from the Christian Library of Turfan, an Eastern Outpost of the Antiochian Tradition." In *The School of Antioch: Biblical Theology and the Church in Syria*, edited by Vahan S. Hovhanessian, 19–40 and 87–97. The Bible in the Christian Orthodox Tradition 6. Bern: P. Lang. Repr. in Dickens 2020a, 216–45.

Dickens, Mark. 2016b. "More Gravestones in Syriac script from Tashkent, Panjikent and Ashgabat." In Tang and Winkler 2016, 105–29. Repr. in Dickens 2020a, 246–71.

Dickens, Mark. 2017. "Syriac Inscriptions near Urgut, Uzbekistan." *Studia Iranica* 46.2: 205–60.

Dickens, Mark. 2020a. *Echoes of a Forgotten Presence: Reconstructing the History of the Church of the East in Central Asia*. OPOe 15. Münster: LIT.

Dickens, Mark. 2020b. "Nestorius, the Misunderstood 'Heretic.'" In Dickens 2020a, 1–24.

Dickens, Mark. 2020c. "*Tarsā*: Persian and Central Asian Christians in Extant Literature." In Tang and Winkler 2020, 9–41.

Dickens, Mark. 2020d. "Yahbalaha the Turk: An Inner Asian Patriarch of the Eastern Christians." In Dickens 2020a, 272–92.

Dickens, Mark, and Nicholas Sims-Williams. 2012. "Christian Calendrical Fragments from Turfan." In *Living the Lunar Calendar*, edited by Jonathan Ben-Dov, Wayne Horowitz, and John M. Steele, 269–96. Oxford: Oxbow Books. Repr. in Dickens 2020a, 120–48.

Dickens, Mark, and Peter Zieme. 2014. "Syro-Uigurica. 1, A Syriac Psalter in Uyghur Script from Turfan." In Heijer, Schmidt, and Pataridze 2014, 291–328.

Ding Guang 丁光. 2019. "Hanxuejia Mu Ade dui Zhongguo jingjiao de yanjiu" 汉学家慕阿德对中国景教的研究 [The Sinologist Arthur C. Moule and His Study of the Luminous Teaching in China]. *SZY*, no. 2: 160–69.

Drake, Francis S. 1935. "Nestorian Literature of the T'ang Dynasty." *The Chinese Recorder* 66.10: 608–17; 66.11: 677–87; and 66.12: 738–42.

Drake, Francis S. 1936–37. "Nestorian Monasteries of the T'ang Dynasty and the Site of the Discovery of the Nestorian Tablet." *MS* 2: 293–340.

Drake, Francis S. 1940a. "Foreign Religions of the T'ang Dynasty: Manichaeism." *The Chinese Recorder* 71.10: 643–49; and 71.11: 675–88.

Drake, Francis S. 1940b. "Foreign Religions of the T'ang Dynasty: Zoroastrianism." *The Chinese Recorder* 71.6: 343–54.

Dresden, Mark J. 1983. "Sogdian Language and Literature." In Yarshater 1983, 1216–29.

Duan Qing 段晴. 2000a. "Dunhuang xin chutu xuliyawen wenshu shidu baogao" 敦煌新出土叙利亚文文书释读报告 [Report on the Interpretation of a Syriac Document Recently Found in Dunhuang]. In *Dunhuang Mogao ku beiqu shiku* 敦煌莫高窟北区石窟 [The Dunhuang Mogao Northern Grottoes], edited by Dunhuang yanjiuyuan 敦煌研究院, 1: 382–90. Beijing: Wenwu chubanshe.

Duan Qing. 2000b. "Dunhuang xin chutu xuliyawen wenshu shidu baogao (xupian)" 敦煌新出土叙利亚文文书释读报告（续篇）[Report on the Interpretation of a Syriac Document Recently Found in Dunhuang: Continuation]. *Dunhuang yanjiu* 敦煌研究 [Dunhuang Research], no. 4: 120–26.

Duan, Qing. 2001. "Bericht über ein neuentdecktes syrisches Dokument aus Dunhuang/China." *OC* 85: 84–93.

Duan Qing. 2002. "Tangdai Da Qin si seng xinshi" 唐代大秦寺、僧新释 [New Explanations of the Da Qin Monasteries and Monks in the Tang Dynasty]. *Dongfangxue yanjiu tongxun* 东方学研究通讯 [Newsletter of Oriental Studies], no. 2: 1–20.

Duan Qing. 2003. "Jingjiaobei zhong 'qishi' zhi shuo" 景教碑中「七时」之说 [Theories about the Expression *qishi* in the Stele of the Luminous Teaching]. In *Yilangxue zai Zhongguo lunwenji* 伊朗学在中国论文集 [Essays on Iranian Studies in China], edited by Ye Yiliang 叶奕良, 3: 21–30. Beijing: Beijing daxue chubanshe.

Durkin-Meisterernst, Desmond. 2004. *Dictionary of Manichaean Texts*, vol. 3.1: *Texts from Central Asia and China: Dictionary of Manichaean Middle Persian and Parthian*. Corpus Fontium Manichaeorum: Subsidia 3. Turnhout: Brepols.

Duvigneau, Aymard-Bernard. 1934. "L'expansion nestorienne en Chine d'après Marco Polo." *BCP* 21, no. 248: 195–207; no. 249: 240–52; no. 250: 304–15; no. 252: 416–29; no. 253: 473–83; no. 254: 541–53; and no. 255: 588–607. Repr. *L'expansion nestorienne en Chine d'après Marco Polo*. Beijing: Imprimerie des Lazaristes, 1934.

Eccles, Lance, and Samuel N. C. Lieu, eds. 2020. 大秦景教流行中國碑: *Stele on the Diffusion of Christianity (the Luminous Religion) from Rome (Da Qin) into China (the Middle Kingdom). 'The Nestorian Monument'* (3 November 2020), <http://www.uai-iua.org/en/projects/73/china-and-the-mediterranean-world> [text and trans. A].

Bibliography

Ecsedy, Ildikó. 1979. "Early Persian Envoys in the Chinese Courts (5th–6th Centuries AD)." In *Studies in the Sources on the History of Pre-Islamic Central Asia*, edited by János Harmatta, 153–62. Budapest: Akadémiai Kiadó.

Edelby, Néophyte. 1952. "Notes sur le catholicosat de Romagyris." *POC* 2: 39–46.

Emmerick, Ronald E. 1987. "Buddhism in Central Asia." In *The Encyclopedia of Religions*, edited by M. Eliade, 2: 400–404. New York: Macmillan.

Emmerick, Ronald E. 1991. "Khotanese *kīrāstānä* 'Christian'?" In *Histoire et cultes de l'Asie centrale préislamique: sources écrites et documents archéologiques. Actes du Colloque international du CNRS, Paris 22–28 novembre 1988*, 279–82. Paris: Éditions du CNRS.

England, John C. 1996. *The Hidden History of Christianity in Asia: The Churches of the East before the Year 1500*. Delhi: ISPCK; Hong Kong: CCA.

England, John C. 1997. "Early Asian Christian Writings, 5th–12th Centuries: An Appreciation." *Asian Journal of Theology* 11.1: 154–71.

Enoki, Kazuo. 1964. "The Nestorian Christianism in China in Mediaeval Time according to Recent Historical and Archaeological Reserches." In *Atti del Convegno Internazionale sul tema: l'Oriente cristiano nella storia delle civiltà (Roma 31 marzo–3 aprile 1963, Firenze 4 aprile 1963)*, 45–77. Problemi attuali di scienza e di cultura 62. Rome: Accademia Nazionale dei Lincei.

Eskildsen, Stephen. 1991. "Christology and Soteriology in the Chinese Nestorian Texts." *B.C. Asian Review* 5: 41–97. Repr. in Malek 2002, 181–218.

Eskildsen, Stephen. [2006?]. "Parallel Themes in Chinese Nestorianism and Medieval Daoist Religion." In Malek [2006?], 57–85.

Fairbank, John K., and Denis Twitchett. 1979. *Cambridge History of China*, vol. 3.1: *Sui and T'ang China, 589–906 (Part 1)*. Cambridge: Cambridge University Press.

Fang Hao 方豪. 1936. "Tangdai jingjiao kaolüe" 唐代景教考略 [Brief Investigation into the Luminous Teaching during the Tang Dynasty]. *Zhongguo shixue* 中國史學 [Chinese Historiography] 1: 120–34. Repr. in *Xibei minzu zongjiao shiliao wengao* 西北民族宗教史料文稿 [Historical Materials and Manuscripts about the Religions of the Northwestern Peoples], edited by Gansusheng tushuguan shumu cankaobu 甘肃省图书馆书目参考部, 862–70. Lanzhou: Gansusheng tushuguan, 1985.

Fang Hao. 1945. "Tangdai jingjiao shigao" 唐代景教史稿 [A Historical Sketch of the Luminous Teaching in the Tang Dynasty]. *Dongfang zazhi* 東方雜誌 [The Eastern Miscellany] 41.8: 31–50.

Fang Hao. 1953–55. *Zhongxi jiaotong shi* 中西交通史 [History of Sino-Western Communications]. 5 vols. Taipei: Zhonghua wenhua chuban shiye weiyuanhui.

Fang Hao. 1970. *Zhongguo tianzhujiao shi renwu zhuan* 中國天主教史人物傳 [Biographies in the History of Chinese Catholicism]. 3 vols. Taizhong: Guangqi chubanshe.

Bibliography

Feng Chengjun 馮承鈞. 1931. *Jingjiaobei kao* 景教碑考 [A Study of the Stele of the Luminous Teaching]. Shidi xiao congshu 史地小叢書. Shanghai: Shangwu yinshuguan.

Feng Qiyong 冯其庸. 2007. "*Da Qin jingjiao xuanyuan zhiben jing* quanjing de xianshi ji qita" 《大秦景教宣元至本经》全经的现世及其他 ["The Nestorian *Xuanyuan Zhiben Jing* Has Been Found"]. *Zhongguo zongjiao* 中国宗教 [China Religion], no. 11: 28–31. Repr. in *Jinian Xi'an Beilin jiubai ershi zhounian huadan guoji xueshu yantaohui lunwenji* 紀念西安碑林九百二十周年華誕國際學術研討會論文集 [Proceedings of the International Symposium to Commemorate the 920th Anniversary of the Beilin Museum], edited by Xi'an Beilin bowuguan 西安碑林博物館, 36–45. Beijing: Wenwu chubanshe, 2008. Also repr. in Ge 2009a, 60–66.

Ferreira, Johan. 2004. "Tang Christianity: Its Syriac Origins and Character." *Jian Dao* 21: 129–57.

Ferreira, Johan. 2007. "Did Christianity Reach China in the Han Dynasty?" *Asia Journal of Theology* 21: 124–34.

Ferreira, Johan. 2014. *Early Chinese Christianity: The Tang Christian Monument and Other Documents*. Early Christian Studies 17. Strathfield: St Pauls Publications [text and trans. A; trans. B].

Fiey, Jean Maurice. 1973. "Chrétientés syriaques du Ḫorāsān et du Ségestān." *LM* 86.1–2: 75–104. Repr. in Fiey 1979.

Fiey, Jean Maurice. 1977. "'Rūm' à l'est de l'Euphrate." *LM* 90.3–4: 365–420.

Fiey, Jean Maurice. 1979. *Communautés syriaques en Iran et Irak des origines à 1552*. Collected Studies Series 106. London: Variorum Reprints.

Fiey, Jean Maurice. 1987. "Une énigme à propos du christianisme au Cachemire." *POC* 37: 58–62.

Fiey, Jean Maurice. 1990. "Hérat." In *Dictionnaire d'histoire et de géographie ecclésiastiques*, vol. 23, edited by Roger Aubert, 1355–56. Paris: Letouzey et Ané.

Fiey, Jean Maurice. 1993. *Pour un Oriens Christianus novus: Répertoire des diocèses syriaques orientaux et occidentaux*. Beiruter Texte und Studien 49. Stuttgart: F. Steiner.

Fiey, Jean Maurice. 1994. "The Spread of the Persian Church." In *First Non-Official Consultation on Dialogue Within the Syriac Tradition*, 97–107. Syriac Dialogue 1. Vienna: Pro Oriente.

Fiey, Jean Maurice. 1995a. "L'expansion de l'Église de Perse." *Istina* 40.1: 149–57.

Fiey, Jean Maurice. 1995b. "Le sceau sassanide d'un catholicos melkite d'Asie centrale." *POC* 45: 6–9.

Foley, Toshikazu S. 2008. "Translating Biblical Texts into Chinese: The Pioneer Venture of the Nestorian Missionaries." *The Bible Translator* 59.3: 113–21.

Foltz, Richard. 2010. *Religions of the Silk Road: Premodern Patterns of Globalization*, 2nd edn. New York: Palgrave Macmillan.

Forte, Antonino. 1976. *Political Propaganda and Ideology in China at the End of the Seventh Century*. Naples: Istituto Universitario Orientale.

Forte, Antonino. 1984. "Il persiano Aluohan (616–710) nella capitale cinese Luoyang, sede del Cakravartin." In Lanciotti 1984, 169–98.

Forte, Antonino. 1992. "Chinese State Monasteries in the Seventh and Eighth Centuries." In *Echō ō Go-Tenjikukoku den kenkyū* 慧超往五天竺國傳研究 [Studies on Huichao's *Record of Travels in the Five Indian Regions*], edited by Kuwayama Shōshin 桑山正進, 213–58. Kyoto: Kyōto daigaku Jinbun kagaku kenkyūsho.

Forte, Antonino. 1995. *The Hostage An Shigao and His Offspring: An Iranian Family in China.* Occasional Papers 6. Kyoto: Istituto Italiano di Cultura, Scuola di Studi sull'Asia Orientale.

Forte, Antonino. 1996a. "A Literary Model for Adam: the Dhūta Monastery Inscription." In Pelliot 1996, 473–87.

Forte, Antonino. 1996b. "The Chongfu-si in Chang'an. A Neglected Buddhist Monastery and Nestorianism." In Pelliot 1996, 429–72.

Forte, Antonino. 1996c. "The Edict of 638 Allowing the Diffusion of Christianity in China." In Pelliot 1996, 349–73.

Forte, Antonino. 1996d. "On the So-called Abraham of Persia: A Case of Mistaken Identity." In Pelliot 1996, 375–428.

Forte, Antonino. 1999–2000. "Iranians in China: Buddhism, Zoroastrianism and Bureaus of Commerce." *Cahiers d'Extrême-Asie* 11: 277–90.

Forte, Antonino. 2003. "Daitoku 大德." In *Hōbōgirin* 法寶義林: *Dictionnaire encyclopédique du bouddhisme d'après les sources chinoises et japonaises*, edited by Sylvain Lévi, Junjirō Takakusu, and Paul Demiéville, 8: 1071–85. Paris: Maisonneuve; Tokyo: Maison Franco-Japonaise.

Foster, John. 1930. "A Nestorian Hymn." *The Chinese Recorder* 61.4: 238–47.

Foster, John. 1939. *The Church of the T'ang Dynasty.* London: SPCK.

Foster, John. 1954. "Crosses from the Walls of Zaitun." *Journal of the Royal Asiatic Society of Great Britain and Ireland*, n.s., 86.1–2: 1–25.

Franzmann, Majella. 2003. *Jesus in the Manichaean Writings.* London: T&T Clark.

Fukushima Megumi 福島恵. 2016. "Tōdai ni okeru keikyōto boshi: Shinshutsu 'Ka Ken boshi' wo chūshin ni" 唐代における景教徒墓誌—新出「花献墓誌」を中心に [Tomb Epitaphs of the Disciples of the Luminous Teaching in the Tang Dynasty: Focusing on the Newly Found "Tomb Epitaph of Hua Xian"]. *Tōdaishi kenkyū* 唐代史研究 [The Journal of Tang Historical Studies] 19: 42–76.

Fukushima Megumi. 2017. *Tōbu Yūrashia no sogudojin: Sogudojin kanbun boshi no kenkyū* 東部ユーラシアのソグド人—ソグド人漢文墓誌の研究 [*Sogdians in Eastern Eurasia: Research on the Sogdians' Tomb Epitaphs in Chinese*]. Tokyo: Kyūko shoin.

Fuller, Michael A. 1990. *The Road to East Slope: The Development of Su Shi's Poetic Voice.* Stanford, CA: Stanford University Press.

Fumagalli, Pier Francesco. 2004. "*Sinica federiciana*: Il fondo antico dell'Ambrosiana." *Aevum* 78.3: 725–71.

Gaibov, Vasif A., and Gennadij A. Košelenko. 2002. "Xristianskie arxeologičeskie pamjatniki na Vostoke (pervoe tysjačeletie n.e.)" [Christian Archaeological Sites in the East (First Millennium CE)]. *Xristianskii Vostok* 10.4: 136–77.

Gaillard, Louis. 1904. *Croix et swastika en Chine*, 2nd edn. Variétés sinologiques 3. Shanghai: Imprimerie de la mission catholique.

Ge Chengyong 葛承雍. 2000. "Cong jingjiaobei shilun Tang Chang'an jingjiao de xingshuai" 从景教碑试论唐长安景教的兴衰 [A Tentative Discussion of the Rise and Decline of the Luminous Teaching in Tang Dynasty Chang'an on the Basis of the Stele of the Luminous Teaching]. *Beilin jikan* 碑林集刊 [Collected Papers of the Forest of Steles] 6: 212–24. Repr. in Ge 2006, 212–31; Ge 2020, 53–75.

Ge Chengyong. 2001. "Tangdai Chang'an yige sute jiating de jingjiao xinyang" 唐代长安一个粟特家庭的景教信仰 [The Faith in the Luminous Teaching of a Sogdian Family in Chang'an in the Tang Dynasty]. *Lishi yanjiu* 历史研究 [Historical Research], no. 3: 181–86. Repr. in Ge 2006, 232–41; Ge 2020, 23–35.

Ge Chengyong. 2004a. "The Christian Faith of a Sogdian Family in Chang'an during the Tang Dynasty." Translated and annotated by Matteo Nicolini-Zani. *Annali Istituto Universitario Orientale di Napoli* 64: 181–96.

Ge Chengyong. 2004b. "Tangdai jingjiao chuanjiaoshi ru Hua de shengcun fangshi yu liuchan wenming" 唐代景教傳教士入華的生存方式與流產文明 ["The Life Style and Lost Civilization of Nestorian Missionaries in the Tang Dynasty"]. *TY* 10: 73–84. Repr. in Ge 2006, 242–51; Malek [2006?], 163–74; Ge 2020, 37–51.

Ge Chengyong. 2006. *Tangyun huyin yu wailai wenming* 唐韵胡音与外来文明 [*Tracing Exotic Civilization in Tang's Rhyme and Hu's Melody*]. Beijing: Zhonghua shuju.

Ge Chengyong, ed. 2009a. *Jingjiao yizhen: Luoyang xin chutu Tangdai jingjiao jingchuang yanjiu* 景教遺珍—洛陽新出土唐代景教經幢研究 [*Precious Nestorian Relic: Studies on the Nestorian Stone Pillar of the Tang Dynasty Recently Discovered in Luoyang*]. Beijing: Wenwu chubanshe.

Ge Chengyong. 2009b. "Xi'an Luoyang Tang liangjing chutu jingjiao shike bijiao yanjiu" 西安、洛陽唐兩京出土景教石刻比較研究 [A Comparative Study of Two Stone Inscriptions of the Luminous Teaching Unearthed in Xi'an and Luoyang, the Two Capital Cities of the Tang Dynasty]. *Wen shi zhe* 文史哲 [Literature, History, Philosophy], no. 2: 17–23. Repr. in Ge 2009a, 122–33; Ge 2020, 97–113.

Ge Chengyong. 2013. "A Comparative Study of Two Nestorian Inscriptions Unearthed in the Two Capital Cities of the Tang Dynasty: Xi'an and Luoyang." In Tang and Winkler 2013, 161–75.

Ge Chengyong. 2014. "Jingjiao tianshi yu fojiao feitian bijiao bianshi yanjiu" 景教天使与佛教飞天比较辨识研究 ["A Comparative Study of the Images of Nestorian Angels and Buddhist Flying Apsaras"]. *SZY*, no. 4: 1–7. Repr. in Ge 2020, 115–35.

Ge Chengyong. 2016. "Luoyang Tangdai jingjiao jingzhuang biaoxian de muai zhuti" 洛阳唐代景教经幢表现的母爱主题 ["The Love Theme Manifested in the

Stone Pillar of Nestorianism in Luoyang in the Tang Dynasty"]. *SZY*, no. 3: 149–54. Repr. in Ge 2020, 137–49.

Ge Chengyong. 2020. *Hu han Zhongguo yu wailai wenming* 胡汉中国与外来文明 [*Han and Hu: China in Contact with Foreign Civilizations*], vol. 4: *Fanseng ru Hua lai: Zongjiao juan* 番僧入华来：宗教卷 [*Religions*]. Beijing: Sanlian shudian.

Geng Sheng 耿昇. 2001. "Zhongwai xuezhe dui Da Qin jingjiaobei de zaoqi yanjiu zongshu" 中外学者对大秦景教碑的早期研究综述 [A Summary of Initial Research on the Stele of the Luminous Teaching of Da Qin by Chinese and Foreign Scholars]. In *Zhongguo zongjiao yanjiu nianjian 1999–2000* 中国宗教研究年鉴 1999–2000 [Annual of Religious Studies in China, 1999–2000], edited by Cao Zhongjian 曹中建, 363–93. Beijing: Zongjiao wenhua chubanshe.

Gernet, Jacques. 2007. "L'inscription de la stèle nestorienne de Xi'an de 781 vue de Chine." *Comptes-rendus des séances de l'Académie des Inscriptions et Belles-Lettres* 151.1: 237–46.

Gernet, Jacques. 2008. "Remarques sur le contexte chinois de l'inscription de la stèle nestorienne de Xi'an." In Jullien, Christelle 2008, 227–43.

Gershevitch, Ilya. 1946. "On the Sogdian St. George Passion." *Journal of the Royal Asiatic Society of Great Britain and Ireland*, n.s., 78.3–4: 179–84.

Gharib, B. 1995. *Sogdian Dictionary: Sogdian-Persian-English*. Tehran: Farhangan Publications.

Gignoux, Philippe. 1969. "L'auteur de la version pehlevie du psautier serait-il nestorien?" In *Mémorial Mgr Gabriel Khouri-Sarkis (1898–1968)*, 233–44. Louvain: Imprimerie orientaliste.

Gignoux, Philippe. 1980. "Sceaux chrétiens d'époque sasanide." *Iranica Antiqua* 15: 299–314.

Gignoux, Philippe. 1991. *Les quatre inscriptions du mage Kirdīr: Textes et concordances*. StIr C 9. Louvain: Peeters.

Gignoux, Philippe. 1995. "The Pahlavi Inscription on Mount Thomas Cross (South India)." In *Solving Riddles and Untying Knots: Biblical, Epigraphic, and Semitic Studies in Honor of Jonas C. Greenfield*, edited by Ziony Zevit, Seymour Gitin, and Michael Sokoloff, 411–22. Winona Lake, IN: Eisenbrauns.

Gignoux, Philippe. 1996. "Zoroastrianism." In Litvinsky, Zhang, and Samghabadi 1996, 403–12.

Gignoux, Philippe. 1999. "Controverses religieuses dans l'Iran sassanide." *Le monde de la Bible* 119: 22–24.

Gignoux, Philippe. 2001a. "L'apport scientifique des chrétiens syriaques à l'Iran sasanide." *JA* 289.2: 217–36.

Gignoux, Philippe. 2001b. "Une croix de procession de Hérat inscrite en pehlevi." *LM* 114.3–4: 291–304.

Gignoux, Philippe. 2002. "Pahlavi Psalter." In EIr Online, <http://www.iranicaonline. org/articles/pahlavi-psalter>.

Gignoux, Philippe. 2008. "Comment le polémist mazdéen du *Škand Gumānig Vīzār* a-t-il utilisé les citations du Nouveau Testament?" In Jullien, Christelle 2008, 59–67.

Gillman, Ian, and Hans-Joachim Klimkeit. 1999. *Christians in Asia before 1500*. Richmond: Curzon.

Godwin, R. Todd. 2016. " 'Eunuchs for the Kingdom of God': Rethinking the Christian-Buddhist Imperial Translation Incident of 787." In Tang and Winkler 2016, 267–82.

Godwin, R. Todd. 2017. *Persian Christians at the Chinese Court: The Xi'an Stele and the Early Medieval Church of the East*. Library of Medieval Studies 4. London: I. B. Tauris [text and trans. A].

Godwin, R. Todd. 2018. "Sacred Sovereigns across the Silk Road: The Church of the East's Gift of Buddhist-Christian Icons to the Chinese Emperor in 781, and Its Relevance to Buddhist-Christian Studies." *Buddhist-Christian Studies* 38: 203–16.

Godwin, R. Todd. 2020. "Da Qin, Tajiks, and Their Doctors: East Syrian Scientists across the Courts of Early Medieval Persia, China and Tibet." In Tang and Winkler 2020, 43–59.

Gong Fangzhen 龚方震. 1992. "Jingjiao: Zhongguohua de jidujiao" 景教：中国化的基督教 [The Luminous Teaching: A Sinicized Christianity]. In Gong Fangzhen, *Ronghe sifang wenhua de zhihui* 融合四方文化的智慧 [The Wisdom of Melding Different Cultures], 27–46. Zhongguo de zhihui congshu 中国的智慧丛书. Hangzhou: Zhejiang renmin chubanshe.

Gong Tianmin 龚天民 (K'ung Tien-min). 1960. *Tangchao jidujiao zhi yanjiu* 唐朝基督教之研究 [Research on Christianity during the Tang Dynasty]. Hong Kong: Jidujiao fuqiao chubanshe [text A, B, C, D, E, F].

Gordon, Elizabeth Anna. 1911. *The Lotus Gospel; or, Mahayana Buddhism and Its Symbolic Teachings Compared Historically and Geographically with Those of Catholic Christianity*. Tokyo: Waseda University Library.

Gordon, Elizabeth Anna. 1914. "Some Recent Discoveries in Korean Temples and Their Relationship to Early Eastern Christianity." *Transactions of the Korea Branch of the Royal Asiatic Society* 5: 1–39.

Gosudarstvennyj Ermitaž (Rossija) and Institut Istorii NAN Kyrgyzstana, eds. 2002. *Sujab Ak-Bešim*. Saint Petersburg: n.p.

Graf, David F. 2018. "The Silk Road between Syria and China." In *Trade, Commerce, and the State in the Roman World*, edited by Andrew Wilson and Alan Bowman, 443–529. Oxford: Oxford University Press.

Grenet, Frantz. 2006–10. "Iranian Gods in Hindu Garb: The Zoroastrian Pantheon of the Bactrians and Sogdians, Second–Eighth Centuries." *Bulletin of the Asia Institute* 20: 87–101.

Grenet, Frantz. 2007. "Religious Diversity among Sogdian Merchants in Sixth-Century China: Zoroastrianism, Buddhism, Manichaeism, and Hinduism." *Comparative Studies of South Asia, Africa and the Middle East* 27.2: 463–78.

Grenet, Frantz. 2015. "Zoroastrianism in Central Asia." In Stausberg and Sohrab-Dinshaw Vevaina 2015, 129–46.

Gropp, Gerd. 1970. "Die Pahlavi-Inschrift auf dem Thomas-Kreuz in Madras." *Archäologische Mitteilungen aus Iran*, n.s., 3: 267–71.

Gu Weimin 顾微民. 1993. "Yesu mentu Duomo lai Hua chuanshuo de zongjiao yiyi" 耶稣门徒多默来华传说的宗教意义 [The Religious Meaning of the Tradition of the Coming to China of Thomas, the Apostle of Jesus]. *Shanghai jiaoyu xueyuan xuebao* 上海教育学院学报 [Journal of the Shanghai Institute of Education], no. 2: 37–43.

Guan Ying 关英. 2002. "Zhouzhi Da Qin si xinkao" 周至大秦寺新考 [New Investigation into the Monastery of Da Qin in Zhouzhi]. *Jidu zongjiao yanjiu* 基督宗教研究 [Study of Christianity] 5: 288–301.

Guan Ying. 2005. *Jingjiao yu Da Qin si* 景教与大秦寺 [The Luminous Teaching and the Monastery of Da Qin]. Xi'an: San Qin chubanshe.

Guglielminotti Trivel, Marco. 2005. "Tempio della Croce – Fangshan – Pechino. Documentazione preliminare delle fonti epigrafiche *in situ*." *OCP* 71.2: 431–60.

Guisso, Richard W. L. 1978. *Wu Tse-T'ien and the Politics of Legitimation in T'ang China*. Program in East Asian Studies Occasional Papers 11. Bellingham, WA: Center for East Asian Studies, Western Washington University.

Gulácsi, Zsuzsanna. 2005. *Mediaeval Manichaean Book Art: A Codicological Study of Iranian and Turkic Illuminated Book Fragments from 8th–11th Century East Central Asia*. Nag Hammadi and Manichaean Studies 57. Leiden: Brill.

Gulácsi, Zsuzsanna. 2009. "A Manichaean 'Portrait of the Buddha Jesus': Identifying a Twelfth- or Thirteenth-Century Chinese Painting from the Collection of Seiun-ji Zen Temple." *Artibus Asiae* 69.1: 91–145.

Gulácsi, Zsuzsanna. 2015. *Mani's Pictures: The Didactic Images of the Manichaeans from Sasanian Mesopotamia to Uygur Central Asia and Tang-Ming China*. Nag Hammadi and Manichaean Studies 90. Leiden-Boston: Brill.

Gyselen, Rika, ed. 2006a. *Chrétiens en terre d'Iran*, vol. 1: *Implantation et acculturation*. StIr C 33. Paris: Association pour l'avancement des études iraniennes.

Gyselen, Rika. 2006b. "Les témoignages sigillographiques sur la présence chrétienne dans l'empire sassanide." In Gyselen 2006a, 17–78.

Hage, Wolfgang. 1978. "Einheimische Volkssprachen und syrische Kirchensprache in der nestorianischen Asienmission." In *Erkenntnisse und Meinungen*, edited by Gernot Wießner, 2: 131–60. Göttinger Orientforschungen: Syriaca 17. Wiesbaden: Harrassowitz.

Hage, Wolfgang. 1982. "Religiöse Toleranz in der nestorianischen Asienmission." In *Glaube und Toleranz: Das theologische Erbe der Aufklärung*, edited by Trutz Rendtorff, 99–112. Gütersloh: G. Mohn.

Hage, Wolfgang. 1988a. "The Christian Community in the Oasis of Turfan." In Hage 1988c, 42–54.

Hage, Wolfgang. 1988b. "Missionary Enterprise of the Church of the East in Central and East Asia." In Hage 1988c, 14–26.

Hage, Wolfgang. 1988c. *Syriac Christianity in the East*. Mōrān ʾEthʾō Series 1. Kottayam: SEERI.

Bibliography

Hage, Wolfgang. 1995–96. "Crosses with Epigraphs in Mediaeval Central and East Asian Christianity." *The Harp* 8–9: 375–82.

Hage, Wolfgang. 2012. "Organisation und Kommunikationsstrukturen der 'Apostolischen Kirche des Ostens.'" In Koschorke 2012, 59–67.

Halbertsma, Tjalling H. F. 2005. "Some Field Notes and Images of Stone Material from Graves of the Church of the East in Inner Mongolia, China." *MS* 53: 113–244.

Halbertsma, Tjalling H. F. 2008. *Early Christian Remains of Inner Mongolia: Discovery, Reconstruction, and Appropriation*. Leiden: Brill.

Hamada Naoya 浜田直也. 2005. "Keikyō kyōten *Isshinron* to sono shisō" 景教経典 「一神論」とその思想 [The Scripture of the Luminous Teaching *Yishen lun* and Its Thought]. *Ajia yūgaku* アジア遊学 [Intriguing Asia] 79: 244–57.

Hamada Naoya. 2007. "Keikyō kyōten *Isshinron* to sono bukkyōteki seikaku ni tsuite" 景教経典「一神論」とその佛教的性格について [On the Scripture of the Luminous Teaching *Yishen lun* and Its Buddhist Character]. *Bungei ronsō* 文芸論叢 [Studies on Japanese and Chinese Literary Arts] 68: 61–75.

Hamada Naoya. 2012. "Zendō no jidai to 'kakugi keikyō'" 善導の時代と 「格義景教」 [The Age of Shandao and the "*Geyi* Luminous Teaching"]. In *Hōnen bukkyō to sono kanōsei: Hōnen Shōnin happyakunen daionki kinen* 法然仏教とその可能性―法然上人八〇〇年大遠忌記念 [Hōnen's Buddhism and Its Possibilities: Commemorating the Eight Hundred Years of Hōnen Jōnin's Death], edited by Bukkyō daigaku sōgō kenkyūjo 佛教大学総合研究所, 117–41. Kyoto: Bukkyō daigaku.

Hambis, Louis. 1961. "Ak-bešim et ses sanctuaires." *Comptes-rendus des séances de l'Académie des Inscriptions et Belles-Lettres* 105.2: 124–38.

Haneda Tōru 羽田亨. 1926. "Keikyō kyōten jotei meishishokyō ni tsuite" 景教經典序聽迷詩所經に就いて ["À propos du *Su-t'ing-mi-che-souo-king*, texte sacré nestorien"]. In *Naitō hakushi kanreki shukuga shinagaku ronsō* 内藤博士還暦祝賀支那學論叢 [Miscellanea of Sinology on the Occasion of the Sixtieth Birthday of Dr. Naitō], 117–48. Kyoto: Kōbundō shobō. Repr. in Haneda 1957–58, 2: 240–69 [text D].

Haneda Tōru. 1929. "Keikyō kyōten shigen anrakukyō ni tsuite" 景教經典志玄安樂經に就いて ["À propos du texte sacré nestorien: *Tche-hiuen-an-lo-king*"]. *Tōyō gakuhō* 東洋學報 [Reports of the Oriental Society] 18.1: 1–24. Repr. in Haneda 1957–58, 2: 270–91 [text E].

Haneda Tōru. 1951. "*Taishin keikyō daishō tsūshin kihōsan* oyobi *Taishin keikyō sengen shihonkyō zankan* ni tsuite" 大秦景教大聖通真歸法讚及ぴ大秦景教宣元至本經殘卷について ["À propos du *Ta-ts'in-king-kiao-ta-cheng-t'ong-tchen-kouei-fa-tsan* et de fragments du *Ta-ts'in-king-kiao-siuan-yuan-tche-pen-king*"]. *Tōhōgaku* 東方學 [Eastern Studies] 1: 1–11. Repr. in Haneda 1957–58, 2: 292–307.

Haneda Tōru. 1957–58. *Haneda hakushi shigaku ronbunshū* 羽田博士史學論文集 [*Recueil des œuvres posthumes de Tōru Haneda*]. Tōyōshi kenkyū sōkan 東方史研究叢刊 3.1–2. Kyoto: Tōyōshi kenkyūkai / Société pour l'étude de l'histoire de l'Extrême-orient, Université de Kyōto).

Bibliography

Hansbury, Mary. 1993. "Nature as Soteric: Syriac and Buddhist Traditions." *Aram* 5.1–2: 197–217.

Hansen, Olaf. 1966. "Über die verschiedenen Quellen der christlichen Literatur der Sogdier." In *Iranian Studies: Presented to Kaj Barr on His Seventieth Birthday June 26, 1966*, edited by Jes Peter Asmussen and Jørgen Læssøe, 95–102. Acta Orientalia 30. Copenhagen: Munksgaard.

Hansen, Olaf. 1968. "Die christliche Literatur der Sogdier." In *Die historische und geographische Literatur in persischer Sprache*, edited by Bertold Spuler, 91–99. HdO I.4.2.1. Leiden: Brill.

Hansen, Valerie. 2012. *The Silk Road: A New History*. Oxford: Oxford University Press.

Hansen, Valerie. 2018. "The Synthesis of the Tang Dynasty: The Culmination of China's Contacts and Communication with Eurasia, 310–755." In Di Cosmo and Maas 2018, 108–22.

Harmatta, János. 1971. "The Middle Persian-Chinese Bilingual Inscription from Hsian and the Chinese-Sāsānian Relations." In *Atti del Convegno internazionale sul tema: La Persia nel Medioevo. Roma, 31 marzo–5 aprile 1970*, 363–76. Problemi attuali di scienza e di cultura 160. Rome: Accademia Nazionale dei Lincei.

Hauser, Stephan R. 2007. "Christliche Archäologie im Sasanidenreich: Grundlagen der Interpretation und Bestandsaufnahme der Evidenz." In *Inkulturation des Christentums im Sasanidenreich*, edited by Arafa Mustafa, Jürgen Tubach, and G. Sophia Vashalomidze, 93–136. Wiesbaden: L. Reichert.

Haussig, Hans Wilhelm. 1979. "La missione cristiana nell'Asia centrale e orientale nei secoli VI e VII e le sue tracce archeologiche e letterarie." In *XXVI Corso di cultura sull'arte ravennate e bizantina: Ravenna, 6/18 maggio 1979*, 171–95. Ravenna: Edizioni del Girasole.

Havret, Henri. 1895–1902. *La Stèle Chrétienne de Si-Ngan-Fou*. 3 vols. Variétés sinologiques 7; 12; 20. Shanghai: Imprimerie de la mission catholique [text and trans. A].

Havret, Henri. 1897. *La stèle chrétienne de Si-ngan-fou: Quelques notes extraites d'un commentaire inédit*. Leiden: Brill.

He Xiangjun 何湘君. 2019. "Neimenggu Heishui cheng chutu huigu jingjiao xieben yanjiu" 内蒙古黑水城出土回鹘景教写本研究 [A Study of the Uighur Manuscripts of the Luminous Teaching Unearthed in Xaraxoto, Inner Mongolia]. *Tulufanxue yanjiu* 吐鲁番学研究 [Turfanological Research], no. 1: 72–84.

Heijer, Johannes den, Andrea Schmidt, and Tamara Pataridze, eds. 2014. *Scripts Beyond Borders: A Survey of Allographic Traditions in the Euro-Mediterranean World*. Publications de l'Institut orientaliste de Louvain 62. Louvain: Peeters.

Heissig, Walther, and Hans-Joachim Klimkeit, eds. 1987. *Synkretismus in den Religionen Zentralasiens: Ergebnisse eines Kolloquiums vom 24.5 bis 26.5 1983 in St. Augustin bei Bonn*. Studies in Oriental Religions 13. Wiesbaden: Harrassowitz.

Hendriks, Olaf. 1958. "L'activité apostolique des premiers moines syriens." *POC* 8: 3–25.

Hendriks, Olaf. 1960. "L'activité apostolique du monachisme monophysite et nestorien." *POC* 10: 3–25; and 97–113.

Herman, Geoffrey, ed. 2014a. *Jews, Christians and Zoroastrians: Religious Dynamics in a Sasanian Context.* Judaism in Context 17. Piscataway, NJ: Gorgias Press.

Herman, Geoffrey. 2014b. "The Last Years of Yazdgird I and the Christians." In Herman 2014, 77–100.

Herman, Geoffrey, ed. and trans. 2016. *Persian Martyr Acts under King Yazdgird I.* Persian Martyr Acts in Syriac: Text and Translation 5. Piscataway, NJ: Gorgias Press.

Hickley, Dennis. 1980. *The First Christians in China: An Outline History and Some Considerations concerning the Nestorians in China during the Tang Dynasty.* London: China Study Project.

Holm, Frits. 1923. *My Nestorian Adventure in China: A Popular Account of the Holm-Nestorian Expedition to Sian-Fu and Its Results.* New York: F. H. Revell.

Holth, Sverre. 1968. "The Encounter between Christianity and Chinese Buddhism during the Nestorian Period." *Ching Feng* 11.3: 20–29.

Hong Ye 洪業. 1932. "Bo jingjiaobei chutu yu Zhouzhi shuo" 駁景教碑出土於盩厔說 [A Rejection of the Theory That the Stele of the Luminous Teaching Was Unearthed at Zhouzhi]. *Shixue nianbao* 史學年報 [Historiography Annual] 1.4: 1–12. Repr. in *Hong Ye lunxueji* 洪業論學集 [Collection of Hong Ye's Essays], 56–63. Beijing: Zhonghua shuju, 1981.

Hopkirk, Peter. 1980. *Foreign Devils on the Silk Road: The Search for the Lost Cities and Treasures of Chinese Central Asia.* Oxford: Oxford University Press.

Hsia, Po-chia Ronnie. 2009. "The Jesuit Encounter with Buddhism in Ming China." In *Christianity and Cultures: Japan and China in Comparison, 1543–1644*, edited by M. Antoni J. Üçerler, 19–43. Bibliotheca Instituti Historici S.I. 68. Rome: Institutum Historicum Societatis Iesu.

Hsü, C. Y. 1986. "Nestorianism and the Nestorian Monument in China." *Asian Culture Quarterly* 14.1: 41–81.

Huang Lanlan 黄兰兰. 2002. "Tangdai Qin Minghe wei jingyi kao" 唐代秦鸣鹤为景医考 ["Qin Minghe Was a Nestorian Doctor in T'ang Dynasty"]. *Zhongshan daxue xuebao (shehui kexue ban)* 中山大学学报（社会科学版）[Journal of Sun Yatsen University: Social Sciences Edition] 42.5: 61–67.

Huang, Paulos Z., Xiaofeng Tang, and Donghua Zhu, eds. 2019. *Yearbook of Chinese Theology 2018.* Yearbook of Chinese Theology 4. Leiden: Brill.

Huang Xianian 黄夏年. 1996. "Jingjiao yu fojiao guanxi zhi chutan" 景教与佛教关係之初探 [Preliminary Discussion about the Relationship between the Luminous Teaching and Buddhism]. *SZY*, no. 1: 83–90.

Huang Xianian. 2000. "Jingjing *Yishen lun* zhi 'hunpo' chutan" 景经《一神论》之「魂魄」初探 [Preliminary Discussion about the Term *hunpo* in the Scripture of the Luminous Teaching *Discourse on the One God*]. *Jidu zongjiao yanjiu* 基督宗教研究 [Study of Christianity] 2: 446–60.

Humbach, Helmut, and Wang Shiping. 1988. "Die pahlavi-chinesische Bilingue von Xi'an." In Sundermann, Duchesne-Guillemin, and Vahman 1988, 73–82.

Hunter, Erica C. D. 1992. "Syriac Christianity in Central Asia." *Zeitschrift für Religions- und Geistesgeschichte* 44.4: 362–68.

Hunter, Erica C. D. 1996. "The Church of the East in Central Asia." *Bulletin of the John Rylands University Library of Manchester* 78.3: 129–42.

Hunter, Erica C. D. 2002. "Converting the Turkic Tribes." In *Walls and Frontiers in Inner-Asian History: Proceedings from the Fourth Conference of the Australasian Society for Inner Asian Studies, Macquarie University, November 18–19, 2000*, edited by Craig Benjamin and Samuel N. C. Lieu, 183–95. SRS 6. Turnhout: Brepols; [Sidney]: Ancient History Documentary Research Centre, Macquarie University.

Hunter, Erica C. D., ed. 2009a. *The Christian Heritage of Iraq: Collected Papers from the Christianity of Iraq I–V Seminar Days*. Piscataway, NJ: Gorgias Press.

Hunter, Erica C. D. 2009b. "The Persian Contribution to Christianity in China: Reflections in the Xi'an Fu Syriac Inscriptions." In Winkler and Tang 2009, 71–85.

Hunter, Erica C. D. 2010. "Syriac Onomastica in the Xian [sic] Fu Inscriptions." *Parole de l'Orient* 35: 357–69.

Hunter, Erica C. D. 2012. "The Christian Library from Turfan: SYR HT 41-42-43, an Early Exemplar of the *Ḥudrā*." *Hugoye: Journal of Syriac Studies* 15.2: 301–51.

Hunter, Erica C. D. 2013. "Traversing Time and Location: A Prayer-Amulet of Mar Tamsis from Turfan." In Tang and Winkler 2013, 25–41.

Hunter, Erica C. D. 2014. "Commemorating the Martyrs and Saints in Turfan." In Zhang Xiaogui 2014, 324–37.

Hunter, Erica C. D. 2016. "Commemorating the Saints at Turfan." In Tang and Winkler 2016, 89–103.

Hunter, Erica C. D. 2020. "The Christian Library from Turfan: Commemorating the Saints in MIK III 45." In Lieu and Thompson 2020, 1–12.

Hunter, Erica C. D., and James F. Coakley. 2017. *A Syriac Service-Book from Turfan (Museum für asiatische Kunst, Berlin MS MIK III 45)*. BTT 39. Turnhout: Brepols.

Hunter, Erica C. D., and Mark Dickens. 2014. *Syrische Handschriften*, vol. 2: *Texte der Berliner Turfansammlung: Syriac Texts from the Berlin Turfan Collection*. Verzeichnis der Orientalischen Handschriften in Deutschland 5.2. Stuttgart: F. Steiner.

Imaeda, Yoshirō. 2008. "The Provenance and Character of the Dunhuang Documents." *Memoirs of the Toyo Bunko* 66: 81–102.

Inglis, James W. 1917. "The Nestorian Share in Buddhist Translation." *Journal of the North China Branch of the Royal Asiatic Society* 48: 12–15.

Ingram, Paul O. 1974. "The Symbolism of Light and Pure Land Buddhist Soteriology." *Japanese Journal of Religious Studies* 1.4: 331–45.

Irving, Christopher. 1919. "A Chinese 'Temple of the Cross.'" *New China Review* 1.5: 522–33.

Iwamoto Atsushi 岩本篤志. 2010. "Kyōu shooku zō *Tonkō hikyū* gaikan: Sono kōsei to kenkyūshi" 杏雨書屋藏「敦煌秘笈」概觀―その構成と研究史 [Overview of the Dunhuang Manuscripts in the Kyōu Library Collection: Structure and

History of Research]. *Seihoku shutsudo bunken kenkyū* 西北出土文獻研究 [Studies on Excavated Documents from Northwestern China] 8: 55–81.

Iwamoto Atsushi. 2016. "Tonkō keikyō bunken to Rakuyō keikyō kyōdō: Tōdai keikyō kenkyū to mondaiten no seiri" 敦煌景教文献と洛陽景教経幢—唐代景教研究と問題点の整理 [The Documents of the Luminous Teaching from Dunhuang and the *Dhāraṇī* Pillar of the Luminous Teaching from Luoyang: Research on the Tang Dynasty Luminous Teaching and Its Problems]. *Tōdaishi kenkyū* 唐代史研究 [The Journal of Tang Historical Studies] 19: 77–97.

Izumi Takeo 泉武夫. 2006. "Keikyō seizō no kanōsei: Seiunji zōden kokūzōgazō ni tsuite" 景教聖像の可能性—棲雲寺藏傳虛空藏畫像について [A Possible Nestorian Christian Image: Regarding the Figure Preserved as a Kokūzō Bosatsu Image at Seiun-ji Zen Temple]. *Kokka* 國華 112.1: 3–17.

Jansma, Taeke. 1975. "The Establishment of the Four Quarters of the Universe in the Symbol of the Cross: A Trace of an Ephraemic Conception in the Nestorian Inscription of Hsi-an fu?" In *Studia Patristica*, vol. 13.2, edited by Elizabeth A. Livingstone, 204–9. Texte und Untersuchungen zur Geschichte der altchristlichen Literatur 116. Berlin: Akademie-Verlag.

Jettmar, Karl. 2003. "Die Aussage der Archäologie zur Religionsgeschichte Innerasiens." In Jettmar and Kattner 2003, 229–309.

Jettmar, Karl, and Ellen Kattner, eds. 2003. *Die vorislamischen Religionen Mittelasiens*. Die Religionen der Menschheit 4. Stuttgart: W. Kohlhammer.

Ji Xiangxiang 計翔翔. 2002. "*Da Qin jingjiao liuxing Zhongguo bei* chutu shijian kaoxi" 《大秦景教流行中國碑》出土時間考析 [An Examination of the Time of Discovery of the *Stele of the Diffusion of the Luminous Teaching of Da Qin in China*]. *WS* 58: 261–68.

Jiang Boqin 姜伯勤. 1994. *Dunhuang Tulufan wenshu yu sichou zhi lu* 敦煌吐魯番文书与丝绸之路 [Dunhuang and Turfan Documents and the Silk Road]. Beijing: Wenwu chubanshe.

Jiang Wenhan 江文汉. 1982. *Zhongguo gudai jidujiao ji Kaifeng youtairen* 中国古代基督教及开封犹太人 [Ancient Christianity in China and the Jews of Kaifeng]. Shanghai: Zhishi chubanshe [text A, B, C, D, E, F].

Jiao Jianhui 焦建辉. 2013. "Longmen shiku Hongshigou Tangdai jingjiao yiji diaocha ji xiangguan wenti tantao" 龙门石窟红石沟唐代景教遗迹调查及相关问题探讨 [Investigation into the Tang Dynasty Relics of the Luminous Teaching in Hongshigou at the Longmen Grottoes and Discussion on Related Issues]. *Shiku si yanjiu* 石窟寺研究 [Study on the Cave Temples] 4: 17–22.

Johnson, Scott Fitzgerald, ed. 2012. *Oxford Handbook of Late Antiquity*. Oxford: Oxford University Press.

Johnson, Scott Fitzgerald. 2017. "Silk Road Christians and the Translation of Culture in Tang China." *Studies in Church History* 53: 15–38.

Johnson, Scott Fitzgerald. 2018. "The Languages of Christianity on the Silk Roads and the Transmission of the Mediterranean Culture into Central Asia." In Di Cosmo and Maas 2018, 206–19.

Jullien, Christelle. 2006. "La minorité chrétienne 'grecque' en terre d'Iran à l'époque sassanide." In Gyselen 2006a, 105–42.

Jullien, Christelle, ed. 2008. *Chrétiens en terre d'Iran*, vol. 2: *Controverses des chrétiens dans l'Iran sassanide*. StIr C 36. Paris: Association pour l'avancement des études iraniennes.

Jullien, Christelle. 2011. "Chrétiens d'Iran entre hagiographie et histoire: Avec une nouvelle proposition sur la croix de Hérat." In *Rabō l'ōlmīn: Florilège offert à Philippe Gignoux pour son 8oe anniversaire*, edited by Rika Gyselen and Christelle Jullien, 175–92. StIr C 43. Paris: Association pour l'avancement des études iraniennes.

Jullien, Christelle. 2019. "Les chrétiens en Iran sassanide." In *Le Coran des historiens*, edited by Mohammad Ali Amir-Moezzi and Guillaume Dye, vol. 1: *Études sur le contexte et la genèse du texte coranique*, 359–91. Paris: Les éditions du Cerf.

Jullien, Christelle, and Florence Jullien. 2002a. *Apôtres des confins: Processus missionnaires chrétiens dans l'empire iranien*. Res orientales 15. Bures-sur-Yvette: Groupe pour l'Étude de la Civilisation du Moyen-Orient.

Jullien, Christelle, and Florence Jullien. 2002b. "Aux frontières de l'iranité: 'nāṣrāyē' et 'krīstyonē' des inscriptions du mobad Kirdīr. Enquête littéraire et historique." *Numen* 49.3: 282–335.

Jullien, Florence. 2008. *Le monachisme en Perse: La réforme d'Abraham le Grand, père des moines de l'Orient*. CSCO 622; Subsidia 121. Louvain: Peeters.

Kaim, Barbara, and Maja Kornacka. 2016. "Religious Landscape of the Ancient Merv Oasis." *Iran: Journal of the British Institute of Persian Studies* 54.2: 47–72.

Kaschewsky, Rudolf. 2002. "Das Sogdische—Bindeglied zwischen christlicher und buddhistischer Terminologie." In *Religionsbegegnung und Kulturaustausch in Asien: Studien zum Gedenken an Hans-Joachim Klimkeit*, edited by Wolfgang Gantke, Karl Hoheisel, and Wassilios Klein, 120–39. Studies in Oriental Religions 49. Wiesbaden: Harrassowitz.

Kaufhold, Hubert. 1996. "Anmerkungen zur Veröffentlichung eines syrischen Lektionarfragments." *Zeitschrift der Deutschen Morgenländischen Gesellschaft* 146: 49–60.

Keevak, Michael. 2008. *The Story of a Stele: China's Nestorian Monument and Its Reception in the West, 1625–1916*. Hong Kong: Hong Kong University Press.

Kern, Iso. 1984–85. "Matteo Riccis Verhältnis zum Buddhismus." *MS* 36: 65–126.

Kessel, Grigory. 2019. "Syriac Medicine." In *The Syriac World*, edited by Daniel King, 438–59. London: Routledge.

Kessel, Grigory, and Nicholas Sims-Williams. 2011. "The *Profitable Counsels* of Šemʿōn d-Ṭaibūtēh: The Syriac Original and Its Sogdian Version." *LM* 124.3–4: 279–302.

Klein, Wassilios. 1995. "Die ostsyrische Mission: Zentralasien." In *Einleitung in die Missionsgeschichte: Tradition, Situation und Dynamik des Christentums*, edited by Karl Müller and Werner Ustorf, 121–30. Theologische Wissenschaft 18. Stuttgart: W. Kohlhammer.

Klein, Wassilios. 1999. "Das orthodoxe Katholikat von Romagyris in Zentralasiens." *Parole de l'Orient* 24: 235–65.

Bibliography

Klein, Wassilios. 2000. *Nestorianische Christentum an den Handelswegen durch Kyrgyzstan bis zum 14. Jh.* SRS 3. Turnhout: Brepols.

Klein, Wassilios. 2004a. "A Newly Excavated Church of Syriac Christianity along the Silk Road in Kyrghyzstan." *Journal of Eastern Christian Studies* 56.1: 25–47.

Klein, Wassilios. 2004b. "Les inscriptions syriaques des républiques d'Asie centrale." In *Les inscriptions syriaques*, edited by Françoise Briquel Chatonnet, Muriel Debié, and Alain Desreumaux, 125–41. Études syriaques 1. Paris: Geuthner.

Klein, Wassilios, and Christiane Reck. 2004. "Ein Kreuz mit sogdischer Inschrift aus Ak-Bešim/Kyrgyzstan." *Zeitschrift der Deutschen Morgenländischen Gesellschaft* 154: 147–56.

Klengel, Horst, and Werner Sundermann, eds. 1991. *Ägypten, Vorderasien, Turfan: Probleme der Edition und Bearbeitung altorientalischer Handschriften.* Schriften zur Geschichte und Kultur des alten Orients 23. Berlin: Akademie-Verlag.

Klimkeit, Hans-Joachim. 1979. "Das Kreuzessymbol in der zentralasiatischen Religionsbegegnung: Zum Verhältnis von Christologie und Buddhologie in der zentralasiatischen Kunst." *Zeitschrift für Religions- und Geistesgeschichte* 31.1: 99–115. Repr. in Malek 2002, 259–83.

Klimkeit, Hans-Joachim. 1985. "Christian-Buddhist Encounter in Medieval Central Asia." In *The Cross and the Lotus: Christianity and Buddhism in Dialogue*, edited by Gary W. Houston, 9–24. Delhi: Motilal Banarsidass.

Klimkeit, Hans-Joachim. 1986a. *Die Begegnung von Christentum, Gnosis und Buddhismus an der Seidenstraße.* Rheinisch-Westfälische Akademie der Wissenschaften. Geisteswissenschaften: Vorträge G 283. Opladen: Westdeutscher Verlag.

Klimkeit, Hans-Joachim. 1986b. "Jesus' Entry into *Parinirvāṇa*: Manichaean Identity in Buddhist Central Asia." *Numen* 33.2: 225–40. Repr. in Malek 2002, 243–57.

Klimkeit, Hans-Joachim. 1988. *Die Seidenstraße: Handelsweg und Kulturbrücke zwischen Morgen- und Abendland.* DuMont-Dokumente. Cologne: DuMont.

Klimkeit, Hans-Joachim. 1991. "Die Kenntnis apokrypher Evangelien in Zentral- und Ostasien." In *Manichaica Selecta: Studies Presented to Professor Julien Ries on the Occasion of His Seventieth Birthday*, edited by Alois van Tongerloo and Søren Giversen, 149–75. Manichaean Studies 1. Louvain: International Association of Manichaean Studies; Lund: Center of the History of Religions.

Klimkeit, Hans-Joachim. 1996a. "Jesus, Mani and Buddha as Physicians in the Texts of the Silk Road." In *Convegno internazionale 1996*, 589–95.

Klimkeit, Hans-Joachim. 1996b. *Manichäische Kunst an der Seidenstraße: Alte und neue Funde.* Nordrhein-Westfälische Akademie der Wissenschaften. Geisteswissenschaften: Vorträge G 338. Opladen: Westdeutscher Verlag.

Klimkeit, Hans-Joachim. 1998a. "Adaptations to Buddhism in East Iranian and Central Asian Manichaeism." In Manfred Heuser and Hans-Joachim Klimkeit, *Studies in Manichaean Literature and Art*, 237–53. Nag Hammadi and Manichaean Studies 46. Leiden: Brill.

Klimkeit, Hans-Joachim. 1998b. "Buddhistische Elemente in der christlichen Literatur Zentralasiens." In *Begegnung von Religionen und Kulturen: Festschrift für Norbert Klaes*, edited by Dorothea Lüddeckens, 135–43. Dettelbach: Röll.

Kōgi, Kudara. 2002. "A Rough Sketch of Central Asian Buddhism." *Pacific World*, 3rd ser., 4: 93–107.

Kohler, Charles, ed. 1906. *Recueil des historiens des croisades: Documents armeniens*, vol. 2: *Documents latins et francais relatifs à l'Arménie*. Paris: Imprimerie nationale.

Kohn, Livia. 2003. *Monastic Life in Medieval Daoism: A Cross-Cultural Perspective*. Honolulu: University of Hawai'i Press.

Kósa, Gábor. 2011. "The Sea of Fire as a Chinese Manichaean Metaphor: Source Materials for Mapping an Unnoticed Image." *Asia Major*, 3rd ser., 24.2: 1–52.

Koschorke, Klaus, ed. 2012. *Etappen der Globalisierung in christentumsgeschichtlicher Perspektive / Phases of Globaliziation in the History of Christianity*. Wiesbaden: Harrassowitz.

Koshelenko, Gennadi A. 1966. "The Beginning of Buddhism in Margiana." *Acta Antiqua Academiae Scientiarum Hungaricae* 14: 175–84.

Koshelenko, Gennadi A., Andrei Bader, and Vassif A. Gaibov. 1995. "The Beginnings of Christianity in Merv." *Iranica Antiqua* 30: 55–70.

Koyama, Noboru. 2013. "Elizabeth Anna Gordon (1851–1925)." In *Britain and Japan: Biographical Portraits*, edited by H. Cortazzi, 8: 351–59. Leiden: Brill.

Krippes, Karl. 1991. "Sociolinguistic Notes on the Turcification of the Sogdians." *Central Asiatic Journal* 35.1–2: 67–80.

Kroll, Paul W. 2001. *Dharma Bell and Dhāraṇī Pillar: Li Po's Buddhist Inscriptions*. Epigraphical Series 3. Kyoto: Scuola Italiana di Studi sull'Asia Orientale.

Kyōu shooku 杏雨書屋, ed. 2009. *Tonkō hikyū: Mokuroku satsu* 「敦煌秘笈」目録冊 [Dunhuang Secret Collection: Catalogue Volume]. Osaka: Takeda kagaku shinkō zaidan.

Kyōu shooku, ed. 2009–13. *Tonkō hikyū: Eihen satsu* 「敦煌秘笈」影片冊 [Dunhuang Secret Collection: Photographic Volumes]. 9 vols. Osaka: Takeda kagaku shinkō zaidan.

Kyōu shooku, ed. 2020. *Tonkō hikyū keikyō kyōten shishu* 「敦煌秘笈」景教経典四種 [The Four Scriptures of the Luminous Teaching in the Dunhuang Secret Collection]. Osaka: Takeda kagaku shinkō zaidan.

La Vaissière, Étienne de. 2005. *Sogdian Traders: A History*. Translated by James Ward. HdO VIII.10. Leiden: Brill.

La Vaissière, Étienne de. 2006. "Chinese-Iranian Relations XIII. Eastern Iranian Migrations to China." In EIr Online, <http://www.iranicaonline.org/articles/chinese-iranian-xiii>.

La Vaissière, Étienne de. 2012. "Central Asia and the Silk Road." In Johnson 2012, 142–69.

La Vaissière, Étienne de, and Eric Trombert, eds. 2005. *Les sogdiens en Chine*. Études thématiques 17. Paris: École Française d'Extrême-Orient.

Bibliography

Labourt, Jérôme. 1904. *Le christianisme dans l'empire perse sous la dynastie sassanide (224–632)*. Bibliothèque de l'einsegnement de l'histoire ecclésiastique. Paris: Lecoffre.

Lala Comneno, Maria Adelaide. 1995. "Cristianesimo nestoriano in Asia centrale nel primo millennio: testimonianze archeologiche." *OCP* 61.2: 495–535.

Lala Comneno, Maria Adelaide. 1997. "Nestorianism in Central Asia during the First Millennium: Archaeological Evidence." *Journal of the Assyrian Academic Society* 11.1: 20–67.

Lala Comneno, Maria Adelaide. 1998. "Archeologia cristiana in Asia centrale: nuove possibilità." In Lavenant 1998, 705–16.

Lalou, Marcelle. 1957. "Influences chrétiennes [au Tibet]." In *Les religions du Tibet*, edited by Marcelle Lalou, 15–19. Mytes et religions. Paris: Presses Universitaires de France. Repr. in Dauvillier 1983, chap. 5.

Lanciotti, Lionello, ed. 1984. *Incontro di religioni in Asia tra il III e il X sec. d.C.* Civiltà Veneziana: Studi 39. Florence: Olschki.

Latourette, Kenneth Scott. 1929. *A History of Christian Missions in China*. New York: Macmillan.

Lavenant, René, ed. 1998. *Symposium Syriacum VII: Uppsala University, Department of Asian and African Languages, 11–14 August 1996*. Orientalia Christiana Analecta 256. Rome: Pont. Institutum Orientalium Studiorum.

Le Coq, Albert August von. 1913. *Chotscho: Facsimile-Wiedergaben der wichtigeren Funde der ersten Königlich Preussischen Expedition nach Turfan in Ost-Turkistan*. Ergebnisse der Kgl. Preussischen Turfan-Expeditionen. Berlin: D. Reimer.

Le Coz, Raymond. 1995. *Histoire de l'Église d'Orient*. Histoire. Paris: Les Éditions du Cerf.

Le Coz, Raymond. 2004. *Les médecins nestoriens au Moyen Âge: Les maîtres des Arabes*. Paris: L'Harmattan.

Leclercq, Henri. 1913. "Chine." In *Dictionnaire d'archéologie chrétienne et de liturgie*, vol. 3.1, edited by Fernand Cabrol and Henri Leclercq, 1353–85. Paris: Letouzey et Ané.

Legge, James. 1888. *The Nestorian Monument of Hsî-an fû in Shen-hsî, China*. London: Trübner [text and trans. A].

Lei Wen 雷聞. 2003. "Lun Tangdai huangdi de tuxiang yu jisi" 論唐代皇帝的圖像與祭祀 [On the Images and Worship of Emperors in the Tang Dynasty]. *TY* 9: 261–82.

Leslie, Donald Daniel. 1981–83. "Persian Temples in T'ang China." *MS* 35: 275–303.

Leslie, Donald Daniel. [1998?]. *Jews and Judaism in Traditional China: A Comprehensive Bibliography*. Monumenta Serica Monograph Series 44. Sankt Augustin: Monumenta Serica Institute.

Leslie, Donald D., and Kenneth H. J. Gardiner. 1996. *The Roman Empire in Chinese Sources*. Studi Orientali 15. Rome: Bardi.

Lewis, Mark Edward. 2009. *China's Cosmopolitan Empire: The Tang Dynasty*. History of Imperial China 3. Cambridge, MA: Harvard University Press.

Li Chongfeng 李崇峰. 2002. "Shaanxi Zhouzhi Da Qin sita ji" 陝西周至大秦寺塔记 ["A Nestorian Pagoda at Zhouzhi, Shaanxi"]. *Wenwu* 文物 [Cultural Relics], no. 6, 84–93.

Li Hongqi 李弘祺. 1985. "Jingjiaobei chutu shidi de jige wenti" 景教碑出土時地的幾個問題 [Some Problems about the Time and the Place of Discovery of the Stele of the Luminous Teaching]. In *Zhongguo shi xinlun: Fu Lecheng jiaoshou jinian lunwenji* 中國史新論—傅樂成教授紀念論文集 [New Essays on Chinese History: A Collection of Essays in Honor of Professor Fu Lecheng], 547–74. Taipei: Fu Lezhi.

Li, Zhu. 2016. "Über die Enkulturation der persisch-syrischen Christen im Tang-zeitlichen China—Am Beispiel der abgewandelten Form der 'Zehn Gebote' im *Buch über Jesus den Messias*." In Tang and Winkler 2016, 367–86.

Li-Layec, Zhu. 2019. "From 'Shiyuan 十願' (Ten Vows) to 'Shijie 十誡' (Ten Commandments): Importance of Absent Elements in Translation as Case Study of Inculturation of Christianity during the Early Tang Dynasty (7th Century)." In Huang, Tang, and Zhu 2019, 143–51.

Liang Yancheng 梁燕城 (Leung In-sing, Thomas). 2010. "Zhouzhi xian Da Qin si wei jingjiao yizhi kaoju" 周至縣大秦寺為景教遺址考據 [A Study of the Monastery of Da Qin in the Zhouzhi District as a Remnant of the Luminous Teaching]. *Wenhua Zhongguo* 文化中國 [Cultural China], no. 1, 99–107.

Liang Yuansheng 梁元生 (Leung Yuen-sang, Philip). 2004. *Shizi lianhua: Jidujiao yu Zhongguo lishi wenhua lunji* 十字蓮花—基督教與中國歷史文化論集 [Cross-Lotus: Selected Essays on Chinese Christianity. Historical and Cultural Perspectives]. Hong Kong: Jidujiao Zhongguo zongjiao wenhua yanjiushe.

Liang Zihan 梁子涵. 1957. "Tangdai jingjiao zhi wenxian" 唐代景教之文獻 [The Documents of the Luminous Teaching of the Tang Dynasty]. *Dalu zazhi* 大陆雜誌 [The Continent Magazine] 15.11: 19–23; and 15.12: 23–32 [text A, B, C, D, E, F].

Liang Zihan. 1963. "Tangdai jingjiao yijing kao" 唐代景教譯經考 [A Study of the Translations of the Scriptures of the Luminous Teaching in the Tang Dynasty]. *Dalu zazhi* 大陆雜誌 [The Continent Magazine] 27.7: 212–19.

Lieu, Samuel N. C. 1987. "Chinese Manichaeism—Transformation or Translation?" *Zeitschrift für Religions- und Geistesgeschichte* 39.4: 337–41.

Lieu, Samuel N. C. 1992. *Manichaeism in the Later Roman Empire and Medieval China*, 2nd edn. Wissenschaftliche Untersuchungen zum Neuen Testament 63. Tübingen: J. C. B. Mohr.

Lieu, Samuel N. C. 1998. *Manichaeism in Central Asia & China*. Nag Hammadi and Manichaean Studies 45. Leiden: Brill.

Lieu, Samuel N. C. 2008. "Manichaean Art and Architecture along the Silk Road." In Parry 2008, 79–101.

Lieu, Samuel N. C. 2009. "Epigraphica Nestoriana Serica." In *Exegisti monumenta: Festschrift in Honour of Nicholas Sims-Williams*, edited by Werner Sundermann, Almut Hintze, and François de Blois, 227–46. Iranica 17. Wiesbaden: Harrassowitz.

Lieu, Samuel N. C. 2012. "Places of Nestorian Presence, Ways of Dissemination: Continental and Maritime 'Silk Roads' in China." In Koschorke 2012, 39–58.

Lieu, Samuel N. C. 2013. "The 'Romanitas' of the Xi'an Inscription." In Tang and Winkler 2013, 123–40.

Lieu, Samuel N. C. 2014. "Epigraphica Nestoriana Serica (II)." In Zhang Xiaogui 2014, 360–80.

Lieu, Samuel N. C. 2016a. "Da Qin 大秦 and Fulin 拂林—The Chinese Names for Rome." In *Between Rome and China: History, Religions and Material Culture of the Silk Road*, edited by Samuel N. C. Lieu and Gunner Mikkelsen, 123–46. SRS 18. Turnhout: Brepols.

Lieu, Samuel N. C. 2016b. "Lost in Transcription?—The Theological Vocabulary of Christian Texts in Central Asia and China." In Tang and Winkler 2016, 349–66.

Lieu, Samuel N. C. 2017. "In the Name of Jesus—Observations on the Term 'Jesus the Messiah' in Christian and Manichaean Texts from Central Asia." In *Gnose et manichéisme: Entre les oasis d'Égypte et la Route de la Soie. Hommage à Jean-Daniel Dubois*, edited by Anna van den Kerchove and Luciana Gabriela Soares Santoprete, 385–98. Bibliothèque de l'École des Hautes Études 176. Turnhout: Brepols.

Lieu, Samuel N. C. 2020a. "From Rome (Daqin 大秦) to China (Zhongguo 中國): The Xi'an 西安 (Nestorian) Monument as a Bilingual and Transcultural Document." In Lieu and Thompson 2020, 121–41.

Lieu, Samuel N. C. 2020b. "Persons, Titles and Places in the Xi'an Monument." In Tang and Winkler 2020, 61–81.

Lieu, Samuel N. C., Lance Eccles, Majella Franzmann, Ian Gardner, and Ken Parry. 2012. *Medieval Christian and Manichaean Remains from Quanzhou (Zayton)*. Corpus Fontium Manichaeorum: Series Archaeologica et Iconographica 2. Turnhout: Brepols.

Lieu, Samuel N. C., and Glen L. Thompson, eds. 2020. *The Church of the East in Central Asia and China*. China and the Mediterranean World 1. Turnhout: Brepols.

Lin Meicun 林梅村. 1995. "Luoyang chutu Tangdai Bosi qiaomin Aluohan muzhi ba" 洛阳出土唐代波斯侨民阿罗憾墓志跋 [A Postscript to the Tomb Inscription of Aluohan, a Persian Residing in China during the Tang]. In *Xueshu jilin* 学术集林 [Collected Scholarly Essays], edited by Wang Yuanhua 王元化, 4: 284–99. Shanghai: Yuandong chubanshe.

Lin Meicun. 1996. "Cong kaogu faxian kan huoxianjiao zai Zhongguo de chuchuan" 从考古发现看火祆教在中国的初传 [A Look at the First Introduction of Zoroastrianism to China from Archaeological Discoveries]. *XY*, no. 4, 54–59.

Lin, Wushu. 1992. "On the Spreading of Manichaeism in Fujian, China." In Wießner and Klimkeit 1992, 342–55.

Lin Wushu 林悟殊. 1995a. *Bosi baihuojiao yu gudai Zhongguo* 波斯拜火教與古代中國 [Persian Zoroastrianism and Ancient China]. Taipei: Xinwenfeng chuban gongsi.

Lin Wushu. 1995b. "Dunhuang yishu *Da Qin jingjiao xuan yuanben jing* kaoshi" 敦煌遺書《大秦景教宣元本經》考釋 [Notes on the Dunhuang Document *Book of the Luminous Teaching of Da Qin on Revealing the Origin and the Foundation*]. *Jiuzhou xuekan* 九州學刊 [Chinese Culture Quarterly] 6.4: 23–30. Repr. in Kelimukaite 克里木凱特 (Hans-Joachim Klimkeit) and Lin Wushu,

Da Jiama yiqian zhongya he dongya de jidujiao 達·伽馬以前中亞和東亞的基督教 [Christianity in Central and Eastern Asia before Vasco de Gama], 212–24. Shijie wenhua congshu 世界文化叢書 [A Series of the Cultures of the World 31]. Taipei: Shuxin chubanshe, 1995. Also repr., with the title "Dunhuang ben *Da Qin jingjiao xuan yuanben jing* kaoshi" 敦煌本《大秦景教宣元本經》考釋 ["Notes on Chinese Nestorian Manuscript Unearthed at Dunhuang *Ta-ch'in Illustrious Religion Sutra on the Origin, Hsüan Yüan Pên Chin*"], in Lin Wushu 2003a, 175–85; Lin Wushu 2011b, 248–58 [text F].

Lin Wushu. 1995c. "Monijiao 'sanchang' kao: Bing lun jingjiaobei 'qi sanchang zhi men' yiju zhi shidu" 摩尼教「三常」考—兼論景教碑「啟三常之門」一句之釋讀 [A Study of the Manichaean Term *sanchang* with a Critical Reading of the Sentence *qi sanchang zhi men* on the Stele of the Luminous Teaching]. *HX* 1: 18–24. Repr. in Lin Wushu 1996, 242–51; Lin Wushu 2005c, 132–41; Lin Wushu 2011b, 113–22.

Lin Wushu. 1996. *Monijiao ji qi dongjian* 摩尼教及其東漸 [Manichaeism and Its Diffusion in the East]. Taipei: Shuxing chubanshe.

Lin Wushu. 1998a. "Jingjiao zai Tangdai Zhongguo chuanbo chengbai zhi wojian" 景教在唐代中國傳播成敗之我見 [Personal Views on the Success and Failure of the Diffusion of the Luminous Teaching in Tang Dynasty China]. *HX* 3: 83–95. Repr., with the title "Tangdai jingjiao chuanbo chengbai pingshuo" 唐代景教傳播成敗評說 ["On the Success and Failure of the Nestorian Mission in China during the Tang Dynasty"], in Lin Wushu 2003a, 85–105.

Lin Wushu. 1998b. "Tangchao sanyijiao zhengce lunlüe" 唐朝三夷教政策論略 [A General Discussion of the Tang Policy towards the Three Persian Religions]. *TY* 4: 1–14. Repr. in Lin Wushu 2003a, 106–19.

Lin Wushu. 1999. "Tangji 'Da Qin muhu xian' kao" 唐季「大秦穆護祆」考 ["A Study of the 'Ta-ts'in Mu-hu Hsien' of the Late Tang Dynasty"]. *WS* 48: 39–46; and 49: 101–12. Repr. in Lin Wushu 2005c, 284–315.

Lin Wushu. 2000a. "Fuwang Qian shi cang jingjiao *Yishen lun* zhenwei cunyi" 富岡謙氏藏景教《一神論》真偽存疑 ["Doubts Concerning the Authenticity of the Nestorian *Discourse on One God* from the Tomeoka Collection"]. *TY* 6: 67–86. Repr. in Lin Wushu 2003a, 186–207; Lin Wushu 2011b, 324–46.

Lin, Wushu. 2000b. "Personal Views on the Success and Defeat of the Nestorian Mission in Tang Dynasty China." *China Archaeology and Art Digest* 4.1: 208–9.

Lin Wushu. 2000c. "Tangdai shousuo jingjiao siyuan kaolüe" 唐代首所景教寺院考略 [A Brief Investigation into the First Monastery of the Luminous Teaching in the Tang Dynasty]. *HX* 4: 275–85. Repr., with the title "Tangdai shousuo jingsi kaolüe" 唐代首所景寺考略 [A Brief Investigation into the First "Luminous Monastery" in the Tang Dynasty], in Lin Wushu 2003a, 48–64.

Lin Wushu. 2000d. "Xi'an jingjiaobei yanjiu shuping" 西安景教碑研究述評 ["A Review of the Studies of the Nestorian Monument in Hsi-an-fu"]. *Zhongguo xueshu* 中国学术 [China Scholarship] 4: 239–60. Repr. in Lin Wushu 2003a, 3–26.

342 Bibliography

Lin Wushu. 2000e. "Xi'an jingjiaobei youguan jingsi shuliang ciju kaoshi" 西安景教碑有关景寺数量词句考释 ["Notes on the Quantity Phrases about Nestorian Monasteries on the Nestorian Monument in Hsi-an-fu"]. *Guoxue yanjiu* 国学研究 [Sinology Research] 7: 97–113. Repr. in Lin Wushu 2003a, 27–47.

Lin Wushu. 2000f. "Zhouzhi Da Qin si wei Tangdai jingsi zhiyi" 盩厔大秦寺为唐代景寺质疑 ["Did Ta-ch'in Monastery in Chou-chih Belong to Nestorianism during the Tang Dynasty?"]. *SZY*, no. 4: 1–12. Repr. in Lin Wushu 2003a, 65–84.

Lin Wushu. 2001a. "Dunhuang ben jingjiao *Zhixuan anle jing* Zuobo luwen zhiyi" 敦煌本景教《志玄安乐经》佐伯录文质疑 ["Questioning Saeki's Restoration of the Dunhuang Document Nestorian *Chih Hsüan An Lo Ching*"]. *Zhongshan daxue xuebao (shehui kexue ban)* 中山大学学报（社会科学版）[Journal of Sun Yatsen University: Social Sciences Edition] 41.4: 1–7. Repr. in *Zongjiao* 宗教 [Religion], no. 6 (2001), 68–73; Lin Wushu 2003a, 146–55; Lin Wushu 2011b, 284–93.

Lin Wushu. 2001b. "Dunhuang hanwen jingjiao xieben yanjiu shuping" 敦煌汉文景教写本研究述评 ["Comment on the Study of Chinese Nestorian Manuscripts from Dun-Huang"]. *Ouya xuekan* 欧亚学刊 [Eurasian Studies] 3: 251–87. Repr., with the title "Dunhuang hanwen jingjiao xiejing yanjiu shuping" 敦煌漢文景教寫經研究述評 ["Comments on the Study of Chinese Nestorian Manuscripts from Dunhuang"], in Lin Wushu 2005c, 161–214.

Lin Wushu. 2001c. "Dunhuang jingjiao xieben P. 3847 zhi zai yanjiu" 敦煌景教寫本 P. 3847 之再研究 [A Further Study of the Dunhuang Manuscript of the Luminous Teaching P. 3847]. *DTY* 5: 59–77. Repr., with the title "Dunhuang jingjiao xieben P. 3847 zai kaocha" 敦煌景教寫本 P. 3847 再考察 ["Re-study on the Chinese Nestorian Manuscript P. 3847 from Dun-Huang"], in Lin Wushu 2003a, 123–45; Lin Wushu 2011b, 225–47 [text B].

Lin Wushu. 2001d. "Gaonan shi cang jingjiao *Xuting mishisuo jing* zhenwei cunyi" 高楠氏藏景教《序聽迷詩所經》真偽存疑 [Doubts about the Authenticity of the *Book of the Lord Messiah* of the Luminous Teaching from Mr. Takakusu Collection]. *WS* 55: 141–54. Repr. in Lin Wushu 2003a, 208–28; Lin Wushu 2011b, 347–68.

Lin Wushu. 2003a. *Tangdai jingjiao zai yanjiu* 唐代景教再研究 [*New Reflections on Nestorianism of the Tang Dynasty*]. Tang yanjiu jijinghui congshu 唐研究基金會叢書 [The Tang Research Foundation Series]. Beijing: Zhongguo shehui kexueyuan chubanshe.

Lin Wushu. 2003b. "Tangdai san yijiao de shehui zouxiang" 唐代三夷教的社会走向 ["The Social Trend of the Three Persian Religions during the Tang Period: Manichaeism, Nestorianism, and Zoroastrism"]. In *Tangdai de zongjiao xinyang yu shehui* 唐代的宗教信仰与社会 [Religion and Society in the Tang Dynasty], edited by Rong Xinjiang 荣新江, 359–84. Shanghai: Shanghai cishu chubanshe. Repr. in Lin Wushu 2005c, 346–74.

Lin Wushu. 2004. "Hanwen monijiaojing yu jingjiaojing zhi hongguan bijiao" 漢文摩尼教經與景教經之宏觀比較 [A General Comparison of the Chinese Manichaean and Nestorian Texts]. In Takata 2004, 131–49.

Bibliography

Lin Wushu. 2005a. "Jin bainian guoren youguan xiyu xianjiao zhi yanjiu" 近百年國人有關西域祆教之研究 ["Comments on the Study of Zoroastrianism in the Western Regions in China for Nearly 100 Years"]. In Lin Wushu 2005c, 229–55.

Lin Wushu. 2005b. "Jingjiao Fuwang Gaonan wenshu bianwei bushuo" 景教富岡高楠文書辨偽補說 ["Additional Notes on the Authenticity of Nestorian Tomioka and Takakusu's Manuscripts"]. *DTY* 8: 35–43. Repr. in Lin Wushu 2005c, 215–26; Lin Wushu 2011b, 369–80.

Lin Wushu. 2005c. *Zhonggu san yijiao bianzheng* 中古三夷教辨證 [*Debate and Research on the Three Persian Religions: Manichaeism, Nestorianism, and Zoroastrianism in Mediaeval Times*]. Zhongwai jiaoliu lishi wencong 中外交流歷史文叢. Beijing: Zhonghua shuju.

Lin, Wushu. [2006?]. "Additional Notes on the Authenticity of Tomioka's and Takakusu's Manuscripts." In Malek [2006?], 133–42.

Lin Wushu. 2007. "Monijiao huaming bianyi" 摩尼教華名辨異 [On the Chinese Names of Manichaeism]. *Jiuzhou xuelin* 九州學林 [Jiuzhou Academy] 5.1: 180–243. Repr. in Lin Wushu 2011e, 51–92.

Lin Wushu. 2008. "Xi'an jingbei youguan Aluoben ru Hua shi bianxi" 西安景碑有關阿羅本入華事辨析 ["Notes on Alopen's Entering Tang China Recorded in the Nestorian Monument of Hsi-an-fu"]. *WS* 82: 149–65. Repr. in Lin Wushu 2011e, 115–37.

Lin Wushu. 2009a. "Jingchuang ban 'sanwei yiti' kaoshi: Tangdai Luoyang jingjiao jingchuang yanjiu zhi san" 經幢版「三位一體」考釋—唐代洛陽景教經幢研究之三 ["On the Trinity: Studies of the Luoyang Nestorian Dharani Pillar of the Tang Dynasty, III"]. *ZWL*, no. 1: 257–76. Repr. in Ge 2009a, 109–21; Lin Wushu 2011e, 211–25.

Lin Wushu. 2009b. "Tangdai jingseng mingzi de huahua guiji: Tangdai Luoyang jingjiao jingchuang yanjiu zhi si" 唐代景僧名字的華化軌迹—唐代洛陽景教經幢研究之四 ["The Sinicization of the Nestorian Monks' Names of Tang: Studies of the Luoyang Nestorian Dharani Pillar of the Tang Dynasty, IV"]. *ZWL*, no. 2: 149–94. Repr. in Lin Wushu 2011e, 226–68 [text A].

Lin, Wushu. 2011a. "A Study on Equivalent Names of Manichaeism in Chinese." In *Popular Religion and Shamanism*, edited by Ma Xisha and Meng Huiying, 55–121. Brill: Leiden.

Lin Wushu. 2011b. *Dunhuang wenshu yu yijiao yanjiu* 敦煌文書與夷教研究 [Dunhuang Documents and the Research on Persian Religions]. Dangdai Dunhuang xuezhe zixuanji 當代敦煌學者自選集. Shanghai: Shanghai guji chubanshe.

Lin Wushu. 2011c. "Jingjiao *Zhixuan anle jing* Dunhuang xieben zhenwei ji luwen bushuo" 景教《志玄安乐经》敦煌寫本真偽及录文補說 [Additional Notes on the Authenticity and the Restoration of Dunhuang Manuscript of the Luminous Teaching *Book on Profound and Mysterious Blessedness*]. *HX* 11: 156–72. Repr. in Lin Wushu 2011b, 294–323 [text E].

Lin Wushu. 2011d. "Tang Song *Sanji jing* zhiyi" 唐宋《三際經》質疑 [Doubts about the *Book on the Three Steps* of the Tang and Song Dynasties]. In Lin Wushu 2011b, 136–45.

Lin Wushu. 2011e. *Zhonggu yijiao huahua congkao* 中古夷教華化叢考 [Collected Studies on the Sinicization of the Persian Religions in Medieval Times]. Ouya lishi wenhua wenku 歐亞歷史文化文庫. Lanzhou: Lanzhou daxue chubanshe.

Lin Wushu. 2014. "Jingjiao 'jingfeng' kao: Yijiao wendian 'feng' zi yanjiu zhi yi" 景教「净风」考—夷教文典「风」字研究之一 [A Study of the Term *jingfeng* in the Luminous Teaching: An Investigation into the Word *feng* in the Documents of the Persian Religions, I]. *XY*, no. 3: 50–64.

Lin Wushu and Rong Xinjiang 榮新江. 1992. "Suowei Li shi jiucang Dunhuang jingjiao wenxian erzhong bianwei" 所謂李氏舊藏敦煌景教文獻二種辨偽 [Two Evaluations of the Authenticity of So-called Dunhuang Documents of the Luminous Teaching from the Li Collection]. *Jiuzhou xuekan* 九州學刊 [Chinese Culture Quarterly] 4.4: 19–34. Repr. in Lin Wushu 2003a, 156–74. Revised edn in Rong Xinjiang, *Mingsha ji: Dunhuangxue xueshushi yu fangfalun de tantao* 鳴沙集—敦煌學學術史与方法論的探討 [Dunhuang Collection: An Academic History and Methodological Discussion of Dunhuang Studies], 65–102. Taipei: Xiwenfeng chuban gongsi, 1999. Revised edn also in Rong 2010, 28–46.

Lin, Wushu, and Rong Xinjiang. 1996. "Doubts Concerning the Authenticity of Two Nestorian Christian Documents Unearthed at Dunhuang from the Li Collection." *China Archaeology and Art Digest* 1.1: 5–14.

Lin Wushu and Yin Xiaoping 殷小平. 2008. "Jingchuang ban *Da Qin jingjiao xuanyuan zhiben jing* kaoshi: Tangdai Luoyang jingjiao jingchuang yanjiu zhi yi" 經幢版《大秦景教宣元至本經》考釋—唐代洛陽景教經幢研究之一 ["Notes on Nestorian *Hsüan yüan chih pên ching* (Sutra on the Essential Teaching) in Dharani Pillar Edition: Studies of the Luoyang Nestorian Dharani Pillar of the Tang Dynasty, I"]. *ZWL*, no. 1: 325–52. Repr. in Ge 2009a, 68–86; Lin Wushu 2011e, 168–91; Lin Wushu 2011b, 259–83.

Lin Wushu and Yin Xiaoping. 2009. "Tangdai 'jingseng' shiyi" 唐代「景僧」釋義 ["The *Jingseng* as Nestorian Priest during the Tang: A New Explanation"]. *WS* 86: 181–204. Repr. in Lin Wushu 2011e, 138–67.

Lin Ying 林英. 2006a. "Fulin seng: Guanyu Tangdai jingjiao zhi wai de jidujiao paibie ru Hua de yige tuice" 拂菻僧—关于唐代景教之外的基督教派别入华的一个推测 [The Fulin Monks: Speculation about Christian Groups Other than the Luminous Teaching Coming to China in the Tang Dynasty]. *SZY*, no. 2: 107–16.

Lin Ying. 2006b. *Tangdai Fulin congshuo* 唐代拂菻丛说 [Collected Theories on Fulin in the Tang Dynasty]. Beijing: Zhonghua shuju.

Lin, Ying. 2007. "Fulin Monks: Did Some Christians Other than Nestorians Enter China during the Tang Period?" *POC* 57: 24–42.

Liščák, Vladimír. 2006. "The Early Christianity in Tang China and Its Scriptures in Chinese." In *Trade, Journeys, Inter- and Intracultural Communication in East and*

West (up to 1250): Papers Presented at the International Workshop (Humboldt-Kolleg), Dolná Krupá, Slovak Republic, June 2–6, 2004, edited by Marián Gálik and Tatiana Štefanovičová, 160–81. Bratislava: Institute of Oriental Studies, Slovak Academy of Sciences.

Liščák, Vladimír. 2008. "Early Chinese Christianity in the Tang Empire: On the Crossroads of Two Cultures." In Parry 2008, 103–25.

Littlejohn, Ronnie. 2014. "First Contact: The Earliest Western Views of Daoism in Matteo Ricci's Journals." In *The Dynamics of Cultural Counterpoint in Asian Studies*, edited by David Jones and Michele Marion, 111–26. Albany: State University of New York Press.

Litvinsky, Boris A., Zhang Guang-da, and R. Shabani Samghabadi, eds. 1996. *History of Civilizations of Central Asia*, vol. 3: *The Crossroad of Civilizations: A.D. 250 to 750*. Paris: UNESCO.

Liu Boyun 柳博贇. 2010. "Zhaoshi yu zhengduan, xiaowang yu huannan: Lun niesituolipai jidujiao de yuanqi, fazhan yiji Tangdai jingjiao de zhongjie" 肇始於爭端，消亡於患難—論聶斯托利派基督教的源起、發展以及唐代景教的終結 ["Nestorian Christianity: Rising from Dispute and Vanishing in Tribulation. Its Origin, Development, and Demise in the Tang Dynasty"]. *Jidujiao wenhua xuekan* 基督教文化學刊 [Journal for the Study of Christian Culture] 24: 217–35.

Liu Shufen 劉淑芬. 1996. "*Foding zunsheng tuoluoni jing* yu Tangdai zunsheng jingchuang de jianli: Jingchuang yanjiu zhi yi" 《佛頂尊勝陀羅尼經》與唐代尊勝經幢的建立—經幢研究之一 ["*Dharani Sutra* and the Growth of Dharani Pillars in T'ang China: Studies on Dharani Pillars, Part I"]. *ZLJ* 67.1: 145–91.

Liu Shufen. 1997. "Jingchuang de xingzhi, xingzhi he laiyuan: Jingchuang yanjiu zhi er" 經幢的形制、性質和來源—經幢研究之二 ["The Form, Nature, and Origins of Dharani Pillars: Studies on Dharani Pillars, Part II"]. *ZLJ* 68.3: 643–725.

Liu Shufen. 2003. "Muchuang: Jingchuang yanjiu zhi san" 墓幢—經幢研究之三 ["Mortuary Pillars and the Cult of the Dead in T'ang–Sung China: Studies on Dharani Pillars, Part III"]. *ZLJ* 64.4: 673–763.

Liu Shufen. 2008. *Miezui yu duwang: Foding zunsheng tuoluoni jingchuang zhi yanjiu* 灭罪与度亡—佛頂尊勝陀羅尼經幢之研究 [Eradicating Sin and Saving the Dead: Studies on the *Foding zunsheng tuoluoni jing* Pillars]. Shanghai: Shanghai guji chubanshe.

Liu, Ts'un-yan. 1976. "Traces of Zoroastrian and Manichaean Activities in Pre-T'ang China." In Liu Ts'un-yan, *Selected Papers from the Hall of Harmonious Wind*, 3–55. Leiden: Brill.

Liu Weimin 劉偉民. 1962. "Tangdai jingjiao zhi chuanru ji qi sixiang zhi yanjiu" 唐代景教之傳入及其思想之研究 [A Study of the Introduction of the Luminous Teaching in the Tang Dynasty and Its Doctrine]. *Lianhe shuyuan xuebao* 聯合書院學報 [Journal of the Hong Kong United College] 1: 1–64.

Liu, Xinru. 1995. "Silks and Religions in Eurasia, c. A.D. 600–1200." *Journal of World History* 6.1: 25–48.

Liu, Xinru. 1998. *The Silk Road: Overland Trade and Cultural Interactions in Eurasia.* Washington, DC: American Historical Association.

Liu, Yang. 2001. "Images for the Temple: Imperial Patronage in the Development of Tang Daoist Art." *Artibus Asiae* 61.2: 189–261.

Liu Yong 刘勇 and Chen Xi 陈曦. 2019. "Tang Wudai Lingnan xibu suteren zongji kao" 唐五代岭南西部粟特人踪迹考 [A Study of the Traces of Sogdians in Western Lingnan during the Tang and the Five Dynasties]. *Zhongguo bianjiang shidi yanjiu* 中国边疆史地研究 [China's Borderland History and Geography Studies], no. 4: 67–76.

Liu, Yu. 2015. "The Dubious Choice of an Enemy: The Unprovoked Animosity of Matteo Ricci against Buddhism." *The European Legacy: Toward New Paradigms* 20.3: 224–38.

Liu Zhenning 刘振宁. 2007. *Shiyu "guaikui" zhongyu "guaikui." Tangdai jingjiao "geyi" guiji tanxi* 始于「乖暌」终于「乖暌」—唐代景教「格义」轨迹探析. Guiyang: Guizhou daxue chubanshe.

Lopez, Donald S., Jr., ed. 1988. *Buddhist Hermeneutics.* Honolulu: University of Hawai'i Press.

Lu Fusheng 盧輔聖, ed. 2000. *Zhongguo shuhua quanshu* 中國書畫全書 [Encyclopaedia of Chinese Calligraphy and Painting]. 14 vols. Shanghai: Shanghai shuhua chubanshe.

Lu Yuan 路远. 1997. "Jingjiaobei yicang Xi'an beilin jingguo" 《景教碑》移藏西安碑林经过 [The Process of Shifting the Stele of the Luminous Teaching to the Xi'an *Forest of Steles*]. *WB*, no. 5: 76–79.

Lu Yuan. 2009. *Jingjiao yu jingjiaobei* 景教与《景教碑》 [The Luminous Teaching and the Stele of the Luminous Teaching]. Xi'an: Xi'an chubanshe.

Luo Xianglin 羅香林 (Lo Hsiang-lin). 1966. *Tang Yuan erdai zhi jingjiao* 唐元二代之景教 [*Nestorianism in the T'ang and Yüan Dynasties*]. Hong Kong: Zhongguo xueshe [text B, C, D, E, F].

Luo Zhao 罗炤. 2007a. "Luoyang xin chutu *Da Qin jingjiao xuanyuan zhiben jing ji chuangji* shichuang de jige wenti" 洛阳新出土《大秦景教宣元至本经及幢记》石幢的几个问题 ["Some Points on the Newly-Discovered Christian Stone Pillar Located in Luoyang City"]. *Wenwu* 文物 [Cultural Relics], no. 6: 30–42. Repr., together with Luo Zhao 2007b, in Ge 2009a, 34–58.

Luo Zhao. 2007b. "Zai tan Luoyang Tangchao jingjiao jingchuang de jige wenti" 再谈洛阳唐朝景教经幢的几个问题 [A New Discussion of Some Points of the Tang Dynasty *Dhāraṇī* Pillar of the Luminous Teaching from Luoyang]. *SZY*, no. 4: 96–102. Repr., together with Luo Zhao 2007a, in Ge 2009a, 34–58.

Luo Zhenyu 羅振玉. 1909. *Dunhuang shishi yishu* 敦煌石室遺書 [Documents from the Dunhuang Caves]. 3 vols. N.p.: Songfenshi, 1909. Repr. in Luo Zhenyu, *Dunhuang ziliao congbian sanzhong* 敦煌資料叢編三種. Vols. 3–5. Beijing: Beijing tushuguan chubanshe, 2000.

Luoyangshi dier wenwu gongzuodui 洛陽市第二文物工作隊. 2009. "Luoyang jingjiao shijingchuang chu tudi de tiaocha" 洛陽景教石經幢出土地的調查 ["Investigation on the Unearthed Spot of the Stele with Lection of Religion Jing of Luoyang"]. In Ge 2009a, 165–71.

Ma Xiaohe 马小鹤. 1999. "Monijiao, jidujiao, fojiao zhong de 'da yiwang' yanjiu" 摩尼教、基督教、佛教中的「大医王」研究 [A Study of the Expression *da yiwang* in Manichaeism, Christianity, and Buddhism]. *Ouya xuekan* 欧亚学刊 [Eurasian Studies] 1: 243–58.

Ma Xiaohe. 2004. "Tangdai Bosiguo da qiuzhang Aluohan muzhi kao" 唐代波斯国大酋长阿罗憾墓志考 [Research on the Epitaph of the Tang Dynasty Persian Chieftain Aluohan]. In *Zhongwai guanxi shi: Xin shiliao yu xin wenti* 中外关系史—新史料与新问题 [The History of Chinese-Foreign Relations: New Historical Materials and New Questions], edited by Rong Xinjiang 荣新江 and Li Xiaocong 李孝聪, 99–127. Beijing: Kexue chubanshe.

Ma Xiaohe. 2014. "Jingjiao yu mingjiao de qishi lichan" 景教与明教的七时礼忏 [The Ritual Repentance Seven Times a Day in the Luminous Teaching and Manichaeism]. In Zhang Xiaogui 2014, 254–67.

Ma, Xiaoyang. 2003. "Conflicts between Roman Catholicism and Buddhism in the Late Ming Dynasty, and Their Effect." *China Study Journal* 18.1–2: 27–40.

Mackintosh-Smith, Tim, and James E. Montgomery, eds. and trans. 2014. *Two Arabic Travel Books: Abū Zayd al-Sīrāfi, "Accounts of China and India" and Aḥmad ibn Faḍlān, "Mission to the Volga."* New York: New York University Press.

Maclean, Arthur John. 1894. "Glossary of Technical Ecclesiastical Terms." In *East Syrian Daily Offices: Translated from the Syriac with Introduction, Notes, and Indices and an Appendix Containing the Lectionary and Glossary*, translated by Arthur John Maclean, 291–301. London: Rivington, Percival.

Maggi, Mauro. 2003. "New Persian Glosses in East Syriac Texts of the Eighth to Tenth Centuries." In Paul 2003, 112–45.

Magone, Rui. 2012. "The Fô and the Xekiâ: Tomás Pereira's Critical Description of Chinese Buddhism." In *In the Light and Shadow of an Emperor: Tomás Pereira, SJ (1645–1708), the Kangxi Emperor and the Jesuit Mission in China*, edited by Arthur K. Wardega and António Vasconcelos de Saldanha, 252–74. Newcastle upon Tyne: Cambridge Scholars Publishing.

Mai, Angelo, ed. and trans. 1825–38. *Scriptorum veterum nova collectio.* 10 vols. Rome: Typis Collegii Urbani.

Mak, Bill M. 2016. "Astral Science of the East Syriac Christians in China during the Late First Millennium AD." *Mediterranean Archaeology and Archaeometry* 16.4: 87–92.

Malek, Roman, ed. 2002. *The Chinese Face of Jesus Christ*, vol. 1. Monumenta Serica Monograph Series 50.1. Sankt Augustin: Institut Monumenta Serica; China-Zentrum.

Malek, Roman, ed. [2006?]. *Jingjiao: The Church of the East in China and Central Asia.* Collectanea Serica. Sankt Augustin: Institut Monumenta Serica.

Mao Yangguang 毛阳光. 2014. "Luoyang xin chutu Tangdai jingjiaotu Hua Xian ji qi qi An shi muzhi chutan" 洛阳新出土唐代景教徒花献及其妻安氏墓志初探 [Preliminary Discussion of the Tomb Epitaph of Hua Xian, a Disciple of the Luminous Teaching, and His Wife Lady An of the Tang Dynasty, Recently Unearthed in Luoyang]. *XY*, no. 2: 85–91.

Marazzi, Ugo. 1999. "Panoramica di storia cristiana in Asia centrale." In *Corso di perfezionamento in storia del cristianesimo antico diretto da Luigi Cirillo e Giancarlo Rinaldi: Atti. Napoli, marzo–giugno 1996*, edited by Nello Del Gatto, 267–71. Serie Didattica 2. Naples: Istituto Universitario Orientale, Dipartimento di Studi Asiatici.

Maróth, Miklós. 1984. "Ein Fragment eines syrischen pharmazeutischen Rezeptbuches aus Turfan." *AoF* 11.1: 115–25.

Maróth, Miklós. 1991a. "Eine unbekannte Version der Georgios-Legende aus Turfan." *AoF* 18.1: 86–108.

Maróth, Miklós. 1991b. "Die syrischen Handschriften in der Turfan-Sammlung." In Klengel and Sundermann 1991, 126–28.

Marsone, Pierre. 2013. "When Was the Temple of the Cross at Fangshan a 'Christian Temple'?" In Tang and Winkler 2013, 205–23.

Mather, Richard B. 1963. "Wang Chin's *Dhūta Temple Stele Inscription* as an Example of Buddhist Parallel Prose." *Journal of the American Oriental Society* 83.3: 338–59.

Mathews, Edward G., Jr. 2000. "Nestorian Monasticism." In *Encyclopedia of Monasticism*, edited by William M. Johnston and Christopher Kleinhenz, 2: 931–33. London: Routledge.

Matsumoto Eiichi 松本榮一. 1938. "Keikyō *Sonkyō* no keishiki ni tsuite" 景教「尊經」の形式に就て [About the Form of the *Book of the Honored* of the Luminous Teaching]. *Tōhō gakuhō* 東方學報 [Journal of Oriental Studies] 8: 21–32 (1–12).

Matsunaga, Alicia. 1969. *The Buddhist Philosophy of Assimilation: The Historical Development of the Honji-Suijaku Theory*. Rutland, VT: Charles E. Tuttle; Tokyo: Sophia University.

Mechelen, Johan van. 2001. "Yuan." In Standaert 2001, 43–111.

Menges, Karl H. 1991. "Manichaeismus, Christentum und Buddhismus in Zentralasien und ihr gegenseitiges Verhältnis." *Central Asiatic Journal* 35.1–2: 81–95.

Messina, Giuseppe. 1932. "Il cristianesimo nascente alla conquista dell'Asia." *La Civiltà Cattolica* 83, no. 1968: 535–43.

Messina, Giuseppe. 1946. "Metodo di propaganda e vicende dell'espansione nestoriana in Asia." *La Civiltà Cattolica* 97, no. 2300: 116–27.

Messina, Giuseppe. 1947. *Cristianesimo, buddhismo, manicheismo nell'Asia antica*. Collana di studi storico-religiosi 1. Rome: N. Ruffolo.

Messina, Giuseppe. 1952. "Al-Biruni and the Beginning of Christianity at Merv." *Indo-Iranica* 5.4: 49–56.

Metzger, Bruce M. 1977. "The Sogdian Version." In Bruce M. Metzger, *The Early Versions of the New Testament: Their Origin, Transmission, and Limitations*, 279–81. Oxford: Clarendon Press.

Bibliography

Michihata Taisei 道籏泰誠. 1927. *Shina no jōdoshū no kaiso Zendō daishi ni ataeshi keikyō (kirisutokyō) no kanka* 支那の淨土宗開祖善導大師に與へし景教（基督教）の感化 [The Influence of the Luminous Teaching (Christianity) on Master Shandao, the Founder of the Chinese Pure Land School]. Tokyo: Gudōsha shuppanbu.

Mikkelsen, Gunner Bjerg. 1995. "Skilfully Planting the Trees of Light: The Chinese Manichaica, Their Central Asian Counterparts, and Some Observations on the Translation of Manichaeism into Chinese." In *Cultural Encounters: China, Japan, and the West. Essays Commemorating 25 Years of East Asian Studies at the University of Aarhus*, edited by Søren Clausen, Roy Starrs, and Anne Wedell-Wedellsborg, 83–108. Aarhus: Aarhus University Press.

Mikkelsen, Gunner Bjerg. 1997. *Bibliographia Manichaica: A Comprehensive Bibliography of Manichaeism through 1996*. Corpus Fontium Manichaeorum: Subsidia 1. Turnhout: Brepols.

Mikkelsen, Gunner Bjerg. 1999. "Manichaean Skilful Means: A Study of Missionary Techniques Used in the Introduction of Manichaeism into China." PhD diss., Århus University, Århus.

Mikkelsen, Gunner Bjerg. 2002. "'Quickly Guide Me to the Peace of the Pure Land': Christology and Buddhist Terminology in the Chinese Manichaean *Hymnscroll*." In Malek 2002, 219–42.

Mikkelsen, Gunner Bjerg. 2005. "Shared Features in the Terminology of Chinese Nestorian and Manichaean Texts." In *Il manicheismo: nuove prospettive della ricerca. Quinto congresso internazionale di studi sul manicheismo, Dipartimento di studi asiatici Università degli Studi di Napoli "L'Orientale," Napoli, 2–8 settembre 2001*, edited by Aloïs van Tangerloo and Luigi Cirillo, 263–75. Manichaean Studies 5. Louvain: Brepols.

Mikkelsen, Gunner Bjerg. [2006?]. "Haneda's and Saeki's Editions of the Chinese Nestorian *Zhixuan anle jing*: A Comment on Recent Work by Lin Wushu." In Malek [2006?], 143–48.

Mikkelsen, Gunner Bjerg. 2014. "Manichaeism Meets Chinese Buddhism: Some Comments on the 'Sutrafication' of the *Sermon on the Light-Nous*." In Zhang Xiaogui 2014, 50–63.

Mingana, Alphonse. 1925. "The Early Spread of Christianity in Central Asia and the Far East: A New Document." *Bulletin of the John Rylands Library* 9: 297–371.

Minov, Sergey. 2014. "Dynamics of Christian Acculturation in the Sasanian Empire: Some Iranian Motifs in the *Cave of Treasures*." In Herman 2014, 159–212.

Mkrtyčev, Tigran K. 2002. *Buddyiskoe iskusstvo Sredney Azii (I–X vv.)* [Buddhist Art of Central Asia (1st–10th Centuries)]. Moscow: Akademkniga.

Mode, Markus. 2003. "Die Religion der Sogder im Spiegel ihrer Kunst." In Jettmar and Kattner 2003, 141–218.

Moffett, Samuel Hugh. 1992. *A History of Christianity in Asia*, vol. 1: *Beginnings to 1500*. San Francisco, CA: Harper.

Morano, Enrico. 1982. "The Sogdian Hymns of *Stellung Jesu.*" *East and West* 32.1–4: 9–43.

Morano, Enrico. 1998. " 'My Kingdom Is Not of This World': Revisiting the Great Parthian Crucifixion Hymn." In *Proceedings of the Third European Conference of Iranian Studies, Held in Cambridge, 11th to 15th September 1995*, edited by Nicholas Sims-Williams, 131–46. Wiesbaden: L. Reichert.

Morano, Enrico. 2010. "Manichaean Middle Iranian Texts Regarding Jesus: Edition of Middle Persian, Parthian and Sogdian Texts from the Berlin Turfan Collection." PhD diss., Università degli Studi di Roma "La Sapienza," Rome.

Moribe Yutaka 森部豊. 2012. "Chūgoku Rakuyō shinshutsu keikyō kyōdō no shōkai to shiryōteki kachi" 中國洛陽新出景教經幢の紹介と史料的價值 [An Introduction to the Luoyang Stone Pillar of the Luminous Teaching and Its Value as Historical Resource]. *Higashi Ajia bunka kōshō kenkyū* 東アジア文化交渉研究 [Journal of East Asian Cultural Interaction Studies] 5: 351–57.

Morita Shinnen 森田眞円. 2011. "Tōsho no keikyō to Zendō daishi" 唐初の景教と善導大師 [The Luminous Teaching in the Early Tang Dynasty and Master Shandao]. *Shinshū kenkyū* 眞宗研究 [Journal of Shinshu Studies] 55: 70–86.

Morris, James H. 2015a. "The Case for Christian Missionary Activity in Japan prior to the 16th Century." *OC* 98: 109–37.

Morris, James H. 2015b. "The Presence of *Jǐngjiào* in Japan as Explored by Ikeda Sakae." *Japan Mission Journal* 69.4: 255–66.

Morris, James H. 2016. "The Legacy of Peter Yoshirō Saeki: Evidence of Christianity in Japan before the Arrival of Europeans." *Journal of Academic Perspectives* 2: 1–22.

Morris, James H. 2017. "Rereading the Evidence of the Earliest Christian Communities in East Asia during and prior to the *Táng* Period." *Missiology* 45.3: 252–64.

Morris, James H., and Chen Cheng. 2020. "A Select Bibliography of Chinese and Japanese Language Publications on Syriac Christianity: 2000–2019." *Hugoye: Journal of Syriac Studies* 23.2: 355–415.

Morrow, Kenneth T. 2019. "Negotiating Belonging: The Church of the East's Contested Identity in Tang China." PhD diss., The University of Texas, Dallas.

Mortari Vergara Caffarelli, Paola. 2004. "Monumenti nestoriani dal Mediterraneo alla Mongolia." In *I Mongoli dal Pacifico al Mediterraneo*, edited by Gabriella Airaldi, Paola Mortari Vergara Caffarelli, and Laura Emilia Parodi, 11–28. Genoa: ECIG.

Moule, Arthur C. 1930. *Christians in China before the Year 1550*. London: SPCK [trans. A, B].

Moule, Arthur C. 1940. *Nestorians in China: Some Corrections and Additions*. Sinological Series 1. London: The China Society.

Mullen, Roderic L. 2016. "The Geographical Context of the Tangtse Inscriptions." In Tang and Winkler 2016, 63–87.

Müller, Friedrich W. K. 1915. "Ein syrisch-neupersisches Psalmenbruchstück aus Chinesisch-Turkistan." In *Festschrift Eduard Sachau zum siebzigsten Geburtstage gewidmet von Freunden und Schülern*, edited by Gotthold Weil, 215–22. Berlin: G. Reimer.

Mustafa, Kawthar. 2001. "Symbolism of Light in Zoroastrianism, Judaism and Christianity." *The Dhaka University Studies* 58.2: 123–31.

Mutō Shinichi 武藤慎一. 2010. "Harahoto shutsudo shiriago bunsho ni okeru Shiria kirisutokyō shisō" ハラホト出土シリア語文書におけるシリア・キリスト教思想 ["Syriac Christian Thought in a Newly Discovered Syriac Manuscript at Khara-Khoto"]. *Daitō bunka daigaku kiyō (jinmon kagaku)* 大東文化大学紀要（人文科学）[Bulletin of Daito Bunka University: The Humanities] 48: 287–99.

Muto, Shinichi. 2012. "Christ's Descent to the Underworld in the Khara-Khoto Syriac Document Found in Inner Mongolia." *The Harp* 26: 313–21.

Muto, Shinichi. 2013a. "The Triune God in the Tripartite World in a Syriac Manuscript Found at Khara-Khoto." In Tang and Winkler 2013, 381–86.

Mutō Shinichi. 2013b. "Zenkindai Hokutō Ajia no kirisutokyō shisō: Harahoto shinshutsudo shiriago bunsho o chūshin to shite" 前近代・北東アジアのキリスト教思想—ハラホト新出土シリア語文書を中心として [Christian Thought in Pre-Modern North-East Asia: Focusing on a Syriac Manuscript Newly Found at Xaraxoto]. *Nihon no shingaku* 日本の神学 [Theological Studies in Japan] 53: 9–23.

Muto, Shinichi. 2016. "The Exorcism in the Newly Found Khara-Khoto Syriac Document." In Tang and Winkler 2016, 147–51.

Muto, Shinichi. 2020. "The Term 'Three-One' (Trinity) in *Jingjiao* in Comparison with That in the Taoist Religion." In Tang and Winkler 2020, 95–112.

Nasrallah, Joseph. 1975. "L'Église melkite en Iraq, en Perse et dans l'Asie centrale [I]." *POC* 25: 135–73.

Nasrallah, Joseph. 1976. "L'Église melkite en Iraq, en Perse et dans l'Asie centrale [II]." *POC* 26: 16–33 and 319–53.

Nasrallah, Joseph. 1977. "L'Église melkite en Iraq, en Perse et dans l'Asie centrale [III]." *POC* 27: 71–78 and 277–93.

Nasrallah, Joseph. 1983. "Réponse à quelques critiques récentes au sujet des catholicosats melchites de Bagdad et de Romagyris." *POC* 33: 160–70.

Nau, François. 1914. "L'expansion nestorienne en Asie." *Annales du Musée Guimet* 40: 193–383.

Naymark, Aleksandr. 2001. "Sogdiana, Its Christians and Byzantium: A Study of Artistic and Cultural Connection in Late Antiquity and Early Middle Ages." PhD diss., Indiana University, Bloomington.

Nicolini-Zani, Matteo. 2006a. "*Christiano-Sogdica*: An Updated Bibliography on the Relationship between Sogdians and Christianity throughout Central Asia and into China." In *Ērān ud Anērān: Studies Presented to Boris Il'ič Maršak on the Occasion of His 70th Birthday*, edited by Matteo Compareti, Paola Raffetta, and Gianroberto Scarcia, 455–70. Venice: Cafoscarina. Available online at <http://www.transoxiana.org/Eran/Articles/nicolini-zani.html>.

Nicolini-Zani, Matteo. [2006b?]. "Past and Current Research on Tang *Jingjiao* Documents: A Survey." In Malek [2006?], 23–44.

Nicolini-Zani, Matteo. 2007. "Gesù Cristo sulla via della Cina: La prima 'cristologia' in dialogo con le religioni e le culture dell'Asia orientale." In *La Rivista del Clero Italiano* 88.12: 859–73.

Nicolini-Zani, Matteo. 2009a. "La ricerca sul cristianesimo siro-orientale nella Cina delle dinastie Tang e Yuan: il contributo della sinologia italiana." In *Quinto Simposio Internazionale di Sinologia dell'Università Fu Jen: "L'incontro fra l'Italia e la Cina: il contributo italiano alla sinologia." 23–24 novembre 2007*, edited by Antonella Tulli and Zbigniew Wesołowski, 623–38 (Chinese trans., 642–54). Xinzhuang: Furen daxue chubanshe.

Nicolini-Zani, Matteo. 2009b. "The Tang Christian Pillar from Luoyang and Its *Jingjiao* Inscription: A Preliminary Study." *MS* 57: 99–140 [text and trans. F].

Nicolini-Zani, Matteo. 2010a. "A New Christian Stone Inscription of the Tang Dynasty from Luoyang, China." *Studi e Materiali di Storia delle Religioni* 76.1: 267–74.

Nicolini-Zani, Matteo. 2010b. "Tang Christianity as Perceived by Jesuit Missionaries and Chinese Converts in the Seventeenth Century." *Sino-Western Cultural Relations Journal* 32: 63–88.

Nicolini-Zani, Matteo. 2013a. "Christian Approaches to Religious Diversity in Premodern China." In *Religious Diversity in Chinese Thought*, edited by Perry Schmidt-Leukel and Joachim Gentz, 99–111. New York: Palgrave Macmillan.

Nicolini-Zani, Matteo. 2013b. "Eastern Outreach: The Monastic Mission to China in the Seventh to the Ninth Centuries." In *Mission and Monasticism: Acts of the International Symposium at the Pontifical Athenaeum S. Anselmo, Rome, May 7–9, 2009*, edited by Conrad Leyser and Hannah Williams, 63–70. Studia Anselmiana 158; Analecta Monastica 13. Rome: Pontificio Ateneo Sant'Anselmo; Sankt Ottilien: EOS.

Nicolini-Zani, Matteo. 2013c. "Luminous Ministers of the Da Qin Monastery: A Study of the Christian Clergy Mentioned in the *Jingjiao* Pillar from Luoyang." In Tang and Winkler 2013, 141–60.

Nicolini-Zani, Matteo. 2014. "Tangdai jidu zongjiao de zongjiao duoyuanhua celüe" 唐代基督宗教的宗教多元化策略 [The Christian Approach to Religious Diversity during the Tang Dynasty]. In Zhang Xiaogui 2014, 312–23.

Nicolini-Zani, Matteo. 2016. "The Dunhuang *Jingjiao* Documents in Japan: A Report on Their Reappearance." In Tang and Winkler 2016, 15–26.

Nicolini-Zani, Matteo. 2017a. "Il cristianesimo nella Cina dei Tang di fronte alla diversità religiosa." In Botta, Ferrara, and Saggioro 2017, 239–48.

Nicolini-Zani, Matteo. 2017b. "Da Seleucia a Chang'an: monaci cristiani sulla Via della seta nel primo millennio." In *Uomini e religioni sulla Via della seta*, edited by Elisa Giunipero, 61–75. La via della seta 3. Milan: Guerini e Associati.

Nicolini-Zani, Matteo. Forthcoming. "Monastic Mission in Dialogue: The Missionary Paradigm of East Syriac Christianity in China. An Historical Perspective." In *La Missio ad gentes delle Chiese Orientali*, edited by Germano Marani, Leonide Ebralidze, and Fabrizio Meroni. Rome: Lipa.

Nicolini-Zani, Matteo, and Roman Malek. [2006?]. "Preliminary Bibliography on the Church of the East in China and Central Asia." In Malek [2006?], 499–698.

Nie Zhijun 聂志军. 2008. "Jingjiaobei zhong 'Yisi' ye shi jingyi kao" 景教碑中「伊斯」也是景医考 [An Investigation into the Possibility That the "Yisi" Mentioned in the Stele of the Luminous Teaching Was Also a Christian Physician]. *DJ*, no. 3: 119–27.

Nie Zhijun. 2010. *Tangdai jingjiao wenxian ciyu yanjiu* 唐代景教文献词语研究 [A Study of the Lexicon Contained in the Texts of the Luminous Teaching of the Tang Dynasty]. Changsha: Hunan renmin chubanshe.

Nie Zhijun. 2011. "'Jingjiao,' 'Bosijingjiao' shi 'jingjiao' de biemingma?" 「经教」、「波斯经教」是「景教」的别名吗？[Are "Scriptural Teaching" and "Scriptural Teaching of Persia" Other Terms for "Luminous Teaching"?]. *Zongjiaoxue yanjiu* 宗教学研究 [Religious Studies], no. 1: 207–12.

Nie Zhijun. 2012a. "Jingjiaobei zhong *qishi* bianzheng ji xiangguan wenti kaocha" 景教碑中「七时」辨正及相关问题考察 ["Research on *Qishi* in Nestorian Monument"]. *Guangxi minzu shifan xueyuan xuebao* 广西民族师范学院学报 [Journal of Guangxi Normal University for Nationalities], no. 6: 65–68.

Nie Zhijun. 2012b. "Tangdai jingjiao *Xuting mishisuo jing* zhong 'Yishu' hanyi shiyi" 唐代景教《序听迷诗所经》中「移鼠」汉译释疑 [Clearing up Doubts about the Chinese Translation "Yishu" in the *Book of the Lord Messiah* of the Tang Dynasty Luminous Teaching]. *Zongjiaoxue yanjiu* 宗教学研究 [Religious Studies], no. 3: 191–96.

Nie Zhijun. 2016. *Tangdai jingjiao wenxian yanjiu* 唐代景教文献研究 [*Studying on the Nestorian Literature of Tang Dynasty*]. Zhongguo shehui kexue boshihou wenku 中国社会科学博士后文库. Beijing: Zhongguo shehui kexue chubanshe.

Nikitin, Alexandr B. 1984. "Xristianstvo v Central'noj Azii: Drevnost' i srednevekov'e" [Christianity in Central Asia: Antiquity and Middle Ages]. In *Vostočnyj Turkestan i Srednjaja Azija: Istorija, kul'tura, svjazi* [Eastern Turkestan and Central Asia: History, Culture, Interrelations], edited by Boris A. Litvinskij, 121–37. Moscow: Nauka.

Nishiwaki Tsuneori 西脇常記. 1988. "*Daishin keikyō sengen chihon kyō* zankan ni tsuite" 「大秦景教宣元至本經」殘卷について [On a Fragment of the *Book of the Luminous Teaching of Da Qin on Revealing the Origin and Reaching the Foundation*]. *Zenbunka kenkyūjo kiyō* 禅文化研究所紀要 [Annual Report from the Institute for Zen Studies] 15: 107–38.

Noyé, Edmond. 1934. "St Thomas et la Chine [I–II]." *BCP* 21, no. 255: 579–88; and no. 256: 640–45.

Noyé, Edmond. 1935. "St Thomas et la Chine [III]." *BCP* 22, no. 257: 28–36.

Okuyama Naoji 奥山直司. 2017. "Monoiu ishi: E. A. Gorudon to Kōyasan no keikyōhi repurika" 物言う石：Ｅ・Ａ・ゴルドンと高野山の景教碑レプリカ [The Stone with a Meaning: E. A. Gordon and the Replica of the Stele of the Luminous Teaching on Mt. Kōya]. In *Shukyō bungei no gensetsu to kankyō* 宗教文芸の言説

と環境 [Theories and Scopes of Religious Literature], edited by Hara Katsuaki 原克昭, 330–35. Tokyo: Kasama shoin.

Okuyama Naoji. 2018a. "E. A. Gorudon no gakumon shisō keisei" E. A. ゴルドンの学問・思想形成 [The Formation of E. A. Gordon's Scholarship and Thought]. *Indogaku bukkyōgaku kenkyū* 印度學佛教學研究 [Journal of Indian and Buddhist Studies] 66.2: 744–38 (231–37).

Okuyama Naoji. 2018b. "E. A. Gorudon to Kōyasan keikyōhi" E・A・ゴルトンと高野山景教碑 [E. A. Gordon and the Stele of the Luminous Teaching on Mt. Kōya]. *Kōyasan daigaku toshokan kiyō* 高野山大学図書館紀要 [Bulletin of the Kōyasan University Library] 2: 1–20.

Orsatti, Paola. 2003. "Syro-Persian Formulas in Poetic Form in Baptism Liturgy." In Paul 2003, 147–76.

Ōsawa, Takashi. "The Acceptance of Syrian Christianity by the Ancient Turks in Central Asia in the Sixth and Seventh Centuries, and the Stone Sculptures Reflecting Their Beliefs." In Teule et al. 2017, 81–106.

Palmer, Martin. 2001. *The Jesus Sutras: Rediscovering the Lost Scrolls of Taoist Christianity*. New York: Ballantine [trans. A, B, C, D, E, F].

Palumbo, Antonello. 2003. "Mani in Cina." In *Il Manicheismo*, edited by Gherardo Gnoli, vol. 1: *Mani e il manicheismo*, 281–316. Scrittori greci e latini. Milan: Fondazione Lorenzo Valla; A. Mondadori.

Pan Shen 潘紳. 1917. *Jingjiao beiwen zhushi* 景教碑文注釋 [Notes and Commentary on the Text of the Stele of the Luminous Teaching]. Shanghai: Shenggonghui [text A].

Pan Zhonggui 潘重規, ed. 1983–84. *Dunhuang bianwenji xinshu* 敦煌變文集新書 [New Collection of "Transformation Texts" from Dunhuang]. 2 vols. Taipei: Zhongguo wenhua daxue zhongwen yanjiusuo.

Panaino, Antonio. 1987–88. "Note sulla lingua e la letteratura cristiano-sogdiana." *Atti del Sodalizio Glottologico Milanese* 29: 18–30.

Panaino, Antonio. 2000. "Il testo del *Padre Nostro* nell'apologetica mazdaica." In *Studi sul Vicino Oriente antico dedicati alla memoria di Luigi Cagni*, edited by Simonetta Graziani, 4: 1937–62. Series Minor 61. Naples: Istituto Universitario Orientale.

Panaino, Antonio. 2004. "La chiesa di Persia e l'Impero sasanide: Conflitto e integrazione." In *Cristianità d'Occidente e cristianità d'Oriente (secoli VI–XI)*, 765–863. Settimane di studio della Fondazione Centro italiano di studi sull'alto Medioevo 51. Spoleto: Centro italiano di studi sull'alto Medioevo.

Panaino, Antonio. 2010. "The 'Persian' Identity in Religious Controversies: Again on the Case of the 'Divided Loyalty' in Sasanian Iran." In *Iranian Identity in the Course of History: Proceedings of the Conference Held in Rome, 21–24 September 2005*, edited by Carlo Giovanni Cereti, 227–39. Orientalia Romana 9. Rome: Istituto Italiano per l'Africa e l'Oriente.

Pang, Garry Moon Yuen. 2009. "*Monumenti Sinici*: A Remarkable Chinese Hymn." In Winkler and Tang 2009, 353–81.

Parry, Ken. 1996. "Images in the Church of the East: The Evidence from Central Asia and China." *Bulletin of the John Rylands University Library of Manchester* 78.3: 143–62.

Parry, Ken. 2005. "The Iconography of the Christian Tombstones from Zayton." In *From Palmyra to Zayton: Epigraphy and Iconography*, edited by Ian Gardner, Samuel Lieu, and Ken Parry, 229–46. SRS 10. Turnhout: Brepols.

Parry, Ken. 2008. *Art, Architecture and Religion along the Silk Roads.* SRS 12. Turnhout: Brepols.

Parry, Ken. 2012a. "The Art of Christian Remains at Quanzhou." In Lieu et al. 2012, 243–62.

Parry, Ken. 2012b. "Byzantine-Rite Christians (Melkites) in Central Asia in Late Antiquity and the Middle Ages." In *Thinking Diversely: Hellenism and the Challenge of Globalisation*, special issue of *Modern Greek Studies (Australia and New Zealand)*, edited by Elizabeth Kefallinos, 91–108.

Parry, Ken. 2016. "Byzantine-Rite Christians (Melkites) in Central Asia and China and Their Contacts with the Church of the East." In Tang and Winkler 2016, 203–20.

Pashazanous, Hamidreza, and Ehsan Afkande. 2014. "The Last Sasanians in Eastern Iran and China." *Anabasis* 5: 139–54.

Paul, Ludwig, ed. 2003. *Persian Origins: Early Judaeo-Persian and the Emergence of New Persian. Collected Papers of the Symposium, Göttingen 1999.* Iranica 6. Wiesbaden: Harrassowitz.

Pauthier, Guillaume. 1858. *L'inscription syro-chinoise de Si-ngan-fou, monument nestorien élevé en Chine l'an 781 de notre ère, et découvert en 1625.* Études Orientales 2. Paris: Firmin-Didot [text and trans. A].

Paykova, Aza V. 1979. "The Syrian Ostracon from Panjikant." *LM* 92.1–2: 159–69.

Payne, Richard E. 2015. *A State of Mixture: Christians, Zoroastrians, and Iranian Political Culture in Late Antiquity.* Oakland: University of California Press.

Pearce, Nick. 2020. "A Nestorian Misadventure: Frits Holm and the Chinese Nestorian Stele." *Journal for Art Market Studies* 4.2: 1–15.

Pelliot, Paul. 1911. "Deux titres bouddhiques portés par des religieux nestoriens." *TP*, 2nd ser., 12.5: 664–70.

Pelliot, Paul. 1912. "Les influences iraniennes en Asie centrale et en Extrême-Orient." *Revue d'histoire et de littérature religieuses*, n.s., 3.2: 97–119.

Pelliot, Paul. 1928. "L'évêché nestorien de Khumdan et Sarag." *TP*, 2nd ser., 25.1–2: 91–92.

Pelliot, Paul. 1930. "Christianity in Central Asia in the Middle Ages." *Journal of the Central Asian Society* 17.3: 301–12.

Pelliot, Paul. 1931. "Une phrase obscure de l'inscription de Si-ngan-fou." *TP*, 2nd ser., 28.3–5: 369–78.

Pelliot, Paul. 1931–32. "Un témoignage éventuel sur le christianisme à Canton au XIe siècle." *Mélanges chinois et bouddhiques* 1: 217–19.

Pelliot, Paul. 1933. "Les Nestoriens en Chine après 845." *Journal of the Royal Asiatic Society of Great Britain and Ireland*, n.s., 65.1: 115–16.

Pelliot, Paul. 1984. *Recherches sur les chrétiens d'Asie centrale et d'Extrême-Orient*, vol. 2.1: *La stèle de Si-ngan-fou*. Œuvres posthumes de Paul Pelliot. Paris: Fondation Singer-Polignac [trans. A].

Pelliot, Paul. 1996. *L'inscription nestorienne de Si-ngan-fou*, edited with supplements by Antonino Forte. Epigraphical Series 2. Kyoto: Scuola di Studi sull'Asia Orientale; Paris: Collège de France, Institut des Hautes Études Chinoises [text and trans. A].

Perrier, Pierre. 2012. *Kong Wang Shan: L'Apôtre Thomas et le Prince Ying. L'évangelisation de la Chine de 64 à 87*. Paris: Éditions du Jubilé.

Perrier, Pierre, and Xavier Walter. 2008. *Thomas fonde l'Église en Chine (65–68 ap. J.-C.)*. Asie. Paris: Éditions du Jubilé.

Petech, Luciano. 1992. "The Silk Road, Turfan and Tun-huang in the First Millenium A.D." In Cadonna 1992, 1–13.

Peters, Curt. 1936. "Der Text der soghdischen Evangelienbruchstücke und das Problem der Pešiṭta." *OC* 11: 153–62.

Pigoulewsky, Nina. 1935–36. "Fragments syriaques et syro-turcs de Hara-Hoto et de Tourfan." *Revue de l'Orient Chrétien* 30 [3rd ser., 10]: 3–46.

Piras, Andrea. 2011–12. "Shared Terminologies between Christianity and Manichaeism." *Nāme-ye Irān-e Bāstān* 11.2: 1–22.

Pirtea, Adrian. 2019. "Isaac of Nineveh, *Gnostic Chapters*." In Sims-Williams 2019, 117–44.

Pirtea, Adrian. 2020. "St. Isaac of Nineveh's Gnostic Chapters in Sogdian: The Identification of an Anonymous Text from Bulayïq (Turfan)." In *Caught in Translation: Studies on Versions of Late-Antique Christian Literature*, edited by Madalina Toca and Dan Batovici, 85–103. Texts and Studies in Eastern Christianity 17. Leiden: Brill.

Pittard, William J., and Nicholas Sims-Williams. 2013. "Fragments of Sogdian Gospel Lectionaries: Some New Identifications." In Tang and Winkler 2013, 43–50.

Platt, Andrew. 2016. "Changing Mission at Home and Abroad: Catholicos Timothy I and the Church of the East in the Early Abbasid Period." In Tang and Winkler 2016, 161–82.

Poggi, Vincenzo. 1985. "Matteo Ripa e la stele di Si-an." In *La conoscenza dell'Asia e dell'Africa in Italia nei secoli XVIII e XIX*, edited by Aldo Gallotta and Ugo Marazzi, 2.1: 211–18. Matteo Ripa 4. Naples: Istituto Universitario Orientale.

Poggi, Vincenzo. 2015. "La chiesa di Persia: Testimonianza, martirio ed espansione missionaria della chiesa siro-orientale." In Alzati and Vaccaro 2015, 113–27.

Pulleyblank, Edwin G. 1992. "Chinese-Iranian Relations I. In Pre-Islamic Times." In EIr, 5.4: 424–31; in EIr Online, <http://iranicaonline.org/articles/chinese-iran ian-i>.

Puri, Baij Nath. 1987. *Buddhism in Central Asia*. Delhi: Motilal Banarsidass.

Pye, Michael. 2003. *Skilful Means: A Concept in Mahayana Buddhism*, 2nd edn. London: Routledge.

"La question de l'apostolat de saint Thomas en Chine." 1925. *BCP* 12, no. 138: 64–69.

Raguin, Yves. 2001. "Xuan Zang, Fa Zang, Jing Jing." In Yves Raguin, *Ways of Contemplation East and West*, 4: 245–64. Taipei: Taipei Ricci Institute.

Raguin, Yves. 2002a. "China's First Evangelization by the 7th and 8th Century Eastern Syrian Monks: Some Problems Posed by the First Chinese Expressions of the Christian Traditions." In Malek 2002, 159–79.

Raguin, Yves. 2002b. "Jesus-Messiah of Xi'an." *Tripod* 22, no. 124: 39–54.

Raschmann, Simone-Christiane. 2009. "Traces of Christian Communities in the Old Turkish Documents." In *Tujue yuwenxue yanjiu: Geng Shimin jiaoshou ba-shi huadan jinian wenji* 突厥语文学研究—耿世民教授八十华诞纪念文集 [Studies in Turkic Philology: Festschrift in Honor of Professor Geng Shimin on His Eightieth Birthday], edited by Zhang Dingjing 张定京 and Abdurishid Yakup, 408–25. Beijing: Zhongyang minzu daxue chubanshe.

Reck, Christiane. 2008. "A Survey of the Christian Sogdian Fragments in Sogdian Script in the Berlin Turfan Collection." In Jullien, Christelle 2008, 191–205.

Reck, Christiane. 2018. *Mitteliranische Handschriften*, vol. 3: *Berliner Turfanfragmente christlichen Inhalts und Varia in soghdischer Schrift*. Verzeichnis der Orientalischen Handschriften in Deutschland 18.3. Stuttgart: F. Steiner.

Rhie, Marylin M. 1999–2002. *Early Buddhist Art of China and Central Asia*. 2 vols. HdO IV.12.1–2. Leiden: Brill.

Ribaud, Pénélope. 2001. "Tang." In Standaert 2001, 1–42.

Ribaud, Pénélope. 2005. "La diffusion des religions du monde iranien en Chine entre le VIe et le Xe siècle." *Études chinoises* 24: 269–83.

Ribaud, Pénélope. 2015. "Le christianisme syriaque à l'époque Tang." In Borbone and Marsone 2015, 41–62.

Riegert, Ray, and Thomas Moore. 2003. *The Lost Sutras of Jesus: Unlocking the Ancient Wisdom of the Xian* [sic] *Monks*. Berkeley, CA: Ulysses Press.

Rist, Josef. 1996. "Die Verfolgung der Christen in spätantiken Sasanidenreich: Ursachen, Verlauf und Folgen." *OC* 80: 17–42.

Rogers, John Michael. 1992. "Chinese-Iranian Relations II. Islamic Period to the Mongols." In EIr, 5.4: 431–34; in EIr Online, <http://iranicaonline.org/articles/chinese-iranian-ii>.

Rong Xinjiang 荣新江. 1995. "Xianjiao chuchuan Zhongguo niandai kao" 祆教初传中国年代考 ["A Study of When Zoroastrianism Was First Introduced to China"]. *Guoxue yanjiu* 国学研究 [Sinology Research] 3: 335–53. Repr. in Rong 2001, 277–300.

Rong Xinjiang. 1997. "Li Shengduo xiejuan de zhen yu wei" 李盛铎写卷的真与伪 [The Li Shengduo Collection: Original or Forged Manuscripts?]. *DJ*, no. 2: 1–18. Repr., with the title "Li Shengduo Dunhuang xiejuan de zhen yu wei" 李盛铎敦煌写卷的真与伪 [The Li Shengduo Dunhuang Collection: Original or Forged Manuscripts?], in Rong 2010, 47–73.

Rong Xinjiang. 1998. "Yige rushi Tangchao de Bosi jingjiao jiazu" 一个入仕唐朝的波斯景教家族 ["A Persian Nestorian Family in Tang China"]. In *Yilangxue zai*

Zhongguo lunwenji 伊朗学在中国论文集 [Essays on Iranian Studies in China], edited by Ye Yiliang 叶奕良, 2: 82–90. Beijing: Beijing daxue chubanshe. Repr. in Rong 2001, 238–57.

Rong Xinjiang. 1999a. "*Lidai fabao ji* zhong de 'mo manni' he 'mishihe': Jiantan tufan wenxian zhong de monijiao he jingjiao yinsu de laili" 《历代法宝记》中的「末曼尼」和「弥师诃」—兼谈吐蕃文献中的摩尼教和景教因素的来历 [Mani and the Messiah in the Chan Buddhist Text *Lidai fabao ji*: With a Discussion on the Source of Manichaean and Nestorian Elements in Old Tibetan Texts]. *Xianzhe xinyan* 贤者新宴 [The Scholars' New Symposium] 1: 130–50. Repr. in Rong 2001, 343–68.

Rong, Xinjiang. 1999b. "The Nature of the Dunhuang Library Cave and the Reasons for Its Sealing." *Cahiers d'Extrême-Asie* 11: 247–75.

Rong, Xinjiang. 2000a. "The Migrations and Settlements of the Sogdians in the Northern Dynasties, Sui and Tang." *China Archaeology and Art Digest* 4.1: 117–63.

Rong Xinjiang. 2000b. "Monijiao zai Gaochang de chuzhuan" 摩尼教在高昌的初传 ["The First Introduction of Manichaeism in Turfan"]. *Zhongguo xueshu* 中国学术 [China Scholarship] 1: 158–71. Repr. in Rong 2001, 369–85.

Rong, Xinjiang. 2000c. "Research on Zoroastrianism in China (1923–2000)." *China Archaeology and Art Digest* 4.1: 7–13.

Rong Xinjiang. 2001. *Zhonggu Zhongguo yu wailai wenming* 中古中国与外来文明 [*Medieval China and Foreign Civilizations*]. Sanlian-Hafo-Yanjing xueshu congshu 三联哈佛燕京学术丛书 [SDX & Harvard-Yenching Academic Library]. Beijing: Sanlian shudian.

Rong, Xinjiang. 2002. "The Li Shengduo Collection: Original or Forged Manuscripts?" In *Dunhuang Manuscripts Forgeries*, edited by Susan Whitfield, 62–83. British Library Studies in Conservation Science 3. London: The British Library.

Rong Xinjiang. 2007. "Tangdai fodao erjiao yan zhong de waidao: Jingjiaotu" 唐代佛道二教眼中的外道—景教徒 [Heretics in the Eyes of Tang Dynasty Buddhism and Daoism: The Disciples of the Luminous Teaching]. *Tianwen* 天问 [Questions on Heaven], 107–21. Repr. in Rong 2015, 334–48.

Rong Xinjiang. 2010. *Bianwei yu cunzhen: Dunhuangxue lunji* 辨伪与存真—敦煌学论集 [*Essays on Dunhuang Studies*]. Shanghai: Shanghai guji chubanshe.

Rong Xinjiang. 2014. "Dunhuang jingjiao wenxian xieben de zhen yu wei" 敦煌景教文献写本的真与伪 [Documents of the Luminous Teaching from Dunhuang: Original or Forged Manuscripts?]. In Zhang Xiaogui 2014, 268–89. Repr. in Rong 2015, 349–68.

Rong Xinjiang. 2015. *Sichou zhilu yu dongxi wenhua jiaoliu* 丝绸之路与东西文化交流 [*The Silk Road and Cultural Interaction between East and West*]. Beijing: Beijing daxue chubanshe.

Rong, Xinjiang. 2018. "Sogdian Merchants and Sogdian Culture on the Silk Road." In Di Cosmo and Maas 2018, 84–95.

Rose, Eugen. 1979. *Die manichäische Christologie*. Studies in Oriental Religions 5. Wiesbaden: Harrassowitz.

Rosenkranz, Gerhard. 1937. "Die älteste Christenheit in China in den nestorianischen Quellenzeugnissen der Tang-Zeit." *Zeitschrift für Missionskunde und Religionswissenschaft* 52: 193–226 and 241–80. Repr. *Die älteste Christenheit in China in den Quellenzeugnissen der Nestorianer-Texte der Tang-Dynastie.* Schriftenreihe der Ostasien-Mission 3/4. Berlin: Verlag der Ostasien-Mission, 1938 [trans. A, B, C, D, E, F, based on Saeki's trans.].

Rubiés, Joan-Pau. 2020. "From Idolatry to Religions: The Missionary Discourses on Hinduism and Buddhism and the Invention of Monotheistic Confucianism, 1550–1700." *Journal of Early Modern History* 24.6: 499–536.

Rui Chuanming 芮傳明. 2014. *Monijiao Dunhuang Tulufan wenshu yishi yu yanjiu* 摩尼教敦煌吐魯番文書譯釋與研究 [Interpretation and Analysis of the Manichaean Documents from Dunhuang and Turfan]. Ouya lishi wenhua wenku 歐亞歷史文化文庫. Lanzhou: Lanzhou daxue chubanshe.

Sachau, Eduard. 1905. "Litteratur-Bruchstücke aus Chinesisch-Turkistan." *Sitzungsberichte der Königlich Preussischen Akademie der Wissenschaften*, no. 47: 964–78.

Sachau, Eduard. 1916. "Vom Christentum in der Persis." *Sitzungsberichte der Königlich Preussischen Akademie der Wissenschaften*, no. 39: 958–80.

Saeki Yoshirō 佐伯好郎. 1911. *Keikyō hibun kenkyū* 景教碑文研究 [Research on the Text on the Stele of the Luminous Teaching]. Tokyo: Tairō shoin.

Saeki, Peter Yoshirō. 1916. *The Nestorian Monument in China.* London: SPCK [text and trans. A, B].

Saeki, Peter Yoshirō. 1934a. "The Sutra on Mysterious Rest and Joy (or Sutra Aiming at Mysterious Rest and Joy)." *Bulletin of the Catholic University of Peking* 9: 105–32.

Saeki, Peter Yoshirō. 1934b. "The Ta-ch'in Luminous Religion Sutra on the Origin of Origins." *Bulletin of the Catholic University of Peking* 9: 133–35.

Saeki Yoshirō. 1935. *Keikyō no kenkyū* 景教の研究 [Research on the Luminous Teaching]. Tokyo: Tōhō bunka gakuin Tōkyō kenkyūsho.

Saeki, Peter Yoshirō. 1936. "Old Problems Concerning the Nestorian Monument in China Re-examined in the Light of Newly Discovered Facts." *Journal of the North China Branch of the Royal Asiatic Society* 67: 81–99.

Saeki, Peter Yoshirō. 1951. *The Nestorian Documents and Relics in China*, 2nd edn. Tokyo: The Toho bunkwa gakuin: The Academy of Oriental Culture, Tokyo Institute [text and trans. A, B, C, D, E, F].

Saeki Yoshirō. 1955. *Chūgoku ni okeru keikyō suibō no rekishi* 中國に於ける景教衰亡の歷史 [A History of the Decline of the Luminous Teaching in China]. Tōhō bunka kōza 東方文化講座 7. Kyoto: Hābādo-Enkyō-Dōshisha Tōhō bunka kōza iinkai.

Saeki, Peter Yoshirō, Herbert Mueller, and Philibert Clément. 1931. "Les croix de Chetze-seu." *BCP* 18, no. 218: 543–47.

Salguero, C. Pierce. 2014. *Translating Buddhist Medicine in Medieval China.* Philadelphia: University of Pennsylvania Press.

Salisbury, Edward E. 1853. "On the Genuineness of the So-called Nestorian Monument of Singan-fu." *Journal of the American Oriental Society* 3.1: 401–19.

Santos, Diego M. 2010. "A Note on the Syriac and Persian Sources of the Pharmacological Section of the *Yǒuyáng zázǔ*." *Collectanea Christiana Orientalia* 7: 217–29.

Savchenko, Alexei. 1996. "Urgut Revisited." *Aram* 8.1–2: 333–54.

Savchenko, Alexei. 2008. "Urgut." In EIr Online, <http://www.iranicaonline.org/artic les/urgut>.

Savchenko, Alexei, and Mark Dickens. 2009. "Prester John's Realm: New Light on Christianity between Merv and Turfan." In Hunter 2009a, 121–35.

Schmidt-Glintzer, Helwig. 1987. "Das buddhistische Gewand des Manichäismus: Zur buddhistischen Terminologie in den chinesischen Manichaica." In Heissig and Klimkeit 1987, 76–90.

Schroeder, John W. 2001. *Skilful Means: The Heart of Buddhist Compassion*. Monographs of the Society for Asian and Comparative Philosophy 18. Honolulu: University of Hawai'i Press.

Schurhammer, Georg. 1930. "Der 'Tempel des Kreuzes' 十字寺." *Asia Major* 5: 247–55.

Schwartz, Martin. 1974. "Sogdian Fragments of the *Book of Psalms*." *AoF* 1: 257–61.

Schwartz, Martin. 1991. "A Page of a Sogdian *Liber Vitae*." In *Corolla Iranica: Papers in Honour of Prof. Dr. David Neil MacKenzie on the Occasion of His 65th Birthday on April 8th, 1991*, edited by Ronald E. Emmerick and Dieter Weber, 157–66. Frankfurt am Main: P. Lang.

Scott, David A. 1985a. "Christian Responses to Buddhism in Pre-medieval Times." *Numen* 32.1: 88–100.

Scott, David A. 1985b. "Manichaean Views of Buddhism." *History of Religions* 25.2: 99–115.

Scott, David A. 1995. "Buddhist Responses to Manichaeism: Mahāyāna Reaffirmation of the 'Middle Path'?" *History of Religions* 35.2: 148–62.

Seah, Ingram S. 1984. "Nestorian Christianity and Pure Land Buddhism in T'ang China." *Taiwan shenxue lunkan* 台灣神學論刊 [Taiwan Journal of Theology] 6: 75–92.

Seckel, Dietrich. 1964. *The Art of Buddhism*. New York: Crown Publishers.

Semenov, Grigori L. 1996a. *Studien zur sogdischen Kulture an der Seidenstraße*. Studies in Oriental Religions 36. Wiesbaden: Harrassowitz.

Semenov, Grigori L. 1996b. "Zum Christentum in Mittelasien: Archäologische Funde in Sogdien." In Semenov 1996a, 57–68.

Semenov, Grigorij L. 2002. "Raskopki 1996–1998" [Excavations 1996–1998]. In Gosudarstvennyj Ermitaž (Rossija) and Institut Istorii NAN Kyrgyzstana 2002, 11–114 ("Summary," 172–73).

Shaked, Shaul. 1990. "Bible IV. Middle Persian Translations of the Bible." In EIr, 4.2: 206–7; in EIr Online, <http://iranicaonline.org/articles/bible-iv>.

Sharf, Robert H. 2002. "On Pure Land Buddhism and Ch'an/Pure Land Syncretism in Medieval China." *TP*, 2nd ser., 88.4–5: 282–331.

Shen, Tsing-song Vincent. 2007. "On the Nestorian Introduction of Christian Monotheism into China (635–845): A Preliminary Evaluation of Its Strategies of Strangification." *Fu Jen International Religious Studies* 1.1: 15–41.

Shenkar, Michael. 2017. "The Religion and the Pantheon of the Sogdians (5th–8th Centuries CE) in Light of Their Sociopolitical Structures." *JA* 305.2: 191–209.

Shi Mingpei 石明培. 2000. "Lüelun jingjiao zai Zhongguo de huodong yu Beijing de jingjiao yiji" 略论景教在中国的活动与北京的景教遗迹 [Discussion of the Activities of the Luminous Teaching in China and the Relics of the Luminous Teaching in Peking]. *Zongjiao* 宗教 [Religion], no. 5: 98–101.

Shih, Joseph. 1998. "Matteo Ricci e le religioni cinesi." In *Le Marche e l'Oriente: Una tradizione ininterrotta da Matteo Ricci a Giuseppe Tucci*, edited by Francesco D'Arelli, 57–71. Rome: Istituto per l'Africa e l'Oriente.

Sims-Williams, Nicholas. 1981. "Syro-Sogdica I: An Anonymous Homily on the Three Periods of the Solitary Life." *OCP* 47.2: 441–46.

Sims-Williams, Nicholas. 1982. "Syro-Sogdica II: A Metrical Homily by Bābay bar Nṣibnāye *On the Final Evil Hour*." *OCP* 48.1: 171–76.

Sims-Williams, Nicholas. 1985. *The Christian Sogdian Manuscript C2*. BTT 12. Berlin: Akademie-Verlag.

Sims-Williams, Nicholas. 1988. "Syro-Sogdica III: Syriac Elements in Sogdian." In Sundermann, Duchesne-Guillemin, and Vahman 1988, 145–56.

Sims-Williams, Nicholas. 1989. "Sogdian." In *Compendium Linguarum Iranicarum*, edited by Rüdiger Schmitt, 173–92. Wiesbaden: L. Reichert.

Sims-Williams, Nicholas. 1990a. "Bible V. Sogdian Translations of the Bible." In EIr, 4.2: 207; in EIr Online, <http://iranicaonline.org/articles/bible-v>.

Sims-Williams, Nicholas. 1990b. "Bulayïq." In EIr, 4.2: 545; in EIr Online, <http://iranicaonline.org/articles/bulayq-town-in-eastern-turkestan>.

Sims-Williams, Nicholas. 1991. "Die christlich-sogdischen Handschriften von Bulayïq." In Klengel and Sundermann 1991, 119–25.

Sims-Williams, Nicholas. 1992a. "Christianity III. In Central Asia and Chinese Turkestan." In EIr, 5.5: 530–34; in EIr Online, <http://www.iranicaonline.org/articles/christianity-iii>.

Sims-Williams, Nicholas. 1992b. "Christianity IV. Christian Literature in Middle Iranian Languages." In EIr, 5.5: 534–35; in EIr Online, <http://www.iranicaonline.org/articles/christianity-iv>.

Sims-Williams, Nicholas. 1992c. "Sogdian and Turkish Christians in the Turfan and Tun-huang Manuscripts." In Cadonna 1992, 43–61.

Sims-Williams, Nicholas. 1993. "The Sogdian Inscriptions of Ladakh." In *Antiquities of Northern Pakistan: Reports and Studies*, edited by Karl Jettmar, 2: 151–63. Mainz: P. von Zabern.

Sims-Williams, Nicholas. 1994. "Traditions Concerning the Fates of the Apostles in Syriac and Sogdian." In *Gnosisforschung und Religionsgeschichte: Festschrift für Kurt*

Rudolph zum 65. Geburtstag, edited by Holger Preißler and Hubert Seiwert, 287–95. Marburg: Diagonal-Verlag.

Sims-Williams, Nicholas. 1995a. "A Sogdian Version of the *Gloria in Excelsis Deo*." In *Au carrefour des religions: Mélanges offerts à Philippe Gignoux*, edited by Rika Gyselen, 257–61. Res Orientales 7. Bures-sur-Yvette: Groupe pour l'Étude de la Civilisation du Moyen-Orient.

Sims-Williams, Nicholas. 1995b. "Christian Sogdian Texts from the Nachlass of Olaf Hansen I: Fragments of the Life of Serapion." *BSOAS* 58.1: 50–68.

Sims-Williams, Nicholas. 1995c. "Christian Sogdian Texts from the Nachlass of Olaf Hansen II: Fragments of Polemic and Prognostics." *BSOAS* 58.2: 288–302.

Sims-Williams, Nicholas. 1996. "The Sogdian Merchants in China and India." In Cadonna and Lanciotti 1996, 45–67.

Sims-Williams, Nicholas. 2000. "Some Reflections on Zoroastrianism in Sogdiana and Bactria." In *Realms of the Silk Roads: Ancient and Modern*, edited by David Christian and Craig Benjamin, 1–13. SRS 4. Turnhout: Brepols.

Sims-Williams, Nicholas. 2002. "A Christian Sogdian Polemic against the Manichaeans." In *Religious Themes and Texts of Pre-Islamic Iran and Central Asia: Studies in Honour of Professor Gherardo Gnoli on the Occasion of His 65th Birthday on 6th December 2002*, edited by Carlo G. Cereti, Mauro Maggi, and Elio Provasi, 399–408. Beiträge zur Iranistik 24. Wiesbaden: L. Reichert.

Sims-Williams, Nicholas. 2004. "A Greek-Sogdian Bilingual from Bulayïq." In *La Persia e Bisanzio: Convegno internazionale (Roma, 14–18 ottobre 2002)*, 623–31. Atti dei Convegni Lincei 201. Rome: Accademia Nazionale dei Lincei.

Sims-Williams, Nicholas. 2009. "Christian Literature in Middle Iranian Languages." In *The Literature of Pre-Islamic Iran*, edited by Ronald E. Emmerick and Maria Macuch, 266–87. London: I. B. Tauris.

Sims-Williams, Nicholas. 2011a. "A New Fragment of the Book of Psalms in Sogdian." In *Bibel, Byzanz und Christlicher Orient: Festschrift für Stephen Gerö zum 65. Geburtstag*, edited by Dmitrij Bumazhnov, Emmanouela Grypeou, Timothy B. Sailors, and Alexander Toepel, 461–67. Orientalia Lovaniensia Analecta 187. Louvain: Peeters.

Sims-Williams, Nicholas. 2011b. "Early New Persian in Syriac Script: Two Texts from Turfan." *BSOAS* 74.3: 353–74.

Sims-Williams, Nicholas. 2012. *Mitteliranische Handschriften*, vol. 4: *Iranian Manuscripts in Syriac Script in the Berlin Turfan Collection*. Verzeichnis der Orientalischen Handschriften in Deutschland 18.4. Stuttgart: F. Steiner.

Sims-Williams, Nicholas. 2013. "A Christian Sogdian Hymn in Sogdian Script." In *Monumentum Gregorianum: Sbornik naučnyx statey pamyati akademika Grigoriya Maksimoviča Bongard-Levina*, edited by Askol'd I. Ivančic, 172–77. Moscow: Granica.

Sims-Williams, Nicholas. 2014a. "An Early Source for the Life of John of Dailam: Reconstructing the Sogdian Version." *Nāme-ye Irān-e Bāstān* 12.1–2: 121–34.

Sims-Williams, Nicholas. 2014b. *Biblical and Other Christian Sogdian Texts from the Turfan Collection*. BTT 32. Turnhout: Brepols.

Sims-Williams, Nicholas. 2015. *The Life of Serapion and Other Christian Sogdian Texts from the Manuscripts E25 and E26*. BTT 35. Turnhout: Brepols.

Sims-Williams, Nicholas. 2016. *A Dictionary: Christian Sogdian, Syriac and English*. Beiträge zur Iranistik 41. Wiesbaden: L. Reichert.

Sims-Williams, Nicholas. 2017. *An Ascetic Miscellany: The Christian Sogdian Manuscript E28*. BTT 42. Turnhout: Brepols.

Sims-Williams, Nicholas. 2019. *From Liturgy to Pharmacology: Christian Sogdian Texts from the Turfan Collection*. BTT 45. Turnhout: Brepols.

Sims-Williams, Nicholas. 2020a. "Sogdian Biblical Manuscripts from the Turfan Oasis." In Lieu and Thompson 2020, 13–21.

Sims-Williams, Nicholas. 2020b. "The Sogdian *Book of Life* Reconsidered." In Tang and Winkler 2020, 113–19.

Sims-Williams, Nicholas, and Desmond Durkin-Meisterernst. 2012. *Dictionary of Manichaean Texts*, vol. 3.2: *Texts from Central Asia and China: Dictionary of Manichaean Sogdian and Bactrian*. Corpus Fontium Manichaeorum: Subsidia 7. Turnhout: Brepols.

Sims-Williams, Nicholas, and James Hamilton. 2015. *Turco-Sogdian Documents from 9th–10th Century Dunhuang*. Translated by Nicholas Sims-Williams. Corpus Inscriptionum Iranicarum II.3.4. London: SOAS.

Sinor, Denis, ed. 1990. *The Cambridge History of Early Inner Asia*. Cambridge: Cambridge University Press.

Skaff, Jonathan Karam. 2003. "The Sogdian Trade Diaspora in East Turkestan during the Seventh and Eighth Centuries." *Journal of the Economic & Social History of the Orient* 46.4: 475–524.

Smelova, Natalia. 2015. "Manuscrits chrétiens de Qara Qoto: nouvelles perspectives de recherche." In Borbone and Marsone 2015, 215–36.

Standaert, Nicolas, ed. 2001. *Handbook of Christianity in China*, vol. 1: *635–1800*. HdO IV.15.1. Leiden: Brill.

Stang, Charles M. 2017. "The 'Nestorian' (*Jingjiao*) Monument and Its Theology of the Cross." In Teule et al. 2017, 107–18.

Starr, S. Frederick. 2013. *Lost Enlightenment: Central Asia's Golden Age from the Arab Conquest to Tamerlane*. Princeton, NJ: Princeton University Press.

Stausberg, Michael, and Yuhan Sohrab-Dinshaw Vevaina, eds. 2015. *The Wiley Blackwell Companion to Zoroastrianism*. New York: Wiley Blackwell.

Stein, Aurel. 1921. *Serindia: Detailed Report of Explorations in Central Asia and Westernmost China*. 5 vols. Oxford: Clarendon Press.

Sugimoto Kazuki 杉本一樹. 2020. "*Tonkō hikyū* keikyō kyōten kamishitsu chōsa hōkokusho"「敦煌秘笈」景教経典紙質調査報告書 [Survey Report on the Paper Quality of the Scriptures of the Luminous Teaching in the Dunhuang Secret Collection]. In Kyōu shooku 2020, 108–14.

Sun, Jianqiang. 2018a. "The Earliest Statements of Christian Faith in China? A Critique of the Conventional Chronology of *The Messiah Sutra* and *On One God*." *Sungkyun Journal of East Asian Studies* 18.2: 133–52.

Sun, Jianqiang. 2018b. "Re-dating the Seven Early Chinese Christian Manuscripts: Christians in Dunhuang before 1200." PhD diss., Leiden University, Leiden.

Sun, Zhenbin. 2015. *Language, Discourse, and Praxis in Ancient China*. Berlin: Springer.

Sundermann, Werner. 1968. "Christliche Evangelientexte in der Überlieferung der iranisch-manichäischen Literatur." *Mitteilungen des Instituts für Orientforschung* 14.3: 386–415.

Sundermann, Werner. 1974. "Einige Bemerkungen zum syrisch-neupersischen Psalmenbruchstück aus Chinesisch-Turkistan." In *Mémorial Jean de Menasce*, edited by Philippe Gignoux and Ahmad Tafazzoli, 441–52. Fondation culturelle iranienne 185. Louvain: Imprimerie orientaliste.

Sundermann, Werner. 1976. "Ein Bruchstück einer soghdischen Kirkengeschichte aus Zentralasien?" *Acta Antiqua Academiae Scientiarum Hungaricae* 24.1: 95–101.

Sundermann, Werner. 1988. "Der Schüler fragt den Lehrer: Eine Sammlung biblischer Rätsel in soghdischer Sprache." In Sundermann, Duchesne-Guillemin, and Vahman 1988, 173–86.

Sundermann, Werner. 1992. "Christianity V. Christ in Manichaeism." In EIr, 5.5: 535–39; in EIr Online, <http://iranicaonline.org/articles/christianity-v>.

Sundermann, Werner. 1996. "Iranian Manichaean Texts in Chinese Remake: Translation and Transformation." In Cadonna and Lanciotti 1996, 103–19.

Sundermann, Werner, Jacques Duchesne-Guillemin, and Feridun Vahman, eds. 1988. *A Green Leaf: Papers in Honour of Professor Jes P. Asmussen*. Acta Iranica 28. Leiden: Brill.

Suter, Rufus. 1938. "The Words *san i fēn shēn* in the Inscription on the Nestorian Monument at Hsi-an fu." *Journal of the American Oriental Society* 58.2: 384–93.

Takahashi, Hidemi. 2008. "Transcribed Proper Names in Chinese Syriac Christian Documents." In *Malphono w-Rabo d-Malphone: Studies in Honor of Sebastian P. Brock*, edited by George Kiraz, 631–62. Piscataway, NJ: Gorgias Press.

Takahashi, Hidemi. 2011. "China, Syriac Christianity in." In Brock et al. 2011, 94–96.

Takahashi, Hidemi. 2013. "On the Transcriptions of Syriac Names in Chinese-Language *Jingjiao* Documents." In Tang and Winkler 2013, 13–24.

Takahashi, Hidemi. 2014a. "Syriac as a Vehicle for Transmission of Knowledge across Borders of Empires." *Horizons* 5.1: 29–52.

Takahashi, Hidemi. 2014b. "Transcription of Syriac in Chinese and Chinese in Syriac Script in the Tang Period." In Heijer, Schmidt, and Pataridze 2014, 329–49.

Takahashi, Hidemi. 2020. "Representation of the Syriac Language in *Jingjiao* and *Yelikewen* Documents." In Lieu and Thompson 2020, 23–92.

Takakusu, Junjirō. 1896. "The Name of 'Messiah' Found in a Buddhist Book; the Nestorian Missionary Adam, Presbyter, Papas of China, Translating a Buddhist Sûtra." *TP* 7.5: 589–91.

Takata Tokio 高田時雄, ed. 2004. *Chūgoku shūkyō bunken kenkyū kokusai shinpojiumu hōkokusho* 中國宗教文獻研究國際シンポジウム報告書 [*Proceedings of the International Symposium "Religions in Chinese Script"*]. Kyoto: Kyōto daigaku jinbun kagaku kenkyūjo.

Takata Tokio. 2014a. "Li Pang yu Bai Jian: Li Shengduo jiucang Dunhuang xieben liuru Riben zhi beijing" 李滂與白堅—李盛鐸舊藏敦煌寫本流入日本之背景 [Li Pang and Bai Jian: The Background of the Coming to Japan of the Dunhuang Manuscripts of the Li Shengduo Collection]. *Xiyu wenshi* 西域文史 [Literature and History of the Western Regions] 9: 333–67. Repr. in Takata 2018, 1–67.

Takata Tokio. 2014b. "Yutian Heng yu Dunhuang xieben" 羽田亨與敦煌寫本 ["Haneda Toru and Dunhuang Documents"]. *Dunhuang yanjiu* 敦煌研究 [Dunhuang Research], no. 3: 184–89. Repr. in Takata 2018, 138–49.

Takata Tokio. 2016. "Riben Dunhuang yishu de laiyuan yu zhenwei wenti" 日本敦煌遺書的來源與真偽問題 [The Problems regarding the Origin and Authenticity of the Dunhuang Documents in Japan]. *Xinan minzu daxue xuebao (renwen shehui kexue ban)* 西南民族大學學報（人文社會科學版）[Journal of the South-West University for Nationalities: Humanistic and Social Sciences Edition], no. 11: 185–92. Repr. in Takata 2018, 149–75.

Takata Tokio. 2018. *Jindai Zhongguo de xueshu yu cangshu* 近代中國的學術與藏書 [Modern China's Scholarship and Book Collections]. Beijing: Zhonghua shuju.

Tam, David. 2019. "The Names of God in the Tang Jingjiao Document *Yishen Lun (A Discourse on God)*." In Huang, Tang, and Zhu 2019, 3–21.

Tan Dawei 譚大衛 (Tam Tai-wai, David). 2018. "Tangdai jingjiao wenxian *Yishen lun Shizun bushi lun* zhong 'shizun' yici zhi shiyi" 唐代景教文獻《一神論·世尊布施論》中「世尊」一詞之釋義 ["The Term *Shizun* in the Tang Jingjiao Document *Shizun Bushi Lun*"]. *DF* 49A: 143–67.

Tang Geng'ou 唐耕耦 and Lu Hongji 陆宏基, eds. 1986–90. *Dunhuang shehui jingji wenxian zhenji shilu* 敦煌社会经济文献真迹释录 [Dunhuang Socio-Economic Documents: Reproduction of the Originals]. 5 vols. Beijing: Quanguo tushuguan wenxian suowei fuzhi zhongxin.

Tang Kaijie 汤恺杰. 2019. "Zhu Qianzhi lun jingjiao de 'yiduan' wenti: Yu Zuobo Haolang de duibi" 朱谦之论景教的「异端」问题—与佐伯好郎的对比 [Zhu Qianzhi on the Question of "Heresy" of the Luminous Teaching: A Comparison with Saeki Yoshirō]. *Shijie zongjiao wenhua* 世界宗教文化 [Religious Cultures in the World], no. 6: 43–50.

Tang, Li. 2002. *A Study of the History of Nestorian Christianity in China and Its Literature in Chinese: Together with a New English Translation of the Dunhuang Nestorian Documents*. European University Studies Series 27: Asian and African Studies 87. Frankfurt am Main: P. Lang [trans. A, B, C, D, E, F].

Tang Li 唐莉. 2004. "Tangdai jingjiao Aluoben wenxian: *Xuting mishisuo jing* ji *Yishen lun*" 唐代景教阿羅本文獻—《序聽迷詩所經》及《一神論》 [Aluoben's Documents of the Luminous Teaching: The *Book of the Lord Messiah* and the

Discourse on the One God]. In *Tangdai wenxue yu zongjiao* 唐代文學與宗教 [Literature and Religion during the Tang Dynasty], edited by Liu Chuhua 劉楚華, 665–82. Hong Kong: Zhonghua shuju.

Tang, Li. 2009a. "A Preliminary Study on the *Jingjiao* Inscription of Luoyang: Text Analysis, Commentary and English Translation." In Winkler and Tang 2009, 109–33.

Tang Li. 2009b. "Luoyang xin chutu Da Qin jingjiao jingchuangwen chushi ji fanyi" 洛陽新出土大秦景教經幢文初釋及翻譯 ["The Newly Unearthed 'Jingjiao' Inscription of Luoyang: Text Analysis, Commentary and Translation"]. In Ge 2009a, 135–56.

Tang, Li. 2014. "Traces of Syro-Persian Christians in Ancient Ceylon." In *Geschichte, Theologie und Kultur des syrischen Christentums. Beiträge zum 7. Deutschen Syrologie-Symposium in Göttingen, Dezember 2011*, edited by Martin Tamcke and Sven Grebenstein, 381–92. Göttinger Orientforschungen: Syriaca 46. Wiesbaden: Harrassowitz.

Tang, Li. 2016. "Critical Remarks on a So-called Newly Discovered *Jingjiao* Epitaph from Luoyang with a Preliminary English Translation." In Tang and Winkler 2016, 27–40.

Tang, Li. 2019. "Monastic Movement as a Driving Force in Syriac Christian Missions along the Ancient Silk Road." In *"Make Disciples of All Nations": The Appeal and Authority of Christian Faith in Hellenistic-Roman Times*, edited by Loren T. Stuckenbruck, Beth Langstaff, and Michael Tilly, 189–98. Tübingen: Mohr Siebeck.

Tang, Li. 2020a. "Christian or Buddhist? An Exposition of a Silk Painting from Dunhuang, China, Now Kept in the British Museum." In Tang and Winkler 2020, 233–43.

Tang, Li. 2020b. "The Liturgical Language of the Church of the East in China." In Tang and Winkler 2020, 121–36.

Tang, Li, and Dietmar W. Winkler, eds. 2013. *From the Oxus River to the Chinese Shores: Studies on East Syriac Christianity in China and Central Asia*. OPOe 5. Münster: LIT.

Tang, Li, and Dietmar W. Winkler, eds. 2016. *Winds of "Jingjiao": Studies on Syriac Christianity in China and Central Asia*. OPOe 9. Münster: LIT.

Tang, Li, and Dietmar W. Winkler, eds. 2020. *Artifact, Text, Context: Studies on Syriac Christianity in China and Central Asia*. OPOe 17. Zürich: LIT.

Tang, Xiaofeng, and Zhang Yingying. 2019. "Fangshan Cross Temple (房山十字寺) in China: Overview, Analysis and Hypotheses." In Huang, Tang, and Zhu 2019, 82–93.

Tardieu, Michel. 1999. "Un site chrétien dans la Sogdiane des Sâmânides." *Le monde de la Bible* 119: 40–42.

Tardieu, Michel. 2008. "Le schème hérésiologique de désignation des adversaires dans l'inscription nestorienne chinoise de Xi'an." In Jullien, Christelle 2008, 207–26.

Teule, Herman, Elif Keser-Kayaalp, Kutlu Akalın, Nesim Dorum, and M. Sait Toprak, eds. 2017. *Syriac in Its Multi-cultural Context: First International Syriac Studies*

Symposium, Mardin Artuklu University, Institute of Living Languages, 20–22 April 2012, Mardin. Eastern Christian Studies 23. Louvain: Peeters.

Tezcan, Mehmet. 2020. "On 'Nestorian' Christianity among the Hephthalites or the White Huns." In Tang and Winkler 2020, 195–212.

Tezcan, Semih. 1974. *Das uigurische Insadi-Sūtra.* BTT 3. Berlin: Akademie-Verlag.

Thacker, Thomas W. 1966–67. "A Nestorian Gravestone from Central Asia in the Gulbenkian Museum, Durham University." *The Durham University Journal* 59 [n.s., 28]: 94–107.

Thompson, Glen L. 2009. "Was Alopen a 'Missionary'?" In Winkler and Tang 2009, 267–78.

Thompson, Glen L. 2013. "How *Jingjiao* Became Nestorian: Western Perceptions and Eastern Realities." In Tang and Winkler 2013, 417–39.

Thompson, Glen L. 2020a. "Strange Teaching from a Strange Land: Foreignness, Heresy, and Our Understanding of the *Jingjiao* and *Yelikewenjiao.*" In Lieu and Thompson 2020, 143–63.

Thompson, Glen L. 2020b. "The Structure of the Xi'an Stele." In Tang and Winkler 2020, 161–93.

Thompson, Glen L. Forthcoming. "Did Christianity (or St. Thomas) Come to First-Century China?" In *Byzantium to China: Religion, History and Culture on the Silk Roads. Studies in Honour of Samuel N. C. Lieu*, edited by Gunner B. Mikkelsen and Ken Parry. Texts and Studies in Eastern Christianity. Leiden: Brill.

Tian Haihua 田海华. 2009. "*Xuting mishisuo(he) jing* zhi 'shiyuan' chuyi" 《序听迷诗所（诃）经》之「十愿」刍议 ["Ten Vows in the Jesus-Messiah-Sutra"]. *Zongjiaoxue yanjiu* 宗教学研究 [Religious Studies], no. 4: 119–22.

Tian Weijiang 田卫疆. 2003. "Shixi Gaochang huigu neibu de sanci zongjiao chuanru jiqi houguo" 试析高昌回鹘内部的三次宗教传入及其后果 ["Analysis of the Religions Introduced among the Uyghurs of Gaochang and Their Effects"]. *Xibei minzu yanjiu* 西北民族研究 [N. W. Minorities Research], no. 1: 102–18.

Tisserant, Eugène. 1931. "Nestorienne (l'Église)." In *Dictionnaire de théologie catholique*, edited by Alfred Vacant, Eugène Mangenot, and Émile Amann, 11.1: 157–323. Paris: Letouzey et Ané.

Tisserant, Eugène. 1946. "Timothée I." In *Dictionnaire de théologie catholique*, edited by Alfred Vacant, Eugène Mangenot, and Émile Amann, 15: 1121–39. Paris: Letouzey et Ané.

Toepel, Alexander. 2005. "Traces of Nestorianism in Manchuria and Korea." *OC* 89: 77–85.

Toepel, Alexander. 2009. "Christians in Korea at the End of the 13th Century." In Winkler and Tang 2009, 279–89.

Toepel, Alexander, and Chung Ju-Mi. 2004. "Was There a Nestorian Mission to Korea?" *OC* 88: 29–35.

Tōhō bunka gakuin Kyōto kenkyūsho 東方文化學院京都研究所, ed. 1931. *Isshinron makidaisan; Jotei meishishokyō ikkan* 一神論第三、序聽迷詩所經一

卷 [*The Chinese Nestorian Scriptures: I, I shên lun; II, Hsü t'ing mi shih so ching*]. Kyoto: Maruzen [text C, D].

Tommasi, Chiara Ombretta. 2014. "'Nestorians' on the Silk Road: Some Notes on the Stele of Xi'an." In *La teologia dal V all'VIII secolo fra sviluppo e crisi: XLI Incontro di studiosi dell'antichità cristiana (Roma, 9–11 maggio 2013)*, 645–69. Rome: Institutum Patristicum Augustinianum.

Tommasi, Chiara Ombretta. 2017. "'La via non ha un nome immutabile, il santo non ha un'apparenza immutabile': Echi letterari nella stele cristiana di Xi'an tra diplomazia e propaganda." In Botta, Ferrara, and Saggioro 2017, 230–38.

Tōno Haruyuki 東野治之. 2020. "*Tonkō hikyū* keikyō kyōten shishu" 「敦煌秘笈」 景教経典四種 [The Four Scriptures of the Luminous Teaching in the Dunhuang Secret Collection]. In Kyōu shooku 2020, 5–18.

Tragan, Pius-Ramon. 1997. "La luce negli scritti giovannei: Percorso di un simbolo biblico." *Servitium* 31.1, no. 109: 33–43.

Tremblay, Xavier. 2001. *Pour une histoire de la Sérinde: Le manichéisme parmi les peuples et religions d'Asie centrale d'après les sources primaires.* Sitzungsberichte 690. Vienna: Verlag der Österreichischen Akademie der Wissenschaften.

Tremblay, Xavier. 2007. "The Spread of Buddhism in Serindia: Buddhism among Iranians, Tocharians and Turks before the 13th Century." In *The Spread of Buddhism*, edited by Ann Heirman and Stephan Peter Bumbacher, 75–129. HdO VIII.16. Leiden: Brill.

Tubach, Jürgen. 1992. "Die Heimat des China-Missionars Alopen." *OC* 76: 95–100.

Tubach, Jürgen. 1995–96. "Der Apostel Thomas in China: Die Herkunft einer Tradition." *The Harp* 8–9: 397–430.

Tubach, Jürgen. 1998. "Abgrenzung und Selbstbehauptung in einer multikulturellen Umwelt: Die christliche Gemeinde von Merw, einer Metropole an der Seidenstraße, in der ausgehenden Sasanidenzeit." In Lavenant 1998, 409–19.

Tubach, Jürgen. 1999. "Die nestorianische Kirche in China." *Nubica et Æthiopica* 4–5: 61–193.

Tubach, Jürgen. 2009. "The Mission Field of the Apostle Thomas." In Winkler and Tang 2009, 291–303.

"Un texte de Marco Polo sur l'existence de chrétiens dans la Chine du Sud depuis le VIe siècle." 1928. *BCP* 15, no. 182: 574–78.

Uray, Géza. 1983. "Tibet's Connections with Nestorianism and Manichaeism in the 8th–10th Centuries." In *Contributions on Tibetan Language, History and Culture: Proceedings of the Csoma De Körös Symposium Held at Velm-Vienna, Austria, 13–19 September 1981*, edited by Ernst Steinkellner and Helmut Tauscher, 399–429. Wiener Studien zur Tibetologie und Buddhismuskunde 10. Vienna: Arbeitskreis für Tibetische und Buddhistische Studien Universität Wien.

Uray, Géza. 1987. "Zu den Spuren des Nestorianismus und des Manichäismus im alten Tibet (8.–10. Jahrhundert)." In Heissig and Klimkeit 1987, 197–206.

Van Esbroeck, Michel. [2006?]. "Caucasian Parallels to Chinese Cross Representations." In Malek [2006?], 425–44.

Van Rompay, Lucas. 2011. "Abraham of Kashkar." In Brock et al. 2011, 8–9.

Vermander, Benoît. [2006?]. "The Impact of Nestorianism on Contemporary Chinese Theology." In Malek [2006?], 181–94.

Vööbus, Arthur. 1958–88. *History of Asceticism in the Syrian Orient: A Contribution to the History of Culture in the Near East*. 3 vols. CSCO 184; 197; 500. Louvain: Sécretariat du CorpusSCO.

Waldschmidt, Ernst, and Wolfgang Lentz. 1926. *Die Stellung Jesu im Manichäismus*. Abhandlungen der Preussischen Akademie der Wissenschaften: Phil.-Hist. Klasse 4. Berlin: Akademie der Wissenschaften.

Walker, Joel Thomas. 2006. *The Legend of Mar Qardagh: Narrative and Christian Heroism in Late Antique Iraq*. Berkeley: University of California Press.

Walker, Joel Thomas. 2012. "From Nisibis to Xi'an: The Church of the East in Late Antique Eurasia." In Johnson 2012, 994–1052.

Walter, Mariko Namba. 2014. "Buddhism in Central Asian History." In *The Wiley Blackwell Companion to East and Inner Asian Buddhism*, edited by Mario Poceski, 21–39. Chichester: Wiley Blackwell.

Wang Changming 王长命. 2018. "Tang Bosi jingjiaotu Li Su chushi Hezhong Jinzhou de shijian ji yuanyou: Bosiren Li Su ji furen Beishi shi muzhiming bukao" 唐波斯景教徒李素出仕河中晋州的时间及缘由—波斯人李素及夫人卑失氏墓志铭补考 [The Time and the Causes for the Persian Christian Li Su's Appointment in Jinzhou, Hezhong, during the Tang Dynasty: A Supplementary Study of the Epitaph of the Persian Li Su and His Wife, Lady Beishi]. *Wenwu shijie* 文物世界 [World of Antiquity], no. 2: 39–41.

Wang Jing 王静. 2006. "Tangdai Zhongguo jingjiao yu jingjiao benbu jiaohui de guanxi" 唐代中国景教与景教本部教会的关系 [The Relationship between the Luminous Teaching in Tang China and the Church Headquarters of the Luminous Teaching]. *Chang'an daxue xuebao (shehui kexue ban)* 长安大学学报（社会科学版）[Journal of Chang'an University: Social Sciences Edition], no. 3: 64–69.

Wang Juan 汪娟 (Wang Chuan). 2018. "Dunhuang jingjiao wenxian dui fojiao yiwen de xishou yu zhuanhua" 敦煌景教文獻對佛教儀文的吸收與轉化 ["The Adaptation of Buddhist Rituals and Liturgical Texts in the Chinese Christian Manuscripts from Dunhuang"]. *ZLJ* 89.4: 631–61.

Wang Lanping 王兰平. 2008. "Yi *Zhixuan anle jing* 'shiguan' weili kan Tangdai jingjiao yu fo dao zhi jian de guanxi" 以《志玄安乐经》「十观」为例看唐代景教与佛道之间的关系 [Looking at the Connections of the Luminous Teaching with Buddhism and Daoism during the Tang Dynasty by Taking the "Ten Contemplations" in the *Zhixuan anle jing* as an Example]. *DJ*, no. 1: 157–62.

Wang Lanping. 2009. "Yi 'shiyuan,' 'shiguan' weili kan Tangdai jingjiao yu fo dao de jiaoshe ronghe" 以「十愿」、「十观」为例看唐代景教与佛道的交涉融合 [Looking at the Blending of the Luminous Teaching with Buddhism and Daoism during the Tang Dynasty Taking the "Ten Vows" and the "Ten Contemplations" as Examples]. In *Zi xi cu dong: Jidujiao lai Hua erbai nian lunji* 自西徂東—基督教來華二百年論集 [*East Meets West: Essay Celebrating the Bicentennial of Protestant Christianity in China*], edited by Li Jinqiang 李金強, Wu Ziming 吳梓明, and Xing Fuzeng 邢福增, 145–59. Hong Kong: Jidujiao wenyi chubanshe.

Wang Lanping. 2014. "Riben Xingyu shuwu zang Tangdai Dunhuang jingjiao xieben *Xuting mishisuo jing* shikao" 日本杏雨书屋藏唐代敦煌景教写本《序听迷诗所经》释考 [A Study of the Tang Dynasty Dunhuang Manuscript of the Luminous Teaching *Book of the Lord Messiah* in the Kyōu shooku Collection in Japan]. *DJ*, no. 4: 27–47.

Wang, Lanping. 2015a. "A Textual Analysis of Chinese Characters with Their Variants in Two Dunhuang *Jingjiao* Manuscripts." *Ching Feng*, n.s., 14.1–2: 23–31.

Wang Lanping. 2015b. "Riben Xingyu shuwu zang Tangdai Dunhuang jingjiao xieben *Zhixuan anle jing* shikao" 日本杏雨书屋藏唐代敦煌景教写本《志玄安乐经》释考 [A Study of the Tang Dynasty Dunhuang Manuscript of the Luminous Teaching *Book on Profound and Mysterious Blessedness* in the Kyōu shooku Collection in Japan]. *DJ*, no. 2: 71–85.

Wang Lanping. 2016a. "Riben Xingyu shuwu zang Fuwang wenshu Gaonan wenshu zhenwei zai yanjiu" 日本杏雨书屋藏富冈文书高楠文书真伪再研究 [Further Research on the Authenticity of the Tomioka and Takakusu Documents in the Kyōu shooku Collection in Japan]. *DJ*, no. 1: 10–33.

Wang Lanping. 2016b. *Tangdai Dunhuang hanwen jingjiao xiejing yanjiu* 唐代敦煌汉文景教写经研究 [Research on the Tang Dynasty Scriptures of the Luminous Teaching in Chinese from Dunhuang]. Dunhuangxue boshi wenku 敦煌学博士文库. Beijing: Minzu chubanshe [text B, C, D, E, F].

Wang Lanping. 2017. *Lishi wenxian yanjiu conggao (jiaji)* 歷史文獻研究叢稿（甲集）[Research Series on Historical Documents: First Collection]. Shanghai: Fudan daxue chubanshe.

Wang, Lanping, and Zhang Qiaosui. 2019. "Review of the Studies on the Research History of Authenticity of *The Discourse on Monotheism* and *The Jesus Messiah Sutra* in Kyou-shooku." In Huang, Tang, and Zhu 2019, 155–62.

Wang Weifan 汪维藩. 2001. "Zhongguo gudai jidujiao jingshen" 中国古代基督教精神 [The Chinese Ancient Christian Spirit]. *Jinling shenxue zhi* 金陵神学志 [Nanjing Theological Review], no. 2: 25–27.

Wang, Weifan. 2002. "Tombstone Carvings from AD 86: Did Christianity Reach China in the First Century?" *Christianity Today* (October 7, 2002). Available online at <https://www.ucly.fr/wp-content/uploads/2019/11/tombstone-carvings-from-ad-86.pdf>.

Wang Xinggong 王行恭. 2011. "You fuhaoxue jiedu jingjiao shizi wenzhang de neihan" 由符號學解讀景教十字紋章的內涵 [The Significance of the Cross Emblem in the Luminous Teaching: A Semiotic Explanation]. *Lishi wenwu: guoli lishi bowuguan guankan* 歷史文物：國立歷史博物館館刊 [Bulletin of the National Museum of History] 21.11: 22–32.

Wang Yao 王堯. 1991. "Dunhuang P. T. 351 tufan wenshu ji jingjiao wenxian xulu" 敦煌 P. T. 351 吐蕃文書及景教文献敘錄 [The Document P. T. 351 in Old Tibetan from Dunhuang and the Description of the Documents of the Luminous Teaching]. In *Di erjie Dunhuangxue guoji yantaohui lunwenji* 第二屆敦煌學國際研討會論文集 [*Papers from the Second International Seminar on Tun-huan* (sic) *Studies*], 539–50. Taipei: Hanxue yanjiu zhongxin.

Wang Yao. 1994. "Tufan jingjiao wenshu ji qita" 吐蕃景教文书及其他 [The Documents of the Luminous Teaching in Old Tibetan and Other Issues]. In Wang Yao, *Xizang wenshi kao xinlu* 西藏文史考信录 [Random Annotations on the Cultural History of Tibet], 208–24. Beijing: Zhongguo zangxue chubanshe.

Wang, Yuanyuan. 2013a. "Doubt on the Viewpoint of the Extinction of *Jingjiao* in China After the Tang Dynasty." In Tang and Winkler 2013, 279–96.

Wang Yuanyuan 王媛媛. 2013b. "Tangdai hanwen monijiao ziliao suo jian zhi 'fawang'" 唐代汉文摩尼教资料所见之「法王」 ["King of the Doctrine" in the Chinese Manichaean Literature of the Tang Dynasty]. In *Hailu jiaotong yu shijie wenming* 海陆交通与世界文明 [Sea-Land Communications and World Civilizations], edited by Chen Chunsheng 陈春声, 215–28. Beijing: Shangwu yinshuguan.

Weinstein, Stanley. 1987. *Buddhism under the T'ang.* Cambridge: Cambridge University Press.

Wellesz, Egon. 1918–19. "Miscellanea zur orientalischen Musikgeschichte: Die Lektionszeichen in den soghdischen Texten." *Zeitschrift für Musikwissenschaft* 1.9: 505–15.

Weng Shaojun 翁绍军. 1996. *Hanyu jingjiao wendian quanshi* 汉语景教文典诠释 [*Sino-Nestorian Documents: Commentary and Exegesis*]. Lidai jidujiao xueshu wenku 历代基督教学术文库. Beijing: Sanlian shudian [text A, B, C, D, E, F].

Wenzel-Teuber, Katharina. 2014. "'Nestorianische' Grabnische in den Longmen-Grotten vermutlich bisher frühester christlicher Grabfund in China." *China heute* 33.1, no. 181: 4–5.

Whitfield, Roderick. 1982–85. *The Arts of Central Asia: The Stein Collection in the British Museum.* 3 vols. Tokyo: Kodansha International.

Whitfield, Roderick, and Anne Farrer. 1990. *Caves of the Thousand Buddhas: Chinese Art from the Silk Road.* London: British Museum Publications.

Whitfield, Susan. 2018. *Silk, Slaves and Stupas: Material Culture of the Silk Road.* Berkeley: University of California Press.

Wickeri, Philip L. 2004. "The Stone Is a Mirror: Interpreting the Xi'an Christian Monument and Its Implications for Theology and the Study of Christianity in Asia." *Quest* 3.2: 37–64.

Widengren, Geo. 1984. "The Nestorian Church in Sasanian and Early Post-Sasanian Iran." In Lanciotti 1984, 1–30.

Wießner, Gernot, and Hans-Joachim Klimkeit, eds. 1992. *Studia Manichaica: II. Internationaler Kongreß zum Manichäismus, 6.–10. August 1989, St. Augustin/Bonn.* Wiesbaden: Harrassowitz.

William, Alan V. 1996. "Zoroastrians and Christians in Sasanian Iran." *Bulletin of the John Rylands University Library of Manchester* 78.3: 37–53.

Williams, Paul. 2009. *Mahāyāna Buddhism: The Doctrinal Foundations*, 2nd edn. London: Routledge.

Williamson, Alexander. 1870. *Journeys in North China, Manchuria, and Eastern Mongolia.* 2 vols. London: Smith, Elder.

Wilmshurst, David. 1990. "The 'Syrian Brilliant Teaching.'" *Journal of the Hong Kong Branch of the Royal Asiatic Society* 30: 44–74.

Wilmshurst, David. 2011. *The Martyred Church: A History of the Church of the East.* London: East & West Publishing.

Wilmshurst, David. 2016. "Beth Sinaye: A Typical East Syrian Ecclesiastical Province?" In Tang and Winkler 2016, 253–66.

Winkler, Dietmar W., and Li Tang, eds. 2009. *Hidden Treasures and Intercultural Encounters: Studies on East Syriac Christianity in China and Central Asia.* OPOe 1. Münster: LIT.

Wong, Dorothy C. 2004. *Chinese Steles: Pre-Buddhist and Buddhist Use of a Symbolic Form.* Honolulu: University of Hawai'i Press.

Wright, Arthur F. 1973. "T'ang T'ai-tsung and Buddhism." In *Perspectives on the T'ang*, edited by Arthur F. Wright and Danis Twitchett, 239–63. New Haven, CT: Yale University Press.

Wu Changxing 吳昶興 (Wu Chang-shing). 2002. "Tangchao jingjiao Da Qin ta de takan yu yanjiu" 唐朝景教大秦塔的踏勘與研究 [Survey and Study of the Tang Dynasty Da Qin Pagoda of the Luminous Teaching]. *ZWL*, no. 4: 80–110. Repr., with the title "Jingjiao Da Qin ta de takan yu pingxi" 景教大秦塔的踏勘與評析 [Survey and Appraisal of the Da Qin Pagoda of the Luminous Teaching], in Wu Changxing 2015b, 267–304.

Wu Changxing. 2007. "Lun jingjiao *Zhixuan anle jing* de anle shijie" 論景教《志玄安樂經》的安樂世界 [The Realm of Blessedness in the Luminous Teaching's *Book on Profound and Mysterious Blessedness*]. *Jinshen xuekan* 浸神學刊 [Taiwan Baptist Theological Seminary Annual Bulletin], 101–28. Repr., with the title "Lun jingjiao *Zhixuan anle jing* de anle zhi dao" 論景教《志玄安樂經》的安樂之道 [The Way of Blessedness in the Luminous Teaching's *Book on Profound and Mysterious Blessedness*], in Wu Changxing 2015b, 211–46.

Wu Changxing. 2010a. "Jingjiao *Xuting mishisuo jing* jingming wenti zai yi" 景教《序聽迷詩所經》經名問題再議 [Another Look at the Issue of Names Contained in the Luminous Teaching's *Book of the Lord Messiah*]. *Zhongtai shenxue lunji* 中台神學論集 [Central Taiwan Theological Seminary Journal] 1: 227–48.

Wu Changxing. 2010b. "Lun jingjiao *Xuting mishisuo jing* zhong de Shangdi, Jidu yu jiushi sixiang" 論景教《序聽迷詩所經》中的上帝、基督與救世思想 [A Discussion of the Concepts of God, Christ, and Salvation in the Luminous Teaching's *Book of the Lord Messiah*]. *Jinshen xuekan* 浸神學刊 [Taiwan Baptist Theological Seminary Annual Bulletin], 3–46.

Wu Changxing, ed. 2015a. *Da Qin jingjiao liuxing Zhongguo bei: Da Qin jingjiao wenxian shiyi* 大秦景教流行中國碑—大秦景教文獻釋義 [The Stele of the Propagation of the Luminous Teaching of Da Qin in China: Explanation of the Documents of the Luminous Teaching of Da Qin]. Hanyu jidujiao jingdian wenku jicheng 漢語基督教經典文庫集成 1. Taipei: Ganlan chuban youxian gongsi [texts A, B, C, D, E, F].

Wu Changxing. 2015b. *Zhenchang zhi dao: Tangdai jidujiao lishi yu wenxian yanjiu* 真常之道—唐代基督教歷史與文獻研究 [*The True and Eternal Way: Bibliographic Research of Assyrian Church of the East in Tang Dynasty*]. Jidujiao xueshu congshu 基督教學術叢書 11. Xinbei: Taiwan jidujiao wenyi chubanshe.

Wu, Chi-yü. 1984. "A Study of the Ching-chiao san-wei meng-tu tsan." In *Proceedings of the Thirty-First International Congress of Human Sciences in Asia and North Africa: Tokyo-Kyoto 31st August–7th September 1983*, edited by Yamamoto Tatsuro, 2: 976–78. Tokyo: Tōhō gakkai [The Institute of Eastern Culture] [text and trans. B].

Wu Liwei 吳莉苇. 2010. "Cong jingjiao yanjiu de wenti kan Zhongxi wenhua jiaoliu shi yanjiu de kuaxueke biyaoxing" 从景教研究的问题看中西文化交流史研究的跨学科必要性 ["Why Should We Value the Cross-Disciplines Approach when Studying the History of Sino-Western Cultural Relationship: A Reflection on the Chinese Study of 'Nestorian Church'"]. *Zhongxi wenhua jiaoliu xuebao* 中西文化交流学报 [Journal of Sino-Western Communications] 2.1: 83–98.

Wu Qiyu 吳其昱 (Wu Chi-yü). 1986. "Jingjiao sanwei mengdu zan yanjiu" 景教三威蒙度讚研究 [A Study of the *Hymn in Praise of the Salvation Achieved through the Three Majesties of the Luminous Teaching*]. *ZLJ* 57.3: 411–38 [text and trans. B].

Wu Qiyu. 2001. "Tangdai jingjiao zhi fawang yu zunjing kao" 唐代景教之法王与尊經考 [Investigation into the "Kings of the Doctrine" and the "Honored Books" of the Luminous Teaching during the Tang Dynasty]. *DTY* 5: 13–57.

Wu Qiyu. 2003. "Dunhuang beiku xuliyawen kejing (Lectionary) shipian canye kaoshi" 敦煌北窟叙利亚文课经 (Lectionary) 诗篇残叶考释 [A Textual Analysis of a Psalm Fragment of the Syriac Lectionary from the Dunhuang Northern Grottoes]. In *Xin shiji Dunhuangxue lunji* 新世纪敦煌学论集 [Collected Papers of Dunhuang Studies in the New Century], edited by Xiang Chu 项楚 and Zheng Acai 郑阿财, 191–233. Chengdu: Bashu shushe.

Wu Qiyu. 2011. "Dunhuang beiqu shiku chutu xuliyawen kejing shipian canpian kaoshi" 敦煌北区石窟出土叙利亚文课经诗篇残片考释 [A Textual Analysis of a Psalm Fragment of the Syriac Lectionary Unearthed in the Grottoes North of Dunhuang]. In *Dunhuang Mogao ku beiqu shiku yanjiu* 敦煌莫高窟北区

石窟研究 [Studies in the Dunhuang Mogao Northern Grottoes], 2: 610–21. Lanzhou: Gansu jiaoyu chubanshe.

Wylie, Alexander. 1856. "On the Nestorian Tablet of Se-gan foo." *Journal of the American Oriental Society* 5.2: 275–336 [trans. A].

Wyngaert, Anastasius van den, ed. 1929. *Sinica Franciscana*, vol. 1: *Itinera et relationes fratrum minorum saeculi XIII et XIV*. Quaracchi: apud Collegium S. Bonaventurae.

Xiang Bingguang 項秉光. 2017. "Dunhuang xiejuan *Xuting mishisuo jing* xieben kao" 敦煌寫卷《序聽迷詩所經》寫本考 ["The Research on The *Hsu T'ing Mi-Shih-So Ching* of Dunhuang Nestorian Manuscripts"]. *DF* 46: 157–87.

Xiang Bingguang. 2019. "Jingjiao Dunhuang zaoqi xiejuan wenben ziju shiyi" 景教敦煌早期寫卷文本字句釋義 ["Words and Sentences in the Dunhuang Nestorian Transcripts"]. *Jidujiao wenhua xuekan* 基督教文化學刊 [Journal for the Study of Christian Culture] 42: 254–73.

Xiang Da 向達. 1957. *Tangdai Chang'an yu xiyu wenming* 唐代長安與西域文明 [Chang'an and the Civilization of the Western Regions in the Tang Dynasty]. Beijing: Sanlian shudian.

Xin Deyong 辛德勇 and Lang Jiedian 郎潔點, eds. 2013. *Chang'an zhi; Chang'an zhitu* 長安志·長安志圖 [Description of Chang'an; Description and Maps of Chang'an]. Xi'an: Sanqin chubanshe.

Xiong, Cunrui Victor. 2000. *Sui-Tang Chang'an: A Study in the Urban History of Medieval China*. Michigan Monographs in Chinese Studies 85. Ann Arbor: Center for Chinese Studies, The University of Michigan.

Xu, Longfei. 2004. *Die nestorianische Stele in Xi'an: Begegnung von Christentum und chinesischer Kultur*. Begegnung 12. Bonn: Borengässer [trans. A].

Xu Pingfang 徐苹芳. 1986. "Yuan Dadu yelikewen Shizi si kao" 元大都也里可温十字寺考 [Investigation into the Christian Monastery of the Cross in Yuan Dadu (Khambalik)]. In *Zhongguo kaoguxue yanjiu: Xia Nai xiansheng kaogu wushinian jinian wenji* 中国考古学研究—夏鼐先生考古五十年纪念文集 [Chinese Archaeological Studies: Collection of Essays in Honor of Mr. Xia Nai on the Fiftieth Anniversary of His Archaeological Activity], 1: 309–16. Beijing: Wenwu chubanshe.

Xu Pingfang. 1992. "Beijing Fangshan Shizi si yelikewen shike" 北京房山十字寺也里可温石刻 [Christian Stone Inscriptions at the Monastery of the Cross in Fangshan, Beijing]. *Zhongguo wenhua* 中国文化 [Chinese Culture], no. 7: 184–89.

Xu Xiaohong 徐晓鸿. 2006. "Tangdai jingjiao renwu kaolüe" 唐代景教人物考略 [A Brief Investigation of Individuals of the Luminous Teaching during the Tang Dynasty]. *Jinling shenxue zhi* 金陵神学志 [Nanjing Theological Review], no. 2: 27–55.

Xu Xiaohong. 2009. "Luoyang jingjiao jingchuang de faxian yu chutan" 洛阳景教经幢的发现与初探 [The Discovery and a Preliminary Discussion of the Luoyang *Dhāraṇī* Pillar of the Luminous Teaching]. *Jinling shenxue zhi* 金陵神学志 [Nanjing Theological Review], no. 3: 16–28.

Yakubovich, Ilya. 2011. "Sogdian." In Brock et al. 2011, 382–83.

Yamada Takahi 山田俊. 2015. "'Anle fa' xiaokao"「安樂法」小考 ["On the 'Comfort'"]. *Daojiao yanjiu xuebao: zongjiao, lishi yu shehui* 道教研究學報：宗教、歷史與社會 [Daoism: Religion, History, and Society] 7: 337–61.

Yan Fu 颜福 and Gao Qian 高倩. 2017. "Facang Dunhuang tufan zhanbu wenshu P. T. 351 yanjiu" 法藏敦煌吐蕃占卜文书 P. T. 351 研究 [A Study of the Dunhuang Divination Document P. T. 351 in Old Tibetan Kept in a French Collection]. *Lanzhou daxue xuebao (shehui kexue ban)* 兰州大学学报（社会科学版） [Journal of Lanzhou University: Social Sciences Edition], no. 1: 59–65.

Yan Wanjun 阎万钧. 1988. "Tangdai zhaowu jiuxing zhi zongjiao de dongchuan" 唐代昭武九姓之宗教的东传 [The Eastward Diffusion of the Religions of Sogdians during the Tang Dynasty]. *SZY*, no. 1: 132–40.

Yang Fuxue 杨富学 and Bao Lang 包郎. 2015. "Xiapu monijiao xin wenxian *Moni guangfo* jiaozhu" 霞浦摩尼教新文献《摩尼光佛》校注 [Xiapu New Manichaean Document *Mani the Buddha of Light*: Edition with Annotations]. *Hanshan si foxue* 寒山寺佛学 [Buddhist Studies of the Hanshan Monastery] 10: 74–115.

Yang, Fuxue, and Xue Wengjing. 2019. "Yishu (Jesu) Worship in Xiapu Manichaean Manuscripts." In Huang, Tang, and Zhu 2019, 97–112.

Yang Rongzhi 楊榮鋕. 1895. *Jingjiao beiwen jishi kaozheng* 景教碑文紀事考正 [Verification of the Facts Recorded in the Text Inscribed on the Stele of the Luminous Teaching]. N.p. Repr. in Wu Changxing 2015a, 335–564.

Yang Senfu 楊森富. 1969. "Jingjiao jingdian zhong de fojiao yongyu bianyi kao" 景教經典中的佛教用語變義考 [Investigation into the Transformed Meaning of the Buddhist Terms Adopted in the Documents of the Luminous Teaching]. *Zhonghua xueshuyuan tianzhujiao xueshu yanjiusuo xuebao* 中華學術院天主教學術研究所學報 [Bulletin of Catholic Research Institute, China Academy] 1: 69–78.

Yang Senfu. 1971. "Youguan jingjiao *Zunjing* zhong de *Sanji jing*" 有關景教尊經中的「三際經」[About the *Book on the Three Steps* among the Honored Books of the Luminous Teaching]. *Furen daxue shenxue lunji* 輔仁大學神學論集 [Collectanea Theologica Universitatis Fujen] 8: 175–82.

Yang Senfu. 1977. "Tang Yuan erdai jidujiao xingshuai yuanyin zhi yanjiu" 唐元二代基督教興衰原因之研究 [A Study of the Causes of the Rise and Decline of Christianity in the Tang and Yuan Dynasties]. In *Jidujiao ru Hua baiqishi nian jinian ji* 基督教入華百七十年紀念集 [Collection of Papers Commemorating the One Hundred Seventy Year Period of Christianity's Entry into China], edited by Lin Zhiping 林治平, 31–79. Taipei: Yuzhouguang chubanshe. Repr. in *Dao yu yan: Huaxia wenhua yu jidu wenhua xiangyu*「道」與「言」—華夏文化与基督文化相遇 [The Dao and the Word: The Encounter between Chinese Culture and Christian Culture], edited by Liu Xiaofeng 劉小楓, 43–73. Shanghai: Sanlian shudian, 1995.

Yang Zengwen 杨曾文. 2018. "Fojiao he yiyaoxue de kaocha yu sikao" 佛教和医药学的考察与思考 [Investigation and Reflection on Buddhism, Medicine, and Pharmacology]. *SZY*, no. 4: 8–17.

Yao Chongxin 姚崇新. 2017. "Shizi lianhua: Tang Yuan jingjiao yishu zhong de fojiao yinsu" 十字莲花—唐元景教艺术中的佛教因素 [The Cross-Lotus: A Study of the Buddhist Elements in the Art of the Luminous Teaching in Tang and Yuan Dynasties]. *DTY* 17: 215–62.

Yao Chongxin 姚崇新, Wang Yuanyuan 王媛媛, and Chen Huaiyu 陈怀宇. 2013. *Dunhuang san yijiao yu zhonggu shehui* 敦煌三夷教与中古社会 [The Three Persian Religions in Dunhuang and Medieval Society]. Lanzhou: Gansu jiaoyu chubanshe.

Yao, Zhihua. 2009. "A Diatessaronic Reading in the Chinese Nestorian Texts." In Winkler and Tang 2009, 153–65.

Yarshater, Ehsan, ed. 1983. *The Cambridge History of Iran*, vol. 3.2. Cambridge: Cambridge University Press.

Yeung, Daniel H. N. 2019. "The Multiple Identities of the Nestorian Monk Mar Alopen: A Discussion on Diplomacy and Politics." In Huang, Tang, and Zhu 2019, 37–49.

Yin Xiaoping 殷小平 and Lin Wushu 林悟殊. 2008. "Chuangji ruogan wenti kaoshi: Tangdai Luoyang jingjiao jingchuang yanjiu zhi er" 幢記若干問題考釋—唐代洛陽景教經幢研究之二 ["Notes on the *Description*: Studies of Luoyang Nestorian Dharani Pillar of the Tang Dynasty, II"]. *ZWL*, no. 2: 269–92. Repr. in Ge 2009a, 92–108; Lin Wushu 2011e, 192–210.

Yoshida, Yutaka. 1996. "Additional Remarks on Sims-Williams' Article on the Sogdian Merchants in China and India." In Cadonna and Lanciotti 1996, 69–78.

Yoshida, Yutaka. 2003. "On the Origin of the Sogdian Surname Zhaowu 昭武 and Related Problems." *JA* 291.1–2: 35–67.

Yoshida, Yutaka. 2015. "Sogdian Literature I. Buddhist." In EIr Online, <http://www.iranicaonline.org/articles/sogdian-literature-01-buddhist>.

Yoshida, Yutaka. 2016. "Sogdian Language I. Description." In EIr Online, <http://www.iranicaonline.org/articles/sogdian-language-01>.

Yoshida Yutaka 吉田豊. 2017. "Chūgoku, Torufan oyobi Sogudiana no sogudojin keikyōto: Ōtani tankentai shōrai saiiki bunka shiryō 2497 ga teiki suru mondai" 中国，トルファンおよびソグディアナのソグド人景教徒—大谷探検隊将来西域文化資料 2497 が提起する問題 [Christian Sogdians in China, Turfan, and Sogdiana: Problems Raised by the Christian Sogdian Text Ōtani]. In *Ōtani tankentai shūshū saiiki kogo bunken ronsō: Bukkyō, manikyō, keikyō* 大谷探検隊収集西域胡語文献論叢—仏教・マニ教・景教 [Essays on the Manuscripts Written in Iranian Languages in the Ōtani Collection: Buddhism, Manichaeism, and Christianity], edited by Irisawa Takashi 入澤崇 and Kitsudō Koichi 橘堂晃一, 155–80. Ryūkoku daigaku saiiki kenkyū sōsho 龍谷大学西域研究叢書 [Ryukoku University Silk Road Studies] 6. Kyoto: Ryūkoku daigaku bukkyō bunka kenkyūjo saiiki bunka kenkyūkai [Research Institute for Buddhist

Culture, Ryukoku University]; Ryūkoku daigaku seikai bukkyō kenkyū sentā [Research Center for World Buddhist Cultures, Ryukoku University].

Young, John M. L. 1969. "The Theology and Influence of the Nestorian Mission to China, 635–1036 (Part I)." *Reformed Bulletin of Missions* 5.1: 1–18.

Young, John M. L. 1970. "The Theology and Influence of the Nestorian Mission to China, 635–1036 (Part II)." *Reformed Bulletin of Missions* 5.2: 1–20.

Young, John M. L. 1984. *By Foot to China.* Tokyo: Radiopress.

Yu Shu 虞恕. 2002. "'Ruhua' yu 'ronghua': bijiao jingjiao yu fojiao dongjian lai Hua de butong zaoyu" 「入华」与「融华」—比较景教与佛教东渐来华的不同遭遇 ["Entry into China" and "Melding with Chinese Culture": A Comparison between the Different Approaches of the Luminous Teaching and Buddhism to Their Diffusion in China]. *Zongjiaoxue yanjiu* 宗教学研究 [Religious Studies], no. 1: 120–23.

Zeng Qingbao 曾慶豹 (Chin Ken-pa). 2011. "Hanyu jingjiao jingdian zhong de 'zhengzhi shenxue' wenti" 漢語景教經典中的「政治神學」問題 ["Jingjiao (Sino-Nestorianism) and Political Theology"]. *DF* 34: 207–32.

Zeng, Qingbao. 2019. "Jingjiao under the Lenses of Chinese Political Theology." *Religions* 10.10: 1–22. doi: 10.3390/rel10100551.

Zeng Yangqing 曾陽晴 (Tseng Yang-ching). 2005a. *Tangchao hanyu jingjiao wenxian yanjiu* 唐朝漢語景教文獻研究 [A Study of the Chinese Documents of the Luminous Teaching from the Tang Dynasty]. Taipei: Huamulan wenhua gongzuofang.

Zeng Yangqing. 2005b. "Xiaodao wenshu zhenwei kao: Li Shengduo shi jiuzang Dunhuang jingjiao wenxian erzhong bianwei zai shangque" 小島文書真偽考—李盛鐸氏舊藏敦煌景教文獻二種辨偽再商榷 [A Research on the Authenticity of the Kojima Documents: A Further Discussion of Two Issues Concerning the Authentification of the Documents of the Luminous Teaching from Dunhuang in the Mr. Li Shengduo Collection]. *Zhongyuan xuebao* 中原學報 [Chung Yuan Journal] 33.2: 253–72.

Zhang Delin 張德麟. 1989. "Dunhuang jingjiao wenxian *Zunjing* zhong de yixie wenti" 敦煌景教文獻《尊經》中的一些問題 [Some Issues in the Dunhuang Document of the Luminous Teaching *Book of the Honored*]. *Kong Meng yuekan* 孔孟月刊 [Confucius and Mencius Monthly] 27.11: 31–36.

Zhang Fengzhen 張奉箴 (Chang, Mark K.). 1970. *Fuyin liuchuan Zhongguo shilüe* 福音流傳中國史略 [*A History of Christianity in China*], vol. 1. Taipei: Sili furen daxue chubanshe [text A, B, C, D, E, F].

Zhang, Guangda. 1994. "Trois examples d'influences mazdéennes dans la Chine des Tang." *Études chinoises* 13.1–2: 203–19.

Zhang, Guangda, and Rong Xinjiang. 1998. "A Concise History of the Turfan Oasis and Its Exploration." *Asia Major*, 3rd ser., 11.2: 13–36.

Zhang Jimeng 張濟猛. 1969. "Riben xuezhe yu jingjiao jingdian" 日本學者與景教經典 [Japanese Scholars and the Scriptures of the Luminous Teaching]. *Dongxi wenhua* 東西文化 [Eastern and Western Cultures] 27: 50–55.

Zhang Naizhu 张乃翥. 2007. "Ba Henan Luoyang xin chutu de yijian Tangdai jingjiao shike" 跋河南洛阳新出土的一件唐代景教石刻 [Postscript to the Stone Inscription of the Luminous Teaching from the Tang Dynasty Newly Found in Luoyang]. *XY*, no. 1: 65–73; no. 2: 132 ("Buzheng shuoming" 補正說明 [Supplements and Corrections]). Repr. in Ge 2009a, 5–16, with English trans., by Pietro De Laurentis: "Note on a Nestorian Stone Inscription from the Tang Dynasty Unearthed in Luoyang," 17–33.

Zhang Naizhu. 2009. "Luoyang jingjiao jingchuang yu Tang dongdu 'Gande xiang' de huren juluo" 洛阳景教經幢与唐东都「感德乡」的胡人聚落 [The Luoyang Pillar of the Luminous Teaching and the Iranian Settlements in Gande Township of the Tang Eastern Capital]. *Zhongyuan wenwu* 中原文物 [Cultural Relics of Central China], no. 2: 98–106.

Zhang, Naizhu. 2013. "The Luoyang Nestorian Pillar and the Gande Township: A Settlement of Foreigners in the Luoyang Area during the Tang Dynasty." In Tang and Winkler 2013, 177–202.

Zhang Naizhu 张乃翥 and Zheng Yaofeng 郑瑶峰. 2014. "Wenhua renleixue shiyu xia Yiluohe yan'an de Tangdai huren buluo: Yi Longmen shiku xin faxian de jingjiao yiku wei yuanqi (I)" 文化人类学视域下伊洛河沿岸的唐代胡人部落—以龙门石窟新发现的景教瘗窟为缘起（上）[The Iranian Tribes along the Yiluo River in the Tang Dynasty from the Perspective of Cultural Anthropology: Taking the Christian Burial Niche Newly Found at the Longmen Grottoes as the Starting Point, I]. *Shiku si yanjiu* 石窟寺研究 [Study on the Cave Temples] 5: 154–74.

Zhang Naizhu and Zheng Yaofeng. 2016. "Wenhua renleixue shiyu xia Yiluohe yan'an de Tangdai huren buluo: Yi Longmen shiku xin faxian de jingjiao yiku wei yuanqi (II)" 文化人类学视域下伊洛河沿岸的唐代胡人部落—以龙门石窟新发现的景教瘗窟为缘起（下）[The Iranian Tribes along the Yiluo River in the Tang Dynasty from the Perspective of Cultural Anthropology: Taking the Christian Burial Niche Newly Found at the Longmen Grottoes as the Starting Point, II]. *Shiku si yanjiu* 石窟寺研究 [Study on the Cave Temples] 6: 255–99.

Zhang, Qiong. 2017. "The Jesuit Heresiological Discourse as an Enlightenment Project in Early Modern China." *Journal of World History* 28.1: 31–60.

Zhang Shuqiong 张淑琼. 2007. "Guangya shuyuan de jingjiao yanjiu" 广雅书院的景教研究 [Studies on the Luminous Teaching in the Guangya Academy]. In *Shiliao yu shijie: Zhongwen wenxian yu Zhongguo jidujiao shi yanjiu* 史料与视界—中文文献与中国基督教史研究 [Sources and Perspectives: Chinese Language Materials and the Study of the History of Christianity in China], edited by Zhang Xianqing 张先清, 315–30. Shanghai: Shanghai renmin chubanshe.

Zhang Xiaogui 张小贵. 2010. *Zhonggu huahua xianjiao kaoshu* 中古华化祆教考述 [A Study of Sinicized Zoroastrianism in Medieval China]. Beijing: Wenwu chubanshe.

Zhang Xiaogui, ed. 2014. *Sanyijiao yanjiu: Lin Wushu xiansheng guxi jinian lunwenji* 三夷教研究—林悟殊先生古稀纪念论文集 [Research on the Three Foreign

Religions: Collected Articles Commemorating Mr. Lin Wushu's Seventieth Birthday]. Ouya lishi wenhua wenku 欧亚历史文化文库. Lanzhou: Lanzhou daxue chubanshe.

Zhang, Xiaogui. 2016. "Why Did Chinese Nestorians Name Their Religion *Jingjiao*?" In Tang and Winkler 2016, 283–309.

Zhang Xiaogui 张小贵 and Zeng Chaoying 曾超颖. 2014. "Zhonggu xianjiao huahua gaishuo" 中古祆教华化概说 [A Survey of the Sinicization of Medieval Zoroastrianism]. In Zhang Xiaogui 2014, 484–503.

Zhang Xiaohua 张晓华. 1999. "Cong fojiao jingjiao chuanbo Zhongguo de chen yu bai kan wailai zongjiao bentuhua de ruogan lilun wenti" 从佛教景教传播中国的成与败看外来宗教本土化的若干理论问题 [Discussion of Some Theoretical Questions about the Indigenization of Foreign Religions on the Basis of Success and Failure in the Diffusion of Buddhism and the Luminous Teaching in China]. *Shixue lilun yanjiu* 史学理论研究 [Historiography Quarterly], no. 4: 60–70. Repr. in *Zongjiao* 宗教 [Religion], no. 1 (2000): 22–30.

Zhang Xiping 張西平, Ma Xini 馬西尼 [F. Masini], Ren Dayuan 任大援, and Pei Zuoning 裴佐寧 [A. M. Piazzoni], eds. 2014. *Fandigang tushuguancang Ming Qing Zhongxi wenhua jiaoliushi wenxian congkan: Di yi ji* 梵蒂岡圖書館藏明清中西文化交流史文獻叢刊：第一輯 [First Collection of Documents about the History of the Sino-Western Cultural Exchanges during the Ming and Qing Dynasties Preserved in the Vatican Library]. 44 vols. Zhengzhou: Daxiang chubanshe.

Zhang Xuesong 张雪松. 2016. "Chuyi xiancun Dunhuang Tangdai jingjiao wenxian de zhenwei wenti" 刍议现存敦煌唐代景教文献的真伪问题 ["The Authenticity of Existing Dunhuang Manuscripts on Nestorianism in Tang Dynasty"]. *Shangrao shifan xueyuan xuebao* 上饶师范学院学报 [Journal of Shangrao Teachers' College], no. 1: 48–52.

Zhang Xushan 張緒山. 2009. "Fulin mingchen yuyuan yanjiu shuping" 拂菻名称语源研究书评 [A Review of Etymological Studies on the Term "Fulin"]. *Shijie lishi* 世界历史 [World History], no. 5: 143–51.

Zhang Yun 张云. 2017. "Jingjiao chuanru Tufan de xiansuo" 景教传入吐蕃的线索 [Clues of the Diffusion of the Luminous Teaching in Ancient Tibet]. In *Shanggu Xizang yu Bosi wenming* 上古西藏与波斯文明 [Ancient Tibet and Persian Civilization], rev. edn, edited by Zhang Yun, 215–19. Beijing: Zhongguo zangxue chubanshe.

Zhao Bichu 趙璧礎. 1990. "Jiu jingjiaobei ji qi wenxian shitan Tangdai jingjiao bensehua" 就景教碑及其文獻試探唐代景教本色化 [A Tentative Discussion of the Indigenization of the Luminous Teaching during the Tang Dynasty on the Basis of the Stele of the Luminous Teaching and Other Documents]. In *Jidujiao yu Zhongguo bensehua: Guoji xueshu yantaohui lunwenji* 基督教與中國本色化—國際學術研討會論文集 [Collection of Papers Presented at the International Academic Symposium "Christianity and Chinese Indigenization"], edited by Lin Zhiping 林治平, 173–91. Taipei: Yuzhouguang chubanshe.

Zhao Jiadong 赵家栋 and Nie Zhijun 聂志军. 2010. "Qianlun Tangdai jingjiao wenxian de zhengli yu yanjiu" 浅论唐代景教文献的整理与研究 ["Discussion on the Nestorian Religion Literature in the Tang Dynasty"]. *Guji zhengli yanjiu xuekan* 古籍整理研究学刊 [Journal of Ancient Books Collation and Studies], no. 6: 8–13.

Zhao Xiaojun 赵晓军 and Chu Weihong 褚卫红. 2007. "Luoyang xinchu Daqin jingjiao shijingchuang jiaokan" 洛阳新出大秦景教石经幢校勘 ["Emendation of the New Stele with Lection of Religion Jing from Daqin Unearthed at Luoyang"]. *Henan keji daxue xuebao (shehui kexue ban)* 河南科技大学学报（社会科学版）[Journal of Henan University of Science and Technology: Social Sciences Edition], no. 3: 29–32. Repr. in Ge 2009a, 157–64.

Zheng Acai 郑阿财. 2013. "Xingyu shuwu *Dunhuang miji* laiyuan, jiazhi yu yanjiu xiankuang" 杏雨书屋《敦煌秘笈》来源、价值与研究现况 ["The Source, Value, and Research Condition of *Secret Dunhuang Documents* Collected in Kyou Shoku"]. *Dunhuang yanjiu* 敦煌研究 [Dunhuang Research], no. 3: 116–27.

Zheng Lianming 鄭連明. 1965. *Zhongguo jingjiao de yanjiu* 中國景教的研究 [Research on the Luminous Teaching in China]. Jidujiao zai Tai xuanjiao bai zhounian jinian congshu 基督教在台宣教百週年紀念叢書. Taipei: Taiwan jidu zhanglao jiaohui.

Zheng Shulian 鄭淑蓮. 2012. "Tangdai jingjiao zai Hua zhi zhengjiao guanxi" 唐代景教在華之政教關係 [The Luminous Teaching in China during the Tang Dynasty and the Connection between Politics and Religion]. *Donghai daxue tushuguan guanxun* 東海大學圖書館館訊 [Tunghai University Library Newsletter] 127: 53–65.

Zheng Xiyuan 郑曦原. 2006. "Niuyue *Da Qin jingjiao liuxing Zhongguo bei* fuzhipin 'shenshi' zhi mi" 纽约《大秦景教流行中國碑》复制品「身世」之谜 [The Riddle of the "Life" of the New York Replica of the *Stele of the Diffusion of the Luminous Teaching of Da Qin in China*]. *WB*, no. 4: 56–59.

Zhongguo shehui kexueyuan lishi yanjiusuo 中国社会科学院历史研究所, Zhongguo Dunhuang Tulufan xuehui Dunhuang guwenxian bianji weiyuanhui 中国敦煌吐鲁番学会敦煌古文献编辑委员会, Yingguo guojia tushuguan 英国国家图书馆, and Lundun daxue Yafei xueyuan 伦敦大学亚非学院, eds. 1990–95. *Yingzang Dunhuang wenxian: Hanwen fojing yiwai bufen* 英藏敦煌文献—漢文佛經以外部份 [Dunhuang Documents in British Collections: Chinese Texts Other than Buddhist Scriptures]. 14 vols. Chengdu: Sichuan renmin chubanshe.

Zhou Zhenxiang 周祯祥. 1993. "Cong jingjiaobei suo juan seng si kan Zhongxi jiaotong he jidujiao zai Zhongguo de chuangbu" 从景教碑所镌僧寺看中西交通和基督教在中国的传佈 ["On the Spread of Christianity and the Exchange between Ancient China and the West from the Inscriptions of Jingjiao Stone Tablet"]. *WB*, no. 5: 21–31.

Zhou Zhenxiang. 1994. "Guanyu 'jingjiaobei' chutu wenti de zhengyi" 关於《景教碑》出土问题的争议 ["Discussion on the Discovering of Jingjiao Tablet"]. *WB*, no. 5: 42–50.

Zhou Zhenxiang. 1996. "Qianshi jingjiaobei jige xuliya wenzi kaoshi zhi qiyi" 浅识景教碑几个叙利亚文字考释之歧異 [A Simple Approach to the Differences in the Interpretation of Some Syriac Words on the Stele of the Luminous Teaching]. *WB*, no. 6: 16–26.

Zhou Zhenxiang. 2003. "Shixi Tangdai jingjiaohui de zuzhi yu zhidu" 试析唐代景教会的组织与制度 [Tentative Analysis of the Organization and Institutions of the Church of the Luminous Teaching in the Tang Dynasty]. *WB*, no. 1: 18–33.

Zhu Donghua 朱東華. 2011. "*Da Qin jingjiao liuxing Zhongguo bei* shufa kaolun" 《大秦景教流行中國碑》書法考論 ["The Nestorian Stele in Tang China: Its Calligraphic Style and the Genealogy of Rubbings"]. *DF* 34: 233–54.

Zhu Donghua. 2013. "Cong yuan fo ru jing jiaodu kan Tangdai jingjiao 'yingshen' zhi 'ying' de jingshi neihan" 從援佛入景角度看唐代景教「應身」之「應」的經世內涵 ["On the Economic Meaning of *Ying* (Nirmana) from the Perspective of Buddhist-Christian Translatability"]. *DF* 39: 219–36.

Zhu Donghua. 2016a. "Jingjing zhuyi zuopin de chuangzuo shixu ji qi sixiang guanxi yanjiu" 景淨著譯作品的創作時序及其思想關聯研究 ["A Chronological and Content Relationship Analysis on Jingjing's Works"]. *DF* 44: 223–37.

Zhu, Donghua. 2016b. "Person and *Shen* 身: An Ontological Encounter of 'Nestorian' Christianity with Confuciansim in Tang China." In *Yearbook of Chinese Theology 2015*, edited by Paulos Z. Huang, 202–13. Yearbook of Chinese Theology 1. Leiden: Brill.

Zhu, Donghua. 2016c. "Ying 應/Nirmāṇa: A Case Study on the Translatability of Buddhism into *Jingjiao*." In Tang and Winkler 2016, 419–33.

Zhu Donghua. 2017. "*Nixiya xinjing* yu jingjiao shenxue" 《尼西亞信經》與景教神學 ["The Nicene Creed and Jingjiao Theology"]. *DF* 47: 27–48.

Zhu Donghua. 2019. "Zhu Qianzhi yu Zhongguo jingjiao de suyuan yanjiu" 朱谦之与中国景教的溯源研究 [Zhu Qianzhi and the Study of the Origins of the Luminous Teaching in China]. *Shijie zongjiao wenhua* 世界宗教文化 [Religious Cultures in the World], no. 6: 35–42.

Zhu, Donghua. 2021. "Chinese Jingjiao and the Antiochene Exegesis." In *The Oxford Handbook of the Bible in China*, edited by K. K. Yeo, 47–62. New York: Oxford University Press.

Zhu Qianzhi 朱谦之. 1993. *Zhongguo jingjiao* 中国景教 [The Luminous Teaching in China]. Zhexue shijia wenku 哲学史家文库. Beijing: Renmin chubanshe [text A].

Zhu Weizhi 朱維之. 1948. "*Xuanyuan ben jing* ji *Zhixuan anle jing* kao" 宣元本經及志玄安樂經考 [A Study of the *Book of the Luminous Teaching of Da Qin on Revealing the Origin and the Foundation* and the *Book on Profound and Mysterious Blessedness*]. *Shenxue zhi* 神學誌 [Theological Review] 1. Repr. in Zhu Weizhi 1951a, 159–77 [text E].

Zhu Weizhi. 1951a. *Wenyi zongjiao lunji* 文藝宗教論集 [*Essays on Literature and Religion*]. Qingnian congshu 青年叢書 [Youth Library Series] II.45. Shanghai: Qingnian xiehui shuju.

Zhu Weizhi. 1951b. "*Xuting mishisuo jing*" 序聽迷詩所經 [*Book of the Lord Messiah*]. In Zhu Weizhi 1951a, 192–217 [text D].

Zieme, Peter. 1974. "Zu den nestorianisch-türkischen Turfantexten." In *Sprache, Geschichte und Kultur der altaischen Völker: Protokollband der XII. Tagung der Permanent International Altaistic Conference 1969 in Berlin*, edited by Georg Hazai and Peter Zieme, 661–68. Schriften zur Geschichte und Kultur des Alten Orients 5. Berlin: Akademie-Verlag.

Zieme, Peter. 1978. "Zwei Ergänzungen zu der christlich-türkischen Handschrift T II B 1." *AoF* 5: 271–72.

Zieme, Peter. 1981. "Ein Hochzeitssegen uighurischer Christen." In *Scholia: Beiträge zur Turkologie und Zentralasienkunde. Annemarie von Gabain zum 80. Geburtstag am 4. Juli 1981 dargebracht von Kollegen, Freunden und Schülern*, edited by Klaus Röhrborn and Horst Wilfrid Brands, 221–32. Veröffentlichungen der Societas Uralo-Altaica 14. Wiesbaden: Harrassowitz.

Zieme, Peter. [2006?]. "A Cup of Cold Water: Folios of a Nestorian-Turkic Manuscript from Kharakhoto." In Malek [2006?], 341–45.

Zieme, Peter. 2009. "Notes on a Bilingual Prayer Book from Bulayık." In Winkler and Tang 2009, 167–80.

Zieme, Peter. 2013. "Turkic Christianity in the Black City (Xaraxoto)." In Tang and Winkler 2013, 99–104.

Zieme, Peter. 2015a. *Altuigurische Texte der Kirche des Ostens aus Zentralasien: Old Uigur Texts of the Church of the East from Central Asia*. Gorgias Eastern Christian Studies 41. Piscataway, NJ: Gorgias Press.

Zieme, Peter. 2015b. "Notes sur les textes chrétiens en vieux-ouïghour." In Borbone and Marsone 2015, 185–98.

Žukova, Ljudmila I., ed. 1994. *Iz istorii drevnix kul'tov srednej Azii: Xristianstvo* [From the History of Ancient Cults in Central Asia: Christianity]. Taškent: Glavnaja Redakcija Enciklopedii.

Zürcher, Erik. 1972. *The Buddhist Conquest of China: The Spread and Adaptation of Buddhism in Early Medieval China*, 2nd edn. 2 vols. Leiden: Brill.

Index of Names, Texts, and Manuscripts

The names in bold character are those of the Christian monks and clerics mentioned in the text of the 781 Xi'an stele inscription.

Aaron. *See* **Qianyou**

Aba I, 8, 11, 35

Abay, 219

Abba Isaiah of Scetis, 41–42

ʿAbdišoʿ, monk. *See* **Taihe**

ʿAbdišoʿ, priest, 219

ʿAbdišoʿ I, 79

ʿAbdišoʿ of Nisibis (ʿAbdišoʿ bar Brika, Ebedjesus), 7, 70, 73, 228n57

Abel, 270n35

Abraham, biblical figure, xiin3, 228n51

Abraham of Kaškar, 8, 34, 203n42

Abraham of Natpar, 34

Abū Zayd al-Sīrāfī, 78

Abū-l-Farağ Muḥammad ibn Isḥāq. *See* Ibn al-Nadīm

Acacius (Aqaq), 34

Accounts of China and India (*Aḫbār al-Ṣīn wa-l-Hind*), 78, 79n92

Acts of Adarparwa, Mihrnarseh, and Mahduxt, 46n189

Acts of Addai, 231n82

Acts of Mar Mari, 5n7

Acts of Mar Qardag, 47

Acts of Martyrs, 42

Acts of Paul, 43

Acts of Peter, 42

Acts of Sergius and Bacchus, 231n86

Acts of the Apostles 3, 229n63, 230n71, 258n146

Adam. *See* **Jingjing**

Adam, biblical figure, 255–56, 258, 269n85

Adam, deacon, 218

Adam, priest. *See* **Fayuan**

Addai, 5, 228n53

Ādurhormazd, 42

Afghanistan, 9, 15, 150, 212n104

Afrasiab. *See* Samarkand

Against the Heathen, 72

Aggai, 5

Agni, 45

Aḥai, 73

Aḫbār al-Ṣīn wa-l-Hind. See *Accounts of China and India*

Ahwaz, al-, 70n54

Ai Tian 艾田, 128n37

Ajvadž, 20

Ak-Bešim (Suyab), 22, 29, 45

Ak-Tepe, 19

Alexandria, 16n56

Allegra, Gabriele M., 153, 173

Altai, 11

Aluoben 阿羅本 (Ardabān), 69, 74, 87–89, 95, 110, 129–30, 147–48, 164–65, 197n1, 204–5, 207, 231

Aluohan 阿羅憾 (Wahrām), 99

Amitābha, 64, 96, 187. *See also* Buddha

Ammō, 48

ʿAmr ibn Mattā, 86

Amu Darya. *See* Oxus

An 安, family, 104, 143, 146

An 安, lady, 91, 146

An Lushan 安祿山 Rebellion, 67, 87, 120, 212n101, 213n107

An Shaolian 安少連, 145

An Shigao 安世高, 54n225

An Yena 安野郍 (Yānakk), 100

Anguo 安國. *See* Bukhara

Anoš. *See* **Lingshou**

Antioch, 3, 5, 15n54, 16n56, 36

Antirrhetikos, 42, 230n69

Anunadhapura, 35

Aphrahat, 62, 229n68

Apocryphal Acts of the apostles, 50

Apocryphal Gospels, 50

Apostolic Canons, 42

Apostolic Constitutions, 229n63

Aprah (Farah), 15

Arabian Peninsula, 9, 79, 110

Ardabān. *See* **Aluoben**

Arnobius of Sicca, 72

Ashurov, Barakatullo, 21

Ásia Extrema, 71

Assemani, Giuseppe Simone, 118

Assyria (Athur), 10

Astana, 14. *See also* Turfan

Athur. *See* Assyria

Avalokiteśvara. *See* Guanyin

Azariah (ʿAzarya), 228

Babel. *See* Baghdad

Babylon, 6

Bacchus, martyr, 42, 227

Bacchus, monk. *See* **Baoguo**

Bacchus, priest. *See* **Chongjing**

Bactria, 9, 11, 45, 53, 76, 84, 87, 207n76, 212n104, 218n136. *See also* Balkh

Baghdad (Babel), 10, 16, 217n129

Bai Yu 白宇, 167

Bairen 柏仁, 144

Balkh, 13, 87, 212n104, 218. *See also* Bactria

Baoda 寶達 (Mšiḥadad), 219

Baoguo 保國 (Bacchus), 221

Baoling 寶靈 (Paul), 221

Baoxin 報信, 228, 231

Bar ʿEbroyo, Grigorios (Barhebraeus), 15, 116

Barbati, Chiara, 39

Barḥadbšabba ʿArbaya, 228n57

Barhebraeus. *See* Bar ʿEbroyo, Grigorios

Baršabba of Merv, 11, 42

Barṣauma of Nisibis, 7

Bartoli, Daniello, 127–28, 130

Behnām, 228n51

Beijing 北京 (Peking), 85, 114, 130

Beilin 碑林 (Forest of Steles), 90, 121, 123, 128

Benedict XV, 133

Berlin-Brandenburgische Akademie der Wissenschaften, 37

Bet ʿAbe, Monastery of, 85–86

Bet Hinduwaye. *See* India

Bet Lašpar. *See* Kurdistan

Bet Madaye. *See* Media

Bet Parsaye. *See* Persia

Bet Qaṭraye, 9

Bet Ṣinaye (al-Ṣin, Ṣin, Ṣinestan, Ṣinistan), 10, 70, 73n68, 79, 86, 88, 198

Bet Ṭaḥoraye. *See* Tocharistan

Bet Tuptaye. *See* Tibet

Bet Ṭurkaye, 10, 12–13

Bethlehem, 43, 47, 277n84

Biblioteca Ambrosiana, 135

Bibliothèque nationale de France, 16n60, 159–60

Bingchen 丙辰, 155, 297n94

Bīrūnī, al-, 16

Biškek, 21, 45

Bodhidharma (Damo 達摩), 72

Book of Giants, 50

Book of Governors, 10, 86n117, 203n42

Book of Life (*Book of the Living*), 42

Book of the Honored. See *Zunjing*

Book of the Lord Messiah. See *Xuting mishisuo jing*

Book of the Luminous Teaching of Da Qin on Revealing the Origin and Reaching the Foundation. See *Da Qin jingjiao xuanyuan zhiben jing*

Book of the Marvels of the World, xinn1–2

Book of the Tower (*Kitāb al-Miǧdal*), 86

Book of Treasures, 228n57

Book on Profound and Mysterious Blessedness. See *Zhixuan anle jing*

Borromeo, Federico, 135

Bosi 波斯. See Persia

Bosi husi 波斯胡寺 (Foreign monastery of Persia). See Bosi si

Bosi si 波斯寺 (Monastery of Persia), 106–7, 110n203, 111–12

Boym, Michał Piotr, 71, 134

Brahmā, 236n15

British Museum, 23n89, 24–25

Buddha, 26–29, 51, 63, 83, 125, 173–74, 179, 181, 185, 198n7, 200n23, 202n35, 209n83, 222n3, 224n13, 226nn25–26, 226n31, 231n83, 242n50, 248n81, 250n87, 259n151, 266n5, 267n18, 269n32, 269n34, 271n40, 272n45, 272n49, 278n99, 282n4, 286nn31–32, 286n37, 288n48, 295n83, 299n11, 300n22. See also Amitābha; Maitreya; Śākyamuni

Buddhoṣṇīṣa vijaya dhāraṇī sūtra. See *Foding zunsheng tuoluoni jing*

Bukhara (Anguo 安國), 11, 19, 21, 44, 90–91, 100, 104, 143, 146

Bulayïq, 14, 17, 22–23, 32–33, 35, 37–38, 41, 43, 114, 172. *See also* Turfan

Bureau of Astronomy. See Sitian tai

Buzheng fang 布政坊 (Buzheng Ward), 111

Byzantine Empire. *See* Roman Empire

C2, Sogdian MS. *See* E27

C5, Sogdian MS. *See* E5

C14, Syriac MS. *See* MIK III 45

C46, Syriac-Sogdian MS. *See* E19

Čač. *See* Sogdiana; Taškent

Cain, 270n35

Cambridge Add. 1982, Syriac MS, 172n169

Canton. *See* Guangzhou

Cao Shibang 曹仕邦, 99n155

Caoguo 曹國. *See* Kaputana

Carlo Horatii da Castorano, 71, 72n63

Catalogue (*Kitāb al-Fihrist*), 79

Catalogue of Authors, 228n57

Cathay, 32, 71–72, 85

Caucasus, 141n81

Cave of Treasures, 228n57

Caves of the Thousand Buddhas. *See* Mogao Caves

Cefu yuangui 冊府元龜, 66n39, 76

Čerčen, 45

Ceylon (Sri Lanka), 12, 35

Chaldean Breviary, 70–71

Chang'an 長安 (Hao 鎬, Khumdan, Kumdan, Xi'an 西安), 12, 63, 65n34, 75, 87–90, 104, 110–12, 117, 121, 123, 128, 150–51, 166, 176, 186–87, 197n1, 207, 212n104, 213n110, 218, 221

Chang'an zhi 長安志, 110n203, 111n209

Chang'er 昌兒, 145

Charlemagne, 129–30

Chen Huaiyu 陳懷宇, 149, 153–54, 166, 170, 172–73, 176, 178, 186–87

Chen Yuan 陳垣, 99n155

Chin Ken-pa. *See* Zeng Qingbao

China Illustrata, 71, 127

Chinese Turkestan. *See* Eastern Turkestan

Chongde 崇德 (Jacob), 221

Chongfu si 崇福寺 (Chongfu Monastery), 151

Chonghe 沖和 (John), 220

Chongjing 崇敬 (Bacchus), 219

Chongsheng si 崇聖寺 (Chongsheng Monastery), 128

Chongyan si bei xu 重嚴寺碑序, 115n229

Chongyi 崇一, 99–100

Choresmia (Khwarazm), 36

Chronicle of Michael the Syrian, 116n233

Chronicle of Se'ert, 6, 15

Chu Suiliang 猪遂良, 165

Church History (by Zechariah the Rhetor), 230n73

Ci huigu kehan shu yi 賜回鶻可汗書意, 77n86

Čimkent, 45

Commentary on the Patriarchs of the Church of the East, 86n119

Confucius, 206n60

Constantine. *See* **Juxin**

Constantinople, 7, 79

Cordier, Henri, 119

Creed, 41, 43

Cruz, Gaspar da, 70

Cui Xing(ben) 崔行本, 144

Cure of the Greek Maladies, 34n126

Cyriacus, monk. *See* **Zhijian**

Cyricus, martyr, 42

Cyrus of Edessa, 228

Da Qin 大秦, 66–69, 74, 76–77, 100–1, 110n203, 115, 129–30, 136, 147–48, 164, 197n1, 201n26, 204–6, 209, 231, 295n84

Da Qin jingjiao dasheng tongzhen guifa zan 大秦景教大聖通真歸法讚 (Kojima manuscript A), 137n70, 148, 154, 165

Da Qin jingjiao liuxing Zhongguo bei 大秦景教流行中國碑 (Xi'an Christian stele), xiin6, xiiin8, 30, 39n146, 60, 63, 65, 68, 69n48, 81n99, 82, 84, 87, 92–98, 101, 106–7, 109, 113–14, 117–37, 141, 146, 147n101, 148, 151, 152n22, 165–66, 168, 170, 188, 193, 196–221, 222n1, 224n13, 224n16, 226n24, 227n38, 227n47, 229n60, 229n64, 244n58, 258n143, 276n83, 295nn83–84, 298n3, 299n12, 299–300nn17–19, 302n37, 303n41

Da Qin jingjiao sanwei mengdu zan 大秦景教三威蒙度讚, 68, 148, 150n114, 152n122, 160–61, 165, 167, 169, 172–73, 175, 178, 194, 198n8, 200n23, 201n30, 202n35, 222–25, 226n24, 230, 256n127, 295n83, 300n19. See also *Glory to God in the Highest*

*Da Qin jingjiao xuanyuan zhiben jing 大秦景教宣元至本經 (collated text), 68, 92, 98, 155, 165, 174, 178, 195, 198n8, 199n17, 214n116, 222n1, 226n24, 227n38, 228, 298–303

Da Qin jingjiao xuanyuan [zhi]ben jing 大秦景教宣元 [至] 本經 (Li Shengduo manuscript), 150n114, 155, 162, 174, 166–69, 195

Da Qin jingjiao xuanyuan zhiben jing 大秦景教宣元至本經 (Luoyang pillar inscription), 141–42, 144, 155, 195

Da Qin jingjiao xuanyuan zhiben jing 大秦景教宣元至本經 (Kojima manuscript B), 137n70, 148, 154, 165

Da Qin jingjiao xuanyuan zhiben jing chuangji 大秦景教宣元至本經幢記, 60n7, 112, 142, 143n86, 144n94, 145n96, 145n98, 214n115

Da Qin si 大秦寺 (Monastery of Da Qin), 66, 74, 88–90, 96, 106–7, 110n203, 111–12, 145, 151, 161, 181, 186, 198n4, 205

Da Qin si ta 大秦寺塔 (Pagoda of the Monastery of Da Qin), 112

Index of Names, Texts, and Manuscripts

Da Tang Yizhou tiexiang beisong bing xu
大唐易州鐵像碑頌并序, 170

Da Tang Zhenyuan xu Kaiyuan shijiao lu
大唐貞元續開元釋教錄, 88n124

Dadišoʿ I, 6, 11

Dadišoʿ Qaṭraya, 42, 229n67

Daizong 代宗, 75, 210, 213n107, 216

Damascus, ix

Damo 達摩. *See* Bodhidharma

Daniel, 227, 264n168

Daodejing 道德經, 201n29, 203n46,
205n53, 205n56, 207n73, 210n89,
210n91, 210n93

Dasheng bensheng xindi guan jing 大乘
本生心地觀經, 167, 173

Dauvillier, Jean, 87n120, 127n33, 193

David, biblical figure, 227, 228

David, metropolitan, 86–87

David, priest, 219

*De christiana expeditione apud Sinas
suscepta ab Societate Jesu*, 71

Deeg, Max, 67, 89n128, 131, 171, 182,
207n75, 217nn128–29

Dejian 德建 (John), 221

Demonstrations, 62, 229

Denḥa I, 85

Dezong 德宗, 103, 120, 150, 167, 169,
210n89, 211n94

Diamond Sutra. See Jingang jing

Dias, Manuel Jr. (Yang Manuo 陽瑪諾),
134–35, 212n104

Diatessaron, 41

Dickens, Mark, 41

Dionysius Exiguus, 262n162

*Discourse of the Venerable One of the
Universe on Almsgiving, Third Part.
See Shizun bushi lun disan*

Discourse on the One God. See Yishen lun

*Discourse on the One Godhead, First Part.
See Yitian lun diyi*

Doctrine of Addai, 231n82

Dong Caoguo 東曹國. *See* Sutrušana

Dongfang Shuo 東方朔, 204n50

Dongshi 東市 (Eastern Market), 108

Dormition of the Virgin, 42

*Doubt-dispelling Exposition
(Škand-gumānīg Wizār)*, 48

Drake, Francis S., 152, 172

Du jingjiaobei shu hou 讀景教碑書後,
131n45

Duan Chengshi 段成式, 101

Dunhuang 敦煌, 14, 18, 23–26, 33,
42–45, 78, 109, 113–14, 142, 146–48,
151, 152n122, 154–60, 165–66, 168–69,
175, 180, 187, 225n20

E5 (formerly C5), Sogdian MS, 39

E19 (formerly C46), Syriac-Sogdian
MS, 149

E27 (formerly C2), Sogdian MS, 37,
42nn162–64

Eastern Turkestan (Chinese Turkestan),
14, 17n67, 22, 30, 43, 49, 52. *See also*
Turkestan

Ebedjesus. *See* ʿAbdišoʿ of Nisibis

Eccles, Lance, 193

Edessa, 7, 228n53

Egyptians, 34

Elam, 10

Elijah, biblical figure, 231

Elijah, priest. *See* **Liben**

Elijah, priest. *See* **Yanhe**

Elijah of Merv, 231n80

Elijah of Nisibis, 231n80

Elišaʿ bar Quzbaye, 34

Eliya of Damascus, 79

Emmanuel. *See* **Mingyi**

Emmerick, Ronald E., 26

ʿEnanišoʿ, 42

Enoki Kazuo 榎一雄, 164

Ephrem, monk. *See* **Xuande**

Ephrem, priest. *See* **Fulin**

Ephrem the Syrian, 62, 231

Eskildsen, Stephen, 186

388   *Index of Names, Texts, and Manuscripts*

Ethiopians, 34, 70

Ethnological Museum "Anima Mundi," 133n50

Eugene, 42

Euphrates, 3

Eustace, 42

Evagrius Ponticus, 42, 230n69

Eve, 269n35

Fang Xuanling 房玄齡, 69, 147, 149, 204, 232

Fangshan 房山, 114

Farah. *See* Aprah

Fars. *See* Persia

Fayuan 法源 (Adam), 221

Fengyi fang 豐邑坊 (Fengyi Ward), 186

Feng Chengjun 馮承鈞, 137

Fengzhen 奉真 (Šubḥalmaran), 221

Fenyang 汾陽, 212n104, 213

Ferreira, Johan, 118–19, 121

Fiqh al-naṣrāniyya. See Law of Christianity

Flower of Histories of the East, 36n137

Foding zunsheng tuoluoni jing 佛頂尊勝陀羅尼經 (*Buddhoṣṇīṣa vijaya dhāraṇī sūtra*), 171

Forte, Antonino, 65, 99n154, 107n189, 111n205, 193

Foster, John, 152, 177

Francis Xavier, 70

Fujian 福建, 64n24

Fulin 拂林, 76, 101, 164, 248n82

Fulin 拂林 (Ephrem), 219

Fushou 福壽 (Moses), 219

Fuzhou 福州, xi, xv

Gabriel (Gabri'el), 76n81, 207n75. *See also* **Jilie**

Gabriel, abbot. *See* **Yeli**

Gabriel, monk. *See* **Guangde**

Gai Bosi si wei Da Qin si zhao 改波斯寺為大秦寺詔, 67n39

Gaillard, Louis, 117–18

Gande 感德, 138, 144

Gansu 甘肅, 24–25, 69, 109, 113, 147, 160

Ganzhou 甘州 (Zhangye 張掖), 113

Gao Lishi 高力士, 74, 208

Gaozong 高宗, 63, 74, 95, 99–100, 108, 111, 137, 206, 207n70, 208n82, 215

Gaozu 高祖, 204n48, 208n82

Gardīzī, Abū Saʿīd ʿAbd al-Ḥayy, 26

Gazā, 228n57

Ge Chengyong 葛承雍, 90, 140

Gengxu 庚戌, 76n82

Gengzi xiaoxia ji 庚子銷夏記, 128n35

George. *See* **Heji**

George (Gigoe, Gigoy, Giwargis), 76n84, 209n85. *See also* **Jihe**

George, martyr, 42, 52, 227,

Gigoy. *See* **Xuanlan**

Gilgit, 12

Gillman, Ian, 57

Gloria in excelsis Deo. See Glory to God in the Highest

Glory to God in the Highest (*Tešbuḥtā d-malakē, Gloria in excelsis Deo*), 41, 114, 166, 172–73. See also *Da Qin jingjiao sanwei mengdu zan*

Gnostic Chapters, 42

Goa, 35

Godwin, R. Todd, 65–66, 82

Gök-Tepe, 19

Golgotha (Gagulta), 280

Gong Tianmin (K'ung Tien-min) 龔天民, 167, 174

Gordon, Elizabeth Anna, 187–88

Gouvea, António de, 71

Greeks, 36, 218

Gregory of Nazianzus, 230n74

Gregory of Nyssa, 230n74

Gregory Thaumaturgus, 230n74

Guangde 廣德 (Gabriel), 221

Guangji 光濟 (Isaac), 220

Guangqing 廣慶 (Michael), 219

Guangxi 廣西. *See* Guilin

Guangzheng 光正 (John), 221

Guangzhou 廣州 (Canton), 12, 78, 103, 156

Guanyin 觀音 (Avalokiteśvara), 179, 202n35, 224n16, 289n51, 295n83

Guilin 桂林 (Guangxi 廣西), 100

Guillaumont, Antoine, 87n120, 127n33

Guiyijun 歸義軍, 78

Guiyijun yanei mianyou poyong li 歸義軍 衙內麵油破用歷, 113n220

Gundešapur, 70n54

Guo Ziyi 郭子儀, 87, 212n101, 212n104, 213

Hage, Wolfgang, 52, 58

Hainei shizhou ji 海內十洲記, 204n50

Haiyao bencao 海藥本草, 102

Hamada Naoya 浜田直也, 178n189

Hami, 45

Han Taihua 韓泰華, 219n140

Hananiah, 228

Haneda Tōru 羽田亨, 152, 158, 167, 195

Hangzhou 杭州 (Wulin 武林), 130, 219n140

Hao 鎬. *See* Chang'an

Harew. *See* Herat

Havret, Henri, 131, 135

Heguo 何國. *See* Kušaṇiyya

Heguang 和光 (Jacob), 221

Heji 和吉 (George), 219

Heming 和明 (Isaac), 221

Ḥenanišoʿ II (Ningshu 寧恕), 217

Hengzhou cishi Ma jun shendao bei 恒州 刺史馬君神道碑, 69n50

Hephthalite Huns, 11

Herat (Harew, Heria), 15, 73

Heria. *See* Herat

Hetʿum, 36

Hezhong 河中, 103

History (by Theophylact Simocatta), 11n34

History of Aḥiqar, 42

History of Mar Aba, 11n33

Holm, Frits V., 122, 132–33

Homilies on the Gospel of John, 34n125

Hong Kong 香港, 153

Hou Han shu 后漢書, 66, 252n106

Hua Xian 花獻, 90–91

Huanchun 還淳 (John), 220

Huang Chao 黃巢, 78

Huang Xianian 黃夏年, 178, 248n79

Ḥudrā (Penqita), 32, 33n118

Huichang 會昌, 77, 139

Huiming 惠明 (Mahdadgušnasp), 219

Huitong 惠通 (John), 219

Hunter, Erica C. D., 95

Hymn in Praise of the Salvation Achieved through the Three Majesties of the Luminous Teaching of Da Qin. See Da Qin Jingjiao sanwei mengdu zan

Hymns for Epiphany, 62

Hymns on Faith, 62

Hymnscroll, 50, 148n105, 223n6, 283n8

Ibn al-Nadīm (Abū-l-Faraǧ Muḥammad ibn Isḥāq), 79

Ibn al-Ṭayyib, 70, 73

Ibrāhīm ibn Yuḥannā, 16

Illustrated Account of the Western Regions. See Xiyu tuji

India (Bet Hinduwaye), 9, 10, 12, 27, 29–30, 33, 35, 70–73, 86, 134, 148n104, 181, 183, 205n55

Indians, 53, 71

Indus, 12

Inner Mongolia, 33, 141

Insādi sūtra, 58

Iran. *See* Persia

Iranians. *See* Persians

Iraq, 8

Isaac, biblical figure, xiin3, 19

Isaac, monk, 221

Isaac, monk. *See* **Guangji**

Isaac, monk. *See* **Yingde**

Isaac, priest. *See* **Heming**
Isaac, priest. *See* **Rijin**
Isaac I, 6
Isaac of Nineveh, 42, 229n67
Išitikhan (Xi Caoguo 西曹國), 104n179
Išoʿdad, monk. *See* **Jingfu**
Išoʿdad, monk. *See* **Wenming**
Išoʿemmeh, monk. *See* **Renhui**
Išoʿyahb III, 73, 85
Izadspas. *See* **Jingzhen**

Jacob, biblical figure, xiin3
Jacob, monk. *See* **Chongde**
Jacob, monk. *See* **Heguang**
Jacob, priest. *See* **Yejumo**
Jacob Baradaeus, 7
Jacobite Church. *See* West Syriac Church
Japan, 9, 26–28, 158, 159n39, 188, 194
Jaxartes, 4
Jerusalem, 16n56, 256n129, 260n156, 277
Jiang Wenhan 江文漢, 165
Jiangsu 江蘇, 72
Jianzhong 建中, 103, 211, 216
Jihe 佶和, 76–77, 87, 112, 209. *See also*
    George (Gigoe, Gigoy, Giwargis)
Jilie 及烈, 75–76, 87, 207. *See also*
    Gabriel (Gabriʾel)
Jin shi 金史, 69n50
Jing 涇, 181
Jingang jing 金剛經, 175
Jingde 敬德 (Job), 219
Jingfu 景福 (Išoʿdad), 61, 221
Jingjing 景淨 (Adam), 61, 68, 88, 109,
    148–50, 164–65, 167–68, 170, 175–76,
    181, 198
Jinglong 景龍, 111n209
Jingtong 景通, 227, 298–99, 303
Jingtong 景通 (Sergius), 61, 88, 220
Jingzhen 敬真 (Izadspas), 220
Jinzhou 晉州, 103
Jiu Tang shu 舊唐書, 76n80, 77, 78n89,
    88n125, 99–100nn155–56, 204n52,
    208n81, 213n107, 232n91, 263n165

Jiwei 己未, 219n140
Job. *See* **Jingde**
Job of Rev-Ardašir, 34
Joel. *See* **Yaoyue**
John, bishop. *See* **Yaolun**
John, deacon. *See* **Huitong**
John, evangelist, 34, 62, 226
John, monk, 221
John, monk. *See* **Chonghe**
John, monk. *See* **Dejian**
John, monk. *See* **Huanchun**
John, monk. *See* **Shouyi**
John, monk. *See* **Xuanzhen**
John, monk. *See* **Yaoyuan**
John, monk. *See* **Zhide**
John, priest. *See* **Guangzheng**
John, priest. *See* **Neicheng**
John Chrysostom, 34
John of Daylam, 42
John the Baptist, 277
John the Solitary, 229n67
Jordan, 277
Joseph, biblical figure, 20
Joseph Ḥazzaya, 229n67
Joseph of Arimathea, 257
Journey to the Eastern Parts,
    32n114, 36n136
Judea, 201n26, 260
Julitta, 42
Justinian, 73
Juxin 居信 (Constantine), 220

Kaifeng 開封, 128n37
Kaiyuan 開元, 76nn80–82, 180
Kaiyuan men 開遠門 (Kaiyuan
    Gate), 108
Kang 康, family, 90, 145
Kangguo 康國. *See* Samarkand
Kapiśi, 150
Kaputana (Caoguo 曹國), 104n179
Karlgren, Bernhard, 196
Kašana (Shiguo 史國), 104n179
Kašgar, 14, 44–45

Index of Names, Texts, and Manuscripts

391

Kaśmir, 27, 29, 53

Kawād I, 34

Kazakhstan, 21

Keevak, Michael, 133n52

Kerala, 35

Khara-Khoto. *See* Xaraxoto

Khorasan, 9, 13, 15–16, 48, 116

Khotan, 26, 45

Khumdan. *See* Chang'an

Kircher, Athanasius, 71, 118, 127, 134–35

Kirdīr, 56

Kitāb al-Fihrist. See Catalogue

Kitāb al-Miǧdal. See Book of the Tower

Kiyono Kenji 清野謙次, 159

Klimkeit, Hans-Joachim, 52, 56n236, 57

Kofu 甲府, 26–28

Kojima manuscript A, Chinese MS. See *Da Qin jingjiao dasheng tongzhen guifa zan*

Kojima manuscript B, Chinese MS. See *Da Qin jingjiao xuanyuan zhiben jing* (Kojima manuscript B)

Kojima Yasushi 小島靖, 148, 165

Kongwangshan 孔望山, 72

Korea, 9

Kottayam, 35

Kōya-san 高野山, 188

Krasnaja Rečka (Saryg), 21

Kuaiyutang tiba 快雨堂題跋, 128n36

Kuča, 45

Kūkai 空海, 188

Kumdan. *See* Chang'an

K'ung Tien-min. *See* Gong Tianmin

Kurdistan (Bet Lašpar), 9

Kušaṇiyya (Heguo 何國), 104n179

Kyoto Imperial University. *See* Kyōto teikoku daigaku

Kyōto teikoku daigaku 京都帝國大學, 158

Kyōu shooku 杏雨書屋, 158–59, 162, 194–95

Kyrgyzs, 49

Kyrgyzstan, 21

Ladakh, 27, 29

Laiwei 來威 (Noah), 220

Lala Comneno, Maria Adelaide, 17n67, 19

Laozi 老子, 170, 198n7, 296n60, 209n83

Laozi huahu jing 老子化胡經, 180, 187

Lateran Museum, 133

Law of Christianity (Fiqh al-naṣrāniyya), 70, 73

Le Coq, Albert von, 14

Leclercq, Henri, 82, 106

Lectionary, 33, 39, 230n71

Legge, James, 131

Letters (by Francis Xavier), 70

Letters (by Išoʿyahb III), 86n115

Letters (by Timothy I), 10n26, 10n28, 12n36, 15n54, 86n116, 86n118

Li Chengqi 李成器 (Li Xian 李憲), 208n78

Li Chongfeng 李崇峰, 112

Li Deyu 李德裕, 77n86

Li Deyu wenji 李德裕文集, 77n86

Li Jingdu 李景度, 61

Li Jingfu 李景伏, 61

Li Jinghong 李景弘, 61

Li Jingliang 李景亮, 61

Li Jingshen 李景佚, 61

Li Jingwen 李景文, 61

Li Pang 李滂, 158

Li Shengduo 李盛鐸, 154–55, 158–59, 162, 297n94

Li Shengduo manuscripts. See *Da Qin jingjiao dasheng tongzhen guifa zan*; *Da Qin jingjiao xuanyuan zhiben jing* (Kojima manuscript B); *Da Qin jingjiao xuanyuan [zhi]ben jing* (Li Shengduo manuscript); *Zhixuan anle jing*

Li Shimin 李世民. *See* Taizong

Li Su 李素, 61, 89, 103

Li Xian 李憲. *See* Li Chengqi

Li Xun 李珣, 101

Li Yong 李邕, 170

Li Zhizao 李之藻, Leo, 130–31

Liangchuan 梁川, 145

Lianyungang 連云港, 72

Liao 遼 (Liaodong 遼東), 252n106

Liben 立本 (Elijah), 221

Liber graduum, 229n67

Lidai fabao ji 歷代法寶記, 187

Lieu, Samuel N. C., 62–63, 185, 193, 196, 197n1

Life of John of Daylam, 32

Life of Saint George, 32, 43

Life of the Melkite Patriarch of Antioch Christopher, 16

Lijian 利見 (Luke), 219

Lilou 李樓, 137

Lin Wushu 林悟殊, 69n48, 94n140, 112, 145n97, 153–58, 161, 165–66, 168–69, 174, 194–95, 229n67

Lingbao 靈寶, 218

Lingde 靈德 (Sergius), 220

Lingshou 靈壽 (Anoš), 220

Lingwu 靈武 (Ningxia 寧夏), 109, 113, 210

Lingyan si beisong bing xu 靈岩寺碑頌并序, 170

Lintao 臨洮, 69

Liquan fang 醴泉坊 (Liquan Ward), 111

List of the East Syriac Episcopal Sees, 79n93

Liu boluomi jing 六波羅蜜經 (*Ṣaṭpāramitā sūtra*), 150

Liyong 利用 (Simeon), 221

Lo Hsiang-lin. *See* Luo Xianglin

Longmen 龍門, 138

Loulan 樓蘭, 45

Lü Xiuyan 呂秀巖, 127–28, 218

Luke, evangelist, 226

Luke, monk. *See* **Lijian**

Luke, monk. *See* **Wenzhen**

Luo Xianglin (Lo Hsiang-lin) 羅香林, 100, 168, 173, 194

Luo Zhenyu 羅振玉, 152n122

Luohan 羅含, 75, 77, 111, 207, 209. *See also* Rahām

Luolong 洛龍, 137

Luoyang 洛陽 (Luo 洛, Sarag, Zhou 周), 87–92, 95, 99, 104, 109–10, 112, 114, 126, 137–45, 155, 207n74, 218

Luoyang Museum, 137, 139–40, 142

Lushan si bei 麓山寺碑, 170

M 104, Parthian MS, 256n131

M 459, Parthian MS, 256n131

M 734, Parthian MS, 256n131

Ma Qingxiang 馬慶祥, 69n50

Macarius the Egyptian, 41

Madras, 35

Magi, 43, 47, 52, 78, 201n27, 276n83

Mahdadgušnasp. *See* **Huiming**

Maitreya, 289n51. *See also* Buddha

Malabar, 71

Maʿna, 34

Maʿna of Širaz, 34

Mani, 30, 48–50, 63, 115, 149n110, 181, 184

Mañjuśrī, 248n81

Manṣūr, al-, 16

Mantota, 35

Mar Aba I. *See* Aba I

Mar Ammō. *See* Ammō

Mar Maron, Monastery of, 10n26, 12

Mar Thomas. *See* Thomas, apostle

Mardānfarrox ī Ohrmazddād, 48

Margiana, 3, 46

Mari, 5

Mark (Marqos). *See* Yahballaha III

Mark, evangelist, 227

Martyrdom of Narseh, 46n189

Mary, 48, 72, 227, 275–76

Maṣin, 198n5

Matsumoto Eiichi 松本榮一, 173

Matthew, evangelist, 227

Matthew, monk. *See* **Mingtai**

Maximian, 227n45

Index of Names, Texts, and Manuscripts

Maymurgh (Miguo 米國), 89–90, 104
Media (Bet Madaye), 3, 9
Melkite Christians. *See* Melkite Church
Melkite Church, 15–17, 36, 101, 115–16
Merv, 3, 9, 11–13, 16, 18–19, 30, 33, 42, 44, 46, 48, 52, 70n54, 84
Mesopotamia, 4–5, 30, 81n99, 94–95, 97
Metaphorical Teaching, Second Part. See *Yu di'er*
Metropolitan Museum of Art, 133
Mi 米, family, 90, 145
Mi Jifen 米繼芬, 89–90, 103, 146n99
Michael. *See* **Guangqing**
Michael I Rabo (Michael the Syrian), 116
Miguo 米國. *See* Maymurgh
MIK III 45 (formerly C14), Syriac MS, 32, 33n118
MIK III 6911, painting, 22n86
Mikkelsen, Gunner B., 175
Milis, 212n104, 218
Mingana, Alphonse, 73n68
Mingdi 明帝, 72
Mingtai 明泰 (Matthew), 219
Mingyi 明一 (Emmanuel), 221
Miran, 45
Mishael, 228
Mizdaxkan, 19, 30
Mogao 莫高 Caves, 147, 159
Mongolia, 30
Moore, Thomas, 136
Morrow, Kenneth T., 84
Moses, biblical figure, 227, 230
Moses, priest, 219
Moses, priest. *See* **Fushou**
Moṣul, 70n54
Moule, Arthur C., 105, 123, 152
Mount Thomas, 35
Mšiḥadad. *See* **Baoda**
Müller, Andreas, 134n56
Murtuq, 149n110. *See also* Turfan
Museum für Asiatische Kunst, 22n86, 23
Mylapore, 35

Naǧran, 79
Nāhīd, 42
Nanshan 南山, 144
Nanshi 南市 (Southern Market), 138
Naymark, Aleksandr, 20
Nazareth, 298
Neicheng 內澄 (John), 221
Nestorius, 7
New York, 132–33
Nie Zhijun 聶志軍, 153, 173, 194
Ning 寧 (Ningguo 寧國), 74, 208
Ningshu 寧恕. *See* Ḥenanišoʿ II
Ningxia 寧夏. *See* Lingwu
Ningxu 凝虛 (Sergius), 220
Nišabur, 9
Nisibene Hymns, 62
Nisibis, 7, 102
Noah. *See* **Laiwei**
Nomocanon, 70, 73n69

Odes of Solomon, 62
Okuno-in 奥之院, 188
On the Wars, 73n67
Ong (the country of the Öngüt), 85
Ornament of Histories, 26n95
Osaka 大阪, 158–59, 162, 194–95
Ōtani 2497, Sogdian MS, 37n139
Ōtani Kōzui 大谷光瑞, 37n139
Oxus (Amu Darya), 4, 11, 36, 212n104

P. 3847, Chinese MS. *See* Pelliot chinois 3847
P. T. 351, Old Tibetan MS. *See* Pelliot tibétain 351
Palestine, 130
Palmer, Martin, xiii, 113, 136
Pamir, 136n134
Pan Shen 潘紳, 131
Pandžikent, 19–20
Pannami 潘那密, 76
Paradise of the Fathers, 42
Paris, 16n60, 122, 159–60

394 *Index of Names, Texts, and Manuscripts*

Pars. *See* Persia

Parthia, 3

Paul, apostle, 201n29, 227, 230

Paul, priest. *See* **Baoling**

Pauthier, Guillaume, 131

Pearl, The, 7

Pei Ju 裴矩, 206n63

Pelliot, Paul, 53, 65n34, 88n124, 93n138, 107n189, 113, 123, 131, 148, 159, 200n18, 200nn20–21

Pelliot chinois 3847 (P. 3847), Chinese MS, 107, 114, 148, 150, 159–61, 168–69, 173, 194, 230n78

Pelliot tibétain 351 (P. T. 351), Old Tibetan MS, 187

Penqita. See *Ḥudrā*

Pērōz (Beilusi 卑路斯), 111

Persia (Bet Parsaye, Bosi, Fars, Iran, Pars), xiv, 4–6, 8–10, 13–17, 33–35, 42, 44, 46–48, 53, 56, 61, 63, 65–68, 70n54, 76–77, 80, 83, 88–89, 94, 101–2, 104, 107, 110–11, 113–14, 181, 201, 214n112, 217n128, 248, 261, 263n165

Persian Empire, 4–6, 7–8, 15–16, 31, 34, 45, 56n238, 65, 67, 69, 75, 80, 82, 99, 102

Persian Gulf, 9

Persians (Iranians), 6, 8n18, 34, 53, 65, 67, 101, 263n165

Peshitta (*Pšiṭṭā*) Bible, 40–41, 115, 202n37

Peter. *See* Yuanyi

Pethion, 42

Pilate, 254–55nn121–22, 279, 280n110

Polo, Maffeo, xi, xv

Polo, Marco, xi, xv, 15

Prajña, 150–51, 167, 173, 181

Procopius of Caesarea, 45n183, 73

Protoevangelium of James, 43

Psalter, xi, xiin3, 33, 35, 38, 40–41

Pseudo-Clement, 47

Pseudo-Dionysius the Areopagite, 97n146

Ptolemy, 231n84

Puji 普濟 (Pusay), 220

Pulleyblank, Edwin G., 196

Pulun 普論, 77, 111, 209

Pure Land (*jingtu* 淨土), 64, 96, 237n16, 283n8

Pusay. *See* **Puji**

Qangli Turks, 12

Qarluq Turks, 12

Qi 齊, village, 137

Qianyou 乾祐 (Aaron), 219

Qin Minghe 秦鳴鶴, 99–100

Qingsu 清素, 145

Qingxu guan 清虛觀 (Qingsu Temple), 186

Qirghiz Turks, 12

Qizil-qiya, 20

Qočo, 14, 22–23, 43, 45, 49, 78, 114. *See also* Turfan

Quan Tang wen 全唐文, 66n39, 115n229

Quanzhou 泉州, 31, 141

Qurutqa, 14, 43. *See also* Turfan

Qushen 去甚 (Salomon), 221

Rahām, 207n75. *See also* **Luohan**

Rajagṛha, 212n104

Relação da propagação da fé no reyno da China, 71

Remaining Traces of Past Centuries, 16n59

Renhui 仁惠 (Išoʿemmeh), 220

Ribaud, Pénélope, 110

Ricci, Matteo, 128, 134, 179

Riegert, Ray, 136

Rijin 日進 (Isaac), 219

Ripa, Matteo, 135

Romagyris. *See* Rumagird

Roman Empire, 4n5, 5–6, 56, 66, 76, 201n26, 248n82, 295n84, 298n1

Rome, 4n5, 6, 76, 133, 248, 254, 260–61, 277

Rong Xinjiang 榮新江, 89, 153–58, 165

Index of Names, Texts, and Manuscripts 395

Ru 汝, prefecture, 145
Rubroek, Willem van, 32, 36
Ruizong 睿宗, 75, 207n70, 207n72, 208n82
Rumagird (Romagyris), 16
Ryukoku University, 37n139

S. 1366, Chinese MS, 113
S. 6551, Chinese MS, 180
S. 6963, Chinese MS, 180
Sabrišoʿ, monk. *See* **Zhaode**
Sabrišoʿ, priest, 218
Šābuhr II, 5–6, 42, 46n189, 261n160
Saeki P. Y. *See* Saeki Yoshirō
Saeki Yoshirō (Saeki P. Y.) 佐伯好郎, xii, 123, 131, 136, 152, 154n128, 155, 165, 173, 188, 194–95
Śākyamuni, 75, 151, 181, 207, 226n26. *See also* Buddha
Ṣaliba Zka, 73
Salisbury, Edward E., 130n43
Salomon. *See* **Qushen**
Samarkand (Afrasiab, Kangguo 康國), 9, 11, 13–14, 19–20, 44–45, 73, 88n125, 90, 104
Samson. *See* **Shenshen**
Sarag. *See* Luoyang
Sarah, martyr, 228
Saryg. *See* Krasnaja Rečka
Sasanian Empire. *See* Persian Empire
Satan (Adversary), 47, 196, 199, 242–44
Ṣatpāramitā sūtra. See *Liu boluomi jing*
Sayings of the Fathers, 41
Seckel, Dietrich, 124
Segestan, 3, 9, 15, 116
Seiun-ji 棲雲寺, 26–28
Seleucia-Ctesiphon, 4, 7, 9, 31, 44, 63n20, 80, 85
Semedo, Álvaro de, 71
Semireč'e (Seven Rivers), 4, 14, 21–22, 45
Septuagint Bible, 17, 40
Serapion, 42

Sergius, chorepiscopus, 87, 218
Sergius, chorepiscopus. *See* **Jingtong**
Sergius, martyr, 42, 227, 231
Sergius, monk. *See* **Lingde**
Sergius, monk. *See* **Ningxu**
Sergius, monk. *See* **Yuanzong**
Sergius of Elam, 10, 15n54, 86n116, 86n118
Sergius of Rešʿayna, 97n146
Serindia, 45, 49, 53
Seven Rivers. *See* Semireč'e
Severians, 15
Severus Sebokt, 231n84
Severus the Great 15n54
Shaanxi 陝西, 90, 127–28, 129n41
Shaanxi History Museum, 128n38
Shaanxi Provincial Museum, 128n38
Shandao 善導, 187
Shanxi 山西, 103
Shaocheng 少誠, 145
Shazhou 沙洲, 78
Shengli 聖歷, 75, 207
Shengshan si 聖善寺 (Shengshan Monastery), 91
Shenshen 審慎 (Samson), 221
Shepherd of Hermas, 50
Shi Gaochang ji 使高昌記, 114n223
Shiguo 史國. *See* Kašana
Shiguo 石國. *See* Taškent
Shizi si 十字寺 (Monastery of the Cross), 114
Shizun bushi lun disan 世尊布施論第三, 163, 250
Shouyi 守一 (John), 220
Shu Yuanyu 舒元輿, 115
Shuipang, 14. *See also* Bulayïq; Turfan
Shuofang 朔方, 87, 102, 212–13
Šila, 73
Silk Road, xiv, 4n3, 11, 15, 18, 26, 28, 32, 36, 44, 45n182, 46, 57n239, 109
Simeon, monk. *See* **Liyong**
Simeon, monk. *See* **Wenshun**

Simeon, priest, 219

Simeon, priest and elder, 221

Simon of Ṭaibuteh, 42, 229n67

Simon Peter, 227, 282–90, 296

Sims-Williams, Nicholas, 42n162

Ṣin, al-. *See* Bet Ṣinaye

Ṣin (Ṣinestan, Ṣinistan). *See* Bet Ṣinaye

Sitian tai 司天臺 (Bureau of
  Astronomy), 103

Siyuan 思圓, 89

Škand-gumānīg Wizār. See
  Doubt-dispelling Exposition

Sleepers of Ephesus, 42

Sogdiana, 9, 11–14, 16–17, 19–21, 28, 30,
  36, 44, 53, 73, 88. *See also* Taškent

Sogdians, 11–15, 36, 49, 54, 104, 138,
  146, 244n59

Sortes Apostolorum, 42, 114n222

Sri Lanka. *See* Ceylon

Stein, Marc Aurel, 23, 45, 113

*Stele of the Diffusion of the Luminous
  Teaching of Da Qin in China*. See *Da
  Qin jingjiao liuxing Zhongguo bei*

Su Shi 蘇軾, 112

Šubḥalmaran. *See* **Fengzhen**

Sumeru (Meru), 286n37, 290n55

Sun Chengze 孫承澤, 128

Sun Jianqiang 孫建強, 78, 165, 169

Sun Yat-sen University, 156

Sutra of the Six Perfections. See *Liu
  boluomi jing*

Sutrušana (Ušrusana, Dong Caoguo
  東曹國), 104n179

Suyab. *See* Ak-Bešim

Suzhou 蘇州, 155, 297n94

Suzong 肅宗, 75, 109, 210, 213, 215

Syria, 4, 6, 66

Syrians, 34

Syro-Malabar Church, 71

Tacitus, ix

Taḥurestan. *See* Tocharistan

Taicu 太蔟, 217

Taihe 太和 (ʿAbdišoʿ), 221

Taiwan 台灣, 153

Taixuan zhenyi benji jing 太玄真一本際
  經, 173, 186, 225n19

Taizhou 台州, 218

Taizong 太宗, 68, 73, 110n203, 148, 204,
  208–9nn82–83, 210n89, 214, 231,
  232n91, 252n106

Tajikistan, 36n134

Takahashi Hidemi 高橋英海, 196,
  262n162

Takakusu Junjirō 高楠順次郎, 88n124,
  155, 159

Takakusu manuscript, Chinese MS. See
  Xuting mishisuo jing

Takeda kagaku shinkō zaidan 武田科学
  振興財団, 158–59, 162, 194–95

Takeda Science Foundation. *See* Takeda
  kagaku shinkō zaidan

Taklamakan, 26n94

Talas. *See* Taraz

Tang huiyao 唐會要, 66n39, 110n203,
  112, 147, 205n59

Tang jingjiao beisong zhengquan 唐景教
  碑頌正詮, 134, 212n104

Tang Li 唐莉, xiii, 145n97, 153, 172

Tang liangjing chengfang kao 唐兩京
  城坊考, 112

Tangtse, 27–29

Taraz (Talas), 21, 45

Tarim, 26n94, 44–45

Taškent (Čač, Shiguo 石國), 11, 16, 45,
  104n179, 138. *See also* Sogdiana

Tešbuḥtā d-malakē. See *Glory to God in
  the Highest*

Tetrabiblos, 231

Theodoret of Cyrus, 34

Theophylact Simocatta, 11

Thomas, apostle (Mar Thomas), 70–72

Thomas of Marga, 10, 73n68, 86, 203n42

Three Steps of the Monastic Life, 229n67

Tianbao 天寶, 74, 208

Tianxue chuhan 天學初函, 131n45

Index of Names, Texts, and Manuscripts 397

Tibet (Bet Tuptaye), 10, 27–28, 30, 187

Tibetan Empire, 10, 45

Tibetans, 10

Tigris, 3, 8

Timothy I, 9–11, 12n36, 14–15, 73n68, 85–86, 217n129

Tisserant, Eugène, 102

Tocharistan (Bet Ṭaḥoraye, Taḥurestan), 136

Tokmak, 21, 45

Tomioka Kenzō 富岡謙藏, 155, 159

Tomioka manuscript, Chinese MS. See *Yishen lun*

Tongdian 通典, 66n39, 101

Tonkō hikyū 敦煌秘笈 (Dunhuang Secret Collection), 158–59, 162, 194–95

Tōno Haruyuki 東野治之, 163, 165, 168

Toutuo si bei 頭陀寺碑, 170

Toyoq, 14, 35. *See also* Turfan

Tractado em que se contam muito por estenso as cousas da China, 70

Transoxiana, 11, 16

Travancore, 35

Trigault, Nicolas, 70–71, 131, 135

Tumšuq, 45

Turfan, 4, 11, 14, 17, 22–23, 30, 32–33, 35–39, 41, 43–44, 46, 49–53, 78, 101, 109, 114, 116, 172, 180, 256n131

Turkestan, 53, 84. *See also* Eastern Turkestan

Turks, 10–13, 15, 36, 54, 84

Uighur kingdom of Qočo, 49, 78, 114

Uighur steppe empire, 49

Urganč, 36

Urgut, 20

Ušrusana (Dong Caoguo 東曹國). *See* Sutrušana

Uzbekistan, 12

Voltaire, 129, 130n43

Wahrām. *See* Aluohan

Wahrām IV, 261n160

Wan/Luan 彎/鸞, monk, 101

Wang Chuan. *See* Wang Juan

Wang Duan 王端, 170

Wang Jin 王巾, 170

Wang Juan (Wang Chuan) 汪娟, 173

Wang Lanping 王蘭平, 153, 158, 194

Wang Wenzhi 王文治, 128

Wang Yande 王延德, 114

Wang Zhixin 王治心, 99–100n155

Wei 渭, 181

Wei Zheng 魏徵, 149, 232

Weng Shaojun 翁紹軍, 153, 170

Wenjian 文簡, 91

Wenming 文明 (Išoʻdad), 220

Wenshun 聞順 (Simeon), 220

Wenzhen 文貞 (Luke), 220

West Syriac Christians. *See* West Syriac Church

West Syriac Church (Jacobite Church), 7, 15, 115–16

Western Paradise, 96

Williamson, Alexander, 135

Wilmshurst, David, 68, 116

Wu 武, king, 207n74

Wu Chang-shing. *See* Wu Changxing

Wu Changxing (Wu Chang-shing) 吳昶興, 153

Wu Chi-yü. *See* Wu Qiyu

Wu Qiyu (Wu Chi-yü) 吳其昱, 153, 172, 178n188

Wu Zetian 武則天, 75, 83, 99, 207n70, 207n72, 207n74

Wu Zibi 吳子苾, 219n140

Wulin 武林. *See* Hangzhou

Wuzong 武宗, 77, 139, 169

Wylie, Alexander, 131

Xaraxoto (Khara-Khoto), 33, 43

Xi Caoguo 西曹國. *See* Išitikhan

Xiabu zan yijuan 下部讚一卷. See *Hymnscroll*

Xi'an 西安. *See* Chang'an

Xi'an Beilin Museum. *See* Beilin

Xi'an Christian stele. See *Da Qin jingjiao liuxing Zhongguo bei*

Xianfeng 咸豐, 219n140

Xiang Da 向達, 112

Xiantian 先天, 75, 207

Xiapu 霞浦, 64n24

Xin Tang shu 新唐書, 204n52, 213n107, 263n165

Xingqing gong 興慶宮 (Xingqing Palace), 77, 111–12, 208n78, 209

Xingtong 行通, 218

Xinhai 辛亥, 111n210

Xinjiang 新疆, 23, 26n94, 49

Xishi 西市 (Western Market), 108

Xiushan fang 修善 (Xiushan Ward), 112

Xiyu tuji 西域圖記, 206n63

Xu Song 徐松, 112

Xuande 玄德 (Ephrem), 221

Xuanlan 玄覽 (Gigoy), 88, 221

Xuanqing 玄慶, 145

Xuanying 玄應, 145

Xuanzhen 玄真 (John), 220

Xuanzong 玄宗, 66, 74, 82, 99, 208, 210n89, 213n107, 215

Xusraw I, 261n160

Xusraw II, 261n160

Xuting mishisuo jing 序聽迷詩所經 (Takakusu manuscript), 155–59, 163–65, 194, 265

Yaghnab, 36n134

Yahballaha I, 6

Yahballaha III (Mark, Marqos), 85

Yama, 271

Yamī, 271n41

Yānakk. *See* An Yena

Yang Manuo 陽瑪諾. *See* Dias, Manuel Jr.

Yang Rongzhi 楊榮鋕, 135

Yang Senfu 楊森富, 229n67

Yanhe 延和 (Elijah), 219

Yaolun 曜輪 (John), 87, 219

Yaoyuan 曜源 (John), 220

Yaoyue 遙越 (Joel), 219

Yarkend, 45

Yazdbōzīd. *See* **Yisi**

Yazdgird I, 5, 46n189

Yazdgird II, 5, 261n160

Yazdgird III, 8, 111

Yejumo 耶俱摩 (Jacob), 220

Yeli 業利 (Gabriel), 218

Yifeng 儀鳳, 111n209

Yiji 義濟 (Zechariah), 221

Yin Xiaoping 殷小平, 94n140, 145n97, 166

Yingde 英德 (Isaac), 220

Yining fang 義寧坊 (Yining Ward), 74, 107–8, 110–11, 121, 129, 186, 205

Yishan xiansheng wenji 遺山先生文集, 69n50

Yishen lun 一神論 (Tomioka manuscript), 155–59, 162–65, 178n189, 194, 233

Yisi 伊斯 (Yazdbōzīd), 87, 88n123, 101–2, 109, 211, 212n104, 213, 214n114, 218

Yitian lun diyi 一天論第一, 163, 233

Yotkan, 26. *See also* Khotan

Young, John M. L., 119

Youyang zazu 酉陽雜俎, 101

Yu di'er 喻第二, 162, 246

Yuan Haowen 元好問, 69n50

Yuanhe 元和, 144

Yuanyi 元一 (Peter), 219

Yuanzhao 圓照, 150, 181

Yuanzong 元宗 (Sergius), 221

Zarang, 15

Zechariah. *See* **Yiji**

Zechariah the Rhetor (of Mytilene), 230n73

Zeng Qingbao (Chin Ken-pa) 曾慶豹, 184

Index of Names, Texts, and Manuscripts
399

Zhang Delin 張德麟, 173

Zhang Gengyu 張賡虞, 130

Zhang Jimeng 張濟猛, 153

Zhang Naizhu 张乃壽, 138n75

Zhangye 張掖. *See* Ganzhou

Zhaode 昭德 (Sabrišoʻ), 220

Zhenguan 貞觀, ix, 69, 110n203, 147–48, 204–5, 231

Zhenyuan xinding shijiao mulu 貞元新定釋教目錄, 88n124, 151n116, 181n199

Zhide 至德 (John), 221

Zhijian 志堅 (Cyriacus), 221

Zhitong 志通, 145

Zhixuan anle jing 志玄安樂經 (Li Shengduo manuscript), xvn12, 64, 150n114, 155, 162, 166, 186, 194, 228n56, 282

Zhongzong 中宗, 75, 207n70, 207n72, 208n82

Zhou 周. *See* Luoyang

Zhouzhi 盩厔, 112, 127–29

Zhu Donghua 朱東華, 153

Zhu Qianzhi 朱謙之, 118n6, 154n128

Zhu Weizhi 朱維之, 176

Zhuangzi 莊子, 205n57

Zieme, Peter, 51n211

Zizhi tongjian 資治通鑒, 111n210

Zong Chuke 宗楚客, 111n209

Zunjing 尊經, 143n87, 148, 160, 194, 226

Zuoʻe 作噁, 216

www.ingramcontent.com/pod-product-compliance
Lightning Source LLC
Chambersburg PA
CBHW072053290825
31867CB00004B/350